D0084979

American Government

Enduring Principles and Critical Choices

To understand contemporary American politics and government students need to see how political ideas, institutions and forces have developed over time. The fourth edition of *American Government* dwells on the seminal role played by political memory and path dependency in shaping contemporary institutions, political forces, and public opinion as well as the critical choices that have caused them to shift course. It provides a comprehensive depiction of current demographic, political, attitudinal, and governmental facts, trends, and conditions. Each chapter begins with a detailed contemporary portrait of its subject.

Marc Landy is Professor of Political Science at Boston College. He also teaches in the Masters in American History and Government Program at Ashland University. He is the coauthor of *Presidential Greatness and The Environmental Protection Agency from Nixon to Clinton.* He has written for many journals, including *National Affairs*, *Political Science & Politics* and *Public Administration Review.*

American Government

Enduring Principles and Critical Choices

Marc Landy
Boston College, Massachusetts

CAMBRIDGE
UNIVERSITY PRESS

University Printing House, Cambridge CB2 8BS, United Kingdom

One Liberty Plaza, 20th Floor, New York, NY 10006, USA

477 Williamstown Road, Port Melbourne, VIC 3207, Australia

314–321, 3rd Floor, Plot 3, Splendor Forum, Jasola District Centre, New Delhi – 110025, India

79 Anson Road, #06-04/06, Singapore 079906

Cambridge University Press is part of the University of Cambridge.

It furthers the University's mission by disseminating knowledge in the pursuit of education, learning, and research at the highest international levels of excellence.

www.cambridge.org
Information on this title: www.cambridge.org/9781108471367
DOI: 10.1017/9781108571418

First published 2019

A catalogue record for this publication is available from the British Library.

ISBN 978-1-108-47136-7 Hardback
ISBN 978-1-108-45783-5 Paperback

Contents

Preface

This book grows out of a friendship that developed from a deep intellectual affinity. Sid Milkis and I met in 1984 when we were put on the same panel at the American Political Science Association meeting. We found that we were both preoccupied by the New Deal. Sid was trying to understand how it gave rise to the modern administrative state. I was trying to figure out how Franklin Roosevelt both embraced the labor movement and staved off the transformation of the Democratic Party into a British-style Labor party. Soon after, Sid came to Brandeis University, where I had become a Fellow of the Gordon Public Policy Center. We had adjoining offices at the center and were able to continue our conversations over lunch and coffee and at the center's seminars. We discovered that our common interests were not limited to Franklin Roosevelt and the New Deal; we had both come to believe that the study of political science had been severed from its historical roots and that our job was to graft the study of contemporary politics back on to those roots. Both of us were already doing this in our American politics teaching with very good results. We saw that students developed a much keener and firmer grasp of current matters when they became aware of the intellectual and institutional connections that the contemporary issues and events had with the past. Sid applied this approach to his book *The President and Parties* and to the textbook he coauthored with Michael Nelson, *The American Presidency: Origins and Development.* Marc applied the approach to essays about the labor movement's impact on the development of American politics. Together, we drew on the American political development framework in our investigations for our book *Presidential Greatness* and our chapter, "The Presidency in History: Leading From the Eye of the Storm," in Michael Nelson's edited volume, *The Presidency and the Political System.* In the meantime, our devotion to connecting past and present came to appear less eccentric; many other scholars also began to find greater meaning and interest in bringing history to bear on the study of American politics. American Political Development (APD) has now established itself as one of the most active and intellectually vibrant movements within political science.

The underlying premise of the APD approach is the conviction that to understand contemporary American politics and governments, students need to understand how political ideas, institutions, and forces have developed over time. In Chapter 1, I invoke what William Faulkner once wrote, "The past is never dead. It's not even past." The past shapes our ideas, attitudes and sentiments endowing the present with meaning. Delving into the past reveals what key political and governmental principles endure and what critical changes have occurred – hence the book's subtitle, "Enduring Principles, Critical Choices". The book dwells on the seminal role played by political memory and path dependency in shaping contemporary institutions, political forces, and public opinion as well as the key decisions that have caused them to shift course. The seminal fourth chapter entitled "Political Development" dwells on those episodes when enduring principles were most profoundly contested. The other chapters likewise elucidate the critical choices that have shaped their specific subject.

Because the very purpose of the APD approach is to shed light on the present, this book provides a comprehensive depiction of present demographic, political, attitudinal, and governmental facts, trends, and conditions. Each chapter begins with a detailed contemporary portrait of its subject. For example, the contemporary portrait segment in "Campaigns, Elections, and Media" includes a detailed description of the 2016 presidential election campaign. The portraits ground the students in the most important facts and analytical principles regarding the chapter subject, and comprise a brief guide to current politics and governments.

There are no separate chapters about civil rights, civil liberties, or public policy because these subjects are so integral to American politics that they form key threads woven into the fabric of the entire book. We do, however, devote an entire chapter to political economy (Chapter 6). We believe that such a chapter is necessary because so much of the substance of political discussion, partisan conflict and policy-making is about economics. As the name, political economy, implies, this chapter highlights the political forces that have shaped the institutional and legal framework in which economic activity takes place. Throughout the book, students are made aware that what they are learning in their history courses complements their political science understanding, and vice versa. Chapter 6 shows them how the study of economics and of political science inform one another as well.

New in the Fourth Edition

This new edition greatly strengthens the book's coverage of political behavior and the media, and is supported by materials on the Cambridge University Press website, www.cambridge.org. Whereas Part IV of the previous editions, entitled "Political Forces," contained two chapters, Part IV of this edition, renamed "Political Life," now contains four. There is an entire chapter devoted to public opinion. Campaigns and elections also have a chapter of their own as do political parties. The consideration of media is now so central to both the campaigns and elections Chapter and the political and civic participation chapter that the word "media" has been added to the titles of both.

The critical choice theme announced in the book's subtitle now receives greater emphasis. In each chapter the critical choices the chapter considers are highlighted. Each critical choice discussion begins with an introductory paragraph that crystallizes the importance of the choice. It ends with a segment entitled "Upshot" that illuminates the contemporary importance of the choice. To stimulate critical thinking, every chapter offers a critical thinking essay question based on a controversial issue the chapter raises. For example, following the sections on the spoils system and civil service reform in the chapter entitled "The Bureaucracy," the following question is posed: "The spoils system distributes government jobs on the basis of party loyalty. The civil service system relies on competitive examination for that purpose. Discuss the strengths and weaknesses of each approach. Which one do you favor?"

This edition provides many more graphs, maps, tables, and timelines than previous editions did. These graphics serve to greatly enrich both the contemporary portrait and the developmental components of each chapter and to strengthen the analytic connection between past and present. They also render the book's content more readable and inviting.

Organization

Each chapter begins with an overview that uses a bullet format to highlight the central themes of the chapter. Each of these bullets serves as a heading for each of the different sections that comprise the chapter. Following the overview there is a brief vignette that provides an evocative introduction to at least one of the key themes bulleted in the overview. For example, the Congress chapter's opening vignette is about Congress' consideration of President Trump's cabinet nominees, revealing how this process exemplifies the growing party polarization of Congress. Next comes the "Contemporary Portrait" section described above. The rest of the chapter is organized developmentally according to the chapter overview bullets. The concluding section is entitled "Looking Forward." It invites the student to make use of insights from the chapter to consider an issue of great present and future importance. For example, the political parties chapter looks at the functions that political parties have historically performed and invites the student to consider which of those functions they still perform; which they do not; and why the loss of certain key functions are of critical importance going forward. The chapter ends with a summary, organized on the basis of the section headings, that focuses on the most important matters the chapter discusses.

Acknowledgments

I thank the coauthor of the previous editions of this book Sidney Milkis for our decades of fruitful intellectual collaboration. The editor of this edition, Robert Dreesen, has been unstinting in his encouragement and support. The developmental editor Brianda Reyes has provided very valuable guidance regarding how to make the book more accessible to students, as well as a host of other helpful suggestions. Jessica Goley, Thomas Goodman, Nick Allmaier, and Peter Wilkin have been gracious, thoughtful, energetic, and diligent in their assistance. I thank my good friend Steve Thomas, for the stimulating conversations we have had about the book and his insights for improving it.

1 Introduction

CHAPTER OVERVIEW

This chapter focuses on:

- **Fundamental concepts of American politics and government.**
- **Why this book approaches the study of American politics and government from the perspective of American political development (APD).**
- **Why the American political system is biased in favor of the status quo.**
- **How critical choices operate to overcome the bias in favor of the status quo and lead to transformative change.**
- **The aims of American government as outlined in the Preamble to the Constitution; a brief introductory sketch of efforts to achieve those aims and some of the most serious current controversies those efforts provoke.**

"I Have a Dream"

On August 28, 1963, 250,000 people marched on Washington to protest discrimination against African Americans and to celebrate the rise of the civil rights movement. Race relations in the South were dominated by so-called Jim Crow laws, enacted at the end of the nineteenth century, which imposed racial segregation in all aspects of life. In *Brown v. Board of Education of Topeka* (1954), the Supreme Court declared the so-called "separate but equal" doctrine in education policy unconstitutional. Nonetheless, many Southern schools remained segregated. Not since the turbulent Reconstruction Era that followed the Civil War had the South been so alienated from the rest of the country.

When, starting in the mid 1950s, civil rights demonstrations broke out throughout the South to protest this racial caste system, local police brutally repressed efforts to break down what the distinguished African American sociologist W. E. B. Du Bois had called the "color line." When African American students tried to enter Little Rock High School in September of 1957, a crowd of white parents cursed and threatened them as the governor of Arkansas, Orval Faubus, blocked the door. The civil rights movement gained great momentum in 1960 when black and white students joined together to sit in at lunch counters throughout the South demanding to be served. The wave of protests continued in 1961 as Northern blacks and whites took bus trips to the South and refused to segregate themselves when they reached Southern bus terminal waiting rooms and restaurants. A particularly ugly confrontation took place in Birmingham, Alabama in September of that year, where one of the civil rights movement's most important leaders, Martin Luther King, Jr., was jailed. President John F. Kennedy had been reluctant to take on civil rights, arguing that it was up to local officials to enforce the law. After Birmingham, however, Kennedy gave his support to a comprehensive civil rights bill making racial discrimination in hotels, restaurants, and other public accommodations illegal and giving the attorney general the power to bring suits on behalf of individuals to speed up lagging school desegregation. The measure also authorized agencies of the federal government to withhold federal funds from racially discriminatory state programs.

To heighten awareness of their cause and to press for passage of Kennedy's bill, civil rights leaders organized the largest single protest demonstration in American history. King's speech at the Lincoln Memorial was its climax. Late in the afternoon, the summer heat still sweltering, King appeared at the microphone. The crowd, restlessly awaiting King's appearance, broke into thunderous applause and chanted his name. King began by praising Lincoln's Emancipation Proclamation as "a great beacon of hope to millions of Negro slaves who had been seared in the flames of withering injustice." But, he continued,

> one hundred years later, we must face the tragic fact that the Negro is still not free. One hundred years later, the Negro is still sadly crippled by the manacles of segregation and the chains of discrimination. One hundred years later, the Negro lives on a lonely island of poverty in the midst of a vast ocean of material prosperity. One hundred years later, the Negro is still languishing in the corners of American society and finds himself an exile in his own land. So we have come here today to dramatize an appalling condition.

This litany of oppression might have elicited anger; indeed, some of King's followers had been growing impatient with his peaceful resistance to Jim Crow and its brutish defenders. But King, an ordained minister, spoke the words of justice, not revenge: "Let us not seek to satisfy our thirst for freedom by drinking from the cup of bitterness and hatred." A reverend might have been expected to invoke the warnings of the biblical prophets in calling America to account, instead King appealed to America's charter of freedom. He called upon Americans to practice the political and social ideals of the Declaration of Independence:

> When the architects of our republic wrote the magnificent words of the Constitution and the Declaration of Independence, they were signing a promissory note to which every

American was to fall heir. This note was a promise that all men would be guaranteed the unalienable rights of life, liberty, and the pursuit of happiness.

King lamented that America had not lived up to those famous words. Even after the Brown case had interpreted the Constitution so as to fulfill the promise of the Declaration of Independence, segregationists prevailed. The promissory note had come back marked "insufficient funds."

Still, he counseled continued faith in the promise of American life. African Americans should "refuse to believe that the bank of justice is bankrupt." At the same time, King warned, their faith in American justice could not last much longer; the time had come "to make real the promises of Democracy." "Now is the time to rise from the dark and desolate valley of segregation to the sunlight path of racial justice." His indictment went beyond the South. "We can never be satisfied as long as a Negro in Mississippi cannot vote and a Negro in New York believes he has nothing to vote for." The crowd shouted and clapped in cadence with him. Inspired by this surge of feeling, King abandoned his prepared text; but even as he spoke "from his heart," in words that would make this address memorable, King's sermon had a familiar ring, drawing again on the Declaration of Independence:

> I say to you today, my friends, that in spite of the difficulties and frustrations of the moment, I still have a dream. It is a dream deeply rooted in the American dream. I have a dream that one day this nation will rise up and live out the true meaning of its creed: "We hold this truth to be self-evident, that all men are created equal." When we let freedom ring, when we let it ring from every village and every hamlet, from every state and every city, we will be able to speed up that day when all of God's children, black men and white men, Jews and gentiles, Protestants and Catholics, will be able to join hands and sing in the words of the old Negro spiritual, "Free at last! Free at last! Thank God almighty, we are free at last!"

Figure 1.1. The Unfinished Word of Martin Luther King. Cartoon by David Granger, 2011.
Source: Political Cartoons Com.

Fundamental Democratic Republican Concepts: Speech, Leadership, Institutions

King's speech is a fine place to begin this text because it shows that politics is not just about power, greed, and ambition but also about the noblest sentiments of the human spirit. It also vividly illustrates what American politics and government are made of, their fundamental concepts. It was a speech and, in a free society, most of political life is lived through speech. The various forms of speech that politics employs – argument, explanation, exhortation, and discussion – are what give it its distinctive character. Just as clay is the medium of sculpture, words are the medium of republican and democratic politics. The brilliance of King's speech stems from his ability to artfully make use of what that medium has to offer – metaphor, adjective, symbol, analogy. The speech was listened to by hundreds of thousands of people. It was a *public event.* Unlike many other activities – friendship, sex, reading or listening to music on an iPhone, politics typically takes place in public. Not everyone is capable of commanding the attention of a crowd the way Martin Luther King did. Those who can command such public attention we call leaders. Followers have a big political role to play as well, but the United States is a very big place and ordinary people have only a very limited capacity to influence political life and make their voices heard. Therefore, they are very dependent on leaders to represent, inspire, and command them. King was not a professional politician. No matter. The key tasks of *political leadership* are frequenly performed by those who do not even think of themselves as politicians and who do not hold political office.

King's speech took place in a very particular context and was intended to achieve very particular goals. King's goal was to pass civil rights legislation. The very need to push hard for that goal implies that there is opposition to it. Other people, and their leaders have other, conflicting, goals. Speech and leadership give politics some of the qualities of theatre – vivid language, evocative acting. But, as the word "goal" suggests, politics also ressembles sports. Competition can be fierce. Foul play occurs and gets penalized if the perpetrators get caught. There are winners and losers. Thus conflict and competition are also central to politics.

Politics also ressembles sports in that it is highly organized. The rules are carefully laid out. Different teams develop a collective identity and persist over time. The term used for the organizations that endure, command loyalty and develop their own collective identities is *institution.* Martin Luther King was not simply speaking to a crowd of individuals on that warm August day, he was speaking to people with strong institutional affiliations – union members, church congregants, lodge brothers, and sorority sisters. And he was appealing to leaders of two powerful political institutions – the Democratic and Republican parties – to press for action by one of the three central national governing institutions, the

United States Congress. King himself was not only the leader of a movement, he was also the head of an important religious institution, the Ebenezer Baptist Church. Chapter 3 will introduce an additional fundamental republican democratic concept: deliberation.

The American Polity: A Democratic Republic

The entire political story of civil rights, of which this speech is such an epochal part, takes place within the frame established by one overarching institution, a polity, the United States. It was the law of the United States that had the ultimate authority to decide the outcome of the civil rights struggle. It was the legislature of the United States that deliberated about and formulated the law. The citizenry of the United States chose the members of that legislature. The United States is a *polity* because it successfully claims the political allegiance of its members. Those members may feel a deeper tie to their church or to some other institution to which they belong, but it is the constitution and the laws of the United States that they are compelled to obey. The governing institutions of the US provide them with their political rights and responsibilities. Once in the history of the United States its claim to being a polity was challenged. Southern states seceded and, temporarily, formed a new polity, the Confederate States of America. It took a brutal war, the Civil War, to defeat secession and restore the US's status as a single polity.

The United States is unusual in that it went through a formal process of constitution writing to become a polity. Many other polities such as Britain, France, China, or Japan did not begin on any specific date, nor did they go through a process of discussion and debate to become a polity. If this were a text on comparative politics, it would be necessary to delve deeply into how those other polities came into being; instead it focuses exclusively on the formation of the American polity. Chapter 2 describes the ideas and beliefs that formed the background to the actual formation of the United States. Chapter 3 focuses specifically on the writing and ratification of that polity's founding document, the United States Constitution. Chapter 4 identifies key moments of constitutional crisis when there were major reconsiderations of the American polity's constitutional underpinning.

In order to claim that speech and choice are the building blocks of a polity, that polity must allow persons to speak freely, to have a say in how the laws are made and to feel secure that those laws will be obeyed. A polity characterized by free speech, rule of law, and collective decision making is called a *republic*. The American Republic, and all modern ones, operate on the basis of representation. The citizenry plays a minor role, if any, in governing. For the most part its role is restricted to electing representatives who do the actual work of governing. Because the representatives are popularly elected the United States is a representative, democratic republic.

American Political Development

Political Memory

Martin Luther King gave a speech in the present in an effort to influence the future and yet so much of it focuses on the past. It refers back to leaders, documents, and songs from long ago – Lincoln, the Declaration of Independence, the framers of the Constitution, a spiritual sung by slaves. This was no accident. King knew that the best way to impress all the audiences for his speech – the crowd on the Mall, the congressmen whose votes he was trying to garner, tomorrow's newspaper readers, the next generation of children reading history textbooks– was to link his thoughts and aspirations to great leaders, ideas, and cultural symbols from the past.

As the great American writer William Faulkner observed, "the past is not dead, it is not even past." It shapes our ideas, attitudes, and sentiments endowing the present with meaning. Stories from the past pervade our imaginations. They provide vivid examples of what to do and what not to do. They help to define our sense of who we are, whom we love, and whom we hate. They supply our minds with a cast of heroes to emulate. Faced with a tough decision, a president or even an ordinary person might not only consider the present facts but also look for moral and intellectual guidance by asking "What would Lincoln have done? What would Martin Luther King have done?"

The pull of the past is demonstrated by the frequency with which historical analogies find their way into political debate. People often make use of such analogies to reason through a problem and to defend their position. Those who favored Obama's stimulus package chose a favorable historical case to compare it to – FDR's New Deal. Those who opposed the War in Iraq often likened it to an unsuccessful prior war – Vietnam. Those who favored it claimed that a failure to attack Iraq would do to the Middle East what the appeasement of Hitler at Munich did to Europe. The manner in which the past influences our thoughts, feelings, and imagination this text calls *political memory.* MLK crafted his words to create the strongest possible connection between his ideas and sentiments and those that serve as the wellsprings of American political memory.

Enduring Principles

This book will show that the political memory of Americans is largely devoted to political principles that were established early in our history and that endure. Those principles are so deeply embedded in American political understanding and so central to its political life that the term *enduring principles* forms half of this book's subtitle. These foundational principles stem from three distinct sources. The commitment to natural rights and limited government stems from the Classic Liberal political philosophers of the seventeenth century. The commitment to local self-government and community solidarity stems from Puritanism and the practical experience of local self-government in the New England townships. The commitment to democracy and equality is rooted in the experience of the American Revolution and the works of such apostles of majority rule as Thomas Paine and Thomas Jefferson. For simplicity sake, the book refers to these three political strands as Classic Liberalism, Communitarianism, and Egalitarian Democracy. The commonalities and tensions between them are discussed in Chapter 2, and the actual political conflicts that those tensions give rise to are highlighted in Chapter 4 and reemerge continually in later chapters.

In the words of leading political scientists Stephen Skowronek and Karen Orren, "because a polity in all its different parts is contructed historically, over time, the nature and prospects of any single part will be best understood within the long course of political formation." They term this approach to studying politics, *political development.* This text takes a political development approach. It shows how the political building blocks discussed in the previous section – speech, leadership, conflict, institutions – have operated over time to shape current American politics and government. How the key political principles mentioned above have faced challenge, how and to what extent they have endured.

As critical as political memory is to understanding present politics, the American Political Development (APD) approach also demonstrates two other crucial avenues by which the past affects the present – *path dependency* and *critical choices.*

Like individuals, political institutions are also heavily influenced by the past. Once a particular way of doing things has been set in motion, considerable inertia develops that encourages the continuation of that course. Political scientists call this phenomenon *path dependency.* A striking everyday example of path dependency is typewriting. When inventor C. L. Sholes built the first commercial typewriter prototype in 1868, the keys were arranged alphabetically in two rows. But the metal arms attached to the keys would jam if two letters near each other were typed in succession. So, Sholes rearranged the keys to make sure that the most common letter pairs such as "TH" were not too near each other. The new keyboard arrangement was nicknamed QWERTY after the six letters that form the upper left-hand row of the keyboard. QWERTY's original rationale has disappeared because keyboards now send their messages electronically. Many typing students find it very hard to master. Despite its shortcomings, QWERTY remains the universal typing keyboard arrangement simply because it is already so widely used and so many people have already taken pains to master it. Future typists might benefit from a change, but they do not buy keyboards; current typists do. Many political institutions and practices are just like QWERTY. Although their original purposes no longer exist, people are used to them and the costs of starting afresh are just too high.

There are countless examples of path dependence in American politics. Perhaps the single most important example is the way in which the United States is carved up into individual states. State boundary lines exist for all sorts of peculiar historical reasons. On the East Coast, they represent, for the most part, the grants given by Britain to specific individuals and groups to establish colonies. On the Pacific Coast and in the Southwest, they represent the boundaries of colonies obtained from Spain. In the Great Plains, they often represent little more than the preference of surveyors for drawing squares and rectangles. One can imagine many good reasons for adjusting state boundaries to accommodate practical realities. Why should Kansas City be split between Kansas and Missouri? The suburbs of northern New Jersey and southwestern Connecticut are dominated culturally and to a large measure economically by New York City and yet they remain part of other states. There have been very few changes in state boundaries over the entire course of American history.

This bias in favor of the status quo is not simply because people are creatures of habit, though indeed they are. It is also because, as a rule, those who benefit from an existing policy will fight harder to keep the policy in place than those who might benefit from a change will fight to alter it. Beneficiaries of existing policies know what they have and what they stand to lose if policies change. Potential beneficiaries can only estimate the benefits that a policy change might bring them. Therefore, politically speaking, fear of loss is a more powerful motivator than hope of gain.

Critical Choices

By showing how the odds favor the status quo, the developmental approach encourages a greater appreciation of what it takes to beat the odds. As passage of the 1964 Civil Rights Act and the 1965 Voting Rights Act so forcefully demonstrate, the powerful inertial biases of American politics are sometimes overcome. A key theme of this book is how and why Americans have made *critical choices* that shifted America's political path. How and why did the antipathy to political parties yield to the establishment of a two party political system? How and why did a strictly limited federal government mushroom into an elaborate administrative state? How and why were voting rights for African Americans and women finally granted after having been denied for so long?

Those critical choices that reshaped the constitutional underpinnings of the Ameican polity the text refers to as conservative revolutions (see Chapter 4). Calling them conservative revolutions is a reminder that such is the power of path dependency that even when when critical change does occur, those changes are decisively shaped by past events.

In sum, this text bases its discussion of American politics on several key building blocks: the interplay of enduring principles and critical choices; the role of political memory and path dependency, the influence of political speech, the role of political leaders, the dynamics of political competition, and the functioning of political institutions.

The Plan of This Book

This book is divided into four parts. The first, "Formative Experiences," contains Chapters 2, 3, and 4, which focus respectively on political culture, constitutional design, and critical episodes in American political development. Chapter 2 examines the formation and meaning of the core political beliefs that Americans profess. It shows how those beliefs coalesce to form what Tocqueville called "habits of the heart," an enduring political culture shaping the political opinions and actions of Americans. Chapter 3 looks at the Constitution: the political debate its creation provoked, the conflicts between rights and democracy that it settled, and those that it left unsettled. It explains why it is so important that the American government was erected on the basis of an original and carefully designed blueprint and how that conscious plan both reflects American political culture and has helped to shape it. Chapter 4 focuses on the major points of transition that have occurred since the constitutional founding.

Part II, "Pivotal Relationships," looks at how the federal government engages with the states and with the economy. The Constitution does not establish fixed boundaries between national and state governmental power, nor does it clearly define the limits of government regulation of private property. The disputes provoked by these uncertain boundaries have proven to be among the most hotly contested controversies in all of American political life and have given it much of its distinctive style and substance. As we shall see, those who fight for greater national power as well as those who resist either in the name of states rights or property rights all invoke the principles of rights and democracy to support their side.

The four chapters that form Part III, "Governing Institutions," each examine one of the three branches of national government – the Congress, the presidency, and the federal judiciary – enumerated in the Constitution, as well as the bureaucracy, which developed, in large measure, outside of formal constitutional arrangements. These chapters describe how those institutions operate now and how they have changed over time. The great debates over the structure and purposes of these institutions demonstrate how political arguments and political decisions shape and alter the "nuts and bolts" of government.

Part IV concentrates on the various phenomena that comprise American political life and the interrelationships among them. It begins with an analysis of contemporary public opinion describing how the opinions that Americans hold both reflect enduring aspects of American political culture and display some disturbing deviations from it. In a representative democracy the primary means for translating opinion into meaningful political participation comes through the act of voting. The next two chapters examine voting, first by looking at the most powerful means for galvanizing and organizing voting behavior, the political party, and then by looking at the impact of political campaigns and of the rules governing elections. The chapter on campaigns and elections includes a detailed account of the 2016 presidential campaign. Although elections are central to the operation of a democratic republic, they are not the sole focal point of meaningful political activity. Chapter 14 examines other critical forms of political behavior: movements, lobbies, and voluntary associations. All of these political actors have been discussed extensively earlier in the book, but always in supporting roles. It would be impossible to have a full-fledged discussion of any of the topics in Parts I through III without paying due attention to their mighty influence. Here they gain center stage. The spotlight is on their development and dynamics and how they have embodied and exemplified key questions of liberty, community, and democracy. The book ends with some reflections on several of the major concepts and principles that permeate the text.

Each chapter begins within an overview of its key themes. A vignette follows that evokes one or more of those themes. Then the chapter provides a contemporary portait of how the chapter's subject actually functions today. After, the chapter traces the political development of that subject to demonstrate the debt that current reality owes to enduring principles and to persistent paths and critical choices that have been forged over time. It provides a concluding statement, and ends with a summary of the most important points the chapter has made.

American Politics and Government: Policies and Programs

There is no better guide to what Americans want and expect from government than the Constitution's Preamble:

> We the People of the United States, in Order to form a more perfect Union, establish Justice, insure domestic Tranquility, provide for the common defense, promote the general Welfare, and secure the Blessings of Liberty to ourselves and our Posterity, do ordain and establish this Constitution for the United States of America.

The following is a brief introductory sketch of programs and policies that have been put in place to implement these high-minded but vague objectives and some of the most serious current controversies surrounding them.

"Form a More Perfect Union"

At present, the United States is the only major nation that refers to itself as a "union." The US was founded as a union of states and, to this day, the individual states have many of the powers that in other countries belong exclusively to the central government. They levy taxes, educate college students, build and maintain roads, and have their own law codes. Most crimes are tried in state criminal courts. Most lawsuits are brought in state civil courts. Those states with capital punishment laws exercise a legal power to kill. States perform a multitude of important regulatory functions. They regulate insurance companies, hospitals, and real estate transactions. All states issue drivers licenses. States also require licenses to engage in a wide variety of professions and businesses. In North Carolina, for example, one must obtain a license in order to engage in any one of more than one hundred and fify occupations including school teaching, practicing law, parachute rigging, embalming, and acting as an agent for a professional athlete.

Each state has its own constitution, which differ greatly from one another. For example, unlike the federal government and forty-nine other states, Nebraska's legislature is not bicameral; it consists solely of one legislative chamber. The Louisiana legal code is derived from France's Code Napoleon, not from British Common Law that serves as the basis for the law codes of all the other states. The complex relationship between the states and the national government is called federalism (see Chapter 5). The US is not the only federal nation. Germany, India, and Canada are among the other nations that grant significant powers to their states or provinces.

The original reason for seeking to establish *a more perfect union* was the weakness of the central government formed by the Articles of Confederation (see Chapter 2). The current national government is at least as strong as those of other nations. It commands the largest and strongest military and spends the most money on defense of any country in the world. Some of its activities – such as running the military, the diplomatic corps, the post office, and the national parks, forests, and public lands, and providing old-age pensions – it does entirely on its own. But many others – providing healthcare and income subsidies to the poor, training workers, regulating air and water pollution, aiding the handicapped and establishing student achievement standards – it does in partnership with state and local governments. Sometimes it funds these policy partnerships through what are called federal grants in aid (see Chapter 5). Sometimes it simply requires the states and localities to do them with their own money through what are called mandates (see Chapter 5).

There is no clear-cut distinction between which powers belong to the states and which to the federal government. This blurriness gives a distinctive cast to American political debate. Here, political conflict occurs not only over *what* government should do, but *who* should do it. For example, the arguments over abortion, gay marriage, and gun control include both the question of what should be done about them and also whether the states or the federal government should control the matter. Before the passage of the No Child Left Behind law (NCLB) in 2002, the federal government had restricted its intervention in K-12 education to enforcing school desegregation and providing various forms of aid to poor school districts. NCLB made it a condition of federal aid that every state establish student achievement standards and test students to ensure that they were meeting those standards. Many parents, teachers, and concerned citizens considered NCLB to be an unwarranted intrusion of the federal government into a matter that ought to remain the exclusive province of the states and localities. In the face of this mass of protest, in 2015 Congress replaced NCLB with the Every Student Succeeds Act, which significantly loosened the national standards, greatly reducing the intrusiveness of the national government in educational matters.

Perfecting the Union pertains not only to harmonizing national and state governments but also to determining which persons can legitimately claim to be a part of it. Other nations traditionally defined their citizenry on the basis of blood. A Frenchman was a Frenchman because he was descended from Frenchmen. The US, being a nation formed by immigrants, did not adopt that approach. Citizenship has been open both to those born here and those who take an oath of allegiance to the United States. Becoming an American means committing one's self to the set of principles that define the *American creed* as that creed is expressed in the Declaration of Independence, the Preamble to the Constitution and the Bill of Rights.

Controversy: Open versus Restricted Immigration

Not everyone has the opportunity to become a US citizen. Current law restricts the number of aliens who can establish residency in the United States and thus become eligible for citizenship. To escape poverty and political oppression, millions of foreigners, most of them from Mexico, the Caribbean, and Central America, enter the country illegally. The Pew Research Center has estimated that as of 2014 there were 11,700,000 illegal aliens in the United States (www.pewresearch.org/fact-tank/2016/09/20/measuring-illegal-immigration-how-pew-research-center-counts-unauthorized-immigrants-in-the-u-s/). The attitude of American citizens toward them is ambivalent. They perform work that American citizens are unwilling to perform – slaughtering cows and hogs, harvesting crops, maintaining lawns – but they also put a great strain on schools, housing, police, hospitals, and welfare systems.

The arguments in favor of exerting tighter control of illegal immigration and in favor of loosening such control are based on different conceptions of how best to perfect the Union. Neither denies that the essence of American citizenship is a commitment to the American creed. But restrictionists insist that the Union can only continue to flourish if the rate of immigration does not exceed the capacity of government and society to successfully absorb and assimilate the newcomers. Anti-restrictions maintain that any serious attempt to keep people out violates the deepest principles of liberty and equality that underlie the Union and thus renders the Union all the more imperfect. As we shall see in Chapter 13, the immigration issue played a big role in the 2016 presidential campaign.

"Insure Domestic Tranquility"

Unlike other countries, the United States has no national police force. The ordinary tasks of "insuring domestic tranquility," such as preventing and solving crimes, regulating traffic, and controlling crowds, are performed by state and local police. States also have their own codes of criminal law covering most ordinary crimes such as burglarly, arson, rape, murder, and assault, and their own courts for enforcing those codes. In 1878, Congress passed the *Posse Comitatus* Act, which is still in effect. *Posse Comitatus* means "power of the county." It forbids the mililtary from conducting domestic law enforcement except for constitutionally explicit or congressionally mandated exceptions. The Insurrection Act of 1807 clarifies the authority of the federal government to use the military to suppress domestic insurrections, as Lincoln did in the South's secession in the Civil War. In the 1950s and 1960s federal troops were used to overcome the refusal of Southern governors to integrate schools as required by decisions of the Supreme Court, and were sent in to control some of the riots that had broken out in the African American neighborhoods of major American cities.

The federal government does perform certain specific law enforcement functions that are beyond the capacity of state and local police. The Federal Bureau of Investigation was formed to cope with crimes that crossed state lines, such as kidnapping, and subsequently expanded the scope of its activities to include the prosecution of organized crime. The Secret Service guards the safety of the president, the vice president, their families, presidential candidates, and visiting world leaders. It also protects the money supply by prosecuting counterfeiting of US currency and bonds. The Coast Guard was granted an exception by the Congress to enable it to fight drug trafficking. But the targeted nature of these assignments attest to how powerful the resistance of Americans is to allowing the federal government to perform ordinary police functions.

Since 9/11, efforts to prevent terror attacks has served to greatly increase federal law enforcement responsibilities. This expansion is signified by the creation of the Department of Homeland Security (DHS), the first new cabinet level department since the Department of Veterans Affairs was established in 1989. Both the Secret Service and the Coast Guard have been transferred to DHS. It also houses the newly created Transportation Security Administration created to protect the nation's airports, railroads and other transportation networks, the Customs Service, the Immigration Service, and various other bureaus and parts of other agencies concerned with domestic preparedness. Although not part of DHS, the FBI has greatly expanded its antiterror efforts.

Controversy: "Insure Domestic Tranquility" versus Civil Liberties

The most serious current controversy about insuring domestic tranquility concerns the clash between protecting citizens against terror attack and protecting the full range of individual rights the Constitution guarantees. Normally a search warrant is required in order for law enforcement to place a tap on a telephone or otherwise listen in on what would otherwise be private communication. In order to obtain information about terror attack planning President George W. Bush ordered the National Security Agency (NSA) to monitor international telephone calls and international email of persons suspected of terrorist ties without first obtaining a search warrant. When news of this practice was leaked to the *New York Times*, many critics claimed that it was a violation of one's right to communicate in private. The administration stressed that the NSA did not eavesdrop on the actual phone conversations or read emails but rather searched for patterns of phone numbers and emails addresses to see who was talking to whom. This did not reassure critics who viewed the compiling of any data about interpersonal telecommunications as a violation of civil liberties. Despite the great outrage expressed, Congress confirmed the president's authority to order these forms of surveillance when it amended the Foreign Intelligence Surveillance Act in 2008.

"Provide for the Common Defense"

The goal of "providing for the common defense" is obvious. Americans want to be safe from foreign threat. But what does "defense" mean? As any football fan knows, offense and defense are inseparable. The other team cannot score if your team has the ball. The same is true for war. The national defense does not consist only of fending off enemy attack. In many cases the best defense consists of keeping one's enemies on the defensive by strengthening one's own offensive capabilities. The United States military is trained and equipped to attack others as well as to defend against attack.

Modern war is horrifically destructive. It is a last resort for protecting national security. Therefore a critical aspect of providing for the common defense involves diminishing the likelihood of war through the conduct of diplomacy. Diplomatic time and effort is devoted to building alliances with other friendly nations and trying to find common ground even with potential enemies via negotiation. The military aspect of providing for the common defense is primarily the responsibility of the Department of Defense and the armed services that it supervises. The diplomatic aspect is primarily the province of the Department of State. These duties are so vital to the safety of the nation that the Secretaries of Defense and State, along with the Secretary of the Treasury, are, after the president, the most powerful and prestigious positions in the executive branch.

Until the Cold War ended in the early 1990s, the United States was one of two world superpowers and was engaged in a costly and dangerous rivalry with the other superpower, the Soviet Union. With the collapse of the Soviet Union, the US has become the world's sole superpower. Its military strength dwarfs that of any other nation. It spends more on defense than the rest of the world combined.

Because it has such a voracious appetite for supplies and technology, it has spawned huge industries devoted to producing weapons, transport, communications systems, and other high-tech equipment for it. In order to maintain its technological edge over other nations, the military invests heavily in scientific and engineering research, much of which is done by universities who, in turn, have become heavily dependent upon the funds they receive from the Defense Department to conduct such studies. Indeed the US spends more on defense research and development than any other nation spends for all its military needs. President Dwight David Eisenhower coined the term "military industrial complex" to refer to this complex network of government, industry, and higher education.

Its size and strength enables the United States to operate on a global basis. No other nation has the wherewithal to do so. Even at the height of the Iraq War, when 160,000 soldiers were fighting in that country and another 12,000 were fighting in Afghanistan, the US maintained what are called combatant commands prepared to wage war almost anywhere in the world. These include: European Command, Pacific Command, and Southern Command, among others. Each command has a well-staffed headquarters and large numbers of troops, with others available to be mobilized in time of war.

Controversy: Superpower or Super Bully?

The most serious controversy involving "the common defense" stems from the United States' superpower status and global reach. Does this overwhelming power really make the country safer or does such strength serve as an almost irresistible temptation to throw its weight around? In recent decades the US has been engaged militarily in places such as Kosovo, Somalia, and Libya where the relationship between the fighting it was engaged in and US national security was tenuous at best.

The War on Terror launched by the Bush administration committed the US to long, costly, and bloody wars in Iraq and Afghanistan. Nations whom the US considers to be allies either opposed these efforts or made only very small troop commitments. Some argue that the US should not be so willing to act on its own. It should work more closely with its allies because that is the best way to maintain peace and the best way to ensure that the burden of fighting is more equally shared should war become unavoidable. Others contend that those allies have become so used to having the US fight their battles for them that they are no longer willing or able to bear their fair share of the load and that, therefore, the US has no choice but to take on the primary responsibility of protecting its national security, and theirs.

"Promote the General Welfare"

The United States took a very different approach to providing for the general welfare than did the nations of Western Europe. It defined "welfare" to mean restricting the intrusion of government rather than providing help to people. This effort to reign in government power is called *limited government.* It assumes that unless the constitution specifically grants government the right to engage in a specific activity, the government is not permitted to do so. Limiting government to only those constitutionally specified activities is called *enumerated powers.* Article I of the Constitution restricts the legislative power of government to only those specific powers enumerated in Article Section 8. Throughout most of its history the national government did not provide student loans, unemployment benefits, aid to the disabled, old-age pensions, medical care for the poor, or any of the other social service programs it now offers.

In the twentieth century American government has greatly expanded its powers beyond those enumerated in the Constitution. As a result, differences between American welfare policy and those of Western Europe have diminished considerably. The major remaining differences relate not to the total amount of welfare aid – the US is now in line with most advanced countries in total welfare funds expended – but rather how and for what purposes welfare aid is provided. The US is much more inclined to *target* specific categories of recipients – the elderly, the disabled, children, and unwed mothers. Whereas many rich countries will provide income to any poor person, in the US a guaranteed income is only accorded to those over 65 and welfare payments only go to poor single parent families, and for a maximum of only five years. In many European countries, college tuition is free or very low. The US national government does not attempt to control college tuition but subsidizes low-income college students and provides low-interest loans to middle class ones. Nor does the US provide free universal day care and preschool as so many of its counterparts do. Rather it funds preschool programs for the poor.

Rather than make direct payments for many welfare purposes, the US prefers to make use of the Federal Tax Code for philanthropic purposes. Gifts to charity are tax deductible. A very sizeable part of funds spent on medical care, scholarship aid, mental health services, and many other welfare programs comes from charitable donations. Low-income working people receive tax credits to offset their income tax obligations. If those credits exceed the taxes owed, they keep the difference.

The federal government also provides for the general welfare by regulating the behavior of the private sector. Federal agencies such as the Environmental Protection Agency, the Food and Drug Administration, the Occupational Safety and Health Administration, the Civil Rights Division of the Justice Department, and the Consumer Product Safety Commission have been established to enforce a variety of regulatory laws passed by Congress. The missions of these various regulatory bodies include, among others: enforcing laws to limit the air, water, and other forms of pollution emitted by factories, power plants, and automobiles; guaranteeing the safety of food, drugs, toys, and workplaces; and combating race, gender, and other forms of discrimination.

The federal government also intensively regulates various aspects of the economy. It does this in two different ways. It oversees the behavior of specific sectors such as banking and stock and bond trading to try to make sure that the firms engaged in those activities provide accurate information to customers and do not engage in excessively risky activities. It also regulates the overall functioning of the economy by controlling the money supply and setting the interest rates the government charges for the sale of government bonds.

Other rich nations engage in these same regulatory activities. But they also take aggressive actions to control labor markets and the conditions of employment. They intervene to set wages for the employees of certain industries, establish a mandatory number of vacation days, and restrict the ability of employers to fire workers. The US restricts itself to establishing a minimum wage that, in practice, only affects the lowest-paid workers. Otherwise companies are free to pay what they wish, hire and fire whom they want, and set whatever vacation policies they desire as long as they do not discriminate among workers on the basis of race, religion, national origin, gender, or age.

Controversy: Welfare versus Self-reliance

What government provides for individuals and businesses they need not provide for themselves. Ever since the creation of old-age pensions in the 1930s, every major proposal for greater government welfare aid has aroused opposition on the grounds that it diminishes the self-reliance and sense of personal responsibility of those receiving the aid. This criticism is at the heart of the controversy that arose from the bailouts of certain banks, investment houses, insurance firms, and automobile companies that took place during the financial collapse and economic recession of late 2008 and early 2009. Opponents argued that by bailing out those who made excessively risky loans, insurance contracts, and investments the government was signaling that it would do so again in the future, thus relieving the perpetrators of these risky practices of the need to act more prudently and responsibly. Likewise, the bailout of Chrysler and General Motors signaled that if a company employs a large enough number of workers, dealers, and suppliers, the government will not let it fail even if it is has failed the market test of supply and demand. Supporters of bailouts do not deny that they give the wrong message to firms; rather they argue that if major banks, insurance companies, and investment houses fail, the stock and bond markets will tumble, credit will disappear, and a wave of home foreclosures will occur. Furthermore, the auto industry is so central to the economy that the failure of the first and third largest auto companies would set off a similar wave of unemployment. So, even if bailouts risk encouraging irresponsibility, they are necessary, and in this instance were the lesser of two evils.

"Secure the Blessings of Liberty"

The American Constitution is made up of seven separate articles and twenty-seven differerent amendments. But when Americans are asked what's in the Constitution they rarely mention either the articles or the last seventeen amendments. For the average American the Constitution *is* the Bill of Rights – the rights to free speech, religion, gun ownership, property, and other liberties granted to persons and to the states in the first ten amendments. Americans have always prided themselves on being a liberty-loving people and they still do. A great theme of American political development is that of the expansion of rights to include full civil and political rights to African Americans and women. Although the Constitution contains no right to old-age pensions, social security has become such an accepted part of American life that it has more or less risen to the status of a right. In recent years, laws have been passed to greatly increase the rights enjoyed by the physically and mentally disabled. The Supreme Court has also declared that the Constitution ensures that every American enjoys a right to privacy.

Controversy: A Right to Healthcare?

In our discussions of immigration and electronic surveillance we have already commented on the problems that arise when rights clash. Another great source of controversy arises from efforts to further expand rights. The current controversy over heathcare reveals differences of opinion about how much of it Americans should have by right. Currently most Americans have health insurance. It is either a benefit they receive from their employer, tax free, or something they purchase for themselves. But many employers do not provide health insurance. Therefore many Americans are uninsured either because they cannot afford to buy it or they are young and healthy enough that they would rather go without it.

Even if one agrees that healthcare is a right of all Americans what does that right actually entitle one to? Breakthroughs in modern medicine have greatly expanded the possible meanings of healthcare. Laser surgery enables tennis players with knee problems to be back on the court in a few weeks. Viagra extends the active sex life of men into their old age. Fertility treatment enables women to get pregnant later in life. Botox eliminates wrinkles. Does everyone have a right to all these forms of healthcare? Some argue that the right to healthcare is limited to "no frills" items like checkups and catastrophic illness or trauma. Others argue that virtually any form of physical or mental correction or enhancement should be available to all Americans regardless of income, especially since the government provides much of the funding that goes into the discovery and development of the chemicals and techniques that make such enhancements possible.

"Establish Justice"

We save "Establish Justice" for last because for two of the three dominant schools of contemporary American political thinking it is very closely tied to goals we have already discussed. *Libertarians* would argue that establishing justice means the same thing as securing the blessings of liberty. They would consider justice to mean what the Declaration of Independence posits as the right to "pursue happiness." Justice is not something that government grants; rather, it is the opportunity to make the best of things on one's own, free of government interference. *Liberals* would link the establishment of justice to providing for the general welfare. They consider that a society is just only if it assists those who have not had a fair chance to pursue happiness because they are poor, female, or members of racial, religious, or ethnic minorities. They demand that government do more than refrain from interfering in the race of life. They want it to act affirmatively to ensure that all handicaps have been removed so that the race is run fairly. Only *conservatives* view the establishment of justice as a distinct aim of politics. Conservatives are often lumped together with libertarians because they too oppose government policies aimed at redistributing wealth and subsidizing the poor. Both fear that such policies undermine self-reliance and personal responsibility. But unlike libertarians, conservatives seek to use government to establish justice by upholding moral virtue and combating moral decay.

Controversy: Permit, Subidize, or Ban Abortion

These differing views of justice crystallize in the debate over abortion. Libertarians support unfettered access to abortion, believing that women should have the freedom to control what is done to their bodies. They oppose the attempts by conservatives to moralize the issue. Most liberals also oppose restrictions on abortion but as a matter of justice they also insist that the government subsidize abortions for those too poor to afford them. Many conservatives consider abortion to be immoral and therefore they want government to ban it or at least establish restrictive conditions to control it, including requiring pregnant minors to discuss the matter with their parents and with the prospective father.

The Institutions of Government

Afer setting out the aims of American government in the Preamble, the Constitution proceeds to establish specific institutions designed to carry out those aims. The Constitution creates three branches of government: the executive, headed by the president (see Chapter 8), the legislative, comprised of two separate branches of Congress – the House of Representatives and the Senate (see Chapter 7) – and the judicial, comprised of a system of federal courts presided over by the Supreme Court (see Chapter 9).

Each of these branches has its own duties, and this allocation of responsibilities is known as the *separation of powers*. Each branch is also granted specific means for intruding into the workings of the others. This system of intrusions is referred to as *checks and balances*. Thus, the president has the power to veto bills passed by Congress. The House of Representatives can *impeach* the president and the Senate may then vote to remove him from office. The Senate must confirm certain presidential appointments, most especially appointments to the federal courts and to the president's cabinet. Although the Constitution does not explicitly provide for it, the Supreme Court has acquired the power to declare acts of Congress and actions of the president unconstitutional.

The following is a brief sketch of each of the three branches of the federal government. The sketches display both continuity and change. They depict critical ways in which the three branches adhere to the constitutional blueprint. They also describe departures from that blueprint and raise the question of whether or not those departures violate the spirit of checks and balances.

Congress

Article I grants *Congress* the exclusive power to legislate. All the laws of the United States must pass both houses of Congress – the *House of Representatives* and the *Senate*. If the president vetoes a bill approved by Congress, both houses must reapprove the measure by a two-thirds vote for it to become law. All bills having to do with raising revenue must first pass the House of Representatives before being eligible for consideration by the Senate. The Senate reviews all cabinet, court, and diplomatic appointments made by the president and must consent to them.

Congresspersons also engage in many activities not discussed in the Constitution. They provide diverse services to their constituents including help with immigration problems and with difficulties in obtaining veterans, social security, and other forms of benefits that constituents believe they qualify for. Congress also engages in extensive oversight of executive agencies. It holds hearings and calls executive officials to testify and to defend their actions. Although the Constitution does not specifically grant such powers to Congress, they may well be defended as constituting important checks on the executive, preventing it from dealing arbitrarily or unfairly with citizens or evading the letter or the spirit of laws passed by Congress. Congress's capacity to adequately check executive excess is more fully discussed in Chapter 7.

The President

Congress legislates, but it no longer serves as the only or even perhaps the most important initiator of legislative proposals. The role of chief legislator has passed to the *president.* He often sets the legislative agenda and uses his enormous political influence to press for passage of legislation he favors and to fight against legislation he opposes.

This shift in the nature of legislative leadership is but one aspect of a broad increase in the expansion of the president's political importance. The president commands the bulk of the attention that the media pays to national political affairs. His speeches are televised. His travels and activities are reported on in minute detail. Presidential elections are by far the most important and celebrated of all national political events. The Constitution makes the president commander in chief of the armed forces, but in addition to acquiring the power of legislator in chief he has now also become political celebrity in chief. Only the most popular entertainers and athletes can claim a similar level of fame.

Celebrity poses both opportunities and problems for the president. It enables him to command public attention more or less at will and thus enables him to communicate more successfully with the citizenry than anyone else. But it also greatly increases the public's expectations of what he can accomplish. If the economy declines, the public is ready to blame him even though he may not necessarily be in a position to do anything about it. The impact of this expansion of the president's role on the system of checks and balances will be discussed more fully in Chapter 8.

The Supreme Court

Article III of the Constitution creates a federal court system, culminating in a *Supreme Court,* that is responsible for "all cases arising under the Constitution." The federal courts do indeed hear and decide cases involving disputes between states, disputes that take place at sea, and a host of other questions that are clearly beyond the capacity of any state court to deal with. But the Supreme Court in particular has also taken on two enormous responsibilities that the Constitution does not specifically give it. It decides whether acts of Congress and of the president are constitutional or not. During the Bush administration the Court overruled actions of both the president and Congress regarding the War on Terror.

The Supreme Court has also taken on the power to declare the existence of rights not enumerated in the Bill of Rights. For example, in declaring unconstitutional a Connecticut law that made it a crime to sell or use contraception because the law violated the right to privacy, it admitted that the Constitution mentions no such right. Rather, it argued, the spirit of a right to privacy pervades the document as a whole. Defenders of these rulings view them as critical both to checking congressional and presidential excess and protecting the people's liberties. Critics charge that these decisions undermine the Constitution by allowing the Court to usurp legislative and executive authority as well as to short-circuit the constitutional amendment process by rewriting the Constitution itself. This controversy over the Court's role in the checks and balances system will be taken up more fully in Chapter 9

A Request

As the reader now proceeds to the fuller account of American government and politics that this chapter has introduced, we urge that in addition to trying to understand how politics works, the reader also try to appreciate politics. Because no person is an island, politics is inescapable. We must live with the collective decisions made in our midst whether we choose to participate in them or not. Inescapable yes, tedious no. Politics combines the suspense of sports with the colorful array of characters found in great literature. Savor its richness, its dramatic intensity, and its capacity to surprise.

CHAPTER SUMMARY

* Key building blocks of American politics include: the influence of political speech, the role of political leaders, the dynamics of political competition, and the functioning of political institutions.
* The American polity is best understood to be a democratic republic.
* The United States is a federal union in which both the states and the national government exercise considerable powers.

* The American Constitution prescribes limited government based on enumerated powers and seeks to create a system of checks and balances between the different branches of government.
* American political development is an approach to the study of politics and government that proceeds historically in order to illuminate how the past affects the present and future.
* The past strongly influences the present because of how political institutions work and how individuals think about politics and government. Three key aspects of political development are: political memory, path dependency, and critical choices.
* Path dependency means that once a way of doing things has been set in motion a considerable inertia develops that encourages the continuation of that course.
* Americans have made critical choices that shifted America's political path.
* The battle over immigration is not one between right and wrong but between different conceptions of rights – the right to enter a free society versus the right of those already there to protect their quality of life by defining the terms and conditions of entry.
* Unlike most other countries, the United States has no national police force. The ordinary tasks of "insuring domestic tranquility" such as preventing and solving crimes, regulating traffic, and controlling crowds are performed by state and local police.
* With the collapse of the Soviet Union, the US has become the world's sole superpower. Its military strength dwarfs that of any other nation.
* Historically, the United States took a very different approach to providing for the general welfare than did other advanced republican democracies, but those differences have diminished considerably in recent decades.
* A great theme of American political development is that of the expansion of rights to include full civil and political rights to African Americans and women. In recent years laws have been passed to greatly increase the rights enjoyed by the physically and mentally disabled.
* A key difference between libertarians, liberals, and conservatives regards their views of justice.

SUGGESTED READINGS

Bryce, James. *The American Commonwealth.* Indianapolis, IN: Liberty Fund, 1996.

Chesterton, G. K. *What I Saw in America.* New York: Dodd Mead, 1923.

Crenson, Matthew A., Ginsberg, Benjamin. *Downsizing Democracy: How America Sidelined its Citizens and Privatized its Public*, Baltimore: Johns Hopkins University Press, 2002.

Croly, Herbert. *Progressive Democracy.* New York: Transaction, 1998.

Hamilton, Alexander, James Madison, and John Jay. *The Federalist Papers*, ed. Charles Kesler. New York: Mentor Books, 1999.

Hartz, Louis. *The Liberal Tradition in America*, 2nd edn. New York: Harvest Books, 1991.

Heclo, Hugh. *On Thinking Institutionally*, Boulder, CO: Paradigm Publishers 2008.

Lowi, Theodore. *The End of Liberalism*, 2nd edn. New York: W. W. Norton, 1979.

McWilliams, Wilson Carey. *The Idea of Fraternity in America*. Berkeley: University of California Press, 1973.

Morone, James. *Democratic Wish: Democratic Participation and the Limits of American Government*, rev. edn. New Haven, CT: Yale University Press, 1998.

Orren, Karen, and Stephen Skowronek. *The Search for American Political Development*. New York: Cambridge University Press, 2004.

Pierson, Paul. *Politics in Time: History, Institutions, and Social Analysis*. Princeton, NJ: Princeton University Press, 2004.

Putnam, Robert *Bowling Alone: The Collapse and Revival of American Community*, New York: Simon & Schuster, 2000.

Schuck, Peter H., and Wilson, James Q. *Understanding America: The Anatomy of an Exceptional Nation*. Washington, DC: Brookings Institution Press, 2006.

Smith, Rogers M. *Civic Ideals: Conflicting Visions of Citizenship in the United States*. New Haven, CT: Yale University Press, 1999.

Storing, Herbert, ed. *The Complete Anti-Federalist*. University of Chicago Press, 1981.

Tocqueville, Alexis de. *Democracy in America*, ed. Harvey Mansfield and Delba Winthrop. University of Chicago Press, 2000.

Part I
Formative Experiences

2 Political Culture

CHAPTER OVERVIEW

This chapter focuses on:

- **A contemporary portait of American political culture.**
- **The cornerstones of American political culture: communitarianism, classic liberalism, and democratic egalitarianism.**
- **The debate about separating from the mother country.**
- **The critical choice to declare a creed.**
- **Violations of the American creed: slavery and denial of women's rights.**
- **The push towards a more powerful union: centralization, nationalism, and mixed government.**

The Declaration of Independence does not say "all *Americans* are created equal." It extends the promise of equality and of the inalienable rights attached to it to all men, meaning all people. In a series of speeches in the days and weeks following September 11, 2001, President George W. Bush argued that the terrorist attacks on the World Trade Center and Pentagon were not merely acts of senseless destruction but direct challenges to the universal principles of human freedom that the Declaration defined.

Three days after the attack, speaking at a prayer service at the National Cathedral, the president explained that the War on Terror was about nothing less than the future of human freedom and that defending freedom was America's oldest responsibility and greatest tradition: "In every generation, the world has produced enemies of human freedom. They have attacked America, because we are freedom's home and defender. And the commitment of our fathers is now the calling of our time."

The following week, addressing a joint session of Congress, he explained why America in particular had been the target of the attacks: "Why do they hate us? They hate us for what we see here in this chamber – a democratically elected government. Their leaders are self-appointed. They hate our freedoms – our freedom of religion, our freedom of speech, our freedom to vote and assemble and disagree with each other."

He told the members of Congress that the War on Terror was not merely to protect American lives and property but to defend the universal principles at the heart of the American creed: "Freedom and fear are at war ... The advance of human freedom now depends on us."

In early November, President Bush addressed the United Nations to impress upon the peoples of the world that America's fight was their fight as well because the natural rights at stake belonged to everyone.

> [T]he dreams of mankind are defined by liberty, the natural right to create and build and worship and live in dignity ... These aspirations are lifting up the peoples of Europe, Asia, Africa and the Americas, and they can lift up all of the Islamic world. We stand for the permanent hopes of humanity, and those hopes will not be denied.

In his January 2002 State of the Union address, he spoke of how America was once again being called upon to play a "unique role in human events," a role first recognized by John Winthrop when he announced that the New World was "a city upon a hill," a beacon of freedom beamed at a world threatened by despotism.

There are many different approaches that Bush could have chosen for explaining to the American people what the problem was and how the government would respond. His decision to so strongly emphasize issues of human freedom and natural rights provides an important clue to just how deeply embedded such ideas are in what this chapter calls American political culture. *Political culture* refers to the core beliefs in a society. These central beliefs forge a people – "We the People," as the preamble to the Constitution reads – from a large and diverse society. The first chapter discussed the concept of path dependence. This chapter describes how these core beliefs that have persisted throughout the course of American political development were forged. After painting a portrait of American political culture, it examines its three cornerstones, *communitarianism*, *classic liberalism*, and *democratic egalitarianism*, and the key differences between them. It examines the debate among the colonists about whether to fight for independence, and invites the reader to decide whether the Loyalists or the revolutionaries made a better case. It explains that unlike other nations, American government is grounded in a creed, stated in the Declaration of Independence. It describes the two great stains on that creed, slavery and the subjugation of women. It shows that in the aftermath of the American Revolution the tensions between the three strands of American political culture bubbled to the surface, and describes how the political crisis arising from those tensions led to a push for a more powerful union.

American Political Culture: A Contemporary Portrait

American political culture is in many respects similar to the United States' sister rich democratic nations in Europe. Like them, Americans believe in a political system that is free, democratic, and respectful of minority rights. They all believe that people should be tolerant of religious ethnic and cultural diversity, and that individuals should be judged on their merits, not on what family they come from or what ethnic group they belong to. They also share a strong skepticism about the national government and other large institutions, especially corporations. However, there are critical cultural, economic, and political matters about which American opinion departs from those of its closest relatives. These departures combine to form a political culture that is highly distinctive and help to account for the critical political and policy differences between the United States and other mature democracies that this book will explore in later chapters.

Americans are far more patriotic than citizens of those countries. They are more likely to display pride in their country and to say that they would prefer to live in America than elsewhere. Americans are also more likely to believe that American culture is superior to other cultures. Germans are almost as likely to proclaim cultural superiority, but only a third of Britons and a quarter of the French do so (www.pewglobal.org/files/2011/11/Trend-Table.pdf).

Americans believe that the fundamental principles and attributes of American society are sound even though they are highly critical of specific governmental institutions, especially Congress and the bureaucracy. Americans are proud of their particular ethnic, religious, and racial identities. And yet most Americans identify themselves as "just Americans" (Jack Cirtrin and David O. Sears, *American Identity and the Politics of Multiculturalism*, Cambridge University Press, 2014, pp. 153–4).

Americans are also more optimistic about their futures than Europeans. This optimism is also reflected in the greater willingness of Americans to bring children into the world. The US birthrate is higher than that of any other developed country except Ireland and New Zealand (www.cia.gov/library/publications/the-world-factbook/rankorder/2054rank.html).

Americans also have a much stronger conviction that they control their own destinies. Only a third of Americans say that "success in life is determined by outside forces" whereas 72 percent of Germans, 57 percent of the French, and 41 percent of the British agree with that statement. Americans differ from their sister democratic republics in their understanding of the proper relationship between the individual and the government. Only about a third of Americans think that the government should play an active role so that nobody is in need whereas almost two-thirds of French and Germans and half of Britons think it should (www.pewglobal.org/files/2011/11/Trend-Table.pdf).

Like their European counterparts, Americans value equality. But they are far more likely to define equality in terms of equal opportunity rather than equal result. Most Europeans claim that government should reduce the gap between the rich and the poor. Most Americans disagree. They are less likely to see income inequality as unfair because they are more likely to interpret such inequality as resulting from differences in talent, ambition, and effort. They are more likely than Europeans to see poverty as resulting from laziness and passivity more than from bad luck. Although they profess an appreciation for diversity, they oppose the use of racial, gender, or ethnic quotas as a means for achieving it. Individual merit is the only acceptable grounds for attaining professional and economic success. Freedom for the individual is considered a superior objective to social equality. Even those racial minorities, African Americans and Hispanics, that have experienced significant economic discrimination are more likely than Europeans to believe that they can and will better themselves economically and that individuals are responsible for their own destiny.

Americans are far more religious than Europeans. Fifty percent of Americans say religion was very important to them compared to only 21 percent of Germans, 17 percent of Britons, and 13 percent of the French (www.pewglobal.org/files/2011/11/Trend-Table.pdf). Americans are also far more likely than Europeans to agree that "it is necessary to believe in God to be moral." They are also far more likely to profess the moral values that religion inspires. In the United States, it is less common for a man and a woman to live together as a couple without being married. Prostitution is illegal in forty-nine states. Many towns and counties ban the sale of alcohol. The differences in moral attitudes between Europe and the US were evident in the public reaction to President Clinton's sexual encounters with a young woman who was serving as his intern. In the United States there was shock and outrage. The case figured significantly in the bill of impeachment brought against him by the House of Representatives. The same news was greeted in Europe with a combination of unconcern and amusement at Americans' lack of sophistication. By European standards, Americans appear "puritanical."

In summary, compared to Europeans, Americans are:

More patriotic
More optimistic
Less positive about an active government
Less concerned about income inequality
More religious
More individualistic

Thus although their levels of education and wealth are roughly equal to those of Europeans countries, Americans are not nearly as "modern" in their beliefs. If by "modern" one means irreligion, a relativistic attitude toward other cultures, a nonjudgemental attitude regarding sexual conduct, and a desire for the government to provide for one's needs. The more traditional religious and moral principles that Americans adhere to are usually associated with premodern social arrangments based on family ties and social caste. One might therefore expect Americans to have stronger ties to family and place, and to expect that their lot in life will be no better than that of their parents. Yet Americans are the most staunchly individualistic, the most likely to move away from home, and have the strongest commitments to free and open economic competition of any rich nation. The answer to how such varied and even contradictory attitudes have come to coexist lies in the origins and early development of American political culture, and the two very different cornerstones on which it has been built.

Communitarianism

The first cornerstone of American political culture was deposited by the original English settlers of Massachusetts, a full century and a half before the American Revolution. They are known as Puritans because of their commitment to purifying Protestantism. Their approach put them at odds with the Church of England, whose members were known as Anglicans. Although Anglicans were also Protestants, they did not accept the radical version of it that the Puritans preached.

Puritan religious understanding was grounded in the thought of the great theologian John Calvin (1509–64), who was born a Frenchman but who lived most of his life in Geneva. Calvin's defining principle was that because humankind was so deeply sinful, individuals could not, on their own, redeem themselves in the eyes of God and bring about their own salvation. Salvation was something that only God could bestow. Calvin condemned the Roman Catholic Church because it preached that through confession, penance, and good works a person could be saved and expect to go to heaven, a view that the Church of England shared. One might imagine that a rejection of good works would cause Calvinists to become selfish and self-indulgent, but the Puritans' interpretation of the impossibility of saving themselves led in just the opposite direction. They determined to create a covenant with God in which they would pledge to act as righteously as possible and to be single-minded in their devotion to Him.

A covenant is not a contract. It puts God under no obligation. The totality of the Puritan commitment came with no strings attached. Individuals did not enter the covenant; it was entered into by the entire congregation, hence the origin of the term "congregationalist." And, because any one member could destroy the covenant, each congregant had to accept responsibility for the behavior of every other member. They were each their brothers' and sisters' keeper. The congregation was comprised of the entire community. The idea of the covenant therefore established a political community in which every person had a critical role to play and the good of the whole took precedence over that of any one individual. Thus what was initially a religious commitment came to have great political significance encouraging high levels of political participation in the Puritan communities and a strong commitment to the principle of the common good. Local self-government was integrally linked to religious virtue.

America appealed to the Puritans precisely because it was a new land that had not been corrupted by the decadent and heretical forms of Christianity that dominated the Church of England. In a speech entitled "A Model of Christian Charity," John Winthrop, the first governor of Massachusetts, gave voice to the Puritan mission, suggesting that England would soon take heed of what they were accomplishing in the New World: "For we must consider that we shall be as a city upon a hill, the eyes of all people are upon us." Thus the Puritan mission was twofold: to establish a religious community pleasing in the eyes of God, and to provide the mother country with a shining example of how she could mend her ways. The Puritans thus bequeathed to later Americans both a strong commitment to democratic solidarity and a deep sense of America as an exemplary nation with a mission to encourage others to adopt its freedom-loving ways.

The Puritans did not dominate American religion. However, their community spirit, denigration of materialism, and commitment to serving as a beacon to the godless became critical elements of American political culture, which was bolstered by the continuing overall strength of American religious life.

Because the American colonies were a haven for religious dissenters, no one church dominated life in the colonies.. Religious freedom strengthened religious influence on American society. It cultivated the belief that churches did not threaten individual liberty, as was the case in feudal Europe, but protected it. Shorn of state sponsorship, churches became strong, independent institutions that contributed significantly to the emergence of a distinctive American culture. The Anglican Church in America, painfully weaned from government support, became the Episcopal Church. After the Revolution, Roman Catholics previously under the administration of the vicar apostolic of England came under the authority of Father John Carroll of Baltimore, named in 1789 the first American Roman Catholic bishop. Lutherans, Presbyterians, Quakers, Jews, Baptists a few decades later, and Methodists thrived along with the Congregationalists.

The strength of American religious institutions and religious attachments tempered the individualism fostered by the second cornerstone of American political culture, Classic Liberalism. Christian principles of fellowship and charity were enfused into daily life. Tocqueville observed, "While the law allows the American people to do everything, there are things which religion prevents them from imagining and forbids them to dare." The actual conditions of life in the colonies reinforced and strengthened the strong sense of community and commitment to local self-government that the Puritans pioneered. Although the colonies were officially subservient to Britain, the vast ocean separating them from Britain, combined with the mother country's preoccupation with European affairs, sapped Britain of the capacity and energy to effectively govern them. They had no choice but to govern themselves.

As Tocqueville observed, this relentless need to cope with the practicalities of their common life helped them develop the "habits of the heart," the feelings of mutual respect, sympathy, and obligation needed to live successfully together. Thus, emotions and sentiments were joined to religious and political principle to encourage successful self-government. No aspect of community life was more important in developing such habits of the heart than the jury. Jury service plucked people out of their ordinary private life and forced them to think and deliberate about matters of great import to the community. Jurors had to decide whether a person was guilty of a crime and should therefore be imprisoned or even executed. In civil matters they had to sort out the relative merits of the claims made by those who brought suit and those against whom the suit was brought. Tocqueville recognized that such a challenging responsibility was the best way for ordinary people to develop the skills and sentiments that self-government required. He called juries "the schoolrooms of democracy."

Classic Liberalism

The second cornerstone of American political culture consisted of a set of political philosophical principles developed by the great seventeenth-century and early eighteenth-century British political philosophers Thomas Hobbes, John Locke, and David Hume and the great French political philosopher Baron de Montesquieu. Its fundamental principles are *natural rights* and government as a *social contract.* It asserts that people live completely freely, on their own, until they chose to make a contract with one another to form a government. They make the contract because on their own they cannot protect their natural rights to live free of oppression and violent death and to enjoy their property. Those entering the contract promise to give up their freedom to do exactly as they wish in return for the promise that government will protect their natural rights. If the government fails to secure their rights, they are free to dissolve the contract and return to their prior natural state of complete freedom.

The term "Classic Liberalism" should not be confused with Liberalism as the term is currently used. Liberalism in its modern guise connotes a belief in using the national government to achieve benevolent purposes. It is directly at odds with Classic Liberalism's stress on limited government. *Modern Liberalism* has far more in common with Progressivism, a political viewpoint we will discuss in Chapter 4. The shift from the older to the newer meaning of liberalism was promoted by Franklin Delano Roosevelt (FDR), who deemed it more politically prudent to shed the "Progressive" label and call his defense of an activist ambitious national government "Liberalism." FDR's impact on American politics will be discussed in Chapters 4 and 8.

Classic Liberalism's rights-based approach was a sharp departure from earlier political philosophical traditions. Like Communitarianism, those had stressed the duties and obligations owed to the political community and/or the Church rather than the rights of individuals. Traditionally, people conceived of themselves as members of a greater whole – a clan, a tribe, a city, a congregation – not as solitary persons. Hobbes and Locke influenced the American Founders to believe that everyone is born endowed with a right to live as one pleases and therefore the community may not trample on those rights unless the individual does harm to others. This view of government as a contract between free individuals was in stark contrast to the Puritan concept of covenant. The purpose of the covenant was to commit to collective obligations. The purpose of the social contract was to protect individual rights. American political culture absorbed both of these contradictory points of view and the tensions between them continue to animate American political life.

Classic Liberals recognized the difficulties of maintaining and perpetuating a political order dedicated to individual freedom. Their knowledge of history informed them that the right to life and liberty was constantly being trampled as a result of the lust of kings and nobles for power and glory and the competing claims of different religions to provide the sole path to salvation. To counter these threats it was necessary to encourage people to find satisfaction in pursuits that did not so readily stimulate them to oppress and kill one another. Therefore, Classic Liberals encouraged people to enjoy their private lives; to seek comfort and happiness from their work and their recreation and to satisfy their competitive instincts by vying with one another in the marketplace rather than on the battlefield. They believed that the pursuit of wealth, comfort, and security would prove less threatening to liberty than the pursuit of glory or salvation.

Previously, the world of business had been looked down upon. Soldiers and churchmen were seen as far nobler than those engaged in "mere" trade. The Classic Liberals sought to elevate the prestige of business in order to encourage ambitious and energetic men to enter this "safe" profession rather than to expend their energies and talents on warmongering and theological disputation. Furthermore, to succeed in business they would need to develop talents and habits far more conducive to political peace and stability than those associated with soldiering and religious disputation. The traits of frugality, prudence, patience, and temperance necessary to commercial success were also more conducive to preserving a decent political order than the swagger and recklessness of the soldier or the intolerant single-mindedness of the religious zealot. Imagination, inventiveness, and ambition were also highly prized as long as they were channeled in a practical, marketable direction, toward increasing human wellbeing and comfort. Thus, even as Americans were encouraged to view themselves as idealistic residents of a "city on a hill," they were also coming to appreciate the value of the private pursuit of gain.

The Classic Liberals sought to organize governmental affairs to protect liberty. Montesquieu in particular stressed the importance of a separation of powers among the executive, legislative, and judiciary. But he also believed that the peaceful and liberty-loving habits created through a devotion to commerce were a necessary complement to political protections if natural rights were to be preserved. A liberal republic would need to be a commercial republic.

Because Americans were highly literate, Classic Liberal ideas spread rapidly and widely during the eighteenth century. Newspapers flourished in all the cities and towns of any size. Large cities established publishing houses of their own. Even if they did not read the actual writings of Hobbes, Locke, Hume, and Montesquieu, the settlers were exposed to classical liberal ideas in a welter of books and articles written by disciples of these philosophers. These popularizations were devoted to making the key principles of classical liberalism accessible and attractive to the ordinary reader. Classic Liberal ideas were especially appealing to British Americans because, unlike the people they left behind, a large percentage of the males among them owned some property and participated in town governments, criminal and civil juries, and colonial assemblies.

These first two cornerstones of American political culture differed in crucial respects. The Puritan community existed to please God and therefore life in common was devoted to spiritual, virtuous ends. Classic liberals conceived of the goals of politics and government in a less exhalted light. People chose to live in common not to achieve noble ends but to preserve their life, liberty, and property. Puritans placed the wellbeing of the community as a whole above that of its individual members. Classic Liberalism was individualistic at its core. The Puritans and the local governments they spawned governed themselves democratically. Town meetings were open to all eligible members of the community, and decisions were made by majority vote. The quintessential local political institution, the jury, was chosen from among the citizenry. By contrast, the most influential Classic Liberal thinker, John Locke, argued that the people could consent to place the hands of government in a monarchy (rule of one), aristocracy (rule of few), or democracy (rule of the many). Fearing that unlimited democracy would lead to mob rule and the deprivation of liberty, he preferred a mixed government in which rule by the many was checked by other institutions that retained monarchic and aristocratic aspects.

Despite the deep differences in outlook between Puritans and Classic Liberals, they also shared important similarities that allowed them to coexist and to influence one another. Unlike supporters of feudalism or hereditary monarchy, they both believed that government was only legitimate if it was based on the willingness of the individual to be governed. Membership in the Puritan

Table 2.1. Puritanism and Classic Liberalism.

Puritanism	Classic Liberalism
• Commitment to community solidarity • Sense of America as an exemplary nation • Impulse to encourage community spirit, denigrate materialism, and serve as a beacon to the godless	• Shifts from focus on duties to focus on rights • Views of government as a contract between individuals based on consent • Promotes pursuit of private interest in the name of protecting liberty

community was voluntary; you could leave it, or you could be expelled from it. In that sense it was not completely different from the liberal idea of a government formed by individuals who have agreed to join in order to protect their rights.

Separation from the Mother Country

The decision to fight for independence from Britain was indeed a difficult one. The vast majority of colonists were of British descent and had always considered themselves to be British. They knew that the English were far freer than any other people and that in the absence of the protection of the British army and navy they would be at great risk of being conquered by a far less benevolent colonial power, most likely France or Spain. Yet, in 1776 the Continental Congress, composed of representatives of the thirteen colonies, voted for independence. By that time the colonists had come to harbor a number of serious grievances regarding their treatment by the mother country. For the first 150 years of their existence they paid no taxes to Britain. Then, in the wake of the French and Indian War, Britain imposed a series of taxes. The first, known as the Stamp Act, imposed a tax on a wide variety of print matter that included playing cards, newspapers, and various documents. Later, the tax on tea precipitated the Boston Tea Party. Another source of resentment on the part of colonists involved the British Parliament's effort to curtail juries. Because it did not believe that colonial juries were sufficiently willing to convict fellow colonists charged with evading paying customs duties, it sought to exempt such cases from jury trial. As we have seen, juries were a pillar of local self-government, and yet the British government was depriving them of much of their importance.

A reasonable case can be made for either the choice to revolt or to remain loyal to Britain. In the French and Indian War, British troops fought to protect American colonists. The war was expensive and therefore Britain felt that it was only fair to make the colonists help pay for it. Smuggling was indeed quite common in the colonies, and juries often did treat such cases with great indulgence. Nonetheless, the two cornerstones of American political culture fed the colonists sense of outrage at such aggressions. According to Classic Liberalism, government was formed to secure rights, including a right to property. Taxes were a form of reducing a person's property and therefore required a person's consent. But the colonists were not represented in the British Parliament and therefore were not granted the opportunity to give or withhold their consent. Colonists were also devoted communitarians and feared that the restrictions Britain had already imposed on local self-government was just the beginning of concerted effort to turn them from citizens into subjects.

Perhaps the most articulate and impressive of those who sought to remain loyal to Britain was Thomas Hutchinson of Massachusetts. Hutchinson was a direct descendant of very early Puritan settlers. He took an active part in the political life of the colony, rising to be governor. He adhered to Classic Liberal principles. Indeed, his opposition to revolution was derived from the deepest of Classic Liberal principles, the protection of personal security. He argued that the real choice for Americans was not between remaining with Britain or becoming independent. As victory in the French and Indian war had so recently demonstrated, Britain was the protector of the safety of Americans. Separating from Britain would not produce anarchy but rather subjugation to a far less benevolent, liberty-loving great power. Hutchinson admitted that taxation without representation was unfair. But he reminded colonists that their protests against the Stamp Act had led Parliament to rescind it. Surely, if the colonists protested responsibly, Parliament could be made to rescind the taxes it had more recently imposed, including the odious tax on tea. And even if those efforts failed, the taxes imposed on the colonies were less than those paid by Englishmen, and were simply not that much of a burden. Colonists remained the freest people in the world. Even unfair taxes and some limits on trial by jury were a small price to pay for the protection required to continue to remain so free. Rights are never absolute. There will always be some limitation on them required for the sake of preserving security. The right to self-preservation is the most basic of natural rights; it is wrong to put one's life in danger simply to prevent some relative limitation of one's other rights.

CRITICAL THINKING QUESTION

Reasonable Americans could and did differ about whether to separate from Britain. The Cambridge University Press website contains excerpts from the writings of prominent supporters of independence, including excerpts from an essay by Hutchinson. You are invited to read these writings, summarize what you consider to be the best arguments made by each side, and explain why you chose to be a Revolutionary or a Loyalist.

CRITICAL CHOICE: DECLARING A CREED – THE DECLARATION OF INDEPENDENCE

The United States was the first nation to declare a creed. It is propounded in the Declaration's second sentence. "We hold these truths to be self-evident, that all men are created equal, that they are endowed by their Creator with certain unalienable Rights, that among these are Life Liberty and the Pursuit of Happiness." Each element of the creed embodies Classic Liberalism. The term "men" in the language of the eighteenth century meant "persons". All persons were equal because they each voluntarily gave up the equal freedom they enjoyed in the state of nature in order to join together to secure their rights. Those rights were unalienable, meaning that no one could legitimately take them away. The first and most basic of those rights was life, the guarantee that government would not harm you and would protect you against threats to your security. Second was liberty, freedom to think and do as one pleased and to take part in a free government. The third is somewhat harder to interpret. Classic Liberals had declared a right to property. Jefferson would have understood "pursuit of happiness" to include a right to protection of one's property. But he wanted to express something more ambitious and exalted, a fair chance to succeed in life. Perhaps the closest modern equivalent of the phrase "pursuit of happiness" would be "equal opportunity." There is no promise that one will succeed, but one is entitled to a fair chance to realize one's ambitions.

The status of the *Declaration of Independence* as the American creed is attested to by the choice of July 4, the date it was issued, as the nation's official birthday, rather than July 2, the date of the Continental Congress vote for independence. Thus, the principles justifying the revolution were exhalted above the revolutionary act itself.

All the members of the Continental Congress signed the Declaration, even though it officially required only the signature of the Congress's president, John Hancock. Hancock's signature was the largest to appear at the end of the Declaration – to save King George III the trouble, he noted cheekily, of putting on his reading glasses. The other members of Congress, embracing their president's rebellious spirit, added their names. After all, the Declaration was no mere official document, but "an avowal of revolution." In making their signatures part of such a dangerous state paper, the members of the Continental Congress took a solemn oath as citizens of a new government. They gave the first official display of the American political community. As the last sentence of the document read, "for the support of this declaration, with a firm reliance on the protection of divine providence, we mutually pledge to each other our lives, our fortunes, and our sacred honor."

The gravity of this pledge was demonstrated by the manner in which the Declaration was publicized. It was read before groups of people in public ceremonies. The mobilization of British soldiers on American soil for the purpose of suppressing the incipient rebellion added solemnity to these occasions. With this menace in mind, Congress directed that the Declaration should be proclaimed not only in all the colonies but also by the head of the army.

On July 9, General George Washington ordered officers of the Continental Army brigades stationed in New York City to obtain copies of the Declaration from the Adjutant General's Office. Then, with the British soldiers "constantly in view, upon and at Staten-Island," as one participant recalled, the brigades were "formed in hollow squares on their respective parades," where they heard the Declaration read.

Enshrining Classic Liberalism in the Declaration of Independence did not force Americans to come down from "the city on a hill." The habits of the heart that the Puritans had first imparted still exerted their influence on political life. American political culture continued to rest on these first two often conflicting cornerstones.

UPSHOT

Although other nations enable immigrants from other countries to become citizens, in practice, immigrants have a very hard time fitting into the lives of nations for whom citizenship has traditionally been based on blood and common culture. In America, slavery excepted, adherence to the political creed embodied in the Declaration of Independence is the defining quality of what it means to be an American.

Violations of the American Creed

Slavery

Neither the Revolution itself nor the Declaration on which it grounded itself did much to remedy the two most glaring violations of the American creed, slavery and the subjugation of women. Nonetheless the Declaration proved invaluable to later advocates for abolition and for women's rights. The Declaration did not say "all white men were created equal." And, in eighteenth-century speech, the term "men" was equivalent to "persons" and therefore included women. Thus the phrase "all men are created equal" became a rallying cry for the advocates of abolition and of womens rights. It enabled them to demonstrate the hypocrisy of those who refused to treat women and African Americans equally and to deprive them of their "unalienable rights."

Virginia was the first of the English colonies, founded in 1607. Unlike Massachusetts, it was founded by seekers of wealth, not religious perfection. No sooner had it been settled than it began to deprive men and women of the fruits of their

Table 2.2. Slave population and percentage of total population of original thirteen colonies, 1770.

Colony	Slave population	Percentage
New Hampshire	654	1
Massachusetts	4,754	2
Connecticut	5,698	3
Rhode Island	3,761	6
New York	19,062	12
New Jersey	8,220	7
Pennsylvania	5,561	2
Delaware	1,836	5
Maryland	63,818	32
Virginia	187,600	42
North Carolina	69,600	35
South Carolina	75,168	61
Georgia	15,000	45

Source: W. W. Norton.

labor. Slavery was introduced in Virginia in 1620 by a Dutch ship that landed twenty Africans on the banks of the James River. Over time it spread to all the British colonies in North America. Virginia's leaders, including such great figures as George Washington, Thomas Jefferson, and James Madison, professed to believe in the key principles of Classic Liberalism, but they also owned slaves. At the time of the outbreak of the American Revolution in 1776 slavery was legal in all thirteen former colonies and there were more than half a million slaves in what was to become the United States.

Thomas Jefferson was painfully aware of the contradiction involved in a slave owner such as himself declaring that "all men were created equal" and that they had an inalienable right to liberty. He knew that slavery was wrong. He hoped that it would die out over time. But he believed that it had become too important to the livelihoods of white Southerners to be abolished. Many Southerners shared his view that slavery was a necessary evil. Jefferson did attempt to abolish the slave trade in his original draft, although Congress removed it in the final version. In a long paragraph, which John Adams admiringly called "the vehement philippic against Negro slavery," Jefferson charged King George III with waging "cruel war against human nature itself, violating its most sacred rights of life and liberty in the persons of distant people who never offended him, captivating and carrying them into slavery in another hemisphere, or to incur miserable death in their transportation thither." Jefferson further accused the British of compounding their crime of introducing slavery into the colonies by sowing seeds of rebellion among slaves. His uncharacteristically venomous prose was aimed at the "Christian king of Great Britain," who, through his subordinates in America, "was now exciting these very people to rise in arms among us, and to purchase that liberty of which he deprived them, by murdering the people upon whom he also obtruded them; thus paying off former crimes committed against the liberties of one people, with crimes which he urges them to commit against the lives of another." These are the most hollow words to be found in the Declaration. Everyone knew that the colonists themselves were responsible for the evils of slavery and therefore had to bear the responsibility for the violence and death that would occur when slaves sought their freedom. The fact that Jefferson felt compelled to deflect the blame for it from the colonists to the King reflects just how badly its claims to liberty and equality were tarnished by the perpetuation of this oppressive institution.

The Southern states resisted emancipation. Even gradual abolition would have violated the "property rights" of thousands of influential men, including Jefferson, and left the South with the unwanted task of devising a new labor system. Moreover, the South was afraid that a large population of free blacks would exact retribution, perhaps violently. Jefferson would write in 1820:

> I can say with conscious truth that there is not a man on earth who would sacrifice more than I would to relieve us from this heavy reproach in a practical way . . . But as it is, we have the wolf by the ears, and we can neither hold him, nor safely let him go. Justice is in one scale, and self-preservation on the other.

Jefferson's fears were tragically realized by the violent slave uprising led by Nat Turner, which originally was planned to begin on July 4, 1831. The revolt actually began on August 22, when a band of eight slaves led by Turner killed five members of the Travis family in Southampton, Virginia. During the next three days, the ranks of the rebels swelled to between sixty and seventy and they killed an additional fifty-eight whites in Jerusalem, Virginia. Militias caught most of the rebels within a few days, and Turner was captured on October 31. He was executed on November 11, 1831.

And yet the crucial significance of declaring "all men are created equal" was not lost on either the defenders or the opponents of slavery. John C. Calhoun of South Carolina, one of slavery's most effective champions, admitted as much in the late 1840s. He lamented that the Declaration had "spread far and wide, and fixed itself deeply in the public mind." The Declaration became a revered document, not only because its message was "popular," as Calhoun thought, but also because it articulated and affirmed the American creed. In 1852, Frederick Douglass, a former slave who had escaped bondage to become an eloquent defender of emancipation, purposely chose the Declaration's July 4th anniversary to remind Americans that they could not enslave African Americans and still be true to their creed.

> What to the American slave, is your 4th of July? I answer; a day that reveals to him, more than all the other days in the year, the gross injustice and cruelty to which he is the

> constant victim. To him your celebration is a sham; your boasted liberty an unholy license; your national greatness, swelling vanity; your sounds of rejoicing are empty and heartless; your denunciations of tyrants, brass fronted impudence; your sermons and thanksgivings, with your religious parade, and solemnity, are, to him, mere bombast, fraud, deception, impiety, and hypocrisy – a thin veil to cover up crimes which would disgrace a nation of savages.

Like Abraham Lincoln and Martin Luther King, Douglass made clear that slavery robbed the Revolution of its true meaning. As the Declaration made abundantly clear, the fight for independence was not just about separating from Great Britain but about establishing a political order devoted to liberty and equality for all.

Denying Rights to Women

When Abigail Adams urged her revolutionary husband John and his fellow rebels to "remember the ladies" or the women would "foment a revolution of their own," he did not take his wife's plea seriously. Politics, he insisted, was "not the Province of the ladies." In truth, Abigail Adams was not advocating political rights; she was advocating fairer treatment for women in the household. "Do not put such unlimited power into the hands of husbands," she wrote. "Remember all men would be tyrants if they could."

Though the Revolution did not directly alter the political status of women, it did improve their legal and educational circumstances. For example, it became somewhat easier for women to obtain divorces in the aftermath of the struggle for independence. During the colonial period, divorces were rare, but easier for men to obtain than for women. The difference did not vanish after the Revolution, but it did diminish. Before independence, no Massachusetts woman was known to have obtained a divorce on the grounds of adultery; thereafter, wives were more likely to sue errant husbands successfully.

The New Englander Judith Sargent Murray urged the cultivation of women's minds to encourage self-respect and "excellency in our sex." Her fellow reformer, Benjamin Rush, gave political expression to this view: only educated and independent-minded women, Rush argued, could raise the informed and self-reliant male citizens that a republican government demanded.This emphasis on "republican motherhood" and its potential to bestow dignity on the democratic individual had a dramatic influence on female literacy. Between 1780 and 1830, the number of colleges and secondary schools, including those for women, rose dramatically. Women's schools and colleges offered a solid academic curriculum. By 1850, there were as many literate women as men. Nonetheless, American women remained excluded from participation in political life. Most Americans considered the female's rightful place to be in the home.

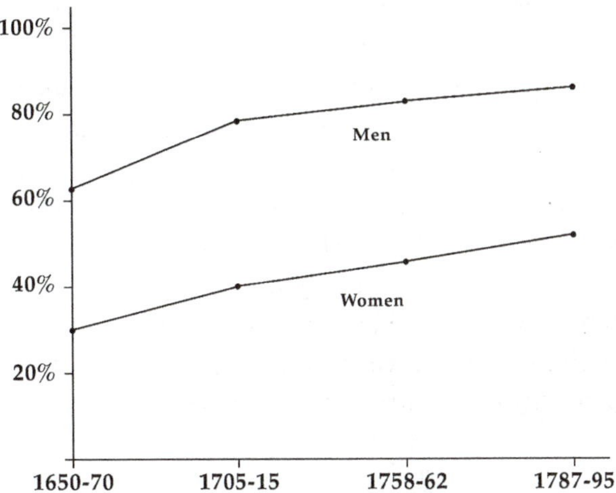

Figure 2.1. Literacy rate in Colonial New England.
Source: W. W. Norton.

Like opponents of slavery, advocates of women's rights found the Declaration a powerful text to enlist on behalf of their cause. The organizers of the first convention for women's rights, in 1848 at Seneca Falls, New York, were veterans of the antislavery movement. In preparing the convention's statement of principles and demands, Elizabeth Cady Stanton invoked the Declaration. "We hold these truths to be self-evident," the proclamation declared, "that all men and women are created equal." The Seneca Falls proclamation went on to submit "facts" to a "candid world" to prove "the history of mankind is a history of repeated injuries and usurpations on the part of man toward woman, having in direct object the establishment of an absolute tyranny over her."

Even some of the convention's leaders, such as Lucretia Mott, felt that the right to vote was too advanced for the times and would lead to ridicule of the nascent women's movement. But, Frederick Douglass, one of thirty men brave enough to attend the Seneca Falls gathering, argued convincingly that political equality was essential if women were to enjoy true freedom. The convention adopted the suffrage resolution by a small majority. The Seneca Falls Statement of Principles, as Stanton observed, "would serve three generations of women" in their fight for natural rights promised by the Declaration.

A Third Cornerstone: Democratic Egalitarianism

The Declaration did not specify the institutional forms that would best protect the rights it proclaimed. The ensuing debate about how the ex-colonies should govern themselves revealed not only ongoing tensions between Communitarianism and Classic Liberalism but also the growing influence of what would become a third political cultural cornerstone, Democratic Egalitarianism. Communitarians and Classic Liberals shared a fear of tyranny of the majority. Although the New England townships had been governed democratically, that democracy had been kept under very tight wraps. Only members of the congregation in good standing could participate. There was no room for the godless, meaning all those other Christians who did not adhere to strict Puritan theological principles. Thus, strict religious conformity served as a powerful check on democratic practice.

Prior to and during the Revolution the fear of majority tyranny receded in favor of a desire to place more power in the hands of the people. Democratic egalitarianism trumpeted majoritary rule as a virtue and adopted a much more inclusive view of who should be eligible to participate in politics.

Common Sense

A democratic understanding of revolution was given a powerful push in January of 1776 by the publication of an enormously influential and widely read political pamphlet called *Common Sense*. It was written by Thomas Paine, a newly arrived English immigrant. It was written in simple and direct language shorn of the flowery trappings characteristic of late eighteenth-century political writing. It succeeded spectacularly in its objective of reaching a mass audience. About 150,000 copies were sold in the critical period between January and July 1776. The population of the colonies at that time was roughly 2.5 million. One in seventeen people bought the pamphlet. To achieve a similar proportion of buyers, a pamphlet today would have to sell more than 15 million copies. It called for a democratic representative government with power concentrated in a large national popular assembly. The primacy of local government and the connection to religious virtue, so central to the communitarianism the Puritans had inspired, was sacrificed in the name of national majority rule. Elections would be frequent, terms short, and rotation in office required. Everything possible should be done to preserve the new government's democratic character and to surpress all monarchic tendencies. Therefore, Paine opposed the creation of any independent executive power. As the size of America grew, so should its assembly, assuring a strong relationship between the people and their representatives.

The fight for independence intensified the celebration of "the People." The line between "gentlemen" and the rest of the society, never as clear in the colonies as it was in the mother country and Europe, was radically blurred by the Revolution and its aftermath. Still, the leaders of the Revolution disagreed about how democratic the new government should be. John Adams encouraged the national and state governments to adopt, in a modified form, the British system of separated powers. Perhaps the united colonies should not have a king, but they needed a strong executive who would share power with separate legislative and judicial institutions. "Without three orders and an effectual balance between them," he wrote in 1786, America "must be destined to frequent unavoidable revolutions." Thomas Paine disagreed. He prescribed a complete departure from the British system, with its clashes between the king, the House of Lords, and the House of Commons. America should be governed by a popular assembly and organized to express the sentiments of the people.

During its first years, the new Union took a democratic direction. In the wake of the Declaration, and its charges against King George III, most of the states wrote constitutions that sought to ensure that executive power would not threaten popular liberty. In some states, the executive office, an outpost of royal administration during the colonial period, was eliminated entirely. Where an executive was provided for, governors were often given little power. They tended to be limited to one-year terms and some were not eligible for reelection. They had no authority to convene or dissolve the legislature; nor could they exercise a veto over laws passed by the assemblies. They were not allowed to appoint state officials or to manage executive branch activities.

The states vested vast authority in popular assemblies. In the spirit of Paine, the great Boston patriot Samuel Adams declared "every legislature of every colony ought to be the sovereign and uncontrollable Power within its own limits of territory." To ensure that legislatures were truly popular, state constitutions put them on a very short leash. They called for annual elections and required candidates to live in the districts they represented. Many states went so far as to assert the right of voters to instruct the men in office on how to vote on specific issues and to elect judges. No state granted universal manhood suffrage, but most substantially reduced the size of the property requirements for voting that had previously been in place.

As John Adams warned, the decisive rejection of the British system of mixed government enabled legislatures to act irresponsibly. Most telling was the inability of many state legislatures to pay their debts and provide for a stable currency. But in the wake of independence, there was little support for antimajoritarian institutional checks and balances. The revolutionary struggle, aroused by pamphlets such as *Common Sense*, made political leaders more conscious of the power of the people. Political leaders competed with each other in demonstrating their sympathy for the people - and in so doing, greatly expanded their public audience.

The Articles of Confederation

Communitarian and democratic egalitarian impulses dominated the first effort to form a national government in the United States. In fact, the Declaration of Independence referred explicitly not to the United States but to these "free and independent states." It envisioned not one large republic, which revolutionary leaders feared would be undemocratic and undermine local self-government, but a loose federation of thirteen. The first national government after the Revolution, formed after the Articles of Confederation ratified in 1781, embodied this desire to retain the full independence of the states, whose governments, as we have seen, were based on highly democratic principles.

The Articles provided for a national legislature modeled on the Continental Congress. It remained the creature of the state legislatures, which chose its members, had the power to remove them at any time, and paid their salaries and expenses. It had the authority to declare war, conduct diplomacy, coin money, regulate Indian affairs, appoint military officers, and requisition men from the states. But it had little power to fulfill these responsibilities. It could neither levy taxes nor regulate trade. The states retained the power of the purse, as well as the ultimate authority to make and administer laws.

The national government had no distinct executive branch. The president was a figurehead, a delegate chosen to preside over congressional sessions. Executive power, such as it was, rested with congressional committees, constantly changing in their membership. With no means for carrying out policies of finance, war, and foreign policy, the national government's power was extremely limited.

The Articles' decentralist approach came under increased criticism due to the various governmental failings that increasingly came to threaten the viability of the Union. The Continental Congress had also relied on the states, but its dependence occurred during wartime, which made the states relatively willing to provide men and money for the common defense. But such a loose alliance of states proved far less practical during peacetime. From 1781 to 1786, for example, Congress requested $15 million from the states to carry out its foreign and domestic responsibilities, but received only $2.5 million.

The absence of national power also weakened national security. No sooner had the 1783 treaty ending the Revolutionary War been signed than British ministers, seeking to exploit the new weak alliance of colonies, surreptitiously instructed the Canadian colony to maintain its forts and trading posts, so they could serve as bases for raids and espionage against the United States. Many frontier settlements suffered terrible losses from Indian attack. Trouble also developed in the southwest where the Spanish closed the Mississippi River to American navigation in 1784. The Confederation's weak response prompted settlers along the western frontier to consider seceding from the Union and joining Spain's empire.

Chaos ensued from the Confederation's inability to control commerce among the states and with foreign nations, aggravating the economic hardship that the war had wreaked. The states imposed competitive duties and tariffs on goods coming from other states and fought with each other over foreign trade. These squabbles enabled Britain to engage in a policy of divide and conquer. British merchants got around the regulations of states that sought to restrict their goods by bringing their products in through states that did not. Britain expanded exports to America while holding imports to a minimum. The Confederation lacked the authority to retaliate.

Economic depression and the unfavorable balance of trade led to increased pressure on states to make life easier for debtors, especially for small farmers who were well represented in democratic state legislatures. Farmers demanded that more paper money be printed to expand the money supply, making it cheaper for them to repay their debts. More than half the states yielded to this pressure between 1785 and 1786. Rhode Island printed so much money that creditors fled the state to avoid being paid in worthless currency. Although this case was extreme, many states experienced the ironic spectacle of debtors hunting down creditors, who hid for fear of being paid!

State legislatures that maintained a sound currency fared no better. Massachusetts's decision to maintain a tight money supply led to an armed rebellion. In the summer of 1786, mobs in its western communities tried to halt farm foreclosures by taking up arms and forcibly closing the debtor courts. The rebellion's leader was Daniel Shays, a war hero who had fought at Bunker Hill. The Massachusetts governor appealed to Congress, but the national government had no legal authority to put down rebellions in the states. When the state government finally mobilized its own troops, with funds raised by frightened private merchants, and sent them to quash the uprising, the rebels attacked the Springfield arsenal. Shays was defeated and fled to Vermont, but the Massachusetts legislature did respond to the rebels' plight by providing some debt relief.

Toward a More Powerful Union: Centralization, Nationalism, and Mixed Government

Centralization

Shays's rebellion greatly strengthened the hand of leaders such as George Washington, Alexander Hamilton, and James Madison, who believed a stronger national government, one less subservient to the popular will, was needed to solve the international and domestic troubles experienced under the Articles of Confederation. Still, there were many Americans, including such prominent patriots as Patrick Henry, John Hancock, and Samuel Adams, who resisted efforts to convene a constitutional convention for the purpose of tightening "the buckle of the continent." Indeed, to do so might jeopardize both the democratic spirit aroused by revolution and the tradition of local self-government that extended back a century and a half before the Revolution.

Jefferson, as a champion of both local self-government and egalitarian democracy, considered active engagement in politics critical to the protection of rights. From Paris, where he was serving as ambassador, he wrote Madison urging him not to overreact to the Massachusetts uprising. Democracy has "its evils," he acknowledged, and the acts of Shays's band were "absolutely unjustifiable." But such popular rebellions, although "evil," were "productive of the good." They prevented "the degeneracy of government" and nourished "a general attention to the public affairs . . . I hold it that a little rebellion now and then is a good thing, and as necessary in the political world as storms in the physical."

Washington and Madison disagreed with Jefferson. "What, gracious God, is man! that there should be such inconsistency and perfidiousness in his conduct," the usually stoic Washington declared after hearing of the Massachusetts riots. "We are fast verging to anarchy and confusion." Still, the supportive response of the Massachusetts legislature to the rebellion showed that Jefferson's sentiments were not merely the musings of a patriot abroad. After all, Shays's rebels were not radicals calling for a redistribution of property, they were former soldiers and respected citizens trying to protect their property.

The disagreement between Jefferson and Washington about Shays's rebellion highlights the uneasy relationship between the newer democratic egalitarian strand of American political culture and the Classic Liberal strand. It challenges the notion that equality and rights, both celebrated in the Declaration, were truly compatible. As the next chapter shows, in the course of creating and ratifying the Constitution the American people displayed a remarkable ability to rise to that challenge.

Fiscal difficulties and Shays's rebellion were not the only forces impelling the states, except Rhode Island, to send representatives to a convention in Philadelphia in the summer of 1787 to redress the weaknesses of the Articles of Confederation. Strong intellectual and political leadership also played a critical role in shifting American political culture in a nationalizing and centralizing direction and toward an appreciation of "checks and balances" as the means for moderating democratic excess. A strong case for mixed government was made by John Adams's three-volume work, *A Defense of the Constitutions of Government of the United States*. Adams proposed strengthening the national government by establishing a two-chamber legislature – one popularly elected, the other based more on aristocratic principles – and a strong, impartial executive who could veto acts of the legislature. The whole system was to be overseen by an independent judiciary. Such a constitution would moderate the sort of raw and disruptive conflict between rich and poor that Shays's rebellion represented and the danger of mob tyranny that it evoked. This notion of separate governing institutions checking one another not only became a fundamental building block of the Constitution; it altered the way Americans came to think about government. The principle of "checks and balances" seeped its way into American political culture.

Nationalism

The cause of creating a stronger union was fostered by a growing sense of American nationalism. Noah Webster's writings served to push American political culture in a nationalist direction. Webster would later become famous for his American dictionary; but during the 1780s his *Spelling Book* made him a household name. The *Spelling Book* emphasized American, as distinct from British, language. Its preface urged Americans to appreciate and further develop their own literature. Webster's *Reader*, published soon thereafter, included selections from the speeches of revolutionary leaders whom Webster praised as orators the equal of Demosthenes and Cicero. Both of Webster's books sold several million copies and remained bestsellers through the nineteenth century.

Webster considered a strong sense of nationality vital to the preservation of the Union. America was not just a collection of localities, and it involved more than political principles and governing institutions. A true spirit of nationality could develop only from distinctiveness in the daily life of the people. It was intimately associated with everyday matters of dress, speech, manners, and education. Cultural independence was the "mortar for the stones of union ... An American ought not to ask what is the custom of London and Paris, but what is proper for us in our circumstances and what is becoming our dignity."

In an influential 1785 tract, Webster joined his appeal to America's sense of national identity to a defense of stronger union. The Articles of Confederation was too "feeble to discharge its debts" and was, therefore, unworthy of a rising nation. It encouraged Americans to think small, clinging to "provincial views and attachments" that arrested the country's development. Some form of allegiance to states and localities was necessary. Provincial liberties were an important part of Americans' sense of themselves as citizens. But the country would only reach its fulfillment if people in the various states recognized and embraced their shared sense of mission: "The citizens of this new world should enquire not what will aggrandize this town or this state, but what will augment the power, secure the tranquility, multiply the subjects, and advance the opulence, the dignity, and the virtues of the United States." Only in this way would American individualism transcend narrow, destructive selfishness.

Webster's celebrity indicates that the people's sense of national identity grew during the 1780s, preparing the country to accept a stronger national government. The Northwest Ordinance of 1787, based on an initial draft written by Thomas Jefferson, reveals this impulse toward a stronger national constitution. This legislation established rules for the Northwest Territory, which included the present-day states of Ohio, Indiana, Illinois, Michigan, and Wisconsin. These states were carved from territory that once belonged to the original colonies, who ceded them to the national government. The western lands, which just a few years before had encouraged conflicts among the states, became a force for unity

Figure 2.2. Northwest Territory.
Credit: Kappamaps.com

once they were given to the national government. In keeping with Jefferson's belief that slavery was an evil that could not be abolished where it already existed but ought not be allowed to spread, the Ordinance banned slavery in the Northwest Territory. Thus, westward expansion was able to proceed in conformity with the inalienable rights proclaimed in the Declaration of Independence.

Popular Heroes

Popular attachment to a strong national government was immeasurably strengthened by the adoption of that cause by America's first great popular heroes, Benjamin Franklin and George Washington. Benjamin Franklin was the first great spokesman for American national unity. As early as 1754, in response to the growing threat to the colonies posed by France, Franklin proposed a plan to place the colonies under a colony-wide government headed by a president general appointed by the king, and a grand council to be composed of representatives of the individual colonies. The plan was approved at a meeting of delegates from the colonies that took place in Albany, New York, but it was then met with overwhelming opposition from both the colonial assemblies and the British government. The individual colonies were not yet ready to give up any substantial part of their autonomy to a central body. The British opposed uniting the colonies into a central government that would be far more capable of resisting British authority than were thirteen separate and warring colonial

Figure 2.3. Join or Die.
Source: Library of Congress.

governments. Franklin's commitment to unity is brilliantly depicted in a cartoon he printed in his newspaper, the *Pennsylvania Gazette.* Entitled "Join or Die," it shows a snake that is cut up into eight separate parts, each representing a separate colony except for the five New England colonies which are fused into a single segment and Georgia and Delaware which are omitted.

Franklin advocated on behalf of the colonies during two prolonged stints in London serving as an agent of the Pennsylvania colonial assembly. He helped draft the Declaration of Independence and, as the US representative to France was instrumental in bringing France into the Revolutionary War on the American side. However, Franklin's greatest fame and popularity came not from his political endeavors but from his remarkable accomplishments in private life. He was a successful businessman, author, philanthropist, scientist, and inventor. His life embodied the virtues and possibilities that Classic Liberalism celebrated and promoted. He was a self-made man, the son of a printer. Everything he accomplished he attributed to hard work, persistence, and a willingness to take risks. He moved from Boston to Philadelphia because he believed that the latter city was more likely to give an ambitious nobody a chance to succeed. In the words of the Declaration, he would be freer to "pursue happiness" there. In a very short period of time, despite being a newcomer without connections, he became one of the city's most influential personages. He was fascinated with science, but as a conscientious liberal, he was not content with acquiring scientific knowledge for its own sake but sought to apply that knowledge to improving the comfort and safety of humankind. Among his many inventions were the lightning rod, the Franklin stove, and bifocal eyeglasses. He was perhaps most celebrated as the author and publisher of the widely popular *Poor Richard's Almanack.* The almanac was a yearly publication that contained weather forecasts, astrological information, poems, and stories, but it was most famous for Poor Richards' sayings, many of which, such as "a penny saved is a penny earned," "Early to bed and early to rise, makes a man healthy wealthy and wise," "God helps them that help themselves," and "Haste makes waste," are quoted in ordinary speech to this day. Consider also "If you would persuade, you must appeal to interest rather than intellect" and "Plough deep while sluggards sleep." Taken as a whole the sayings are a compendium of the virtues that comprise the Classic Liberal commercial republic – patience, self-reliance, self-interest, hard work, and frugality. Franklin the writer as well as Franklin the man was the embodiment of those virtues.

George Washington was the greatest of all early American heroes, both for what he was and for what he was not. His extraordinary leadership talents kept the revolutionary army together despite the immense suffering and numerous defeats it endured, and eventually enabled it to emerge victorious. He was a person of immense dignity with the ability to inspire awe and respect from all who came in contact with him. But he was a new kind of military hero, one who did not seek to remain in power once the war was over. At the height of his influence, after the successful conclusion of the Revolution, he voluntarily returned to private life. His retirement from power had a profound effect everywhere in the Western world. The greatest English military heroes such as Cromwell, William of Orange, and Marlborough had sought political rewards commensurate with their political achievements. In contrast, Washington was sincere in his desire for all soldiers "to return to our Private Stations in the bosom of the free, peaceful and happy country." Thus he practiced the Classic Liberal commandments he preached. Even the greatest leader should not cling to power for its own sake. Once he had done what was necessary to ensure the liberty and security of his countryman, he should return to the comforts and pleasures of private life.

When these two heroes agreed to attend the Constitutional Convention in Philadelphia, they bestowed those proceedings with invaluable legitimacy. Washington, in fact, agreed to serve as the president of the convention, to preside over what was sure to be a contentious debate over the country's future. His unifying presence in Philadelphia did not discourage that debate, but it surely gave it more prestige and enhanced the prospect that the final document would receive a fair hearing from the American people. The cause of creating "a more perfect Union" and of the deepening national attachment it involved was immeasurably strengthened by the personal commitments that America's two greatest heroes made to achieving it.

Chapter 3 examines the Constitutional Convention and the constitution it produced. Considering that it was meant to serve as the blueprint for a government, that document is remarkably brief. But its few pages outline a set of governing principles and institutions that are remarkably diverse and seemingly incompatible. It provides for both a central government and a union of states; a government of strict limits and immense powers; democratic accountability and antidemocratic insularity; and guarantees of liberty and protections for slavery. Its complexities and tension reflect the complexities and tensions that characterize the political culture in which it was produced.

Looking Forward

As this chapter shows, from the beginning of European settlement America was not just a place to escape to, but a place to build a "city on a hill." It would give the people back home something to look up to and emulate. And, the "city" would be governed by those who lived in it, its cit(y)zens. However, such noble aspirations did not preclude involuntary servitude for others. From its inception, America had to cope with the anomalous combination of high ideals and dreadful oppression. Nor did a strong sense of mutual obligation and community spirit preclude an equally strong commitment to the rights of individuals, including a right to property, and the flowering of a spirit of enterprise and self-reliance. To this day Americans struggle with the warring tensions between civic commitments and selfish concerns, between belief in equality and toleration of persisting inequalities that were present from the beginning. Looking forward, American political culture will continue to struggle with the ambivalent forces that set it on its path.

CHAPTER SUMMARY

Contemporary portrait:

* Americans are more patriotic, optimistic, individualistic, religious, moralistic, and committed to a competitive free enterprise economy than citizens of other advanced democratic republics. They are also more tolerant of income inequality and less supportive of using government to provide a guaranteed income to individuals.

Cornerstones of American political culture:

* The cornerstones of American political culture were formed by three often conflicting influences: Puritanism, Classic Liberalism, and Democratic Egalitarianism.
* The Puritans stamped American political culture with a strong strain of commitment to community solidarity and to serving as an example for other nations to follow.
* Classic Liberalism, developed by political philosophers in the seventeenth and eighteenth centuries, stamped American political culture with a commitment to

natural rights, freedom of the individual, separation of powers, and limited government.

* The term Classic Liberalism should not be confused with Liberalism as the term is currently used. Liberalism in its modern guise connotes a belief in using the national government to achieve benevolent purposes. It is directly at odds with Classic Liberalism's stress on limited government.

Separating from the mother country:

* Both Loyalists and revolutionaries defended their decisions on Classic Liberal grounds.

Declaring a creed – the Declaration of Independence:

* The colonies did not simply rebel against Britain, they claimed that they had a right to do so on the basis of Classic Liberal principles. Thus they fought not just for independence but for a set of political-philosophical beliefs. They declared a political creed based on Classic Liberal principles.

Violations of the American creed:

* The establishment of slavery and the lack of equal rights for women created a profound contradiction in American political culture. Christian, Classic Liberal, and Democratic Egalitarian principles warred with an acceptance of the most thoroughgoing dehumanizing oppression and victimization of a large minority of the population and a subordinate status for half the people.

A third cornerstone: democratic egalitarianism:

* Prior to and during the Revolution the fear of majority tyranny receded in favor of a desire to place more power in the hands of the people. Democratic egalitarianism trumpeted majority rule as a virtue and adopted a much more inclusive view of who should be eligible to participate in politics.
* The Articles of Confederation rested on strong communitarian and democratic egalitarian premises and provided for a very weak central government.

Towards a more powerful union: centralization, nationalism, and mixed government:

* The cause of creating "a more perfect Union" was immeasurably strengthened by the nationalist writings of Noah Webster and the personal commitments that two of America's great heroes, Benjamin Franklin and George Washington, made to achieving it.

SUGGESTED READINGS

Almond, Gabriel, and Sidney Verba. *Civic Culture: Political Attitudes and Democracy in Five Nations*. Princeton, NJ: Princeton University Press, 1963.

Du Bois, W. E. B. *The Souls of Black Folk*. New York: Penguin, 1996.

Franklin, Benjamin. *The Autobiography of Benjamin Franklin and Other Writings*, ed. Ormond Seavey. New York: Oxford University Press, 1998.

Howe, Daniel Walker. *The Political Culture of American Whigs*. University of Chicago Press, 1984.

Kloppenberg, James. *The Virtues of Liberalism*. Cambridge, MA: Harvard University Press, 2000.

Maier, Pauline. *American Scripture: How America Declared its Independence from Britain*. New York: Random House, 2002.

McWilliams, Wilson Carey. *The Idea of Fraternity in America*. Berkeley: University of California Press, 1973.

Meyers, Marvin. *The Jacksonian Persuasion*, rev. edn. Stanford, CA: Stanford University Press, 1990.

Miller, Perry. *The New England Mind: The Seventeenth Century*. Cambridge, MA: Belknap Press, 1983.

Morone, James. *Hellfire Nation: The Politics of Sin in American History*. New Haven, CT: Yale University Press, 2003.

Paine, Thomas. *Common Sense*. New York: Penguin, 1976.

Schuck, Peter H., and Wilson, James Q. *Understanding America: The Anatomy of an Exceptional Nation*. New York: Public Affairs, 2008.

Smith, Roger M. *Civic Ideals: Conflicting Visions of Citizenship in the United States*. New Haven, CT: Yale University Press, 1999.

Tocqueville, Alexis de. *Democracy in America*, ed. Harvey Mansfield and Delba Winthrop. University of Chicago Press, 2000.

Wood, Gordon. "The Democratization of Mind in America." In *The Moral Foundations of the American Republic*, 2nd edn., ed. Robert H. Horowitz. Charlottesville: University Press of Virginia, 1979.

The Creation of the American Republic, 1776–1787. Chapel Hill: University of North Carolina Press, 1998.

3 Contesting the Constitution

CHAPTER OVERVIEW

This chapter focuses on:

- **A contemporary portrait of the American Constitution.**
- **Madison's new political science and the opposition to it.**
- **The role of leadership and deliberation in making the constitutional convention a success.**
- **The critical choices to create the Senate and to protect slavery.**
- **The creation of a strong executive.**
- **The key elements of the constitutional framework the Convention established.**
- **The ratification of the Constitution.**

Benjamin Franklin remarked at the 1787 Constitutional Convention that the President's chair depicted a "rising sun and not a setting sun," indicating his high hopes for the fledgling US government.

> While the last members were signing [the Constitution] Doctor Franklin, looking towards the President's Chair, at the back of which a rising sun happened to be painted, observed to a few members near him, that painters had found it difficult to distinguish in their art a rising sun from a setting sun.

Benjamin Franklin spoke these famous words at the Constitutional Convention while the delegates who labored during the summer of 1787 to draft the Constitution were coming forward to sign their names to the document. His remarks expressed the grave doubts that even the most optimistic Founders felt about whether the people would approve the new Constitution. Even if they did, would the result, as the preamble promised, "form a more perfect Union"? Franklin himself confessed that "there are several parts of this constitution which I do not at present approve." It was, after all, the product of many compromises, made necessary by the diverse interests represented at the convention. Moreover, the Constitution – embodying an attempt to serve the competing traditions of liberalism and democracy – represented a novel experiment in self-rule, one that was bound to be controversial.

As the oldest man at the convention, Franklin was aware of just how daunting a task it was to launch not only a new government but also a new way of governing. The Framers of the Constitution had invented the large-scale federal democratic republic. Before the establishment of the United States, the ideas of democracy and republicanism had been applied only to small places, such as ancient Athens and the small American states under the Articles of Confederation. Large places were governed by kings or queens. Franklin trembled at the possibility that this effort to tie size to liberty might well fail.

In spite of his doubts, Franklin saw the sun rising over America because he believed that the Constitution gave institutional form to the values that aroused the Revolution and pushed the country toward the creation of a national community. Today, more than 200 years later, Americans have reason to share Franklin's sense of accomplishment and possibility. Despite dim and dark moments, the sun has never set on the American experiment in large-scale constitutional democracy.

The essential governing structure and key governing principles established at that convention remain in place to this day. The next chapter will examine the critical challenges and reconsiderations of the Constitution that have taken place at key moments in American political development. However, none of those great constitutional moments pushed the US off the central path that the Constitution paved. Indeed, the most important of those moments, the Civil War and the end of slavery, is best understood as a fulfillment of the promise made in the Declaration of Independence "that all men are created equal." As Lincoln understood, the Declaration and the Constitution are inextricably bound together. Even those sections of the Constitution most at variance with the spirit of the Declaration, those that condoned slavery, never sought to justify it.

This chapter focuses on the designing of the constitutional path the country still follows, and the critical choices the Convention delegates faced. It explores the key controversies that emerged in the debate over the Constitution's ratification by the states, and how those conflicts were rooted in the tensions stemming from the different cornerstones of American political culture. It describes the process of invention that took place at the Constitutional Convention held in Philadelphia in the summer of 1787. There was no precedent in all of history for the endeavor the Framers had embarked upon. Therefore they had to carefully consider a wide variety of alternative institutional forms and principles. That consideration, reflected both in the debates at the Constitutional Convention and in the subsequent debates over ratification, was the fullest and freshest exploration of how best to organize a free government that has ever taken place.

The last chapter concluded with a discussion of the debate that arose during the 1780s between those who believed that liberty was best preserved by an active and competent citizenry and those who believed that protecting liberty required limiting political participation in order to prevent mob rule. This quarrel

Figure 3.1. In Defense of the Constitution.
Source: Library of Congress.

was at the heart of the conflict between those who framed and championed the Constitution, who came to be called *Federalists*, and those who opposed it, the *Anti-Federalists*. But it was a lovers' quarrel. The two sides had much in common, most especially a deep and abiding love of country and of freedom and pride in having thrown off the yoke of British rule. Both adhered to the basic tenets of Classic Liberalism: natural rights, the social contract, and limited government (see Chapter 1). Like a lovers' quarrel, the fierceness of their disputes stemmed from the passionate attachments binding them together. The Anti-Federalists believed that Classic Liberal principles could best be protected by relying on a vigilant and active citizenry, not by the limitations on popular rule proposed by the Federalists. In particular the Anti-Federalists opposed the most radical principle the Constitution contained, the notion that a large republic offered better protection of liberty than a small one. Their defense of a small republic meant that despite their adherence to Classic Liberalism, the Anti-Federalists continued to also champion the virtues of locality and community that American political culture derived initially from the Puritans and that we have labeled as Communitarianism. Tom Paine also opposed the Constitution, but on democratic egalitarian rather than communitarian grounds. He opposed the Senate, which he viewed as an elitist body, one that was inegalitarian since the small states would be overrepresented. He also felt that the torturous nature of the amendment process made it too difficult for the majority to exert its will.

Like most quarrels, neither side came away entirely satisfied with the outcome. On the whole, the Constitution was a victory for the Federalists. Its central premise, the creation of a strong national government, ensured that America would be a large republic that emphasized natural rights and placed obstacles in the path of majority rule, the key principle of democratic egalitarianism. Key aspects of the Constitution – most notably the Senate and the Supreme Court – were adopted despite telling criticisms about how antidemocratic they were. But the Constitution did not close the door on either democracy or decentralized government. It gave the greatest degree of responsibility for funding the government to the most democratic element of the government, the House of Representatives. The Federalist effort to centralize power in the hands of the national government was tempered by the *Bill of Rights,* which, as first enacted, was viewed not as a list of individual entitlements but instead as a constraint on the power of the national government – as a bulwark of local self-rule. In particular, the Tenth Amendment's guarantee that "The powers not delegated to the United States by the Constitution, nor prohibited by it to the States, are reserved to the States respectively, or to the people" offered powerful protection against the destruction of the existing forms of local and state politics that the Anti-Federalists cherished.

The Constitution of the United States: A Contemporary Portrait

What we take most for granted about the Constitution is actually its most remarkable quality, its unbroken span of existence for a period of more than two hundred years. As it did in 1788, the American government still consists of a bicameral legislature, an independent judiciary, an independently elected

Table 3.1. Codified constitutions of Western nations.

Country	Date of Adoption
United States	June 21, 1788
Netherlands	August 24, 1815
Belgium	February 7, 1831
Italy	December 27, 1947
Germany	May 12, 1949
France	October 4, 1958
Switzerland	April 18, 1999

Source: CIA World Factbook.

executive, and a division of governing authority between the federal government and the states. As later chapters will discuss in detail, every one of these elements and the relationships among them has gone through considerable change over time. But this does not undermine the extraordinary stability of the constitutional framework that has endured for more than two centuries. The Constitution was never intended to provide a detailed enumeration of how politics and government ought to act or how they do act. Rather, it provides a broad framework for political and governmental action and establishes a set of fundamental principles to guide that action.

No other nation has displayed anywhere near this high level of constitutional stability and continuity. In 1787 France was still a monarchy. Since 1789 it has had five different constitutions. In 1787, Britain was a monarchy with actual governing authority distributed among the monarch, the Lords and the Commons. Now the monarch's tasks are almost entirely ceremonial and the Lords has been stripped of virtually all its governing authority. Germany and Japan have constitutions that date back a mere half-century: they only came into existence after World War II.

Although the 1787 format remains in place, the current Constitution does differ from the original in a few profound ways. Most important of all, the Thirteenth Amendment, ratified in 1865, freed the slaves. The Fifteenth Amendment ratified in 1870 guarantees the right to vote to all citizens regardless of race or color. The Nineteenth Amendment, ratified in 1920, extends full voting rights to women. The Fourteenth Amendment forbids the states from depriving their citizens of rights that the federal constitution guarantees. It states, in part:

> No State shall make or enforce any law which shall abridge the privileges or immunities of citizens of the United States; nor shall any State deprive any person of life, liberty, or property, without due process of law; nor deny to any person within its jurisdiction the *equal protection of the laws.*

Prior to its ratification, the Bill of Rights only applied to the actions of the federal government, not the states. Even after the Fourteenth Amendment's adoption,

Table 3.2. Critical constitutional changes since the 1791 ratification of the Bill of Rights.

Twelfth Amendment	1803	Required electors to cast a separate vote for president and vice president. Reduced from five to three the number of candidates from whom the House of Representatives could choose if no candidate got an electoral vote majority
Thirteenth Amendment	1865	Abolished slavery
Fourteenth Amendment	1866	Forbade the states from abridging the privileges and immunities of US citizens or of denying them due process or the equal protection of the laws
Fifteenth Amendment	1869	Prohibits the denial of the right to vote based on race, color, or previous condition of servitude
Seventeenth Amendment	1913	Provides for the direct election of senators by popular vote
Nineteenth Amendment	1919	Guarantees women the right to vote

many states placed great obstacles in the path of its full implementation. Over time, however, the Supreme Court has interpreted the amendment as requiring states to abide by the most important aspects of the Bill of Rights.

Originally, the Constitution required that senators were to be elected by individual state legislatures. The Seventeenth Amendment, ratified in 1913, required that senators be elected by the citizens of their respective states. As the original Constitution established that the president be chosen by electors comprising the *Electoral College*, rather than by a nationwide popular vote, each state was granted a number of electors equal to their number of congressional districts plus two additional electors for their two senators. The states were free to choose those electors any way they wished. To win, a candidate had to obtain an electoral vote majority, otherwise the choice went to the House of Representatives, who chose among the top five finishers (House members do not vote as individuals; rather, each state delegation votes separately and each state is granted one vote). The Electoral College remains in place, but the Twelfth Amendment changed the process by which electors vote. The original Constitution called for each elector to vote for two different candidates, one of whom must not be from the elector's home state. The Twelfth Amendment requires electors to cast only one vote for president and a second vote for vice president, and, in the absence of an electoral majority the House of Representatives, chooses among the top three finishers. The Twenty-second Amendment limits the president to two terms in office.

Taken as a whole, these changes redefine American government and politics in ways that expand both its Classic Liberal and democratic aspects. As a result of empowering ex-slaves and women and insisting on the popular election of senators, the overall political system has become far more democratic. It includes virtually the whole adult citizenry. By requiring states to incorporate key aspects of the Bill of Rights it seeks to ensure that the Classic Liberal principle of natural rights be universally enforced. By establishing separate and single ballots for president and vice president, it improves the odds that a single candidate will gain a majority of electoral votes and therefore the presidential choice will be made by the voters and not by the House of Representatives. By limiting the president to two terms, it diminishes the risk of a president becoming a despot.

As the judiciary chapter will demonstrate, Americans love to argue about the meaning of their rights. The extent and nature of the rights contained in the Bill of Rights is at the heart of public debate about and judicial consideration of issues as diverse as gay marriage, gun control, the treatment of terror suspects, and the extent of the government's right to interfere with the rights of property owners. Given how much debate takes place about the meaning of the Constitution, it is especially remarkable to note how little of that debate revolves around the governing structure as outlined in the Articles of the Constitution as opposed to the proliferation of argumentation that surrounds the Bill of Rights. Indeed, the only serious constitutionally based arguments regarding the structure of national governing institutions occurred in the wakes of the 2000 and 2016 presidential elections, when the popular vote and the electoral vote diverged, and prominent politicians and opinion makers urged that Article II be amended to abolish the Electoral College and have the president chosen by national popular vote. These calls did not result in any widespread movement to amend the Constitution. However, Democrat legislators in many states are supporting an effort to change state law to achieve the goal of national popular election in the absence of constitutional change.

Eleven states and the District of Columbia have passed a law that commits their state's electoral votes to the presidential candidate who wins the national popular vote regardless of how the popular vote in the *state* was cast. Thus, in a state whose voters chose, say, the Democratic candidate, the state's votes would be cast for the Republican candidate if he or she had won the national popular vote. The law would only go into effect when enough states have enacted identical legislation to create the 270 electoral vote majority necessary to elect a president. The same bill has been introduced in all the other state legislatures. If the 270 majority is reached, the issue of whether a state's right to choose electors includes the right to bind those electors based on results in other states is a matter that will undoubtedly be settled in court. So far, the plan has only gained support in Democrat-leaning states. In order to win support in enough states to reach the 270 electoral goal, it will need to win support from Republican-leaning states, and those states have so far shown no inclination to support the measure.

Table 3.3. Declaration of independence to adoption of constitution timeline.

July 4, 1776	Declaration of Independence
March 1, 781	Ratification of the Articles of Confederation
September 3, 1783	Treaty of Paris ends the Revolutionary War
May 25, 1787	Constitutional Convention begins
September 17, 1787	Delegates sign the Constitution
June 21, 1788	Constitution is ratified
March 4, 1789	The government established by the Constitution begins operation

Source: Library of Congress.

Madison's New Political Science and the Opposition to it

The Federalist Papers

The contest over the Constitution was waged not only indoors, in the Philadelphia convention and state ratifying conventions, but "out of doors" as well, through the media. The New York ratification contest led to the most famous and influential explanation and defense of the Constitution, the eighty-five separate essays that compose *The Federalist Papers*. They were written by John Jay, James Madison, and Alexander Hamilton using the pseudonym Publius (a Roman statesman who championed the cause of the people).

Publius acknowledged that a full-fledged defense of the constitution demanded nothing less than "a new science of politics." In *Federalist* 10, Madison laid out the principle that most clearly separated not only the Federalists from the Anti-Federalists but the new political science from the old. He refuted the Anti-Federalist belief, shared by all previous republican thinkers, that a good republic was a small republic. He argued that a large republic was better suited for maintaining liberty because it discouraged the creation of a single majority faction capable of dominating the minority and depriving it of its rights. Madison understood faction to be "a number of citizens, whether amounting to a minority or majority of the whole, who are united by some common impulse of passion, or of interest, adverse to the rights of other citizens, or to the permanent and aggregate interests of the community." As was pointed out in Chapter 2, Madison's concerns about unreliable majorities were not merely theoretical; they were based on the terrible clashes between creditors and debtors that arose in the 1780s culminating in Shays's rebellion.

Madison, like all previous great republican thinkers, feared tyranny of the majority. But he parted company with them by denying that the problem of majority tyranny could best be solved by abolishing faction. Madison's analogy was that liberty bears the same relationship to faction that air does to fire. It is possible to snuff out a fire by depriving it of air, but then the people cannot breathe either. Likewise, faction can be destroyed, but only at the price of snuffing out liberty for everyone.

According to Madison, previous thinkers had failed to appreciate that a large republic deals with faction better than a small one does. The larger the republic, the more separate factions it will contain. As factions multiply, they become less able to coalesce into a stable and coherent majority capable of tyrannizing others. Size and diversity, traditionally the enemy of republics, turn out to be its dearest friends.

The sheer arithmetic of large republics dictated that the actual work of government be carried out not by the people themselves but by their representatives. In *Federalist* 10, Madison argued that representation is what enables popular government both to remain popular and to avoid the otherwise inescapable difficulties posed by popular rule. Caught up, as they inevitably are, in the task of earning a living and tending to their families, subject to prejudice and passion, ordinary people are simply not capable of assuming the burdens of governance. Even if they were all geniuses, their vast numbers and the sheer size of the districts they lived in meant they could not all gather in one place and deliberate for days on end. Therefore, the best they can do is make reasonably good choices about who should govern for them and whether the record of those who govern is worthy of their continuing support.

Properly structured, the process of electing representatives enables ordinary people to hold their government accountable but does not place unreasonable burdens on them. Here again, size comes to the rescue. Bigger electoral districts are better than small ones because they contain a larger number of individuals fit to assume the mantle of leadership. They provide voters with a richer array of talent from which to choose. The keys to the new science of politics are therefore size and representation.

But what was to prevent representatives themselves from forming a faction that would tyrannize the populace? To answer this puzzle, Madison built on John Adams's idea of checks and balances. Although each branch would enjoy distinctive powers, none would enjoy a monopoly of power. Each branch – the president, Congress, and the judiciary – would be granted some power to meddle in the affairs of the others, ensuring that government power remained dispersed. Madison stated this view in a famous passage from *Federalist* 51:

> [T]he great security against a gradual concentration of the several powers in the same department consists in giving to those who administer each department the necessary constitutional means and personal motives to resist encroachments of the others ... Ambition must be made to counteract ambition. The interest of the man must be connected with the constitutional rights of the place ... If men were angels, no government would be necessary. If angels were to govern men, neither external nor internal

controls on government would be necessary. In framing a government which is to be administered by men over men, the great difficulty lies in this: you must first enable the government to control the governed; and in the next place oblige it to control itself.

The Anti-Federalist Critique

The opponents of the Constitution, known as Anti-Federalists, rejected the new science of politics on which it was based. They clung to key aspects of the Puritan cornerstone of American political culture that this new science rejected. They opposed the large republic. Small size was necessary for democracy, they believed, because all self-government relies on friendship and trust among the citizens. Like the Federalists, they also feared tyranny of the majority, but, like their Puritan forebears, they sought to avoid it by nurturing ties of mutual affection and common interest among the community, not by multiplying faction. To trust and empathize with another person, one has to know that person's character. Such knowledge is possible only in small places. As anyone who lives in a small town knows, not everyone has to be on a first-name basis with everybody else. But there can be no real strangers. By consulting a friend, or the friend of a friend, one can obtain a rich assessment of the character of a person that one does not know personally. This knowledge does not imply that everyone likes and trusts one another. Even in the smallest of towns, one is likely to make enemies. But because there is so much knowledge of one another, one knows whom to trust and whom not to trust. Although grudges and feuds are bound to develop, their importance in the overall scheme of things is likely to be small compared to the sense of mutual responsibility, affection, and solidarity that small places instill.

In a large place, people remain anonymous and are therefore incapable of disciplining one another. Small places are nosy and gossipy. This lack of privacy can be aggravating, but because people are so knowledgeable about each other, they can anticipate political problems before those problems mushroom into open conflict. The Anti-Federalists counted on the capacity of citizens in small republics to exercise mutual vigilance to nip the formation of oppressive faction in the bud.

Small republics are also better at political education. Schools made citizens literate, but a complete democratic education required active participation in the affairs of state. The Anti-Federalists considered citizenship to be like a muscle: it could only become strong through exercise. Only by partaking in the myriad tasks of local governance could people learn the hard lessons of citizenship: how to speak in public; how to listen carefully to others; how to know when to hold fast to principle and when to compromise. Because Anti-Federalists counted on the people themselves to preserve and protect the republic, they were much more concerned than the Federalists were about the character and outlook of citizens.

Table 3.4. Federalists versus Anti-Federalists.

Federalists	Anti-Federalists
• Extended republic • Feared tyranny of majority above all • Believed in the advantage of many competing factions • Wanted representatives to be superior, distinguished men	• Small republic • Feared tyranny of government above all • Believed in preventing faction • Wanted representatives to be like the people

Left to themselves, Americans would retreat to private concerns, especially since the proposed Constitution would spawn a large, diverse society more concerned with trade and pleasure-seeking than civic virtue. Corrupt and decadent people would be incapable of being good citizens. Therefore, the Anti-Federalists believed that a constitution should sanction vice and promote virtue. Because religion is such a powerful source of good conduct and also a potential source of terrible factional discord, the Anti-Federalists believed that government had to both support and regulate it. Some Anti-Federalists favored the establishment of an official church and the punishment of religious dissent. They believed that successful democracy required the limitation of some forms of personal liberty, and they were prepared to pay that price.

The Anti-Federalists failed to prevent adoption of the Constitution. However, as the following chapter will show, their fears regarding the destructive implications of the new science of politics that the Constitution embodied, particularly as it affected community cohesion and trust and friendship among citizens, would continue to resonate throughout the course of American political development.

The Role of Leadership and Deliberation in making the Constitutional Convention a Success

Nearly 200 years later, the historian Catherine Drinker Bowen used the term "miracle" to describe the success of the Constitutional Convention in producing a single constitutional blueprint. But the miraculous events in Philadelphia were distinctively practical, the result of political debate, compromise, and decision. The convention succeeded because most of the delegates displayed a great talent for deliberation, and a few showed a great talent for leadership. Studying the Philadelphia convention allows students to see the workings of these two key political principles – leadership and deliberation – that are so central to the success of a large, complex republic.

Deliberation

Deliberation is the art of reasoning together. Political deliberation is the application of this art to public decision making. It is not enough to have good talks; political deliberation is successful only when an assembly comes to a decision about whatever public issue is at stake.

Political deliberation involves a complex set of skills and attitudes. The key attitude is open-mindedness. Whatever one's preconceived ideas, one must be open to changing one's mind. This may not happen often. But if one remains close-minded, the other debaters will see that efforts at persuasion are hopeless and they too will be tempted to close their minds. The deliberation will turn into irreconcilable conflict. If the constitutional deliberation had degenerated into a stalemate, it would have been a contest with no winners. Those delegates who sensed they were losing the debate would have diverted their energies either to sabotaging the convention or to convincing the voters in the several states not to ratify the document that was produced. Because delegates allowed themselves to be influenced by other delegates, creative solutions were found to problems that at first seemed intractable. Today's government was born out of the painstaking and imaginative political deliberation engaged in by the men who wrote the Constitution and worked for its ratification.

To encourage deliberation, the convention delegates took the drastic step of adopting a secrecy rule: nothing spoken within Philadelphia's convention hall was "to be printed, or otherwise published or communicated without leave." The convention took place without visitors, journalists, or even public discussions by the delegates in earshot of nonparticipants. Citizens who suspected that the convention would strengthen the central government beyond what a democracy could tolerate complained that such a "Dark Enclave," as Patrick Henry put it, could only be the work of conspirators.

Even Thomas Jefferson, in Paris at the time, who thought the convention "an assembly of demigods," complained of the "abominable . . . precedent . . . of tying up the tongues" of the delegates. His criticism expressed the principle that democracy is strengthened by, as Woodrow Wilson would later put it, "open covenants, openly arrived at." Public deliberations, these men believed, allow citizens to judge representatives and the arguments brought to bear in support of their positions. Moreover, public debates educate and improve public judgment.

Still, the convention delegates adopted the secrecy rule easily and never wavered from their decision to hold meetings behind closed doors. Reflecting on that hot summer in Philadelphia many years later, Madison insisted that "no Constitution would ever have been adopted by the convention if the debates had been public." The secrecy rule encouraged the delegates to take controversial positions, discuss them freely, change their minds, and work out compromises without fear of challenging received wisdoms, such as the sovereignty of the states, and without temptation to play to any gallery save that of posterity.

The enduring union that the Constitution achieved required more than the luxury of secret deliberations; it also required leadership. Madison and Washington provided that crucial leadership. Each had his own gifts and style, but collectively they gave the convention a sense of direction. Like most serious deliberations, the Constitutional Convention risked having to consider too many options in too little time. Madison and Washington controlled the agenda to ensure that the initial choices that were made would shape and guide later choices. They provoked the other delegates when the deliberation became listless, and they calmed their colleagues when it became overheated. They took initiative when others were timid and suggested compromise when others were intransigent.

George Washington made his greatest leadership contribution simply by showing up. As we noted in Chapter 2, he was the most famous and celebrated man in America. He had led the Continental Army to victory, and in the wake of that victory, he refused to help disgruntled army veterans overthrow the feckless national government and make him king. Having seen Washington's commitment

Table 3.5. Delegates to the Constitutional Convention.

State	Number of delegates	Names of delegates
Connecticut	3	Oliver Ellsworth, William Johnson, Roger Sherman
Delaware	5	Richard Bassett, Gunning Bedford, Jr., Jacob Broom, John Dickinson, George Read
Georgia	4	Abraham Baldwin, William Few, William Houstoun, William Pierce
Maryland	5	Daniel Carroll, Daniel of St. Thomas Jenifer, Luther Martin, James McHenry, John Mercer
Massachusetts	4	Elbridge Gerry, Nathaniel Gorham, Rufus King, Caleb Strong
New Hampshire	2	Nicholas Gilman, John Langdon
New Jersey	5	David Brearly, Jonathan Dayton, William C. Houston, William Livingston, William Paterson
New York	3	Alexander Hamilton, John Lansing, Robert Yates
North Carolina	5	William Blount, William Davie, Alexander Martin, Richard Spraight, Hugh Williamson
Pennsylvania	8	George Clymer, Thomas Fitzsimons, Benjamin Franklin, Jared Ingersoll, Thomas Mifflin, Gouverneur Morris, Robert Morris, James Wilson
South Carolina	4	Pierce Butler, Charles Pinckney, Charles Cotesworth Pinckney, John Rutledge
Virginia	7	John Blair, James Madison, George Mason, James McClurg, Edmund Randolph, George Washington, George Wythe
Rhode Island	None	

Source: Teaching American History.

to republican rule, no citizen could believe that he would use the convention for selfish political purposes. At no other time in American history has one person towered over all others in terms of public affection and respect. The public was keenly aware that he was putting his great reputation at risk by agreeing to participate in this uncertain venture. Thus his very presence at the convention greatly increased its prestige and legitimacy. It was a foregone conclusion that Washington would chair the convention. As the presiding officer, he was called not chairman but president.

Agenda Setting, Conflict, and Compromise

The delegates were slow to arrive in Philadelphia. Eleven days elapsed between the scheduled start of the convention, on May 14, 1787, and its actual opening, on May 25, when enough delegates had finally arrived to produce the minimum number of seven states required for official business to begin. Because Madison insisted, the Virginia delegation, including Washington, arrived on time. Madison had more than punctuality on his mind. He used the spare eleven days to work with the Virginia delegation to gain its united support for his plan. The session opened with Virginia's plan as the only one on the table and with a Virginia delegate as the presiding officer. Under these favorable circumstances, the Virginia Plan became the framework for the convention's subsequent discussions. The final document retained the most essential features of Madison's plan: three separate branches of government, federalism, and a bicameral legislature.

If all the delegates had arrived on time, there would have been no fully formed proposal to claim first place on the agenda. The delegates may well have chosen to begin with a broad discussion of the state of the country and wrangled about how best to revise the Articles. Such a meandering discussion might have produced only minimal changes especially since the mandate given by Congress to the Convention was to revise the Articles not to write a new document. Instead, the Virginia Plan, which clearly and self-confidently challenged Congress's instructions, put the delegates on the spot. They would immediately have to decide whether to abide by their instructions from Congress or write a new and powerful constitution. Because the choice was posed so starkly and because the Virginia Plan was so comprehensive and compelling, the convention made its most decisive choice first, to face the full challenge of constituting a national government.

The heart of the Virginia Plan was contained in a resolution that Edmund Randolph, delegate from Virginia, proposed on May 30 "that a national government ought to be established consisting of a supreme legislature, judiciary, and executive." It would enjoy supremacy over the states and possess broad powers. Had the delegates been able to avoid such a stark choice so early in the convention,

Table 3.6. The Virginia Plan versus the New Jersey Plan.

Virginia Plan	New Jersey Plan
• New plan for national government • Three branches of government • Federalism • Bicameral legislature	• Revision of Articles of Confederation • One-state-one-vote legislature • No claim of national supremacy

a majority might have chosen to do so. But faced with an either–or decision, they chose to accept Randolph's challenge, and his resolution passed easily. For the next several weeks, the deliberations of the convention focused on the Virginia Plan. Although many of its specific elements were changed or rejected, there was no retreat from the principles encapsulated in Randolph's May 30th resolution. The fork in the road heading toward a new constitutional order had been taken.

On June 15th the opponents of the Virginia Plan finally introduced the New Jersey Plan. It was framed as a series of amendments to the Articles of Confederation and called for a revision, not a transformation, of the existing government. It left intact the one-state-one-vote legislature and made no broad claim about national supremacy. Had this scheme served as the initial basis of discussion, the convention's product might have been far less revolutionary. It is a testament to the political skill of the Virginians – Washington and Madison in particular – that the New Jersey Plan now seemed, by comparison to their plan, excessively tame, even though it did include proposals to give Congress power to tax and regulate commerce, to establish a supreme court, and to create an executive authorized to compel states to obey federal law.

THE CRITICAL CHOICES TO CREATE THE SENATE AND PROTECT SLAVERY

In addition to the deep divide between delegates who favored a strong central government and those who opposed it, two other profound political divisions existed among the delegates. Those from the small states feared that if government was nationalized and consolidated, the views and interests of the large states – Massachusetts, Pennsylvania, and Virginia, in particular – would prevail. Slaveholders feared that the new nation's non-slaveholding states would try to persuade Congress to inhibit slavery. On the other hand, delegates from the large states argued that it was unjust to give the smaller states as much power as those that were so much more heavily populated. The Convention made the critical choice to guard the interests of the small state by the creation of a separate branch of the legislature in which they would be granted equal representation. It guarded the interests of the slave states by writing protections for slavery into the Constitution.

Even if delegates from the small states and from the slave states agreed in principle that the United States was a full-fledged union, not merely a compact of states, they recognized that reserving strong powers for the individual states was still the best way to protect their specific interests, and they did not believe that allowing the lower house to choose the members of the upper house did so. They were not persuaded by the argument that the states would be adequately protected because the new national government was to be one of strictly enumerated powers. In principle, the idea of strict enumeration ensured that all matters not delegated to the national government would be reserved to the states, but the small-state delegates realized that such delegations of authority would never be entirely clear-cut. The national government would always be tempted to interpret its power in the most expansive manner possible. Indeed, nationalists could draw on general language, such as the final clause of Article I, Section 8, which authorized Congress "To make all Laws which shall be necessary and proper for carrying into Execution the foregoing Powers," to consolidate their influence.

The most dramatic moment of the entire proceedings occurred on July 16, 1787, when a majority of state delegations were persuaded to support the compromise over representation in the bicameral legislature, a plan based on Benjamin Franklin's motion. Franklin's plea for "the assistance of Heaven" had helped to restore a deliberative atmosphere in which delegates could consider the most difficult issue confronting them.

The Great Compromise

The Great Compromise provided for two houses. The lower house, called the House of Representatives, would provide representation proportional to each state's population. In order to provide some tilt in importance to this lower house, it was stipulated that all bills relating to the raising of revenue would have to originate there. The upper house was called the Senate, and its members would be chosen by the states. Each state, regardless of its size, would be entitled to two senators. As a result of this compromise, the bicameral legislature came to embody the two opposing views of what role states should have in the new constitutional order. In the Senate, the states would continue to be represented as distinct and equal polities, whereas in the House they would be reduced to nothing more than the sum of their allotted representatives.

Protecting Slavery

The other major compromise, involving the toleration and protection of slavery, marked a major exception to the lovers' quarrel typical of the constitutional debates. How could such otherwise ethically progressive and sophisticated people abet this evil? The question is all the more perplexing because so many of them, including some slave owners, recognized the evil of slavery. They acquiesced because they feared that to oppose slavery would foment a greater evil, the dissolution of the Union. Slavery's advocates, a majority in all the slave states, had made it clear that they would oppose the Constitution if they perceived that it would threaten either the present or the future of slavery. Therefore, even those delegates most opposed to slavery were obliged to consider what life would be like if that threat were carried out. Their willingness to compromise with slavery came from their considered conclusion that to do so was the lesser of two evils.

The Union had almost no chance of survival if the Southern states left. Already, the young fragile nation faced a hostile power, Britain, on its northern border. West of the Mississippi lay the French and Spanish empires. If the South seceded, the Union would be reduced to little more than a strip of coastline that extended southward only as far as Pennsylvania (Delaware would remain a slave state until the ratification of the Thirteenth Amendment in 1865). And it would share a long southern border with what might then prove to be a hostile country. To make matters worse, the easiest route west went through the South. The North was hemmed in by the Appalachian Mountains and powerful, hostile Indian nations. The most active western settlement was occurring in the slave-owning territories of Tennessee and Kentucky. In the near future, the South was likely to become larger and more powerful than the North. Therefore, the Northern delegates recognized that they had no practical choice but to appease the South on the issue that it regarded as most important, namely slavery.

The Constitution contained three clauses protecting slavery. The first dealt with how slaves were to be counted for purposes of apportioning congressional districts. The white population of the Southern states was insufficient to maintain voting parity with the North in the House of Representatives. Therefore, in order not to be outvoted by the North, the Southern states required that slaves be counted in the census, on which the apportionment of seats in the House would be based. Ironically, this demand forced them to admit that slaves were indeed human beings, but they were prepared to live with this awkwardness for the sake of protecting their political strength. The opponents of slavery were unwilling to count slaves on an equal basis with non-slaves, but they compromised by allowing each slave to be counted as three-fifths of a person for the purposes of congressional apportionment.

The second proslavery clause guaranteed the continuation of the importation of slaves for a period of twenty years. To ensure that this protection would not be abridged, this clause was declared non-amendable. This provision was politically the most complex because it did not have the unified support of all slaveholders. States such as Virginia, that already had more slaves than were needed to run their plantations, would have been happy to ban the importation of slaves as a way to increase the value of their slave property. But states such as South Carolina and Georgia, that needed more slaves for their plantations, had strong interests in continuing the international slave trade in order to keep the price of slaves down. In the end, the greater intensity of feeling on the issue among the deep Southerners enabled them to prevail.

The third provision, and the one that was to cause the most enduring controversy, was the fugitive slave provision. This provision required all states, including those that prohibited slavery, to return escaping slaves to their owners. The fugitive slave provision in the Constitution states, "No person held to service or labor in one state, under the laws thereof, escaping into another, shall, in consequence of any law or regulation therein, be discharged for such service or labor, but shall be delivered up on claim of the party, to whom such service or labor may be due." The original proposal from the South Carolina delegation required "slaves and servants to be delivered up like criminals." The final version makes no reference either to slaves or criminals, only to persons "held to service or labor." Another version required that fugitive persons be delivered up to the person "justly claiming" their labor. The final version makes no reference to the justice of the claim. Instead of "justly claiming," it substitutes "to whom such service or labor may be due" and therefore ignores the issue of whether that claim is just. And the convention's committee on style changed the definition of a fugitive from one "legally held to service or labor" to a person held "to service or labor in one state, under the laws thereof." This wording thereby removed any direct constitutional endorsement of the legality of the practice of slavery. If indeed a promise to return fugitive slaves was a necessity, it is difficult to imagine how such an endorsement could have been worded to offer less support for slavery in principle.

The fugitive slave provision of the Constitution represents the fine line the Framers walked between codifying slavery and denying its moral legitimacy. As dreadful as these concessions and compromises with slavery were, they could have been worse. While allowing the continuation of slavery and even abetting it by promising to help catch fugitive slaves, the Constitution ostentatiously refrained from providing slavery with a moral stamp of approval. The term "slavery" is never even mentioned in the document. The embarrassed delegates resorted to euphemisms such as "persons held to service," a tacit acknowledgment of their feelings of shame in acquiescing to it.

One cannot entirely exonerate the antislavery delegates, because it is impossible to say for sure that their willingness to go along with these three provisions

Table 3.7. Constitutional compromises.

Two legislative houses:
- House of Representatives, with representation proportionate to each state's population, where all bills pertaining to revenue must originate.

Senate, with two representatives from each state:
- Compromise over slavery:
  Three-fifths clause
  Guaranteed importation of slaves for twenty years
  Fugitive slave provision

was indeed the absolute minimum degree of cooperation required to placate the proslavery delegates. After all, quitting the Union would have exacted a high price from the South as well; the South, too, had an incentive to compromise to keep the Union intact. But if one accepts the premise that abiding with slavery was necessary to preserve the Union, then the Northerners may be given credit for not making a far worse deal, one that indicated positive approval for slavery and provided it with moral legitimacy.

Obviously, scrupulous attention to the wording of proslavery provisions provided no solace for those doomed to remain in chains. But the Constitution's wording, which deprived the defenders of slavery of any additional moral ground to stand on, provided later opponents of slavery with a crucial moral advantage. If the document had directly endorsed slavery, Abraham Lincoln would not have been able, decades later, to claim that the cause of the Union, a cause rooted in the Constitution, required that slavery be curtailed. The convention's insistence on treating slavery as a necessary evil, rather than a positive good, enabled Lincoln to argue that the Framers intended to confine slavery in the expectation that it ultimately would die. This expectation, Lincoln insisted, demonstrated their belief that "a house divided against itself could not stand"; and it justified Lincoln's position that a defense of the Constitution required that slavery was wrong and must ultimately be abolished.

UPSHOT

The small state–big state divide at the root of the establishment of the Senate is no longer central to American politics. Nonetheless, the Senate continues to serve as a vital bulwark of American federalism and gives the states a strong voice in national decision making. Although protecting slavery was probably necessary to get the slave states to ratify the Constitution, it served to bolster and perpetuate an institution that mocked the liberal principles on which the new republic was founded and ultimately resulted in a war that produced the most deaths of any war in American history.

The Creation of a Strong Executive

For the most part, the completed Constitution was based on the initial Virginia Plan as modified by the defenders of the states and of slavery, but there was one critical deviation from Madison's initial blueprint. The Virginia Plan was quite vague about the executive. It allowed for either an individual or a committee. Neither Madison nor his Anti-Federalist critics envisaged the establishment of a strong executive branch of government as came to be provided for in Article II of the Constitution. Indeed, before the Constitution was written, the conventional wisdom held that strong executive power and democracy did not mix. Initially, Madison preferred to rely on the Senate to perform those tasks normally assigned to an executive. A few delegates, most notably Alexander Hamilton, Gouverneur Morris, and James Wilson, favored a strong and independent executive. But early on, they were a distinct minority. The establishment of a strong executive owes its existence to the deliberative activity of the convention itself. Opposition to a strong executive melted slowly. As the overall shape and format of the national government became clearer, the majority of the delegates began to recognize that such a bold effort needed a single identifiable person in charge as well as the means to make that person accountable and responsible. Thus, the delegates agreed to a single person rather than a committee because no one would be able to figure out whom to hold responsible if several different people participated in an executive decision.

Presidential Selection

The delegates had great difficulty deciding how the president was to be chosen. Eight of the twelve states that sent delegates to the convention relied on the legislature to select the executive, and that was the method Madison included in the Virginia Plan. This decision reflected Madison's deep fear of despotism. Independence had come in a war against a king. Like most of the other delegates, even those who favored a strong national government, he feared creating another king. Allowing the people to choose the president heightened that risk. The public was too ignorant and too susceptible to demagogic appeals to be trusted to reliably choose someone who did not harbor monarchic ambitions. Throughout most of the Convention, legislative choice remained the preferred option.

Proponents of legislative choice recognized it risked undermining the principle of checks and balances, but they believed they had a solution to that problem. The president would serve only one fixed term and his compensation would also be determined in advance. Once elected, he would be free of congressional influence, since it could not offer him reelection nor change his salary.

The opponents of legislative selection placed more faith in the people and less in Congress. Whereas particular segments of the public might be swayed by irrational appeals, there was safety in large numbers. The public at large, encompassing a vast number of voters, could be trusted to make a wise decision. They were confident that certain individuals would make such great contributions to public life that they would be celebrated nationwide. Therefore, the national electorate would be sufficiently well acquainted with them to know whom best to choose. They dubbed such individuals "continental characters."

Congress could not be trusted to make this choice. Congressmen might be better informed than ordinary voters, but they were also much more likely to support candidates on a self-interested basis. Cliques of congressmen would form, each seeking to choose the person most likely to advance their interests and ambitions. Also, legislative choice would likely succumb to corruption. Compared to a national electorate, the congressional electorate would be very small and therefore a majority could be bought for a reasonable price. Congress might be less likely than the public at large to choose a despot, but it was far more likely to chose a weak, subservient, venal person.

Neither of these options fully satisfied delegates from the smaller states because the choice was between direct majority rule if based on national popular vote, or indirect majority rule if decided by the House of Representatives. The compromise method of election finally adopted by the Convention found a way to address their concerns while also satisfying the proponents and opponents of congressional selection of the executive.

The compromise created a two- or potentially three-step process for choosing the president. The first step involved the choice of electors who would comprise the Electoral College. These electors would be chosen on a state-by-state basis. Each state would be awarded the number of electors that matched the number of House districts the state contained plus two additional electors, matching the number of senators each had. Each state would be free to decide how to choose those electors. The electors would not meet as a national college. Rather, those chosen by each state met as a group to decide how that state would cast its electoral votes. Electors would cast two ballots, one of which would have to be for a person from outside their state. The person receiving the most electoral votes would become president but only if he received an outright majority of electoral votes. Otherwise the choice was to be made by the House of Representatives from among the top five finishers. However, the House's determination was not made on the basis of majority vote. Instead, each state's delegation would meet together to determine how the state would vote and each state would have only one vote.

As is the case with any serious political compromise, those involved had to give up something that they dearly wanted in order to obtain things they wanted even more. Thus, for the opponents of legislative selection the price of keeping the initial selection process out of the hands of Congress was to give up their demand for national popular election. Nor were they guaranteed that each state would choose its electors on a popular basis. Each state was free to choose its electors as it wished. The legislative choice opponents concluded that placing the choice in the hands of electors who had to cast at least one of their ballots for someone outside their state would accomplish their primary goal of encouraging the selection of "continental characters" and so they sacrificed their goals regarding popular election. They were also pleased that the compromise placed no limit on reeligibility. They believed that only if the president was allowed to run for reelection would he feel obliged to remain in the good graces of the public and therefore have sufficient incentive to serve the public interest.

The advocates of congressional choice were consoled by their belief that rarely if ever would a single candidate succeed in obtaining a majority of electoral votes. Therefore, Congress would retain control of the actual selection. Small states delegates were appeased by the guarantee that their states would have at least three electoral votes, since they each had at least one House member as well as two Senators. Furthermore, if the selection process moved to the House of Representatives, each state delegation, regardless of its size, would have an equal voice in the outcome.

Although these various elements of the executive were considered during the course of the entire convention, they were assembled into a single package only at the last minute by a committee appointed to propose final solutions for the important matters that the convention deliberations had left unresolved. When the overall proposal was presented to delegates, they approved it overwhelmingly. The only change they made to the committee proposal was to substitute the House of Representatives for the Senate as the legislative body to choose the president if no candidate received an absolute majority of electoral votes. In the course of a few months, most of them had traveled an enormous political distance, from opposing any independent executive to endorsing one that had a single person in control, was eligible for reelection and, if able to obtain an Electoral College majority, would be elected independently of the legislature. On no other question was the cumulative impact of all that deliberating so great.

CRITICAL THINKING QUESTION

The Cambridge University Press website contains excerpts from the Convention debates about presidential selection. You are invited to read these speeches, summarize what you consider to be the best arguments made by each side, and then address two questions: (1) Do you favor popular election or choice by the legislature?; and (2) Do you approve of the compromise that was reached regarding the Electoral College and the role allotted to Congress? (If not, what better alternative do you propose?)

The Key Elements of the Constitutional Framework the Convention Established

Popular Representation and Checks and Balances

The fruit of the Constitutional Convention's deliberations was a document that established a set of governing institutions and a pattern of relationships between those institutions that gave practical form to the Federalists' "new science of politics." The independent executive, independent judiciary, and bicameral legislature it created embodied both the principles of popular representation and of checks and balances. The *House of Representatives* was intended to be the more popular of the two houses. Its members would be kept relatively close to the people because they would have to run for election frequently, every two years, most likely from districts that were relatively small. (The Constitution does not mention district elections for the House, and they were not mandated by law until 1842.)

By contrast, the *Senate* would be comprised of two members from each state who would be elected for six-year terms. The Senate would not simply uphold states' rights, but would also check the excesses of the more popular House. Six-year terms would insulate senators somewhat from the ebb and flow of popular passions. The system of staggered elections, by which only one-third of the Senate could change in any given election, would further enhance the ability of its members "to refine and enlarge the public views." Those senators from the bigger states would be especially free from popular pressure. The large size of their constituencies meant that they would represent a diverse set of interests and would not slavishly serve any one narrow point of view.

Because they enjoyed freedom from constituency pressure and because their house was of manageable size, senators would be able to consider public questions in a "cool and deliberate" fashion. They could be calm and reasonable in ways that members of the House could not, providing them, in Madison's view, with a special responsibility:

> Stimulated by some irregular passion, or some illicit advantage, or misled by the artful misrepresentations of interested men, [the people] may call for measures which they themselves may afterwards be the most ready to lament and condemn ... [At such times, they need] the interference of some temperate and respectable body of citizens ... to check ... the blow mediated by the people against themselves, until reason, justice, and truth can regain their authority over the public mind.

For a bill to become a law it had to be passed by both houses. Likewise, a presidential veto could only be overcome by a two-thirds vote of both houses. Thus each house of Congress would exert an independent check on the other as well as on the actions of the other branches.

The Constitution gave the separate branches sufficient power so that the ambitions of each could act to stalemate the ambitions of the others. Congress checks the other two branches through its role in judicial and executive appointments, presidential selection, treaty making, impeachment, and its control over taxing and spending. The Senate has final approval over the president's choices for judges, members of the Supreme Court, and members of the cabinet. If no presidential candidate garners a majority of the Electoral College, the House of Representatives elects the president. The House determines whether a judge, an executive official, or the president should be subject to an impeachment trial. If the House impeaches, then the Senate decides whether to remove the impeached person from office. Any treaty negotiated by the president with a foreign power must be ratified by a two-thirds vote of the Senate. And, the executive branch can only spend money that Congress has budgeted for it.

The president's greatest power over Congress resides in the ability to *veto* legislation. This power is far from absolute, however, because Congress can override that veto by a two-thirds vote of each house. The president also appoints the members of the Supreme Court and other federal courts and members of the cabinet, all subject to Senate approval. The importance of the president in making the complex system of representation work further reveals the Founders' objective of moderating democracy.

The Constitution was not explicit in providing checks for the judiciary over the other two branches. Indeed, as is described in Chapter 9, the issue of whether the Supreme Court had the power to declare acts of Congress unconstitutional remained hotly contested even after the Constitution was adopted. In *Federalist* 78, however, Alexander Hamilton argued that the court did have such power and that its ability to declare laws unconstitutional was a crucial aspect of the checks and balances system. Because even a presidential veto could be overridden by Congress, the court needed this authority in order to prevent congressional despotism. Hamilton recognized that granting such great power to judges appointed for life was highly undemocratic. But he argued that because the judiciary was inherently the weakest branch of government, it was not in a position to abuse that power. Hamilton further argued that judges alone had the knowledge and institutional means to uphold the law. Only they were fully competent to interpret the Constitution, and their lack of executive authority meant that they would not do so in a dictatorial fashion.

Federalism

In addition to the checks and balances among the institutions of the federal government, the Constitution also provided for checks and balances between the federal and state governments. The system of *federalism* made for a "compound republic," Madison observed, in which "the power surrendered by the people is first divided between two distinct governments, and then the apportion allotted to each subdivided among separate and distinct departments." The system of federalism thus ensured "a double security" in protecting "the rights of the people." As we have seen, the states are central to the configuration of both the Senate and the Electoral College. In addition, Article V of the Constitution grants them an important role in the amendment process. Constitutional amendments, which required approval by two-thirds of both the House and Senate, also had to be ratified by three-fourths of the states. The Constitution also provided an alternative amendment method by which two-thirds of the states may call for a constitutional convention that would have the authority to propose amendments.

Classic Liberalism and the New Science of Politics

The Framers' "new science of politics" was not entirely new. It was grounded in the Classic Liberal doctrines propounded a century earlier. Government existed only to enable people to live freely and securely. Therefore, strict limits had to be imposed on it. From this perspective, the two most important words in the Constitution appear in Section 1 of Article I. The whole section reads "All legislative powers herein granted shall be vested in a Congress of the United States, which shall consist of a Senate and House of Representatives." The words "herein granted" proclaim the limited extent of federal power. If powers are not herein granted, meaning that if they are not enumerated in the following sections of Article I, then the federal government does not have them. This principle of enumerated powers, bolstered by the checks and balances already described, gives practical meaning to the concept of limited government.

The Ratification of the Constitution

In order for the draft Constitution to go into effect, to be *ratified*, it had to be adopted by nine states. The outcome of the state-by-state voting was by no means certain. All the states had prominent Anti-Federalists.

Anti-Federalist Objections

As the Anti-Federalist Patrick Henry forcefully argued at the Virginia ratifying convention, the opponents of the Constitution rejected the wording "We, the People" in favor of "We, the States." They recognized that the Constitutional Convention had gone against the instructions issued by the Continental Congress and that the very first words of the preamble had revolutionary consequences. Their preference was to marginally strengthen the national government without a major alteration of the Articles of Confederation.

Despite their preference for direct citizen involvement, the Anti-Federalists did recognize the need for political representation. Even state capitals were too far away to enable most citizens to participate in state government. But their innate distrust of representation led them to take a very different view of national government than did the Federalists. The Anti-Federalists' goal was to minimize the separation, both physical and psychological, between representative and constituent. Therefore representative districts should be as small as possible, enabling the representative to stay in touch with each constituent. Elections should be held yearly, giving constituents frequent opportunity to oust an incumbent who did not adequately reflect their concerns. No matter that the result would be a House of Representatives so large as to be unwieldy and whose members would serve such brief terms that they would not have a chance to become knowledgeable and competent. The loss of effectiveness and deliberative capacity, argued the Anti-Federalists, were small prices to pay to preserve democratic accountability.

The Anti-Federalists loathed the Senate. They recognized that its small size and infrequent election would encourage a strong sense of collegiality among its members. This was not the type of classroom or the kind of mutual instruction they favored. Anti-Federalists took the word "represent" literally. The task of the representative was to *re-present* the views of constituents to the representative body. The Anti-Federalists envisaged representatives returning home frequently to districts small enough to enable them to instruct constituents about the events taking place at the national capital and to receive instruction about how best to represent their constituents.

The Anti-Federalists similarly feared and loathed the proposed presidency. Having severed from a king, why now voluntarily succumb to a monarch? They opposed not only a commander in chief, but also the very idea of a standing army available for such a commander to lead. They admitted that the Union might face military danger, but they much preferred placing responsibility for defense in citizen militias, mobilized by the states, whose sole purpose was to respond to a military emergency. When the emergency passed, the militias would disband, and the country would not then have to worry about how to cope with the threat inevitably posed to its freedom by a standing army led by a powerful commander.

Ironically, Anti-Federalists attacked the Constitution both for protecting and inadequately securing slavery. Southern Anti-Federalists such as Patrick Henry also warned that a strong centralized government made possible the abolition of slavery, which would cripple the South's economy. Conversely, the Massachusetts Anti-Federalist, Consider Ames, who had participated in Shays's rebellion, indicted the new Constitution for sanctioning and protecting an institution that denigrated the core principle of the Declaration. Massachusetts had outlawed slavery by judicial decree just a few years earlier. Ames feared that the Constitution's necessary and proper clause could be interpreted so as to undermine the antislavery efforts of individual states.

Table 3.8. Constitutional ratification by state.

State	Date of ratification	Margin
Delaware	December 4–7, 1787	30–0
Pennsylvania	November 20 – December 12, 1787	46–23
New Jersey	December 11–18, 1787	38–0
Georgia	December 25–31, 1787	26–0
Connecticut	January 3–9, 1788	128–40
Massachusetts	January 9 – February 6, 1788	187–168
Maryland	April 21–26, 1788	63–11
South Carolina	May 12–23, 1788	149–73
New Hampshire	June 18–21, 1788	57–47
Virginia	June 2–25, 1788	89–79
New York	June 17 – July 26, 1788	30–27
North Carolina	November 16–21, 1789	194–77
Rhode Island	May 26–29, 1790	34–32

Source: Teaching American History.

The Federalist Triumph

The debates that preceded the ratification votes were long and heated. What ultimately enabled the Federalists to triumph was the same advantage they possessed in the Philadelphia convention: they had a specific, comprehensive, and detailed plan for governing the nation, and their opponents had none. Therefore, the Anti-Federalists were continually on the defensive, criticizing this or that feature of the Constitution but offering no broad alternative for how the new nation would sustain itself in the future.

The Federalists were politically astute enough not to trumpet the radical innovations that the document contained but rather to emphasize its fundamental compatibility with the ideas and principles that Anti-Federalists held dear. This shrewd combination of arguments is shown to best advantage in *The Federalist Papers*, written, as we have noted, for the express purpose of gaining support for the Constitution in the politically volatile state of New York. Each paper concentrated on either a particular reason for seeking change in the status quo, a particular advantage offered by the new Constitution, or a refutation of some criticism about the Constitution levied by the Anti-Federalists.

Taken as a whole, *The Federalist Papers* provided a systematic and comprehensive case for the necessity of revamping the Articles and for adopting a strong central government. They also persuasively argued that the new government would preserve the most essential features and virtues of the existing system, most important, the power and influence of the states. Then, as now, a political campaign is usually won by whoever can most successfully appeal to the undecideds. The Federalists won because they could convince citizens in the middle that their plan was both radical enough to solve the problems posed by the weakness of government under the Articles of Confederation and conservative enough to protect the sovereignty of the states.

A Bill of Rights

The Federalists found it wise to make an additional concession during the ratification debates. They pledged that if the Constitution were adopted, they would support the addition of a bill of rights in the form of a series of constitutional amendments. Many state constitutions already contained bills of rights. In some cases, these rights were listed in the preamble of the state constitution, as if to show that the details of institutional design that followed should be viewed as the specific devices by which the goals set out in the bill of rights were to be achieved.

The leading architects of the federal Constitution, including Madison and Hamilton, had opposed including a bill of rights. They claimed to oppose it because such a list was unnecessary for a government whose authority was expressly limited to its enumerated powers. But this argument cannot be taken at face value because in various parts of the Constitution this principle of relying on enumeration is violated and specific protections against government excess are provided. The deeper reason the Federalists opposed a bill of rights may have been that the government they were trying to put in place would not be strong enough and that its enemies would make use of a bill of rights to weaken it still further.

Supporters of a bill of rights saw it as an essential means for explaining to citizens what the purposes of the new government were and how the public should judge it. This explanation was especially important to wavering Anti-Federalists who acknowledged the need for a stronger union but found the proposed constitution devoid of any clear statement about how it was to serve the greater goal of protecting liberty. They feared that later generations would not fully realize that behind the Constitution lay the Declaration of Independence. In their minds at least, the Constitution was worthless if its various institutional contrivances were not explicitly dedicated to "unalienable rights." Therefore, they insisted that the Constitution be amended to enumerate the most essential components of those rights to ensure that future generations would be fully informed about what it was that their government had been established to protect.

The key rights enshrined in the Bill of Rights are as follows:

- No established religion; free exercise of religion
- Free speech; press; assembly
- Right to petition government for a redress of grievances
- Right to bear arms
- No unreasonable search and seizure
- No double jeopardy or compulsion to testify against oneself

- No taking of private property without just compensation
- Right to due process of law
- Right to trial by jury

The enduring importance and success of the Bill of Rights, its special place in the hearts of Americans, proved that its supporters were right. It is fitting that the lovers' quarrel among Americans over adoption of the Constitution should have led in the end to such a critical improvement in the nature of their relationship.

The Bill of Rights is one demonstration of the critical role played by the Anti-Federalists as well as the Federalists in founding the new government. The quarrels between these rivals were mostly resolved in favor of the Federalists. Not only did they succeed in convincing the Convention to do more than amend the Articles of Confederation; they also prevailed over the Anti-Federalists on two of the most contentious issues: the extended republic and the establishment of a direct connection between citizens and federal government. But the Anti-Federalists' enduring contribution both to the creation of the Constitution and to the subsequent development of American politics and government should not be underestimated. Even at the Convention itself, where their ranks were thin, delegates with Anti-Federalist sympathies succeeded in forcing the Federalists to provide a much more powerful role for the states than delegates such as Madison or Washington were initially inclined to accept.

The inclusion of a Senate elected by and with equal representation of the states was a compromise forced on Federalists. Likewise, giving the states such a prominent role in the amendment process and providing for the election of the president by an electoral college organized on a state-by-state basis were also grudging concessions made to win over the support of wavering delegates with Anti-Federalist sympathies. These specific provisions add up to the creation of a new form of federalism that represented one of the Constitution's most imaginative and daring innovations.

Although the more extreme Federalists, such as Hamilton, had hoped to use the Constitution to enshrine the dominance of centralized national authority, they did not succeed. The Constitution itself left the relationship between central and local politics in a purposefully ambiguous tension. Sadly, this ambiguity would eventually result in civil war. But it also provided the opportunity for democratic politics to survive and thrive within a constitutional context. As the American republic developed in the nineteenth century, the national government remained small and relatively insignificant while state and local politics flourished. State constitutions were rewritten to permit and encourage democratic participation to an extent that would have warmed the hearts of Anti-Federalists (see Chapter 5). Democratic impulses gained a far greater grip on the national imagination than the Federalists expected or hoped. The key success in the framing of the Constitution was not to settle the differences between Classic Liberalism, democratic egalitarianism, and communitarianism, but rather to create a strong and resilient framework within which they could continue to fruitfully collide and coexist.

Looking Forward

Because the Constitution purposely sets up a test of wills between the different branches and between the national government and the states, it is not surprising that these different governing institutions have been and continue to be frequently at odds with one another. Presidents claim that their executive power gives them the right to make decisions that Congress claims really amount to lawmaking, and complain that Congress oversteps its bounds in trying to "micro-manage" presidential efforts to implement the laws. Congress hurls similar charges at decisions of the Supreme Court. All three branches of the national government assail the states for violating national policy, and the states return the compliment by claiming that the national government has exceeded the enumerated powers designed to limit it. Subsequent chapters will explore how these constitutional collisions have played out over time, the contests of opinion they have inspired, and, looking forward, which new ones are likely to emerge. They will reveal how such contests embody the tensions between Classic Liberal, communitarian, and democratic egalitarian principles depicted in Chapter 2. For example, will a democratic/egalitarian demand for popular national election of the president spell the end of the Electoral College? Should a concern for decentralized government restrict the national government's reliance on the commerce clause to intrude into what had been considered state prerogatives? Are sensitive issues relating to gender identity best decided by federal courts and federal agencies, or should they be left in the hands of local communities?

CHAPTER SUMMARY

Contemporary portrait:

* The most important changes to the Constitution that have taken place since the passage of the Bill of Rights are: the Thirteenth, Fourteenth, and Fifteenth Amendments abolishing slavery, granting African Americans the right to vote, and forbidding the states from depriving citizens of due process and equal protection of the laws; the Seventeenth Amendment requiring the popular election of senators and the Nineteenth Amendment extending voting rights to women.

Madison's new political science and the opposition to it:

* Madison refuted the Anti-Federalist belief, shared by all previous republican thinkers, that a good republic was a small republic. He argued that a large republic was better suited for maintaining liberty because it discouraged the creation of a single majority faction capable of dominating the minority and depriving it of its rights.
* To prevent the representatives themselves from forming a faction that would tyrannize the populace, Madison relied on the principle of checks and balances. Although each branch would enjoy distinctive powers, each would be granted some power to meddle in the affairs of the others, ensuring that government power remained dispersed. Thus, "Ambition must be made to counteract ambition. The interest of the man must be connected with the constitutional rights of the place."
* The Anti-Federalists opposed the large republic because they believed that only small republics were capable of promoting the civic virtues necessary to prevent tyranny.

The role of leadership and deliberation in making the Constitutional Convention a success:

* Deliberation is the art of reasoning together. It involves a complex set of skills and attitudes.
* Madison, Washington, and Franklin each provided leadership that was critical to the success of the Convention.
* Washington lent his great prestige to the effort and then exerted control over the deliberations in his role as chair.
* Madison's skill in agenda setting ensured that his plan, the Virginia Plan, would become the framework for the Convention's subsequent discussions.
* At a moment of great crisis and contention, Franklin restored a deliberative atmosphere that made possible the passage of the Great Compromise.

The critical choices to create a Senate and protect slavery:

* The Great Compromise consisted of a House of Representatives, which would provide representation proportional to each state's population, and a Senate, which would be chosen by the states. Each state, regardless of its size, would be entitled to two senators.
* The Constitution protected slavery by requiring the return of fugitive slaves, guaranteeing the continued importation of slaves for a period of twenty years and bolstering slave states' representation in the House of Representatives by allowing them to add three-fifths of their slave population to their census for purposes of apportioning House districts.

The creation of a strong executive:

* The presidential selection process adopted by the Convention was a compromise between those who favored selection by the legislature, those who favored

popular election, and those who favored selection by the states. Electors are chosen by the states but roughly in proportion to their populations. The House of Representatives elects the president if an electoral college majority is not forthcoming.

The key elements of the constitutional framework the Convention established:

* The Constitution gave practical form to the Federalists' "new science of politics." The independent executive, independent judiciary, and bicameral legislature it created embodied both the principles of popular representation and of checks and balances (see Chapters 7, 8, and 9).
* The Constitution also created what Madison termed a "compound republic" in which both the national government and the state government enjoyed distinct spheres of authority (see Chapter 5).

The ratification of the Constitution:

* Among the Anti-Federalists' reasons for opposing the Constitution were: the congressional districts were too large; House and Senate elections were too infrequent; the presidency would become tyrannical.
* What ultimately enabled the Federalists to triumph was the same advantage they possessed in the Philadelphia convention: they had a specific, comprehensive, and detailed plan for governing the nation, and their opponents had none. They also persuasively argued that the new government would preserve the most essential features and virtues of the existing system, most important, the power and influence of the states.
* The Bill of Rights was a concession the Federalists made to win the support of those who viewed it as an essential means for reinforcing the principle proclaimed in the Declaration of Independence that the deepest purpose of the new government was to protect inalienable rights.

SUGGESTED READINGS

Bailyn, Bernard. *The Ideological Origins of the American Revolution.* Cambridge, MA: Harvard University Press, 1992.

Bowen, Catherine Drinker. *Miracle at Philadelphia: The Story of the Constitutional Convention, May to September, 1787.* New York: Book of the Month Club, 1966.

Chernow, Ron. *Alexander Hamilton.* New York: Penguin Books, 2004.

Fallon, Richard. *The Dynamic Constitution: An Introduction to American Constitutional Law.* New York: Cambridge University Press, 2004.

Farrand, Max, ed. *The Records of the Federal Convention of 1787*, 4 vols. New Haven, CT: Yale University Press, 1966.

Hamilton, Alexander, James Madison, and John Jay. *The Federalist Papers*, ed. Charles Kesler. New York: Mentor Books, 1999.

Jensen, Merrill. *The Articles of Confederation.* Madison: University of Wisconsin Press, 1963.

McDonald, Forrest. *The Formation of the American Republic*. New York: Penguin, 1967.
Rakove, Jack. *Original Meanings: Politics and Ideas in the Making of the Constitution*. New York: Knopf, 1997.
Rossitor, Clinton. *1787: Grand Convention*. New York: Macmillan, 1966.
Siemers, David. *The Anti-Federalists: Men of Great Faith and Forbearance*. Lanham, MD: Rowman & Littlefield, 2003.
Storing, Herbert, ed. *The Complete Anti-Federalist*, 7 vols. University of Chicago Press, 1981.
Storing, Herbert, *What the Anti-Federalists Were For*. University of Chicago Press, 1981.
Wood, Gordon. *The Creation of the American Republic*. New York: W. W. Norton, 1982.
The Americanization of Benjamin Franklin. New York: Penguin, 2004.

4 Political Development

CHAPTER OVERVIEW

This chapter focuses on:

- **The critical choice to democratize the Constitution in the early 1800s.**
- **The critical choice to promote mass democracy in the Jacksonian era.**
- **The critical choice to inaugurate a new birth of freedom during the Civil War.**
- **The Progressive Era's anticipation of the modern state.**
- **The critical choice to create the modern state during the New Deal.**
- **Continuity and change since the New Deal.**

In January of 1830 the United States Senate began debate on a motion by Senator Samuel Foote of Connecticut calling for a temporary halt to federal government sales of lands in the West. What followed was no mere debate about the wisdom of such a step but a great debate about the nature and meaning of the Constitution. Senator Robert Hayne of South Carolina rose in opposition to Foote's motion. But rather than confining himself to the lands question, he launched a tirade against oppression of the states by the national government.

> I am opposed, therefore, in any shape, to all unnecessary extension of the powers or the influence of the legislature or executive of the union of the states; and, most of all, I am opposed to those partial distributions of favors whether by *legislation* or *appropriation*, which has a direct and powerful tendency to spread corruption through the land – to create an abject spirit of dependence – to sow the seeds of dissolution – to produce jealousy among the different portions of the union, and, finally, to sap the very foundations of the government itself.

Hayne had a lot more than land sales on his mind in issuing this diatribe. Congress had recently passed a tariff law that was highly detrimental to the South Carolina economy. A tariff is a tax imposed on a good that is imported from abroad. Because it raised tariffs on manufactured goods, thus aiding Northern manufacturers, it invited South Carolina's European trading partners to retailiate by raising tariffs on the state's agricultural exports. Southerners in general and South Carolinians in particular feared that this act of regional discrimination was only the beginning of Northern aggression against the South. They feared that eventually Northerners would attempt to use the power of Congress to limit or even abolish slavery. Hayne used the occasion of the land sale moratorium, bitterly opposed by Westerners, to forge an alliance with the West in opposition to all unwanted federal intrusion.

Senator Daniel Webster of Massachusetts responded to Hayne that the Union was no mere alliance of convenience but something to be cherished and revered.

> I know that there are some persons in the part of the country from which the honorable member comes, who habitually speak of the union in terms of indifference, or even of disparagement ... They significantly declare, that it is time to calculate the value of the union, and their aim seems to be to enumerate and to magnify all the evils real and imaginary, which the government under the union produces. The tendency of all these ideas and sentiments is obviously to bring the union into discussion, as a mere question of present and temporary expediency – nothing more than a mere matter of profit and loss. The union to be preserved while it suits local and temporary purposes to preserve it; and to be sundered whenever it shall be found to thwart such purposes. Union, of itself, is considered by the disciples of this school as hardly a good. It is only regarded as a possible means of good; or, on the other hand as a possible means of evil. They cherish no deep and fixed regard for it, flowing from a thorough conviction of its absolute and vital necessity to our welfare.

Hayne retorted that Webster misunderstood the intentions of the Constitution's framers.

> The object of the framers of the constitution ... was not to draw power from the states, in order to transfer it to a great national government, but, in the language of the constitution itself, "to form a more perfect Union"; – and by what means? By "establishing justice, promoting domestic tranquillity, end securing the blessings of liberty to ourselves and our posterity." But, according, to the gentleman's reading, the object of the constitution was, to *consolidate the government*, and the means would seem to be, the promotion of injustice, causing domestic *discord*, and depriving the states and the people "of the blessings of liberty" forever.

Webster replied that it was Hayne, not he, who misunderstood the Framers. "I deem far otherwise of the union of the states, and so did the framers of the constitution themselves What they said I believe ... that the union of the states is essential to the prosperity and safety of the states ... I would strengthen the ties that hold us together."

Hayne supported his view of the Constitution by describing it as a compact between the states and that it was up to each state to decide whether or not a particular national government action violated the compact. In that case the state had every right to refuse to obey.

The constitution of the United States was formed by the sanction of the states, given by each in its sovereign capacity. It adds to the stability and dignity, as well as to the authority, of the constitution, that it rests upon this legitimate and solid foundation. The states, then, being the parties to the constitutional compact, and in their sovereign capacity, it follows of necessity that there can be no tribunal above their authority to decide. In the last resort, whether the compact made by them be violated and consequently that, as the parties to it, they must themselves decide, in the last resort, such questions as may be of sufficient magnitude to require their interposition.

Webster pointed to the chaos that would result from Hayne's view that a state could refuse to abide by a federal government mandate.

Four-and-twenty interpreters of constitutional law, each with a power to decide for itself, and none with authority to bind anybody else, and this constitutional law the only bond of their union! What is such a state of things but a mere connection during pleasure, or, to use the phraseology of the times, *during feeling*? And that feeling, too, not the feeling of the people, who established the Constitution, but the feeling of the State governments.

He also derided the constitutional theory upon which such an absurd result rested.

This absurdity . . . arises from a misconception as to the origin of this government and its true character. It is, Sir, the people's Constitution, the people's government, made for the people, made by the people, and answerable to the people. The people of the United States have declared that this Constitution shall be the supreme law. We must either admit the proposition, or dispute their authority. The States are, unquestionably, sovereign, so far as their sovereignty is not affected by this supreme law. But the State legislatures, as political bodies, however sovereign, are yet not sovereign over the people. So far as the people have given power to the general government, so far the grant is unquestionably good, and the government holds of the people, and not of the State governments. We are all agents of the same supreme power, the people. The general government and the State governments derive their authority from the same source. Neither can, in relation to the other, be called primary, though one is definite and restricted, and the other general and residuary. The national government possesses those powers which it can be shown the people have conferred on it, and no more. All the rest belongs to the State governments, or to the people themselves. So far as the people have restrained State sovereignty, by the expression of their will, in the Constitution of the United States, so far, it must be admitted, State sovereignty is effectually controlled.

He ended his defense of the Union with a paean of praise to its many blessings.

Every year of its duration has teemed with fresh proofs of its utility and its blessings; and although our territory has stretched out wider and wider, and our population spread farther and farther, they have not outrun its protection or its benefits. It has been to us all a copious fountain of national, social, and personal happiness . . . "Liberty and Union, now and for ever, one and inseparable!"

This debate between two powerful and prestigious senators epitomizes the great contests of opinion that have periodically threatened to either unravel the Union itself or undermine its capacity to function. On the one hand these contests have been about very particular policy questions – tariffs, the extension of slavery to western territories, old-age pensions. But, as Webster and Hayne both demonstrated, those specific policy differences have been linked to the deepest questions about the nature and meaning of the Constitution.

This chapter focuses on the great contests of opinion and the critical choices stemming from them that have periodically surfaced in the course of American political development. It reinforces the arguments made in the previous chapter that the constitutional order has remained fundamentally unchanged. Key founding principles endure. It combines this claim of stability with the equally valid claim that the American political system has undergone several critical reconsiderations and transformations. It attempts to reconcile these claims about continuity and change through its depiction of each of these critical episodes of reconsideration and transformation as a *conservative revolution*. Each was revolutionary in that it resulted in some major shift in the understanding of individual rights, the meaning of democracy and equality, and the relationship between local and national power. It was conservative in its fidelity to fundamental constitutional norms and principles.

The first section of this chapter connects Chapter 3's study of the Constitution with the critical political episodes that form the core of this chapter. The subsequent sections focus on those episodes that are central to the development of the American nation: the democratization of the Constitution, the rise of mass democracy, the new birth of freedom, and the creation of a modern state. Finally, the chapter explores key political developments that have occurred since the creation of a modern state in the 1930s.

CRITICAL CHOICE: DEMOCRATIZING THE CONSTITUTION

The first conservative revolution took place between 1800 and 1808, during Thomas Jefferson's two terms as president. It promoted democracy, liberty, and decentralization by defending and promoting free speech, legislative supremacy, and states' rights. It was inextricably connected to two new forms of political communication and political organization: a popular press and a political party.

Federalists and Republicans

No sooner had the Constitution been ratified than Americans began to fight over its meaning. This contest led to the emergence of two fiercely divided parties, the Federalist Party and the Republican Party, that became engaged in a heated contest of principle. The Federalists, led by Alexander Hamilton, and the Republicans, led by Thomas Jefferson, both spoke the language of rights and accepted the "self-evident" truth that government existed to protect property and free enterprise. But the two parties disagreed fundamentally about the relationship between liberty and democracy and the relative importance of local self-government. Federalists believed that republican government rested in the deliberations of political representatives held at a considerable distance from popular opinion. Republicans championed both the democratic egalitarian principle that the people should rule and the communitarian principle that they should do so, for the most part, locally.

Constitutional struggle broke out during George Washington's first term, thwarting his desire to place the presidency and the Constitution above partisan conflict. Washington's two most brilliant cabinet ministers – Alexander Hamilton, secretary of the treasury, and Thomas Jefferson, secretary of state – differed over Hamilton's program to strengthen government's finances. At the request of the first Congress, Hamilton issued a series of reports between 1790 and 1791 that called on the legislature to fund the national debt, assume the war debts of the states, encourage manufacturing through the creation of a system of tariffs, and create a national bank. Jefferson opposed the national bank because he feared it would establish an unhealthy concentration of power in the national government, creating a dangerous tie between the capital and the country's wealthiest citizens, and because it was unconstitutional. Jefferson believed that democracy required a predominant agricultural sector, comprising small landholders of roughly equal wealth. Hamilton's commercial republic, Jefferson claimed, would breed inequality and moral decay, thus destroying the moral foundation of a free society.

Hamilton and his allies, identifying themselves as the respectable defenders of constitutional order, called themselves Federalists. Washington refused to adopt the label but tilted toward Hamilton. The Jeffersonians rejected the name Anti-Federalist and instead called themselves Republicans. They opposed the expansion of the national government because this would inevitably force Congress to delegate more power to the executive branch. The Republicans believed that such an "administrative republic" would make the more decentralized and popular institutions – Congress, the states, and the localities – subordinate to the executive, would frustrate the popular will, enshrine a privileged elite, and push the United States toward a British-style monarchy.

The Republican attack on the Washington administration was not confined to the councils of government; it was also communicated directly to the public through newspapers. In early 1791, Hamilton helped start the *United States Gazette*. Jefferson and James Madison aided in the establishment of a competing Republican newspaper, the *National Gazette*, which appeared in October 1791. As the political struggle between the Republicans and Federalists intensified, the number of newspapers expanded dramatically, from fewer than 100 in 1790 to more than 230 in 1800. By 1810, Americans were buying 22 million copies of 376 newspapers annually, the largest newspaper circulation in the world.

Madison's essays in the *National Gazette*, published in 1791 and 1792, demonstrated his opposition to the Federalists' concentration of executive power. Previously, Madison's fears of majority tyranny led him to support the Constitution's institutional arrangements for dividing and filtering the voice of the people. But now he sought to arouse a "common sentiment" against the consolidation of government power. Formerly a defender of nationalism, Madison became a champion of the states as agents for mobilizing public opinion against excessive consolidation. By working with Jefferson to organize the Republican Party, Madison championed the political centralization that building a national political party entailed as the best way to defend state and local interests against governmental centralization.

Previously, Madison had opposed Jefferson's notion that the "Constitution belongs to the living." He had warned against frequent public appeals about constitutional issues, fearing that popular contests over them would "carry an implication of some defect in the government" and thus "deprive the [Constitution] of that veneration which time bestows on everything." Continual constitutional discord would prevent the Constitution from establishing itself as the American political religion. But Madison came to believe that the Federalists had undermined the Constitution's system of checks and balances and had created a struggle between the many and the few. Now it was necessary to provoke just the sort of popular constitutional debate he had previously opposed.

The terms of this debate were illustrated by the different ways in which Republicans and Federalists chose to celebrate the Fourth of July, which became a national holiday during the 1780s. The Federalists emphasized nationalism and made few, if any, references to the Declaration of Independence, whose anti-British character embarrassed Federalists who now sought economic and political reconciliation with the mother country. Also, the claim that all men were created equal seemed too democratic. Federalists preferred to celebrate the Constitution – whose more perfect Union was dedicated to moderating America's democratic impulses – rather than to praise Jefferson's handiwork.

Republicans, by contrast, celebrated the Declaration as a "deathless instrument," written by "the immortal Jefferson." They eagerly invoked its indictments of the British monarchy and recalled America's great debt to its sister republic, France. Above all, they stressed the Declaration's opening paragraphs – proclaiming that all men were "created equal" with "unalienable rights" – which they celebrated as America's creed. The essence of that creed, one Republican newspaper claimed, was not to be celebrated merely "as affecting the separation of one country from the jurisdiction of another; but as being the result of rational discussion and definition of the rights of man, and the ends of civil government."

The Republican triumph over the Federalists in the 1800 election strengthened the democratic character of the Constitution. This shift toward democratic principles did not dismantle republican government, but it did put an end to Federalist efforts to restrain popular opinion and to secure ordered liberty through the creation of an administrative establishment in the nation's capital. Jefferson was the first president to invoke the authority of the "will of the majority." He denied that the president, not to mention the judiciary, could claim authority that did not rest ultimately with "the people in mass."

"Absolute acquiescence in the decisions of the majority," Jefferson declared in his first inaugural address, "is the vital principle of republics, from which there is no appeal but force, the vital principle and immediate parent of despotism." Representatives' views, even those of presidents, should not be privileged over ordinary Americans, for when the voices of democratic citizens were added together they represented the ultimate sovereign. These combined voices represented public opinion – a concept that would soon come to dominate American political culture.

The Revolution of 1800

The great change that the Republicans wrought in politics and government when they came to power is often called the Revolution of 1800. It was dedicated to strengthening the decentralist and democratic institutions of the Constitution – the states and the House of Representatives. The Republicans sought to limit the scope of central government authority so that it rarely touched people's lives. They cut taxes and spending. Jefferson pardoned everyone (mostly Republican newspaper editors) convicted under the recently expired Sedition Act.

But the Revolution of 1800 was a decidedly conservative one. Republican faith in democracy was not absolute. Office was sought as a matter of honor, on the basis of accomplishments and service to one's country, not through active campaigning. Full citizenship rights, including the vote, were limited to men with property. Property qualifications were relatively modest – about two in three white males could vote in America compared to one in four in England – but most Republicans considered property to be an important barometer of independence and responsibility. Except for changing how the Electoral College voted for president, the Republicans presided over no formal constitutional changes. Despite their criticisms of the undemocratic nature of the judiciary, they left it intact. Likewise, they did not fully dismantle the Federalists' economic program. The National Bank remained until 1811, when its charter expired. In 1816, after the War of 1812 with Britain made clear the need for some sort of monetary control, the Republicans chartered a second bank.

Jeffersonians did not advocate a permanent mass party system. The Republican Party was a temporary expedient for defeating the Federalists and restoring

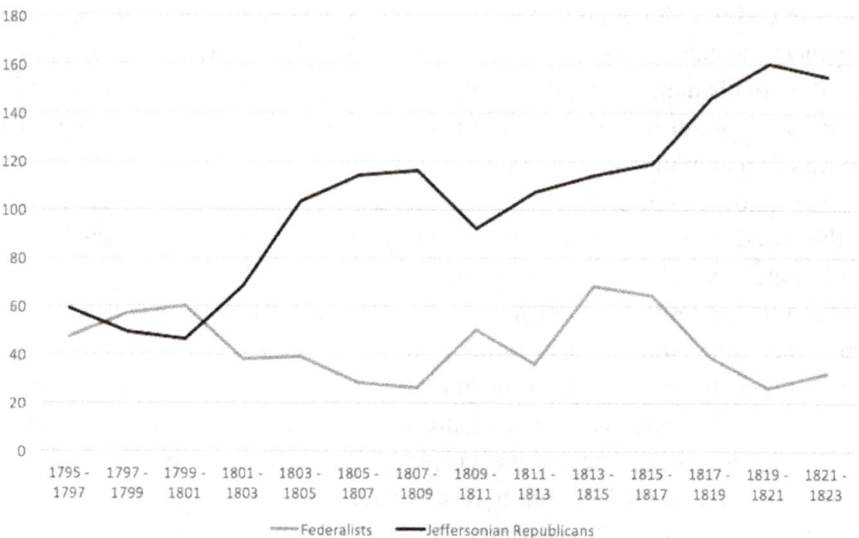

Figure 4.1. Party strength in US House of Representatives, 1795–1823.
Source: Office of the Clerk of the US House of Representatives.

balance to the constitutional order. Having accomplished those tasks, it could safely wither away, restoring the nonpartisan character of the Constitution. Jefferson's first inaugural address made overtures to Federalists, promising constitutional continuity and political moderation: "every difference of opinion is not a difference of principle . . . We have all called by different names brethren of the same principle. We are all republicans – we are all federalists." Jefferson's overture was remarkably successful, leading as it did to the gradual disintegration of the Federalist Party. Figures 4.1 and 4.2 chart the decline of the Federalists and the ascendancy of the Republicans in Congress from the 1790s to the early 1820s

The Louisiana Purchase

Jefferson's purchase of Louisiana, a territory encompassing not only New Orleans but most of the Great Plains and much of what is now the Northwest, doubled the country's size, adding some 830,000 square miles. The Constitution made no provision for acquiring foreign territory and incorporating it into the Union. But constitutional niceties were overlooked so that this vast southwest territory could be added to "make room for the generations of farmers yet unborn," strengthening the rural and therefore democratic character of the republic. Jefferson reconciled this effort to preserve the agrarian character of the country with his fear that America could thus become an empire on the order of France or Great Britain by declaring that this vast addition of empty space would enable

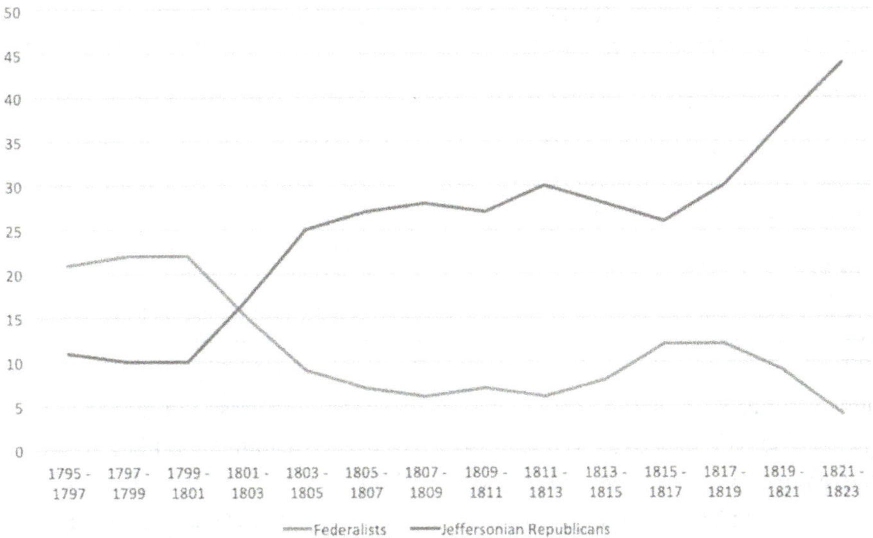

Figure 4.2. Party strength in US Senate, 1795–1823.
Source: United States Senate.

Figure 4.3. The Louisiana Purchase.
Credit: Granger Collection, NYC – All rights reserved.

Table 4.1. First conservative revolution: Jefferson's democratization of the Constitution.

Changes	Continuities
• Cut taxes and spending • Established first political party • Vast expansion of the size of the country as a result of the Louisiana Purchase	• White male suffrage with property qualifications persisted • No formal constitutional changes implemented • Judiciary left intact, despite Republican criticisms • National Bank was not abolished

America to become an "Empire of Liberty." The terrible consolidation of power that had resulted from the formation of the European empires woud be avoided because the new territory would quickly be divided into self-governing units set on a path toward statehood. In that manner, the US would remain decentralized with political primacy remaining in the states and localities.

UPSHOT

The Revolution of 1800 strengthened the democratic character of the Union. It reversed the centralizing efforts of the Federalists and ensured the political dominance of the states and localities, a path that would last well into the twentieth century (see Chapter 5). The "Empire of Liberty" resulting from the Louisiana Purchase preserved the agrarian character of the United States and reconciled its vast expansion with the maintenance of decentralist government.

CRITICAL CHOICE: PROMOTING MASS DEMOCRACY

Like the Jeffersonians, Jackson and his political allies sought to strengthen the democratic egalitarian tradition that the Constitution had sought to tame and to defend local and state government against national power. But the Jacksonians' political philosophy encouraged a much bolder assault on the principles and institutions of republican government that sought to restrain majority rule. By the 1830s, the word "democracy" largely supplanted "republicanism" as a description of the American political system. Indeed, the Jacksonians changed their party's name from Republican to Democrat. The constitutional battles between Republicans and Federalists obscured their agreement about the need to moderate democracy through institutional checks and balances. The Jacksonians sought to reverse this equation and make the Constitution and its institutional arrangements servants of public opinion. They did not displace liberalism. They remained committed to limitied government and natural rights. Rather, Jacksonians sought to render those republican principles compatible with a highly mobilized, competitive, and locally oriented democracy.

Andrew Jackson embodied this version of democracy. He was the first "outsider" president. His predecessors were highly educated and had undergone extensive apprenticeships in national politics and diplomacy. A self-made man, Jackson had little formal education, only brief experience in Congress, and no experience in the executive branch. In his first inaugural address, he stated the matter forthrightly: "The majority is to govern."

The most powerful expression of Jackson's egalitarian instinct was his decision to veto the rechartering of the Second Bank of the United States. He believed that destroying the bank did not threaten a free economy but instead honored it. He hoped to unleash the commercial spirit of the people from the shackles of government-created monopolies such as the bank, which favored idle speculators over the productive members of society: farmers, laborers, and mechanics. The clarion call of Jacksonian democracy, "equal rights to all and special privileges to none," promised political and economic independence to the producing "bone and sinew of the country." Jackson coupled his attack on economic centralization with an attack on governmental consolidation. He vetoed federally funded road projects. He cut the federal budget creating a revenue surplus. He used the surplus to pay off the national debt and returned what was left over to the states.

Jackson's championing of the will of the people greatly increased the pressure to open up the political process. By the late 1820s, most states had eliminated property qualifications for officeholding and had expanded suffrage to include all adult white males. Voter turnout soared. In 1824, only 27 percent of the eligible voters bothered to go to the polls. By 1828, when Jackson was elected, turnout doubled to 56 percent. In 1840, 78 percent of eligible voters cast ballots, a remarkable rate of participation that did not decline until the end of the nineteenth century.

The Party System

The party system arose as a means to both stimulate and discipline this extraordinary burst of democratic vitality. The Jefferson-led Republicans had viewed their party as a temporary expedient for defeating the Federalists' program of "consolidation." Their successors, the Jackson-led Democrats, defended not just parties but a *party system* as a critical extraconstitutional device to make democracy work (see Chapter 11). Parties were the only means for cultivating strong attachments between the people and the fundamental law. "Political parties are the schools of political science," a Jacksonian newspaper editorialized, "and no principle can be safely incorporated into the fabric of national law until it has been digested, limited, and defined by the earnest discussions of two parties ... [Parties] diffuse knowledge, cultivate the popular mind, and as they tend to give the people larger liberties, prepare them for enjoyment."

The Democratic Party itself embodied key decentralizing principles. During the Jeffersonian era, national politics centered on the congressional caucus, which had the power to nominate candidates for president and vice president. As we discuss in Chapters 8 and 14, the Democrats replaced "King Caucus" with national nominating conventions dominated by state party conventions made up of delegates from the localities.

To extend these decentralist political principles into government, the Jacksonians were committed to rotation in government office. The president woud use his appointment and removal power to give jobs to members of state and local Democratic organizations that had supported him. Thus, rotation in office tied the national government to the grassroots by employing officeholders loyal both to the president and to the local political leaders who had recommended them. Political power flowed in two directions. The president could deprive local leaders of the ability to place their loyalists, but if a sufficient number of local leaders felt aggrieved, they could act together to deprive the president of renomination.

Awarding jobs on the basis of political loyalty is often called "patronage." The credo of this patronage system, coined by Senator William Marcy, a militant Jacksonian, was "to the victors belong the spoils of the enemy." By the end of the nineteenth century, reformers would attack the spoils system as a corrupting influence on government. But rotation in office was conceived originally to extend the people's control over the executive branch As Jackson put it in his first annual message to Congress, "The duties of all public officers are, or at least admit of being made, so plain and simple that men of intelligence may readily qualify themselves for their performance." Virtually anybody was qualified to serve, as long as they had the proper political loyalties.

Patronage did not always serve democratic principles well. The lust for government jobs could exalt party organization as an end in itself – to the detriment of firm attachments to principles and programs. Nonetheless, the mechanism of periodic replacement of a substantial part of the government established the material basis for a mass party that mobilized large turnouts in presidential elections and thus counteracted "general indifference" to political life, which Tocqueville identified as the greatest threat to liberty in the United States. Prior to the 1830s, the spoils of office usually referred to the benefits that legislators bestowed on their constituents. Following the rise of the Democratic Party, spoils came to refer to the perquisites that party leaders lavished on campaign workers.

The Jacksonians radically transformed the practice of American politics, but they also hewed to critical conservative principles. They did not alter the Constitution. Most importantly, they adhered to the principle of limited government that the Constitution set forth and the Jeffersonians reinforced. They distributed

Table 4.2. Second conservative revolution: mass democracy.

Changes	Continuities
• Celebration of majority rule • Promoted mobilized, localized democracy • Promoted "common man" politicians over educated elites • Vetoed rechartering of national bank • Rejected federally funded public works projects • Embraced party system as crucial for democracy (not as temporary expedient)	• No formal constitutional changes • Vision of democracy promoted within the framework of making the existing Constitutional structure more effective, not as a radical departure • Whigs exercised checks on Jacksonian democrats in the name of their preference for a stronger and more active federal government • Neither party challenged the other's legitimacy

jobs on the basis of party loyalty but they did not use the spoils system as a rationale for increasing the size and scope of government. Indeed, they left the national government smaller than they found it. Thus, they defended communitarian as well as democratic and constitutional principles.

Decentralist, patronage-based democracy became so dominant that the Whigs, the opposition party formed in opposition to Jackson's bank veto, also committed themselves to it. They, too, claimed descent from Jefferson and praised his celebration of the dignity of the democratic individual. To avoid appearing elitist, Whig leaders such as Henry Clay of Kentucky and Daniel Webster of Massachusetts sought to convey the impression that they were less well educated and privileged than they actually were.

The Whigs set the precedent for how an opposition ought to behave in a party system. They did maintain and express important political differences from the Democrats. They believed in a much stronger federal government than did the Jacksonians. They supported a federally controlled national banking system and federal funding of roads, canals, and other forms of internal improvements. They also sought to strengthen Congress and keep a stronger check on the executive. But in the midst of these differences, they did not challenge the core Jacksonian commitment to local self-government. Nor did they question the legitimacy of the other party, tacitly admitting that both they and the Democrats were loyal supporters of the Constitution.

UPSHOT

The party system the Jacksonians provoked into being remains a central aspect of the American political system (see Chapter 12). Since 1836, control of the presidency and the Congress has been in the hands of one or the other of the two major parties. Indeed, since 1856 every president, and almost every congressperson, has been either a Republican (the successor to the Whigs) or a Democrat. For the next hundred years, the parties would operate according to the decentralist principles the Jacksonians established and the Whigs emulated.

CRITICAL CHOICE: A NEW BIRTH OF FREEDOM

The effort by a whole region of the country to secede posed the most serious threat to the preservation of the Union it has ever confronted. In the face of that threat, Abraham Lincoln sought both to fully establish the supremacy of the national government and to do so on a basis that reconciled the Constitution with the principles of liberty and equality the Declaration of Independence proclaimed.

Avoiding the Issue

Neither Whigs nor Democrats sought to engage Americans in a contest of opinion over slavery. Both were national parties, and their leaders feared that such a sectional struggle would fracture the Union. But the party system could not long suppress such a profound moral issue. Fittingly, the movement against slavery grew out of the churches. Evangelical Christianity, today considered a conservative force, was then a powerful reform agent. Animated by the religious revival efforts of the 1830s, called the Second Great Awakening, religious groups organized Sunday schools, spread the Gospel, opposed drinking, worked for peace, and fought slavery.

Abolitionists (see Chapter 14) sought to extend their influence through religious societies. There were 47 abolitionist societies in 1833, and more than 1,000 by 1837. Antislavery preachers moved from town to town, organizing new chapters and enlisting reform-minded church members, especially women, in petition drives to place antislavery motions before Congress. Although abolitionists operated outside regular political channels, they benefited from the spread of mass democracy. Appealing to a public already accustomed to following national political debates, the abolitionists flooded the country with newspapers, pamphlets, tracts, and pictures calculated to arouse African Americans, free and slave, and Northern public opinion against forced servitude.

The Jacksonian Democrats sought to repress abolitionism. In his 1835 annual message to Congress, President Jackson, whose hero, Jefferson, had fought against censorship, called for a national law barring "incendiary" materials from the mails. When Congress did not pass the law, Jackson imposed it administratively, ordering postmasters to remove antislavery material from the mails. Jackson's action drew little opposition from the political establishment. Even in the North, most Democratic and Whig newspaper editors viewed abolitionism as a threat to peace and union. But Jacksonian democracy had unleashed popular forces beyond its leaders' control. Hundreds of petitions with tens of thousands of signatures poured into Congress, pressing for the abolition of slavery in the nation's capital and asking that neither Florida nor Texas be added to the Union as slave states.

In a last, desperate attempt to stifle debate, House leaders proposed a "gag rule" that prohibited the House from discussing or even mentioning the antislavery petitions. The gag rule passed in 1835 with Jackson's strong support, and was tightened in 1840 during the term of his successor, Martin Van Buren. This affront to democracy was turned to the advantage of the antislavery forces by Jackson's old political rival, John Quincy Adams, who had been elected to the House in 1834. Adams adroitly exploited reverence for the Declaration of Independence and popular rule to defeat the gag rule. In January 1842, Adams presented an antislavery petition from a town in his district and ordered the House clerk to read the Declaration of Independence – reminding the House that popular rule rested on unalienable rights that slavery defiled. Adams exploited the gag rule controversy to remind white people that the basic right of free speech was also under attack. Thus, he was able to enlist support from Americans who, regardless of their views on slavery, believed that the House should remain a free and open arena for democratic debate. The House repealed the gag rule in 1844.

The Great Debate

A national debate over slavery exploded with the enactment of the Kansas–Nebraska Act of 1854. Sponsored by Senator Stephen Douglas and supported by President Franklin Pierce, this act repealed the Missouri Compromise that had adopted a specific line of longitude above which all territories that had been part of the Louisiana Purchase would be admitted as free states, and allowed the Kansas and Nebraska territories to adopt slavery if they chose to do so. This new formula permitting territories to decide for or against slavery by popular vote was called *popular sovereignty*. It passed Congress because of Pierce's heavy-handed use of patronage and was justified as a logical extension of the Democrats' commitment to majority rule.

In his debates with the Republican candidate, Abraham Lincoln, during the 1858 Illinois senatorial election, Stephen Douglas justified Northern Democratic defense of popular sovereignty on communitarian as well as democratic grounds. He argued that government in the United States was "formed on the principle of diversity in the local institutions and laws, and not on that of uniformity ... Each locality having different interests, a different climate, and different surroundings, required different local laws, local policy and local institutions, adopted to the wants of the locality."

Lincoln mocked Douglas's majoritarian claim as hypocritical since so-called "popular sovereignty" enabled one part of the population to enslave another part who had no say in the matter. He granted that the national government had no right to interfere with slavery where it was already established because that ignoble institution was protected by the Constitution. Lincoln venerated the Constitution. Constitutional veneration was a key theme of his speeches. Therefore he felt obligated to couple his opposition to slavery with fidelity to the Constitution. Fortunately, the Constitution only protected slavery where it already existed. Indeed, as Chapter 3 discussed, the word "slavery" does not appear in the Constitution and no principled defense of it is offered. Therefore slavery could be banned from the territories without violating the Constitution. Because such action was constitutional, it must be done in order to abide by the moral foundation of the Constitution, the Declaration of Independence.

Drawing on a verse from the Bible's Book of Proverbs – "A word fitly spoken is like apples of gold in pictures of silver" – Lincoln praised the Declaration's principle of "liberty to all" as the essence of American political life.

> This principle was the word fitly spoken which has proven an apple of gold to us. The Union, and the Constitution, are the picture of silver, subsequently framed around it. The picture was made, not to conceal, or destroy the apple; but to adorn and preserve it. The picture was made for the apple – not the apple for the picture.

Before Lincoln, Thomas Jefferson and Daniel Webster had invoked the Declaration as the nation's creed and had shown the link between its moral principles and the institutional arrangements of the Constitution. But Republicans were less willing to compromise this relationship than Jefferson or the Whigs had been. In the Gettysburg address, Lincoln purposely changed the wording of the Declaration of Independence; instead of saying "we hold these truths to be self-evident that all men are created equal" he said that the nation "was dedicated to the proposition that all men are created equal." As historian Daniel Walker Howe has observed, Lincoln reinterpreted Jefferson to make "the proposition that all men are created equal . . . a positive goal of political action, not simply a pre-political [or natural] state that government should preserve by inaction."

Douglas insisted that the "signers of the Declaration had made no reference to the Negro whatever, when they declared all men to be created equal," instead reserving such equality for whites. Lincoln retorted that denying African Americans a share in the Declaration threatened to transform slavery from a necessary evil into a positive good, a moral right, and thus risked "a gradual and steady debauching of public opinion." In the United States, where public opinion was everything, the consequences of such a change in the public mind would be devastating. Douglas's impropriety was compounded in 1857 by the *Dred Scott* decision (see Chapter 9).

In part, the debate between Lincoln and Douglas involved a struggle for the soul of Jacksonian democracy. Douglas supported the worst side of

Jacksonianism, the commitment to white supremacy; Lincoln championed the best side, commitment to the rights of the common American. Like his hero Jefferson, Lincoln sought to engage the American people in another profound constitutional reconsideration, revolutionary in the magnitude of its constitutional change but conservative in its rededication to unalienable rights and its preservation of the Union.

A War for Freedom

In the middle of the war, Lincoln redefined the war's aim: it did not seek to preserve the Union and prevent the expansion of slavery, but to preserve the Union and abolish slavery. He went about this radical transformation in a decidedly conservative manner. His Emancipation Proclamation only freed slaves who were being held by the enemy. He did not claim that slaves had a constitutional right to be free. Instead he claimed that as commander in chief he had the authority to weaken the enemy by confiscating its property. Slaves were enemy property. A full-scale emancipation of slaves required a constituitional amendment, which he endorsed shorly after being renominated in 1864. Congress passed it in 1865, before his assassination, and it was ratified by the end of the year. Only then did the equality promised by America's scripture, the Declaration of Independence, become a formal constitutional obligation, one adopted by proper constitutional means. That obligation was further extended by the Fourteenth Amendment, also ratified in 1868, which granted all Americans the "privileges and immunities of citizens of the United States," "due process," and "equal protection of the laws." The Fifteenth Amendment, added in 1870, proclaimed that the "right of citizens of the United States to vote shall not be abridged by the United States or any State on account of race, color, or previous condition of servitude." The three Civil War amendments changed the course of constitutional development and expanded government's obligation to protect the rights of the common citizen.

Rhetorical Leadership

The importance Lincoln placed on informing and rousing public opinion led him to focus on rhetoric. Lincoln was perhaps the greatest political orator in American history; much of his leadership ability derived from his ability to use language to justify and ennoble his political actions. His speeches endowed the Union with a religious aura, incorporating the principles of the Declaration into America's political and constitutional practices.

Lincoln used his 1863 *Gettysburg Address* to define the war's aim not as a quest for military glory but as a defense of America's constitutional heritage, a devotion that required the country to adopt a steady, measured course toward a new founding. Its opening lines, "Four score and seven years ago our forefathers brought forth on this continent a new nation, conceived in Liberty, and dedicated to the proposition that all men are created equal," established the Declaration, not the Constitution, as the nation's founding document. In 272 carefully chosen words, he expressed the larger purpose of the sacrifices made on the hallowed Gettysburg battlefield:

> From these honored dead we take increased devotion to that cause for which they gave the last full measure of devotion – that we here highly resolve that these dead shall not have died in vain – that this nation, under God, shall have a new birth of freedom – and that government of the people, by the people, for the people, shall not perish from the earth.

As political theorist Wilson Carey McWilliams has pointed out, Gettysburg established a storyline for the development of the nation. Americans were not "born free"; rather, their rights depended on an honored past and a collective will to fight for those rights. The American story that Lincoln told at Gettysburg thus honored not only the Founders and those soldiers who died there but also the dignity of democratic individuals willing to acknowledge their debts to the people they had wronged, the enslaved Americans who had been denied "the fruits of their own labor." The Gettysburg Address, recited in public schools and etched in stone at the Lincoln memorial, became what legal scholar George P. Fletcher calls the "secular prayer" of post-Civil War America, giving new prominence to the Declaration's self-evident truths as the foundation of a new constitutional order.

Lincoln's last great utterance, his *Second Inaugural*, was aimed at educating his fellow Unionists about how they should act once victory was achieved. They, as well as their Confederate enemies, were Christians and even in their moment of triumph they must behave like Christians. To prepare themselves to display the proper humility and generosity of soul, they must first own up to their own complicity in the evils wrought. Then they would be in a position to accept their religious obligation to forgive, to assist those whom they have vanquished and to bend all their efforts toward healing the wounds the terrible war has inflicted on the body politic.

> Both read the same Bible and pray to the same God, and each invokes His aid against the other . . . Woe unto the world because of offenses; for it must needs be that offenses come, but woe to that man by whom the offense cometh . . . If we shall suppose that American slavery is one of those offenses which, in the providence of God, must needs come, but which, having continued through His appointed time, He now wills to remove, and that He gives to both North and South this terrible war as the woe due to those by whom the offense came . . . With malice toward none, with charity for all, with firmness in the right as God gives us to see the right, let us strive on to finish the work we are in, to bind up the nation's wounds.

Equality Deferred

Lincoln neither expected nor intended that emancipation would secure the rights of black Americans quickly. As the language of the Second Inaugural suggests, he planned to carry out his conservative revolution gently, preferring to address the prejudices of Americans with persuasion rather than force. He did not envisage a wholesale substitution of national for local authority. But his assassination, and his bigoted successor Andrew Johnson, severely limited Lincoln's constitutional refounding. The presidential election of 1876 effectively ended Reconstruction, the attempt of the national government to restructure government in the former confederate states and to protect the rights of the former slaves. The Democrat, Samuel Tilden, won the popular vote, but if the Republican, Rutherford B. Hayes, carried the electoral vote of four disputed states – South Carolina, Louisiana, Florida, and Oregon – he would win the election. Unlike the 2000 election, which was decided by the Supreme Court, the 1876 election was resolved by an electoral commission consisting of eight Republicans and seven Democrats. The commission awarded the election to Hayes on a straight party vote. To make this controversial decision acceptable to the Democrats, Hayes agreed to remove military troops from the South. This agreement enabled white majorities in Southern states to enact Jim Crow laws, a system of forced segregation that prevented enforcement of the Fourteenth and Fifteenth Amendments and that denied African Americans a full share of American citizenship for nearly a century. Thus, a debased form of Jacksonian local self-determination, not the form that Lincoln intended, returned to American politics.

UPSHOT

Bloodshed accomplished what politics could not, the end of slavery and the preservation of the Union. The freedom-loving principles the Civil War Amendments embodied and the exhalted rhetorical defense Lincoln gave of them set the United States on a path toward a new birth of freedom. Yet, it took a full century for the federal government to remove the segregationist barriers with which Southern states blocked that path.

Table 4.3. Third conservative revolution: contest over slavery.

Changes	Continuities
• Constitutional changes in the form of the ratification of Thirteenth, Fourteenth, and Fifteenth Amendments, which abolished slavery and expanded the government's obligation to protect the rights of common citizens	• Preservation of the Union in the face of the threat of dissolution • Changes implemented by the Civil War Amendments and Reconstruction did not have real effect for decades

Anticipating the Modern State: Progressivism

The fourth conservative revolution took place in two stages. In the first two decades of the twentieth century a new set of political ideas that came to be known as Progressivism entered American political life, generating some important political changes. Then in the 1930s a full-fledged political transformation occurred based largely on Progressive principles. Of the three preexisting bedrocks of American political culture – liberalism, communitarianism, and democracy – Progressivism favored only democracy. It sought to break the nation free of parochial attachments and it did not want to allow limits on governmental authority to stand in its way, but rather sought to rally the public in favor of an active and ambitious national government dedicated to public improvement.

The Birth of Progressivism

The initial Progressive assault on the post-Civil War, decentralized republic was motivated by indignation against economic injustice. The US population doubled between 1870 and 1900. Urbanization and immigration increased at rapid rates and were accompanied by a shift from local, small-scale manufacturing and commerce to large-scale factory production and mammoth national corporations. Technological breakthroughs and frenzied searches for new markets and sources of capital caused unprecedented economic growth. From 1863 to 1899, manufacturing production rose by more than 700 percent. But this dynamic growth also generated profound economic and social problems that challenged the capacity of the decentralized republic to respond.

As we discuss in Chapter 6, by the turn of the century, economic power had become highly concentrated, threatening the security of employees, suppliers, and customers. Many Americans believed that great business interests had captured and corrupted government. Those people who fought to reform the economy and the government became known as Progressives. No event so aroused their ardor as the nationwide celebration, in 1909, of the 100th anniversary of Lincoln's birth. A Progressive magazine editorial rejoiced:

> Coming as it did in the flood tide of the most dangerous and determined reaction from fundamental democratic ideals and principles that have marked our history, it has given a new inspiration and hope to thousands who were all but despairing of the success of popular rule in the presence of the aggressive, determined and powerful march of feudalism and privileged wealth, operating through political bosses and money controlled machines, and the pliant tools of predatory wealth in state, press, school and church.

Yet this celebration of Lincoln went hand in hand with an attack on the decentralized republic that he had supported. Forgetting that Lincoln and the

Republicans had defended localized parties as critical agents of "government of the people, by the people, for the people," Progressives scorned party leaders as servants of special interests and usurpers of the Constitution. They championed the creation of direct mass democracy, of "government at first hand: government of the People, directly by the People." Among the tools they sought to introduce to undermine parties were the direct primary and the allocation of government jobs on the basis of objective examinations rather than patronage.

In their attack on intermediary organizations such as political parties and interest groups, Progressives supported women's suffrage; the direct primary, in which voters, not party leaders, would choose candidates; and direct election of senators. They also championed methods of "pure" democracy, such as the initiative, by which a bill could be forced to the attention of legislatures by popular petition, and the referendum, which allowed the electorate to overrule decisions of state legislatures. Especially controversial was the idea of subjecting constitutional questions to direct popular control, including referenda on laws that state courts had declared unconstitutional. Direct democracy became the centerpiece of the insurgent Progressive Party campaign of 1912, which pledged a "covenant with the people," making the people "masters of their constitution."

Progressive's also sought to defeat the special interests and party bosses by handing over the management of public policy to disinterested experts. At the national level, scientific knowledge could then replace political favoritism as the basis for making decisions about such crucial matters as food and drug safety, railroad rates and regulating the currency. At the local level a key element of Progressive reform was the advent of the city manager form of government. Instead of relying on politicians to run cities, cities would be managed by nonpartisan experts trained in the science of urban planning and administration. These efforts to place government on a scientific basis mirrored reforms that efficiency expert Frederick W. Taylor was advancing for private industry – systematic and "scientific" forms of management from the head office to the shop floor. To bring such reform to government, Taylor urged the president to put an efficiency expert in the cabinet.

Progressives blamed the celebration of property rights, celebrated by Classic Liberalism and zealously guarded by the Constitution, for the perversions of the industrial age. Consequently, they stressed collective responsibilities and duties rather than rights. Despite their reverence for Lincoln, they did not emulate his devotion to the Declaration of Independence. Instead, they invoked the Preamble of the Constitution to assert their purpose of making "We the People" effective in strengthening the national government's authority to regulate the society and economy.

The Progressive reformers' idealism owed much to religion. They saw the Progressive party and other reform associations as political expressions of the movement to promote Christian social action. The Progressives' celebration of national democracy dovetailed with the social gospelers' religious devotion, which downplayed, if it did not scorn, particular theological doctrines and denominations. "We have been a wasteful nation," argued Walter Rauschenbusch, the esteemed social gospeler, in a speech praising the Progressive Party. "We have wasted our soil, our water, our forests, our childhood, our motherhood, but no waste has been so great as our waste of religious enthusiasm by denominational strife. The heed of social service is seen in the fact that as the social spirit rises the sectarian spirit declines." The social gospelers thereby invested religious fervor in Progressivism's crusade for political reform.

Whereas Jeffersonian democracy and the principles set forth in the Declaration of Independence dominated the nineteenth century, a more democratic version of Hamiltonianism, dedicated to an energetic national government, came to prevail in the beginning of the twentieth century. In the words of the first Progressive president, Theodore Roosevelt (TR), "I have never hesitated to criticize Jefferson; he was infinitely below Hamilton; I think the worship of Jefferson a discredit to my country." Yet TR was no blind disciple of Hamilton. Unlike Hamilton, who supported an energetic executive in order to curb popular influence, TR viewed the president as the visionary champion of social and economic reform. In the words of TR's confidant reformer Herbert Croly, the aim of progressive nationalism was "to give democratic meaning and purpose to the Hamiltonian tradition and method."

TR lost the 1912 election because the incumbent Republican president, William Howard Taft, refused to bow out in his favor. Because Taft and TR split the Republican vote, the election was won by the Democrat, Woodrow Wilson. In the campaign, Wilson championed a form of Progressivism, which he labeled *The New Freedom*, that was less trusting of centralized authority than TR's version, *The New Nationalism*. Nonetheless, once elected, Wilson supported national economic control initiatives, such as the creation of a federal trade commission with broad responsibilities for overseeing business practices, much like the one TR had proposed. Wilson also supported creation of the Federal Reserve System to administer national banking and currency activities (see Chapter 6).

The policy changes wrought by TR and Wilson exposed deep tensions between the Progressive celebration of democracy and the greatly enhanced power of experts and of the new bureaucracies created to implement those policies. In fact, Progressive reforms made government services less connected to elected officials and more tied to administrative agencies and bureaucracies over which voters had little control. Nor did the Progressives recognize the contradiction inherent in trying to give the people more power via direct democracy and placing more power in the hands of experts whose authority did not come from popular accountability but from their claim to specialized knowledge.

Figure 4.4. Historic voter turnout as percentage of estimated eligible voters.
Source: Matt Stiles, *The Daily Viz.*

Thus, despite Progressivism's championing of mass democracy, its attack on political organizations and its commitment to expertise and administrative management conspired to make American politics and government seem more removed from the everyday lives of citizens.

Progressive democracy actually decreased voter turnout, which was lower in 1920 and 1924 than at any time since the emergence of mass democracy in the 1830s. "Early in the 19th century, soaring turnout among white men reinforced the impression of The People governing," Robert Wiebe has observed; "early in the 20th, falling turnouts reinforced the impression of people being governed."

Progressive Democracy and Liberalism

The Progressive faith in majoritarian democracy dealt severe blows to the liberal principle of equal rights. TR and Taft tolerated racial segregation in the South because they acknowledged its political popularity. Woodrow Wilson, a native Virginian elected to the White House in large part because of white Southern support, allowed his administration to actively promote it. He permitted a number of federal departments to segregate their employees in Washington and to demote or fire their black federal workers in the South.

Progressive indifference to individual rights was not limited to Southern issues. Immigration restrictions and racial segregation were often supported

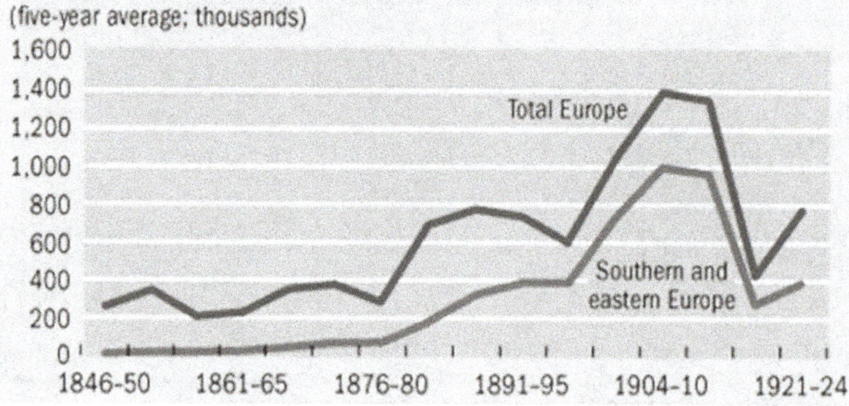

Figure 4.5. On the go: European emigrants before and after the US imposition of quotas.
Source: I. Ferenczi and W. F. Willcox, *International Migrations*, vol. I (New York: National Bureau of Economic Research, 1929).

by "reformers," who viewed the growing diversity of America as a threat to national unity. By 1920, to disenfranchise immigrants, nine Northern states passed literacy tests for voting and eleven states repealed older laws permitting aliens to cast ballots once they pledged to become citizens. The United States and Japan reached a so-called gentlemen's agreement in 1907 that excluded Japanese immigrants. In 1920, Congress passed the most restrictive immigration bill in the nation's history.

Nativist sentiment – which scorned beer drinking as a vice of German, Irish, and Italian immigrants – led to the 1919 ratification of the Eighteenth Amendment to the Constitution, which prohibited the manufacture, sale, and transportation of intoxicating liquors. As the political scientist James Morone has written, "Prohibiting liquor looked like one more progressive social amelioration, blending easily into the movement's disdain for inferior people and corrupt politics."

Progressive Democracy and War

The repressive tendencies of Progressive democracy were revealed dramatically during World War I. President Wilson's war aim was to make the "World Safe for

Democracy." To convey the message to the American people, Wilson formed the Committee on Public Information (CPI), which enlisted 75,000 speakers to "persuade" the public that the war was a crusade for freedom and democracy against the Germans, a barbarian people bent on world domination. Most Americans supported the war. But a significant minority opposed it, including German and Irish Americans whose ethnicity caused them to doubt the cause of the Allied powers, and Progressive reformers such as the prominent social worker Jane Addams, who thought American democracy would be corrupted by the necessities and cruelties of total war. The CPI and a number of self-styled "patriotic groups" sought to discourage, and sometimes repress, this dissent. People who refused to buy war bonds were often exposed to public ridicule and even assaulted. People with German names, scorned as hyphenate Americans, were prosecuted indiscriminately. Some school boards outlawed the teaching of the German language.

Wilson's Progressive democracy did not deter this oppression. Indeed, his view that the war was a moral crusade – to "make the world safe for democracy" – inspired intolerance. Wilson signed the Espionage Act of 1917, which imposed fines of up to $10,000 and jail sentences ranging to twenty years on persons convicted of aiding the enemy or obstructing military recruitment. He banned seemingly treasonable or seditious material from the mails. In May 1918, he signed the Sedition Act, which made it a crime to "utter, print, write, or publish any disloyal, profane, scurrilous, or abusive language" about the government, the Constitution, or the uniform of the Army and Navy, or "say anything" to discourage war bond purchases. Socialist leader Eugene V. Debs was sentenced to ten years in prison for making an antiwar speech.

CRITICAL CHOICE: CREATING THE MODERN STATE

The Great Depression that began in 1929 was the worst economic cataclysm in American history. Out of its ruins rose the New Deal, the defining political episode of the twentieth century. The New Deal built on the two pillars of Progressive democracy – mass politics and national administration – but it added a critical dimension, a new understanding of rights. It marked a critical departure in governing principles, political alignments, institutional arrangements, and public policy. Franklin Delano Roosevelt (FDR) gave legitimacy to Progressive ideas by imbedding them in the language of constitutionalism and interpreting them as a fulfillment rather than a subversion of natural rights. The task of statesmanship, FDR insisted, was to redefine the rights of the Declaration in terms of a "changing and growing social order."

New Deal Liberalism

FDR was the first president to call himself a "liberal," adding the word to the common political vocabulary. In doing so, he reworked - or, as his political enemies claimed, "perverted"- Classic Liberalism. To FDR, the Great Depression made painfully obvious that it was necessary to rewrite the social contract to take account of a national economy remade by industrial capitalism and economic concentration. This new contract would establish a stronger national state to countervail concentrated economic power. As FDR put it, "The day of enlightened administration has come." The traditional emphasis on self-reliance should give way to an acceptance of the need for government to guarantee individuals protection from the uncertainties of the market. A fourth self-evident truth, Security, was added to the litany of "Life, Liberty and the Pursuit of Happiness."

When FDR took the oath of office on March 4, 1933, about a third of the workforce, 15 million workers, were unemployed. In thirty-two states, all the banks were closed; in sixteen more, banking operations were severely curtailed. That morning, the New York Stock Exchange closed its doors. But the New Dealers looked beyond the immediate crisis. They sought to accomplish not only economic recovery but also enduring political and economic reform. Unlike the Progressives, they recognized that American politics could not be remade unless political and economic transformation was interwoven with traditional constitutional principles, especially the guarantee of rights.

The new understanding of the Declaration and Constitution was the principal message of FDR's reelection bid in 1936, and his success was the decisive triumph that established the Democrats as the majority party in American politics for more than a generation.

Lincoln, as this chapter has pointed out, defended the Declaration as America's founding document, claiming that the centrality of the rights it proclaimed justified a "new birth of freedom." The 1860 Republican platform championed the Declaration of Independence as America's founding document. The 1936 Democratic platform, drafted by FDR, was written as a pastiche of the Declaration and thus emphasized the need for a fundamental reconsideration of rights. "We hold this truth to be self-evident," it said, "that government in a modern civilization has certain inescapable obligations to its citizens." Among these new responsibilities was "to erect a structure of economic security for its people, making sure that this benefit shall keep step with the ever increasing capacity of America to provide a high standard of living for all its citizens."

The 1936 election validated FDR's redefinition of the social contract. He won every state but Maine and Vermont. The 1936 Republican platform declared that "America is in peril" and dedicated the party to "the preservation of ... political liberty," which "for the first time" was "threatened by government itself." But FDR successfully defended the New Deal in terms of enhancing liberty. Harking back to the American Revolution, FDR defined his opponents as "economic royalists" who

> have conceded that political freedom was the business of government, but they have maintained that economic slavery was nobody's business. They granted that the Government could protect the citizen in his own right to vote, but they denied that government could do anything to protect the citizen in his right to work and his right to live . . . If the average citizen is guaranteed equal opportunity in the polling place, he must have equal opportunity in the marketplace.

The New Deal, building on what the Progressives had begun, was the first conservative revolution to emphasize national administrative power. Its predecessors had not challenged Classic Liberalism's commitment to private property rights, limited government, and administrative decentralization. Even the Civil War, the most serious constitutional crisis of American history, did not lead to a departure from this consensus. As we explain in Chapter 8, FDR managed to push through Congress political reforms that led to the creation of the White House office, the hub of the executive office of the president. The reconstituted executive office deprived party leaders of the very tasks that gave them status and influence: linking the president to interest groups, staffing the executive branch, developing policy, providing campaign support, and linking the White House to public opinion.

Programmatic Rights

New Deal political reforms sought to embed Progressive programs – which were considered tantamount to rights – in a bureaucratic structure that would insulate reform and reformers from party politics, conservative presidents, and even, to a point, public opinion.

The most important of these new programmatic rights was Social Security. The 1935 Social Security Act provided old-age insurance, unemployment insurance, and Aid to Families with Dependent Children (AFDC), popularly known as welfare. Unlike old-age insurance, unemployment compensation and AFDC were jointly administered by the national and state governments. Social Security was carefully nurtured by FDR to appear as a right, the cornerstone of the economic constitutional order. He insisted that it be financed by a payroll tax rather than by general revenues: "We put those payroll contributions there so to give the contributors a legal, moral right, and political right to collect their pensions. With those taxes in there, no damn politician can scrap my social security program."

And none did. By the 1950s, Social Security was the "third rail" of American politics, bringing political death to those who challenged it. By European standards, the Social Security program was quite limited. It did not include any support for healthcare, and its levels of welfare spending were low. It left considerable discretion and funding responsibility to the states, which dealt out social justice unevenly. Nevertheless, the program marked a watershed in the national government's assumption of the responsibility to protect individuals from the uncertainties of the market. Its programs, especially old-age pensions, grew over the years, so that Social Security became the largest of all federal programs.

The National Labor Relations Act of 1935 established another economic right, that of unions to bargain collectively. The act created a National Labor Relations Board (NLRB) to ensure fair collective bargaining elections, a move that transformed American society and economy (see Chapter 6). When the New Deal began, few factory workers belonged to labor unions, which left them vulnerable to workplace abuses and business cycle uncertainties. By the late 1930s, industrial unionism was firmly in place.

In his 1944 State of the Union message, FDR called for a new bill of rights that provided adequate food, clothing, recreation, employment, housing, and education to all, "regardless of station, race, or creed," and that provided protection from the economic fears of old age, sickness, and accident. These new rights did not officially become part of the Constitution, but they formed the foundation of a new public philosophy that redefined the role of the national government. The previous understanding of rights – which was dedicated to limiting government – gradually gave way to a more expansive understanding of rights that presupposed the creation of a large and powerful executive establishment capable of securing them.

To ensure that these newly established rights would survive his leadership, FDR sought to protect the many appointees he had brought to Washingtron to staff the newly created welfare and regulatory state from being fired by his successors. Through executive orders and legislation, FDR extended so called *merit protection* to 95 percent of federal service employees by 1941. Since Jefferson, federal appointments had been used to nourish parties; the New Deal, FDR's civil service reforms, deprived parties of that opportunity. Federal bureaucrats would now be controlled by the rules governing the programs they administered, not by party leaders. This change did much to enshrine an administrative state dedicated to perpetuating the programmatic rights the New Deal had established.

Civil Rights

In the midst of the New Deal's expansion of rights, the right to racial equality proclaimed in both the Thirteenth and Fifteenth Amendments continued to languish. As late as 1938, the Federal Housing Administration Act had required the home mortgages that it insured to have racially restrictive covenants. But, as the threat of world war worsened, the Roosevelt administration took actions that served as critical precedents for the later triumph of civil rights. In 1940, the Roosevelt administration established the Fair Employment Practices Commission

(FEPC), which was charged with eliminating discrimination in the employment of workers in the defense industry or in government because of "race, color, creed, or national origin." As the wartime internment of Japanese Americans and the continued racial segregation of the armed forces showed, the government was still in support of many racist policies. Nor was the FEPC an adequate response to racial discrimination. Nevertheless, it was the first federal government effort since Reconstruction that was specifically aimed at alleviating racial discrimination.

These administrative efforts were joined to judicial politics. At FDR's behest, his attorney general, Frank Murphy, set up the Civil Liberties Section of the Justice Department in 1939. Later called the Civil Rights Section, this office played a critical part in bringing and successfully adjudicating Supreme Court cases that challenged white supremacy in the South. The most important case, *Smith v. Allwright*, decided in 1944, declared the white primary, a critical foundation of Jim Crow electoral practices, unconstitutional. FDR's successor, Harry Truman, went further. His 1948 executive order demanded that "there shall be equality of treatment and opportunity in the Armed Services without regard to race, color, or national origin."

Liberal Internationalism

New Deal Liberalism also had a critical international dimension. Progressives had championed internationalism to make the world safe for democracy. New Deal rhetoric stressed international rights. As FDR put it in his famous 1941 Four Freedoms speech, the traditional liberal freedoms of speech and religion were to be supplemented by two new freedoms. "Freedom from want" was a commitment to "economic understandings which will secure to every nation a healthy peace time life for its inhabitants." "Freedom from fear" was dedicated to "a world-wide reduction of armaments to such a point and such a fashion that no nation will be in a position to commit an act of physical aggression against any neighbor."

In his draft of the 1941 Atlantic Charter, FDR committed the Allies to "respect the right of all peoples to choose the form of government under which they will live" and "to see sovereign rights and self-government restored to those who have been forcibly deprived of them." Believing that rejection of imperialism was crucial to defeating the Axis powers, FDR persuaded a nervous Winston Churchill to endorse the charter even though the language might be, and eventually was, used against the British Empire.

Of course, FDR's idealism frequently gave way to practical considerations. In his negotiations with Stalin toward the end of the war, FDR failed to prevent Soviet dominion over Eastern Europe. Likewise, the internment of Japanese Americans in concentration camps revealed all too clearly that New Deal rights did not provide ironclad protection for minorities against xenophobic hysteria.

Still, liberal internationalism proved more resilient, at home and abroad, than did the Progressive ambition to promote democracy. World War I stifled Progressive domestic reform and fueled nativist attitudes. World War II strengthened the sense of entitlement, thereby justifying New Deal reforms, and advanced an inclusive popular nationalism and a readiness to use the federal government to secure prosperity and meet important domestic and international responsibilities. As Lincoln showed, words are more important than battles. After the war, the rights rhetoric that FDR pioneered was used effectively against imperialist and discriminatory impulses.

Domestic and international commitments merged to enhance the influence of modern liberalism on American life. For example, in 1944, Congress enacted the GI Bill of Rights that entitled war veterans to home loans, business loans, unemployment compensation, and subsidies for education and training. This legislation did not provide for the broad security and employment programs that FDR championed, but it did greatly expand the economic and educational benefits available to a very large and significant portion of the population, returning veterans and their families.

The conservative aspect of the New Deal consists in what it did not do. The economic collapse of the early 1930s caused many to question the very premises underlying America's free market system (see Chapter 6). Communists gained a foothold in the labor movement. Louisiana Governor Huey Long sought to lead a national movement premised on the radical redistribution of the wealth. Charles Coughlin, a Catholic priest, echoed Hitler in accusing the Jews of masterminding the financial collapse. Like Hitler he preached a form of national socialism that severely restricted property rights, opposed free markets and put the government in charge of controlling economic output and deciding which companies would

Table 4.4. Fourth conservative revolution: the New Deal and the triumph of liberalism.

Changes	Continuities
• Created a new understanding of rights, including establishment of programmatic rights • Gave legitimacy to Progressive ideas by seeking their source in constitutional principles • Dramatically expanded role of executive and federal government and solidified direct relationship between the president and the people • Built on Progressive commitment to a liberal international order • Set precedents for progress on civil rights	• In the face of the crisis of the Great Depression, preserved the fundamental structure of the constitutional order • Essential aspects of free market economy remained intact

be allowed to remain in business. FDR and his political allies faced down these threats. Though the New Deal wrought major changes in the relationship between government and the economy, it did not attempt to confiscate private property or impose government control of the means of production. The free market economy and the risks and rewards attendant upon it remained essentially intact.

UPSHOT

The New Deal created the essential features of the strong and ambitious centralized state that we live with today. As Chapter 8 will discuss, it established the president as the dominant figure in our political life. It also greatly encouraged the framing of public policy debate in terms of rights. The successful assertion of a right to income security set the stage for contemporary claims of a right to healthcare and to a clean and safe environment, among others.

Political Development Since the New Deal: Challenges and Continuities

The post-New Deal era witnessed two significant challenges to it: one to move beyond it; the other to curtail it. An ambitious effort to use government to improve society took place during the 1960s, spearheaded by President Lyndon Baines Johnson (1963–68). The regime of Ronald Reagan (1980–88) sought to reign in government expansion. However, neither of these serious challenges served to significantly alter the governmental and public policy framework the New Deal established. The two decades following Reagan, the administrations of Presidents Bush and Bill Clinton, displayed far more in the way of continuity than change. President Obama was more aggressive in pushing a Progressive agenda, and he did succeed in passing a major healthcare reform. However, his ambitions were curtailed by the fact that he lost control of Congress after only two years in power.

The Great Society

In the signature speech of his presidency, a May 1964 commencement address at the University of Michigan, Lyndon Baines Johnson (LBJ) pointed to the New Deal's promise to end poverty and racial justice as "just the beginning." Challenging the students and parents to embrace more ambitious goals for America, LBJ described his vision of "a Great Society . . . where the city of man serves not only the needs of the body and the demands of commerce but the desire for beauty and the hunger for community."

The eminent Progressive philosopher, John Dewey, had prophesied that Progressive reforms would reach fulfillment in a "Great Community" that would "order the relations and enrich the experience of local associations." Reformers in the 1960s hoped that the Great Society would produce the same thing. Their ambitions were fueled by the success of the civil rights movement. This movement called not merely for a fulfillment of rights promised African Americans, but also for direct action to overcome the bureaucratic inertia of the New Deal state. Its success "demonstrated not only the power and possibility of organized protest, but the unsuspected fragility of resistance to liberating changes," claimed Richard Goodwin, who drafted LBJ's University of Michigan speech.

Indeed, the civil rights movement was a model for the social movements that grew out of the 1960s, including organized opposition to the Vietnam War, feminism, consumerism, and environmentalism. In the early days of the Great Society, LBJ and influential aides such as Richard Goodwin supported these movements (except for the antiwar protests), viewing their clarion call for participatory democracy as paving the way for a new generation of reform.

The Great Society's deepest ambitions were never realized. Its important achievements in civil rights, consumer protection, and education did not increase participatory democracy. Steeped in the rights talk popularized by FDR, it led rather to an explosion of new entitlements proclaimed by groups competing with one another for recognition and for government programs to remedy the historic injustices they had suffered. Rights of women, gays and lesbians, the disabled, consumers, and welfare recipients followed logically from the New Deal idea of a just society. The New Deal promised security in the face of the uncertainties of the business cycle and the unintended hazards created by a dynamic capitalism. The rights revolution expanded on those ideas to encompass protections against the prejudices of private citizens, the risks of congenital disabilities, environmental degradation, and the consequences of poverty and family decomposition. Endowing those rights with practical programmatic meaning necessarily implied the expansion of the government's administrative apparatus.

The Reagan Era

This expansion of claims on the government provoked political opposition rooted in Classic Liberal adherence to limited government. Growing hostility culminated in Ronald Reagan's 1980 election to the White House. Reagan's message as candidate and president was but a variation of the theme he first developed in a nationwide address on behalf of the 1964 Republican presidential candidate, Barry Goldwater. Reagan invoked Paine, Jefferson, and Jackson as he proclaimed that citizens must not be denied the means of exercising their right of rebelling against a despotic government.

The New Deal state, Reagan argued, gave an especially pernicious turn to government oppression, cloaking its intrusiveness in the language of the Declaration. By acting "outside of its legitimate function," Reagan insisted, "natural unalienable rights" were presumed to be a "dispensation of government," which stripped people of their self-reliance and their capacity for self-government. "The real destroyer of liberties of the people," said Reagan, "is he who spreads among them bounties, donations, and benefits." In his inaugural address, the first in more than fifty years to appeal for limited government, he sounded the same theme: "In the present crisis, government is not the solution to our problem; government is the problem." Reagan promised to shrink government and restore the vitality of a democracy based on limited government and decentralized politics.

But Reagan's policies did not redefine the New Deal social contract and therefore did not amount to a conservative revolution. Despite his antigovernment rhetoric, Reagan managed only to halt the expansion of programmatic rights. He had little success in cutting back middle-class entitlements such as Social Security and Medicare, a healthcare program for the elderly created in 1965. Reagan's efforts to loosen regulatory standards for civil rights, environment, and consumer protection were successfully resisted by public interest groups and their allies in Congress and the courts.

In fact, the Reagan administration upheld many aspects of the New Deal, especially its commitment to liberal internationalism, which had lost much support among Democrats since the Vietnam War. Ironically, Reagan's greatest accomplishment may have involved an act of perpetuation. Finishing what Harry Truman began, Reagan prosecuted the Cold War to a successful conclusion. The demise of the Soviet Union occurred for many reasons, but Reagan's tough talk – he dubbed the Communist power an "evil empire" – steered American policy away from detente, the position of accommodation that had prevailed since the early 1970s. This rhetorical hard line justified the extensive arms buildup that put great technological and economic pressure on the Soviet Union and contributed to its ultimate collapse.

Even when championing "conservative" causes, Reagan defended an activist presidency that belied his promise to "get the government off our backs." The conservative movement that helped bring him to power was aroused in no small part by the abortion controversy, which led Reagan and many of his supporters to defend the rights of the unborn in a way that required extending the power of government. Posed in opposition to the rights of pregnant women as championed by the women's movement, the Reagan administration contemplated prohibiting women from having abortions, or in certain cases, even getting counseling from birth control clinics. For example, in early 1988 the Department of Health and Human Services issued a regulation declaring that federal funds could not go to clinics that provided abortion counseling. In the post–New Deal era, when conservatives challenge liberal policies, they do so in the name of new rights that presuppose discretionary use of national administrative power.

Conservative Liberalism, Compassionate Conservatism

Although the twenty years following the Reagan presidency were fraught with political conflict and controversy, they also displayed a compelling magnetic attraction toward the political center. The two Republican presidents, George Bush father and son, were far less critical of big government than Reagan had been. George W. Bush (2000–08) coined the term "compassionate conservatism" to signal his willingness to deploy government to help people as long as the type of help proferred was consistent with conservative values. The Democratic president, Bill Clinton (1992–2000), declared himself a "New Democrat," distancing himself from what he deemed to be the excessive reliance on big spending and subsidizing of special interests characteristic of the old Democrats. The first Democrat to occupy the White House in sixteen years appeared to ratify the "Reagan revolution" when he proclaimed "the era of big government is over." After the Republicans, led by the militant conservative Newt Gingrich, won control of both houses of Congress in 1994 – the first time this had happened in forty years – Clinton signed a welfare reform bill that vastly reduced the number of persons receiving public assistance and constructed a bipartisan coalition in support of a balanced budget.

But Clinton was no Reaganite. Indeed, he revived his presidency and fended off the aggressive leadership of Speaker of the House Gingrich by defending New Deal and Great Society programs. Clinton was reelected in 1996, the first time a Democratic president had been returned to office by the voters since FDR. The crux of his reelection campaign was his dedication to perpetuating Medicare, Medicaid (a healthcare program for the disadvantaged), education spending, and stringent environmental regulation. Clinton – not his opponent, Kansas senator Robert Dole – was the real conservative in this campaign, because he fought to preserve the status quo, the programmatic rights that were the legacy of FDR and the New Deal, from Republican efforts to scale it back.

George W. Bush energetically used national government power and revenue in pursuit of his "compassionate conservative" goals. Nine days after being sworn in as president, he issued an executive order that aimed to increase the ability of religious organizations to avail themselves of federal funds in order to provide social services to those in need. He signaled the importance that he attached to this project by locating the new office responsible for implementing the program in the White House. Bush's major legislative priority during his first year in office was also aimed at achieving compassionate conservative goals. Entitled "No Child Left Behind," it sought to create a national testing system that would make teachers more accountable for the success of their students. Although states were not compelled to participate, they risked losing federal aid if the did not. Bush also supported a new federal program that subsidized prescription drugs for the elderly. It was the most expensive new federally funded entitlement program since the passage of Medicare in 1965.

As we discussed in Chapter 1 and will discuss again in Chapter 10, the terror attacks of September 11, 2001 pressed Bush to endorse another major government expansion, the addition of a new cabinet-level Department of Homeland Security. The department is immense; it has more than 180,000 employees. It signifies a major new consolidation of national government power because it places a whole array of domestic law enforcement and investigatory responsibility under national auspices that had previously rested with the states and localities.

Progressivism Returns

As the presidency chapter discusses in greater detail, the Obama administration adopted a more unabashedly progressive agenda than the president's Democratic Party predecessor, Bill Clinton. During the brief period in which the Democrats had control of both the legislative and executive branches – 2009–11 – they passed the most ambitious expansion of the welfare state since the 1960s, the Affordable Care Act (ACA). After losing control of Congress, Obama attempted to wield his discretionary executive power in a Progressive direction. He issued executive orders and his departments promulgated decrees aimed at achieving ambitious environmental goals, liberalizing immigration, raising labor standards, and extending rights to the transgendered. In the 2016 election campaign, Donald Trump opposed these policies. He promised to repeal the Affordable Care Act. Trump and his cabinet appointees also vowed to rescind many of the Obama administration's aggressive executive actions in the fields of immigration, the environment, and transgender rights.

Critical Question

This chapter has described a number of critical debates about the very nature, limits, and purpose of government that have taken place in the course of American political development. The political debates occurring today also raise critical questions about the nature, limits, and purposes of government. Pick a contemporary political controversy and show how it raises some if not all of these questions. Do you find that some of the arguments made in the debates discussed in this chapter are useful for helping you form your own opinion regarding the controversy you have chosen? If so, explain why? If not, explain why this controversy is so different that previous arguments are not relevant.

Looking Forward: Future Conservative Revolutions

More than eighty years have passed since the onset of the nation's last conservative revolution. The critical choices regarding the adoption of new programmatic rights and the vast expansion of an administrative state to implement them set the American government on a path to which it continues to adhere. Never before have so many years gone by without such a profound contest over the meaning of the Constitution and the role of the national government. In the wake of the most serious challenge to New Deal principles, led by Ronald Reagan, there has been no retreat from the programmatic rights and centralized governmental administration the New Deal embodied.

Is there a conservative revolution on the horizon? The 2008 election gave cause for optimism to modern Progressives seeking a broad expansion of programmatic rights along the lines established in most other wealthy nations. For the first time since 1964, a Democratic president was elected with large majorities in both houses of Congress. Indeed, the Obama administration did pass a major new healthcare bill that went a long way to making health insurance coverage universal. It also spent billions of dollars rescuing the banking system, bailing out Chrysler and General Motors, and attempting to stimulate the depressed economy. When FDR engaged in such expansionary efforts, the voters rallied to his defense, but the public reacted negatively to Obama's policies. The Tea Party movement that arose in 2009 to fight against "big government" was the most energetic dissident force to arise in many years (see Chapter 14). In 2010, the Democrats suffered staggering losses in the congressional, gubernatorial, and state legislative elections, losing control of the House of Representatives. In 2014, Republicans regained the Senate as well. The country seemed poised to turn in a conservative direction. Indeed, in 2016 a Republican, Donald Trump, was elected president and the Republicans also gained control of both houses of Congress. However, Trump hardly proved to be a traditional Republican conservative. Rather than stressing hallowed conservative themes of reducing spending and decentralizing government, he has championed a powerful national government that will restore national greatness, aggressively prosecute illegal aliens, maintain law and order, fight unfair foreign competition, and pressure American companies into building factories at home, not abroad.

Conservatives had long claimed that the media was biased in a liberal direction. But Trump greatly expanded that claim, adopting a belligerent and accusatory stance aimed at undermining its credibility. "I think the media is the opposition party in many ways," Trump said in an interview shortly after he took office: "I'm not talking about everybody . . . But a big portion of the media, the dishonesty, the total deceit and deception makes them certainly partially the opposition party" (www.realclearpolitics.com/video/2017/01/27/donald_trump_the_media_is_the_opposition_party.html). His attack encompassed what he characterized as a liberal establishment that has come to dominate not only the media but a wide array of prominent institutions including the federal bureaucracy, foundations, the universities, and even segments of the corporate world. Trump's approach is often called populist, although it is a far cry from the populist movement of the late nineteenth century that we will discuss in later chapters. He is called a populist because he claims to represent ordinary people and to fight on their behalf not only against unfair foreign economic competition but also against the elite institutions at home that denigrate their beliefs and ignore their concerns.

Thus, in the wake of the Trump election, contemporary political discourse has added a form of populism to the bipolar debate between progressives and conservatives. "Fog of war" is a term used to describe the extreme uncertainty and chaos that soldiers experience during battle. Often they cannot even tell if they are winning or losing it. All they know for sure is that bullets are buzzing overhead. Likewise, when one is in the midst of a great political conflict the outcome is impossible to predict. A profound three-way contest of opinion is currently underway. Only in retrospect, years from now, will the fog of political warfare lift sufficiently to reveal whether or not a conservative revolution has resulted from this epic political struggle.

CHAPTER SUMMARY

Critical choice: democratizing the Constitution:

* The first conservative revolution took place between 1800 and 1808, during Thomas Jefferson's two terms as president. It promoted democracy by endorsing and nurturing those political institutions and constitutional principles that Jefferson and his followers considered to be most democratic in character, such as free speech, legislative supremacy, and a powerful defense of states' rights. And, it was inextricably connected to two new forms of political communication and conflict: a popular press and political parties.

Critical choice: promoting mass democracy:

* The second conservative revolution, presided over by Andrew Jackson, sought to make the Constitution and its institutional arrangements servants of public opinion. Democracy did not displace liberalism in the Age of Jackson. Rather, Jacksonians sought to capture liberalism for the people. Demands for rights had to come to terms with a highly mobilized, competitive, and locally oriented democracy.

Critical choice: a new birth of freedom:

* The third conservative revolution, ending slavery, was revolutionary in the magnitude of its constitutional change but conservative in its rededication to "unalienable" rights and its preservation of the Union.

* The importance that Lincoln placed on informing and rousing public opinion led him to focus on rhetoric. His speeches endowed the Union with a religious aura, incorporating the principles of the Declaration into America's political and constitutional practices.

Anticipating the modern state, Progressivism:

* The Progressive Era did not constitute a full-fledged conservative revolution but it did generate political ideas and precedents that have remained critically influential. It began the process of national government expansion that proved to be the most crucial political development of the twentieth century.

Critical choice: creating the modern state:

* The New Deal was built on the two pillars of Progressive democracy, mass politics and national administration, but it added a new understanding of rights. FDR gave legitimacy to Progressive ideas by imbedding them in the language of constitutionalism and interpreting them as a fulfillment rather than a subversion of natural rights.
* New Deal political reforms were directed not just at creating presidential government but also at embedding Progressive programs – which were considered tantamount to rights – in a bureaucratic structure that would insulate reform and reformers from party politics, conservative presidents, and even, to a point, public opinion. The most important of these new programmatic rights was the right to economic security in old age as embodied in the Social Security Act of 1935.

Political development since the New Deal: challenges and continuities:

* The most significant effort to go beyond the New Deal took place during the 1960s during the presidency of Lyndon Baines Johnson (1963–68). Although it did not constitute a full-fledged conservative revolution, it did have important consequences regarding the expansion of the administrative state and Americans' understanding of their rights.
* Reagan promised to shrink government and restore the vitality of a democracy based on limited government and decentralized politics. But his policies did not redefine the New Deal social contract and therefore did not amount to a conservative revolution. Despite his antigovernment rhetoric, Reagan managed only to halt the expansion of programmatic rights. In fact, the Reagan administration upheld many aspects of the New Deal, especially its commitment to liberal internationalism, which had lost much support among Democrats following the Vietnam War.
* Bill Clinton used the term "New Democrat" to indicate that he was leading his party away from an excessive reliance on big government. George W. Bush called himself a "Compassionate Conservative" to show his willingness to use big government for what he considered to be legitimate conservative ends.

Thus, despite the high level of partisan conflict that characterized the post-Reagan era, the presidential leaders of both parties achieved a high degree of convergence regarding the size and role of government.

* The Obama administration increased commitment to Progressivism, while the election of the populist, Donald Trump, has set up the current three-way political competition between Progressives, conservatives, and populists.

SUGGESTED READINGS

Ackerman, Bruce. *We the People: Foundations.* Cambridge, MA: Harvard University Press, 1991.

We the People: Transformations. Cambridge, MA: Harvard University Press, 1998.

Bensel, Richard. *Yankee Leviathan: The Origins of Central State Authority in America, 1858–1877.* Cambridge University Press, 1990.

Burnham, Walter Dean. *Critical Elections and the Mainsprings of American Politics.* New York: W. W. Norton, 1971.

Derthick, Martha. *Policymaking for Social Security.* Washington, DC: Brookings Institution Press, 1979.

Eisenach, Eldon. *The Lost Promise of Progressivism.* Lawrence: Kansas University Press, 1994.

Gerstle, Gary. *American Crucible: Race and Nation in the Twentieth Century.* Princeton, NJ: Princeton University Press, 2002.

Jaffa, Harry. *Crisis of the House Divided: An Interpretation of the Issues in the Lincoln–Douglas Debates, with a new Preface.* University of Chicago Press, 1982.

A New Birth of Freedom: Abraham Lincoln and the Coming of the Civil War. Lanham, MD: Rowman & Littlefield, 2000.

Keller, Morton. *Affairs of State: Public Life in Late Nineteenth Century America.* Cambridge, MA: Belknap Press, 1977.

Kennedy, David. *Freedom from Fear: The American People in Depression and War, 1929–1945.* New York: Oxford University Press, 1999.

Landy, Marc, and Martin Levin, eds. *The New Politics of Public Policy.* Baltimore, MD: Johns Hopkins University Press, 1995.

Lowi, Theodore. *The End of Liberalism: The Second Republic of the United States*, 2nd edn. New York: W. W. Norton, 1979.

McConnell, Grant. *Private Power and American Democracy.* New York: Vintage Books, 1970.

McMahon, Kevin J. *Reconsidering Roosevelt on Race: How the Presidency Paved the Road to Brown.* University of Chicago Press, 2004.

Mettler, Suzanne. *Soldiers to Citizens: The G. I. Bill and the Making of the Greatest Generation.* New York: Oxford University Press, 2005.

Milkis, Sidney M., and Jerome Mileur, eds. *The New Deal and the Triumph of Liberalism.* Amherst: University of Massachusetts Press, 2002.

Milkis, Sidney M. *The President and the Parties: The Transformation of the American Party System since the New Deal.* New York: Oxford University Press, 1992.

Morone, James. *The Democratic Wish: Popular Participation and the Limits of American Government.* New Haven, CT: Yale University Press, 1998.

Hellfire Nation: The Politics of Sin in American History. New Haven, CT: Yale University Press, 2003.

Patterson, James. *Grand Expectations: The United States, 1945–1974*. New York: Oxford University Press, 1996.

Sanders, Elizabeth. *The Roots of Reform: Farmers, Workers, and the American State, 1877–1917*. University of Chicago Press, 1999.

Skocpol, Theda. *Protecting Soldiers and Mothers: The Political Origins of Social Policy in the United States*. Cambridge, MA: Harvard University Press, 1992.

Skowronek, Steven. *Building a New American State: The Expansion of National Administrative Capacities, 1877–1920*. New York: Cambridge University Press, 1982.

The Politics Presidents Make: Leadership from John Adams to Bill Clinton. Cambridge, MA: Harvard University Press, 1993.

Young, James Sterling. *The Washington Community: 1800–1828*. New York: Columbia University Press, 1965.

Part II
Pivotal Relationships

5 Federalism

CHAPTER OVERVIEW

This chapter focuses on:

- **A contemporary portait of American federalism.**
- **The critical choice to impose dual federalism.**
- **The critical choice to impose national supremacy.**
- **The rise of cooperative federalism.**
- **The progressive advocacy of direct democracy.**
- **The critical choice to establish the national government: federalism's senior partner.**
- **The critical choice to secure civil rights for African Americans.**
- **The complexities and contradictions of modern federalism.**

In 1992, a twelfth-grade student arrived at Edison High School in San Antonio, Texas, carrying a concealed .38-caliber handgun and five bullets. He was arrested and eventually charged with violating a federal law, the Gun Free School Zones Act of 1990. In 1995, in the case of *United States v. Lopez*, the US Supreme Court overturned his conviction. The court did not dispute the prosecution's account. Lopez did in fact have a pistol in school. Nor did the court deny that guns in school are a bad thing deserving of punishment. Instead, the court found that the national government did not have the authority to make laws regarding guns in schools. It determined that the Constitution made this issue a state and local one, not a federal one.

In America, disputes over what the government ought to do frequently turn into disputes over where the decision should be made. The gravest crisis in all of American history, the Civil War, was fought both about the issue of slavery and about whether the national government was supreme over the states. One hundred years later, when federal courts imposed crosstown busing as the remedy for racial segregation in the schools, opponents claimed that the federal government had unconstitutionally usurped the power to make education policy. The fight over what turns into a fight over where because the Constitution does not fully clarify the dividing line between state and federal power.

Federalism: A Contemporary Portrait

If all one knew of the Constitution was the preamble's promise to "insure domestic tranquility and promote the general welfare," it would seem perfectly clear that the federal government had the right to put Lopez in jail. Few people would dispute that tranquility and the general welfare are better served when schools are free of guns. However, if all one knew of the Constitution was the *Tenth Amendment's* requirement that "the powers not delegated to the United States by the Constitution nor prohibited by it to the States, are reserved to the states," Lopez would be set free and a whole range of national government activity would be clearly unconstitutional. Where does the Constitution say that the federal government can set safety standards for drinking water or require colleges to provide equal funding for women's sports?

As we discussed in Chapter 3, this lack of clarity about the limits of national power exists because at the time of the founding the country was divided between those who wanted a strong national government and those who did not. Although both sides in this dispute mostly adhered to Classic Liberal principles, the defenders of states' rights were more imbued with communitarian impulses as they sought to preserve greater decision-making authority for the states and localities. In order to obtain consent for the establishment of a strong national government, its supporters agreed to give the states a direct role in national governance via the Senate and the Electoral College, both of whose members are elected on a state-by-state basis and to support ratification of the Tenth Amendment.. These compromises did not end the argument about how to divide power between the states and the federal government. That debate continues to this day. But the argument is not between enemies. The current relationship between the states and the national government would be better characterized as a partnership. Partners recognize that they need one another and that they must cooperate. But this does not stop them from quarreling, from exerting their individuality and from trying to dominate one another. The relationships between the federal government, the states, and the localities likewise exhibit cooperation, conflict, and competition for dominance.

Since the 1930s, the federal government has clearly become the senior partner. There is no longer any sphere of public policy where the localities or the states enjoy exclusive power. Nonetheless, states and localities continue to dominate certain policy spheres. Local government dominates K-12 education, policing, fire fighting, zoning of property, libraries, and construction and maintenance of local streets, sidewalks, public buildings, and recreation facilities. States build and maintain state highways and police those roads as well as the interstates. They regulate and license certain businesses and professional services. These include: contractors, plumbers, electricians, doctors, and lawyers as well as banks, insurance companies, electrical generators, and hospitals. Almost all public universities, colleges, and community colleges are run by the states. Only a very few cities have their own colleges and junior colleges. The service academies are virtually the only federally run undergraduate institutions. States remain the dominant partners in the making and enforcing of both civil and criminal law. Most ordinary disputes between individuals and between firms are decided in state courts on the basis of state law. With the exception of treason, terrorism, counterfeiting, kidnapping, and certain types of financial fraud, perpetrators of most other types of crime are also tried in state courts on the basis of state law. Of the more than 2 million Americans currently imprisoned, more than half are in state correctional facilities. Local and county jails account for another third. Federal prisons house only one-sixth of the prison population including convicts in state prisons.

However, the federal government retains the right to involve itself in any or all of these state activities. It forces local police to abide by Supreme Court edicts regarding the searching of homes, the surveillance of phone conversations, and the informing of criminal suspects of the right against self-incrimination and their right to an attorney. Title 9 of the federal Equal Opportunity Education Act forbids sex discrimination in schools athletics programs. The Every Student Succeeds Act requires schools to administer achievement tests written by the states. Local zoning rules and state licensing requirements can be overturned if a federal judge finds them to be racially discriminatory. Libraries, city halls, swimming pools, and other municipal buildings must provide ramps and elevators for the handicapped as required by the federal Americans with Disabilities Act. Federal courts reserve the right to hear appeals from those whom states courts have ruled against. All levels of education depend heavily on funding from the federal government.

Even in those vast areas in which the federal government dominates - such as environmental regulation, unemployment assistance, welfare, healthcare for the poor, and job training - the states continue to play a key role. In these spheres and many other as well, Congress writes the statutes, federal agencies issue rules and guidelines for interpreting the law, but the states implement those laws and regulations. State agencies perform the actual work of inspecting facilities, imposing penalties, and issuing contracts. For example, the federal Clean Air Act sets the standards for how clean the air must be, but the actual work of coming up with specific plans for meeting those standards including the inspection of factories and fining those who are not in compliance is left to the states.

Table 5.1. Outlays for federal grants to state and local governments, by function, selected FY1902–FY2015 (nominal $ in millions).

Fiscal year	Total ($)	Health ($)	Income security ($)	Education, training, employment, and social services ($)	Transportation ($)	Community and regional development ($)	Other ($)
2015 est.	628,153	354.031	105,095	65,215	64,378	16,672	22,762
2014	576,965	320.022	100,869	60,485	62,152	13,232	20,205
2013	546,171	283,036	102,190	62,690	60,518	16,781	20,956
2012	544,569	268,277	102,574	66,126	60,749	20,258	24,585
2011	606,766	292,847	113,625	89,147	60,986	20,002	30,159
2010	608,390	290,168	115,156	97,586	60,981	18,908	25,591
2009	537,991	268,320	103,169	73,986	55,438	17,394	19,684
2008	461,317	218,025	93,102	58,904	51,216	19,221	20,849
2007	443,797	208,311	90,971	58,077	47,945	20,653	17,840
2006	434,099	197,347	89,816	60,512	46,683	21,285	18,456
2005	428,018	197,848	90,885	57,247	43,370	20,167	16,501
2000	285,874	124,843	68,653	36,672	32,222	8,665	14,819
1990	135,325	43,890	36,768	21,780	19,174	4,965	8,748
1980	91,385	15,758	18,495	21,862	13,022	6,486	15,762
1970	24,065	3,849	5,795	6,417	4,599	1,780	1,625
1960	7,019	214	2,635	525	2,999	109	537
1950	2,212	123	1,123	484	429	0	53
1940	967	22	271	238	165	0	271
1930	100	0	1	22	76	0	1
1922	116	0	1	7	92	0	8
1913	12	0	2	3	0	0	7
1902	7	0	1	1	0	0	5

Source: Congressional Research Service.

States are now very dependent on the federal government to help pay their bills. Federal grants-in-aid to the states now constitute a quarter of all the money states spend. Table 5.1 shows the vast expansion in federal aid to the states that has occurred since 1902, which has more than doubled since 2000. It also reveals how much of a shift there has been in what that aid is spent on. As of 1960, the largest federal grants were for roads. By 1970, healthcare had become by far the largest recipient of federal aid and income security (often called "welfare") was narrowly exceeding transportation. As of 2014, healthcare accounted for more than half of all federal grants-in-aid to the states receiving over three times more than the second place recipient, income security, and over five times more than the fifth place recipient, transportation. In view of this

Table 5.2. The relationship between the states and the federal government.

Federal government the senior partner	States still retain pivotal role in the following
• States dependent on the federal government to pay bills • Federal grants-in-aid, predominantly for healthcare • Federal government involvement in local matters	• Primary education, policing, highways, public universities, and state and local jail facilities • Implementation of federal laws and regulations
All states have a constitution, executive, legislature, and judiciary yet remain distinctive in their forms of government, cultures, partisan affiliations, economies, and population size	

massive subsidy, it is no surprise that states now spend more on healthcare than on any other purpose, even more than they spend on education.

Table 5.2 summarizes the relationship between the states and the federal government.

State Politics

The fifty states form fifty very distinct political and economic worlds. One might expect Vermont and New Hampshire to ressemble one another politically. They border one another. Neither contains a large city. Tourism and recreation are critical to their economies. Nonetheless, the two states govern themselves quite differently. Vermont has among the strictest land use regulations in the nation. State law restricts where new homes and commercial establishments can be built. It also has relatively high state taxes. New Hampshire has no state income tax and does not try to control land use to anywhere near the same degree that Vermont does. Its state motto, "Live free or die," captures its traditional aversion to intrusive government. Its congressional delegation is split between the two parties. Vermont's congressional delegation has no Republicans and one of its Senators, Bernard Sanders, calls himself a democratic socialist.

All fifty states mimic the federal government in that they have a constitution, an executive, a legislature, and a judiciary. But the forms and powers granted by their constitutions to those three branches of government differ greatly. Nebraska's legislature is unicameral. There is no upper chamber. The governors of New Hampshire and Vermont serve only two-year terms. California, Michigan, New York, and Pennsylvania have well-staffed legislatures that are frequently in session and whose members view serving in the legislature as virtually a full-time job. At the other extreme, North Dakota, South Dakota, Utah, Wyoming, Montana, and New Hampshire have legislators who receive little pay, have few staff, and must maintain other jobs to enable them to earn a living.

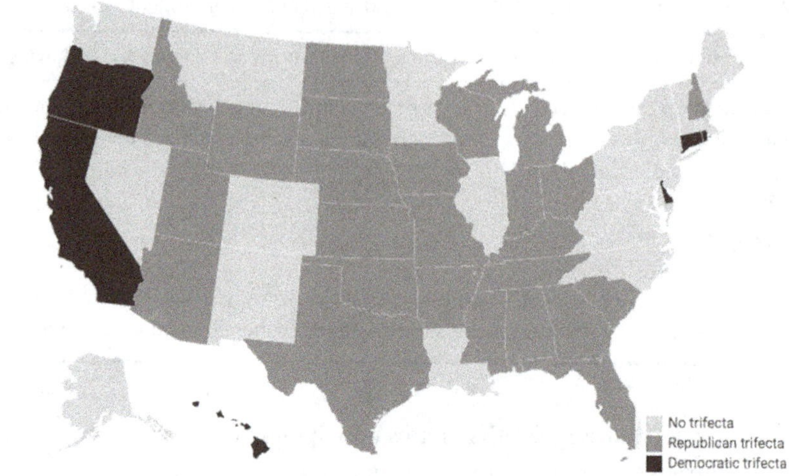

Figure 5.1. State trifectas, post-2016 elections.
Source: Ballotpedia.

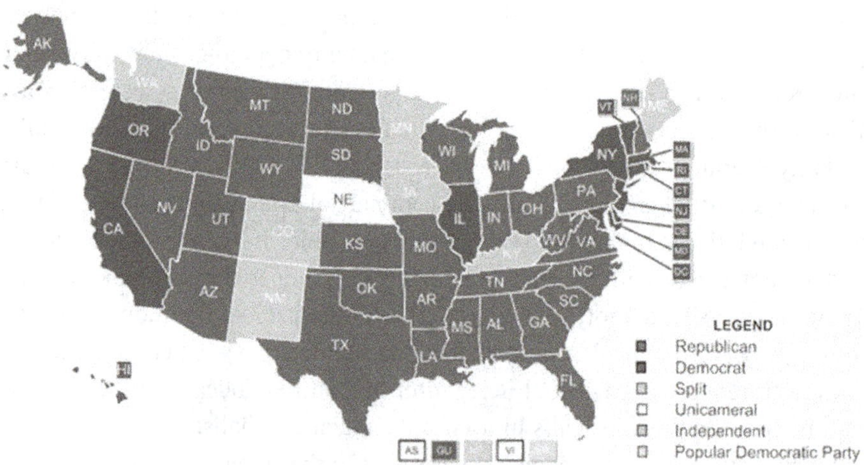

Figure 5.2. Legislative partisan composition, 2016.
Source: National Conference of State Legislatures.

States differ in the degree to which they capture the loyalty and attention of their citizens. When someone from one of the five boroughs calls herself a New Yorker, she is undoubtedly referring to her identification with the city not the state of New York. Sports fans in Massachusetts are far more likely to watch the Boston Celtics or the Boston Red Sox than the University of Massachusetts Minutemen. By contrast, on a Saturday afternoon during

Table 5.3. Median household income by state, 2015.

State	Median income	State	Median income	State	Median income
United States	56,516	Kentucky	42,387	Ohio	53,301
Alabama	44,509	Louisiana	45,922	Oklahoma	47,077
Alaska	75,112	Maine	50,756	Oregon	60,834
Arizona	52,248	Maryland	73,594	Pennsylvania	60,389
Arkansas	42,798	Massachusetts	67,861	Rhode Island	55,701
California	63,636	Michigan	54,203	South Carolina	46,360
Colorado	66,596	Minnesota	68,730	South Dakota	55,065
Connecticut	72,889	Mississippi	40,037	Tennessee	47,330
Delaware	57,756	Missouri	59,196	Texas	56,473
Washington D.C.	70,071	Montana	51,395	Utah	66,258
Florida	48,825	Nebraska	60,474	Vermont	59,494
Georgia	50,768	Nevada	52,008	Virginia	61,486
Hawaii	64,514	New Hampshire	75,675	Washington	67,243
Idaho	51,624	New Jersey	68,357	West Virginia	42,824
Illinois	60,413	New Mexico	45,119	Wisconsin	55,425
Indiana	51,983	New York	58,005	Wyoming	60,925
Iowa	60,855	North Carolina	50,797		
Kansas	54,865	North Dakota	57.415		

basketball season in Kentucky or football season in Alabama, the attention of the state is riveted on the Wildcats or the Crimson Tide. In those states, it is quite common to think of oneself as a Kentuckian or an Alabaman. This strong identification is reflected in the amount of coverage state politics and government receives in those states compared to what it receives in the *New York Times* or the *Boston Globe*.

States differ markedly in their attachments to political parties. In 2016, twenty-eight states had one-party control of both houses of the state legislature and the governorship. Twenty-five of those states were controlled by Republicans.

As Table 5.3 shows, states also vary economically. In the two richest states, Connecticut and Maryland, families earn twice as much as in the poorest state, Mississippi. In the ten richest states, families make more than $60,000 a year while in the eight poorest they make less than $45,000.

US Census

As Table 5.4 shows, states also differ dramatically in the size of their population. Roughly one of every ten Americans lives in California, whereas forty-two states are less than a quarter its size.

Table 5.4. States ranked by population.

Rank	State	Population
	All United States	308,745,538
1	California	37,253,956
2	Texas	25,145,561
3	New York	19,378,102
4	Florida	18,801,310
5	Illinois	12,830,632
6	Pennsylvania	12,702,379
7	Ohio	11,536,504
8	Michigan	9,883,640
9	Georgia	9,687,653
10	North Carolina	9,535,483
11	New Jersey	8,791,894
12	Virginia	8,001,024
13	Washington	6,724,540
14	Massachusetts	6,547,629
15	Indiana	6,483,802
16	Arizona	6,392,017
17	Tennessee	6,346,105
18	Missouri	5,988,927
19	Maryland	5,773,552
20	Wisconsin	5,686,986
21	Minnesota	5,303,925
22	Colorado	5,029,196
23	Alabama	4,779,736
24	South Carolina	4,625,364
25	Louisiana	4,533,372
26	Kentucky	4,339,367
27	Oregon	3,831,074
28	Oklahoma	3,751,351
29	Connecticut	3,574,097
30	Iowa	3,046,355
31	Mississippi	2,967,297
32	Arkansas	2,915,918
33	Kansas	2,853,118
34	Utah	2,763,885
35	Nevada	2,700,551
36	New Mexico	2,059,179
37	West Virginia	1,852,994
38	Nebraska	1,826,341
39	Idaho	1,567,582
40	Hawaii	1,360,301
41	Maine	1,328,361
42	New Hampshire	1,316,470
43	Rhode Island	1,052,567
44	Montana	989,415

Table 5.4. *(cont.)*

Rank	State	Population
45	Delaware	897,934
46	South Dakota	814,180
47	Alaska	710,231
48	North Dakota	672,591
49	Vermont	625,741
50	Washington, D.C.	601,723
51	Wyoming	563,626

Federalism and American Political Development

The essential federal principle enshrined by the Constitution – that the United States is a compound republic composed of state governments as well as the federal government – remains in place. But in the course of American political development that constitutionally established path has been considerably recontoured. This section describes the critical choices that have served to both reinforce and redirect Federalism's path

CRITICAL CHOICE: THE IMPOSITION OF DUAL FEDERALISM

The election of 1800, pitting Thomas Jefferson and John Adams, provided a clear-cut choice between Adams's adherence to Federalist principles and Jefferson's commitment to the "Empire of Liberty." Jefferson prevailed. Jefferson's presidency set the US on the path of dual federalism. The essence of dual federalism was the strict separation of powers and duties between the national government and state government and the curtailment of national government power. Jefferson rejected the Hamiltonian spirit that had crept into the interpretation of governmental powers during the first twelve years of the new nation. He abandoned the ambitious projects that Hamilton had embarked on; he cut the federal budget; and he made clear that the initiative for domestic public policy making would reside with the individual states.

After the ratification of the Constitution the next great contest in American political life was fought over the relative political strength of the federal government and the states. The Federalists who dominated the administrations of both Washingon and Adams were unapologetically elitist. Although they accepted the idea that the people were the ultimate source of authority, they sought to make popular rule as indirect as possible. Because the central government was further removed from the citizenry than were the states and localities, Federalists were more confident that it could be made to function in a stable and reliable manner. They pressed for the establishment of a strong federal bureaucracy, a well staffed professional army and navy and an ambitious national bank capable of promoting national economic development

These aggressive efforts to aggrandize the federal government sparked the growth of an opposition party, the Republicans. Led by Thomas Jefferson and James Madison, it believed in majority rule. Republicans viewed the Federalists not merely as elitists and centralists but as monarchists in the making. They saw no possibility of preserving constitutionally guaranteed liberties in the face of a strong central state. Their understanding of enumerated powers was much more severe in its limitation on government. They were deeply suspicious of the two least democratic aspects of the constitutional order, the Senate and the Supreme Court.

Jefferson's hostility to central government did not undermine his commitment to the nation. But he was convinced that the greatness of the American nation rested in the beliefs and sentiments of the people, which included a deeply felt aversion to a strong national government. As we discussed in Chapter 4, Jefferson envisaged America as a vast "Empire of Liberty" ruled not by soldiers and bureaucrats but by the shared commitment to great governing principles, the rights to "life, liberty, and the pursuit of happiness." The Empire of Liberty would be the first in all humankind not to be ruled from a single center. He was committed to preventing New York or Philadelphia from controlling this empire the way Rome, Paris, and London had become the controlling forces of the Roman, French, and British empires.

Respect and affection between the scattered provinces of this empire would be insufficient to hold such a large entity together unless those sentiments were complemented by common material interests. If shared reverence for the principles of the Declaration of Independence was the ideological glue for holding the empire of liberty together, the practical adhesive was commerce. Trading with people in other parts of the country would enable Americans to develop ties of trust, respect, and reciprocity. Because people in different parts of the far-flung nation needed goods produced in other parts, buying and selling provided an avenue for developing a national outlook that politics, an essentially local activity, did not.

At the same time that he decentralized policy making, Jefferson spearheaded the greatest territorial expansion in American history. As a result of his purchase of the Louisiana Territory from France in 1803, the nation more than doubled in size. Although much of the newly acquired territory was thought to be uninhabitable, the sheer magnitude of the additions changed Americans' understanding of themselves from a country dominated by the eastern seaboard to a nation of truly continental proportions. As Jefferson's theory of an empire of liberty dictated, these territories would not become colonies. Each would establish its own government and quickly be absorbed into the vast nation of states where it would essentially govern itself just as the existing states did.

After Jefferson, centralization made a comeback. The Second National Bank of the United States was chartered in 1816. The election of John Quincy Adams in 1824 promised to greatly increase the power of the central government. Adams vowed to use the national government to build roads and canals and even to establish its own university. Adams failed to get much of his program adopted. Having defeated Adams in 1828, Andrew Jackson set about restoring limited, decentralized government. Lying on his sickbed in the spring of 1832, Jefferson's disciple, President Andrew Jackson, vowed, "The bank is trying to kill me, but I will kill it."

With that, Jackson set about to veto the rechartering of the Second National Bank of the United States, an act that most vividly symbolized his determination to radically curtail the power of the national government. He objected to the bank on democratic-egalitarian grounds. Jackson was convinced that the bank granted "exclusive gratuities and privileges" that "made the rich richer and the potent more powerful."

The bank controlled the money supply and was the dominant lender in America, making 20 percent of all commercial loans. This extraordinary combination of powers enabled it to crush rival banks by manipulating their reserves and to curry favor with Congress by granting legislators loans at favorable rates. Jackson was not inclined to reform the bank. He was suspicious of the very idea of a national bank, fearing that so much financial power placed in a single institution would inevitably lead to privilege and corruption. Better to abolish it and disperse its functions among state banks, he believed. The best way to make the national government democratic was to give it as little to do as possible.

Jackson's actions were consonant with the growing democratic sentiment of the time and with the principle that democracy could best be encouraged locally. In the 1820s and 1830s, many states rewrote their constitutions primarily in order to make them more democratic. Property qualifications for voting were eliminated, thereby expanding the size of the electorate to include virtually all white males. State offices, including judicial posts that had previously been appointed, became directly elected by the people.

Jackson's decentralist convictions were so thoroughgoing that he opposed some national government projects even though he approved of their aims. In 1830, he vetoed federal aid for construction of the Maysville Road. Although the road was supposed to be a link of the national road, it was to be built entirely within the state of Kentucky. Jackson did not believe that the federal government's interstate commerce powers encompassed a project that was essentially local in nature. The road was probably a good idea, but if the people of Kentucky wanted it, Jackson asserted, they should build it.

UPSHOT

For the first 150 years of the life of the United States, the states and localities dominated. Indeed, for the first sixty years of the United States' existence, it was not clear that the Union would prevail. That question was decisively settled only by the Civil War. Even after the Civil War, local self-government, supported by the more decentralizing institutions of the Constitution – Congress and the states – remained the most prominent feature of American political life. The national idea and the constitutional structure that frames it were preserved in the absence of a powerful central state. Only in the middle of the twentieth century, as a result of the New Deal and the Second World War, did Americans come to view national governance as dominant in their political lives.

CRITICAL CHOICE: NATIONAL SUPREMACY, WITHIN LIMITS

Lincoln's decision to use military force to suppress the secession of Southern states from the Union was the critical choice that not only enabled the Union to endure but also that firmly established the supremacy of the federal government over the states. However, Lincoln and the Union would not have prevailed were it not for previous critical choices made on behalf of federal supremacy. In a series of unanimous decisions over a period of almost thirty-five years, the Supreme Court under the leadership of Chief Justice John Marshall established the principle of the supremacy of the federal government over the states and limited the states' ability to interfere with economic competition, property rights, and the sanctity of contracts. President Andrew Jackson's readiness to use federal troops to quell South Carolina's effort to nullify a federal law was a vital precedent for Lincoln's successful assertion of national supremacy.

As we discuss in Chapter 9, Marshall's opinion in *McCulloch v. Maryland* (1819) clearly established the supremacy of the federal government over the states. In that case, the Supreme Court voided a tax that the state of Maryland had imposed on the Second National Bank of the United States. Marshall asserted that the Constitution was derived from the people, not the states. Although limited to those powers specifically enumerated by the Constitution, the federal government's authority was supreme within those limits. The Constitution does not mention the chartering of a national bank, but according to Marshall, such a financial institution was obviously "necessary and proper" for carrying out the enumerated powers to tax and to regulate commerce and was therefore rendered constitutional by the "Necessary and Proper Clause" in Article I of the Constitution. Although states also have the right to tax, they do not have the right to tax federal functions. As the Maryland example demonstrated, such taxes have the power to hamper and indeed to destroy legitimate federal activities.

In *Gibbons v. Ogden* (1824), the court ruled that New York's granting of a monopoly for steamboat service violated the federal government's right to protect the freedom of interstate commerce. Marshall took a broad view of commerce, claiming that it included all aspects of trade, including shipping. He argued that the commerce affected by the New York steamboat monopoly was interstate in character even though the monopoly applied only to the New York portion of waterways. Those waterways, coastal and inland, extended beyond the borders of New York and were therefore aquatic avenues of interstate commerce. It was the constitutional responsibility of the federal government to ensure that trade remained free at all points along those interstate routes.

Marshall's success was based on the power of his reasoning and his self-discipline. He knew that the combined strength of the legislative and executive branch could defeat him by passing constitutional amendments that voided the court's decisions, by impeaching him and his allies, or by defying the court's rulings. Therefore, he picked his opportunities carefully. The court refused to entertain any important cases regarding the two most controversial issues of the time, slavery and the tariff, because feelings about those two issues were so strong that any decision the court might choose to render would risk tearing the country apart. Marshall's court confined itself to cases in which some disagreement existed among its erstwhile opponents, the Republicans. For example, many Republicans were so deeply committed to free enterprise that they shared Marshall's opposition to New York's establishment of steamboat monopoly. Likewise, many Republicans appreciated the positive economic contribution of the Second National Bank and were therefore opposed to the efforts of specific states to hamper its activities. Thus, the rulings that the court handed down were relatively uncontroversial; their great importance lay in the precedents they established. Because his political opponents were so preoccupied by the immediate implications of the rulings, they underestimated the long-term implications.

Unlike his idol Jefferson, Andrew Jackson did not believe in the compact theory of the Constitution. He took the phrase "We the People" literally. His vision of national power was that its scope of responsibility was very limited, but within that scope it reigned supreme. While attending a dinner in honor of Jefferson's birthday, Jackson was disturbed to hear Robert Hayne, senator from South Carolina, offer a toast to "the Union of the States and the Sovereignty of the States." In his own toast, Jackson responded "Our Federal Union, it must be preserved." Sensing that South Carolina was on the verge of passing a nullification ordinance in which it would refuse to pay federally imposed tariffs, Jackson told a South Carolina congressman: "Please give my compliments to my friends in your state, and say to them that if a single drop of blood shall be shed there in opposition to the laws of the United States, I will hang the first man I can lay my hand on engaged in such treasonable conduct, upon the first tree I can reach." When Senator Hayne asked Senator Thomas Hart Benton of Missouri whether Jackson would really do such a thing, Benton replied, "When Jackson begins to talk about hanging, they can begin to look out for ropes."

Jackson responded to South Carolina's Nullification Ordinance of 1832 with a Nullification Proclamation in which he explained his refusal to accept the ordinance and his willingness to call out federal troops to quell any attempt by South Carolina to enforce it. South Carolina backed down. Although Jackson and Democrats in Congress conceded to a reduction in the tariff, the president succeeded in his objective of teaching his fellow partisans the difference between states' rights and nullification of legitimate national policy. Had Jackson failed to defend federal supremacy, it would have no longer served as a premise of American constitutional government and Lincoln's later defense of it would have proved impossible.

Presidential leadership prevented a rebellion over tariffs, but it could not do so over the expansion of slavery. As we discussed in Chapter 4, none of the compromises over the spread of slavery were able to stave of the Civil War. Because slavery was constitutionally protected, ending it would require constitutional change to enable the national government to impose abolition on the slave states. The Thirteenth, Fourteenth, and Fifteenth Amendments to the Constitution committed the national government to forcing the former slave states to grant civil and political rights to African Americans. War and constitutional amendment achieved the supremacy of the national government over the states that the Supreme Court had proclaimed in *McCulloch*.

In the immediate aftermath of the war, it appeared that African American civil and political rights would indeed be secured through the vigorous exertion of national power. The United States established, for the first and only time, a powerful military government to rule on domestic soil. Reconstruction involved thousands of troops and was led by thirty-five generals. The South was divided into five military districts. Generals were empowered to void state and local elections; dismiss governors and mayors; and participate in the selection of tax collectors, sheriffs, judges, and other local officials. The military staffed and led the key Reconstruction agency, the Freedman's Bureau, which provided food and medical assistance to both blacks and whites and established schools for 500,000 children. Federal troops maintained law and order while Southern states rewrote their constitutions to provide slaves with full civil and political rights. But the Reconstruction effort became increasingly halfhearted over time. The South remained unalterably opposed and the political enthusiasm for it among Northerners waned. The number of troops stationed in the South declined, as did the size and ambition of the Freedman's Bureau. Resistance by white Southerners

Table 5.5. Federal supremacy timeline.

1819 *McCulloch v. Maryland*
Struck down Maryland tax on charter of the national bank
National Bank was constitutional use of Congress's power to tax
1824 *Gibbons v. Ogden*
New York steamboat monopoly violated interstate commerce protections
Coastal and inland waterways all under the purview of federal responsibility to maintain free trade
1832 South Carolina Nullification Crisis
Jackson argues South Carolina's refusal to enforce tariff violated federal government supremacy
Threatened to use force to execute the law

took many forms, including terrorism and murder. The Ku Klux Klan was a powerful symbol and organizational weapon for this resistance.

UPSHOT

Never again would there be a concerted effort at disunion. The Union victory created a foundation for the emergence of the US as a great nation. However, the failure of Reconstruction allowed the South to evade both the letter and the spirit of the Fourteenth and Fifteenth Amendments by erecting the complex and comprehensive system of racial oppression nicknamed Jim Crow. State laws and administrative practices prevented African Americans from voting and other forms of political participation, forbade them from eating at restaurants or staying at hotels patronized by whites, and relegated them to inferior facilities at theaters and on streetcars. States and localities established separate schools and separate prisons. Mobs tortured and hanged African American suspects with no police interference and no national government intervention. The federal government did not even begin to attack Jim Crow until the middle of the next century.

Cooperative Federalism

After the Civil War, although dual federalism remained the dominant path of state–federal relations, a new path was cleared, that of cooperative federalism, which enabled the federal government to come to the aid of the states. Even earlier, the federal government had provided some assistance. The father of dual federalism, Thomas Jefferson, had permitted Treasury Secretrary Albert Gallatin, to give grants of land to the states for the support of public schools. Jefferson did not object to this form of federal involvement in his empire of liberty because he felt that it was noncoercive. Land was preferable to cash as a form of subsidy, believed Jefferson, because the federal government owned so much land.

During the second half of the nineteenth century cooperative federalism became a fully accepted and critically important form of intergovernmental relations. It was the driving force in the creation of the American system of state universities. The Morrill Act of 1862 gave land grants to states to establish colleges that taught agriculture, mechanical arts, military science, natural science, and classical studies. Only seventeen state universities existed before 1862. Over the next fifty years, the Morrill Act led to the creation of over fifty more.

Modern agricultural and transportation policies have also been framed by cooperative federalism. The Smith Lever Act, enacted in 1914, created the Department of Agriculture's Extension Service. Rather than impose technical advice on wary farmers, the Extension Service functions as a partnership between the Department of Agriculture and the state land grant colleges. Federal employees work with federally subsidized state specialists to develop programs of technical assistance geared to the specific needs and preferences of local farmers.

Figure 5.3. The Public Highway of the Future.
Source: Granger Collection, NYC –

Road building is one of the most important but also most politically sensitive responsibilities of government. Decisions about where to put roads and where to locate entrances and exits to limited-access roads can determine which communities prosper and which ones die. Washington proved reluctant to make such decisions, leaving them to the states. Since the 1920s, federally subsidized road building and repair have been among the most important activities of the states.

Direct Democracy

In Chapter 3 we discussed the great impact that Progressivism had on American political development. Because state constitutions and municipal charters were far more easily changed than the US Constitution, Progressivism had a more decisive impact on state than on federal politics and governance. The Progressives were able to convince many states to adopt party primary elections, and citizen-initiated referenda, initiatives, and recalls, all of which were defended on democratic egalitarian grounds. Primary elections substituted the will of party voters for that of political leaders in determining whom the party would nominate for state and federal office. The referendum enabled voters to bypass the state legislature and vote directly for or against specific policy proposals. The recall allowed the voters to remove governors and judges from office. These Progressive-inspired changes reflected a critical choice in favor of direct democracy at the expense of representative democracy. The vast size of the national polity and the key provisions of the US Constitution that bolster the representative form of government have prevented the national government from moving toward direct democracy the way the states have. As a result the critical choice in favor of direct democracy altered the path of state but not of federal government.

CRITICAL CHOICE: THE NATIONAL GOVERNMENT – FEDERALISM'S SENIOR PARTNER

The New Deal fundamentally altered the relationship between the states and the national government. Policies championed by the Roosevelt administration and critical Supreme Court decisions greatly expanded the reach of national policy and placed the states in a subordinate position. States emerged from the New Deal with many more functions and far greater administrative capacity with which to perform them. But the relationship between the states and the federal government was irrevocably altered. The federal government had become the senior partner.

Table 5.6. States that have adopted the referendum and/or the initiative.

	Statutes			Constitution	
State	Initiative	Citizen petition referendum	Legislative referendum	Initiative	Legislative referendum
Alaska	D*	Yes	No	None	Yes
Arizona	D	Yes	Yes	D	Yes
Arkansas	D	Yes	Yes	D	Yes
California	D	Yes	Yes	D	Yes
Colorado	D	Yes	No	D	Yes
Florida	None	No	No	D	Yes
Idaho	D	Yes	Yes	None	Yes
Illinois	None	No	Yes	D	Yes
Kentucky	None	Yes	Yes	None	Yes
Maine	I	Yes	Yes	None	Yes
Maryland	None	Yes	Yes	None	Yes
Massachusetts	I	Yes	Yes	I	Yes
Michigan	I	Yes	Yes	D	Yes
Mississippi	None	No	No	I	Yes
Missouri	D	Yes	Yes	D	Yes
Montana	D	Yes	Yes	D	Yes
Nebraska	D	Yes	Yes	D	Yes
Nevada	I	Yes	Yes	D	Yes
New Mexico	None	Yes	Yes	None	Yes
North Dakota	D	Yes	Yes	D	Yes
Ohio	I	Yes	Yes	D	Yes
Oklahoma	D	Yes	Yes	D	Yes
Oregon	D	Yes	Yes	D	Yes
South Dakota	D	Yes	Yes	D	Yes
Utah	D&I	Yes	Yes	None	Yes
Washington DC	D&I	Yes	Yes	None	Yes
Wyoming	D*	Yes	No	None	Yes
US Virgin Islands	I	Yes	Yes	I	Yes

Table 5.7. Cooperative federalism and direct democracy timeline.

Federal land grants to states for public schools and colleges
- Morrill Act, 1862
  - Established agricultural colleges
- Smith Lever Act (1914)
  - Technical assistance provided for needs of local farmers

Federal funding for states to build highways
- State-based Progressive reforms for more direct democracy
- Direct party primaries
- Citizen-initiated referenda
- Initiative
- Recalls

"Strings Attached" Federalism: Federalism Meets the Modern Administrative State

The New Deal of the 1930s made cooperative federalism less simply cooperative by requiring the states to abide by federal dictates in order to receive the funds that the federal government made available. Federal aid to the states greatly increased, but that aid now came with numerous and often onerous demands on what states had to do to qualify for the grants and limitations on how the states could use the grant money. Therefore, we call this new relationship between the national and state government strings attached federalism.

New Deal welfare grants required states to match federal contributions with monies of their own and to designate a single agency to be responsible for receiving and spending welfare aid. Many states had no existing agency capable of performing such a task and were compelled to create state welfare departments. Even those that already had welfare departments were required to expand and professionalize the operations of those agencies in order to meet federally imposed standards. States were "blackmailed" into administering the federal unemployment compensation scheme because a 3 percent tax would be levied on all employers in states that did not assume this administrative burden.

States emerged from the New Deal with many more functions and far greater administrative capacity with which to perform them. But the relationship between the states and the federal government was irrevocably altered. The federal government had become the senior partner. Goals and strategies for an ever-wider sphere of policies were set in Washington. The states were left with the task of implementing those policies according to rules and regulations dictated to them from above. If they failed to abide by federal guidelines they risked losing those grants.

States responded to their roles as junior partners in different ways. Some sought to make the New Deal programs their own by vigorously endorsing and expanding them. These states created "little New Deals" in which state government took on the same expansive and experimental character that the national government did. Led by Governor Philip La Follette, Wisconsin increased taxes on the rich, expanded aid to education, and reorganized state agencies. Some states sought to resist federal encroachment. In Georgia, Governor Eugene Talmadge actually reduced state spending for highways, daring the federal government to cut highway assistance in response. He also refused to cooperate with the mandates of federal welfare and agricultural assistance programs. The fear that this approach would actually cause the federal government to stop helping Georgians led to Talmadge's defeat for reelection in 1936.

In general, the wealthier industrial states of the East and Midwest tried to cooperate with and even emulate FDR's New Deal whereas the poorer states, primarily those in the South, resisted change to the extent they could without endangering their access to federal help. Despite the strings it imposed, the New Deal did not succeed in unifying policies across the states. Indeed, the differing states' responses to it in many ways served to accentuate the political and policy differences among them.

Expansive Judicial Intepretations

During the New Deal the Supreme Court abandoned what had previously served as the most important brake on federal government intervention in the affairs of the states, the commerce clause of the Constitution, which limits the federal government's regulatory role to "interstate and foreign commerce." Prior to the New Deal, the Court had interpreted the word "commerce" to exclude other related economic activities such as manufacturing. It had also interpreted "interstate" narrowly to mean the direct exchange of goods between states. The New Deal defined commerce far more loosely to mean almost any form of production, employment arrangement, sale or transport of goods or services.

In 1942, *Wickard v. Filburn*, the Supreme Court erased the distinction between intrastate and interstate commerce altogether. In order to drive up wheat prices, the Congress had passed the Agriculture Adjustment Act, which imposed limits on how much wheat a farmer could grow. Roscoe Filburn claimed that the act did not apply to him because his wheat was not for sale. He was growing it exclusively to feed his own chickens. Nonetheless, the Court ruled that Filburn was subject to the Act because a decision by farmers to grow more of their own wheat for feed would increase the wheat supply and thus lower its price. Therefore, this form of wheat-growing did indeed affect interstate commerce and Filburn must abide by his production limit. For the next fifty years the Supreme Court did not overturn a single federal statute, on commerce clause grounds or for any other reason.

UPSHOT

The New Deal did not destroy federalism. The national government did not yet intrude in most of the realms in which the states and localities had traditionally dominated. Nonetheless, the relationship between the national government and the states and localities was transformed. Henceforth, the national government could and would use the commerce clause as a rationale for vastly expanding national government intervention in what had previously been the exclusive realm of the states and localities. And, it could and would require the states to obey its directives as the price for obtaining its generous assistance.

CRITICAL CHOICE: REASSERTING NATIONAL SUPREMACY – CIVIL RIGHTS FOR AFRICAN AMERICANS

Although the New Deal profoundly altered the relationship between the states and the federal government by requiring the states to accept federal regulation of aid, this shift did not affect Jim Crow. The Southern states remained free to deprive African Americans of voting rights and of equal access to job opportunities, education and public facilities. Starting in the 1950s and culminating in the 1960s, the federal government revived the Fourteenth and Fifteenth Amendments to overturn the state laws and state administrative practices that promoted and enforced racial segregation.

In the 1940s FDR and Truman had taken steps to racially integrate federal employment practices and, most significantly, to racially integrate the armed forces. But the first serious blow to state laws and practices was imposed by the Supreme Court in 1954. In *Brown v. Board of Education*, it declared all state and local efforts to racially segregate schools to be unconstitutional. In 1964, Congress, aggressively prodded by President Johnson, passed the first major Civil Rights Act since Reconstruction, outlawing discrimination in public accommodations, housing, and employment. The following year it passed the Voting Rights Act, which not only overturned state laws that prevented African Americans from voting but also empowered the Justice Deparment to intervene to enable African Americans to freely exercise their voting rights.

These critical choices were the result of pressure from a grassroots movement, shifts in public opinion, and aggressive political leadership. African Americans borrowed the tactics of nonviolent resistance from the Indian independence movement led by Mohandas Gandhi and the US labor union struggles of the 1930s. They organized peaceful sit-ins at segregated lunch counters, bus terminals, and other segregated public facilities in the South. Black and white protestors would refuse to give up their seats when asked to leave and would then submit peacefully to the beatings and arrests to which they were then subjected.

The civil rights struggle was the first serious political conflict to be fully televised. Americans all over the country watched Southern sheriffs and police officers beat and bully well-mannered young African American men and women for the "crime" of ordering food at a whites-only lunch counter or helping to fill out voter registration papers. Americans saw Southern governors blocking the schoolhouse doors that African American children were politely trying to enter. These dramatic moments tarnished the image of state and local government in the minds of many Americans. Although they might continue to respect the leadership in their own state, they increasingly came to question whether important policy matters should be left in the hands of states whose own troopers used cattle prods to disperse peaceful civil rights demonstrators.

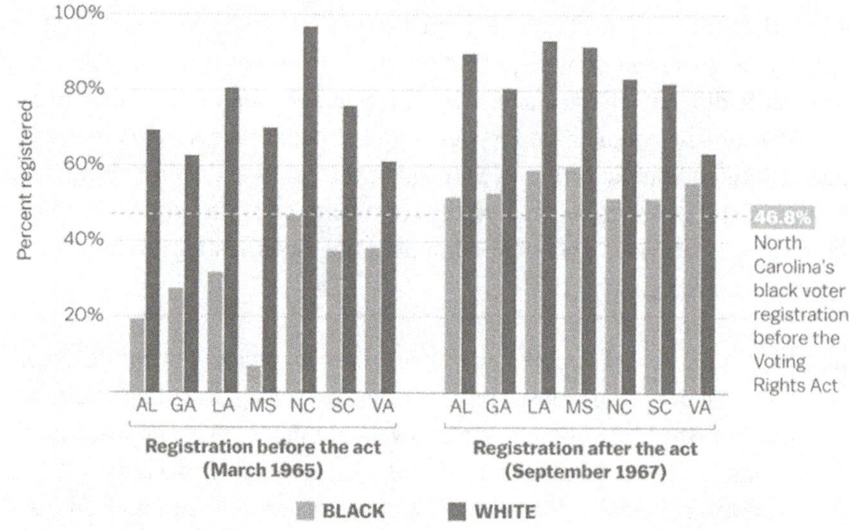

Figure 5.4. Voter registration levels.
Source: Anand Katakam/Vox.

The initial wave of resistance to integration of school and public facilities and to African American voter registration efforts seemed to confirm the skepticism of those Americans who doubted that racial attitudes could be changed by federal legislation. But in the face of persistent and aggressive national intervention, the resistance soon crumbled. Although racial politics would continue to roil American politics for many years, schools and facilities in the South were desegregated and African Americans achieved comparability with whites in terms of voter participation, the promise of the Fourteenth and Fifteenth Amendments was finally fulfilled.

UPSHOT

For almost a hundred years amendments to the Constitution had been in place that appeared to guarantee full civil rights to African Americans. However, in the absence of federal enforcement of those rights, African Americans living in the South were denied them. As a result of the Brown v. Board *decisions and the Civil Rights laws of the 1960s, the federal government made the critical choice to end racial discrimination in public accomodations, voting, and public education, and to make some strides in improving access to housing and employment.*

In order to do so, the Justice Department and the federal courts acquired vast new powers to alter state and local policies and practices. For example, federal judges went beyond rejecting local plans to actually devise plans on their own and impose them on the localities. As a result of these laws and subsequent intepretations of them by the Justice Department, federal courts removed some prison systems from state control and put them in the hands of a federally appointed receiver. Later on, many local police departments, in the North as well as the South, *were required by federal courts to negotiate consent decrees with the Justice Department. Those decrees specified in great detail what changes the police had to make to prevent punitive action by the federal government. As of 2017, fourteen police departments were operating under a consent decree. Thus the cause of Civil Rights has radically transformed the federal–state–local relationship.*

The Complexities and Contradictions of Modern Federalism

Tightening the Federal Screw: Process Federalism and Mandates

In the late 1960s and early 1970s, the rights revolution spread beyond issues of voting to include an entire host of policy issues such as the environment, job safety, mental health, education, and the rights of people who are disabled. Although this rights revolution was inspired by the Civil Rights crusade, the national government's response to it was critically different. No federal marshals showed up to enforce national environmental or occupational safety and health laws. No dramatic confrontations occurred between state governors and national authorities. Instead, the national government relied, for the most part, on the states to implement the new array of federally imposed mandates. Although the states rarely disagreed with the broad purpose of the federal mandates, they often adamantly opposed the specific regulations that dictated the pace at which the mandates would be implemented. No longer did Washington simply point the states in a particular policy direction; it now provided detailed timetables for meeting specific objectives and penalties for failing to attain them in the time allotted.

To press states to comply with federal objectives, Washington also devised a new form of string to attach to its grants to the states. It now threatened to take money away from one grant category if the states failed to comply with a totally different one. For example, the Clean Air Act of 1970 requires states to bring noncompliant metropolitian areas into compliance. Failure to do so makes the states liable to lose federal highway subsidies even though there is no direct connection between the program they are required to comply with, the Clean Air Act administered by the EPA, and the subsidy they are threatened with losing, which comes from a totally different program administered by a different federal agency, the Department of Transportation (DOT).

In addition to threatening to withhold funds, Congress has sometimes chosen to simply mandate the states to accomplish congressionally determined objectives without providing any funds to the states and localities to implement those goals. This approach is particularly appealing to Congress because it enables the central government to gain the credit for accomplishing popular policy goals without having to pay the large costs that such policies incur. Federal statutes established the goals to be accomplished and then required others to pay the cost of meeting them. For example, local school systems have to pay for the installation of federally mandated elevators that improved accessibility for disabled students. Municipalities have to install expensive new equipment at their own expense to meet more stringent federally mandated drinking water standards. In the mid 1990s, the city of Columbus, Ohio, conducted a study demonstrating that federal mandates were costing the city hundreds of millions of dollars a year.

Process Federalism

The Supreme Court provided a strong judicial underpinning to this increased exercise of national power. In *Garcia v. San Antonio Metropolitan Transit Authority* (1985), it appeared to give a blanket endorsement to virtually any form of national government intrusion into the domain of the states and localities. It offered a new theory of federal–state relations known as process federalism. This new doctrine argued that the meaningful constitutional protections for the states are not provided either by the Tenth Amendment or by the principle of enumerated powers, but by the structure of the national government itself. The most important of these structural protections is the US Senate, whose members are chosen by the states. This opinion implied that the Court would not object to any imposition by the national government on the states as long as the Senate approves it.

The Supreme Court Pushes Back

Although, on the whole, the federal government has become ever more intrusive and dominant in state matters, recent decades have also witnessed important countervailing trends. The Supreme Court has made some decisions that push back the boundaries of federal authority. In important instances, the federal government has been induced to give states a great deal more leeway in meeting federal guidelines. And in at least one area where gridlock prevails at the federal level, a group of states have banded together to act on its own.

In the *Lopez* decision, with which this chapter began, the Court retreated from the process federalism principle of *Garcia*. The majority argued that the very principle of enumerated powers underlying the Constitution meant that the commerce clause was intended to exclude *something*. If interstate commerce could be used to justify all manner of congressional intrusion regardless of how tenuous the connection between the problem at hand and the flow of interstate commerce, then the commerce clause was meaningless.

In 1996 and 1997, the court issued a series of decisions that reinforced the defense of states' rights begun by *Lopez*. The Eleventh Amendment to the Constitution forbids the federal judiciary from entertaining any suit against a state by a citizen of another state. In *Seminole Tribe v. Florida* (1996), the court interpreted the Eleventh Amendment to mean that states enjoy *sovereign immunity*, meaning that states cannot be sued by any private party. The court did not declare this immunity to be absolute; it is limited by the due process and equal protection guarantees of the Fourteenth Amendment. But if those civil rights protections are not at stake, a state is immune from suit.

In *Printz v. United States* (1997), the Supreme Court invalidated a section of the Handgun Violence Protection Act, popularly known as the Brady Bill, which required local law enforcement officials to conduct background checks on people seeking to buy guns. The Court interpreted the Tenth Amendment to mean that local and state officials cannot be compelled to do the national government's business.

In 2012, the Supreme Court overturned the Medicaid provision of President Obama's healthcare reform (Patient Protection and Affordable Care Act). It declared that threatening to take funds away from one state subsidy program if a state failed to comply with a totally different one was an unconstitutional form of coercion of the states by the federal government. If the Court remains firm in sticking to this precedent, then the federal government will no longer be able to employ this powerful weapon for coercing state compliance with federal dictates.

Negotiated Federalism

While the strings attached to federal aid have mostly grown tighter and more numerous, there are important examples of states negotiating with the federal government to loosen strings. Such negotiated federalism has taken two forms. One form involves waivers. In some instances, states have convinced their federal overseers that they can accomplish the goals that tight strings are intended to make them attain while avoiding much of the red tape and wasteful effort that so many specific and detailed requirements requirements inevitably produce (see Chapter 10 for an explanation of "red tape"). In those cases, states produce a comprehensive plan for accomplishing what federal law demands and the federal government gives the state a waiver from the specific guidelines it has written to accomplish those aims. These negotiations do no signal a return to a purely cooperative relationship. The federal government remains the senior partner dictating what must be accomplished. But such negotiations promise to give the states a great deal more leeway in how best to attain the goals the federal gobvernment establishes.

One of the first and still perhaps the most significant example of a waiver regards federal welfare policy. In 1994, Wisconsin obtained the first of a series of waivers from the Department of Health and Human Services that allowed it to establish an innovative statewide program called W-2. Instead of using strict income criteria to determine who was eligible for welfare payments as federal policy required, Wisconsin was allowed to adopt a job-readiness standard. Regardless of how little income a person had, if a person was deemed to be job ready, they were required to find work rather than be given welfare. To help in that process, the state greatly expanded its capacity to help job-ready people find work. Those low-income people who were not considered job ready were required not simply to train for jobs, as HHS demanded, but to actually perform community services jobs. Nor did W-2 adjust the level of assistance it offered to take account of family size. Thus, eligible mothers did not receive extra payments for having more children. W-2 proved so successful both in slashing welfare rolls and in assisting previously eligible persons to find jobs that it served as the model for the federal law, the Personal Responsibility and Work Opportunity Reconciliation Act of 1996, popularly known as Welfare Reform.

A waiver from ordinary federal requirements was likewise essential to the most ambitious state effort at healthcare reform, embarked upon by Massachusetts in 2006. The goal of the reform was to provide universal healthcare coverage by mandating that every resident have health insurance. Prior to the reform, Massachusetts received federal funds to reimburse hospitals and doctors for providing care to the poor. In order to find a way to enable poor people to obtain insurance, it convinced the Department of Health and Human Services to use much of that money to subsidize the purchase of health insurance by the poor. Because nearly everyone would then have insurance, hospitals and doctors would no longer have to treat patients for nothing and therefore they would no longer need to be compensated by the government for so doing. As a result of the waiver, Massachusetts was able to devise a plan that provides health coverage to 93 percent of its residents, by far the highest coverage percentage of any state.

Another form of negotiated federalism occurs when states, with the support of powerful lobbying groups, convince Congress that an existing law places an excessive burden upon them. A critical example of this form of negotiated federalism regards the reauthorization of the Elementary and Secondary Education Act (ESEA). This Act is the most important source of federal funding for public schools. When it was revised in 2001, it placed a great many demands on states. It required them to devise statewide standards in reading and mathematics,

Table 5.8. Forms of federalism.

Dual federalism	• Introduced with election of Jefferson in 1800, endured until New Deal of 1930s • Emphasized decentralization and separate roles for federal and state government
Cooperative federalism	• Became more dominant in the midst of the federal government's refusal to enforce the protections of Reconstruction • The federal government subsidizes state projects
Strings attached federalism	• Made possible by administrative state born out of the New Deal • States must abide by federal requirements in order to receive certain funds • Expanded during rights revolution
Contemporary/ negotiated federalism	• Includes features of all forms of federalism • Waivers loosen strings attached

to test all students annually in grades 3 through 8, and to meet annual statewide progress objectives ensuring that all groups of students reach proficiency within twelve years. States that failed to abide by those guidelines were subject to loss of federal aid. Many school districts, state education agencies, mayors, and governors found these requirements to be excessively burdensome, and they were supported in their criticism by important teacher and parent organizations. In 2015, this coalition was successful in convincing Congress to greatly reduce those federal impositions. The new version of ESEA, called the Every Child Succeeds Act, still requires that states test all students in math, reading, and science. But, it gives states great leeway in deciding how those scores are to be used to measure school district success and how best to hold districts and teachers accountable. Most importantly, it removes the threat of depriving districts of federal aid if they fail to comply.

State Initiative

States have taken the lead in developing policy initiatives in areas where they consider federal policy to be inadequate. This new path has some precedent in the innovative policy initiatives that some states took during the Progressive Era. Both Wisconsin and New York developed old-age pension schemes before the federal government did. Louis Brandeis was so impressed by these efforts to test out policies that could later be adopted by the federal government that he referred to the states as "Laboratories of Democracy." Wisconsin and Massachusetts' creative use of federal waivers to forge innovative welfare and healthcare policies fit this mold.

What distinguishes the most ambitious of the current state efforts, lowering CO_2 emissions in an effort to reduce climate change, is that it is a coordinated effort among many states. Twelve states took the US Environmental Protection Agency to court to force the federal government to regulate climate change more aggressively. The attorneys general of those states did not argue that EPA's failure affected their states in particular; rather, they claimed that their role as legal guardians of their states required them to take action when the national government failed to protect the nation as a whole, of which their states are obviously a part. In April 2007, the Supreme Court ruled five to four that the Environmental Protection Agency violated the Clean Air Act by improperly declining to regulate new-vehicle emissions standards to control the pollutants that contribute to global warming and required the agency to develop policies to reduce CO_2 emissions.

To reduce CO_2 emissions from generators of electricity, ten New England and mid-Atlantic states have banded together to establish the the Regional Greenhouse Gas Initiative (RGGI). This project is innovative both in its involvement of many states and also in the manner in which it seeks to achieve reductions. To do so in the most efficient manner possible RGGI employs a market-based "cap-and-trade" approach. It puts a "cap" on allowable CO_2 emissions. Initially each electric power generator is given an allowance equal to 90 percent of their current emissions. To reach the goal of that 10 percent reduction they either reduce on their own or buy excess allowances from other generators who have reduced by more than 10 percent and therefore have extra allowances to sell. This system encourages efficiency because it gives an incentive to those generators that can achieve their reductions most cheaply to keep doing so beyond the 10 percent requirement because they can sell those reductions at a profit to those who cannot reduce as cheaply. So far, Congress has not chosen to alter federal policy in response to this laboratory experiment by the Northeastern states.

Not everyone views the adoption by the federal government of ambitious state policies in a positive light. Critics claim that some such efforts are really examples of some states exploiting the federal government to impose their policy preferences on others. George Mason Law School professor Michael Greve calls such efforts "cartel federalism". He borrows the term "cartel" from economics, where it refers to a group of firms that seek to keep prices high by limiting competition. The difficulty cartels face regards enforcing such limits. Those not included in the cartel can gain business by offering lower prices, and even cartel members are tempted to cheat by lowering their prices for the same reason. Therefore, a successful cartel usually requires government to enforce its anti-competitive practice. For example, city governments protect the taxicab cartel by restricting the number of taxis that are allowed to operate and setting the prices taxis can charge. Greve argues that those states that want to impose expensive regulations on private industry also try to form cartels. They seek to avoid having businesses migrate to states with less expensive regulations by having the federal government impose their version on all states. For example, states with severe air pollution problems such as California require automobile manufacturers to put very costly antipollution devices in their cars. States that do not have such serious air problems are capable of meeting federal air quality standards without requiring such expensive equipment. Therefore, drivers in those states could buy cheaper cars without deteriorating the air to unacceptable levels. Nonetheless, the federal law requires that all cars sold in the United States adopt expensive pollution devices regardless of the state in which they are licensed.

Looking Forward

The "empire of liberty" that Jefferson envisaged has not disappeared. An American traveling abroad is struck by how much more intrusive and pervasive government is elsewhere. In many other democratic countries, citizens must carry identity cards. If they move, they must inform the government. Government permission may be required for activities, like laying off a worker, that Americans consider to be matters of strictly private concern. Texans have a legal right to carry concealed handguns and, as we learned in *Lopez*, the federal government has no right to keep those handguns away from schools. Other countries have national police forces whose jurisdiction extends as far as the nation's borders. In this country, ordinary police work is done by local police forces whose powers cease at the city and county limits. We have all seen movies in which the police have to give up chasing the crook because he gets across the county line. The willingness to put up with this ridiculous outcome is eloquent testimony to how deeply Americans cherish the idea of local government. As Chapter 11 shows, polls continue to demonstrate strong public support for local government even as support for the federal government has declined.

Nonetheless, the federal government will, in all likelihood, remain the senior partner in the state–federal relationship. The states cannot match the federal government's revenue-raising capabilities and therefore the states will continue to accept stringent federal strings attached to the aid they receive. Healthcare already exemplifies this trend. It is not only the largest item in state budgets, but is also the item that receives the greatest amount of federal subsidy. And, even in those policy realms where states and localities enjoy the greatest autonomy there are strong forces pushing for greater national involvement and national uniformity. Education is a prime example. Schools are increasingly looked upon as the most important means for creating a national workforce capable of ensuring American economic competitiveness. The greater the emphasis on this goal, the less patience there will be to put up with local school systems that are not effectively contributing to this vital national effort, and the more pressure there will be for stricter national intervention and oversight.

CHAPTER SUMMARY

Contemporary portrait:

* In order to obtain consent for the establishment of a strong national government, its supporters made concessions to those who feared a strong national government. They agreed to limit its powers to those that were expressly delegated to it, reserving all other powers to the states. They also agreed to give the states a direct role in national governance via the Senate and the Electoral College.
* Path dependency and critical choice are critical concepts for understanding the political development of American federalism. Contemporary federalism bears the marks of all the different pathways previously established.
* States and the national government have formed a partnership. Partners recognize that they need one another and that they must cooperate. But this does not stop them from quarreling, from exerting their individuality and from trying to dominate one another. Over the course of American political development, the federal government has emerged as the senior partner.
* The fifty states form fifty very distinct political worlds. They differ in the degree to which they capture the loyalty and attention of their citizens and in the structure and content of their constitutions.

Critical choice: imposing dual federalism:

* Dual federalism was imposed by the Jefferson administration, reinforced by the Jackson administration, and remained the dominant federalism pathway until the Civil War. The essence of dual federalism was the strict separation of powers and duties between the national government and state government and the curtailment of national government power.

Critical choice: national supremacy, within limits:

* In a series of unanimous decisions over a period of almost thirty-five years, the Supreme Court under the leadership of Chief Justice John Marshall established the principle of the supremacy of the federal government over the states and limited the states' ability to interfere with economic competition, property rights, and the sanctity of contracts.
* Andrew Jackson's suppression of South Carolina's nullification effort was a critical precedent for Lincoln's effort to preserve the Union.
* Lincoln's decision to use military force to suppress the secession of Southern states from the Union was the critical choice that established the supremacy of the federal government over the states in practice as well as in principle.
* The failure of Reconstruction demonstrated the limits of national supremacy.

Aiding the states, empowering citizens:

* During the second half of the nineteenth century the national government became more willing to provide aid to the states. Cooperative federalism did not replace the predominant pattern of dual federalism, but in certain specific policy areas it made the stark division of responsibility characteristic of dual federalism less clear cut.
* Influenced by Progressivism, many states chose to incorporate forms of direct democracy into their constitutions.

Critical choice: the national government, federalism's senior partner:

* The New Deal of the 1930s altered cooperative federalism by "attaching strings" to federal grants, thus requiring the states to abide by federal dictates in order to receive the funds that the federal government made available.
* During the New Deal the Supreme Court abandoned what had previously served as the most important brake on federal government intervention in the affairs of the states, the commerce clause of the Constitution.

Critical choice: reasserting national supremacy: civil rights for African Americans:

* In 1954, the Supreme Court's *Brown v. Board of Education* decision declared all state and local efforts to racially segregate schools to be unconstitutional.
* The 1964 Civil Rights Act outlawed racial discrimination in public accommodations, housing and employment. The 1965 Voting Rights Act overturned state laws that prevented African Americans from voting and empowered the Justice Department to intervene to enable African Americans to freely exercise their voting rights.
* The critical choice to end Jim Crow was the result of pressure from a grassroots movement, shifts in public opinion, and aggressive political leadership.

The complexities and contradictions of modern federalism:

* The imposition of detailed timetables and the threat to withhold funds from other grant categories placed greater pressure on the states to abide by federal guidelines.
* Congress has sometimes chosen to simply mandate the states to accomplish congressionally determined objectives without providing any funds to the states and localities to implement those goals.
* In *Garcia v. San Antonio Metropolitan Transit Authority* (1985) the Supreme Court invoked the doctrine of Process Federalism, which argued that the meaningful constitutional protections for the states are not provided either by the Tenth Amendment or by the principle of enumerated powers, but by the structure of the national government itself, especially by the existence of the Senate.

* In its *Lopez* decision the Supreme Court reasserted that the Commerce Clause does place real limits on the federal government's authority to intervene in state matters.
* The federal government has sometimes loosened the strings attached to the states by amending federal law or by granting them waivers that permit them greater flexibility in achieving federally defined goals.
* States have taken the lead in developing policy initiatives in areas where they consider federal policy to be inadequate, most notably with regard to climate change.
* The high tide of process federalism was reached in the 1980s.
* Beginning in the 1970s, the federal government imposed unfunded mandates on the states and localities as a means of accomplishing federal government goals with the costs borne by the states and localities.
* While the strings attached to federal aid have mostly grown tighter and more numerous, there are important examples of states negotiating with the federal government to loosen strings.
* States have taken the lead in developing policy initiatives in areas such as climate change, where they consider federal policy to be inadequate.

Looking forward:

* The national government's superior revenue-raising ability as well as strong forces pushing in the direction of national involvement and uniformity ensure that the federal government will remain the senior partner in the state–federal partnership.

SUGGESTED READINGS

Beer, Samuel. *To Make a Nation: The Rediscovery of American Federalism*, rev. edn. Cambridge, MA: Belknap Press, 1998.

Conlan, Timothy. *From New Federalism to Devolution: Twenty-Five Years of Intergovernmental Reform*. Washington, DC: Brookings Institution Press, 1998.

Derthick, Martha, ed. *Dilemmas of Scale in America's Federal Democracy*. New York: Cambridge University Press, 1999.

Keeping the Compound Republic: Essays on American Federalism. Washington, DC: Brookings Institution Press, 2001.

Diamond, Martin. *As Far as Republican Principles Will Admit: Essays by Martin Diamond*. Washington, DC: AEI Press, 1992.

Donahue, John D. *Disunited States*. New York: Basic Books, 1998.

Ehrenhalt, Alan. *Democracy in the Mirror: Politics, Reform, and Reality in Grassroots America*. Washington, DC: CQ Press, 1998.

Elazar, Daniel. *American Federalism: A View from the States*, 3rd edn. New York: Harper & Row, 1984.

Feeley, Malcolm, and Rubin Edward, *Federalism: Political Identity and Tragic Compromise*, Ann Arbor, MI: University of Michigan Press, 2008.

Greve, Michael. *The Upside-Down Constitution*, Cambridge, MA: Harvard University Press, 2012.

McDonald, Forrest. *States Rights and the Union: Imperium in Imperio, 1776–1876.* Lawrence: Kansas University Press, 2000.

Nugent, John. *Safeguarding Federalism: How States Protect their Interests in National Policymaking*, Norman: University of Oklahoma Press, 2009.

Peterson, Paul E. *The Price of Federalism.* Washington, DC: Brookings Institution Press, 1995.

Walker, David B. *The Rebirth of Federalism: Slouching Toward Washington.* New York: Chatham House, 2000.

6 Political Economy

CHAPTER OVERVIEW

This chapter focuses on:

- **A contemporary portrait of American political economy.**
- **The critical choice to set the liberal economic path.**
- **The great debates that have taken place concerning the role of government in the economy.**
- **The critical choice to create a regulatory state.**
- **The complex pattern of regulation, deregulation, and rights expansion that occurred after World War II.**

In February 2016, in the midst of the presidential campaign, the Carrier corporation, a maker of heating and cooling equipment, announced plans to close its Indianapolis, Indiana gas furnace plan and move gas furnace production to Mexico. All the plant's 1,400 workers would lose their jobs. Donald Trump opened his Indiana primary campaign with a blistering attack on Carrier's decision and a promise to keep the Indiana plant open. "You're going to bring it across the border, and we're going to charge you a 35 percent tax," he said. "Now within 24 hours they're going to call back. 'Mr. President, we've decided to stay. We're coming back to Indianapolis'" (www.indystar.com/story/news/politics/2016/04/20/trump-takes-aim-carrier-republican-nominating-process-and-media/83291370/).

Likewise, in September 2016, in the midst of the general election campaign, the Ford Motor Company announced that it would build a new plant in Mexico and move its small car production there from Michigan. Trump denounced this move. While campaigning in Flint, Michigan he declared, "We shouldn't allow it to happen. They'll make their cars, they'll employ thousands and thousands of people, not from this country . . . and we'll have nothing but more unemployment in Flint" (www.freep.com/story/news/politics/2016/09/14/donald-trump-flint-bethel-church/90354890). As he did with Carrier, Trump threatened to impose a 35 percent tax on Ford car imports from Mexico.

After winning the election, Trump reiterated his promise to convince Carrier to keep the Indianapolis plant open. In late November, the company issued the following statement:

> Carrier has had very productive conversations in recent days with President-elect Trump and Vice President-elect Pence. We have negotiated an agreement with the incoming administration that we believe benefits our workers, the state of Indiana and our company. We are announcing today that Carrier will continue to manufacture gas furnaces in Indianapolis, in addition to retaining engineering and headquarters staff, preserving more than 1,000 jobs. (www.carrier.com/carrier/en/us/news/news-article/carrier_statement_regarding_indianapolis_operations.aspx)

To persuade Carrier, Trump relied on a combination of threats and promises. Carrier's parent company, United Technologies, is a major defense contractor. Trump let it be known that he would make sure that it did not receive much federal government business in the future. At the same time, he supported the efforts of Mike Pence, soon to be Vice President but still governor of Indiana, to provide incentives to Carrier to stay. The final deal contained $7 million worth of such grants and tax credits from the state of Indiana to the company.

Weeks later, Ford announced that it was canceling its plans to build a new car plant in Mexico and would instead invest $700 million in expanding a plant in Flat Rock, Michigan that would add 700 new jobs. The head of Ford, Mark Fields, denied that he had made a deal with Trump. Rather, he said the decision was a "vote of confidence" in the pro-business environment Trump was establishing (http://money.cnn.com/2017/01/03/news/economy/ford-700-jobs-trump/).

Trump's demands that Carrier and Ford abandon their investment plans reveals that relations between business and government can display deep tensions between the different strands of American political culture described in Chapter 2. Carrier and Ford sought to open plants in Mexico to take advantage of the international labor market. An American autoworker earns between $20 and $30 an hour whereas a worker in Mexico makes less than $6. A car or a gas furnace is much cheaper to build in Mexico, and therefore Ford and Carrier can sell them at a lower price, benefitting consumers. The Classic Liberal defense of free markets cherishes such labor market competition. Trump's effort to block it appeals to communitarian values since losing those plants threatens to impoverish the communities in which the displaced workers live. Indeed, Trump owed his election to the votes he received in the declining industrial regions of Pennsylvania, Michigan, and Wisconsin.

Other contemporary economic policy debates also reveal deep political cultural tensions. Government efforts to regulate business are often justified on democratic egalitarian grounds, protecting ordinary people from the greedy and corrupt practices of giant banks, investment houses, and industrial corporations. Opponents of those regulations claim that such government interference undermines free market principles and destroys competition. Imposing higher taxes on the rich is rationalized as a democratic–egalitarian initiative, redistributing income from an economic elite to the rest of us. Those who oppose such taxes offer the Classic Liberal defense that economic growth depends upon a ready supply of capital, which only the rich can supply. Raising the minimum wage is justified as a necessary means for preventing the exploitation of low-income workers. Opponents argue that forcing firms to pay higher wages causes them to hire fewer workers thereby reducing employment opportunities for the very people the minimum wage is aimed at helping. This chapter explores how these political cultural tensions involving economic policy have played out over time; the critical choices that have been made about American political economy, and why those tensions and those choices provide necessary context for understanding contemporary political economy and debates about it. But first we provide a contemporary portrait of the relationship between government and the economy.

A Contemporary Portrait of American Political Economy

Risk Protection

The government is deeply involved in the world of industry, commerce, and finance. It insures against risk, subsidizes favored economic activities, and punishes misbehavior. Its insurance efforts are geared to fight fear. One of the greatest enemies of economic prosperity is fear. People fear to put money in banks if they are concerned that the banks might not give them back their money when they ask for it. At the more than 8,000 banks that pay premiums to it, the *Federal Deposit Insurance Corporation* insures deposits of up to $250,000 per depositor. Therefore depositors can feel good about leaving their money in the bank. Banks need not worry that too many depositors will withdraw their money at one time and therefore they can be more aggressive in lending money.

The federal government also provides insurance to workers who lose their jobs. Currently, workers who are laid off or fired from their jobs receive a stipend from the government. The program is administered by the states and therefore benefits differ somewhat state by state. Typically, unemployed workers will receive half their normal weekly paycheck tax free. The length of the payment period varies according to state law, but depending on overall economic conditions might extend to six months, a year, or even longer. The effect of this insurance is to lessen the fears that inevitably strike when one loses one's job: How will I pay the mortgage? How will I buy groceries? In addition to the psychological damage instilled by such fears, they also have a negative economic impact. They impel unemployed workers to take the first available job, even if that job is a poor match for their skills and ambitions. Unemployment insurance allows them to take the chance to hunt for jobs that are more challenging and make fuller use of their talents. As a result, the economy enjoys a more talented and motivated workforce.

The large federal government insurance programs are known as entitlements. The two largest are aimed at the elderly. Social Security old-age pensions provide income to older Americans who have worked for a specified number of years in the course of their lives. Social Security is the single largest federal government outlay. As of 2016, it accounted for 24 percent of all federal spending. Medicare provides health insurance for older Americans. In 2016, it accounted for 16 percent, roughly the same as what the government spent on Defense. Social Security and Medicare are available to virtually all older Americans. Other entitlement programs are means tested and are only available to low-income Americans. They include: health insurance (Medicaid), subsidized food purchases (the Supplemental Nutritional Assistance Program), and payments to the disabled (Supplemental Security Income). The federal government also provides assistance to low-income single parents (TANF), but those payments are not full entitlements because one can only receive them for a maximum of five years. TANF is the only major means-tested program whose outlays have been significantly curtailed in recent decades; all the others have been greatly expanded. The average American pays more than $8,000 a year to fund entitlement programs. One hundred and fifty thousand Americans, more than 49 percent of the population, receive at least one form of entitlement benefit (www.aei.org/wp-content/uploads/2016/07/Prepared-Statement-Eberstadt-July-6-2016-final.pdf). Figure 6.1 shows how the federal government spends taxpayers' money.

Subsidies

The federal government provides huge subsidies to encourage economic behavior that it deems to be in the public interest. These subsidies are either paid directly to the recipient or are provided indirectly in the form of lower tax payments. The largest direct subsidy the government provides is to the farmers of certain specified crops. The governments spends more than $20 billion a year on farm subsidies, most of which goes to corn, wheat, rice, and cotton farmers (www.economist.com/news/united-states/21643191-crop-prices-fall-farmers-grow-subsidies-instead-milking-taxpayers). They receive a specified amount per bushel and an additional subsidy based on a price level that the government guarantees them. Thus, if the government guarantees a price of $2 a bushel for corn but the price falls to $1 90¢, the corn farmer receives and extra 10¢ per bushel. If the price remains above $2, no

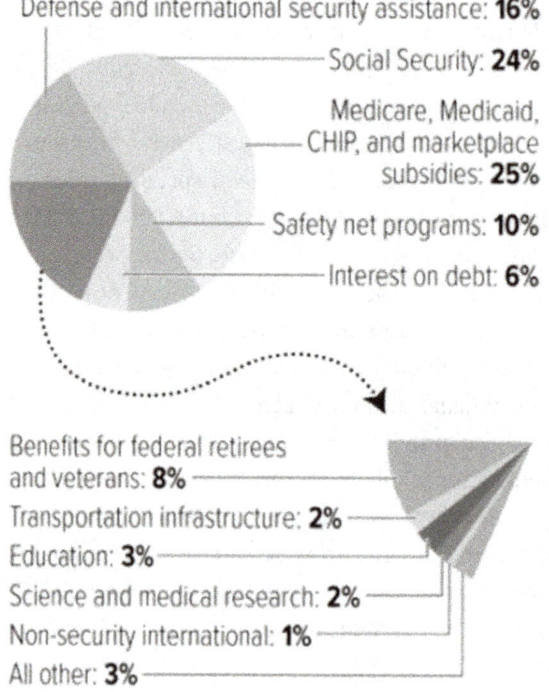

Figure 6.1. How taxpayers' money is spent: 2015 figures from the Office of Management and Budget, FY 2017 Historical Tables.
Source: US Federal Spending – CBO.

extra subsidy is paid. These subsidies keep food prices low because they encourage farmers to grow more crops than they would if they were just paying attention to the market price. It also helps farmers to survive market downturns.

The largest indirect subsidies dwarf the direct ones. They are provided via the tax code and are therefore known as tax expenditures. In 2015, tax expenditures reduced federal income tax revenue by more than a trillion dollars and were therefore more expensive than either Social Security, Medicare, or Defense (www.cbpp.org/research/federal-tax/policy-basics-federal-tax-expenditures). The largest tax expenditures are for employee health benefits, home ownership, and retirement savings. Homeowners may deduct the interest they pay on their mortgages from their taxable income. If one makes $50,000 a year and pays $4,000 a year in mortgage interest, one will be taxed as if one only made $46,000 a year. If one is in the 25 percent tax bracket, meaning one pays a quarter of one's taxable income in tax, one saves $1,000. In 2015, this subsidy cost the federal government more than $100 billion a year in tax revenue sacrificed.

Workers do not pay tax on the money they and their employers place in retirement plans or health insurance plans. Indeed, tax expenditures for employee health benefits constitute the single greatest source of tax expenditure: in 2015 it amounted to $210 billion (www.fas.org/sgp/crs/misc/R44333.pdf). Tax expenditures for retirement plans total $159 billion. Retirement plans are not only important because of the income security they provide. They also constitute the chief source of investment capital for the US economy. These plans use the contributions that workers and employers make to invest in stocks, bonds, and real estate. The profits these investments earn enable the plans to accumulate wealth that greatly exceeds the value of the contributions made by those workers and their employers (www.taxpolicycenter.org/briefing-book/how-large-are-tax-expenditures-retirement-saving).

Taxpayers may also deduct the contributions they make to private charities. These donations fund hospitals, churches, private education, the arts, and many social services. When the tax expenditures for charity, health insurance, and retirement plans are added to publicly provided Social Security, healthcare, veterans benefit, and welfare, it turns out that the United States spends roughly the same amount on social programs as a percentage of Gross Domestic Product (GDP) that Europeans spend. The difference is that in Europe the vast majority of social program expenditures are made directly by government whereas in the United States they represent a combination of budgetary items and tax expenditures.

The tax code provides thousands of other specific subsidies for various forms of business investment. For example, producers of wind energy receive a corporate income tax credit of .019 cents for every kilowatt hour of energy they produce during the first ten years that a particular wind energy facility is in production. A credit is more valuable than a deduction because it is subtracted not from taxable income but rather from the actual tax one would otherwise pay. If the facility produces a million kilowatt hours a year, it would save $19,000 in taxes.

Regulation

The federal government polices many aspects of the behavior of industry, transport, communications, advertising, banking, and securities. This function of government is called *regulation*. Most of this policing is done through regulatory agencies. These regulators are either lodged in federal departments, including Labor, Justice, and Transportation, or in independent agencies such as the Environmental Protection Agency (EPA), the Consumer Product Safety Commission (CPSC), the Federal Trade Commission (FTC), and the Securities and Exchange Commission (SEC). The aim of such regulation is to improve market performance by insuring the provision of adequate information, forcing producers to bear the full social cost of production, punishing efforts to restrict competition and protecting civil rights. For example, the SEC requires the issuers of stocks and bonds to provide a full and accurate statement of what their companies are worth so that prospective buyers have sufficient information to make an informed decision about whether or not to purchase securities in that company. The Food and Drug Administration (FDA) requires food manufacturers to list the ingredients in their produce so consumers know what they are getting. Pharmaceutical manufacturers must list the most frequent side effects of the medications they sell so that doctors and patients can have a fuller picture of the risks specific drugs pose.

Environmental regulation is largely devoted to forcing producers to bear the full costs of production. Producers choose to pollute because it is cheaper for them to do so than to employ cleaner techniques. But pollution is not really cheap, its actual costs are paid by others – those who breathe the dirty air or drink the poisoned water the polluters have emitted. By requiring producers to employ cleaner production methods, environmental regulators diminish the gap between the costs polluters pay for and the full social costs imposed by their production practices.

The Federal Trade Commission and the Department of Justice work to protect free and fair market competition by punishing those who try to use unfair practices to eliminate competition or who try to monopolize a market. The Equal Employment Opportunity Commission protects civil rights by suing employers who engage in discriminatory hiring or firing on the basis of race, color, religion, sex, national origin, age, disability, or genetic information. The Fish and Wildlife Service protects the rights of endangered species to survive by preventing land development that threatens the habitats of those species.

Macroeconomic Policy

These regulatory efforts are aimed at the micro level, the functioning of specific markets and the behavior of firms engaged in those markets, and are referred to as *microeconomic* policy. Through its powers to tax, spend, and manage the currency, the federal government also intervenes at the *macroeconomic* level, the economy as a whole, in order to encourage price stability, full employment prosperity, and growth. Such efforts are referred to as macroeconomic policy. The Federal Reserve, whose members are appointed by the president, is in charge of monetary policy. It tries to manage the money supply primarily through selling government securities to banks and buying them from banks. When it sells, it reduces the amount of money the banks have. Since banks are required by law to keep a certain portion of their money in reserve, the Fed has lessened the amount of money they have available to lend. Because they have less money to lend, they will charge more by raising the interest rate on their loans. When the Fed buys securities, it pours more money into the banking system and therefore increases the amount banks can lend, thereby lowering the interest rate.

The government can also try to control overall economic activity by means of its taxing and spending policies. This is called fiscal policy. If it spends more than it takes in through taxes it runs a deficit. Advocates of deficit spending believe that its spurs economic activity because it raises aggregate demand, meaning the total demand for goods and services of the economy as a whole. Government demand stays high because the tax cuts do not produce commensurate cuts in government spending. Private demand rises because tax cuts raise taxpayers' incomes, which encourages them to consume more. If government chooses to run a surplus by taxing more than it spends, the opposite result is supposed to come about. Government buys less than it takes in and consumers spend less because their incomes have declined. Fiscal policy is controversial. Some economists doubt whether it works. And, it is rarely used as a vehicle for reigning in demand. Politicians find it too politically risky to raise taxes or cut spending for any reason, let alone as a speculative attempt to cool down the economy.

CRITICAL CHOICE: SETTING THE LIBERAL ECONOMIC PATH

The adoption of the Constitution, including the Bill of Rights, was the critical choice that set the US firmly on the path of economic liberalism. It commits the US government to sustaining the essentials of a liberal economy. Most important of all is the limitation placed on the scope of government by restricting it to the enumerated powers "herein granted" in Article I and the forbidding of government from impinging on the rights established in the Bill of Rights. A government thus limited has no authority to intrude itself into the private economy by any means that the Constitution does not explicitly grant it.

Economic Liberalism

Acknowledging the many ways that government intervenes in the economy should not obscure the fact that the central path followed by American political economy has been one of private property and free markets as set out by the Classic Liberal philosophers discussed in Chapter 2. When Thomas Jefferson drafted the Declaration of Independence, he borrowed from John Locke's *Second Treatise*, which argued that government could only be legitimate if it rested on the consent of the governed and protected the "natural rights" of "life, liberty, and estate." But Jefferson changed "estate," by which Locke meant "property," into "the pursuit of happiness." This wonderfully enigmatic phrase captures the essence of the liberal political economic system the Founders envisioned. The phrase is based on rights, not results. It does not promise happiness but, rather, a fair chance to pursue that dream, equal opportunity rather than equal results. It hints at the complex amalgam of striving, optimism, and uncertainty that form the distinctively American economic quest.

The *liberal economy* that embodies this understanding of the pursuit of happiness has three essential aspects: private property, competition, and promise keeping. Jefferson did not want to list property among the three most essential inalienable rights, but he did not intend to deny its importance. The right to property enables persons to keep what possessions they have and to know that if they make investments or do work, they can keep the fruits of those risks and labors. The right to property also means that government is obliged to protect people's property against theft and that government itself cannot rob people of their hard-won assets.

The liberal economy is inherently competitive; it depends on producers vying with one another for the patronage of consumers by offering better goods and cheaper prices. The liberal economy is like a track meet in which everyone is given an opportunity to run the race. The competition is not entirely fair, because some runners are better trained, coached, and equipped. But once at the starting line, everyone must obey the same rules or face disqualification. In the economic version of the race, contracts are kept, debts are paid, thieves and counterfeiters are caught and punished, and the list of ingredients printed on the package is accurate. Government officiates; it writes the rules and enforces them.

A liberal economy requires people to keep their word as well as do their work. Such trust cannot develop in an atmosphere of deceit. I lend money to you only if I believe your pledge to repay it. If we sign a contract together, it is because we trust each other to live up to the bargain.

Constitutional Safeguards

In addition to the protections offered by the principle of enumerated powers and the Bill of Rights, the Constitution contains specific clauses that safeguard the key components of economic liberalism: private property, the sanctity of contract, and economic competitiveness. Article I forbids states from impairing the obligation of contracts. It protects inventors and authors by allowing them to patent their works to prevent others from copying those works for specified length of time. The Fifth Amendment forbids government from taking a person's property without due process of law and without just compensation. Other constitutional clauses enable the Congress to create the ground rules and enforcement powers on which a liberal economy depends: to coin money, punish counterfeiting, and establish uniform weights and measures.

Table 6.1. The Constitution and the economy: the key clauses.

Article I, Section 1

All legislative Powers *herein granted* shall be vested in a Congress of the United States . . .

Article I, Section 8

The Congress shall have Power To:

Regulate Commerce with foreign Nations, and among the several States, and with the Indian Tribes;

Establish uniform Laws on the subject of Bankruptcies throughout the United States;

Coin Money, regulate the Value thereof, and of foreign Coin, and fix the Standard of Weights and Measures;

Provide for the Punishment of counterfeiting the Securities and current Coin of the United States;

Promote the Progress of Science and useful Arts, by securing for limited Times to Authors and Inventors the exclusive Right to their respective Writings and Discoveries

Article I, Section 10

(No state shall pass any) law impairing the Obligation of Contracts

Fifth Amendment

(No person shall be) deprived of life, liberty, or property, without due process of law; nor shall private property be taken for public use, without just compensation.

The key to sustaining economic competitiveness is the grant of power to Congress in Article I to regulate interstate and foreign commerce. Indeed, in the minds of many Framers, federal oversight of interstate and foreign commerce was the most compelling reason for creating the Union in the first place. Lack of such authority under the Articles of Confederation raised such dangerous possibilities as coastal states blackmailing landlocked ones into paying for permission to ship products overseas, or downstream states imposing tariffs on goods shipped from states upstream. Only the federal government could prevent such anticompetitive behaviors from occurring. Table 6.1 lists those clauses in the Constitution that are most important for sustaining a liberal economy.

UPSHOT

As the contemporary portrait shows, US private enterprise does not enjoy free reign. However, the path of economic liberalism that the Constitution established is different from the one trod by other prosperous democratic nations. The US places far fewer restrictions on how business operates and how people dispose of their property. For example, in the US when a renter's lease expires, a landlord is generally free to rent to someone else. The lease is a contract and the sanctity of contract means that when its terms are fulfilled neither party is under any further obligation. In most other rich countries, the law goes to great lengths to protect renters and it is extremely difficult for landlords to evict them, lease or no lease.

Perhaps the greatest difference between the US and the rich countries of Europe and Asia relates to the degree of government intervention in the labor market. The US does intervene. In addition to enforcing fair employment practices, it regulates worker pension programs, limits child labor, protects worker safety and health, sets a minimum wage, and enables workers to join labor unions. Most rich countries do much more. In some, government involves itself directly in negotiations between unions and employers. In the US, government's role is limited to sometimes requiring "cooling off" periods before strikes are called. In general, private employers and unions negotiate on their own. Many European countries prescribe the number of vacation days workers are entitled to. More importantly, they make it extremely difficult to fire workers. Workers in other relatively rich countries enjoy much greater government-mandated job security than in the United States. This has the perverse effect of making firms in those countries more reluctant to hire new workers since once they hire them it is virtually impossible to lay them off. This effect is most severe on young workers, those who are just entering the world of work. As a result, the youth unemployment rate is much higher in most other advanced economies than it is in the United States.

Debating the Role of Government

The United States remained on the constitutionally prescribed path of economic liberalism but this did not prevent deep political divisions from emerging about the concrete meaning of "the pursuit of happiness" and how much leeway the government enjoys to intervene in that pursuit. In the early nineteenth century, the deepest differences emerged regarding the role of government. Those who favored active government intervention argued that it was necessary to maximize both economic progress and protect national security. Those who opposed such intrusions did so on Classic Liberal as well as communitarian and democratic grounds. As Classic Liberals they were convinced that such intervention would undermine limited government and thus lead to tyranny. As communitarians and democrats they believed that such intervention would privilege the rich and powerful at the expense of the common people and serve the interests of the great cities to the detriment of smaller localities.

In the late nineteenth century the issue of government intervention in the economy resumed center stage but the nature of the debate was transformed.

Now it was those who opposed greater government intervention who did so on Classic Liberal grounds. They argued that such intervention would undermine property rights and economic competition. Proponents of government intervention adhered to democratic and communitarian principles. They argued that in the face of the massive economic power concentrated in a few banks and corporations and in the nation's largest cities, government intervention was the necessary means to protect the common people and the communities in which they lived.

Hamilton versus Jefferson

During the early years of the life of the United States, the chief advocate of greater government involvement in the economy was Secretary of Treasury Alexander Hamilton. His interventionist strategy was composed of four essential elements, the first and second of which derived from the power granted to Congress to borrow money (Article I, Section 8). First he sought to have the new central government assume the debts incurred by the states during the Revolution. Even though the states had promised to repay bondholders, many had not done so. Hamilton argued that the US would be able to borrow in the future only if it maintained an unsullied record of paying off the debts it had already incurred. He also recognized that if the national government took over state debt it would cement itself as the dominant force in financial affairs and thereby increase its power and prestige.

Second, Hamilton proposed that the debts be repaid through the issuance of new federal government bonds. This approach is called *funding the debt.* In addition to simply providing a mechanism for paying off the state debts the federal government had assumed, it had a great political advantage. Rich Americans would buy bonds because they paid a decent interest and looked like a good investment opportunity. Therefore it was good for the nation to remain permanently indebted. Hamilton mistrusted the rich, fearing that they would always put their private interests above their patriotic obligations. Funding the debt was a means to bind their public and private interests together. For, if the nation floundered, the bonds held by the rich might not be redeemed. Figure 6.2 shows the evolution of the national debt from the 1790s to the present.

The third element of Hamilton's strategy was intimately connected to the first two. He argued that managing the debt, when added to the many other critical financial tasks to perform, required the government to create a national bank. He admitted that the Constitution did not provide for a national bank but it did grant Congress the power "To make all Laws which shall be necessary and proper for carrying into Execution the foregoing Powers, and all other Powers vested by the Constitution in the Government of the United States." Surely a bank was a necessary and proper means for carrying out such diverse financial

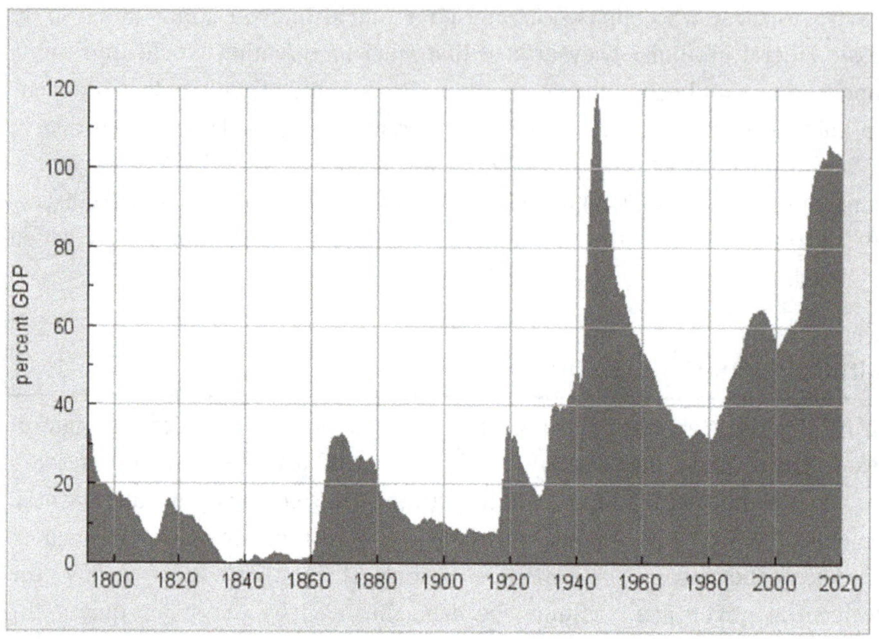

Figure 6.2. Accumulated gross federal debt, FY 1792–FY 2020.
Source: Christopher Chantrill, Usgovernmentspending.com

responsibilities as raising revenue, borrowing money and coining currency. Congress chartered the First National Bank of the United States in 1791.

The final element of Hamilton's plan was to use federal banking and tariff policy to promote US manufactures. A tariff is a tax placed on imported goods. Congress had asked Hamilton to investigate manufactures as a way "to render the United States independent of foreign nations for military and other essential supplies." Hamilton argued in his *Report on Manufactures* that even more than providing essential military supplies, manufactures would help forge the strong sense of national identity that makes a country feel secure. He encouraged trade between South and North as a way to develop closer ties between the two regions and to promote a common sense of nationality. But Southern states would sell their products in the North instead of Europe only if the North could replace Europe as the South's source of manufactured goods. Therefore, argued Hamilton, national security required federal support for manufactures. To promote manufacturing, Hamilton supported not only a national bank to supply capital to manufacturing enterprises, but also subsidies to manufacturers in the form of high tariffs on imported manufactures and a government commission to award bounties for the establishment of new industries and prizes for the encouragement of inventions, particularly of labor-saving machinery.

The leader of the opposition to Hamilton's scheme was Secretary of State Thomas Jefferson. He opposed federal assumption of state debt because he believed it rewarded greed. Many people who bought state bonds to finance the war had come to doubt that the bonds would ever be repaid, so they sold them at a loss to those who could afford to wait and see what the government would eventually do. Jefferson sympathized with the original bondholders who would now have lost money twice, first by selling the bonds at a loss and then by paying additional taxes in order to pay off the bonds in full.

Jefferson opposed the national bank on constitutional grounds. He interpreted the term "necessary" in the "necessary and proper clause" to mean "essential," not merely "helpful." A bank would indeed facilitate the implementation of financial policies but it was not essential for so doing and therefore it was unconstitutional. Jefferson was also convinced that the bank would increase the power of the central government, which was inherently less democratic and more despotic than the state and local governments, and it would discriminate against the credit needs of ordinary people in favor of making loans on favorable terms to Hamilton and his rich and powerful friends.

Jefferson did not agree that the nation would benefit by promoting manufactures. He believed that a free republic needed to be based on farming. Farmers owned their own property. Unlike manufacturing laborers, they did not develop the servile and resentful attitudes that come about when one has to work for a boss. Farmers also developed a wide range of skills and talents and learned to be stewards of the land. They cultivated the art of self-government and were therefore not only stewards of their property but of the localities in which they lived. Workers forced to live in crowded decadent cities enjoyed no such opportunities. Therefore, Jefferson bitterly opposed Hamilton's scheme for privileging manufactures over agriculture.

Hamilton's plans achieved mixed results. He succeeded in convincing Congress to assume state debts, to fund the debt, and to establish a nation bank. Jefferson dropped his opposition to debt assumption in exchange for obtaining Hamilton's support for Jefferson's plan to site the nation's capital on the Virginia–Maryland border rather than in either of the nation's two most populous and commercial cities – New York or Philadelphia. Congress failed to recharter the bank and it went out of business in 1811. Then, in 1816, in the aftermath of the War of 1812, it chartered the *Second Bank of the United States*. However, as the next section describes, the bank did not last. Congress failed to implement Hamilton's financial subsidy schemes for manufacture. However, it did agree to raise tariffs periodically during the following decades and such tariff rises did indeed favor certain manufacturing sectors.

Critical Question

Do you agree with Madison or Jefferson regarding the role that government should play in the economy? Specifically, should the government have assumed the debt? Should Hamilton's plan for promoting manufactures have been adopted? Was Jefferson right to claim that farmers had civic virtues that laborers lacked?

Destroying the "Monster"

In 1832, President Andrew Jackson declared war on the "monster" Second Bank of the United States. Like Jefferson, Jackson's bitter opposition was rooted in the liberal principle of equal opportunity and in resentment against speculators and influence peddlers. The small farmer and the Westerner did not enjoy access to the bank's loans, which went to those Hamilton had hoped they would go to, Eastern commercial and industrial bigwigs. Also, the bank threatened democracy by lavishing money on its political allies and by subverting democratic essentials – honest toil and social solidarity. Its credit manipulation created an artificial economy of phony paper assets and speculation that threatened the health of the real economy, the one based on hard work, honest exchange, and neighborliness.

Jackson vetoed the bank's recharter. By supporting his subsequent reelection, a majority of voters voiced their own qualms about economic privilege. Like Jackson, they preferred a tangible, manageable economy in which profit and competition blended with affection for customers, confidence in partners, respect for rivals, and trust in coworkers. Jackson called the people who live this kind of economic life – "the farmer, the mechanic, and the laborer" – the "bone and sinew of the country." This decisive tilt in the direction of unfettered competition did not come free of charge. Credit and currency controls remained very weak until after the turn of the twentieth century. The federal government lacked the tools to cope with rampant speculation and the periodic financial crises it sparked.

Free Labor

The Republican Party, founded in the mid 1850s, added a vital new element to the debate about political economy by introducing a democratic egalitarian modification to Classic Liberal doctrine. Its crucial slogan was "free labor." It justified its opposition to the spread of slavery to the territories on the grounds that slaves would provide unfair competition to non-slave workers. Although such a strong emphasis on getting ahead by working hard was perhaps implicit in Classic Liberal doctrine, it was the Republicans who placed it at the core of their political project and linked it to the wellbeing of the common people. As Chapter 11 shows, getting ahead through hard work is a principle deeply embedded in American public opinion.

The Impact of War

The Civil War tilted the debate about the proper role of government in an interventionist direction. It greatly accelerated demand for manufacturing production and labor. Armies need uniforms, weapons, ammunition, wagons, cooking utensils, and more. At the same time, taking so many young men away from their jobs drastically reduced the industrial labor supply. To produce more with less, industry invented new labor-saving techniques, including steam-powered equipment and other forms of mechanization.

To ensure the security of war supplies, Congress in 1861 enacted a very high tariff on imported goods. Southern states, fearing that European countries would revenge themselves by imposing similarly high tariffs on their cotton exports, had opposed the protective tariff. But during the war and its aftermath, the South was unable to influence Congress to protect its economic interest. Therefore, high tariffs survived long into the postwar period, increasing the profitability of American manufacturing and greatly accelerating its growth. National security likewise provided a strong rationale for the building of the transcontinental railway. Because it would take years for sufficient freight traffic to develop to make the railway profitable, Congress provided enormous subsidies in the form of land grants to the two railroads that were partners in the project.

CRITICAL CHOICE: CREATING THE REGULATORY STATE

In the late nineteenth century, the debate about the role of government in the economy was transformed. Those who had championed government intervention in the name of economic growth now came to favor unfettered economic competition. Those who sought a more democratic, egalitarian economy went from opposing greater government intervention in the economy to embracing it. The growing political and economic dominance of large corporations had, indeed, been fostered by government. They now determined that the only way to countervail such concentrated economic power was to bring the force of government to bear on the other side. The growing political power of the Progressive movement (see also Chapters 4 and 12), preceded by the Populists (see also Chapter 12), resulted in a critical choice in favor of granting the federal government broad regulatory power over various aspects of the economy.

Fostering Corporate Growth

By the 1880s, as Hamilton had hoped, the United States had become a major manufacturing power. But no longer was the economy characterized by small companies. Whole sectors of the economy – oil, steel, sugar refining, and others – came to be dominated by one or few huge corporations. To some extent the shrinking number of individual firms in a given industry was the result of the superior efficiency of the firms that came to dominate. But the creation of huge economic entities capable of controlling entire industries was also greatly facilitated by government. Perhaps the most important such action was the willingness of state legislatures to change their laws governing incorporation to adopt the principle of limited liability. Unlike an ordinary firm, the owners of a limited liability corporation, its shareholders, could not be held responsible for paying its debts. If the corporation failed, the liability of its shareholders was limited to the amount they had invested. Limited liability meant limited risk. Potential investors could calculate how much money they could afford to lose and limit their stock purchase to that amount.

Limited liability was defended on democratic grounds. The great Massachusetts senator Daniel Webster explained why limited liability served vital democratic purposes. Industrial expansion provided more jobs and cheaper products, but it was hindered by lack of investment funds. America lacked a large class of very wealthy people who could afford to take great investment risks. To encourage ordinary people to invest, the system needed to limit their risk by enabling them to calculate in advance how much they could possibly lose. Thereby, limited liability democratized the investment process.

But this vast expansion in the capacity to raise money also permitted corporations to grow to previously unimaginable sizes. And because their potential loss was limited, investors had less cause to pay attention to what corporate management was actually doing and therefore became more tolerant of the ruthless practices that were often required to dominate an industry. Not only were these corporations large and powerful, but, since their liability was limited, no actual person could be held accountable for the promises they made. At the stroke of a pen, a corporation could go out of business and leave suppliers, customers, and creditors with nobody to hold responsible for what was owed to them. The moral sensibility of ordinary people was violated in the name of economic growth.

The US Supreme Court likewise fostered the growth of corporate power and economic concentration. In *Wabash, St. Louis, and Pacific Railroad Company v. Illinois* (1886) it forbade states from regulating railroads. The Court decreed that corporations were legally "persons" entitled to the Fourteenth Amendment's guarantees of equal protection and due process of law, protections that would be violated if different states adopted different rules for governing railroad fares, taxes, and labor standards.

In 1890, Congress attempted to prevent monopolies from forming by passing the Sherman Antitrust Act, which made it a crime for companies to attempt to do so. The constitutional basis for this statute was the commerce clause of the Constitution granting Congress the right to regulate interstate and foreign commerce. But the Supreme Court interpreted the commerce clause so narrowly as to

Figure 6.3. Devouring the Railroads.
Source: Granger Collection, NYC –

render the law virtually impotent. In *United States v. E. C. Knight Co.* (1895), the Court said that the interstate commerce only referred to the buying and selling of products across state lines and did not include the manufacturing of products. E. C. Knight was a manufacturer, a sugar refiner, and therefore it was not covered by the Sherman Act.

The Populists

Railroads were the lightning rods for popular discontent with the new corporate order. They needed government help to acquire property along proposed routes and to subsidize construction costs. To obtain such assistance, they bribed state legislatures and other government officials. Railroads' tentacles crossed state lines, which thwarted a state's ability to discipline them. Thus, the states had proven unable to exercise meaningful discipline of the railroads even before the Supreme Court's *Wabash* decision deprived them of the legal right to do so. Railroads were able to exert monopoly power over the farmers who depended on the railroads to haul their crops. Farmers were lucky to have even one railroad nearby; therefore, they could not credibly threaten to ship their crops on a rival line. Thus the railroads could charge them exorbitant rates compared to those lucky enough to have access to alternative transportation options. Such *price discrimination* fed farmers' fear of being held hostage to the whim of the "monster." Ignoring the extent to which they relied on government, railroads tried to evade government regulation and control by arguing that such interference was a violation of their economic freedom.

In the late 1870s a grassroots effort arose among farmers in such Great Plains states as South Dakota, Kansas, and Iowa to demand that the federal government intervene to protect them from the railroads. This movement called itself the People's Party but it soon became known as the *Populists.* The Populists demanded that the federal government take over the railroads because of the monopoly power these leviathans were exercising, but generally speaking, they were not socialists. They did not challenge the essential principles of economic liberalism but rather sought to rid it of its antidemocratic and anti-Christian tendencies. In 1887, Populist agitation was an important source of the political pressure on Congress to create the first significant federal regulatory initiative, the Interstate Commerce Commission (ICC). The ICC was granted the power to prevent railroads from setting rates that discriminated against small farmers in favor of large shippers and to investigate charges of illegal railroad practices.

In 1896, the Populist leader William Jennings Bryan was nominated by the Democrats for president (see Chapter 11). At the nominating convention, Byran defended free enterprise, claiming that the measure of a businessman was not money or property but productiveness, like a farmer who "by the application of brain and muscle to the natural resources of the country creates wealth". He scolded adherents of laissez faire for undemocratically depriving most hard-working Americans of the status they had earned:

> We say to you that you have made the definition of a businessman too limited in its application. The man who is employed for wages is as much a businessman as his employer; the attorney in a country town is as much a businessman as the corporation counsel in a great metropolis; the merchant at the crossroads is as much a businessman as the merchant in New York. ... We come to speak for this broader class of businessmen.

Bryan recognized that "the broader class of businessmen" were mostly debtors. Therefore, in addition to calling for regulation of the railroads, he also sought to ease the plight of debtors by inflating the currency, taking the US off a currency standard that was strictly gold and onto a standard that would include silver as well. Since silver was more plentiful than gold, this change would increase the money supply, making money cheaper and debts easier to pay. Bryan transformed this seemingly technical question about currency into a titanic religious struggle by denouncing his opponents in starkly religious terms: "You shall not press down upon the brow of labor this crown of thorns, you shall not crucify mankind upon a cross of gold."

In defending the Gold Standard, Bryan's opponents made a similar argument to that made by Alexander Hamilton in favor of the federal government's assumption of the Revolutionary War debt. They invoked the principle of promise keeping. If borrowers cheapen the value of money when their debt comes due, Gold Democrats claimed, they are cheating on their promise to pay back their debt in full, an action that is both immoral and economically destructive. If creditors doubt that their loans will be fully repaid, they will be less likely to make loans and economic activity will decline. Bryan and the Silver Democrats did not dispute the importance of promise keeping. Rather, they stressed other virtues that the liberal emphasis on promise keeping ignored - justice, forgiveness, charity, the survival of country towns. They believed that the farmer who could not pay his loan because his crops failed was not a sinner, but that the banker who called in the loan was, because he ignored the Christian duty to be charitable and the democratic duty to help a neighbor.

Progressive Regulation

Bryan lost the 1896 election and the political strength of Populism waned. But its efforts to reign in big business were sustained by a more widespread and successful political movement, Progressivism (see Chapters 4, 5, and 12). Under the leadership of presidents Theodore Roosevelt and Woodrow Wilson, the federal government embarked upon extensive regulation of the economy. The Hepburn Act greatly increased the regulatory power of the Interstate Commerce Commission by allowing it to set ceilings on the freight rates that railroads could charge their customers. In 1906, Congress passed legislation establishing the Food and Drug Administration (FDA) to protect consumers from rotten food and impure pharmaceuticals. In 1914, it created the Federal Trade Commission (FTC) to provide more effective regulation of unfair business competition by supplementing judicial enforcement with the active intervention of an executive agency.

The shift in attitude toward government intervention extended to banking as well. In 1907, the third largest New York bank failed. In response to the ensuing panic, Republicans proposed a banking federation resembling a European central bank. The Democrats were opposed, but once they regained control of the House of Representatives, in 1910, they felt obliged to come up with an alternative. In 1913, Congress passed the Federal Reserve Act that created a decentralized federation of twelve regional reserve banks, each a private institution owned and operated by its members' banks. Each regional reserve bank acquired capital by requiring its members to spend 3 percent of their own capital to buy its stock.

Regional reserve banks had three tools with which to regulate the money supply. First, they could change the *discount rate*, the interest rate that member banks paid to borrow money from them. The higher the discount rate, the more expensive it was for members to borrow money and the higher the rate that

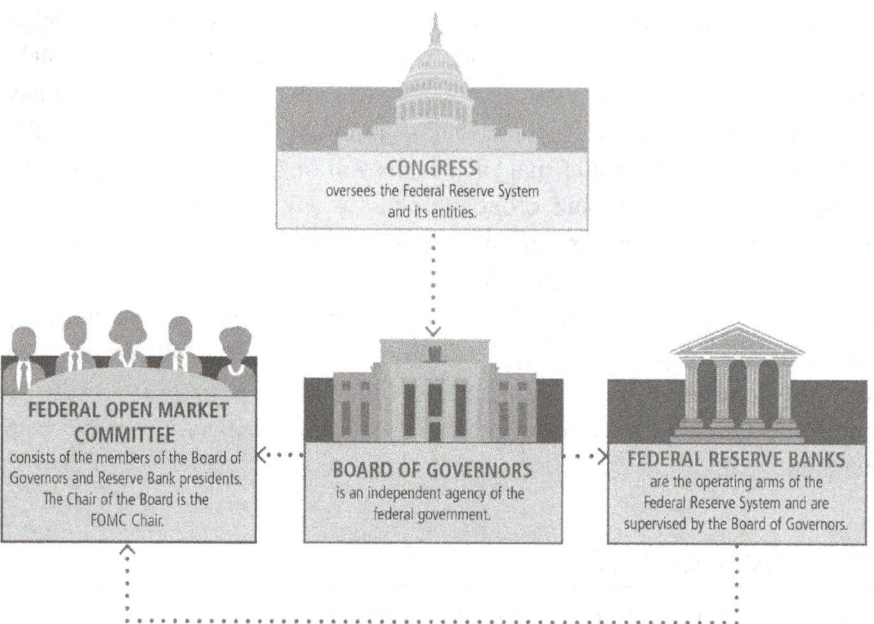

Figure 6.4. Federal Reserve system.

members would charge to lend money to customers. Raising the discount rate made money more expensive, thereby lowering demand for it. Second, regional reserve banks could change the reserve requirements imposed on members. If banks had to keep more assets in reserve, they could make fewer loans, thereby shrinking the amount of money in circulation. Third, reserve banks could engage in open market operations, buying and selling government bonds and notes. When the reserve banks sold notes and bonds, the money used to pay for them was taken out of circulation, thereby reducing the money supply. During a panic, a reserve bank might use all three tools – buying bonds and notes, lowering the discount rate, and reducing reserve requirements – to rapidly expand the money supply and make more funds available to threatened banks. The Federal Reserve was a distinctively American solution to the problems posed by an inflexible money supply. It created institutions for manipulating money and credit but did not cede control to either Washington or Wall Street. The twelve regional banks were responsive to their members and to the *Federal Reserve Board* (the Fed), whose members were appointed by the president but had staggered terms so that no single president could appoint a majority.

New Deal Regulation

FDR's New Deal was both an extension of Progressive regulatory principles to other branches of the economy – securities, radio, chain stores, trucking, airlines, and coal mining – and a critical choice in favor of a vastly more ambitious view of government economic involvement. As we discussed in Chapter 4, it also went far beyond Progressive principles by instilling a new concept of a right to economic security. The new programmatic rights aimed at protecting economic security were embodied in the Social Security Act and the National Labor Relations Act, both passed in 1935 and discussed in Chapter 4. In addition, the *Federal Deposit Insurance Corporation* (FDIC) provided a government guarantee that depositors could reclaim their bank deposits, up to a certain limit, if a bank failed. The FDIC encouraged them to leave their money in the bank, which bolstered the economy by increasing the amount of capital available for banks to lend. The New Deal also established an unemployment compensation program providing income for a period of time to those who lost their jobs. Because unemployed workers knew they had a cushion, they could spend more time finding the right job rather than taking the first one that came along. This government-supported flexibility improved labor market efficiency by emboldening workers to find the best outlet for their talents.

Taxation

To pay for this vastly more expansive notion of government the New Deal imposed far greater tax burdens on the wealthier segments of the populace than had previously been in place. The Constitution had imposed strict limits on federal taxing power. Those limits were not eased until 1913 when the Sixteenth Amendment to the Constitution was adopted that permitted the imposition of an income tax. The 1935 Revenue Act expanded the income tax's democratic egalitarian character. It turned the income tax into a far more progressive *tax*, meaning that as a person's income increased, so did the percentage of tax paid by that person. For example, today, married couples who make between $18,550 and 75,300 pay 15 percent of their income in federal tax while those making between 75,300 and 151,900 pay 25 percent. Table 6.3 shows all the tax brackets and the tax rates associated with them.

In practice, the degree of progressivity was lessened because the government allowed many income deductions, including, as we have seen, the deduction for interest paid on home mortgages and for gifts made to charity. Nonetheless, the progressive tax did force the rich to pay a larger share of their income in taxes than those less well off and it did raise an enormous amount of revenue. Because those in the high tax brackets paid such a high percentage of their income in tax, the value of tax deductions was greatly increased. Ever since, tax deductions have become a major tool of government economic policy because they provide such a strong incentive for the wealthy to invest in tax deductible endeavors.

Table 6.2. Key regulatory agencies established during the Progressive Era and the New Deal.

Progressive Era	
Food and Drug Administration (FDA) (1906)	Regulate the safety and purity of food and drugs
Federal Trade Commission (FTC) (1914)	Regulate competitive practices of businesses
Federal Reserve (1913)	Regulate money supply
New Deal	
Securities and Exchange Commission (SEC) (1934)	Regulate the securities industry
Federal Communications Commission (FCC) (1934)	Regulate broadcasting
Federal Aviation Administration (FAA) (1938) (originally the Civil Aeronautics Administration)	Regulate civil aviation

Table 6.3. 2016 Taxable income brackets and rates (estimated), 2016.

Rate (%)	Single filers	Married joint filers	Head of household filers
10	$0 to $9,275	$0 to $18,550	$0 to $13,250
15	$9,275 to $37,650	$18,550 to $75,300	$13,250 to $50,400
25	$37,650 to $91,150	$75,300 to $151,900	$50,400 to $130,150
28	$91,150 to $190,150	$151,900 to $231,450	$130,150 to $210,800
33	$190,150 to $413,350	$231,450 to $413,350	$210,800 to $413,350
35	$413,350 to $415,050	$413,350 to $466,950	$413,350 to $441,000
39.6	$415,050+	$466,950+	$441,000+

Source: Kyle Pomerleau, TaxFoundation.org

Macroeconomics

As we discussed in Chapter 4, the Progressives not only sought democratic reform; they also advocated a greater role for technical and professional expertise in the making and the carrying out of public policy. Since the New Deal, a vital aspect of policy making, known as macroeconomics, has been the virtually exclusive province of experts. The founder of the study of macroeconomics was an Englishman, John Maynard Keynes. He recognized that the overall performance of an economy was not just the sum of its parts. It depended on the expectations of businesspeople about the future performance of the economy. If expectations were high, businesses would invest in new equipment, add supplies, and hire more workers. If expectations were low – even if business was good at the time – they would reduce inventory, eliminate new investment, and fail to hire additional workers. Keynes saw that worldwide economic depression made businesspeople pessimistic about the future, which created a self-fulfilling prophecy. To create business optimism, the government needed to put more money into the hands of the non-rich. If the wealthy were given more money, they might save some of it. The non-wealthy would spend a higher proportion because they had more pressing material wants. Giving the non-rich money, regardless of how, was therefore the most efficient way to stimulate a rise in consumer demand that would encourage businesses to purchase new resources and equipment and hire more workers to satisfy it. As unemployment declined, purchasing power would increase and consumer demand would continue to grow. A new, optimistic, self-fulfilling prophecy would be established.

FDR was reluctant to embrace *Keynesianism* because it required government to spend money it did not have and therefore to operate at a deficit. Government had engaged in *deficit spending* in the past, but only in wartime. Purposely going into debt in peacetime seemed immoral. Initially, FDR allowed for deficit spending only as an emergency measure. When the economy showed signs of recovery, he cut federal spending to reduce the deficit. The economy declined. When spending was increased because of the imminent threat of World War II, the economy rebounded.

The New Deal also deepened government involvement in macroeconomics by centralizing monetary policy making. The 1935 Banking Act shifted decision-making power from the regional reserve banks to the Federal Reserve Board and its chairman, Mariner Eccles. This change was accompanied by a new understanding of the Fed's mission. It was no longer merely an instrument for adjusting seasonal changes in credit demands and for averting bank panics; it was now a full-fledged partner in manipulating the economy to stimulate economic growth. Eccles invoked the Fed's credit-expanding authority because he realized that the stimulative effect of deficit spending would be blunted unless interest rates were kept low. Low interest rates allowed businesses to borrow money in order to expand their production in response to the increased demand for their goods brought on by increased government spending.

Keynesianism did not become official government doctrine until 1946, when President Harry Truman signed the Full Employment Act, committing government to maintaining a growing economy using all available means, including Keynesian tactics. The act created a *Council of Economic Advisors*, professional economists who would provide the president with technical expertise in maintaining high levels of employment and steady economic growth. The Keynesian approach to the macroeconomy was adopted by presidents such as Kennedy and Obama. They sought to stimulate economic growth and prosperity by increasing government spending while holding taxes steady or even reducing them.

Ronald Reagan also made use of the macroeconomic tools of taxes, government spending and control of the money supply but not entirely in the manner prescribed by Keynes. He hoped to stimulate the economy not by encouraging greater consumption but by increasing the supply of capital available for investment. This approach came to be known as *Supply-side Economics.* More investment would create more business activity and more employment, which in turn would lead to greater prosperity. He convinced Congress to adopt massive tax cuts, primarily for business and the wealthy. Reagan's policies did indeed enliven a sluggish economy but it unclear whether or not this was a result of the supply-side theory. In the absence of compensating budget cuts, his tax reductions led to unprecedented peacetime budget deficits. Deficit spending to increase demand is the classic Keynesian solution for addressing economic recession. Thus the boom that took place starting in 1983 could have been the result of either a supply-side stimulus resulting from tax cuts on businesses and the wealthy or a demand-side stimulus resulting from deficit spending, or both.

UPSHOT

Progressivism and the New Deal greatly expanded government involvement in the economy, but in a distinctive manner. In contrast to other rich nations, the US government does not, for the most part, conduct business on its own. There is no government-owned airline, freight railway, television, or radio station. Nor does it become a partner with private stockholders in manufacturing airplanes and automobiles. Instead, the US chooses to regulate private activities. It sets rules for business behavior, monitors that behavior (in cooperation with the states) and punishes those firms who break the rules. It uses the tax code to engage in a modest redistribution of income and to subsidize some forms of economic activity. It also employs macroeconomic tools to maintain economic stability. Thus, government intrudes into virtually all aspects of economic life but, for the most part, it does not substitute public for private control.

The Postwar Political Economy: Regulation, Deregulation, Rights Expansion

Although economic policy went through many changes in the second half of the twentieth century, it remained on the Classic Liberal path established at the founding as modified by the democratic–egalitarian reforms of the Progressive and New Deal eras. In Classic Liberal fashion, the government removed impediments to domestic and international market competition. In a democratic and egalitarian spirit, it broadened access to healthcare and education and created new programmatic rights regarding health education and the environment.

Expanding Rights

The path of providing greater economic security pioneered by the New Deal's Social Security Act was extended to include medical care as well as old-age pensions. In 1965, Congress passed Medicare (see Chapter 4), which provides all Americans over the age of 65 with government-funded healthcare. It also established Medicaid (see Chapter 5), a program for providing healthcare to the poor. The cost of Medicaid was shared with the states. Old-age and medical benefits were also greatly expanded via the tax code. Normally, workers might be expected to prefer higher wages to fringe benefits such as health insurance or old-age pension. But changes in the federal tax codes enacted during World War II exempted benefits from taxes. Because wages were taxed and benefits were not, workers preferred receiving the same amount of additional money in the form of benefits. Employers, with the support of labor leaders, could buy more worker loyalty and contentment per dollar by expanding benefits. Therefore, many workers came to enjoy low-cost healthcare as well as pensions that were far larger than what Social Security provided.

Ever since the Revolutionary War, the US government had paid various forms of pensions and bonuses to war veterans. This tradition was continued in the wake of World War II but with a novel twist. The 1944 GI Bill of Rights did not simply provide veterans with cash. Rather, it entitled them to attend universities and specialized training programs of all sorts at government expense. It thus served to benefit not only the veterans themselves, but the economy as a whole. The skills of the American workforce were greatly improved at no cost to employers. The pool of well-educated workers expanded dramatically, raising labor productivity and increasing the proportion of workers in high-paying jobs. Just as the United States was the first nation in history to enable most young people to go to school, it was also the first to provide mass higher education. Thanks in part to the GI Bill, the number of students enrolled in college jumped from less than 1.5 million in 1941, representing just 16 percent of high school graduates, to almost 2.5 million in 1949, representing 40 percent of high school graduates. Enrollment dipped somewhat in the later 1950s as the number of new veterans declined, but it never again dropped below 25 percent of high school graduates. In the Fall of 2017, more than 20 million students were enrolled in college, representing more than 40 percent of those between the ages of 18 and 24, and 65.9 percent of high school graduates.

The 1970s witnessed the expansion of regulation to include the environment, consumer protection and occupational safety and health. The Clean Air Act of 1970, the Clean Water Act of 1972, and the Resource Conservation and Recovery Act of 1976 required firms to reduce the amounts of chemicals and other pollutants they were emitting into the air and water and burying in the land. The Occupational Safety and Health Act of 1970 required employers to make sure that they provided a safe and healthy workplace for their employees. The Consumer Product Safety Act of 1972 established a commission charged with making sure that the toys, electronic equipment, clothing, appliances, and other products purchased by consumers were safe.

These new regulations used the same tools adopted by their Progressive predecessors – commands to regulated firms to change their practices – inspections to make sure those commands were obeyed, penalties imposed on those who disobeyed. But they added an additional rationale for imposing regulation. Environmental and occupational health regulations were defended both on the grounds that they corrected imperfections in the market *and* that they protected fundamental rights. In the same spirit that FDR had justified the Social Security Act by proclaiming Americans' right to economic security, the leading congressional environmental spokesman, Senator Edmund Muskie (D Maine), declared that clean air and water laws were necessary to protect Americans' right to a safe and healthy environment. The right of workers to enjoy a safe and healthy workplace underpinned the passage of OSHA. Rights claims have dominated every subsequent debate over environmental policy. The current debate over the regulation of CO_2 and Methane in order to reduce the greenhouse gases implicated in global warming actually extends the rights rationale to a global scale. Advocates of stringent regulation propound a universal human right to protection from the threats posed by climate change.

Finance Regulation

The twenty-first century witnessed an expansion of the efforts to control corrupt business practices that had been so prominent during the Progressive Era and the New Deal. Both the financial collapse of 2008 and a wave of fraud induced corporate failures at the turn of the millennium led to major new initiatives regulating financial activity. As a result of the widespread participation of ordinary workers in stock-owning pension funds and the great increase of mass participation in buying and selling stocks that occurred during the 1980s and 1990s, most Americans had become stockholders. Therefore the health of the stock market became of much wider public concern. That health was threatened beginning in the late 1990s by the discovery of massive financial fraud at such major corporations as Tyco, WorldCom, Global Crossing, Adelphia, and Enron, all of which went out of business as a result. By July of 2002, the Dow Jones Industrial Average, a major stock market index, had dropped 25 percent from its historic high in March of 2000. The stock market lost an estimated $7 trillion. This collapse riveted public attention on the variety of accounting techniques that these corporations had used to overstate profits, minimize losses, and otherwise exaggerate how economically healthy they were. There were also disturbing revelations about the extent to which the outside accountants hired by corporations to audit the company books had abetted these fraudulent practices. Likewise, these companies had bribed stock analysts to encourage their clients to buy the companies' stock.

In 2002 Congress passed a major new regulatory initiative aimed at curbing such abuses. It was named the Sarbanes–Oxley Act in honor of its sponsors, Congressman Michael Oxley (R–OH) and Senator Paul Sarbanes (D–MD). The act imposed federal rules regarding the composition, structure, and operation of corporate governing boards. Formerly, such matters had been dealt with by state corporation law, and dealt with very loosely. Sarbanes–Oxley required public corporations to appoint an Audit Committee and a Compensation Committee composed entirely of independent directors, thus excluding the corporation's own management. The audit committee was granted sole responsibility for hiring and approving the work of the outside auditors. The compensation committee determined how much management was to be paid.

Sarbanes–Oxley also required the Chief Executive Officer (CEO) and the Chief Financial Officer (CFO) to personally attest that the corporation's financial statements were accurate and complied with the accounting rules the new law set in place. The CEO also had to certify that the company's own accounting practices were capable of detecting and preventing fraud. Making top corporate CEO executives personally liable for the quality and accuracy of their companies' financial statements inspired a massive reorganization and reformation of internal accounting and reporting procedures. The Act also established the Public Company Accounting Oversight Board (PCAOB) to devise and enforce federal accounting rules that auditors must abide by.

As we discussed in the beginning of the chapter, the essential rationale for using taxpayer money to save major banks, investment firms, and insurance companies from bankruptcy was that they were "too big to fail." These mega corporations played such a dominant role in the overall banking and investment system that the failure of any one of them could cause the entire system to unravel. In 2010 Congress passed the Dodd–Frank Wall Street Reform and Consumer Protection Act, named for its sponsors Congressman Barney Frank (D–MA) and Senator Thomas Dodd (D–CT). The Act creates the Financial Stability Oversight Council chaired by the Treasury Secretary to monitor threats to financial stability especially those caused by those giant firms "too big to fail." If the Council concludes that such a firm is in danger of failing it can order a government takeover of the company in order to dismantle the firm in a deliberate and orderly manner so as not to endanger the overall financial system. Thus, the market would retain the ability to punish "too big to fail" companies that made bad risks, but government control over the process of liquidating them would prevent a destructive chain reaction involving other large financial companies. Dodd–Frank also attempted to reduce the likelihood of failures by forcing big banks to adopt more conservative loan practices requiring them to keep more of their assets in reserve against the possibility of loan defaults.

Table 6.4. Postwar regulation: major new regulatory statutes and agencies.

Environmental Protection Agency (1970)	Regulate air, water, and toxics pollution
Occupational Safety and Health Administration (1971)	Regulate occupational safety and health
Consumer Product Safety Commission (1972)	Regulate consumer product safety
Sarbanes–Oxley Act (2002)	Regulate the composition, structure, and operation of corporate governing boards; establish the Public Company Accounting Oversight Board (PCAOB) to devise and enforce federal accounting rules that auditors must abide by; make corporate CEOs executives personally liable for the quality and accuracy of their companies' financial statements
Dodd–Frank Wall Street Reform and Consumer Protection Act (2010)	Create the Financial Stability Oversight Council to monitor threats to financial stability, especially those caused by those giant firms "to big to fail"

Opening Markets

Even as it was exerting stricter control over certain aspects of economic life, the United States was freeing up other aspects. Although the United States has been involved in world markets from the beginning, it has also erected significant barriers to free international trade. From the Civil War until the end of World War II, high tariffs were in place on many manufacturing products. In 1930, the average tariff on imported goods was 50 percent of their price. But the US was the only major industrial economy left intact by World War II. As a consequence, it had a great opportunity to increase its manufacturing exports and little to fear from foreign manufacturing competition. By lowering its tariffs it hoped to induce other nations to lower theirs. By 1951, average tariffs had fallen to 12.5 percent and by the end of the 1990s to approximately 5 percent. The lowering of US tariffs and other forms of trade barriers has continued even as other nations restored and expanded their industrial capacity and as specific sectors of the US economy, such as steel, textiles, garments, and toys, have been decimated by foreign import competition.

US commitment to free trade has national security as well as strictly economic roots. As the Cold War intensified, the United States sought to enlist other countries as allies in that worldwide struggle. It recognized that efforts to induce those nations into military and mutual security agreements would be greatly hampered if, at the same time, the US was limiting importation of those nations' goods. Therefore, it coupled its international alliance-building initiatives with proposals to expand world trade. In 1994 the United States joined the *World*

Trade Organization (WTO), a new international body with extensive powers to settle trade disputes, and endorsed the most recent *General Agreement on Tariffs and Trade* (GATT). GATT reduced tariffs by 40 percent by phasing out quotas on textiles and apparel and by extending copyright and other forms of protection to intellectual property, including recordings and books. Although the Cold War has ended, the US still considers the expansion of worldwide free trade and the increased prosperity it brings to be a crucial tool for enhancing peaceful international relations.

The US has been especially active in promoting free trade among its hemispheric neighbors in North, Central, and South America. In 1993, President Clinton signed the *North American Free Trade Agreement* (NAFTA), which eliminated tariff barriers and other trade constraints between the United States, Mexico, and Canada. This free-trade zone encompassed a $6.5 trillion market containing 350 million consumers. The following year, in 2005, the US Congress approved the Dominican Republic–Central American Free Trade Agreement (DR-CAFTA). DR-CAFTA eliminated all tariffs imposed by the US on manufactured goods from the other DR-CAFTA signatories – Costa Rica, the Dominican Republic, El Salvador, Guatemala, Honduras, and Nicaragua.

On the domestic front, the deregulation of trucking, telephone, and airlines that took place during the 1970s was designed to foster competition in those businesses. As a result of previous government regulation, one company, American Telephone and Telegraph Company (ATT), enjoyed a virtual monopoly in providing telephone service. Federal price regulation of airline fares discouraged new competitors from providing air passenger service. Regulatory restrictions on routes and loads hampered trucking competition. These deregulatory efforts were a tacit admission that the New Deal regulations they were undoing had actually worked against the interests of consumers by discouraging competition. Since these regulatory protections benefited the existing companies and their workers, deregulation had been considered politically impossible. However, the defensive advantage enjoyed by these employer–employee coalitions was overcome by the ability of the president, congressional leaders, and professional economists to convince ordinary Americans that they had something at stake in the outcome, namely lower prices. The bias in favor of the status quo that we discussed in Chapter 1 was overcome.

Looking Forward

Chapter 4, on political development, ended by characterizing contemporary political debate as embodying a three-way conflict between Progressivism, Conservatism, and Populism. Economic policy provides a principal focus for that debate. Chapter 14 describes how an important modern social movement, the Tea Party, reflected Classic Liberal opposition to government intrusion in the real estate market, and how another, Occupy Wall Street, made a democratic egalitarian appeal to deploy government against greed, corruption, and privilege. In 2016 two political insurgencies took place. The Trump campaign was largely a populist movement seeking to protect American workers and the communities they lived in against efforts by their employers to send their jobs abroad and by immigrants to compete for their jobs. But it also echoed the Tea Party commitment to reducing government regulation. The Bernie Sanders campaign embodied the democratic egalitarian convictions of Occupy Wall Street. But it also echoed Trump's populist commitment to protectionism. The protectionist stances of both Trump and Sanders were opposed by the establishments of their respective political parties, who staunchly supported Classic Liberal adherence to free trade. Thus neither of the two parties now projects an unambiguous set of political economic alternatives. Therefore the future course of American economic policy will be determined by lively political debate and conflict within the parties as well as between them.

CHAPTER SUMMARY

Contemporary portrait:

* Current American economic policy ensures against risk; subsidizes favored economic activities; punishes misbehavior; and intervenes at the macroeconomic level, the economy as a whole, in order to encourage price stability, full employment, prosperity, and growth.
* The greatest difference between the US and the rich countries of Europe and Asia is that the US does less to control the labor market.

Critical choice: setting the liberal economic path:

* The essential aspects of economic liberalism are: private property, competition, and promise keeping.
* The adoption of the Constitution, including the Bill of Rights, was the critical choice that set the US firmly on the path of economic liberalism. In addition to the protections offered by the principle of enumerated powers and the Bill of Rights, the Constitution contains a number of specific clauses that safeguard a liberal economy.

Debating the role of government:

* In the nineteenth century those who argued for a more democratic egalitarian economy opposed government intervention.
* The specific policy debates that arose regarding banks, debt, and promotion of industry embodied deep differences of opinion about the nature and purposes of republican government.

* The doctrine of free labor was an important addition to the economic principles of Classic Liberalism.

Critical choice: creating the regulatory state:

* In the late nineteenth century, the court and the state legislatures made critical decisions that fostered corporate growth.
* Beginning with the Populists in the late nineteenth century, those who argued for a more democratic egalitarian economy came to favor government intervention.
* Federal government regulation of economic activity took hold during the Progressive Era and was expanded during the New Deal.
* The principle of economic rights was introduced during the New Deal. Initially this principle was limited to providing economic security for the elderly.
* The New Deal also greatly expanded the progressive income tax and pioneered the use of macroeconomic policy.

The postwar political economy: regulation, deregulation, rights expansion:

* During the 1960s the principle of economic rights was extended to providing healthcare for the elderly.
* The 1970s witnessed the expansion of regulation to include the environment, consumer protection, and occupational safety and health.
* In the twenty-first century major new regulations of corporations and banks were enacted
* After World War II the US liberalized its international trade policies by reducing tariffs and eliminating other import and export barriers.
* In the 1970s the US deregulated a series of economic activities including trucking, telephone, and airlines (but not airline safety).

Looking forward:

* Protectionism has reentered contemporary economic policy debate. It is being championed on democratic egalitarian grounds.

SUGGESTED READINGS

Chandler, Alfred Dupont. *Scale and Scope: The Dynamics of Industrial Capitalism.* Cambridge, MA: Belknap Press, 1990.

The Visible Hand: The Managerial Revolution in American Business. Cambridge, MA: Belknap Press, 1977.

Derthick, Martha, and Paul J. Quirk. *The Politics of Deregulation.* Washington, DC: Brookings Institution Press, 1985.

Friedman, Milton. *Capitalism and Freedom.* University of Chicago Press, 1963.

Hacker, Jacob. *The Divided Welfare State: The Battle Over Public and Private Social Benefits in the United States.* New York: Cambridge University Press, 2002.

Harris, Richard, and Sidney M. Milkis. *The Politics of Regulatory Change: A Tale of Two Agencies, 2nd edn.* New York: Oxford University Press, 1996.

Hawley, Ellis. *The New Deal and the Problem of Monopoly: A Study in Economic Ambivalence.* New York: Fordham University Press, 1995.

Howard, Christopher. *The Hidden Welfare State: Tax Expenditures and Social Policy in the United States.* Princeton, NJ: Princeton University Press, 1997.

McCoy, Drew R. *The Elusive Republic: Political Economy in Jeffersonian America.* Chapel Hill: University of North Carolina Press, 1996.

McCraw, Thomas K. *Prophets of Regulation: Charles Francis Adams, Louis D. Brandeis, James M. Landis, Alfred E. Kahn.* Cambridge, MA: Belknap Press, 1984.

Samuelson, Robert. *The Great Inflation and its Aftermath: The Past and Future of American Affluence.* New York: Random House, 2008.

Sellers, Charles. *The Market Revolution: Jacksonian America, 1815–1846.* New York: Oxford University Press, 1991.

Skidelsky, Robert. *Keynes: The Return of the Master.* Philadelphia: Public Affairs, 2009.

Stein, Herbert. *Presidential Economics: The Making of Economic Policy from Roosevelt to Clinton,* 3rd rev. edn. Washington, DC: AEI Press, 1994.

Stiglitz, Joseph E., *Freefall: America, Free Markets, and the Sinking of the World Economy*: New York: W. W. Norton, 2010.

Part III
Governing Institutions

7 Congress

CHAPTER OVERVIEW

This chapter focuses on:

- **A contemporary portrait of the US Congress.**
- **The key constitutional provisions relating to Congress.**
- **The era of congressional dominance.**
- **The critical choices that transformed Congress.**
- **The resurgence of Congress, the rise of institutional combat, and the increase in party polarization.**

Article II, Section 2 of the Constitution gives the Senate the power to approve those executive branch appointees whom the Congress designates as requiring such confirmation. In the past fifty years, the Senate has turned down only one presidential nominee, although others have withdrawn from consideration in the face of serious Senate opposition. In most instances, the Senate fulfills its constitutional obligation by subjecting nominees to close scrutiny and then approving them. The ordinary understanding has been that the president is entitled to select the executive team that he feels will best serve him. But 2016 was different. Ultimately, all but one of President Trump's nominees were confirmed but only because his party held a narrow 52–48 senatorial majority. Not a single Democrat supported Trump's nominees for Attorney General, Secretrary of Health and Human Services, or Secretary of Education. When two Republicans voted against Secretary of Education Betsy DeVos, creating a 50–50 tie, it required the intervention of the vice president to break the tie in her favor. This was the first time in history that a vice president availed himself of his constitutional power to do so.

This heightened party discord in Congress marked a further advance in the party polarization that has come to characterize the legislative branch in recent times. This chapter examines how Congress has struggled to retain its capacity to deliberate in the face of increased polarization and of the rising power and prestige of the presidency. After sketching a contemporary portrait of Congress, it examines the crucial questions the Framers confronted when they set out to create an independent legislature. It then looks at each crucial phase of congressional development: Congress' emergence as the dominant branch of government in the nineteenth century; its transformation in response to the rise of activist national government in the twentieth century and its resurgence, accompanied by intensified institutional combat with the president, that began in the late 1960s. The final section focuses on the the remarkable political impact of four extraordinary midterm elections – 1994, 2006, 2010, and 2014 – that promoted both polarization within Congress and conflict between Congress and the executive.

The Contemporary Congress – A Portrait

The Constitution grants the legislative power to Congress. No law can be established unless passed by Congress. In principle, the Constitution restricts the legislative power to those specific matters "here in granted" in Article I. As we discussed in Chapter 3, these specific grants of authority known as enumerated powers are the critical tools by which the Constitution establishes a limited government. However, in modern times the courts have greatly expanded the meaning of some of those enumerated powers, especially the power to regulate commerce (see Chapter 9), and the limitations on what Congress can pass laws about have greatly eased. The 114th Congress, which met from 2015 to 2017, enacted statutes regarding such diverse subjects as a nuclear deal with Iran, a major revision of federal education policy, a ban on taxation of internet access, and an increase in funding for highways.

Congress does a great deal more than pass laws. Two of its most important contemporary functions, neither of which is mentioned in the Constitution, are oversight of the executive branch and constituency service. The source of congressional power over executive departments is its power of the purse. It can reward or punish executive agencies by either increasing or reducing their budgets. Thus, it uses its legislative power to obtain executive influence. Its budgetary power is so great that it rarely has to directly threaten to invoke it. For example, if influential congresspersons believe that the Environmental Protection Agency is being too aggressive in closing down dry cleaners who violate clean air regulations, they can threaten to reduce the EPA's enforcement budget unless the agency adopts a less aggressive policy. The committee and subcommittee staffs conduct extensive investigations of the agencies that fall within their jurisdiction. Those investigations are often followed by committee or subcommittee oversight hearings at which the members subject agency officials to extensive cross-examination about agency activities. Based on what they learn from staff reports and hearings testimony, the committees may choose to direct the agency to make changes. In order to avoid even the whisper of budgetary retribution, agency officials are highly responsive to those congressional directives.

For similar reasons, agency officials are receptive to requests from well-placed congresspersons to give special consideration to constituents or to other persons whom those representatives wish to help. Often, congressmen ask nothing more than that an agency official search for and retrieve a license application, social security check or visa request that has somehow gotten lost in the bureaucratic maze. Indeed, the members employ staffers who do nothing but work with the bureaucracy on these sorts of issues. This function is known as "constituency service." But there is no clear line between this type of problem solving and the exertion of undue pressure on agencies to show favoritism. For example, in 2009 Congresswoman Maxine Waters (D–CA), a member of the House Banking Committee, arranged a meeting between government officials and a group of bankers to discuss applications made by the banks for financial assistance under the bank bailout program (TARP) that Congress had passed. Among the banks represented was OneUnited, in which her husband was an investor. When she was accused of using her power over the banking industry to help her husband, she denied the charge. All the banks at the meeting were experiencing serious financial difficulties and were owned by racial minorities. She claimed that she had pushed for the meeting to help all those minority-owned banks, not OneUnited in particular. The Office of Congressional Ethics determined that she was guilty of a conflict of interest and recommended that she be disciplined by the House Ethics Committee. The committee disagreed and decided not to charge her with an ethics violation. It determined that she had not crossed the line between constituency service and undue favoritism.

In addition to the influence over the executive that derives from its legislative powers, the Senate, but not the House, also has constitutionally mandated executive powers. Article I requires the Senate to confirm the appointments that the president makes to the federal courts and to high-level executive positions. It must approve all treaties that the president enters into with foreign governments.

The Legislative Process

When a proposal for a new law is introduced into Congress, it is referred to as a "bill" and assigned a number. If it is first introduced by a senator, the number is given the prefix S. For example, in 2015 a bill to approve the Keystone pipeline was first introduced in the Senate and was labeled S1. If a bill is first introduced by a House member, the number is given the prefix HR. In the same congressional session, a bill to reauthorize the federal terrorism insurance program was first introduced in the House and designated HR3210. Executive departments also draft bills, as do various lobbying organizations. But no bill becomes a law unless it is introduced by a congressperson, passed by both houses of Congress, and signed by the president. If the president vetoes the bill, it must be repassed by a two-thirds majority in each house of Congress in order to become a law, a move that is known as a "veto override."

Each bill is first assigned to the committee or committees that have jurisdiction over the issues the bill deals with. The more complex the bill the more likely it will be assigned to more than one committee. Most senators and congressmen keep their same committee assignments from session to session. They become expert in the matters their committees deal with. Before the whole committee deliberates on the bill, it will usually receive extensive consideration by a subcommittee that has particular expertise regarding the matter at hand. When a bill is reported out of committee and onto the House or Senate floor, non-committee members often depend heavily on the views and opinions of the committee members they most trust in deciding how to cast their votes. It is usually the case that the most important decisions regarding the shape and scope of a particularly bill are made in committee, not on the floor.

The various committees responsible for writing laws are known as authorizing committees. But one House and one Senate committee do not write laws. They spend money. Those Committees are known as the House and Senate Appropriations Committees. Their various subcommittees decide how much of the money that the authorization committees allow for should actually be spent in a given year. This process of appropriating is necessary in order to bring total congressional spending in line with the total amount of money that the annual budget has available. The appropriations process does not guarantee that revenue and spending will balance. Often the federal government runs a deficit. But without the work of the appropriations committee and its subcommittees there would no means for disciplining congressional spending.

Committee assignments, and the appointment of committee chairs, are made by the members of the party that controls the House or Senate, the majority party caucus. This caucus is much more unwieldy in the 435-member House than in the Senate, where it could be as small as 51. In order to enable the House majority caucus to function effectively, it grants a great deal of control to its leader, the Speaker of the House. As a result of the speaker's critical role in choosing the people who control the crafting legislation and perform other vital roles as well, the speaker enjoys great power. Another critical avenue for exerting control is the House Rules Committee. Because there is not enough time in a session of Congress to deal with all the bills that the committees approve and because the leadership may have additional reasons for keeping a bill from coming to a floor vote, the Rules Committee decides which bills will indeed reach the floor. Because the speaker controls the appointment of the Rules Committee and of its chair, the Speaker of the House determines which bills will be voted on and which will not.

If a proposal deals with revenue, the Constitution requires that the House first considers the proposal. If the proposal covers any other topic, the Senate is free to consider it first. Because the Senate has fewer members, however, it cannot scrutinize as many proposals as the House can. Therefore, the Senate often allows the House to act first, using the lower chamber as a filter to determine which issues really merit further attention. Often, each chamber will pass a significantly different version of a bill. To reconcile these differences, the House and Senate leadership each appoint members to a joint conference committee. The conference committee tries to achieve compromises regarding the major issues in dispute. If it succeeds, the conference version goes back to each house to be ratified or defeated. If both houses approve of the compromise bill, it is sent to the president's desk for a signature.

Frequently, serious disagreements arise within each delegation as well as between the two. The Speaker of the House and the speaker's staff play a key role in brokering compromise within the House delegation, so it can speak with one voice in its negotiations with the Senate. Nancy Pelosi, House Speaker from 2006 to 2010, was instrumental in obtaining passage of the healthcare reform legislation that became law in 2010. Repeatedly, she found ways to compromise deep differences that surfaced among members of the House and between House committees, and to pressure members whose support for the legislation was wavering.

Unlike the House, the Senate does not adopt time limits for the consideration of statutes, treaties, or presidential nominees. Therefore, a senator or group of senators can prevent the Senate from voting on a statute or nominee simply by engaging in a filibuster, continuing to talk and refuse to yield for a vote. It takes sixty votes to end a filibuster. Therefore, controversial legislation that comes before the Senate needs more than the support of a majority. If the majority is less than sixty the minority may well succeed in blocking the legislation by filibustering. The mere threat of filibuster is often enough to force the majority to make significant concessions to the minority regarding the content of the legislation.

A good example of how the legislative process operates is provided by the landmark financial regulatory statute, the Dodd–Frank Wall Street Reform and Consumer Financial Protection Act that became law in 2010. It is named for its Senate and House sponsors Thomas Dodd (D–CT) and Barney Frank (D–MA). After extensive discussion with the Department of the Treasury, Congressman Barney Frank introduced his financial regulatory proposal to the House as HR4173 on December 2, 2009. The bill was then referred to the Houses Financial Services Committee chaired by Frank, as well as to several other committees whose jurisdictions encompassed some particular aspect of what Frank was proposing. On December 8, 2009, the Rules Committee proposed a rule that would bring the bill to the floor. The rule provided for three hours of general debate. The House passed the rule and then proceeded to debate the bill. It considered a number of amendments offered by various House members, some of which passed and some of which failed. On December 11, a vote was taken and HR4173 passed by a vote of 223 to 202.

On January 12, 2010, HR4172 was received by the Senate and referred to the Committee on Banking, Housing, and Urban Affairs chaired by Senator Dodd. On May 20, 2010 that committee discharged it and it was taken up for debate on the Senate floor. The Senate then voted to substitute the version of the bill written by Dodd's Committee. The Senate Banking Committee version passed the Senate by a vote of 59 to 39. The Senate then requested a conference with the House to reconcile the differences between the two versions. The leaders of both Houses selected the members for the conference. The conference held nine sessions to hammer out a compromise, which was then reported to both houses on June 29, 2010. The following day the House agreed to accept the conference compromise by a vote of 237 to 192. The Senate followed suit two weeks later, passing the conference version by a vote of 60 to 39.

In summary, Congress performs the following functions:

- Passes laws
- Raises revenue
- Appropriates revenue
- Oversees the executive branch
- Provides constituency service
- Approves executive and judicial appointments (Senate)
- Approves treaties (Senate)

The Supporting Cast

The sheer amount of work that Congress must undertake pursuant to its legislative, oversight, and constituency services burdens is far more than 435 representatives and 100 senators can handle on their own. In response to this ever-growing workload, Congress has transformed itself into a large, complex organization. It now employs more than 17,000 people. Congressmen are heavily dependent on the personal staffs, committee staffs, and research organizations that compose a large part of this workforce.

House members are limited to a personal staff of eighteen. The size of Senate staff varies according to the size of the state the senator represents. A typical senator from a large state employs between forty-five and fifty staffers. A congressperson's staff conducts research, writes speeches, drafts bills, fields requests and complaints from constituents, and badgers the bureaucracy. The representative reserves his/her own work time for the public and the politically delicate aspects of the job. Staffers cannot substitute for the representative when it comes to making speeches, attending campaign events and committee meetings, giving press interviews, or negotiating with other members or with prominent White House officials and constituents.

Each congressional committee and subcommittee has a staff of its own. These staffs are responsible for keeping committee members informed about the

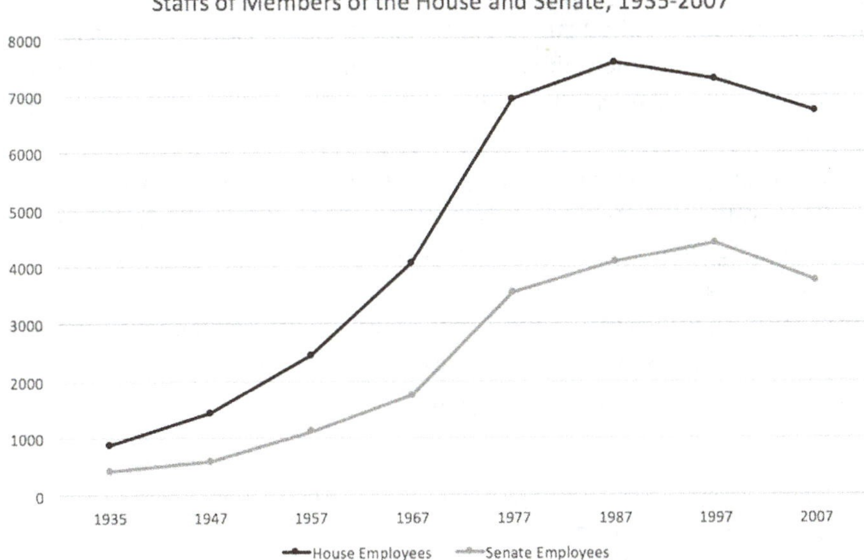

Figure 7.1. Congressional staff.
Source: Brookings Institute.

specialized policy questions about which the committee legislates and the activities of the executive agencies over which it has oversight. Committee staff drafts the specific language that transforms the decisions the committee makes into actual legislation. It also plans and schedules committee hearings and writes committee reports. The average number of committee staff is sixty-eight in the House and forty-six in the Senate. Figure 7.1 charts the growth in the size of congressional staff from the 1930s to the twenty-first century.

Congress has also established research organizations of its own to serve the informational needs of the individual members, the committees, and staffers. The three most important of these are: The Congressional Budget Office (CBO), the Government Accountability Office (GAO), and the Congressional Research Service (CRS). The CBO's mandate is to provide the Congress with "objective, nonpartisan, and timely analyses to aid in economic and budgetary decisions on the wide array of programs covered by the federal budget." Later on in this chapter we will see how important the CBO has become in the policy-making process. The Speaker of the House of Representatives and the president pro tempore of the Senate jointly appoint the CBO director, after considering recommendations from the two budget committees. The term of office is four years, with no limit on the number of terms a director may serve. The CBO currently employs about 235 people.

The GAO is the chief investigative agency supporting congressional efforts to oversee the executive branch. It audits the spending of federal agencies and performs other types of analyses and investigations designed to measure agency performance and unearth agency misdeeds. The head of the GAO, the Comptroller General of the United States, is appointed to a fifteen-year term by the president from a slate of candidates Congress proposes. The GAO has 3,350 employees.

The CRS is an all-purpose research agency performing whatever type of information gathering that a member or a committee requests of it. It provides policy analyses briefings and seminars as well as confidential memoranda and expert testimony at congressional hearings. The CRS is part of the Library of Congress, the head of which is the Librarian of Congress, who is appointed by the president and confirmed by the Senate. It has approximately 600 employees.

In summary, the supporting cast includes:

- Personal staff
- Subcommittee and committee staff
- Congressional Budget Office
- Government Accountability Office
- Congressional Research Service

The Size and Shape of Congress

Since the Constitution grants every state two senators, the size of the Senate only changes when new states are added to the Union. This last happened when Alaska and Hawaii became states in 1958 and 1959 respectively, increasing the total number of states from 48 to 50 and the size of the Senate from 96 to 100 members. The Constitution does not set the size of the House of Representatives. It merely guarantees that each state will have at least one representative; each congressional district will have at least 30,000 persons, and that the districts will be apportioned among the states on the basis of population. In 1790, each member of the House of Representatives represented about 34,000 residents. Today, the House has more than quadrupled in size, and each member represents about ninteen times as many constituents. In 2000, each member of the House of Representatives represented a population of about 647,000. The 2010 census showed a 9.7 percent increase in the size of the US population, and therefore each congressional district grew by approximately that same percentage. The current size of 435 representatives was established in 1911.

In order to ensure that each congressional district has more or less the same number of people, congressional seats are reapportioned in response to the population shifts discovered by the census, which is conducted every ten years. The 2012, House elections were the first ones conducted according to the 2010

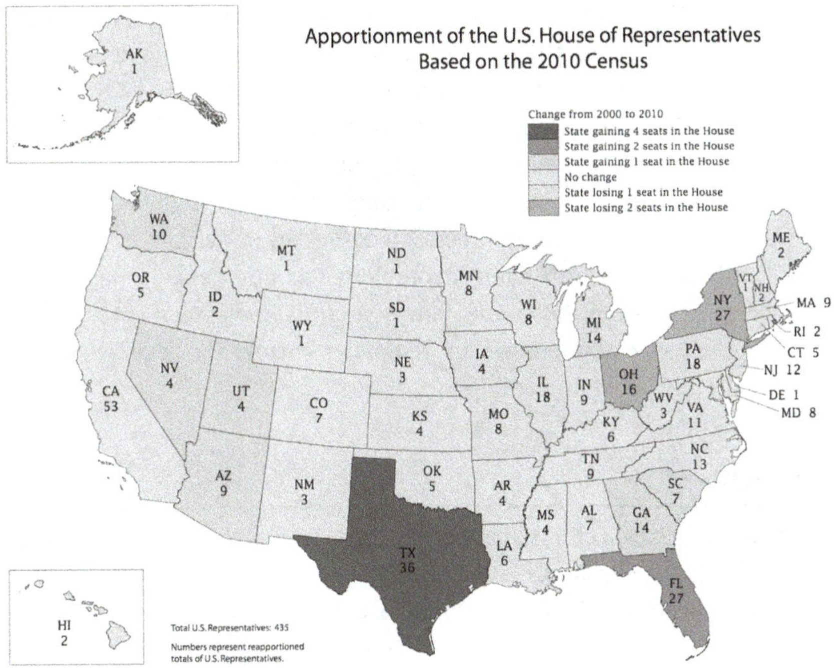

Figure 7.2. Congressional Apportionment.
Source: US Census.

census, which requires that eleven seats be reapportioned among the states (see Figure 7.2).

The states gaining seats are: Texas (4), Florida (2), Arizona (1). Georgia (1), South Carolina (1), Nevada (1), and Utah (1). The states losing seats are: New York (2), Ohio (2), Massachusetts (1) Pennsylvania (1), Michigan (1), Illinois (1), Iowa (1) Missouri (1), Louisiana (1). Notice that all the gainers are in the South and West and all the losers, except Louisiana, are in the North and Midwest. Louisiana's population loss is due to very special circumstances, the devastating effect of Hurricane Katrina in 2005. This shift of population from the North and East to the South and West was also detectable in the 2000 census when twelve seats were reapportioned. Because population growth and decline happens unevenly within as well as between states, states are also obligated to redraw their congressional boundaries even if they do not gain or lose seats. In most states, redistricting is the responsibility of the state legislature. How those districts are drawn has a huge impact on who wins and who loses. Every incumbent and every likely challenger wants their district to be dominated by voters favorable to them. This goal may well put them at odds with leaders of their own party. Each political party wants the districts drawn to maximize the number of seats they are likely to win. Whereas the incumbent wants to stack his/her district with likely supporters, party leaders do not want any one district to have so many favorable voters that it deprives the party of the ability to win in the other districts. They would rather spread their partisan supporters around, giving them an ability to win more seats by slimmer margins rather than a smaller number of seats by large margins. Thus, the redistricting process is highly politically charged. The parties fight between themselves but even within each party, incumbents battle to retain or to gain favorable voters and party leaders battle with incumbents to spread favorable voters around. Seventeen states have attempted to depoliticize this process by removing it from the legislature and assigning it to an independent commission.

2016 Election

The 2016 congressional elections marked the first time since 2008 that voters gave control of both the legislative and executive branches to the same party. The Republicans had controlled the House since 2010 and the Senate since 2014. In addition to winning the presidency, they retained a majority in each house, although by reduced margins. They lost two Senate seats leaving them with a four seat majority of 52 to 48. Their House margin declined by six seats leaving them with a 241–194 majority. The two Republicans who were defeated, Ayotte of New Hampshire and Kirk of Illinois, both came from states that supported Clinton over Trump. The other victorious Republican incumbents who were considered vulnerable came from states that Trump carried.

The 115th Congress that took office in January 2017 was the most racially diverse in congressional history. It had more Hispanics, African Americans, Asian Americans, and women of color than ever before. The number of women, 104, comprising 19 percent of Congress, stayed the same, but the number of women of color was four times greater than in the previous Congress. African Americans increased from 46 to 49. Hispanics members increased to 38.

Congress and the Constitution

Article I of the Constitution established Congress as the preeminent branch of government, granting it seventeen legislative powers, including the most important of all governmental powers: taxation, regulation of commerce, and declaration of war. These enumerated powers are followed by the "necessary and proper clause," which grants Congress whatever additional powers are required to exercise its specific responsibilities, assuming those powers do not expressly violate the Constitution. Article I, Section 2 designates the speaker as the principal officer of the House of Representatives. Article I,

Section 3 declares the vice president to be the presiding officer of the Senate, and designates a president pro tempore to preside in the absence of the vice president.

Having granted so much power to the legislature, the Convention delegates sought to avoid the intemperate and irresponsible behavior of their own state legislatures during the currency crisis of 1785. Americans went on such a buying spree after the Revolutionary War – importing such luxuries as clocks, glassware, and furniture from Great Britain – that gold and silver became scarce and the value of money was driven up. Indebted farmers were able to convince several state legislatures to loosen the money supply by printing vast sums of money. The price inflation that followed proved economically disastrous.

This irresponsible behavior of state legislatures was aggravated by the impotence of the central government under the Articles of Confederation. The national legislature lacked authority to regulate interstate commerce and could not impose more responsible economic policies on the states. Members of Congress were chosen by the state legislatures, which paid their salaries and had the power to remove them at any time. Therefore, congressional representatives were afraid to take actions that their state legislatures disapproved of for fear of losing their positions or having their pay reduced. To craft a Congress capable of more enlightened statesmanship and better public policy making than could be found in the state legislatures, the Framers carefully considered how best to select representatives; how many should be chosen; and what checks to establish between House and Senate, Congress and the states, and Congress and the other two branches of the federal government.

Selection and Size

To select better representatives, the Framers determined to draw them from a bigger pool. House districts would be large; senators would be chosen by entire states. State legislators were often elected for periods of a year or even six months. By creating longer congressional terms – two years for the House, six for the Senate – the Framers hoped to insulate representatives from volatile changes in public opinion.

To promote deliberation, Congress was to be a relatively small body. The House of Representatives would initially have only sixty-five members and the Senate twenty-six. By contrast, the legislature of Massachusetts had more than 300 members. Anti-Federalists protested that the small size of the legislature made it insufficiently representative. So intent were the Framers on maintaining distance between House members and their constituents that until the very last day of the Constitutional Convention they fought to maintain a ratio of one member per 40,000 citizens. Fearing that such a high ratio would offend democratic sentiments, George Washington stepped down from the chair – the only time he did so – to defend reducing the minimum from 40,000 to 30,000. The Convention had debated and rejected this proposition several times in the preceding weeks, but once Washington endorsed it, debate ceased and it passed unanimously.

Bicameralism

The Framers feared the democratic character of the House, which, if left to its own devices, would become all too responsive to popular whims and passions. They sought, as Madison put it, to refine popular passions by "successive filtrations." The first line of defense was bicameralism, the creation of two separate houses of Congress with all laws having to be passed by both. The House would be the popular branch its members elected directly by the people every two years. The Senate would be a much smaller body whose members would enjoy greater distance from the people by virtue of their longer, six-year terms and because their method of election would be determined by the state legislatures. As the Framers hoped, most state legislatures opted to elect the senators themselves rather than leaving the choice to the mass of voters.

All revenue bills had to originate in the House. This concession to the House shows the Framers' commitment to giving the primary power over the operations of the federal government to its most democratic element. But the House would be moderated by the more discerning attention of the Senate. As befit the chamber's "cool and deliberate sense of the community," the Senate was given a privileged part in foreign affairs and government staffing. It was granted sole authority to ratify foreign treaties, confirm presidential nominations to the executive branch and judiciary, and try public officials impeached by the House.

Midterm Elections

Even as they were checking excessive democratic responsiveness by creating a bicameral legislature, the Framers were promoting democratic responsiveness by providing for midterm congressional elections. In the midst of the president's four-year term, the Constitution requires the entire House of Representatives as well as one-third of the Senate is subject to stand for reelection. Thus, the Congress can change its political character *in between* presidential elections. No other republican democracy has midterm parliamentary elections. As we shall see in the last section of this chapter, congressional midterm elections have proven to be critical devices for ensuring democratic accountability. By shifting control of Congress to the minority party, they have forced both the president and the Congress to alter course in a direction more in line with the public will.

CRITICAL THINKING QUESTION: SEPARATION OF POWERS

Later in this chapter there will be considerable discussion of the conflicts that have arisen between the legislative and executive branches. In a parliamentary system such as exists in Canada and Great Britain there is no division between the executive and the legislature. After you have read the entire chapter, consider whether or not the framers of the Constitution made a mistake in dividing power between the Congress and the president. Would the US have been better served by a system that combines the two?

Congressional Dominance

For more than half of the United States' political development, Congress served as the chief national policy-making body. As we shall see in the next chapter, the president did not dominate the legislative process in the nineteenth century as he would later on. Nor had he yet become the single focal point of national political attention. The scope and reach of federal departments and agencies were far narrower and more limited than they would become in the twentieth century and, therefore, administrative policy making was far less important than congressional law making. In the course of the nineteenth century, Congress developed the strong internal organization and leadership necessary for maintaining its political dominance.

Organizing Congress: The Emergence of the Party Caucus

Chapter 11 describes the Framers' fear of political parties as factions that would incite class, religious, or racial conflict and thereby endanger liberty. The Constitution's system of separation of powers, operating in a large and diverse society, was intended to inhibit the emergence of a strong two-party system. Ironically, it was that very party system that enabled Congress to perform its constitutional responsibilities. In 1800, the Republicans triumphed over the Federalists and installed Thomas Jefferson as the nation's third president. This critical election empowered a party dedicated to constraining the president and strengthening Congress and the states.

In order to perform its democratic function of passing laws that reflect majority sentiment and its republican function of holding executive power in check, Congress needed a unifying force that, as Jefferson saw, could only be provided by political parties. Presidents can be strong and appear "above party."

Congress, however, is a large collection of individuals. Although members of Congress may achieve celebrity and popularity outside of parties, Congress as an institution can rival the president's claim to public confidence only if it can be held collectively accountable. Accountability requires that parties reward and punish members based on their adherence not only to collective decisions of the party but also to the tactics adopted by the party leadership implementing those decisions.

Unlike Washington and Adams, therefore, Jefferson deemphasized his formal powers and governed instead through his extra-constitutional role as party leader. He helped build a disciplined party organization in Congress and relied on *party leaders* in the House and Senate to advance his program. Jefferson himself sometimes presided over the meetings of the congressional Republican representatives, known as *party caucuses*.

Leading Congress: The Speaker of the House

The Constitution does not enumerate the Speaker of the House's responsibilities and powers. Nor was there any significant discussion of these questions at the Constitutional Convention. Until Henry Clay of Kentucky was elected speaker in 1808, party leadership in the House was shared by several floor leaders. The speaker acted as merely a moderator. A strong president such as Jefferson could dominate such diffuse congressional leadership. Clay displaced the president as the leader of the majority party in the House. He extended party control over congressional committees, which became, in Woodrow Wilson's celebrated phrase, "little legislatures," meaning that the committees performed the real work of formulating legislation.

Like most great legislative leaders, Clay derived his success in large part from his extraordinary personality. John C. Calhoun, a fierce rival, said, "I don't like Henry Clay, he is a bad man, an imposter, a creator of wicked schemes. I wouldn't speak to him, but, by God, I love him." The leadership strength of the House Speaker has ebbed and flowed over the course of American political development. But many speakers, including recent ones such as Newt Gingrich, speaker from 1994 to 1998, and Nancy Pelosi, speaker from 2006 to 2010, have exerted powerful control over the House.

Clay emerged as the dominant national political leader during the controversy with Britain that led to the War of 1812. Clay was one of the most influential of the "Warhawks," a congressional faction that favored making aggressive demands on Britain and going to war if those demands were not met. Unifying the Republican caucus behind him, Clay strengthened the House's capacity to meet its broader legislative obligations by expanding the number and influence of its committees, which enabled each representative to specialize in a specific policy area such as finance or foreign policy. Clay was especially careful to appoint Warhawks to key posts including the chairmanship of the foreign affairs committee. Clay and his allies forced a reluctant Madison to deliver a war message to Congress. On June 18, 1812, President Madison signed the first declaration of war in American history.

Unfortunately, Congress proved far more eager to declare war than to prepare for it. Traditional Republican hostility to centralized power caused Congress to slash tax revenues and military appropriations, leaving the military both understaffed and undersupplied. Legislative dominance deprived the country of the solid benefits that the Framers expected from a unified and energetic executive. The inability of Congress to match its talent for deliberation and debate with administrative competence would continue to bedevil national governance throughout the nineteenth century.

A Citizen Legislature

Congress benefited greatly from the expanded importance of political parties during the 1830s and 1840s. The rise of the mass-based, decentralized party system that we discussed in Chapter 4 and will elaborate on in Chapter 12 knitted congressional representatives more closely to their constituents. Congress became a more vibrant institution, one that registered competing democratic voices. Unlike the contemporary Congress, viewed by the public as the keystone of an unresponsive government establishment, the nineteenth-century Congress became a "citizen legislature."

The most striking feature of this citizen legislature was the very rapid turnover of its members. For much of the twentieth century, power in the Congress was acquired through *seniority*, which encourages long congressional careers. But in the nineteenth century, the House had 30 to 60 percent turnover at every election. The Senate's longer and overlapping terms gave it a more stable membership than the House, but it too saw far more turnover in the nineteenth century than it does today. Before the Civil War, members rarely made the Senate a career. Until the end of the century, the average senator did not even finish one term, completing only three to four years of service. Figure 7.3 shows how the average tenure in office has increased since the mid nineteenth century.

One cause of the high turnover was the unpleasantness of life in Washington. Unlike the first two capital sites, New York and Philadelphia, Washington lacked culture and creature comforts. Members of Congress felt stranded in this primitive new city, described by the historian Merrill Peterson as "a village pretending to be a capital, a place with a few bad houses, extensive swamps, hanging on the skirts of a too thinly peopled, weak and barren country." Another disincentive to long congressional service was the limited role that the national government played in the political life of the country. The triumph

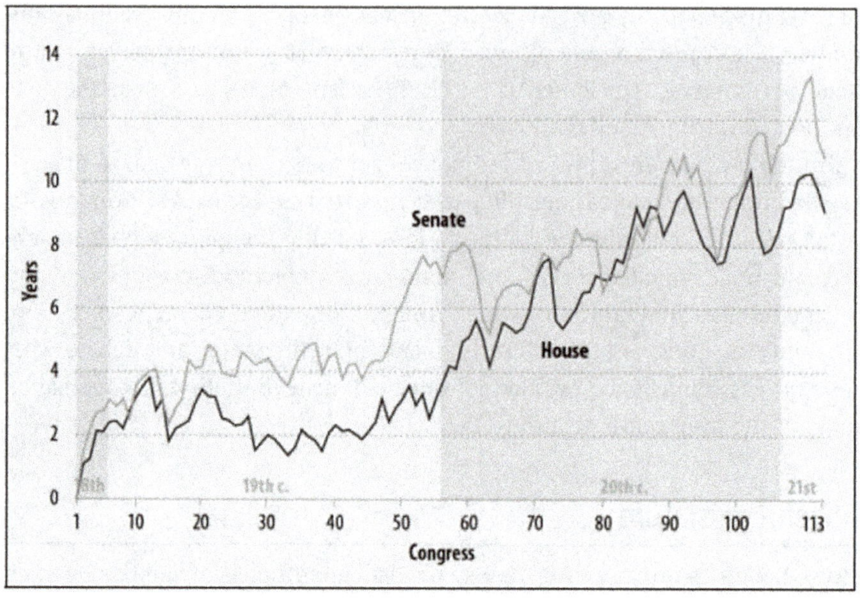

Figure 7.3. Congressional service tenure.
Source: CRS analysis of ICPSR and proprietary data. Inter-university Consortium for Political and Social Research, and Carroll McKibbin, *Roster of United States Congressional Officeholders and Biographical Characteristics of Members of the United States Congress, 1789–1996: Merged Data* [computer file] 10th ICPSR edn. (Ann Arbor: MI: Inter-university for Political and Social Research [producer and distributor], 1997).

of the Jacksonians over the Whigs had restored the primacy of state and local government.

Another key characteristic of the citizen legislature was a high level of partisan competition. The two political parties were evenly balanced during most of the nineteenth century, and therefore House elections tended to be close, which threatened reelection prospects. State legislative elections were also close. Because the Senate was chosen by the state legislatures, senatorial elections were likewise highly competitive. State legislative candidates would often run for office pledged to a particular senatorial candidate. This is why the famous 1858 Lincoln–Douglas debates took place all over the state of Illinois. Each candidate was trying to help elect legislative candidates pledged to vote for him.

Partisan competition and member turnover combined to create a lively Congress. It became the great national theatre in which passionate and lively debate over such critical issues as slavery, tariff policy, the bank, and the money supply took place. Congressional drama reached a fever pitch in May of 1856. Senator Charles Sumner (R–MA) delivered a two-day speech entitled "The Crime against Kansas" that accused the South of conspiring to admit Kansas to the Union as a slave state. Among those members of Congress singled out for insult and ridicule was Andrew P. Butler (D–SC), who Sumner described as "Don Quixote who had

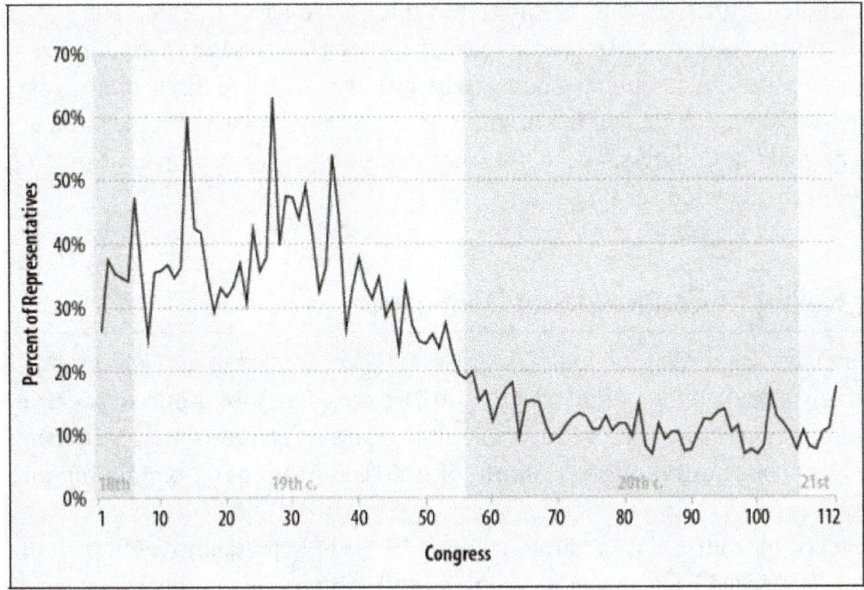

Figure 7.4. Congressional retention.
Source: CRS analysis of ICPSR and proprietary data. Inter-university Consortium for Political and Social Research, and Carroll McKibbin, *Roster of United States Congressional Officeholders and Biographical Characteristics of Members of the United States Congress, 1789–1996: Merged Data* [computer file] 10th ICPSR edn. (Ann Arbor: MI: Inter-university for Political and Social Research [producer and distributor], 1997).

chosen a mistress to whom he has made his vows, and who . . . though polluted in the sight of the world, is chaste in his sight – I mean the harlot slavery."

Congressman Preston Brooks (D–SC), a kinsman of Butler's, decided to avenge his family's honor. Brooks approached Sumner, who was seated at his desk mailing copies of the offending speech to his constituents. Calling the speech a "libel on South Carolina, and Mr. Butler, who is a relative of mine," Brooks brought his cane down on Sumner's head, neck, and shoulders repeatedly and with increasing force, until the cane shattered. Sumner tried to rise from his desk, ripping up the heavy screws that bolted it to the floor. Blinded by blood, he staggered down the center aisle of the Senate chamber.

The South declared Brooks a hero. The North viewed Sumner as a martyr. Southern opposition prevented the two-thirds majority necessary to expel Brooks from the House, but he resigned anyway. South Carolinians immediately sent him back to Washington with triumphant unanimity. Sumner stayed away from the Senate for three years – recuperating, his supporters said; hiding, claimed his enemies. During that time the Massachusetts legislature reelected him as a symbolic rebuke to the "barbarism of slavery." His empty seat in the Senate chamber remained a visible symbol of the deepening sectional divide.

The Sumner–Brooks incident was hardly part of the deliberative process that the Founders of the Constitution prescribed for the Congress, but it shows how the national legislature had become the center of American democratic life, a forum that helped draw Americans into struggles about the most fundamental political issues. John Quincy Adams (when he was in the House), Henry Clay, Daniel Webster, John C. Calhoun, and Charles Sumner shaped the debate over slavery, making Congress, as the historian Henry Jones Ford observed, "a school of political education for the nation."

The Height of Congressional Dominance

In the post-Civil War period, Congress achieved an even greater political dominance than it had enjoyed prior to the presidency of Andrew Jackson. This dominance was achieved by combining strong congressional leadership with greater political party control of the congressional nomination and election process.

Leadership control was far stronger in the House of Representatives than in the Senate. It reached its peak late in the nineteenth century due to the leadership of Thomas B. Reed of Maine. Unlike previous celebrated legislators such as Adams, Clay, Webster, and Calhoun, Reed was single-mindedly concerned with the process of governing. He defined a statesman as "a politician who is dead," and he displayed a wit and cynicism that animated a ruthless insistence on streamlining the House's chaotic proceedings in order to eliminate obstruction and delay.

House rules required that a majority of members, a quorum, be present in order for the House to meet. In an effort to thwart Reed's authority, the minority Democrats sat mute during attendance call, preventing a quorum. Reed counted them present anyway. Reed appointed himself chair of the Rules Committee, enabling him to determine when and how a bill would be considered. In 1891, the Supreme Court sanctioned the transformation of the House into a more disciplined legislative body by upholding the constitutionality of these and other "Reed rules" aimed at controlling members' behavior.

The Democrats opposed the increase in discipline, contending that the Constitution intended Congress to be a body of individuals representing various localities. Reed countered that "a majority under the Constitution was entitled to legislate, and that, if a contrary practice has grown up, such practice is unrepublican, undemocratic, against sound policy, and contrary to the Constitution." He was expressing the Jacksonian principle that political parties were a critical agent of popular rule and that grassroots party control of Congress upheld the democratic character of American republican government. Before becoming speaker, Reed had written in a national magazine, "Our government is founded on the doctrine that if one hundred citizens think one way and one hundred and one think the other, the one hundred one are right."

Figure 7.5. Senatorial Courtesy: an 1893 cartoon of the Senate filibuster.
Source: www.senate.gov/artandhistory

Democrats nickname him "Czar" Reed and made his "tyranny of the House" a major campaign theme in the 1890 congressional elections. After winning an overwhelming victory, they repealed most of Reed's rules. But Reed, now in the minority, launched a retaliatory campaign of obstruction designed to persuade

Democrats to acknowledge that his procedural innovations had been necessary to allow the House to function. Although many Democrats remained unhappy with the quorum rule and other procedures that centralized power in the House, they grudgingly reinstituted similar procedural tools for maintaining majority party control. By the end of the nineteenth century, the House was a highly centralized institution, dominated by a powerful speaker who could restrict obstructionist tactics on the floor, control committee assignments, and, through the Rules Committee, exercise influence over the legislative agenda.

The Senate did not achieve a similar degree of leadership control. Its party leaders were less likely to remove a committee member for disloyalty. The Senate rules allowed "legislative holdups" by which a member could prevent a bill from coming to the floor for full debate. Also, individual senators could filibuster. Still, by the late nineteenth century it too had become far less tolerant of obstruction and delay. Finance Committee chairman Nelson Aldrich (R–RI) and other influential Republican senators succeeded in imposing a previously unknown degree of partisan and procedural discipline in the Senate. These efforts were reinforced in 1917 when the Senate, at the suggestion of President Woodrow Wilson, adopted a rule (Rule XXII) allowing it to end debate with a two-thirds majority vote – a motion known as "cloture" (in 1975 it reduced the number of votes needed for cloture to sixty).

Although party control was justified on the basis of majority rule, critics charged that it worked against the interests of the many. The close identification of the Republican Party with big business made the Congress vulnerable to control by the great corporations that were coming to dominate American politics in the late nineteenth century. The protective tariff became the party's signature policy (see Chapter 6). Laws such as the McKinley Tariff of 1890 strengthened the Republican Party's business connections. The identification with business would later become a liability, but during the prosperous times of the late nineteenth century it was politically advantageous. Congress, under the tight grip of party leadership, did not engage in vital debate over industrial capitalism as it had over slavery. Party organization existed to pass legislation, not discuss it.

THE CRITICAL CHOICES THAT TRANSFORMED CONGRESS

In response to the challenge posed by the expansion of presidential power and desirous of freeing itself from such strict leadership control, Congress made several critical choices to transform itself. It changed its organization and practices to make legislators into policy specialists. Party organization gave way to narrowly focused autonomous committees enabling representatives to acquire expertise in programs that served their ambition. They made Congress their career as they functioned as "policy entrepreneurs," that is, formulators and

Table 7.1. Congressional committees.

Senate committees	House committees	Joint committees
Aging	Agriculture	Commission on Security and Cooperation in Europe
Agriculture, Nutrition, and Forestry	Appropriations	Joint Committee on Printing
Appropriations	Armed Services	Joint Committee on Taxation
Armed Services	Budget	Joint Committee on the Library
Baking, Housing, and Urban Affairs	Education and the Workforce	Joint Economic Committee
Budget	Energy and Commerce	
Commerce, Science, and Transportation	Ethics	
Energy and Natural Resources	Financial Services	
Environment and Public Works	Foreign Affairs	
Ethics	Homeland Security	
Finance	House Administration	
Foreign Relations	Intelligence	
Health, Education, Labor, and Pensions	Judiciary	
Homeland Security and Governmental Affairs	Natural Resources	
Indian Affairs	Oversight and Government Reform	
Intelligence	Rules	
Judiciary	Science, Space, and Technology	
Rules and Administration	Small Business	
Small Business and Entrepreneurship	Transportation and Infrastructure	
Senate Caucus on International Narcotics Control	Veterans' Affairs	
Veterans' Affairs	Ways and Means	

Source: GovTrack.

stewards of new policies and programs for their constituencies and for the organized interests with whom they were allied. Table 7.1 provides a list of current House and Senate committees.

By the end of the nineteenth century the party model of congressional government had become obsolete. Acquisition of the Philippines and greater influence over Cuba, brought about by victory in the Spanish-American War in 1898, broadened America's international obligations and muted partisan differences. William McKinley, a former member of the House elected president in 1896, noted how the emergence of the United States as a world power freed the president from collective party responsibility: "I can no longer be called the

President of a party; I am now the President of the whole people." Greater attention to foreign affairs expanded executive discretion and diminished the role of lawmaking. In Chapter 8 we examine additional sources of the rise of presidential power and popularity in the early twentieth century, particularly the impact of Progressivism. Through these combined factors, the presidency threatened to displace Congress as the principal agent of popular rule.

The first phase of Congress's transformation was directed at the congressional leadership, not at the president. Desirous to obtain greater decision-making authority, legislators sought to gain more control over their personal electoral fortunes. Therefore, they supported progressive reforms such as the direct primary, which replaced partisan campaigns with candidate-centered campaigns (see Chapters 11 and 12). They also sought changes in the power structure of Congress to better enable them to influence public policy in ways that would serve their districts and states and thus enhance their prospects for reelection.

A Revolution in the House

The attack on congressional party leadership began in 1910 with a revolt against third-term Speaker of the House Joseph Cannon (R–IL). A disciple of Czar Reed, "Uncle Joe" Cannon managed the House with an iron fist.

Cannon was a standpat Republican, meaning that he resisted popular economic and political reforms. Like Henry Clay, he prevailed over a weak president. He opposed President William Howard Taft's tariff reduction efforts and pushed the Paine–Aldrich tariff, which raised rates on many items, through the House in 1910. But unlike Clay's command during Madison's occupation of the executive mansion, Cannon's dominance of Taft incited a rebellion that stripped the office of much of its influence.

Cannon retaliated against three Republicans who voted against the Paine–Aldrich tariff by removing them as committee chairmen. Incensed by this and other dictatorial acts, Progressive Republicans joined with the Democrats to strip the speaker of his powers to appoint committee chairs and members to control the Rules Committee as well as many of his other means for controlling the business of the House.

The Progressive revolt spread rapidly to the Senate, where it was led by Robert La Follette (R–WI), elected in 1906. He was so despised by the leadership that he was denied the minimal courtesies extended to a freshman senator. Instead of being granted a seat on the Committee on Interstate Commerce, a fine vantage point for taking on the railroads, which reformers viewed as the most egregious of the Trusts, La Follette was appointed chair of the Committee to Investigate the Condition of the Potomac River Front, which never had a bill referred to it or even held a meeting.

But this effort to humiliate La Follette backfired. With the help of the press, he took his case for railroad regulation as embodied in the Hepburn Bill directly to the people, arousing popular opposition to corporate power and the Senate leadership that served it. Only President Theodore Roosevelt, who also stumped for the bill (see Chapter 8), played a more important part in mobilizing support for it. The Hepburn Bill was enacted despite the efforts of Senate leaders to kill it.

La Follette's successful insurgency signaled the emergence of a new kind of senator, one who stood apart, who resolutely attacked parties and private interests, who was celebrated by the press. La Follette's celebrity contributed not only to economic reform but also to the downfall of the most powerful Republican senator, Nelson Aldrich, who like Speaker Cannon was deprived of legislative control by a coalition of Progressive Republicans and Democrats. The Progressive attack also aroused public sentiment for the direct election of senators. Enacted in 1913, the Seventeenth Amendment provided that senators be elected by voters, not state legislatures. This change further undermined *party discipline* because candidates now had to depend on their own electioneering ability rather than on party control of state legislatures.

The Emergence of Committee Government

After the downfall of Cannon and Aldrich, and continuing well into the twentieth century, committees dominated Congress. They held hearings and wrote legislation in the privacy of their chambers. Committee chairs were virtually legislative barons, controlling committee agendas, hiring staff, and scheduling hearings. Party strength remained important because it determined the relative number of Democrats and Republicans on each committee and whether the senior Democrat or Republican would be chair. For example, when Senator Jeffords quit the Republicans, committee chairs and membership majorities shifted to the Democrats. But party leaders did not choose chairs. Instead, a seniority system allocated leadership positions and committee assignments based on length of congressional service.

The seniority system remained in place until 1974. It enabled members of Congress to plan long careers on a particular committee without fear of being removed by party leaders. Individual members, no longer subject to collective partisan responsibility, became policy makers in their own right. They used this influence to benefit constituents, thereby improving their reelection prospects. Thus, committee government reduced the number of competitive districts, and turnover of both House and Senate seats declined.

Committee government made Congress a less representative institution. In the party-dominated system, members of Congress could be disciplined by party leaders and lose cherished committee assignments. The new seniority system ensured that committee chairs would remain in office even if they thwarted congressional majorities, held meetings in secret, and denied access to dissenting groups. Therefore, the task of popular representation fell increasingly to the president, who, as Chapter 8 describes, was becoming more closely tied to public opinion even as Congress became more insulated. The two branches traded constitutional roles. The people looked to the president for democratic innovation, whereas the House and Senate applied restraint.

The primary responsibility for Congress in this revised constitutional order was to oversee administration of public policy. It used committee hearings, investigations, and individual member or staff interrogations to try to hold the executive accountable. Individual legislators developed policy expertise to match the bureaucrats who staffed the burgeoning executive branch. Committee organization mirrored that of departments and agencies. Thus, for example, the Senate Foreign Relations Committee oversaw the State Department, and the Labor and Human Resources Committee oversaw the Department of Health and Human Services.

The 1946 Legislative Reorganization Act codified and rationalized congressional oversight. It reduced the number of committees and subcommittees and clarified their *jurisdictions*. It made Congress's oversight responsibility explicit and called on it to engage in "continual watchfulness" over the activities of administrative agencies. It provided individual representatives and committees with large staffs, which enhanced Congress's capacity to oversee the bureaucracy. Committee staff grew from 103 in 1891 (41 in the Senate and 62 in the House) to 483 in 1947 (290 in the House and 193 in the Senate). As congressional staff continued to expand in the post-World War II era, staff members came to perform a variety of crucial roles. The greatest prestige went to committee, and later subcommittee, staff. They were, and still are, policy specialists. But even they cannot master all the issues that come before their committee, so they reach out to experts from universities, think-tanks, and lobbying organizations. The staff's job is largely to synthesize those expert opinions in a manner that makes them comprehensible to the members. Once a subcommittee reaches agreement on specific issues, its staffers produce a draft that is sent up to the full committee. Committee staffs perform similar tasks for the committee as a whole and also become involved in negotiating with the staffs of other committees, particularly the Rules Committee, to resolve issues of jurisdiction and scheduling.

This shift toward oversight brought with it a new set of constitutional difficulties. In the late 1940s and early 1950s the most publicized and controversial use of congressional investigations was for the purpose of uncovering domestic subversion. In the late 1940s, as the power of the Soviet Union grew, Americans began to worry about threats to national security posed by communist espionage. Several different members of the House and Senate made use of their leadership positions on committees or subcommittees to launch investigations into domestic communist subversion. The most prominent of these investigators was Senator Joseph McCarthy (R–WI). His inquisitorial methods and blatant disregard for the civil liberties of the subjects of his investigations became so notorious that the term McCarthyism entered the language as a synonym for unfair and obnoxious intrusion into the private lives and political views of citizens. Despite his highly publicized and extensive investigations, McCarthy unearthed few if any serious instances of security breaches. Such breaches did occur and spies were caught and convicted, but not by McCarthy or by his committee's most influential House counterpart, the House Committee on Un-American Activities.

The witch-hunt wilted by overreaching itself. Beginning in April of 1954, Senator McCarthy's Subcommittee on Investigations of the Committee on Government Operations began televised hearings on charges of communist subversion in the US Army. Such sustained exposure to McCarthy's bullying tactics, rude behavior, and the weakness of his evidence eroded popular support. A critical moment in McCarthy's political demise occurred when he implied that a young lawyer named Fred Fischer, who worked for the law firm of the army's special counsel, Robert Welch, had communist leanings. Welch replied: "Until this moment, Senator, I think I never gauged your cruelty or recklessness ... Have you no sense of decency, sir?" Welch's calm and measured response to McCarthy's brutalities struck a responsive chord. The audience in the gallery burst into applause. McCarthy's day as a popular leader was done. McCarthy's ignominious political demise served as a salutary cautionary tale. His successors have only rarely wielded congressional investigatory power in ways that threaten civil liberties.

UPSHOT

By the middle of the twentieth century, Congress had changed in a number of critical ways. Senators were now popularly elected rather than being chosen by state legislatures. Committees became far more autonomous, providing members a greater opportunity to function as policy entrepreneurs. Committee chairs were chosen on the basis of seniority, thereby reducing the power of the leadership. Personal and committee staffs were greatly expanded, enabling Congress to engage in much more aggressive oversight of the executive branch and to conduct more numerous and ambitious investigations. These changes improved Congress's ability to oversee the activities of the executive branch and to serve local districts and states. But they sapped its vitality as a representative institution capable of forging consensus among the nation's diverse voices.

The Resurgence of Congress, the Rise of Institutional Combat, and the Increase in Party Polarization

Curbing Presidential Power

Starting in the late 1960s, the relationship between the president and Congress went through further changes, leading over the course of the decade to a significant resurgence of congressional power and a major increase in institutional combat between the two branches. Much of this resurgence was due to growing fears that the presidency was becoming too powerful. The failure of the United States to achieve "peace with honor" in Vietnam, discussed in more detail in Chapter 8, fostered public cynicism about the merits of presidential policies and a greater inclination by the press to challenge the wisdom and veracity of presidential statements and proposals. Even champions of a strong presidency became concerned about presidential imperialism and more appreciative of Congress's constitutional responsibility to represent public views and to refine and imbed them in settled, standing law.

Concerns about presidential excess were greatly aggravated by the presidency of Richard Nixon. Nixon was the first new president since Zachary Taylor in 1848 to be elected without a party majority in either house of Congress. Nonetheless, he unilaterally extended the Vietnam War and bombed Cambodia. In further disregard of Congress, Nixon impounded, refused to spend, funds appropriated by Congress. Presidential impoundments had previously been exercised only for reasons of economy and efficiency, but Nixon's were an attempt to undermine the legislative process. In an effort to curtail his predecessor Lyndon Johnson's "War on Poverty," he impounded funds that Congress had appropriated to one of its signature policies, the Community Action Program (see Chapter 8). The impoundment was subjected to judicial challenge and ultimately overturned. In 1974, Congress would pass legislation curbing the president's ability to impound funds.

The Watergate scandal caused Congress to go beyond curbing the president to actively seeking his removal. For the first time in history, a president resigned from office, a direct consequence of the House Judiciary Committee's recommendation that the full House vote to impeach him. The Watergate scandal was named for the building that housed the Democratic National Committee headquarters, which was broken into by operatives of the Republican Committee to Re-Elect the President during the 1972 presidential campaign. The key issue was whether Nixon knew about the break-in and tried to cover up his connection to it. The Senate Select Committee on Presidential Campaign Activities, known as the Watergate Committee, ordered Nixon to hand over tapes that he had made of his Oval Office conversations and sued him when he refused to do so. The special prosecutor Archibald Cox, who had been appointed by President Nixon to investigate the matter, was also denied access to the tapes.

Nixon claimed executive privilege, a president's right to withhold information from Congress. Committee chairman Senator Sam Ervin (D-NC) countered that executive privilege could be defended under some circumstances, such as those dealing with national security, but could not be invoked when dealing with possible criminal activities. Nixon argued that "inseparably interspersed in the tapes are a great many very frank and very private comments wholly extraneous to the committee's inquiry."

Partisanship gave way to institutional loyalty, as even Nixon's staunchest congressional defenders demanded that he produce the tapes. Senator Howard Baker (R–TN), committee vice chairman, who had long been a friend and advisor to the president, contended that the tapes contained material "essential if not vital, to the full inquiry mandated and required by this committee." Baker and Ervin's engagingly telegenic presences did much to reassure the nation that the confrontation between the president and Congress could be resolved through regular constitutional procedures. Ervin's country lawyer image and his passionate but calm invocations of the separation of powers made him a folk hero. His judicious committee leadership served to remind the American people of Congress's critical constitutional responsibility to hold the president accountable.

On July 24, 1974, in *US v. Nixon*, the Supreme Court unanimously ruled against the president. Chief Justice Warren Burger, a Nixon appointee, stated that "To read the Article II powers of the President as providing an absolute privilege against a subpoena essential to enforcement of criminal statutes ... would upset the constitutional balance of a 'workable government' ... and cut deeply into the guarantee of due process of law." On the heels of the court's decision, the House Judiciary Committee voted to impeach Nixon. His chances of surviving a Senate trial suffered when he admitted that the tapes did implicate him in the Watergate cover-up. Also, a gap was discovered in one of the tapes during what appeared to be a crucial conversation about the break-in between Nixon and key aides. Even Nixon's Republican supporters on the Judiciary Committee conceded that the president had virtually confessed to obstruction of justice. On August 9, 1974, Nixon announced his decision to resign, becoming the first president forced from office. The scandal further jeopardized confidence in the integrity of the presidential office.

Asked in 1959 whether the president or Congress should have "the most say in government," a representative sample of Americans favored the president by 61 to 17 percent. Watergate shattered that virtual consensus. A similar survey in 1977 showed that 58 percent of Americans believed Congress should have the most say; only 26 percent supported presidential primacy. For the first time since the heady days of Czar Reed and Nelson Aldrich, Congress seemed poised to assume its place as the primary representative institution.

The Watergate scandal provoked Congress to pass a multitude of laws curbing the president's powers, including the Congressional Budget and Impoundment Control Act of 1974, which required the president to obtain Congress's approval before impounding any funds. The act also created budget committees in both houses to coordinate and strengthen legislative involvement in fiscal policy making, and it established the Congressional Budget Office (CBO) to provide

president's preeminence in legislative and administrative matters. As political scientist R. Shep Melnick has written:

> No longer would Congress respond to calls for action by passing vague legislation telling the executive to do something. Now Congress was writing detailed statutes, which not infrequently deviated from the president's program. Subcommittees were also using oversight hearings to make sure that administrators paid heed not just to the letter of legislation but to its spirit as well.

The new vitality that was created by subcommittee government is best illustrated by the outpouring of congressionally initiated environmental, consumer protection, worker safety, and civil rights laws that took place during the 1970s. These initiatives were not the sort of measures one would expect from the keystone of a conservative Washington establishment.

Greater party caucus influence in organizing the House and Senate did not return the speaker and Senate majority leader to the preeminence they lost during the Progressive insurgency, but the two positions did acquire more power to control the federal budget, make committee assignments, and control the flow of legislation. The new budgetary process, in particular, increased centralization in both the House and Senate. It gave the majority party dominant influence over the budget committees and enabled the speaker, in consultation with the Senate's president pro tempore, to appoint the director of the Congressional Budget Office.

Table 7.3. Post-Watergate reforms.

The 1974 Congressional Budget and Impoundment Control Act	Requires the president to obtain Congress's approval before impounding any funds. It also created budget committees in both houses and established the Congressional Budget Office (CBO).
The 1972 Case Act	Requires that all executive agreements, be reported to Congress.
The 1973 War Powers Resolution	Requires that after sixty days troops committed to battle by the president must be removed unless Congress votes to declare war or otherwise approve their continued deployment.
The 1973 Legislative Reorganization Act	Requires recorded votes on all floor amendments in the House.
The 1973 "Subcommittee Bill of Rights"	Shifted the power to select subcommittee chairs from the committee chairs to the majority members of the committee.
During the 1970s	The House and Senate leadership acquired more power to control the federal budget, make committee assignments, and control the flow of legislation.

Divided Government – Institutional Combat

Congress's resurgence was accompanied by a rise in the level and bitterness of institutional combat with the president. From 1968 to 1992, Republicans held the presidency for all but four years. By contrast, Democrats controlled the House of Representatives for that entire twenty-six-year period and the Senate for all but six. This recurring partisan divide, the longest period of almost continual divided government in the nation's history, greatly aggravated relations between the executive and the legislature. Republican efforts to enhance the unilateral powers of the executive and to circumvent legislative restrictions on presidential conduct were matched by Democratic initiatives to burden the executive with smothering oversight by congressional committees and statutory limits on presidential power.

The main forum for partisan conflict was a series of investigations in which the Democrats and Republicans sought to discredit one another. From the early 1970s to the mid 1980s there was a tenfold increase in the number of indictments brought by federal prosecutors against national, state, and local officials, including more than a dozen members of Congress, several federal judges, and a number of high-ranking executive officials. This heightened legal scrutiny was partly a response to the Watergate scandal. In what became known as the "Saturday night massacre," Nixon fired special prosecutor Archibald Cox, who had been charged with investigating the scandal.

To prevent future "massacres," Congress passed the 1978 Ethics in Government Act. It provided for the appointment of independent counsels to investigate allegations of criminal activity by executive officials. Not surprisingly, divided government encouraged the exploitation of the act for partisan purposes. In the 1980s, congressional Democrats were able to demand criminal investigations and possible jail sentences for their political opponents. When Bill Clinton became president in 1992, congressional Republicans turned the table with a vengeance. Political disagreements were readily transformed into criminal charges, culminating in the impeachment of the president.

Polarization

The most important congressional development in recent decades has been the ever growing discord between the majority and minority parties. They have increasing difficulty finding common ground. The art of compromise has been in decline. The ideological gap between members of one party and those of the other has widened. Liberal Republicans and conservative Democrats have virtually disappeared, and there are fewer moderates. With very few exceptions, the Democrats in Congress are liberals and the Republicans are conservatives. Political scientists refer to this widening ideological gap as polarization. Figure 7.6

In Congress as Well as Public, the Center Increasingly Cannot Hold

Ideological scores of senators and representatives based on roll-call votes. Negative numbers represent liberal views and positive numbers conservative views

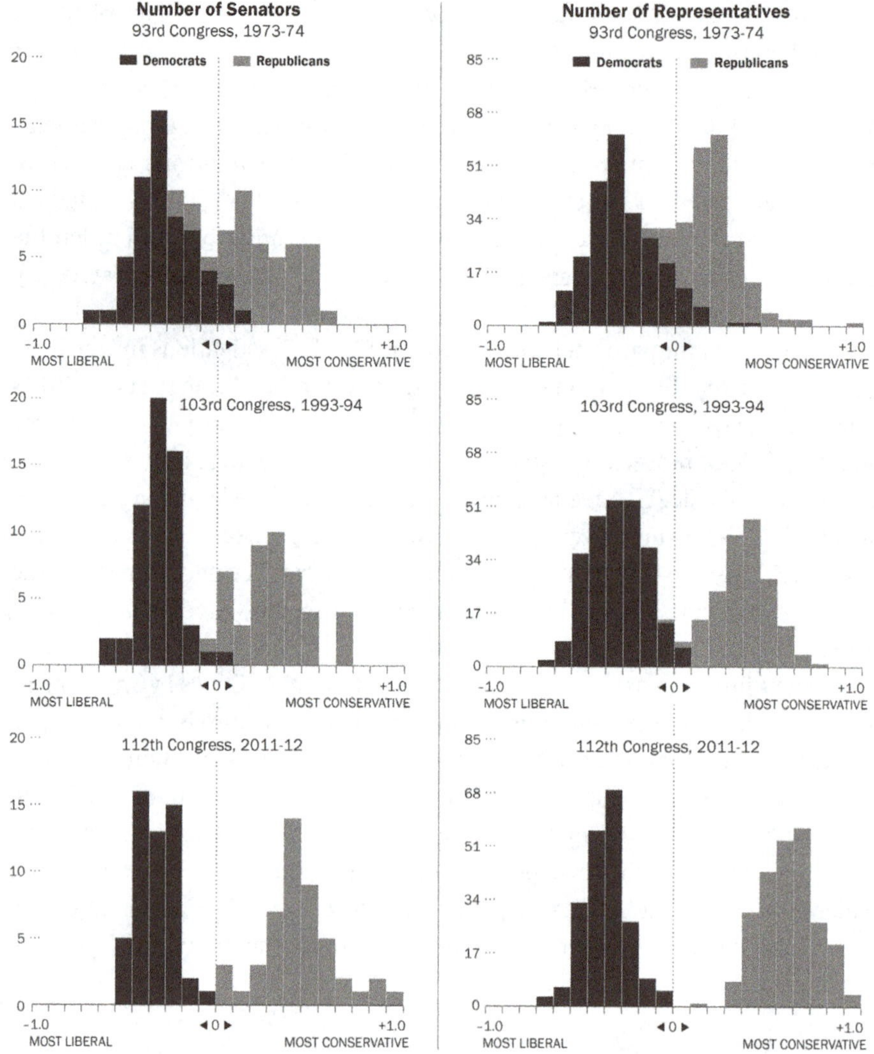

Sources: Royce Carroll, Jeff Lewis, James Lo, Nolan McCarty, Keith Poole and Howard Rosenthal.

Figure 7.6. Party polarization.
Source: Pew Research Centre.

shows the decline in overlap between liberals and conservatives that occurred between the 1960s and 2007.

These deep differences have given rise to much greater institutional combat as each party tries to make use of whatever rules and procedures they can find to undermine the other party and press for their own agenda. Because partisan polarization has coincided with long periods of divided government, institutional combat has also repeatedly broken out between Congress and the president. Since 1994 this combat has resulted in a presidential impeachment, repeated threats to shut down the government, and passage of a landmark piece of legislation without a single vote from the minority party.

The long periods of divided government experienced in recent decades have served to heighten polarization, giving each of the parties an institutional base from which to attack the other. The beginning of this chapter emphasized the importance of midterm elections as devices for enabling the public to register its disapproval with the direction in which the president was leading the country. Between 1994 and 2014, midterm election victories by the party out of power dramatically served that purpose. Remarkably however, none of these spectacular changes in voter preference led to a sustained period of undivided government. A mere two years after gaining control of both houses of Congress for the first time in half a century, the Republicans were defeated in the presidential election of 1996. In 2010, only four years after regaining control of Congress, the Democrats suffered the worst loss of seats in the House of Representatives since 1938, losing control of that body and seats in the Senate as well. In 2014, two years after President Obama's reelection, the Republicans regained both the House and Senate.

In 1994 Republicans gained control of both houses of Congress for the first time since the 1952 election. Sensing that Bill Clinton's efforts to expand government and raise taxes had become highly unpopular, the second-ranking House Republican, minority whip Newt Gingrich, persuaded more than 300 House candidates to sign a "Republican Contract with America" that promised to restore limited government by eliminating programs, lightening regulatory burdens, and cutting taxes. Although exit polls – surveys of voters after they voted – suggested that few voters had actually heard of the Republican manifesto, Clinton's attack on the contract during the campaign unwittingly served the Republican objective of turning the congressional elections into a national referendum on his presidency and the Democratic Party. The president's assault backfired, serving only to abet Republicans in their effort to highlight his failure to move Democrats toward the center and to mute partisan division in Washington.

In a sign that it planned to move in a more conservative direction, the new House Republican majority chose Gingrich, a staunch conservative, to be speaker. He viewed Congress as a key part of the corrupt Washington establishment and therefore sought to radically change how it functioned. He set out to reform House rules, promising to restore its constitutional responsibility to foster democratic debate and resolution. The number and size of committees were reduced, as were their staffs. Term limits were imposed on the speaker and on committee and subcommittee chairs. Closed-door hearings and unrecorded votes were prohibited. Gingrich pledged a renewed emphasis on legislative debate that would "promote competition between different political philosophies." Yet the basic thrust of the Republican reforms was to centralize power in the hands of the party leadership. Party leaders strengthened their hold over committee chairmen, who in turn were empowered over subcommittee leaders. For the first time since Cannon was shorn of his powers, the Speaker of the House presumed to command the counsels of government, restoring Congress as the first branch of government. As Gingrich seized control of the legislative initiative during the early months of the 104th Congress, Clinton issued a plaintive reminder that "the President is relevant here."

The House Republicans provoked a fierce battle over the budget by advancing a bold plan to balance it by 2002. Clinton rejected key specifics of the plan, especially an effort to scale back the growth of Medicare by encouraging beneficiaries to enroll in health maintenance organizations and other privately managed healthcare systems. To pressure Clinton into accepting its budget-cutting priorities, Congress refused to extend government borrowing privileges, thereby shutting down government offices and threatening to put the US treasury into default. These tactics backfired. Clinton's December 1995 veto of a sweeping budget bill that overhauled Medicare and revised decades of federal social policy roused popular support. Neither the Contract with America nor Speaker Gingrich's bravado had prepared the country for such a fundamental assault on the welfare state. In attacking Medicare and popular educational and environmental programs, Republicans went beyond their 1994 campaign promises. They, not Clinton, appeared to be the radicals in this budgetary brinkmanship. Clinton's triumph paved the way for his reelection victory a year later.

Clinton's reelection did not serve to dampen the House Republicans' partisan zeal. Rather, it goaded them into overreaching once again by impeaching him. In 1994 President Clinton asked the Justice Department to appoint a special prosecutor to investigate allegations against both him and his wife, Hillary Rodham Clinton, stemming from their involvement in a failed real estate development scheme called Whitewater. In January 1998, Congress authorized independent counsel Kenneth Starr to expand the "Whitewater" inquiry to pursue allegations that the president had had an affair with White House intern Monica Lewinsky, and that he and his friend Vernon Jordan had encouraged her to lie about it under oath. Clinton not only denied the affair with Lewinsky but accused Starr, a prominent Republican, and his supporters in Congress of orchestrating a slanderous, partisan campaign to weaken the president.

Starr's relentless investigation uncovered evidence that forced Clinton to admit he had had an "improper relationship" with Lewinsky. In September 1998, Starr issued a report compiling a devastating chronicle of the president's adulterous affair and his months of subsequent lies. The House of Representatives, voting largely along party lines, approved a resolution calling for a full inquiry into possible grounds for impeachment. But the public continued to express overwhelming approval of Clinton's performance in office: Americans appreciated his successful management of the economy; disapproved of Starr's prosecutorial tactics; and were disgusted by the Republicans' sensationalization of the prosecutor's findings. Defying opinion polls, the House voted to impeach Clinton on charges of perjury and obstruction of justice. The vote split along partisan lines, with only six Democrats voting for any of the articles of impeachment and only one Republican voting against them. After a five-week trial, on February 12, 1999, the Senate failed to produce the 2 to 3 vote needed to convict Clinton on any of the charges.

In 2006, Democrats scored massive gains in the House of Representatives and impressive gains in the Senate to regain full control of Congress for the first time since 1994. Because the Democrats lacked a veto-proof majority in the Senate, their landslide victory did not immediately result in any major legislative victories. The 1994 Republicans were much more fortunate because much of their ambition lay in *preventing* the passage of Clinton administration initiatives, whereas the 2006 Democrats sought new policy reforms which President Bush could still prevent by exercising his veto. The most important short-term consequence of the Democratic victory was the election of Nancy Pelosi (D–CA) as Speaker of the House. Pelosi proved to be the most powerful speaker since Gingrich. Like Gingrich, she came from the more extreme, not the moderate, wing of her party. Her great influence would not be felt until the 2008 election put a Democrat, Barack Obama, in the White House.

With control of Congress and the presidency in Democratic hands, the period 2008–10 would witness the greatest outpouring of new and ambitious policy changes since the heyday of LBJ's Great Society, in 1964–66. In order to cultivate close ties to the House leadership and ensure passage of his top legislative priority, healthcare reform, the president put the chief responsibility for crafting the legislation in the hands of Congress. Pelosi showed extraordinary leadership ability as she kept her fractious supporters in line behind a truly ambitious path-breaking bill. However, she paid an enormous price for this singleness of purpose. She failed to obtain the vote of a single Republican for the measure. By contrast, Republicans supported the Social Security Act of 1935 by a margin of better than 3 to 1 in the Senate and better than 5 to 1 in the House. A majority of House Republicans supported Medicare. Thirteen Senate Republicans also voted for it, while seventeen were opposed. Each of these landmark pieces of legislation could make a credible claim to having been passed on a bipartisan basis. The Healthcare Reform law of 2010 could make no such claim.

Final passage of the Healthcare Act was only achieved because the House and Senate Democratic leaders resorted to an irregular and highly controversial procedural maneuver. On November 7, 2009 the House passed its version of health reform by 220 to 215 votes. On December 24, 2009 the Senate cut off a filibuster and passed its own version of health reform by a vote of 60 to 39. But before a conference committee could forge a compromise and obtain passage from both houses, the Senate lost the sixty-member majority they needed for cloture against the filibuster the Republicans had promised to mount against a compromise bill. Senator Edward Kennedy (D–MA) died leaving the Democrats with a Senate majority of only fifty-nine. A special election held to replace him was won by a Republican, Scott Brown, who had pledged to support a Republican filibuster. To thwart the Republicans, the House and Senate leadership found a way to avoid the need for a cloture vote. They adapted a procedure designed for dealing with strictly budgetary issues called reconciliation to enable the Senate to pass the measure by majority vote. No piece of legislation as important as the healthcare bill had ever been adopted by the Senate in this manner. The Senate Parliamentarian ruled that using reconciliation for this purpose did not violate Senate rules. Nonetheless, Republicans called it a violation of Senate tradition, likening it to the "nuclear option" for circumventing the Democrats' filibuster of Bush's judicial nominees that they had refrained from invoking when they were in the majority. The nuclear option would have been to change the Senate rules to end a filibuster by a simple majority vote. Because the healthcare measure proved to be unpopular with the public, the Republicans benefited politically from their unqualified opposition to it. Another major Democratic initiative, the nearly $800 billion stimulus package aimed at resuscitating the economy in the wake of the financial collapse of 2008, likewise received no Republican votes in the House and only three in the Senate.

If public opinion had been strongly in support of these initiatives, the lack of minority party support might not have proven so politically damaging. But opinion polls revealed a majority of the public opposed both of them. The Democrats gambled that once the bills passed, their popularity would improve, but this was not the case. The unambiguous opposition to these measures shown by the Republicans established a clear choice in voters' minds. If one opposed these new laws, one should vote for the Republicans, and in the 2010 congressional elections a great majority of voters did just that. Republicans regained control of the House of Representatives, gaining fifty-five seats. They also picked up six seats in the Senate. Lacking a Senate majority, the Republicans could not repeal Obamacare. However, as the new program began to display significant difficulties, they refused to cooperate with the Democrats to revise it, sticking to their pledge to repeal the policy in its entirety whenever they could gain the power to do so.

The heightened level of polarization was further evidenced by the House Republican leadership's threat to shut down the government unless President Obama agreed to eliminate funding for Planned Parenthood, a nongovernmental organization that distributed birth control and conducted abortions. At the very last minute, just before the federal government was to run out of money, a compromise was reached and the Republicans agreed to authorize spending for the rest of the fiscal year.

After obtaining control of both houses by winning back the Senate in 2014, the Republicans further extended their policy of noncooperation with President

Table 7.4. Critical midterm elections.

1994	Republicans regain the House for the first time in fifty years, and also gain control of the Senate
2006	Democrats regain control of both houses of Congress
2010	Return to divided government, Republican regain the House
2014	Republicans regain the Senate

Obama. The chairs of the House and Senate Budget committees announced that they would refuse to consider the president's budget request and not even hold hearings on it. In a joint statement, they showed just how polarizing the budgetary process had become:

> Nothing in the president's prior budgets – none of which have ever balanced – has shown that the Obama administration has any real interest in actually solving our fiscal challenges or saving critical programs like Medicare and Social Security from insolvency ... Rather than spend time on a proposal that, if anything like this administration's previous budgets, will double down on the same failed policies that have led to the worst economic recovery in modern times, Congress should continue our work on building a budget that balances and that will foster a healthy economy.

Likewise, when Supreme Court Justice Antonin Scalia died unexpectedly in February of 2016, Senate Republicans refused to consider confirming Merrick Garland, Obama's choice, to be Scalia's successor. Majority leader Mitch McConnell argued that since the vacancy had occurred in a presidential election year, the choice of a new justice should rest with the newly elected president.

Looking Forward

As Chapter 3 described, the Constitutional Convention succeeded in large measure because of the capacity of the delegates to deliberate. Deliberation is the art of reasoning together. It involves a complex set of skills and attitudes on the part of those engaged in arriving at a collective decision. Most importantly, deliberators must respect those with whom they disagree and keep an open mind about the possible avenues for settling differences. Like the Constitutional Convention, Congress is a representative body whose members' interests and political views differ. However, as Jefferson said in his first inaugural speech, "Every difference of opinion is not a difference of principle." Growing ideological and political polarization makes Congress ever less capable of operating deliberatively. Instead of deliberating amongst themselves, the polarized congressional parties increasingly rely on elections to determine policy outcomes. Whichever party gains a majority, imposes its will on the minority. The minority party waits until the next election in the hope of becoming the majority. Then it can undo key policy decisions made during the previous two years. If each party controls one house, or if the president is of a different party than the one that controls either or both houses, polarization insures stalemate.

To restore a deliberative atmosphere requires a willingness to sacrifice short-term policy gains. This requires leadership. Majority leaders would need to impress upon their members the importance of encouraging the minority to offer policy suggestions; to take those suggestions seriously and to modify policy proposals even when they could achieve victory without compromise. Likewise, minority leaders would need to encourage their members to respond favorably to such outreach, even at the cost of whatever political advantage might be gained by outright opposition.

Polarization not only discourages deliberation, it also reduces Congress's ability to check the executive. As the Watergate scandal showed, Congress is best able to act against the president when the two parties display a common front. A divided legislative branch will struggle in its effort to countervail the branch that is by its very nature unified. Again, the capacity to unite to check the executive depends on leadership. *Federalist* 51 argued that in order for Congress to exert such a salutary check, "Ambition must be made to counteract ambition. The interest of the man must be connected with the constitutional rights of the place." In other words, the ambitions of congressional leaders must remain grounded in the success of Congress. Their own power and influence is thus tied to the power and influence of Congress as a whole. The future independence and strength of Congress rests on the willingness of congressional leaders to accept the dictates of *Federalist* 51 and place their institutional responsibility ahead of strictly partisan and ideological motives and tie their ambition to the wellbeing of the branch they lead.

CHAPTER SUMMARY

A contemporary portrait of the US Congress:

* Two of Congress's most important contemporary functions, neither of which is mentioned in the Constitution, are oversight of the executive branch and constituency service.
* The most important decisions regarding the shape and scope of a particularly bill are usually made in committee, not on the floor.
* Congressmen are heavily dependent on their personal staffs, committee staffs, and congressional research organizations.

Congress and the Constitution:

* The Framers designed the Congress both to provide for democratic accountability and to limit the threat to liberty and stability resulting from an excess of democracy.

* Article I of the Constitution established Congress as the preeminent branch of government, granting it seventeen legislative powers, including the most important of all governmental powers: taxation, regulation of commerce, and declaration of war.
* Even as they were checking excessive democratic responsiveness by creating a bicameral legislature, the Framers were promoting democratic responsiveness by providing for midterm congressional elections.

The era of congressional dominance:

* For more than half of the United States' political development, Congress served as the chief national policy-making body.
* Henry Clay exploited his position as Speaker of the House to exert powerful leadership and discipline of that body.
* Party organization of Congress helped it fulfill its obligation to embody majority sentiment and hold the executive in check.
* During the mid nineteenth century Congress became the forum for passionate and lively debate over such critical issues as slavery, tariff policy, the bank and the money supply, helping to draw the public into struggles about the most fundamental political issues.
* After the Civil War, Congress achieved its highest level of dominance by combining strong congressional leadership with even greater political party control of the congressional nomination and election process. The tight grip of party leadership deprived Congress of its ability to serve as the primary arena for debating the great issue of the time, as it had done before the Civil War.

The critical choices that transformed Congress:

* The increasing prominence of the presidency caused Congress to find ways to maintain its power.
* The Progressive revolt of the early twentieth century deprived party leaders of the power to choose chairs. Instead, committee assignments and chairmanships were based on seniority.
* Congresspersons increasingly came to see themselves as "policy entrepreneurs," the formulators of new policies and programs for their constituencies and for the organized interests with whom they were allied.
* Congress became increasingly devoted to the task of overseeing the administration of public policy. It used committee hearings, investigations, and individual member or staff interrogations to try to hold the executive accountable.

The impact of institutional combat, divided government, and party polarization:

* Starting in the late 1960s, a resurgence of congressional power was spurred by dissatisfaction with presidential leadership of the war in Vietnam and by President Nixon's abuses of executive power.

* In the 1970s Congress reformed its own internal procedures. Both chambers reduced the power of committee chairs. Power flowed upward to party leaders and downward to subcommittees and individual members.
* Between 1994 and 2010, the party out of power won three overwhelming midterm election victories. These results vividly demonstrate the importance of midterm elections as devices for enabling the public to register disapproval with the political direction in which the president was leading the country.
* The most important congressional development in recent decades has been the ever-growing polarization between the majority and minority parties.

SUGGESTED READINGS

Cooper, Joseph, ed. *Congress and the Decline of Public Trust.* Boulder, CO: Westview Press, 1999.

Dodd, Lawrence C., and Bruce Ian Oppenheimer, eds. *Congress Reconsidered,* 7th edn. Washington, DC: CQ Press, 2000.

Dodd, Lawrence C., and Richard Schott, eds. *Congress and the Administrative State.* New York: John Wiley, 1979.

Fenno, Richard E. *Congressmen in Committees.* Boston: Little, Brown, 1973.

Home Style: House Members in Their Districts. Boston: Little, Brown, 1978.

Fiorina, Morris. *Congress: Keystone of the Washington Establishment,* 2nd edn. New Haven, CT: Yale University Press, 1989.

Ginsberg, Benjamin, and Martin Shefter. *Politics by Other Means: Politicians, Prosecutors, and the Press from Watergate to Whitewater,* 3d edn. New York: W. W. Norton, 2003.

Hibbing, John R., and Elizabeth Theiss-Morse. *Congress as Public Enemy: Public Attitudes Toward American Political Institutions.* New York: Cambridge University Press, 1996.

Jacobson, Gary. *The Politics of Congressional Elections,* 5th edn. New York: Addison-Wesley, 2000.

Mayhew, David. *Congress: The Electoral Connection.* New Haven, CT: Yale University Press, 1986.

Peters, Ronald M., Jr. *The American Speakership: The Office in Historical Perspective,* 2nd edn. Baltimore, MD: Johns Hopkins University Press, 1997.

Rohde, David W. *Parties and Leaders in the Postreform House.* University of Chicago Press, 1991.

Schickler, Eric. *Disjointed Pluralism: Institutional Innovation and the Development of the U.S. Congress.* Princeton, NJ: Princeton University Press, 2001.

Sundquist, James L. *The Decline and Resurgence of Congress.* Washington, DC: Brookings Institution Press, 2002.

Theriault, Sean. *Party Polarization in Congress.* New York: Cambridge University Press, 2008.

Wilson, Woodrow. *Congressional Government.* Boston: Houghton Mifflin, 1885.

Wirls, Daniel, and Stephen Wirls. *The Invention of the United States Senate.* Baltimore, MD: Johns Hopkins University Press, 2004.

8 The Presidency

CHAPTER OVERVIEW

This chapter focuses on:

- **A contemporary portrait of the US presidency.**
- **The critical choices made by Washington, Jefferson, Jackson, and Lincoln.**
- **The critical choices involved in the creation of the personalized presidency.**
- **The impact of the Cold War and television.**
- **The opportunities and hazards posed by the personalized presidency.**

On September 22, 1993, in the midst of his battle to overhaul the US healthcare system, President Bill Clinton gave a critical speech to a joint session of Congress. The president considered this speech the most important one of his life, the moment at which he would launch a titanic struggle to enact a program that would affect the lives of every citizen and one-seventh of the US economy. Understandably, Clinton felt great pressure as he looked out on the assembled dignitaries, but tension nearly dissolved into panic when he found the wrong speech displayed in the teleprompter. He furtively signaled to Vice President Al Gore, sitting behind him on the dais, and then proceeded to improvise. After seven harrowing minutes, the president's aides, notified by the vice president of the mishap, managed to insert the right speech.

Clinton's prepared remarks called for government to "guarantee all Americans a comprehensive package of [healthcare] benefits over an entire lifetime." He brandished a red, white, and blue "health security card" – similar to the Social Security card Americans carry – to symbolize that this plan would be the greatest extension of the welfare state since enactment of Social Security in 1935. The program would mandate employer-paid insurance, provide benefits to nonworkers, and create federal purchasing alliances to regulate managed care and control costs.

The president's speech was very well received in the hall. Clinton's pollster, Stanley Greenberg, reported that the Dayton, Ohio, focus group he had convened to provide instantaneous public reaction was also highly favorable to both Clinton's impromptu and planned remarks. The president and his aides would have been shocked to discover that this spine-tingling oratorical episode would prove to be the high point of their battle for healthcare reform. The teleprompter gaffe foreshadowed more serious and irremediable problems. Ensuring that "No American will go without healthcare" was a popular idea, but the complexity of the 1,342-page plan and the prospect of government controls on such a large and pervasive industry eventually turned the public and Congress against it. In September 1994, almost a year to the day after Clinton introduced the Health Security Act with such fanfare, Senate majority leader George Mitchell declared the president's bill dead.

Clinton's healthcare debacle illustrates that surveys and focus groups can be a very unreliable basis of support for presidential causes. A president, particularly one as politically gifted as Clinton, can dominate the national political agenda. But as both of his successors, George W. Bush and Barack Obama would also discover, the president's powerful public presence does not necessarily enable him to achieve his policy goals.

This chapter begins with a contemporary portrait of the presidency. It then analyzes how the presidency was intended to fit into the overall constitutional order and how the first, precedent-setting president interpreted his constitutional mandate. Next, it looks at the democratization of the office, especially as it was accomplished by Thomas Jefferson and Andrew Jackson. It discusses how Abraham Lincoln harnessed the democratic energy that was now attached to the office to produce a new public philosophy, a "new birth of freedom" that ended slavery and revised the Constitution to guarantee civil rights. Then the chapter charts the rise of the modern presidency after its post-Lincoln recession, with special attention to the role of the Progressive movement. The focus shifts to Franklin D. Roosevelt and the New Deal to show the flowering of the modern presidency. The rest of the chapter describes the presidency as it developed since FDR. The focus here is on the growing personalization of the presidency, how it has come increasingly to serve as the very personification of government and the opportunities and pitfalls that this rise in the prominence of the office has created.

The Presidency: A Contemporary Portrait

Article II of the Constitution vests the *executive power* in the president. However, unlike Article I, which limits the power of Congress to the legislative powers "herein granted," there is no such restriction placed on the executive power. Thus, there is no explicit definition of what the executive power is and how far that power extends. Therefore, the nature and extent of executive power have been contested throughout the course of American political development and remain so to this day. This contemporary portrait examines how presidents exercise the formal grants of power Article II assigns as well as the many other exercises of formal and informal authority an expansive understanding of executive power has enabled them to perform.

National Security and Diplomacy

> *The President shall be Commander in Chief of the Army and Navy of the United States, and of the Militia of the several States, when called into the actual Service of the United States . . .*

As commander in chief, the president presides over a vast military establishment. As of 2017, 1,281,900 persons served in the active military plus an additional 801,200 people in reserve units. In 2016, the defense budget amounted to 580.3 billion.

Although the Constitution grants Congress the power to declare war, World War II was the last war that received such a declaration. In many instances, presidents have insisted that their commander-in-chief power is sufficient for committing American troops into battle. Thus, the president has acquired considerable autonomy in determining how and when the United States will use the considerable force at its disposal.

> *He shall have Power, by and with the Advice and Consent of the Senate, to make Treaties, provided two thirds of the Senators present concur.*

Over the course of American political development, the president has signed and Congress has ratified more than a thousand treaties, among the most notable in recent decades being the North American Free Trade Agreement (see Chapter 6), entered into with Canada and Mexico, and the treaty to reduce stockpiles of nuclear weapons that President Obama signed with Russia in April 2010.

However, the most important international agreement of recent years, the 2015 Iran nuclear deal, whose official name was the Joint Comprehensive Plan of Action, was not subject to congressional approval. This deal called for Iran to reduce its nuclear capabilities in exchange for the elimination of the economic sanctions that had been imposed. The Obama administration claimed that even though it involved complex agreements regarding matters of enormous import, it was not a treaty at all but rather an executive agreement. Therefore, it could be entered into by the president alone pursuant to his executive power.

In the face of congressional criticism, Obama agreed to give Congress some ability to review the agreement. He signed a bill enabling Congress to disapprove the pact by a majority vote of each house. But this bill gave Congress far less power than a treaty proposal would have granted. To pass a treaty, two-thirds of the Congress must agree and the president has no opportunity to exercise a veto. Since his proposal took the form of an ordinary bill, Obama could exercise his veto over it and then it would require two-thirds of each house to override his veto. Rather than requiring the support of two-thirds of the Senate, he only needed the support of one-third plus one of either house to allow the deal to remain in place. Both houses of Congress were in Republican hands when the deal was signed, and therefore it was politically far more expedient for the president to treat the matter as an executive agreement rather than a treaty.

There is no clear line between what constitutes a treaty and what constitutes an executive agreement. Presidents have often chosen to treat international negotiations as executive agreements rather than treaties in order to avoid the cumbersome and potentially unsuccessful effort to get the Congress to go along. In theory, an executive agreement has less standing than a treaty because it is only binding on the president who signed it. But, in practice, governments are very reluctant to renege on deals made with foreign governments, even if there is no strict legal barrier to doing so. As this example indicates, in diplomacy as well as war-making, modern presidents have granted themselves a great deal of decision-making autonomy.

Legislator in Chief

> *He shall from time to time give to the Congress Information on the State of the Union, and recommend to their Consideration such Measures as he shall judge necessary and expedient.*

Presidents do far more than make specific recommendations to Congress. Indeed, they have become the dominant force in setting the congressional legislative agenda and in serving as the chief advocate for the matters they place on that agenda. Regardless of the Constitution's vesting of legislative power in Congress, in practice the chief executive now functions as legislator in chief. He makes use of the televised State of the Union Address, delivered in February of each year, to outline and advocate for that agenda.The federal budget, although it requires congressional approval, is drafted by an executive agency, the Office of Management and Budget. Although congressional committees and congressional leaders play an active role in the crafting of statutes, it has fallen to the president to serve as the chief instigator and promoter of landmark legislation.

The president's role as legislator in chief is exemplified by the passage of the Affordable Care Act (ACA) in 2010. The ACA is one of the most ambitious new social programs adopted in modern times. Congress passed it, but the president was its champion. He took the lead in mobilizing public opinion to pressure Congress to act.

President Obama launched his healthcare campaign by hosting the White House Forum on Healthcare Reform, attended by senior members of Congress and leaders of such prestigious and powerful lobbying organizations as the Teamsters Union, the American Association of Retired People, the US Chamber of Congress, and the Children's Defense Fund. The only other speaker to address the entire gathering was not a healthcare expert nor a prominent politician, but rather an ordinary citizen, a firefighter and emergency medical technician from Dublin, Indiana, Travis Ulerick. Ulerick had served as a host at one of the hundreds of healthcare community discussions that the White House had sponsored and that were attended by 30,000 people. The reason for featuring him was to demonstrate to members of Congress that Obama's healthcare plan had the strong support of people who were just like the voters in their home districts.

The energy and effort that President Obama put into galvanizing public opinion for healthcare reform exceeded what any previous president had expended on a single legislative proposal. In June 2009, ABC News televised *Questions for the President: Prescription for America.* On a Wednesday night, during the coveted primetime hour between 10 and 11 p.m., President Obama answered questions about his healthcare proposal from an audience chosen by ABC to represent a cross section of ordinary people. The White House organized nine events with a similar format that it called "Town Meetings" in towns and cities in various parts of the country. In addition, President Obama gave fifty-four speeches and public statements on healthcare reform and devoted thirteen of his Saturday radio and internet addresses to the topic.

Presidential Vetoes

> *Every Bill which shall have passed the House of Representatives and the Senate, shall, before it become a law, be presented to the President of the United States: If he approve he shall sign it, but if not he shall return it, with his Objections to that House in which it shall have originated . . .*
>
> *If any Bill shall not be returned by the President within ten Days (Sundays excepted) after it shall have been presented to him, the Same shall be a Law, in like Manner as if he had signed it, unless the Congress by their Adjournment prevent its Return, in which Case it shall not be a Law . . .*

The rarity with which vetoes are overridden testifies to what an important source of strength they are for the president. The mere threat of a veto may often prove sufficient to impede the passage of a bill the president disapproves of. Ordinarily,

Table 8.1. List of presidents showing how they have varied greatly in their use of the veto power.

Congresses	President	Regular vetoes	Pocket vetoes	Total vetoes	Vetoes overridden
1st–4th	George Washington	2	–	2	–
5th–6th	John Adams	–	–	–	–
7lh–10lh	Thomas Jefferson	–	–	–	–
11th–14th	James Madison	5	2	7	–
15th–18th	James Monroe	1	–	1	–
19th–20th	John Quincy Adams	–	–	–	–
21st–24th	Andrew Jackson	5	7	12	–
25th–26th	Martin Van Buren	–	1	1	–
27th	William Henry Harrison	–	–	–	–
27th–28th	John Tyler	6	4	10	1
29th–30th	James K. Polk	2	1	3	–
31st	Zachary Taylor	–	–	–	–
31st–32nd	Millard Fillmore	–	–	–	–
33rd–34th	Franklin Pierce	9	–	9	5
35th–36th	James Buchanan	4	3	7	–
37th–39th	Abraham Lincoln	2	5	7	–
39th–40th	Andrew Johnson	21	8	29	15
41st–44th	Ulysses S. Grant	45	48	93	4
45th–46lh	Rutherford B. Hayes	12	1	13	1
47th	James A. Garfield	–	–	–	–
47th–48th	Chester A. Arthur	4	8	12	1
49th–50th	Grover Cleveland	304	110	414	2
51st–52nd	Benjamin Harrison	19	25	44	1
53rd–54th	Grover Cleveland	42	128	170	5
55th–57th	William McKinley	6	36	42	–
57th–60th	Theodore Roosevelt	42	40	82	1
61st–62nd	William H. Taft	30	9	39	1
63rd–66th	Woodrow Wilson	33	11	44	6
67th	Warren G. Harding	5	1	6	–
68th–70th	Calvin Coolidge	20	30	50	4
71st–72nd	Herbert C. Hoover	21	16	37	3
73rd–79th	Franklin D. Roosevelt	372	263	635	9
79th–82nd	Harry S. Truman	180	70	250	12
83rd–86th	Dwight D. Eisenhower	73	108	181	2
87th–88th	John F. Kennedy	to	9	21	–
88th–90st	Lyndon B. Johnson	16	14	30	–
91st–93rd	Richard M. Nixon	26	17	43	7
93rd–94th	Gerald R. Ford	48	18	66	12
95th–96th	James Earl Carter	13	18	31	2
97th–100th	Ronald Reagan	39	39	78	9
101st–102nd	George H. W. Bush	29	15	44	1
103rd–106th	William J. Clinton	36	1	37	2
107th–110th	George W. Bush	12	–	12	4
111th–114th	Barack H. Obama	10	–	10	1
Total		1506	1066	2572	111

the president has ten days within which to issue a veto. However, if a bill reaches the president less than ten days before Congress adjourns, he can keep it from becoming law simply by refusing to sign it. That is what is meant by a "pocket veto." The most common reason for casting vetoes is that the opposition party controls Congress and is therefore in a position to pass bills that the president opposes.

The veto has two significant limitations. First, it cannot be used selectively. If a president approves of certain provisions of a bill but opposes others, he has no choice but to either sign the whole bill or veto it in its entirety. Many state governors can exercise a line item veto, meaning they can select out individual parts of a bill and veto only those sections. But the Supreme Court ruled in *Clinton v. City of New York* (1998) that the president has no such power. Second, the veto is a purely negative instrument of power: it does not enable the president to force Congress to act affirmatively. President Bush relied on signing statements to minimize the first limitation by appending signing statements to statutes. President Obama tried to overcome the second limitation by issuing executive orders to make policy changes that Congress had refused to enact.

When a president signs a bill into law he may append a written statement to it. Such statements are often relatively innocuous, but they can also announce a president's reservations about the constitutionality of one or another of the law's provisions, thus exempting the chief executive from Article II's requirement to "faithfully execute the laws." George W. Bush used signing statements more aggressively than any previous president to indicate his unwillingness to enforce aspects of laws that he considered to be unconstitutional. The 130 signing statements he issued contained 1,100 challenges to provisions of congressional legislation that he signed into law. Critics of Bush's use of signing statements said that they were tantamount to the exercise of a line item veto since they announced his intention of selectively implementing a law.

Barack Obama's response to congressional unwillingness to act on proposals he considered to be crucial was to issue them as executive orders. Executive orders are written instructions that the president issues for the purpose of informing his subordinates as to how he expects them to implement and enforce laws. For example, in 2014, frustrated by Congress's inability to pass immigration reform legislation, Obama issued an executive order preventing the deportation of more than 4 million illegal immigrants. These were the parents of children who were legal by virtue of having been born in the United States. Obama justified his action on the basis of what is called "prosecutorial discretion." This principle acknowledges the reality that law enforcement officials must retain some latitude in deciding which violators of the law to prosecute and which not to prosecute. The president claimed that he was simply instructing government lawyers about whom not to prosecute. Critics claimed that this executive order exceeded the bounds of permissible prosecutorial discretion because it exempted such a numerous class of people from deportation. They also pointed out that it did not merely prevent deportation but also took positive steps to aid this class of illegal immigrants by issuing them work permits. A federal court sided with the critics and the Obama order did not go into effect.

In his first few weeks in office, President Trump likewise made aggressive use of executive orders. His most controversial order was to impose a temporary ban on travel to the US from seven Muslim countries. He also reinstated the Keystone Pipeline that President Obama had refused to authorize, ordered a hiring freeze in certain segments of the federal government, and authorized construction of a wall along the US–Mexico border.

Managing the Executive Branch

> *He shall nominate, and by and with the Advice and Consent of the Senate, shall appoint Ambassadors, other public Ministers and Consuls, Judges of the supreme Court, and all other Officers of the United States, whose Appointments are not herein otherwise provided for, and which shall be established by Law . . .*

The president appoints between 1,200 and 1,400 people to offices subject to Senate confirmation. This number includes the heads of departments and key federal agencies; federal judges, including members of the Supreme Court; ambassadors; and the Chairman of the Joint Chiefs of Staff as well as the chiefs of each of the armed services. It also includes key departmental subordinates who play a variety of different roles and have a variety of different names including: undersecretary, assistant secretary, deputy secretary, and general counsel. In addition, the president makes over 300 appointments that are not subject to Senate approval. Many of these are to commissions and councils that have little power, but roughly a third of them are to the Executive Office of the President (EOP), where they provide critical administrative support to the president. Considering that there are almost 3 million federal employees, the number subject to presidential appointment is quite small. The rest of the federal workforce operates under civil service regulations that insulate them from politics (see Chapter 10).

The heads of the fifteen executive departments comprise the president's cabinet. These departments are listed in Table 8.2. Unlike in a parliamentary system, the cabinet is not an official policy-making body. The president is not obligated to ask it for its collective opinion, nor to go along with those opinions. Presidents vary in how frequently they call the cabinet into session. Reagan held thirty-six cabinet meetings while Clinton held only six. Presidents often find it far more useful to speak informally to those few cabinet members who have deep

Table 8.2. Executive departments.

US Department of Agriculture
US Department of Commerce
US Department of Defense
US Department of Education
US Department of Energy
US Department of Health and Human Services
US Department of Homeland Security
US Department of Housing and Urban Development
US Department of Justice
US Department of Labor
US Department of State
US Department of the Interior
US Department of the Treasury
US Department of Transportation
US Department of Veterans Affairs

Source: Whitehouse.gov

knowledge of a particular problem he is facing, than to call the entire group into session for a formal meeting. Two of the most important federal positions, Director of the Office of Management and Budget and National Security Advisor, are not included in the cabinet, and the latter is not even subject to Senate approval.

The president elect sets about the business of selecting presidential appointees immediately after election. Indeed, presidential candidates choose trusted advisors to make preparations for the transition of power long before an election takes place. In May 2016, even before he was officially the Republican nominee, Donald Trump chose New Jersey governor Chris Christie to lead his transition team. In August of 2016, Hillary Clinton chose former interior secretary Ken Salazar to head her team. Nonetheless, the actual appointments process is invariably chaotic and contentious. The number of would-be appointees far outnumbers the positions available. The president is forced to choose among qualified persons all of whom have been active in the campaign. And, despite his desire to reward the deserving, he may well decide that the special expertise and experience required to fill certain posts requires him to appoint people who did not support him, including some who supported his opponents.

> *He may require the Opinion, in writing, of the principal Officer in each of the executive Departments, upon any Subject relating to the Duties of their respective Offices.*

This is the only clause in the Constitution that describes how presidential appointees relate to the president. It gives no indication of the breadth and depth of executive branch responsibilities, nor of the president's deep immersion in the attempt to direct and manage executive branch activities. Federal judges and many members of independent regulatory commissions are appointed by the president but cannot be fired by him, thus he exerts direct control over an even smaller number of federal employees than his appointments power would seem to indicate. Nor does he have automatic authority to rearrange the bureaus, agencies, commissions, and departments that comprise the executive branch. Under current law, such reorganizations must pass Congress. President Bush undertook two major reorganizations: the creation of the Department of Homeland Security as authorized by the Homeland Security Act of 2002 and the reorganization of the intelligence services as authorized by the Intelligence Reform and Terrorism Prevention Act of 2004. President Obama did not embark on any reorganizations.

As the size, complexity, and scope of the executive branch has grown, the challenge of controlling it has grown apace. As we shall see later in this chapter, it was only in the late 1930s that Congress created an Executive Office of the President, providing him with staff to help him manage the federal bureaucracy. In Chapter 10 we will discuss two of its most important managerial tools, the Office of Management and Budget and the National Security Staff.

The EOP is now so large that most of it is housed next door to the White House in the Eisenhower Executive Office Building. But, because the president needs a great deal of staff assistance on a minute-to-minute basis, the offices of some of his closest aides are in the West Wing of the White House. Each president has his own distinctive approach to governing and therefore the precise nature and composition of the West Wing changes with each

Table 8.3. Executive Office of the President.

Council of Economic Advisers
Council on Environmental Quality
Office of Management and Budget
Office of National Drug Control Policy
Office of Science and Technology Policy
Executive Residence
National Security Council
Office of Administration
Office of the Vice President
Office of the United States Trade Representative
White House Office
President's Intelligence Advisory Board

Source: Whitehouse.gov

presidential administration. However, certain key aspects remain constant. The West Wing always includes a press secretary and a staff of speech writers to manage the president's relations with the media and to produce drafts of speeches and messages. It also includes the White House Chief of Staff, who supervises and coordinates the West Wing as a whole. That person may also serve as the president's personal chief of staff, working closely with him to plan political and legislative strategy and how best to manage the president's time. However, the closest and most trusted aide to the president may hold some other post in the West Wing. Valerie Jarrett was widely considered to be the advisor whom Obama most relied on. Her official title was Senior Advisor to the President and Assistant to the President for Intergovernmental Relations and Public Engagement.

The Vice President

Article II of the Constitution also provides for a vice president but does not specify the vice president's duties. That role had shrunk to virtual insignificance during the nineteenth century. Martin Van Buren (1837–41) was the last incumbent vice president elected president until George H. W. Bush (1989–93). Other nineteenth-century vice presidents - often chosen to provide geographical balance to the presidential ticket - succeeded to the presidency because of the death of the president, but not one of these "accidental presidents" was elected to a full term. It was not until the election of 1904 that an "accidental" president, Theodore Roosevelt, was elected on his own.

When FDR died, it was obvious that he had failed to fully prepare Vice President Harry Truman to take over. This dilemma created sufficient public anxiety to encourage future presidents to confide more fully in their vice presidents and provide more extensive briefings, particularly about national security. Eisenhower initiated this new relationship by giving Vice President Richard Nixon extensive diplomatic responsibilities. Reagan made Vice President George H. W. Bush head of a taskforce to provide regulatory relief for business. Clinton put Vice President Al Gore in charge of a major initiative to reform the federal bureaucracy. George W. Bush relied on Vice President Dick Cheney with regard to a whole raft of domestic and national security matters. Cheney is widely believed to have been the most powerful vice president ever.

President Obama also chose to give his vice president, Joseph Biden, very important and visible responsibilities. In 2009 he put Biden in charge of implementing the $787 billion stimulus package passed by Congress to bring the economy out of the doldrums created by the 2008 financial crisis. Obama also called upon the foreign policy expertise Biden had garnered as chairman of the

Senate Foreign Relations Committee. Biden was a major participant in President Obama's extended deliberations regarding the decision to send 30,000 additional troops to Afghanistan. He also served as the lead administration official in dealing with Iraq.

Party and Celebrity

The Framers of the Constitution abhorred political parties and feared that the president might become so personally popular as to overturn the constitutional balance and become, in fact if not in name, a king. Nonetheless, the president now serves as party leader and has become a dominant public celebrity. Presidents are their party's most effective fundraisers and they dominate its national committee. The president often campaigns for party candidates.

The president commands virtually constant media attention. The public is kept informed of his activities, even those that would normally be considered private. Not only did the public learn that the Obamas had a dog but it knew that it was a male, neutered, Portuguese water dog named Bo. President Bill Clinton told an MTV audience about his underwear preference, briefs not boxers. Donald Trump was a prominent celebrity even before taking office. As president, he has made an unprecedented effort to dominate the news cycle. His adversarial stance vis-à-vis the media makes him the subject of constant media attention, as does his continual use of Twitter to comment on a wide range of topics ranging from foreign affairs to complaints about media treatment of himself and his family.

CRITICAL THINKING QUESTION: ADMIRABLE QUALITIES IN A PRESIDENT

In the rest of this chapter you will read about many presidents. When you have finished the chapter, pick the president you most admire and explain why.

CRITICAL CHOICE: SETTING PRECEDENTS

The description of presidential powers and responsibilities in Article II of the Constitution is remarkably short. The first president, George Washington, made a number of crucial decisions regarding how the chief executive would actually function and how broadly he should construe his authority.

As we discussed in Chapter 3, the decision to establish a president and to grant him significant powers was made grudgingly. The only reason that many doubters about the wisdom of granting a single man so much power supported this decision was their certainty that the first president would by George Washington. Not only was he most respected and beloved American, but he had already proven that he could be trusted to protect and preserve republican government. In 1783 his emotional address to the officers at army headquarters in Newburgh quelled an attempt to stage a coup against the Continental Congress. As the doubters hoped, Washington in office firmly established its republican character. However, as the proponents of a strong executive hoped, he also showed that the president was no mere clerk. He asserted the president's right to create a link directly to the people. And, as the president's oath of office demanded, he also proved that the president could respond swiftly and decisively to threats to the nation's security thereby "preserving and protecting the Constitution."

Washington's determination to maintain the republican character of the office was evident in the very first controversy that arose regarding the president: what to call him? A committee of the House of Representatives wanted to address him simply as "the President of the United States." But the Senate, at the behest of Vice President John Adams, rejected the house committee's report. Because "titles and politically inspired elegance were essential aspects of strong government," Adams insisted he be addressed as "His Highness the President of the United States and Protector of Their Liberties." Madison led House opposition to what he took to be this anti-republican terminology. He was supported by President Washington, who made known his annoyance at Adam's efforts "to bedizen [him] with a superb but spurious title." The Senate proposal was defeated. The chief executive would have no more august title than "the President of the United States." Adams's efforts to give the presidency aristocratic airs led him to be nicknamed "His Rotundity."

Washington rejected the substance as well as the trappings of monarchy. Hamilton had argued in *Federalist* 73 that the president should veto bad laws. But Washington disagreed. He cast only two vetoes, both on constitutional grounds. One was in response to a measure he considered unconstitutional. The other was in response to a bill that undermined national security and therefore, as commander in chief, required his veto. Most importantly, Washington voluntarily stepped down after completing his second term, although the Constitution did not require him to do so, thereby establishing an enduring precedent for peacefully and lawfully relinquishing presidential power.

Washington strengthened the presidency even as he preserved its republican character. The Constitution does not empower the president to address the people. Indeed, his duty to preserve the presidency in the face of popular intemperance might be understood to preclude such direct address. Nonetheless, early in his term Washington issued a proclamation honoring Thanksgiving Day. This seemingly innocuous gesture established the tradition of direct popular communication that provides much of the modern president's power and prestige.

Although far more circumspect than Clinton's or Obama's pleadings for health-care reform, Washington's proclamation supported his conviction that communication between the nation's first citizen and its people was a vital form of civic education.

Washington also defended the president's capacity to manage the executive branch. As we have seen, the Constitution grants the president extensive appointment powers as well as the right to obtain in writing the views of the principal executive officers. But it does not declare the president to be in control of those departments, nor does it give the executive a clear directive to treat employees as subordinates. If Washington had not insisted that all members of the executive branch were in fact his "deputies," the president might have become, as the name suggests, a mere "presider" who ceded actual control over executive affairs to individual department heads acting in conjunction with their senior associates and powerful members of Congress.

The Constitution requires the president to obtain the advice and consent of the Senate when appointing department heads. Many representatives assumed that, by implication, Senate confirmation was also necessary for the president to fire an executive official. Washington disagreed. In a bill establishing the Department of State, Congress decided to allow the president to fire executive officials on his own, to grant him removal power, but only after Vice President Adams broke a tie in the Senate. If the president had been a less universally admired and trusted figure than Washington, at least one more senator would probably have voted no, and the deputy theory would not have become part of the unofficial Constitution.

Washington asserted presidential authority regarding both domestic insurrection and foreign threat. Several western Pennsylvania towns resisted a federal whiskey excise tax and drove away the tax collectors. Washington summoned troops to quell the uprising, commanding them himself. He risked his prestige to enforce the principle of national supremacy. In the face of a Washington-led army, the rebellion dissolved.

The Constitution gave the president no authority to dissolve treaties nor to declare peace, a power that seemed intimately related to Congress's power to declare war. Washington determined that the mutual defense treaty with France threatened war with Britain, so he broke it, issuing the Neutrality Proclamation of 1793 (see Chapter 4). Alexander Hamilton aggressively defended Washington's right to issue the proclamation in a series of newspaper articles under the pseudonym Pacificus. He distinguished between the vesting clause in Article I, which states that, "All legislative Powers herein granted shall be vested in a Congress of the United States," and the vesting clause in Article II, which states that, "The executive Power shall be vested in a President of the United States of America." The absence in Article II of the words "herein granted," Hamilton argued, clearly indicated that the executive power of the nation was lodged exclusively in the president, "subject only to the exceptions and qualifications which are expressed in the Constitution." In foreign affairs, wrote Hamilton, explicit constitutional restrictions on presidential power extended no further than the right of the Senate to ratify treaties and Congress to declare war and did not hinder the executive in other foreign policy matters that were "naturally" his domain.

Madison, writing under the name Helvidius – a Roman patriot who had been the victim of tyranny – replied to Hamilton. He denied that foreign policy was "naturally" an executive power. The tasks of foreign policy – to declare war, to conclude peace, and to form alliances – were among "the highest acts of sovereignty; of which the legislative power must at least be an integral and preeminent part." In foreign as in domestic affairs, wrote Madison, republican government confined presidential power to the execution of the laws; otherwise, the executive would acquire legislative power. Madison lost the argument. The Neutrality Proclamation established the precedent that the president can act unilaterally in foreign affairs except where the Constitution provides specific exceptions and limitations.

UPSHOT

Washington set critical precedents regarding the nature of the presidency that survive to this day. Although presidential power expanded dramatically in the twentieth and twenty-first centuries, it is still true that the president is a commoner and not a king. But Washington established that the president is no mere clerk. He can remove subordinates from office and he can communicate directly with the people. For almost a 150 years presidents emulated Washington by voluntarily leaving office after a maximum of two terms. Franklin Roosevelt broke that precedent but very quickly the country responded with a constitutional amendment that made mandatory what Washington had done voluntarily. The expansive power in matters of war and peace that Washington's Neutrality Proclamation embodied remains very much in place. Not all of Washington's precedents survive. Presidents feel free to veto laws they think are wrong-headed, even if those laws are constitutional.

CRITICAL CHOICE: DEMOCRATIZING THE PRESIDENCY – JEFFERSON AND JACKSON

Washington had asserted the presidents' right to communicate with the people but this did not imply that he felt himself reliant upon their support, or obligated to do their bidding. He did not view himself as the people's representative.

Jefferson and Jackson did see themselves in that light. They took critical steps to democratize the office.

Thomas Jefferson was the first president to argue that the strength of the executive office depended not only on its constitutional authority but also on "the affections of the people." He asserted that he had a direct tie to them. Indeed, he was uniquely well placed to do their bidding because unlike any individual congressman or senator whose constituencies were limited to specific districts or states he represented all the people. Only he could "command a view of the whole ground."

Jefferson also made the president look like a democrat. He jettisoned the presidential coach and rode his own horse. At presidential dinners, he flouted distinctions in rank and purposely ignored diplomatic protocol in the reception of foreign envoys. He believed that a presidential appearance before Congress resembled too much a speech from the throne, which would threaten to interfere with the deliberations of the people's representatives. He began the century-long practice of sending the president's annual State of the Union message to Congress in writing to be read aloud by the clerk of the House.

Jefferson also democratized the presidency by connecting it to a political party. The Republican Party linked the president and the people. Nomination and election by a mass political party made the president both a popular spokesman and accountable to a collective organization that enlarged even as it restrained presidential ambition. It restrained the president because he was as beholden to the party leaders of the various states as they were to him. The Revolution of 1800 could not have occurred without Jefferson's and Madison's sustained party-building efforts during the 1790s. As the beloved author of the Declaration of Independence, Jefferson might well have been elected in 1800 in the absence of party. But without its support and discipline, he would have either become a prisoner of the status quo or prey to schismatic pressures. He initiated the replacement of incumbent federal officials with party loyalists that would later acquire the title, the spoils system (see Chapter 4). Federal appointments would become the staple of party organization in the nineteenth and early twentieth centuries, thereby adding a practical underpinning to principled loyalties.

The president now derived power directly from the people through a party program. Washington's dream of an executive who stood apart from factions had proved unrealistic. Ironically, Jefferson shared Washington's antipathy to party politics. Once the Republican Party triumphed over the Federalists, he expected it to dissolve and nonpartisan constitutional government to be restored. But Jefferson was a better politician than a prophet. As president, he continued to function as a party leader. He encouraged party discipline in Congress and relied on House and Senate floor leaders to advance his programs. He made extensive use of party caucuses – meetings of leaders from the executive and legislative branches – to formulate policy and to encourage party unity. Jefferson constructed a highly centralized partisan system within the government.

Andrew Jackson, a disciple of Jefferson, was even bolder in his assertion of the democratic character of the presidency. Because he was the only official elected by the whole people, he considered himself to be uniquely responsible for their welfare. He was the tribune of the people, devoted to shrinking the federal government to prevent it from becoming excessively powerful and threatening the people's economic and political independence. He stopped federal funding of internal improvements – the building of roads and canals – because he saw no constitutional basis for them. The army was reduced. Expenditures shrank. The Second Bank of the United States was dismantled, and its deposits were reinvested in selected state banks. In carrying out these reductions, Jackson exercised presidential power more aggressively than Jefferson. Federalist and Republican presidents had abided by Washington's view that a veto should be cast only if the president believed that a piece of legislation was unconstitutional. But in 1832, Jackson justified vetoing the bank partly on the grounds that the recharter was bad policy.

Jackson combined his support for limited government with an abiding commitment to the Union. When South Carolina threatened to refuse to abide by a new tariff law passed by Congress, Jackson made clear that he himself would lead the military force that would invade the state and force it to abide by its constitutional obligation to obey federal law (see Chapters 5). It is inconceivable that Lincoln could have defeated the much more potent secession threat he faced if Jackson had succumbed to South Carolina.

No president between Jackson and Lincoln was able to emulate Jackson's close identification with the people. But even Jackson did not personify government to the extent that modern presidents do. For all his personal popularity, he did not shift governmental authority toward the executive branch nor even toward the federal government. Like his idol Jefferson, Jackson wielded presidential power in the cause of a government of limited power in which the states and localities were preeminent.

UPSHOT

Jefferson and Jackson asserted that the president has the strongest claim to be the representative of the people and to act as the people's tribune. This claim served as a crucial precedent for the even more ambitious democratic assertions that we will examine when we look at the twentieth-century transformation of the office. They also gave the president a more democratic persona that more closely identified him with the common people. They played a crucial role in the creation of a crucial democratic institution, the political party. Not all subsequent presidents have been the leaders of their party, but the most impressive and important ones have been party leaders and have used the party as a critical source of their power.

CRITICAL CHOICE: AGENT OF CONSTITUTIONAL CHANGE – ABRAHAM LINCOLN

The precedents that Washington, Jefferson, and Jackson established endowed the office with sufficient strength and legitimacy to enable Abraham Lincoln to embark upon the most momentous of all presidential endeavors – reconstituting the Union. He was not a folk hero like Jackson, but he too sought to establish a strong link to the common man. He cultivated the image of himself as a rail splitter who was born on the frontier in a log cabin. But as president, he aimed not merely to serve the people but to educate the people about the very meaning of their constitutional rights. He provided new and provocative answers to fundamental political questions about the proper role of executive power and how to reconcile the Constitution as a legal document with democratic principles and practice. And, in no small measure due to Washington's assertion of the role of commander in chief and Jackson's suppression of nullification, Lincoln possessed sufficient executive authority to defeat a determined internal enemy.

Lincoln argued that the Constitution embodied the American democratic tradition because it was inextricably connected to the Declaration of Independence. Stephen Douglas's concept of popular sovereignty (see Chapter 4) deviated from the Declaration and the spirit of the Constitution because it tolerated the expansion of slavery. This error was compounded by the Supreme Court's 1857 *Dred Scott* decision, authored by the militant Jacksonian Roger Taney, which declared unconstitutional any act of Congress or the territorial legislatures that abolished slavery. Lincoln feared that Douglas's and Taney's doctrines would transform slavery from a necessary evil into a positive good, a moral right, producing "a gradual and steady debauching of public opinion." The consequences of such a change in the public mind would be devastating.

Lincoln's indictment of slavery, and the constitutional changes stemming from that indictment, brought forth a new, more positive view of liberty that obliged government to ensure equality under the law. Thus, Lincoln and his party lessened the inherent tension between liberalism and democracy. They incorporated the Declaration of Independence into the Constitution by abolishing slavery (Thirteenth Amendment), promising that American citizens could not be denied the right to vote "on account of race, color, or previous condition of servitude" (the Fifteenth Amendment), and guaranteeing all Americans the "privileges or immunities" of citizenship, "due process," and "equal protection of the laws" (the Fourteenth Amendment). These amendments altered the course of constitutional development. Eleven of the first twelve constitutional amendments limited national government powers; six of the next seven expanded those powers at the expense of the states and localities.

At Lincoln's insistence, the Republicans made the Thirteenth Amendment, which emancipated the slaves, "the keystone of its 1864 platform." His Emancipation Proclamation only freed slaves held on enemy territory, Lincoln claimed that it was strictly a measure to aid the war effort and therefore something he could order using his war powers. But he had no right to abolish slavery altogether. Because the Constitution protected slavery, it could only be ended by constitutional amendment.

Reelected by large majorities, Lincoln and congressional Republican leaders pushed the amendment through a reluctant Congress. The Constitution does not require a presidential signature on constitutional amendments, but Congress sent it to the president to sign anyway. This oversight, deliberate or not, testifies to Lincoln's importance as a popular party leader. The Thirteenth Amendment was self-consciously based on the Northwest Ordinance, supporting Lincoln's claim that the Northwest Ordinance symbolized the Framers' hostility to slavery (see Chapter 2). Its passage further vindicated Lincoln's position that the Republicans, not the Democrats, were the true heirs of Jeffersonian democracy.

The magnitude of Lincoln's conservative revolution was limited by his identification with Jeffersonian principles. His view of the limits of federal government powers was quite narrow compared with those of most twentieth-century presidents. Like the Whigs before them, Lincoln's Republicans favored a stronger national government than the Democrats did. But by modern standards their view of the federal government remained quite limited. They remained tightly bound by the Classic Liberal commitment to private property, limited government, and administrative decentralization. They demonstrated their commitment to what Lincoln called "a fair race of life" by ending slavery and enhancing "free labor" through policies such as the 1862 Homestead Act (see Chapter 6). With these principles firmly in place, there was no longer a need for the dynamic and aggressive presidential leadership that had secured them. The obscurity of the presidents who served between Lincoln and Theodore Roosevelt is a testimony to the limits that congressional party leadership placed on presidential power and therefore upon the prestige and popularity of those who held the office.

UPSHOT

Lincoln's conservative revolution – ending slavery while remaining faithful to the Constitution – was described in Chapter 4. This remarkable accomplishment took the presidential office to new heights. Lincoln showed that the president could serve as the agent of constitutional change and constitutional perpetuation, and as the key defender of the American creed (see Chapter 2).

CRITICAL CHOICE: CREATING THE PERSONALIZED PRESIDENCY

In the twentieth century a critical change took place in the public's perception of the presidency. He came to personify government. The older understanding of America as a decentralized political order in which the drama of politics was played out primarily in the states and localities, was replaced by a sense that grand political theatre took place only in the nation's capital with the president cast in the leading role. We call this transformation of the presidency the "personalized presidency."

The personalized presidency began to take shape during the Progressive Era, the period of reform spanning the last decade of the nineteenth century and the first two decades of the twentieth century (see Chapter 4). In response to massive economic, cultural, and social changes that occurred during this period, pressures mounted for a more expansive national government and a more systematic administration of public policy. The late nineteenth-century polity, which could accommodate decentralized party organizations, political patronage, and a dominant Congress, began to give way to a new order that depended on consistent and forceful presidential leadership.

Theodore Roosevelt

The vigorous expansion of presidential power began with Theodore Roosevelt (TR). TR proclaimed that the president was "a steward of the people." He was bound to actively and affirmatively do all he could for the people, and not content himself with the negative merit of keeping his talents 'undamaged in a napkin." TR's conviction that the president possessed a special mandate from the people made him a self-conscious disciple of Jackson. Unlike Jackson, however, TR wanted to join popular leadership to a greater sense of national purpose. He trumpeted a "New Nationalism" that foretold an unprecedented expansion of government's responsibility to secure the nation's social and economic welfare. The New Nationalism was indebted to Hamilton's original understanding of a great American nation. TR also relied on the defense of a broad discretionary authority for the president that Hamilton articulated to justify Washington's Neutrality Proclamation. Washington, Jackson, and Lincoln had all taken a broad view of presidential authority in times of national crisis. But TR was the first president to apply the Hamiltonian principle to the day-to-day administration of government. But he turned Hamilton on his head. Hamilton supported an energetic executive because he thought it would curb popular influence and implement policies geared toward aiding the commercial and business elite to foster economic development. TR devoted his energy to social and economic reform dedicated to helping ordinary people. As a self-proclaimed disciple of Lincoln, he asserted that "Men who

Figure 8.1. Astride the World: a 1905 cartoon depicting the "Big Stick Policy" of President Theodore Roosevelt.
Source: Granger Collection –

understand and practice the Lincoln school of American political thought are necessarily Hamiltonian in their belief in a strong and efficient National Government and Jeffersonian in their belief in the people as the end of government."

Jefferson and especially Jackson had sought to establish closer ties between the presidency and the public, but they had worked through their party organizations to do so. Similarly, Lincoln had relied heavily on the Republican Party to mobilize support for the war and his Reconstruction policies. But TR's Republican Party was badly divided regarding a bill to regulate railroad rates that he considered vital to public wellbeing. When this bill stalled in the Senate, TR toured the country to stir up support for it. The public pressure that his rhetoric stimulated overcame Senate resistance. The president of the Rock Island railroad confided to Secretary of War William Howard Taft that senators he had counted on for "allegiance," although privately opposed to the Hepburn bill, so named after its Senate sponsor, yielded because the president had "so roused the people that it was impossible for the Senate to stand against the popular demand." The Hepburn Act marked not only the first significant strengthening of national administrative power to regulate the economy since Washington, but also the first time a president successfully forced the hand of Congress through a direct appeal to the people. TR thus advanced the Progressive cause by establishing the president as the principal agent of popular rule.

TR not only spoke directly to the public in support of policies he favored, he also exploited the newly emerging mass-circulation newspapers and magazines to go over the heads of party leaders and establish direct links with the people. He ushered in what has been called the "rhetorical presidency," an approach to presidential leadership that relied primarily on direct communication with the public. He described the presidency as a "bully pulpit" from which he could and should vigorously promoted himself as the leader of public opinion.

Wilson

TR's successor, Woodrow Wilson, expanded the concept of the rhetorical presidency, announcing in his first inaugural address that presidential rhetoric was the "high enterprise of the new day." In his 1913 address to Congress on tariff reform, he revived the practice, abandoned by Jefferson, of addressing Congress in person. Even TR had not dared to abandon this precedent, which, like the two-term tradition, was viewed as a bulwark against despotism. But Wilson believed that Progressive democracy required the president to take advantage of congressional messages to influence public opinion. The rise of the mass media increased the focus of public attention on such events and enabled the president to use them to bring public pressure to bear on Congress. Although diehard Jeffersonian Democrats resented it, the speech was well received by Congress and the public, aiding Wilson to launch the first successful campaign for tariff reform since before the Civil War. By 1914, Wilson had won congressional approval for a series of other Progressive reforms including the establishment of the Federal Trade Commission and the Federal Reserve banking system. However, he also suffered an epochal defeat. His effort to overcome Senate opposition to the League of Nations by taking his case directly to the people was a dismal failure.

FDR

Franklin Delano Roosevelt (FDR) further expanded the personalized presidency by creating a new and more intimate mode of public communication and by attempting to increase the personal power of the president at the expense of the Court, rival party leaders, and the two-term tradition that Washington and Jefferson had established. In an effort to allay public anxiety about such massive new government programs as Social Security, FDR invented a new rhetorical form, the "Fireside Chat." By the early 1930s radios were widely available and most homes had one. FDR realized that radio demanded a very different speaking style than did large public rallies. Over radio he was not speaking to vast crowds but rather to families sitting comfortably and quietly in their own living rooms or kitchens. Such an audience would respond far better to a calm conversational speaking style than to a formal passionate speech. Therefore, FDR spoke to them

Table 8.4. Fireside chats.

Sunday, March 12, 1933	On the Banking Crisis
Sunday, May 7, 1933	Outlining the New Deal Program
Monday, July 24, 1933	On the National Recovery Administration
Sunday, October 22, 1933	On Economic Progress
Thursday, June 28, 1934	Achievements of the 73rd US Congress and Critics of the New Deal
Sunday, September 30, 1934	On Government and Capitalism
Sunday, April 28, 1935	On the Works Relief Program and the Social Security Act
Sunday, September 6, 1936	On Drought Conditions, Farmers and Laborers
Tuesday, March 9, 1937	On the Reorganization of the Judiciary
Tuesday, October 12, 1937	On New Legislation to be Recommended to Congress
Sunday, November 14, 1937	On the Unemployment Census
Thursday, April 14, 1938	On the Recession
Friday, June 24, 1938	On Party Primaries
Sunday, September 3, 1939	On the European War
Sunday, May 26, 1940	On National Defense
Sunday, December 29, 1940	On the "Arsenal of Democracy"
Tuesday, May 27, 1941	Announcing Unlimited National Emergency
Thursday, September 11, 1941	On Maintaining Freedom of the Seas and the Greer Incident
Tuesday, December 9, 1941	On the Declaration of War with Japan
Monday, February 23, 1942	On the Progress of the War
Tuesday, April 28, 1942	On Our National Economic Policy and Sacrifice
Monday, September 7, 1942	On Inflation and Progress of the War
Monday, October 12, 1942	Report on the Home Front
Sunday, May 2, 1943	On the Coal Crisis
Wednesday, July 28, 1943	On the Fall of Mussolini
Wednesday, September 8, 1943	On the Armistice with Italy and the Third War Loan Drive
Friday, December 24, 1943	On the Tehran and Cairo Conferences
Tuesday, January 11, 1944	On the State of the Union
Monday, June 5, 1944	On the Fall of Rome
Monday, June 12, 1944	Opening the Fifth War Loan Drive

Source: FDR Library.

as if he was seated in their midst, warming himself by the fireside. He explained complex new policies to them in simple terms using homey examples. These "chats" proved to be greatly successful in reassuring the public that the president knew what he was doing and that the fears these major departures had instilled in them were groundless.

The Limits of Presidential Expansion

During his second term, FDR launched four major initiatives aimed at expanding presidential power: "court packing," "the purge campaign," a plan for reorganizing the executive branch, and a campaign to win an unprecedented third term in office. He did get elected to a third and even a fourth term, and each of the other initiatives also had a measure of success. But each also ended up setting enduring limits on the expansion of executive power.

Court Packing

Shortly after he was sworn in for his second term, FDR announced his court-packing plan, enabling the president to appoint an additional Supreme Court justice for every existing one who failed to retire within six months of reaching the age of 70. Six of the nine current justices were 70 or older, which meant that FDR could enlarge the Court to fifteen justices, thereby overcoming the Court's resistance to New Deal policies.

Jefferson, Jackson, and Lincoln had each fought with the Court, but the intensity of the opposition to FDR's plan was unprecedented. Although the new rights that FDR championed had broad popular support, the public was hostile to the plan's audacious aggrandizement of executive power. By controlling the judiciary, the final constitutional barrier to expansion of government and of the presidency would be eliminated.

Humphrey's Executor v. United States and *Schechter Poultry Corp. v. United States*, both handed down on "Black Monday," May 27, 1935, severely constrained presidential authority. *Humphrey* forbade the president from firing members of independent regulatory commissions, a power the Court had affirmed in 1926. *Schechter* declared the National Recovery Administration's discretionary powers to regulate prices, wages and other business conditions to be an unconstitutional delegation of legislative authority. Thus, FDR's effort to extend power over the judiciary was more than simply a ploy to amplify his own power or to win disputes over particular policies. It was also an effort to preserve the powers that he felt the president needed to create and maintain the new economic constitutional order.

Much to FDR's surprise, the court-packing plan provoked an outpouring of public and congressional opposition. Although literally constitutional, critics recognized that it represented an effort of the president to control the Court and therefore it was a frontal assault on two of the deepest principles underlying the Constitution, checks and balances and separation of powers.

As we shall see with regard to each of the four initiatives, court packing was not an unmitigated failure. Shortly after FDR introduced it, the Supreme Court abruptly ceased overturning New Deal initiatives. Since 1937, it has not invalidated any significant federal statute regulating the economy. The expansion of federal government power the New Deal ushered in survived the court-packing campaign intact but so did the existence of the Supreme Court as an independent branch of government that has on several important occasions reigned in presidential power.

To provide the president with the managerial tools needed to run the enlarged federal bureaucracy, FDR asked Congress to approve a major executive branch reorganization and to provide him with greater staff resources. The most ambitious part of the proposal called for taking the vast number of independent commissions, bureaus and agencies that had been created during the Progressive Era and the New Deal and integrating them into the existing cabinet departments. This reorganization would have enabled the president, through the cabinet secretaries that he appointed, to direct and control such key activities as food and drug, securities, communications, and railroad regulation that remained largely outside his span of authority. Congress refused to grant him such powers. It preferred to retain the greater degree of influence it enjoyed with such agencies precisely because they were not within the president's grip. Congress did however recognize that the president lacked sufficient managerial resources. Therefore, it did enable him to hire additional staff. It also created the *Executive Office of the President* (EOP), which contains the White House Office (the so-called West Wing), the nerve center of the modern executive establishment. It enhanced his budgetary control by moving the Bureau of the Budget, later the Office of Management and Budget (OMB), from the Treasury to the Department to the EOP (for a detailed discussion of OMB, see Chapter 10).

The third initiative was FDR's purge campaign. As the New Deal wore on, many Southern Democrats, and some Northern Democrats as well, became increasingly hostile to the great increase in federal government power that it entailed. The Southerners were especially worried that the New Dealers might decide to try use these new powers to end the discrimination against African Americans that pervaded Southern life. During the 1938 midterm elections, FDR intervened in one gubernatorial and several Senate and House primaries in a bold effort to replace conservative Democrats with 100 percent New Dealers. Although Wilson and Jefferson had dabbled with the idea, no president had ever challenged his own party on such a scale. The press nicknamed FDR's effort the "purge," evoking Adolph Hitler's murder of Nazi dissenters and Joseph Stalin's elimination of suspected opponents within the Soviet Communist Party. Although bloodless, FDR's aggressive intervention challenged the very foundation of the party system as a check on presidential ambition. FDR won only two of his twelve purge attempts. This largely failed effort showed that even a president as popular as FDR could not succeed in dominating his party. No subsequent president has launched such an ambitious effort to challenge intraparty rivals and opponents.

Only FDR himself knew why he chose to break with tradition and run for a third term. Certainly his inability to purge conservatives from his party as well as the growing threat emanating from Nazi Germany entered into his calculations. Whatever his motives, his election to a third, and then to a fourth, term set a new precedent with the potential to vastly enhance presidential power. But the precedent proved short-lived. The Twenty-second Amendment to the Constitution,

Table 8.5. Limits on expansion of presidential power.

- Congress refuses to support court packing
- FDR fails to unseat prominent conservative Southern senators
- Congress refuses to give FDR the power to reorganize the executive branch
- The Twenty-second Amendment limits the president to two terms

which limited presidents to two terms, was ratified in 1951. It made mandatory what Washington and all his predecessors prior to FDR had done voluntarily.

UPSHOT

The personalized president went beyond the earlier claim to represent the people. It took responsibility for the people's wellbeing, to be the people's steward. To that end, the president adopted a broad reading of the Constitution, feeling free to engage in any endeavor that the document did not explicitly forbid. If Congress did not follow his lead, he would appeal over its head directly to the people, making extensive use of mass media.

The personalized presidency has had a variety of critical consequence for the office. Aides to the president have displaced party leaders as formulators of policy, organizers of campaigns, liaisons with interest groups, and communicators with the public. The party is no longer the controlling element in presidential elections and governance. Presidents have campaigned and governed as the heads of their own personal organizations. Increasingly, the public has come to hold the president responsible for government action, even for economic and social developments beyond the executive's authority.

America's emergence as a world power during and after WWII further widened the scope of responsibilities and further increased his prominence and visibility. This expanded understanding of the presidency does not imply that the president has always been triumphant. As the defeat of the League of Nations Treaty, the failure of court packing, and the poor result of the purge campaign demonstrate, personalizing the presidency presents pitfalls as well as opportunities. This chapter's opening story of Bill Clinton and healthcare reform further demonstrates that placing the president on such a pedestal has not necessarily served to enhance presidential authority, nor to ensure the adoption of his policies.

Later in the chapter there will be further examples of the public turning on the incumbent president, using midterm elections to hamstring his initiatives by electing a hostile congressional majority.

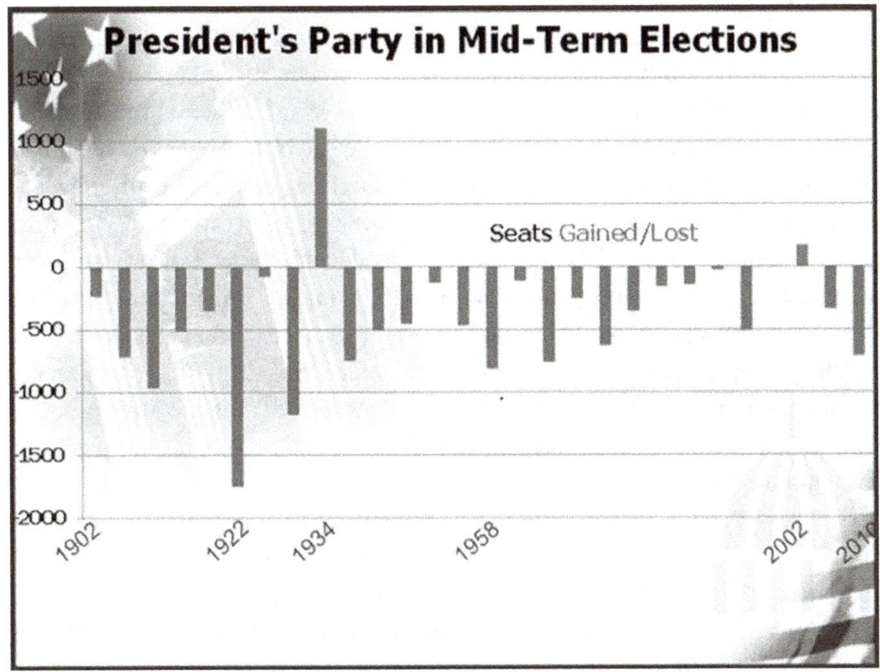

Figure 8.2. Midterm elections updated.
Source: Tim Storey, NCSL.

> *Distrust of his motives and disgust at his behavior impelled the House of Representatives to impeach a president, Clinton, and to force another from office because it was on the verge of impeaching him, Nixon. In the entire previous history of the Republic, it had impeached only one and never forced one from office. Even where presidential power had come to seem most sacrosanct, war-making, the Congress, in 1973, passed the War Powers Resolution whose purpose was to curtail the ability of the president to initiate hostilities, and the Supreme Court issued a series of rulings aimed at forcing the president to alter his conduct of the War on Terror. The ever-present image of the president, and the public's preoccupation with him, have also made him more subject to public rebuke and to efforts by the other branches to curtail his powers.*

The Impact of the Cold War and Television

Two critical postwar events, the Cold War and television, served to further increase the personalization of the presidency.

The Cold War

As early as 1937, FDR began to challenge the mood of isolationism that had dominated the United States since the end of World War I. Whereas the Supreme Court through 1936 had resisted his domestic policy reforms, it abetted his internationalism. In *US v. Curtiss-Wright Export Corporation* (1936), the court upheld a 1934 law authorizing the president to forbid the sale of weapons to countries engaged in armed conflict. This law had been passed with the so-called Chaco War between Bolivia and Paraguay in mind, and FDR quickly forbade arms sales to both countries. Weapons merchants challenged the measure as an unconstitutional delegation of legislative authority to the president. A federal district court agreed, but a near unanimous Supreme Court held that the president is the government's "sole organ" in international relations, and therefore his actions do not require a specific grant of power from either the Constitution or Congress.

The Curtiss-Wright case established as constitutional doctrine the sweeping defense of the executive's prerogative in foreign affairs that Hamilton had offered in 1793 to defend Washington's Neutrality Proclamation. This principle was reinforced by *US v. Belmont* (1937), which approved the president's right to reach executive agreements with other countries without Senate ratification. These court decisions made it virtually impossible to challenge FDR's increasingly internationalist policies on constitutional grounds.

The advent of the Cold War meant that the US did not return to peacetime in the aftermath of WWII. Therefore, the president retained much of the power and dominance he had only previously enjoyed during wartime. After the advent of nuclear weapons, his personal role was greatly enhanced, at least in the popular mind, because he and he alone had his "finger on the button." Only the president could make the decision to drop "the bomb." To calm public fears of nuclear holocaust, the Soviet and American governments installed a special telephone, called the "hotline," that would permit the US president and the Soviet premier to communicate directly in the event that either suspected the other of provoking a war. During the periods of greatest tension Soviet and US leaders met in what were billed as "summit meetings" to try to find ways to ease tensions between the two superpowers. The intense publicity that surrounded summit meetings and the installation of the hotline promoted the image of the Cold War as a personal duel between the president and his Soviet counterpart.

Television

The advent of television meant that the face as well as the voice of the president entered the nation's living rooms. Dwight Eisenhower (1953–61) was the first president to appear on television regularly, but John F. Kennedy (1961–63) was the first to master the new medium. Convinced that viewers were bored by formal speech-making, Kennedy relied more on press conferences. Previous presidents, notably TR and FDR, had used press conferences to cultivate the journalistic fraternity. Kennedy used television to turn them into the visual equivalents of FDR's fireside chats: informal, intimate means for going over the heads of Congress and journalists to reach the public directly. Public opinion surveys gave Kennedy a 91 percent approval rating for his press conference performances. The key was his careful preparation and an ability to appear comfortable and in command on television.

Kennedy's very success compounded the modern president's problems. Because they were such effective communicators, Reagan and Clinton were tempted to promise more than they could deliver. As they became increasingly cut off from Congress and party, modern presidents had great difficulty satisfying the very reform demands they helped stimulate. Kennedy's personalization of the presidency greatly accentuated its separation from the other centers of political power.

The Personalized Presidency: Opportunities and Hazards

Strength and Fragility: LBJ

Of all the post-FDR presidents, Lyndon Johnson (LBJ) most clearly exemplified both the extraordinary prospects and the fragile authority of the personalized presidency. His greatest achievement came in the struggle for civil rights. More than any of his predecessors, he identified himself with that struggle and enlisted the full force of his rhetorical and legislative gifts in its service. By persuading Congress to enact the 1964 and 1965 civil rights laws, LBJ accomplished what Lincoln could not – statutory protection for African American political participation, employment opportunity, and access to public accommodations.

Like the Social Security Act and the Wagner Act, the 1960s civil rights acts became endowed with quasiconstitutional status. Although racial issues remain controversial, the specific rights that these two landmark statutes propound have become as unexceptional as free speech, free assembly, or free practice of religion. Obviously, the enactment of these laws was not all LBJ's doing. He was responding to powerful political and moral pressures exerted by the civil rights movement under the unofficial but inspired leadership of Martin Luther King, Jr. LBJ also built on the initiatives of Kennedy, who after a period of indecision had decided to support the civil rights struggle. But LBJ aggressively exploited the political opportunity provided by Kennedy's assassination to press a reluctant Congress to pass the 1964 bill, and then availed himself of the huge congressional majority obtained in the 1964 election to pass the 1965 Voting Rights Act.

Taking further advantage of this immense electoral victory, Johnson expanded the New Deal vision of programmatic rights by winning passage of Medicare which provided the elderly with a right to healthcare. He also obtained congressional approval of a program to give healthcare to the poor, Medicaid (1965), and a law providing educational opportunities for the disadvantaged, the Elementary and Secondary Education Act (1965).

But LBJ was not content to deliver on promises made by Lincoln and FDR. He heralded a Great Society that went beyond the "pursuit of happiness" – as propounded in the Declaration of Independence – to the promise of happiness itself (see Chapter 4). At its most grandiose, the Great Society sought not to enlarge the liberal tradition but to transcend it. LBJ's vision gave rise to a legislative program of remarkable breadth. Policies dedicated to enhancing the quality of American life included pollution reduction, urban redevelopment, consumer protection, and preschool education. These policies of the "spirit rather than the flesh" were also expected to restore a sense of citizenship to political life that had been sapped by bureaucratic indifference and the crass consumerism of mass society.

The Johnson administration launched new social initiatives to foster "participatory democracy." Those people affected by government programs were to be directly involved in policy formulation and implementation. This promise of political self-determination marked a renewal and intensification of the Progressive principle of direct democracy. Participatory democracy was central to LBJ's War on Poverty, which was administered by local community action programs and was required to involve the "maximum feasible participation of residents of the areas and the groups served."

The Great Society did not fulfill its ambitions to supersede the New Deal. Local elected officials threatened by the support given to grassroots movements in their cities and towns appealed to Congress to rein in participatory democracy. The Great Society's hallmarks, those programs that went beyond providing civil and programmatic rights, were killed or gutted. Indeed, by failing in its most grandiose ambitions to restore direct democracy, the Great Society served to increase public skepticism about both the sincerity of governmental intentions and the capacity of government to act effectively. As the personal embodiment of these great ambitions, the prestige of the presidency suffered accordingly.

Although rhetorically committed to grassroots democracy, LBJ's early years in power were the apex of "presidential government." Major policy departures were conceived in the White House, hastened through Congress by the legislative skill of LBJ and his sophisticated congressional liaison team, and administered by new or refurbished executive agencies highly responsive to the president's directives. LBJ also established a personal governing coalition that reached beyond his party. This personalized presidency proved his undoing. His domination of the political process ensured that he, not Congress, would be blamed when his Great Society programs failed, victims of hasty packaging and unrealistic goals.

The war in Vietnam demonstrated even more starkly both LBJ's personal shortcomings and the more troubling aspects of modern presidential government itself. He extended the American commitment in Vietnam because, as a progressive internationalist in the tradition of TR, FDR, and JFK, he believed that the righteous use of force was necessary in foreign affairs to make the world safe for democracy. In Korea, Harry Truman could claim to be carrying out the United Nations' dictate. In Vietnam, however, no treaty or other obligations required the United States to intervene. Nor did Congress authorize a "police action" of a magnitude justifying the commitment of 500,000 troops (the size of the American force fighting in Vietnam by the end of 1967). The Johnson administration's claim that such action was authorized by the 1964 Gulf of Tonkin Resolution was dubious. In truth, LBJ believed and stated publicly that he had constitutional authority to deploy troops in Vietnam without congressional authorization.

By early 1968, LBJ was trapped, unable to withdraw troops for fear of being damned as the first American president to lose a war, yet lacking the popular support to undertake more aggressive military action. Attacked by left and right, he shocked the nation by announcing in a televised address on March 31, 1968, that he would not seek reelection.

Disciplining Richard Nixon

Despite growing mistrust of the presidency, the welfare state continued to expand. During the 1970s Congress passed a host of new environmental, special education, and consumer protection initiatives as well as a major expansion of the Social Security Act that pegged Social Security payments to the consumer price index, thereby insulating millions of old-age pensioners from the risk of inflation. But these popular new initiative did not serve to increase trust in the president.

Public mistrust grew in response to LBJ and Nixon's conduct of the war and by the evidence of presidential misconduct revealed in the Watergate Scandal (see Chapter 7). As we discussed in Chapter 7, Congress sought to curb presidential abuse of power by impeaching President Nixon and passing the War Powers Resolution over Nixon's veto. As we also discussed in Chapter 7, the courts also acted to curb presidential power by ruling against Nixon's impoundments of funds appropriated by Congress and against his assertion of executive privilege as a rationale for withholding the Watergate tapes from Congress, rulings with regard to impoundments and executive privilege.

The Personalized President as a Conservative: Ronald Reagan

Although all the Republican presidents of the postwar period considered themselves to be conservatives, only Ronald Reagan mounted a serious effort to halt the expansion of the federal government. He convinced Congress to make major tax cuts. There were no commensurate reductions in spending, nonetheless, the sheer size of the reductions in revenue resulting from the tax cuts put a severe damper on Congress's programmatic ambitions. However, except for the tax cut, all of Reagan's efforts to cut government were accomplished through acts of presidential discretion that short-circuited the legislative process. Although done in the name of limited government, Reagan's approach to reform was as president-centered as that of FDR and LBJ. Even reductions in environmental and consumer protection were done by administrative action, not legislative change.

To obtain the Republican congressional majority required to mount a full-scale assault on the New Deal, Reagan would have needed to put his popularity and rhetorical ability in the service of winning votes for Republican congressional candidates. Forging such partisan loyalty was precisely what FDR accomplished in 1936. Confident of his own reelection, FDR risked alienating voters by demanding that they support Democratic congressional candidates as well. Instead of defusing partisan conflict, FDR crystallized it. He did not take the safe road of simply rehearsing his administration's accomplishments and taking credit for economic recovery. Instead, he castigated New Deal opponents in harsh, provocative terms as "economic royalists" and "privileged princes of the economic dynasty." He turned the election from a personal contest into a partisan conflict, which, given the popularity of the New Deal, he knew he could win.

Reagan did just the opposite. His 1984 reelection campaign was geared to maximize his personal appeal at the price of draining the election of broader political meaning. Its theme, "Morning in America," provided a soft focus that failed to clarify the choice between Democrats and Republicans. Campaign advertising stressed the virtues and charms of Reagan the man rather than pressing voters to elect representatives and senators who supported his programs. The result was a stunning victory for the president. He defeated Walter Mondale by a larger popular vote margin than any presidential victor has been able to accomplish since. He carried every state except Minnesota, Mondale's home state. But this personal victory was bought at the price of foreswearing partisan advantage. Republicans gained just fourteen House seats, leaving Democrats still in control, and lost two seats in the Senate, retaining a very slim majority. In 1986, Democrats took the upper chamber as well. Failing to gain control of Congress, Reagan had no hope of advancing his agenda during his second term.

Although Reagan opposed many of the domestic policies of his Democratic predecessors, on the foreign policy front he steadfastly continued the policy of containing the Soviet Union begun by Democrat Harry Truman (1946–52) and brought it to fruition by winning the Cold War. He expanded the military buildup begun by his immediate Democratic predecessor, Jimmy Carter (1977–81) in response to the Soviet Union's war in Afghanistan. Containment was the policy of exerting continuing pressure on the Soviet Union by stationing troops on its borders and actively preventing its efforts to expand militarily. Containment required vast expenditures on defense, much of which were devoted to remaining technologically superior. Even before Reagan began his offensive, the Soviets were experiencing severe internal difficulties. But to bring them down, he capitalized on what otherwise might have proved only a temporary setback. The enormity of the economic and technological challenge posed by his military buildup and the staunchness of his rhetoric may have sapped the Soviets of the vigor that otherwise might have proved sufficient for them to stage a comeback. Figure 8.3 shows the pattern of defense spending from 1950 to 1990.

Unfortunately, Reagan's foreign policy also confirmed the personalized presidency's extraordinary isolation and its tendency to ignore constitutional limits. In November 1986, the nation learned that with the president's approval, National Security Council staffers had sold weapons to Iran and that, with or without the president's knowledge, some of the proceeds had been used to assist the Contras, opponents of the socialist Nicaraguan government. Congress had passed the Boland Amendment that expressly forbade arming the Contras, and it would have prohibited selling arms to Iran if it had any inkling such sales were being contemplated. In reaction to the scandal, Reagan's approval rating fell from 67 percent to 46 percent in one month. Although Reagan later reclaimed some of his popularity, his administration never recovered from the institutional estrangement that the Iran–Contra affair instigated.

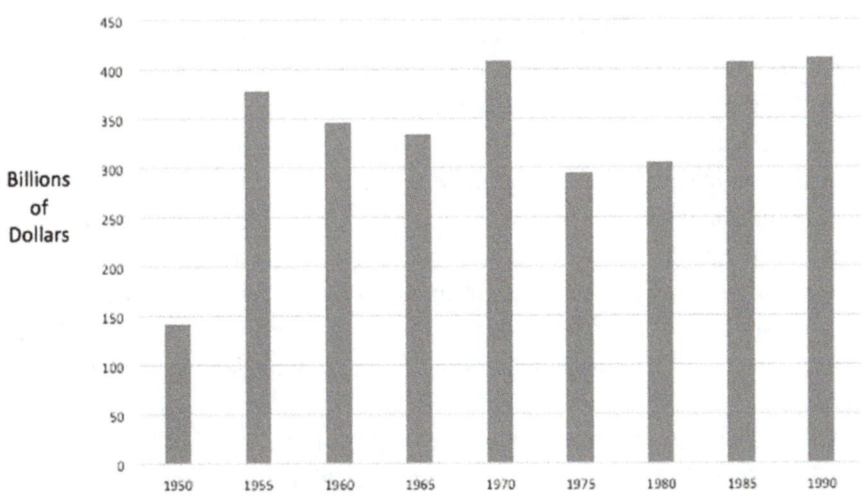

Figure 8.3. Defense spending, 1950–1990.
Source: Center for Defense Information.

Personal Victories, Policy Defeats: Bill Clinton

The presidency of Bill Clinton also displayed both the problems and the opportunities created by the increased personalization of the office. In the words of the great presidential scholar, Richard Neustadt, Clinton's greatest mistake was to think that he won the 1992 election. Of course, he got elected, but he only received 43.3 percent of the popular vote, beating George W. Bush by slightly less than 6 percent. It is impossible to tell how the election would have turned out were it not for the enormous impact of third-party candidate Ross Perot, who relentlessly attacked Bush, not Clinton, and who received 19 percent of the vote, the best showing by a third-party candidate since Theodore Roosevelt in 1912. Neustadt's point is that Clinton misinterpreted the election results. He had not won over a majority of voters and that should have given him cause for caution. He should have realized that the fame and adulation that go along with winning a presidential election are not in themselves sufficient to push Congress to adopt major new initiatives.

In the manner of the personalized presidency, Clinton did not involve his congressional allies in the formulation of the massive new healthcare proposal whose demise we discussed at the beginning of this chapter. Instead, he entrusted the task to a nonelected individual who had no appointive position in the administration and had therefore never undergone senatorial confirmation, his wife Hilary Clinton. She in turn appointed a taskforce of healthcare experts who met in secret and handed Congress a fully articulated program package for its consideration. This lack of prior consultation offended senior Democratic congressmen on whom the administration had to rely to obtain congressional passage. Because it had received no political vetting, Republican congressional leaders suspected that the public could be turned against it. Thus, they chose to oppose it in its entirety rather than seek to modify it. This decision was critical to their success in winning both houses of Congress in 1994.

Remarkably, this political humiliation did not foreclose Clinton's reelection in 1996. He also withstood his impeachment, provoked by the Monica Lewinsky sex scandal, and served out his second term (see Chapter 7). Both these victories were due to Clinton's personal political skills. He regained strength with the voters by shrewdly cooperating with the Republicans on initiatives he knew to be popular with the voters. Despite protests from fellow Democrats, he signed the Republican-sponsored Welfare Reform. But he staunchly opposed Republican initiatives he knew to be unpopular, such as revamping Medicare and Social Security.

Clinton's bipartisan efforts won him few friends on the Republican side of the aisle and the Republican majority voted to impeach him. The Republicans eagerly embraced the report of Independent Counsel Kenneth Starr, which found that the president had lied under oath to a grand jury regarding his sexual relations with

White House intern Monica Lewinsky. Starr had been appointed as an independent counsel by a panel of three federal judges pursuant to a law passed in 1994 and signed by President Clinton.

Clinton survived impeachment by convincing the majority of the public that special prosecutor Kenneth Starr's vendetta against him was a greater evil than his own immoral sexual behavior. In the face of such staunch public support, the Senate vote fell far short of the two-thirds majority required to oust the president from office. Clinton faced two separate charges: perjury and obstruction of justice. Ten Republican senators joined all forty-five of the Senate Democrats to acquit Clinton of the charge of perjury by a vote of 55 to 45. Five Republicans joined the Democrats to acquit him of the obstruction of justice charge by a 50–50 vote. Thus Clinton combined three great personal victories - two presidential electoral victories and impeachment acquittal - with major policy defeats and the loss of control of both houses of Congress for six of his eight years in office.

Reasserting Party Leadership: George W. Bush

George W. Bush was the first president since FDR to actively and successfully reassert the president's role as party leader. During the Clinton era, Republicans not only took control of Congress, they also captured the governorships of all the most heavily populated states except California - Texas, New York, Florida, Pennsylvania, Illinois, Michigan, Ohio, New Jersey, and Massachusetts. Recognizing that a defeat of Democratic nominee Al Gore would require them to promote a moderate candidate, these large-state Republican governors united behind Governor George W. Bush of Texas. This display of solidarity shows that even though candidate-centered politics and declining party cohesion emerged as powerful trends after the New Deal, it was still possible, at least for Republicans, to put party wellbeing above personal ambition.

As president, Bush built upon the party effort that had won him nomination. His active and energetic campaigning on behalf of Republican congressional candidates in 2002 was critical to the party's success in regaining control of the Senate and garnering additional seats in the House. In preparation for 2004, Bush and his advisors launched what could be called the first "national party machine" in American history. It was an elaborate network of campaign volunteers concentrated in the sixteen most competitive states. Instead of focusing on so-called "swing" voters, those who were still on the fence between the two candidates, the 2004 Bush–Cheney grassroots organization reached out to "lazy Republicans." These were people predisposed to vote for Republicans at all levels but who needed to be prodded to go to the polls.

Bush reaped enormous benefits from his reinvigoration of presidential party leadership. He was the first president since Franklin Roosevelt to be reelected while his party also gained seats in both the House and Senate and the first Republican president to do so since Calvin Coolidge in 1924. Bush's three most recent Republican predecessors – Dwight Eisenhower in 1956, Richard Nixon in 1972, Ronald Reagan in 1984 – and Bill Clinton in 1996 won reelection by much larger margins than he did. But theirs were "lonely landslides" in which the president did well but his party suffered in the congressional elections. In contrast, Bush's 2004 reelection spearheaded a partisan victory.

Personalizing a War: Bush and Iraq

In contrast to his successful party leadership, Bush's conduct of the War on Terror revealed him to be a victim of the personalized presidency. Like LBJ, he was unable to maintain public support for his war policies. Like Richard Nixon, his unilateral efforts caused him to run afoul of the Supreme Court.

Bush's initial response to 9/11 gave no indication of the political difficulties to come. Like a true Progressive, Bush emphasized that the War on Terror was not only an effort to protect American lives and property but also a "crusade" to protect liberal and democratic values. In words reminiscent of FDR, Bush told a joint session of Congress on September 20, 2001,

> Freedom and fear are at war . . . The advance of human freedom, the great achievement of our time, now depends on us. Our nation, this generation, will lift a dark threat of violence from our people and our future. We will not tire, we will not falter, and we will not fail.

Bush's estrangement from public opinion was traceable to his decision to invade Iraq. He did obtain congressional endorsement, an Authorization for the Use of Military Force in Iraq. But the rationale for the invasion was based in large measure on the threat Iraq posed by virtue of its possession of weapons of mass destruction. Post invasion, no such weapons were found. This failure fed the cynicism of Bush's critics who claimed that Bush was aware that Iraq had no such weapons. Although the invasion itself went smoothly, the US was unsuccessful in establishing a new government capable of suppressing armed resistance. As American casualties mounted, the war became ever more unpopular with the American public. Like LBJ, Bush was unable to make a persuasive case to the American people that the gains from pacifying Iraq were worth the loss of life. Hence the 2006 electoral defeat in which the Democrats recaptured control of both houses of Congress. His foreign policy failure robbed him of the fruits of his party building successes.

Bush also faced rebuke from the Supreme Court. In June 2006, the Supreme Court ruled in *Hamdan v. Rumsfeld* that the Bush policy of holding illegal enemy combatants at Guantanamo Bay, Cuba, and having them tried by military tribunals with no right of habeas corpus, was illegal because it had not been authorized by Congress. The right of habeas corpus is a hallowed legal protection that compels the government to bring anyone charged with a crime before a civilian judge. In response, Bush obtained congressional passage of the Military Commissions Act authorizing the use of military tribunals and the denial of habeas corpus. Then the Supreme Court shifted its grounds for opposing military tribunals. In *Boumediene v. Bush* it ruled that regardless of congressional approval, the denial of habeas corpus to illegal enemy combatants was unconstitutional. The practical meaning of this seemingly far-reaching decision is hard to evaluate. Although President Obama promised to close the Guantanamo Bay detention facility, President Trump has pledged to keep it open, and military tribunals are still in place. When the Obama administration announced its intention to try the alleged mastermind of the 9/11 attacks in a civilian court, however, the outcry against this decision caused it to delay the trial indefinitely.

Personalization and Polarization: Barack Obama

Barack Obama's presidential career eerily paralleled his Democratic predecessor Bill Clinton's presidency in that it combined a great personal electoral victory – reelection in 2012 – with major defeats, namely the loss of control of both houses of Congress for six of his eight years in office and the political repudiation that comes when one's successor is defeated and the presidential office is assumed by the other party. The comparison is not perfect, however, in that Obama did not suffer the indignity of impeachment and scandal, and he did succeed in obtaining passage of his number one policy priority, healthcare reform.

Hillary Clinton was the presumptive front runner for the 2008 Democratic presidential nomination. However, Barack Obama's challenge to her did not represent a full-fledged insurgency akin to TR, McGovern, Sanders, or Trump, all of whom mounted aggressive and vehement challenges to party orthodoxy (see Chapter 13). Indeed, no sharp policy divisions emerged from Clinton and Obama's nomination contest. On what would become the signature domestic initiative of his presidency, healthcare reform, Obama took a much more moderate position than Clinton during the campaign.

Obama's triumph resulted from both his greater identification with opposition to the War in Iraq and his message of "hope and change." Clinton had also come to oppose the war, but she had initially cast her Senate vote for the Authorization of Military Force (AUMF). Obama had opposed it from the beginning. His hope and change message was meant to emphasize that he was a relative newcomer to Washington and therefore, unlike Hillary Clinton, he was not tainted by the bitter partisan discord that had welled up since the Clinton impeachment resulting from the 2000 election result and the Iraq War. His message resonated with an electorate that had grown tired of the atmosphere of petty vindictiveness that seemed to dominate Washington and was looking for a president who could create a more cooperative and positive political climate.

Obama's key strategic decision upon taking office was to make healthcare reform his top domestic priority. He jettisoned his relatively modest campaign proposal in favor of a far more ambitious plan that resembled the one Hillary Clinton had put forward during the campaign. In particular, Obama now supported Clinton's idea that those who did not already have health insurance would be required to purchase a government-approved health insurance policy. Those who refused would have to pay a fine. Obama and his advisors decided that this provision, called a mandate, was necessary in order to induce insurance companies to offer policies at a reasonable price. In the absence of a mandate, healthy people might choose to remain uninsured. Insurance companies would be stuck providing insurance mostly to those with health problems and therefore they would have to charge much higher prices or lose money.

Obama put the full weight of his office behind the push for passage of this the most ambitious domestic policy reform in many decades. His personal involvement was so great that the reform measure, the Affordable Care Act (ACA), came to be nicknamed "Obamacare." The "Contemporary Portrait" section of this chapter describes some of the specific steps he took to mobilize public support for this audacious initiative. Congressional Republicans objected to many features of the proposal, most especially the mandate. They recalled that the previous effort of a Democratic president, Bill Clinton, to pass an ambitious healthcare proposal had led to such a backlash that they were able to gain control of Congress. Therefore, the Republican leadership determined not to seek compromise but to oppose the proposal in its totality. Not a single congressional Republican supported it. Because the Democrats controlled both houses of Congress, they were able to gain passage. The healthcare reform was the first major piece of policy reform legislation in modern times to pass with no support from the opposition party. Hopes for an end to the poisonous atmosphere of partisan discord were dashed.

Although the Republicans could not prevent passage of Obamacare, they won the public opinion battle. They scored a tremendous victory in the 2010 midterm elections, winning back control of the House of Representatives and reducing the Democrat margin in the Senate by five seats. Never again during the six remaining years of his presidency would Obama enjoy a majority in the House of Representatives. Thus, he would not be able to gain congressional approval for any of his major policy initiatives. In the 2014 midterm elections Obama suffered another resounding defeat, losing control of the Senate to the Republicans as well as an additional thirteen seats in the House.

Obama's Foreign Policy

Obama's foreign policy departed in significant ways from that of his predecessor. He vigorously prosecuted efforts to counter the threat of domestic terrorism but reduced the level of rhetorical aggressiveness. Unlike Bush, Obama did not speak of a "War on Terror." Nor did he invoke the term "Radical Islam" with regard to the terror threat. To make clear his determination to alter the United States' posture toward the Arab world, he chose Cairo as the venue for his first major foreign policy address. Thus, he honored a promise he had made during the campaign to give a major address to Muslims from a Muslim capital during his first few months as president. The title of the speech was "A New Beginning," indicating his intention to reach out to the Arab world and establish a greater rapport with it. The democratic uprisings that began in 2010, known as the Arab Spring, appeared to vindicate this rhetorical shift. In a similar vein, he called for a "reset" in relations between the United States and Russia. His speech delivered in Moscow called for "a sustained effort among the American and Russian people to identify mutual interests, and expand dialogue and cooperation that can pave the way to progress."

Unlike any of his predecessors, Obama displayed ambivalence about the United States' dominant role in world affairs. Speaking at the 2010 nuclear summit attended by forty-seven nations, Obama declared: "Whether we like it or not, we remain a dominant military superpower." Such a statement is in stark contrast to Democratic predecessor Bill Clinton's statement in his 1997 inaugural address that America stands alone as the world's "indispensable nation." In a similar vein, Obama took many occasions to apologize for past American misdeeds. The overall impression he sought to convey was that the United States should see itself less as a "city on a hill" (see Chapter 2) bringing freedom and democracy to the rest of the world, than as a member of a community of nations of more or less equal moral stature.

Obama's policies differed from his predecessors' in substance as well as tone. For example, he supported efforts to oust Egypt's authoritarian ruler, Hosni Mubarak, despite the fact that Mubarak had been a staunch ally of the United States. His most decisive break with Bush's policies involved Iraq. In December of 2011, he completed the withdrawal of US forces from Iraq. True, the Bush administration shortly before leaving office had agreed to withdraw US forces by that date. However, Bush had agreed to the 2011 deadline way back in 2007. A four-year window remained to alter the agreement if circumstances warranted. As the date neared, many foreign policy experts, including Obama's Secretary of Defense Leon Panetta and some other members of Obama's foreign policy team, were of the opinion that the military situation in Iraq had deteriorated to such an extent that keeping American troops there was now imperative. Panetta thought that Obama could have pressed the case harder with the Iraqis to obtain their permission to remain and that the US had sufficient leverage with the Iraqis to force them to do so. In view of Bush's strong commitment to victory in Iraq, he would most likely have opted to have the troops remain. Obama's decision to go ahead with the actual pullout, therefore, represented a significant departure from previous policy.

Obama also departed both rhetorically and substantively from previous policy toward Iran. In his 2002 State of the Union address, Bush declared that Iran, along with North Korea and Saddam Hussein's Iraq, formed an "axis of evil." To combat Iran, Bush imposed very harsh economic sanctions designed to coerce Iran into abandoning its efforts to develop nuclear arms. Obama chose a different tack. He abandoned all talk of an axis of evil. Instead, he sought to engage Iran in negotiations regarding its nuclear arms. The result was an executive agreement (see "Contemporary Portrait" above) in which the US and five other nations that were also imposing sanctions agreed to lift them. In exchange, Iran promised to limit its nuclear development program and agreed to certain forms of inspection of the program's facilities. The deal reflected Obama's shift away from demonizing Iran in his belief that Iran could become a constructive force in the Middle East, and his greater reliance on negotiations as opposed to ongoing coercion.

Because the Arab Spring failed, Obama was unable to improve relations with Arab countries. In the face of Russia's invasion of Crimea and its subsequent efforts to destabilize the Ukraine, Obama abandoned the "Russian reset" and joined a number of other nations and international organizations in imposing sanctions. But these specific setbacks should not be taken to minimize the change in America's foreign policy posture that Obama brought about. Most importantly, he sought to place less emphasis on American world dominance and emphasize instead friendship, partnership, and cooperation with other nations.

In summary, Obama's departures from Bush's foreign policy can be summarized thus:

- Reduction in the level of rhetorical aggressiveness regarding terrorism
- "Reset" in relations between the United States and Russia.
- Air strikes in Libya
- Withdrawal of US forces from Iraq
- Iran Nuclear Deal

Looking Forward

The Framers neither intended nor expected the president to personify government in the public mind. Such personification smacks of monarchy not republican government. FDR's four-term reign so frightened Republican political leaders that they spearheaded the ultimately successful campaign to pass a constitutional amendment limiting the president to two terms. President Nixon's efforts to centralize power in the White House and to cover up the Watergate scandal led to a liberal outcry against the "imperial presidency" and to a spate of congressional initiatives designed to restrict presidential discretion. As we have discussed, the Supreme Court also moved against the president, demanding that he release his secret White House tapes. The Court continued to curb presidential power by depriving him of the line item veto. In *Clinton v. New York City* (1998) the Supreme Court ruled that the Constitution does not give the president such a power. As we have already discussed, the Court overturned the Bush administration's effort to deny the right to habeas corpus of illegal enemy combatants. A federal court stayed President Obama's executive order on immigration.

This pushback from the Court and Congress shows that the president is not yet a king. Despite the quasi-royal glamour the office radiates, the American president has, so far, been subject to effective institutional constraint. However, strong political forces are at work that threaten to undermine those checks. The intensifying polarization of the electorate has made the presidential election into an increasingly heated ideological struggle. The winner wants to claim that he represents all the people. However, increasingly he is perceived as the champion of one set of strongly held views that is in confrontation with its polar opposite. Therefore, he is impelled to press harder and harder to achieve the policy objectives his supporters crave, and to do so unilaterally if necessary. In the face of such pressure it is very difficult to be scrupulous about respecting constitutional boundaries, even if he were disposed to do so. Like his predecessor, President Trump has engaged in audacious unilateral actions. The ideological stakes are unlikely to diminish in the foreseeable future, and thus it is doubtful that Trump's successors will prove more reticent. Looking forward, the key question is whether Congress and the courts can prove sufficiently strong and vigilant to ensure that presidential leadership stays within constitutional bounds.

CHAPTER SUMMARY

The presidency, a contemporary portrait:

* The vesting clause in Article II of the Constitution grants all executive power to the president, leaving considerable room for controversy about just how broad the president's powers really are.
* President Trump and all his modern predecessors have displayed legislative and managerial authority far beyond what the Constitution explicitly grants them.
* The president functions as legislator in chief.
* The president enjoys the greatest degree of autonomy with respect to national security and diplomacy.
* The size, complexity, and scope of the executive branch presents a great managerial challenge to the president.
* The president serves as party leader and has become a dominant celebrity.
* In recent times, the president has assigned a variety of different roles to the vice president. Overall, the vice presidency has become more important and more prestigious.

Critical choices: Washington to Lincoln:

* George Washington established critical precedents for presidential conduct.
* Thomas Jefferson and Andrew Jackson both acted to democratize the presidency.
* Abraham Lincoln demonstrated that the president could serve as an agent of constitutional change. He provided new and provocative answers to fundamental political questions about the proper role of executive power and how to reconcile the Constitution as a legal document with democratic principles and practice.

Critical choice: creating the personalized presidency:

* In the twentieth century the president came to personify government.
* Theodore Roosevelt and Woodrow Wilson pioneered the personalized presidency and Franklin Delano Roosevelt (FDR) added further critical rhetorical and political dimensions to it.

The impact of the Cold War and television:

* The advent of the Cold War meant that the president retained much of the power and dominance he had only previously enjoyed during wartime. After the advent of nuclear weapons, his personal role was further enhanced because he alone had his "finger on the button."
* The advent of television meant that the face as well as the voice of the president entered the nation's living rooms.

The personalized presidency: opportunities and hazards:

* Of all the post-FDR presidents, Lyndon Johnson (LBJ) most clearly exemplified both the extraordinary prospects and the fragile authority of the personalized presidency.
* Although all Republican presidents of the postwar period considered themselves to be conservatives, only Ronald Reagan mounted a serious effort to halt the expansion of the federal government. Although done in the name of limited government, Reagan's approach to reform was as president-centered as that of FDR and LBJ.
* Although they both served two full terms, the programmatic ambitions of both Presidents Clinton and Obama were checked by their party's inability to keep control of the Congress.
* The presidency of George W. Bush marked both an expansion of the personalized presidency via his approach to fighting terrorism and an effort to reduce presidential isolation through his reassertion of party leadership.
* The Supreme Court and Congress took important steps to limit President Bush's and President Obama's assertions of executive authority. Disputes among the branches regarding the proper extent of presidential power are ongoing.
* Obama's foreign policy marked a major shift away from his predecessor's foreign policy.

SUGGESTED READINGS

Arnold, Peri. *Making the Managerial Presidency*, 2nd rev. edn. Lawrence: University Press of Kansas, 1998.

Binkley, Wilfred E. *The President and Congress.* New York: Knopf, 1947.

Ceaser, James. *Presidential Selection: Theory and Development.* Princeton, NJ: Princeton University Press, 1979.

Cornwell, Elmer, Jr. *Presidential Leadership of Public Opinion.* Bloomington: Indiana University Press, 1965.

Corwin, Edward. *The President: Office and Powers, 1787–1984*, 5th rev. edn. New York: New York University Press, 1989.

Crenson, Matthew, and Benjamin Ginsberg. *Presidential Power: Unchecked and Unbalanced.* New York: W. W. Norton, 2007.

Howell, William. *Power Without Persuasion: The Politics of Direct Presidential Action.* Princeton, NJ: Princeton University Press, 2003.

Landy, Marc, and Sidney M. Milkis. *Presidential Greatness.* Lawrence: University Press of Kansas, 2000.

Lowi, Theodore. *The Personal President.* Ithaca, NY: Cornell University Press, 1995.

Milkis, Sidney M., and Michael Nelson. *The American Presidency: Origins and Development, 1776–2007*, 7th edn. Washington, DC: CQ Press, 2016.

Nelson, Michael, ed. *The Presidency and the Political System*, 8th edn. Washington, DC: CQ Press, 2005.

Neustadt, Richard. *Presidential Power and the Modern Presidents: The Politics of Leadership from Roosevelt to Reagan.* New York: Free Press, 1991.

Paludan, Phillip S. *The Presidency of Abraham Lincoln.* Lawrence: University Press of Kansas, 1994.

Rudalevige, Andrew. *The New Imperial Presidency: Renewing Presidential Power after Watergate.* Ann Arbor: University of Michigan Press, 2005.

Skowronek, Stephen. *The Politics Presidents Make: Leadership from John Adams to Bill Clinton.* Cambridge, MA: Harvard University Press, 1997.

Tulis, Jeffrey. *The Rhetorical Presidency.* Princeton, NJ: Princeton University Press, 1987.

9 The Judiciary

CHAPTER OVERVIEW

This chapter focuses on:

- **A contemporary portrait of the federal judiciary, particularly the Supreme Court.**
- **The critical choice to establish judicial review and establish the Court as the guardian of national supremacy.**
- ***Dred Scott* and the false path to reinforce slavery.**
- **The Court and the regulation of commerce.**
- **The Court's redefinition of rights.**
- **The path dependency involved in reaffirming the rights revolution and the path deviation involved in reconsidering federalism.**

At about ten o'clock in the evening on Tuesday, December 12, 2000, more than a month after election day, the Supreme Court issued a dramatic decision that ended the historic dispute over the presidential election and enabled Republican governor George W. Bush of Texas to become president of the United States. The court's decision was the last act in a legal drama that began the day after the election when Americans awoke to discover that the contest between Bush and his Democratic opponent, Vice President Al Gore, was still undecided. Gore defeated Bush in the popular vote by almost half a million votes, but in the Electoral College (see Chapter 3). Gore led Bush by 266 votes to 246 votes, short of the majority needed to win. The outcome would be determined by the vote in Florida, where Bush held a popular vote margin of less than 2,000 of the nearly 6 million votes cast. If Florida's 25 electoral votes went to Bush, he would have 271 electoral votes, a bare majority of the 538 total, and would become president despite losing the popular vote.

A discrepancy between the popular and electoral vote had not occurred since 1888, when Republican Benjamin Harrison won despite receiving fewer popular votes than Democrat Grover Cleveland. The 2000 election was a reminder that the Constitution does not provide for majority rule but for republican government, which moderates, or frustrates, majorities in the name of minority rights and local self-government. But the import of this discrepancy was largely disregarded amid the dispute over Florida's votes.

Claiming that machines had failed to count all his votes, Gore called for a hand recount in four counties with high Democratic totals that were controlled by Democratic election commissions. The crux of Gore's legal challenge, supported by the Florida Supreme Court, was that voting machines, and therefore official ballots, were flawed, especially in Democratic counties. A hand count would show the true intent of voters and, in all likelihood, overcome Bush's lead, which had shrunk to 327 votes after the November 10 statewide machine recount required by Florida law for such close elections. As a complex and bitter legal process played out, Americans sought comic relief in stories of how chads, cardboard dots that Florida's voters punched out in casting their ballots, clung stubbornly to ballots, disguising the real intention of voters.

Discerning voter intent was the subject of the Supreme Court decision in *Bush v. Gore*. The court ruled that the Florida Supreme Court's order requiring manual recounts of every under vote in Florida (that is, every ballot in the state for which

Figure 9.1. An Imperfect Balance: a 2005 cartoon by Hanson and Dagbladt depicting the judicial contest between Bush and Gore for the United States Presidency.
Source: Political Cartoons.com

a machine failed to register a vote for president) was unconstitutional. By failing to establish a standard by which counties across the states would judge voter intention, the Florida court violated the Fourteenth Amendment's requirement that states protect the right of individuals to equal protection and due process of the law. Seven of the nine justices agreed that the Florida court had violated basic Fourteenth Amendment rights.

But the Supreme Court divided more closely and bitterly on the second, decisive part of its ruling. By a 5–4 vote, the court ruled that the Florida court had also violated the Constitution in overruling the state legislature. The legislature had invoked a federal law that insulates a state's electors from challenge so long as they are certified by December 12. A proper recount simply could not be conducted by that date, and an attempt to do so violated "the constitutional prerogative of the state legislature to determine how electors are chosen."

Gore conceded. But this surrender did not take place without considerable protest. Justice John Stevens criticized the court's majority for emphasizing the need to certify votes by December 12 rather than enforcing Florida's obligation to determine voter intent. In the interest of "finality," Stevens charged, "the majority effectively orders the disenfranchisement of an unknown number of voters whose ballots reveal their intent – and are therefore legal votes under state law – but were for some reason rejected by ballot-counting machines."

Chief Justice William Rehnquist's majority opinion replied that the Supreme Court's first obligation was to the Constitution, not the voters: "the individual citizen has no federal constitutional right to vote for electors for the President of the United States"; that privilege, according to Article II of the Constitution, exists at the pleasure of the state legislatures. The Florida state legislature had a constitutional right to resolve any controversy over the final selection of electors in order to meet the December 12 deadline imposed by Congress.

In his concession speech, Gore congratulated Bush on "becoming," not on "being elected," the forty-third president of the United States. Gore's distinction hinted at the daunting challenge Bush faced of ruling without a popular mandate. But Bush benefited greatly from the people's faith in the Supreme Court as the proper interpreter, the guardian, of the Constitution. Although many militant Democrats viewed the decision as a crude conservative power play, surveys indicated that most people wanted the courts to decide the contest. They accepted Bush as the legitimate president.

It is hard to imagine public officials and citizens in other representative democracies allowing judges to decide the outcome of a national election. Americans' acceptance of *Bush v. Gore* speaks to the extraordinary power of the independent judiciary to influence virtually every aspect of American political life. The power of the judiciary is one of the most distinctive characteristics of the American constitutional order. It was often the first thing a foreign visitor noticed about American government. As early as the 1830s, Alexis de Tocqueville observed, "There is hardly a political question in the United States which does not sooner or later turn into a judicial one." American judges, he noted, did not simply interpret an existing body of law, as they did in France or Great Britain; nor were they limited to arbitrating legal disputes. They played a very large part in the development of law and public policy itself.

How is it that a people with a strong democratic tradition have given so much authority to nine unelected judges? This chapter explores the fundamental constitutional debate about the judiciary in relation to the elected branches. It traces the development of that relationship and the strains it has caused. After painting a contemporary portrait of the judiciary, the chapter considers the origins and growth of judicial authority. It then examines the failed efforts of the Court to impose its will on two great national controversies - slavery and government regulation of the economy. Next it examines the Court's role in the redefinition of the meaning of rights that has occurred since the New Deal and the political consequences of that redefinition. Finally it looks at the Court during the last three decades to understand the complex web of retrenchment, extension and reaffirmation of rights it has spun.

The Judiciary: A Contemporary Portrait

The Rule of Law

The contemporary judiciary deals with several different kinds of law. Civil law establishes a framework for overseeing the rules that govern the relationships between private parties, individuals, associations, and firms. When one party believes itself aggrieved by another, it brings a civil action that petitions the judiciary to rule against the other party and provide relief. The party bringing a civil action is called a plaintiff. The other party is the defendant. The most common forms of civil actions involve contracts and torts. A contract is a binding agreement between those who sign it, its signatories. A signatory sues when they believe that another signatory has violated the terms of the contract. For example, if a sawmill promises to deliver 1,000 two by fours to a lumberyard and only delivers 900, the lumberyard might sue the sawmill for breach of contract. A tort is a harm done to one party by another. If one believes that someone else has done damage to one's property or person, one brings a tort action seeking compensation for that injury. For example, if someone slips on a banana skin in the supermarket and breaks an ankle, if that person sues the supermarket claiming the market bore responsibility for the fall, the case would be considered a tort.

Whereas civil actions involve disputes among persons or organizations, criminal actions involve offenses against the people as a whole. The criminal law enumerates and describes what constitutes such public offenses. Offenses are ranked in terms of their severity. Misdemeanors are composed of petty crimes such as vandalism and the theft of inexpensive objects. Felonies are composed of more serious offenses such as murder, rape, assault, robbery, and theft of expensive objects. Because a crime is an offense against all of us, the government, not the person or persons directly harmed, acts as the plaintiff.

As we discussed in Chapter 2, one of the most serious grievances brought by the American colonists against the British Crown concerned restrictions placed on trial by jury. To guard against such a threat in the future, the Constitution grants criminal defendants a right to a jury trial and the Seventh Amendment extends that right to civil cases as well. Likewise, state constitutions guarantee this right in criminal trials and every state except Louisiana also guarantees it in civil trials. Relatively few Americans can expect to serve as public executives, legislators, or judges, but most can expect to be called for jury duty. The difficult judgments regarding guilt and responsibility jurors are called upon to make may well be the most important and demanding forms of public service that citizens are ever called upon to perform.

Public law concerns those cases in which the government or the constitutional rights of citizens are involved. Constitutional law is that form of public law that involves judicial scrutiny of government or private action in terms of whether it violates the Constitution. Most of the cases discussed in this chapter relate to constitutional law. Administrative law is the form of public law that relates to the conduct and rulings of administrative agencies in determining whether they are in conformity with the will of Congress and whether the rights accorded to those subject to administrative rulings are being protected. For example, if the Occupational Safety and Health Administration issues a regulation requiring all metal workers to wear safety glasses and the owner of a metal-working factory thinks that some metal-working machines are so safe that the owner should not have to provide glasses to the operators of those machines, the owner can sue OSHA in federal court claiming that the regulation is "arbitrary and capricious" and therefore it needs to be modified.

A key difference between a court and a legislature regards the matter of standing. Anyone can petition a legislature to request that it take up an issue. But to be heard in court one must have standing. One must show that one has been directly harmed by the entity one is suing; one cannot sue simply to make a political point or because one is sympathetic to the problems of others. Later on, we will see that with regard to a whole host of federal laws and regulations, Congress has chosen to relax the rules of standing and make it far easier to claim that one has been harmed by a polluter or a destroyer of natural resources.

The Structure of the Judiciary

The American judicial system is made up of two parallel systems: federal courts and state courts. State courts vary enormously, as befits the differences in state constitutions. Some states elect their judges, including their state Supreme Court justices. In other states, the system of district, appeal, and supreme courts are appointed. Most ordinary civil and criminal matters are handled, under state law, by state courts.

Generally speaking, a case goes to federal rather than state court if the federal government is directly involved, if a federal statute is at issue, if a claim of a violation of the US Constitution is made, or if a civil suit is brought that involves citizens from more than one state. The federal system is composed of three tiers: district courts, appeals courts, and the Supreme Court. District courts are where ordinary civil and criminal federal trials take place. Nationwide, there are ninety-four district courts handling in excess of 200,000 civil cases and 45,000 criminal cases a year. Each state has at least one federal district court. The nation is carved up into eleven separate courts of appeals. There is a twelfth one for the District of Columbia, and the thirteenth is the US Court of Appeals for the Federal Circuit, which specializes in patents and financial claims against the government. Appeals courts deal only with cases brought to them on appeal either from the district courts or federal administrative agencies. The latter type of appeal goes to the DC circuit, which has thus acquired a particular expertise in administrative law. Figure 9.2 shows a map of the federal appeals and district courts.

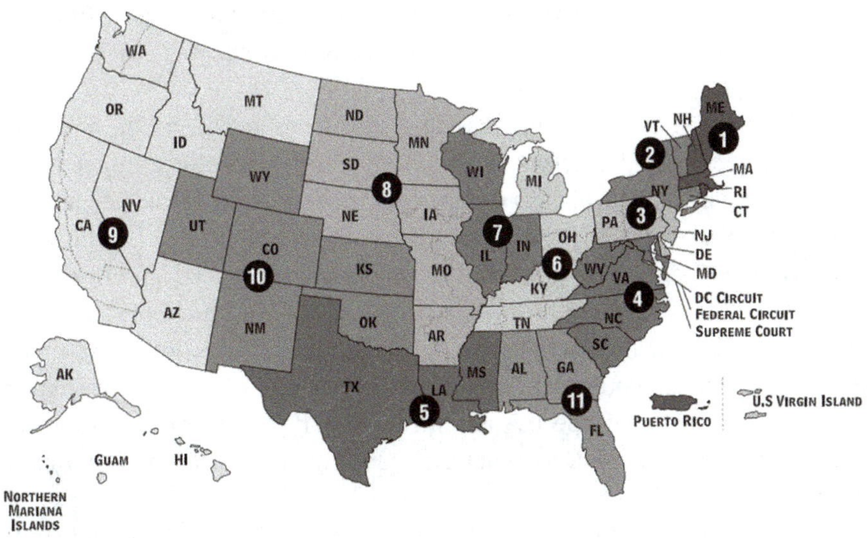

Figure 9.2. Federal Appeals Courts.
Source: US Courts.

The Supreme Court takes cases that arise on appeal from the federal appeals courts; the highest court of a state; or that the Constitution specifically assigns to it, its sphere of original jurisdiction. That sphere includes disputes between: citizens from different states; a state and the federal government; two or more states; or cases involving foreign diplomats. Unlike the lower courts, the Supreme Court is free to decide which cases it wants to hear and which it does not. For a case to be accepted by the Supreme Court at least four justices must agree that it involves "a substantial federal question"; if so, the Court issues a writ of certiorari – Latin for "made more certain" – which brings the case before the court. The court refuses to hear far more appeals than it accepts. It tends to accept those cases that raise issues about which different lower courts have issued contradictory opinions. In such an instance it attempts to establish a clear-cut set of principles and standards in order to provide guidance to the lower courts in order to encourage them to arrive at a consistent set of decisions regarding those issues. But it may also choose to accept other sorts of cases in which at least four of the justices believe that a ruling by the court is useful and important for the wellbeing of the nation.

US district courts try hundreds of thousands of cases each year, the overwhelming number of them are civil. Federal courts of appeals review less than 20 percent of their cases. In recent years the Supreme Court has only heard about seventy-five cases a year. Among the important and controversial questions raised by cases the Court accepted in its 2015–16 term were whether the state of Texas was unreasonably restricting access to abortion clinics; whether the healthcare plans offered by religion-sponsored nonprofit corporations would have to include birth control services as prescribed by the Affordable Care Act; and, whether an African-American man sentenced to death by an all-white jury in Georgia was entitled to a new trial because the prosecution had stricken every black prospective juror from the case.

Federal judges are chosen by the president, who relies heavily on the advice of the attorney general and other members of the president's political inner circle. These designees are almost always from the same party as the president. Judicial nominees come from a variety of legal backgrounds. Many have had previous careers as state judges and prosecutors. Others have been law professors or prominent attorneys. Because these selections must be confirmed by a majority vote in the Senate, its members have a great deal of influence in the selection process. The president, before making a judicial nomination, asks for the support of the senators from the prospective nominee's state, if they are of the president's party. This custom is known as senatorial courtesy. The Senate will normally reject a candidate if those senators object.

Once the president nominates a federal judge, the Senate Judiciary Committee conducts hearings during which its members interrogate the nominee and also hear from a wide variety of interest groups who seek to influence the Senate vote.

Table 9.1. Justices of the Supreme Court.

Name	Year appointed	Nominated by
Anthony Kennedy	1988	Reagan
Clarence Thomas	1991	George H. W. Bush
Ruth Bader Ginsburg	1993	Clinton
Stephen Breyer	1994	Clinton
John Roberts*	2005	George W. Bush
Samuel Alito	2006	George W. Bush
Sonia Sotomayor	2009	Obama
Elena Kagan	2010	Obama
Neil Gorsuch	2017	Trump

* Roberts was appointed as Chief Justice after the death of William Rehnquist

The committee then votes on whether or not to recommend the nominee to the full Senate. Then the Senate debates the nomination and votes to either approve or disapprove the nomination.

Currently the Supreme Court has nine members, the chief justice, and eight associate justices. The number is not set in the Constitution. It is set by Congress and has varied over time. However, Congress has left the number at nine since 1869. Scholars of the court divide its history into distinct eras named in honor of the chief justice. John Roberts is the current chief justice and so the contemporary court is called "the Roberts Court." Later on the chapter will discuss especially the Marshall, Warren, Burger, and Rehnquist Courts.

Figure 9.3 charts the changes in the size of the court up through 1869 when in reached its current size of nine.

When the Supreme Court agrees to hear a case, it accepts briefs from the contending parties and from outside groups whom the litigants ask to submit amicus curiae, or "friend of the court," briefs. A brief is a written explanation of the legal reasons why the Court should rule in a particular way. Then the Court schedules oral arguments, during which the two sides present their case directly to the justices and the justices questions the presenting attorneys. Afterwards, the justices meet in secret conference to discuss the case and vote on it. After the case has been decided, the chief justice assigns an associate justice to write the majority opinion unless the chief justice is on the losing side, in which case the assignment is made by the most senior justice voting with the majority. Every justice is free to write a dissenting opinion, that is, an opinion that opposes the majority, or justices can write opinions that concur with the majority but that offer different reasons for their vote or take up issues not addressed in the majority opinion.

At every stage of a case's consideration except the conference, the Court is assisted by its clerks. In the 2015–16 session there were thirty-four clerks, each

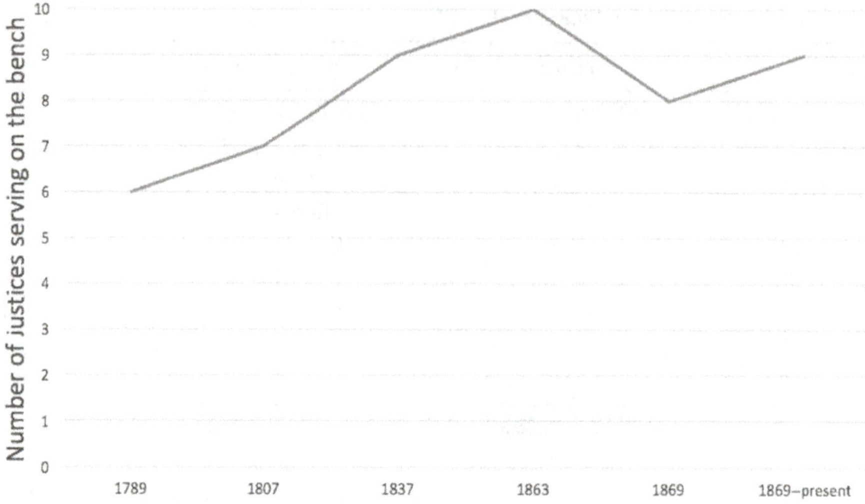

Figure 9.3. Size of the Supreme Court.
Source: Federal Judicial Center.

assigned to a specific justice. Because clerking for the Supreme Court is a highly prestigious post, these clerks, who are all law school graduates, usually have outstanding academic records and come from top-ranked law schools. They scrutinize petitions for certiorari and make recommendations to the justices they work for. They also do the bulk of the research and help draft the justices' opinions.

Defining Rights

As this chapter will explore, two of the most significant functions the Supreme Court performs are to interpret the meaning of the rights mentioned in the Bill of Rights and to rule on the constitutionality of laws enacted by Congress. This latter function is known as judicial review. In recent years the Court has exercised both these vital functions.

The four most significant recent Bill of Rights cases were *McDonald v. Chicago*, which dealt with the Second Amendment right to bear arms; *Citizens United v. Federal Election Commission*, which dealt with the free speech provision of the First Amendment; *Hosanna-Tabor Church v. Equal Employment Opportunity Commission*, which involved the religious liberty provision of the First Amendment; and *Obergefell v. Hodges*, which explored whether or not same-sex couples have a right to marry.

The Second Amendment states "A well-regulated militia, being necessary to the security of a free state, the right of the people to keep and bear arms, shall not be infringed." In 2008 the Court ruled in *District of Columbia v. Heller* that this language meant that government could not infringe on the right of citizens to self-defense and therefore Washington DC's law that banned the possession of handguns in the home was unconstitutional. The majority opinion in that case claimed that the intentions of the Framers made clear that the right to keep and bear arms is fundamental to the American system of ordered liberty and that therefore citizens enjoyed the right to defend themselves.

The question in *McDonald* was whether the Second Amendment applied to the states. The City of Chicago had adopted a ban on handguns in the home similar to that in Washington DC. As we shall see later on, the Supreme Court has decided to extend to states and localities an ever-expanding list of Bill of Rights protections that were originally intended to apply only the federal government. It has interpreted the Fourteenth Amendment's assertion that no state can deny equal protection and due process of law to mean that many critical Bill of Rights protections must extend to states and localities as well. In the majority opinion, Justice Samuel Alito noted that self-defense is a fundamental right, recognized by many legal systems from ancient times to the present day: "In *Heller*, we held that individual self-defense is 'the central component' of the Second Amendment. The right to keep and bear arms was considered no less fundamental by those who drafted and ratified the Bill of Rights." Therefore, he concluded, the right to bear arms was as fundamental as the other rights enumerated in the Bill of Rights that the Court had previously determined deserved to be incorporated with regard to the states. Alito admitted that allowing people to keep handguns in their homes might have negative public safety implications. However, he pointed out that "the right to keep and bear arms . . . is not the only constitutional right that has controversial public safety implications." Restricting the power of the police to conduct searches, to eavesdrop, and to interrogate criminals may likewise threaten public safety, and yet the Court had determined that in the protection of individual liberty such risks be borne. If a fundamental right exists it cannot be denied because its exercise will sometimes cause harm. In his dissent, Justice Stevens denied that the Chicago law constituted the denial of a fundamental right. The Chicago ordinance did not deny the right of citizens to own weapons, even handguns. It simply said they could not keep them in the house.

> The notion that a right of self-defense implies an auxiliary right to own a certain type of firearm presupposes not only controversial judgments about the strength and scope of the (posited) self-defense right, but also controversial assumptions about the likely effects of making that type of firearm more broadly available. It is a very long way from the proposition that the Fourteenth Amendment protects a basic individual right of self-defense to the conclusion that a city may not ban handguns.

The issue of free speech emerged in relation to the provision of the BiPartisan Campaign Finance Reform Act of 2002 (commonly called McCain Feingold) prohibiting corporations and unions from spending their own money on "electioneering communication" within thirty days of a primary or general election. In January 2008, Citizens United, a nonprofit corporation, released a documentary criticizing then Senator Hillary Clinton, who was seeking the Democratic presidential nomination.To promote this documentary, Citizens United produced television advertisements to run on broadcast and cable television. Because its promotion efforts would occur while presidential primaries were taking place, Citizen's United feared that they would be considered "electioneering communications" and therefore kept off the air. Citizens United sought relief in federal court seeking to prevent the Federal Elections Commission from enforcing the applicable provision of the Campaign Finance because it was an unconstitutional limit on free speech. The lower courts dismissed the Citizens United petition and the case went to the Supreme Court.

Justice Kennedy, writing for the five-justice majority, agreed with Citizens United. He noted that the First Amendment categorically declared that the Congress "shall make no law . . . prohibiting or abridging the freedom of speech." The amendment did not limit who had the right to exercise such speech and therefore the Congress could not exempt corporations, unions, or any other entity from exercising free speech. He did not claim that freedom of speech was absolute. He did not deny Justice Holmes famous dictum that freedom of speech did not allow someone to "shout fire in a crowded theatre." But he insisted that there had to be a "sufficient governmental interest" to justify "limits on the political speech of nonprofit or for-profit corporations." He denied that any such interest had been demonstrated in this case. In his dissent, Justice Stevens denied that the First Amendment

> Required that corporations must be treated identically to natural persons in the political sphere . . . Although they make enormous contributions to our society, corporations are not actually members of it. They cannot vote or run for office. Because they may be managed and controlled by nonresidents, their interests may conflict in fundamental respects with the interests of eligible voters.

Because corporations pose a serious threat to the holding of free elections they constituted just the sort of sufficient government interest that the majority said was lacking as a rationale for limiting speech in this instance: "The financial resources, legal structure, and instrumental orientation of corporations raise legitimate concerns about their role in the electoral process. Our lawmakers have a compelling constitutional basis, if not also a democratic duty, to take measures designed to guard against the potentially deleterious effects of corporate spending in local and national races."

The First Amendment also forbids Congress from making any law respecting the establishment of religion (the establishment clause) or prohibiting the free exercise of religion (the free exercise clause). In *Hosanna-Tabor Church v. Equal*

Employment Opportunity Commission, the Court declared, based on those two clauses, there existed a "ministerial exemption" preventing the government from enforcing federal employment discrimination law against a religious body.

Cheryl Perich was a teacher at a school in Redford, Michigan run by the Hosanna-Tabor Church, which belonged to the Lutheran Church–Missouri Synod, the second-largest Lutheran denomination in the United States. She suffered from narcolepsy, a disease that caused her to unpredictably fall into sudden and deep sleeps from which she could not be awakened. She began the 2004/05 school year on disability leave but sought to return to work midyear. The school had already hired a replacement and refused her request. She was asked to resign in exchange for the school continuing to pay part of her health insurance premiums. Perich refused to resign and after persisting in trying to return to work she was warned that she risked being fired. She then informed the school that she had spoken to a lawyer and was planning to sue for reinstatement. The church then fired her stating that her threat to take legal action violated church policy. She reported her firing to the US Equal Employment Opportunity Commission, which then sued the church on her behalf claiming that her firing violated the Americans With Disabilities Act.

In ruling against the EEOC the Court did not address the question of whether indeed the firing violated the act. Rather, it determined that the language of the First Amendment prevented the government from interfering in the hiring and firing of anyone who could plausibly be viewed as a minister of a church. Although Ms. Persich mostly taught secular subjects, she did devote forty-five minutes of her workday to religious subjects. She was trained as a teacher of religion and was considered by the church to be a minister. Therefore, the church was entitled to treat her as a minister and the government could not consider whether or not she was the victim of discrimination based on her disability. The importance of the decision was reinforced by the fact that it was unanimous. Writing for the united Court, Justice Roberts declared: "The establishment clause prevents the government from appointing ministers … the free exercise clause prevents it from interfering with the freedom of religious groups to select their own."

In July 2013, James Obergefell married John Arthur in Maryland. They chose Maryland rather than their native state of Ohio because Ohio had a law that banned same-sex marriage. Ohio did indeed refuse to recognize their marriage and so they brought suit against the state in order to have their union recognized. The case found its way to the Supreme Court.

The US Supreme Court supported Obergefell and Arthur. In a 5–4 decision issued in June of 2015 it held that "The fundamental liberties protected by the Fourteenth Amendment's due process clause extend to certain personal choices central to individual dignity and autonomy, including intimate choices defining personal identity and beliefs." Marriage was among those intimate choices central to dignity and autonomy.

Table 9.2. Pivotal Bill of Rights cases of the Roberts Court.

Year	Case	Ruling	Majority	Dissenting
2010	*McDonald v. Chicago*	5–4	Roberts, Scalia, Kennedy, Thomas, Alito	Stevens, Ginsburg, Breyer, Sotomayor
2010	*Citizens United v. Federal Election Commission*	5–4	Roberts, Scalia, Kennedy, Thomas, Alito	Stevens, Ginsburg, Breyer, Sotomayor
2012	*Hosanna-Tabor Evangelical Lutheran Church and School v. EEOC*	9–0	Roberts, Scalia, Kennedy, Thomas, Ginsburg, Breyer Alito, Sotomayor, Kagan	
2015	*Obergefell v. Hodges*	5–4	Kennedy, Ginsburg, Breyer, Sotomayor, Kagan	Roberts, Scalia, Thomas, Alito

Source: Oyez, IIT Chicago-Kent College of Law.

In his dissent, Justice Roberts did not question whether or not same-sex marriage was a good idea, but he claimed that it was not a constitutionally guaranteed right. Because the Constitution does not anywhere mention a right to "individual autonomy and liberty" no court can legitimately assert such a right. He claimed that because the court majority favored same-sex marriage, it had based its decision on rights that did not exist. By requiring states to grant same-sex marriage, the members of the majority were acting as legislators not judges. Many states, such as Maryland, had enacted same-sex marriage laws. The others were free to do likewise but were under no obligation to do so.

Judicial Review

The most significant recent exercise of judicial review came in the Court's 2012 decision in *National Federation of Independent Business v. Sebelius* upholding the individual mandate provision of President Obama's signature 2010 healthcare reform plan, the Affordable Care Act (ACA). The mandate provision required most Americans who did not have healthcare coverage to purchase it by 2014. Those who did not would be required to pay a specified amount of money to the federal government. Although it would be paid to the government's tax-collecting agency, the Internal Revenue Service, the ACA stated that it was a penalty, not a tax. The plaintiffs, led by the National Federation of Independent Business, claimed the mandate was unconstitutional. They pointed out that no provision of Article I of the Constitution gave the federal government authority to force individuals to buy something. The commerce clause had never been interpreted by either Congress or the Court as granting it such a power. They did not deny that

Congress has the power to tax individuals, but, since the ACA created a penalty not a tax, the taxing power was inapplicable.

Chief Justice John Roberts's majority opinion upheld the mandate provision but did so in such a way as to serve a warning to the national government regarding the limits of its legislative authority. He agreed with the plaintiffs that the commerce clause could not be invoked as a rationale for the mandate: "The power to regulate commerce presupposes the existence of commercial activity to be regulated." He did not read the word "regulate" as including the power to "create." Such an expansive reading would rob the commerce clause of virtually any capacity to restrict what the federal government did. For example, the obesity that stems from poor eating habits imposes far greater costs on the healthcare system than the failure of some to buy health insurance: "Under the Government's theory, Congress could address the diet problem by ordering everyone to buy vegetables" and impose a penalty on those who did not obey that mandate.

Nonetheless, Roberts ruled for the defendants on the grounds that regardless of the language of the law, the fee imposed for not buying insurance was a tax not a penalty and therefore fell under the taxing power granted in Article I. Roberts saved the mandate by demonstrating that the administration's claim on its behalf was mistaken:

> if the concept of penalty means anything, it means *punishment for an unlawful act or omission.* While the individual mandate clearly aims to induce the purchase of health insurance ... *neither the Act nor any other law attaches negative legal consequences to not buying health insurance* ... [If] someone chooses to pay rather than obtain health insurance, they have fully complied with the law. Indeed, it is estimated that four million people each year will choose to pay the IRS rather than buy insurance. We would expect Congress to be troubled by that prospect if such conduct were unlawful. (italics the author's)

In Roberts's mind, the job of the Court was not to rule on public statements by the president, nor even on rationales stated in the law, but rather to evaluate whether the Constitution permitted the exercise of the specific activity under challenge. Because this activity functioned like a tax, not a penalty, it *was* a tax and therefore it was constitutional. The Court upheld the ACA by a 5–4 vote. The dissenters, all Republican appointees, agreed with Roberts's effort to reign in the commerce clause but claimed that the mandate was a penalty not a tax. The rest of the majority, all Democratic appointees, disagreed with Roberts's narrow reading of the commerce clause.

CRITICAL CHOICE: JUDICIAL REVIEW AND GUARDIANSHIP OF NATIONAL SUPREMACY

The Constitution does not say that the Supreme Court is entitled to determine the constitutionality of acts of Congress, nor that it may overrule acts of the states.

In two critical cases, *Marbury v. Madison* and *McCulloch v. Maryland,* the Supreme Court successfully asserted its powers of judicial review and of protecting the supremacy of the national government from challenge by a state.

Those Framers who favored granting the Supreme Court the power of judicial review claimed that it was granted implicitly on the basis of the special status that federal judges are accorded in the document. Judges are chosen by the executive with the advice and consent of the Senate. They serve for life unless they commit an impeachable offense. These conditions endowed the judiciary with a unique capacity to protect individual rights and the rule of law. George Mason of Virginia voiced the view of many Framers that the judiciary could be a "restraining power," protecting the fundamental law against the designs of unruly majorities and popular demagogues. But many other Framers disagreed. They denied that judges had any special wisdom to offer and feared giving too much power to unelected officials. They echoed the sentiments of the Anti-Federalists, who believed that if judges decided important moral and political questions, representative government would become a farce.

The Constitutional Convention defeated every attempt to endow the Supreme Court with powers to overturn the decisions of other branches. As we shall soon see, the power of judicial review came into being only after a bitter struggle between the Court and President Thomas Jefferson. Before the adoption of the Constitution, Americans viewed the protectors of their rights to be local governments and elected assemblies, not a nonelected judiciary. Even after the Constitution's adoption, the courts did not immediately obtain authority to interpret the Constitution. The Court's refusal to challenge the constitutionality of the 1798 Sedition Act, which made it a crime to publish anything that could be taken as derogatory about the government, raised doubts about its willingness to protect fundamental constitutional rights. The act blurred the distinction between conspiracy and legitimate political opposition and seemed to violate the First Amendment's prohibition against any law abridging freedom of speech or press. Its enforcement was marred by partisan intolerance. Most sedition cases were tried in 1800 and were tied directly to that year's presidential election between incumbent Federalist John Adams and Republican Thomas Jefferson. Federal judges, most of them Federalists, were enthusiastic in their prosecution of Republicans who dared to criticize the Adams administration.

Establishing Judicial Review: *Marbury v. Madison*

Republican concerns about the judiciary were reinforced by the Judiciary Act of 1801, enacted just before Jefferson was inaugurated. It created many new federal judgeships that were hurriedly filled via "midnight" appointments by the outgoing Adams administration. The Federalists, having lost control of the other two branches of government, hoped to maintain some governmental control by entrenching a pro-Federalist judiciary protected by life tenure. Among these last-minute appointments was that of staunch Federalist John Marshall as chief justice. This final insult convinced the Republicans to plan a campaign against the judiciary, lest the people's will, as expressed in the 1800 election, be denied.

Jefferson insisted that each branch of government, and state governments as well, share equally in deciding matters of constitutionality. The Court's constitutional rulings would hold only for specific cases in question and would not obligate the executive or Congress to treat them as legal precedents. The Sedition Act had expired the day before Jefferson took office, but to underscore his fierce opposition to it, he pardoned everyone (mostly Republican newspaper publishers) whom it had convicted. He declared that the law had been unconstitutional, underscoring his conviction that the president as well as the courts had the right to make such a determination.

These issues of power and principle came to a head in the 1803 case of *Marbury v. Madison.* Adams's secretary of state, John Marshall, in his rush to assume his new duties as chief justice of the Supreme Court, had failed to deliver commissions to seventeen of Adams's last-minute judicial appointments, including one for William Marbury as justice of the peace in the District of Columbia. Marbury's appointment now rested with the new secretary of state, James Madison, who, seeking to prevent it, withheld delivery of the commission. Jefferson supported Madison on the grounds that the previous administration had not fully executed Marbury's commission and the new administration was under no obligation to do so. Marbury and three others who had been denied their offices petitioned the Supreme Court for a writ of mandamus - a court order to a cabinet official to comply with a legal obligation - that would require Madison to deliver the commission. The court was authorized to issue such a writ by the Judiciary Act of 1789. Jefferson made clear he would order Madison not to comply.

The court lacked the prestige to stand up to a popular president. To order Madison to deliver Marbury's appointment would expose not only the court's inability to enforce its own rulings but also its fragile standing in the country. Yet, to deny Marbury's petition would confirm the president and Congress's freedom from judicial oversight. Writing for a unanimous court, Marshall declared that Jefferson and Madison had abused their offices by refusing to deliver an appointment signed by a president, confirmed by the Senate, and sealed by a secretary of state. Jefferson was abrogating a lifetime appointment and thus violating the principal foundation of the judiciary's constitutional independence. Marshall insisted that the protection of constitutional rights required such independence.

But after scolding the president, Marshall sidestepped a direct political confrontation by denying Marbury his writ. Marshall did so, however, by exercising and defending judicial review. He ruled that Section 13 of the Judiciary Act of

1789, under which Marbury had brought suit, was unconstitutional. The section gave the Supreme Court original jurisdiction in the matter, even though the Constitution insists that the Court's jurisdiction is appellate in all but a few kinds of cases. In adding to the court's original jurisdiction, the Judiciary Act violated the Constitution.

Marshall's opinion avoided a bitter political controversy that he could not win. He gave Jefferson a free hand to bar Federalist appointees from office, but only if the president accepted the court's power to interpret the Constitution. Like Hamilton, Marshall argued that a constitution embodying the rights and privileges of the American people required an independent judiciary to guard it.

Jefferson did not accept this argument, but Marshall's ruling was so adroit that the president had no way to disobey it. After all, the Court had refused Marbury his appointment. In the final analysis, Jefferson's attack on the courts failed because the Republicans were not sufficiently aroused against the judiciary to destroy its independence. Marshall had disarmed them by holding his partisan fire in the service of the court as an institution. By doing so, he displayed just the sort of impartiality the judiciary's special constitutional status called for.

John Marshall's Leadership of the Court

Jefferson's Revolution of 1800 (see Chapters 4 and 8) placed the presidency in the service of democratic rather than liberal principles, which invited a struggle between Republicans and Federalists. Marshall's statecraft preserved the Court's impartiality in the face of this great party contest and thereby strengthened its authority and prestige. The Court was raised from third-rate power to coequal branch of government and obtained the special constitutional status its champions had sought. With both president and Congress enmeshed in a party struggle, only the judiciary remained above the partisan fray. As Hamilton anticipated, because the Court was an independent, small, cohesive body whose members enjoyed life tenure, it could maintain a long-term view, which gave it a decided advantage over a scattered and divided opposition. Marshall fulfilled Hamilton's hopes. Under his leadership the Court successfully defended the Hamiltonian principles of national supremacy and judicial review.

To defend Hamiltonian principles, it was first necessary to enhance the prestige and authority of the Court itself. Marshall took advantage of his position as chief justice to cultivate the distinctive qualities of the Court and gave it institutional identity and standardized its procedures. He led discussion and directed the order of business in private conferences. He either wrote the Court's opinions or assigned that task to another justice. Getting the Supreme Court to speak with one voice would enhance its prestige. Marshall worked skillfully to forge consensus and persuade those in the majority not to write their own opinions but to sign on to the "opinion of the Court." He wrote an overwhelming number of opinions himself, even when he disagreed with the ruling.

As Jefferson and his Republican successors made appointments to the bench, achieving unanimity became more difficult. But the Court did not return to the fractious practices that preceded Marshall's arrival. Jefferson's first appointment, Justice William Johnson of South Carolina, persuaded Marshall to appoint someone to deliver the opinion of the Court, but to leave the rest of the judges free to voice their dissents. The Court still adheres to that procedure. Still, Marshall's firm yet deft hand kept the Court from dividing along partisan lines. The example of judicial restraint that he set during his long tenure, which lasted until his death in 1835, enabled the Court to fully grasp the role of interpreter of the Constitution.

Putting the Court in Support of National Supremacy: *McCulloch v. Maryland*

Marshall interpreted the Constitution in a more centralizing direction than the Jeffersonians and their successors, the Jacksonians, were comfortable with. He thereby moderated their communitarian and democratic egalitarian inclinations in favor of a strong national government. His most important defense of national supremacy related to the national bank controversy that we discussed in Chapters 4 and 6. With Washington's support, the government chartered the Bank of the United States in 1791. The Republicans let it expire in 1811, but some of them, including Jefferson and Madison, had second thoughts after the War of 1812, in which the American military effort was hampered by the national government's reliance on state banks. Consequently, Congress created the Second Bank of the United States in 1816 with another twenty-year charter. Continued state-level opposition gave the Marshall Court its opportunity to address the constitutional issues raised by the bank controversy in the landmark 1819 case of *McCulloch v. Maryland* (see Chapter 5). Maryland enacted a law that imposed a $15,000 tax ($229,000 in 2006 currency) on any bank not chartered by the state. The Bank of the United States, the only financial institution operating in Maryland that was not chartered by the state, and thus clearly the target of the law, refused to pay the tax. Maryland filed suit against James McCulloch, the cashier of the Baltimore branch of the national bank.

The federal government argued in *McCulloch* that Maryland's tax on the bank was unconstitutional. Maryland replied that Congress had no power to incorporate a bank, and in any event, states could tax as they willed within their own borders. Speaking for a unanimous court, Marshall upheld the bank's constitutionality and gave the classic statement of the doctrine of national supremacy.

Challenging the Jeffersonian notion that the states were the repositories of popular rule, the chief justice responded that the Constitution belonged, as the preamble made clear, to "We, the People": "In form and in substance it emanates from them. Its powers are granted by them, and are to be exercised directly on them, and for their benefit." Although the Constitution limited the powers of the national government, it also clearly established the central authority as "supreme law of the land." Therefore, the national government must retain sufficient powers to carry out the great responsibilities vested in it. And those means must be understood flexibly, lest the Constitution be laden with the sort of policy detail that would bog down a great experiment in self-rule. "We must never forget it is a constitution we are expounding . . . intended to endure for ages to come," wrote Marshall.

Marshall admitted that the Constitution did not list a bank as one of the enumerated powers. But a bank was a useful tool for powers that the Constitution did enumerate: collecting taxes, borrowing money, regulating commerce, and supporting armies and navies. Therefore, as the Constitution provides, the bank was "necessary and proper" for implementing those powers. The final part of Marshall's opinion followed from this generous interpretation of national sovereignty. Maryland's tax was unconstitutional because the "power to tax involves the power to destroy." To uphold the tax would empower an inferior to destroy a superior.

Jefferson and Madison had come to accept the bank as a necessary evil, so they accepted the Court's holding. But, they abhorred Marshall's expansive interpretation of national power and the pressure toward governmental consolidation that it created. In 1819, Jefferson said "after twenty years' confirmation of the federal system by the voice of the people, declared through the medium of elections, we find the judiciary on every occasion, still driving us into consolidation." Marshall saw no reason why the Court should be bound by Jefferson's vision of states' rights; he claimed a "mandate" to uphold the nationalist principles that "We the People" had established in 1787. In deftly positioning itself as the guardian of the people's Constitution, the Marshall Court established a tradition of judicial independence and elevated the position of chief justice to a status that would rival the power and prestige of the executive.

UPSHOT

As the Civil War would soon demonstrate, the Court's assertion of national supremacy would not go uncontested. Likewise, there remained considerable disagreement about whether the Supreme Court should be considered the ultimate determiner of the meaning of the Constitution. Nonetheless, Marbury *and* McCulloch *served as key precedents establishing the Court's power. Based on these vital precedents, the Supreme Court did establish itself as the decisive voice in determining the constitutionality of congressional statutes and, post Civil War, as guardian of national supremacy.*

A False Path: *Dred Scott* and the Reinforcement of Slavery

The Supreme Court's ability to chart a course for the country was temporarily set back by its attempt to impose a settlement of the slavery controversy that was wracking the nation during the 1850s. Fearing they would eventually lose if the slavery issue were decided by Congress, proslavery politicians – including President James Buchanan, a Democrat from Pennsylvania who had been elected in 1856 – yearned to have the Court set a clear proslavery path for the country. The case the Court chose to "settle" the matter of slavery was *Dred Scott v. Sandford* (1857). Buchanan's wish to defer to the Court stemmed from his prior knowledge of how the case would be decided. A majority of the justices were from the South. Buchanan knew that they would take a proslavery position. But Buchanan believed that the decision would lack credibility in the North unless a Northern justice voted with the Southerners. He privately lobbied a fellow Pennsylvanian, Justice Robert Greer, to side with those who wanted to deny both Congress and the territorial legislatures the right to prohibit slavery. Greer succumbed, giving the Court false hope that its opinion would have the appearance of a national, not a sectional, ruling.

Dred Scott had been taken as a slave into Illinois and into the northern part of the Louisiana Purchase. Illinois law forbade slavery. Congress had prohibited slavery in the northern part of the Louisiana Territory in the Missouri Compromise of 1820. Scott, now living in the slave state of Missouri, sued his present owner, arguing that prolonged visits to a free state and territory made him a free man. The case came to the Supreme Court on appeals from the Missouri Supreme Court and the federal appeals court, both of which had ruled against Scott.

Chief Justice Roger Taney's majority opinion supported Missouri's contention that Scott was a slave and that the Supreme Court was bound by Missouri law in this case. But, as Buchanan had hoped, the opinion went much further in that it denied that African Americans were citizens in the eyes of the Constitution and stated that they therefore could not sue in federal court. It also declared that Scott's journey to a free territory was meaningless in any case because Congress did not have authority to prohibit slavery in the territories.

But the "cult of the robe" could not resolve the slavery controversy. The Supreme Court's claim to authoritatively interpret constitutional disputes rested on public perception that its judgments were impartial. In attempting to judge a profound political issue, the Court forfeited that claim. Its diminished influence was confirmed by the triumph of Abraham Lincoln and the Republicans in the 1860 election. Lincoln refused to accept *Dred Scott* as a binding precedent. He insisted that the great issues raised in the case had to be resolved by the American people. Chief Justice Taney had denied African Americans citizenship on the grounds that the grand words of the Declaration of Independence that "all men are created equal" did not include "the enslaved African race." But Lincoln insisted that the Declaration's meaning, and its relationship to the Constitution, was not a narrow legal issue. It raised the most basic questions about the nature of American rights and responsibilities. Lincoln granted that the *Dred Scott* decision was binding on the parties to the suit, but he would not allow it to determine the future course of slavery policy. If the Supreme Court were going to settle vital political questions, "the people will have ceased to be their own rulers, to that extent, practically resigned their government, into the hands of that eminent tribunal." Lincoln and the Union's triumph in the Civil War ensured that *Dred Scott* would not stand and that the Court would not rule the nation.

The Court and the Regulation of Commerce

Restraining Government

As we discussed in Chapter 6, in the aftermath of the Civil War the nation faced a great new challenge, the expansion and concentration of economic power. Until the late 1930s the Court was concerned to brake the government's efforts to curb and regulate that power. As it had done during the Marshall era, the post-Civil War judiciary served as the "aristocratic" anchor on America's democratic sail, this time as the protector of property rights. It successfully blocked state and federal efforts to regulate the economy, fearing that such efforts would destroy the free enterprise system. Its success in these efforts rested on the ability of the Republican Party to dominate presidential and congressional politics from the 1870s to the 1930s and thus to control Supreme Court appointments during this long period (see Chapters 4 and 11).

The Supreme Court based its opposition to most forms of economic regulation on its reading of two critical constitutional provisions: the commerce clause in Article I and the due process clause found in both the Fifth and Fourteenth Amendments. In *United States v. E. C. Knight Co.* (1895), the Court rested its gutting of the Sherman Antitrust Act (see Chapter 6) on its interpretation of the commerce clause. The Sherman Act made it illegal for business to contract, combine, or conspire to create a trust or monopoly for the purpose of restraining free trade and monopolizing interstate or foreign commerce. *E. C. Knight* involved the American Sugar Refining Company, which already controlled a majority of American sugar refining companies. It sought to purchase control of four additional ones, including E. C. Knight, and thus acquire 98 percent of refining capacity. The Department of Justice asked for a court order that forbade the purchase, contending that the companies were combining in restraint of trade. The Court disagreed, holding that the Sherman Act did not apply to monopolies in manufacturing, because *manufacturing*, no matter how large the companies were or how widely distributed their goods were, was not part of interstate *commerce*. The Court confined the term "commerce" to its most literal meaning, "trade." Manufacturing had only an indirect impact on trade, and regulating it was a matter for the states.

The due process clause had traditionally been interpreted to mean that government action, national or state, was beyond judicial review so long as fair procedures had been followed. But lawyers and judges who opposed economic regulation fastened on the idea of *substantive due process*. This concept declared that intruding on a fundamental right, such as the right of contract, was a violation of due process of law no matter what procedural niceties had been observed. A New York law required bakery employees to work no more than ten hours per day or sixty hours per week. In *Lochner v. New York* (1905) the Supreme Court declared that this use of New York's police power violated "the right of contract between employer and employees" and was therefore a violation of the due process clause.

Unleashing Government

The Court's suppression of economic regulation was not complete. Both Theodore Roosevelt and Woodrow Wilson succeeded in championing railroad regulation, food and drug safety, and some other forms of government intrusions into economic life (see Chapter 6). But the full-scale defeat of the Court's efforts to constrain government economic intervention did not occur until the New Deal (see Chapter 6). New Deal efforts to lift the Great Depression and to promote economic security caused it to intrude into virtually all realms of economic endeavor – banking, stock and bond trading, labor practices, food supply. The court – *Dred Scott* excepted – had usually restrained itself during national emergencies. But by 1935, a majority of justices resolved to make a stand against what they took to be a massive assault on economic liberty.

The four justices who anchored that resistance – James McReynolds, Willis Van Devanter, George Sutherland, and Pierce Butler – were determined to protect the Constitution no matter how great the public clamor for change. For a time, they were joined by two others, Owen Roberts and Chief Justice Charles Evans Hughes. The result was that during the 1935–36 term the Court struck down more important national laws than in any comparable period in American history, and a number of important state laws as well.

In *Schechter Poultry Corporation v. United States* (1935), the Court declared the National Industrial Recovery Act (NIRA) unconstitutional. Schechter operated slaughterhouses in New York City. The company received live chickens from outside the state, slaughtered them, and then sold them to local stores. It was convicted in federal court of violating a number of standards set under NIRA, including hours and wage regulations. The Court used *E. C. Knight* as a precedent to claim that such regulation of hours and wages exceeded the national government's commerce power. Moreover, it claimed NIRA to be an unconstitutional delegation of authority to the executive branch, violating the separation of powers.

The Court had never before declared an act of Congress unconstitutional for delegating legislative power to the executive. As such, *Schechter* was a direct challenge to the modern administrative state, whose expansion, in the face of terrifying economic insecurity, seemed inevitable. The decision was unanimous. Even Justice Louis Brandeis, whose righteous anger against big business led his political friends to call him Isaiah, voted with the majority. In *Morehead v. New York, ex rel. Tipaldo* (1936), the court voted 5–4 to overrule a New York law that set a women's minimum wage, reaffirming the due process clause of the Fourteenth Amendment as a barrier to assaults on the liberty of contract. Justice Butler announced an unyielding rule of substantive due process, arguing: "the state is without power by any form of legislation to prohibit, change or nullify contracts between employers and adult women workers as to the amount of wages to be paid." This case created, FDR explained, a "no man's land": it showed that the court majority was opposed to all economic reform regardless of whether it was federal or state.

As we discussed in Chapter 8, FDR responded to these threats to the New Deal by launching his court packing plan. Although the plan failed, the Hughes Court chose not to emulate the Taney Court and to shift ground in the direction of self-restraint. Justices Hughes and Roberts adopted pro-New Deal positions in a series of critical cases. In *West Coast Hotel v. Parrish* (1937), issued less than two months after FDR's court plan (see Chapter 8) appeared, the Court retreated from substantive due process, ruling 5 to 4 that a Washington state minimum wage law was constitutional. Justice Roberts switched from the position he had taken in *Tipaldo* just ten months earlier. Because the Washington law protected women, Chief Justice Hughes, writing for the majority, could have resorted to the specific women's exemption the Court had established in a previous case. Instead, he defended the general authority of state government to protect all vulnerable citizens against the uncertainties of the market.

Only two weeks later, in *National Labor Relations Board v. Jones and Laughlin Steel Corporation*, the Court upheld the National Labor Relations Act. In so doing, it extended the notion of commerce to include manufacturing and also declared that the federal government could regulate intrastate commerce if it had a "close and substantial relation to interstate commerce." Just how loosely the majority of justices were willing to define "close and substantial" was revealed in *National Labor Relations Board v. Friedman–Harry Marks Clothing Co.* (1937). In this case, the Court ruled against a Richmond, Virginia clothing company whose production, unlike the Jones and Laughlin steel empire, had only a minimal effect on interstate commerce.

In *Steward Machine Co. v. Davis* (1937), the Supreme Court upheld the New Deal's centerpiece, the Social Security Act. Justices Roberts and Hughes once again cast the deciding votes in a 5–4 opinion, delivered by Justice Benjamin Cardozo, that sustained the unemployment compensation system despite the act's requirement that state laws meet national standards to be eligible for federal funds. Speaking for six justices, Cardozo also upheld the old-age pension system in *Helvering v. Davis* (1937) even though the pensions were funded by a special tax. A year earlier, the Court had ruled that using taxes to promote public welfare intruded on the reserved powers of the states and violated the Tenth Amendment, which reserves to the states and the people those powers not delegated to the national government. By upholding the Social Security Act, the Court apparently had given up its commitment to so-called dual federalism, an interpretation of the Tenth Amendment that strictly limited the powers of the national government to constitutionally enumerated powers and that viewed the national and state governments as sovereign and equal in their respective spheres of influence (see Chapter 5).

FDR solidified the Court's transformation. As a result of retirements and deaths, he was able to appoint eight justices in the next six years, all of whom were selected less for their distinguished jurisprudence than for their devout loyalty to the New Deal. Thus, despite his plan's defeat, FDR eventually "packed" the Court. After winning a third term, he even had the pleasure of replacing his arch-enemy, Justice McReynolds, who between 1937 and 1941 had dissented from pro-New Deal opinions 119 times. These new appointments caused what historian William Leuchtenburg has called "the constitutional revolution of 1937," a full acceptance of the New Deal constitutional order. Since then, the Court has not struck down a single piece of significant economic legislation. Nor has it judged any law (with the exception of the Line Item Veto Act passed in 1996) to be an unconstitutional delegation of authority to the executive.

Table 9.3. Roosevelt Supreme Court appointments.

Appointed Justice	Outgoing Justice	Year
Hugo Black	Willis Van Devanter	1937
Stanley Reed	George Sutherland	1938
Felix Frankfurter	Benjamin Cardozo	1939
William Douglas	Louis Brandeis	1939
Frank Murphy	Pierce Butler	1940
James Byrnes	James McReynolds	1941
Robert Jackson	Harlan Stone (Elevated to Chief Justice)	1941
Wiley Rutledge	James Byrnes	1943

Source: US Senate.

CRITICAL CHOICE: REDEFINING RIGHTS

Beginning in the 1950s, the Supreme Court expanded the rights to which Americans are entitled. Most importantly, it ruled that racial segregation of schools and unequal apportionment of state legislatures were unconstitutional and it declared a right to privacy according to which a woman has a right to have an abortion.

FDR used the term "liberalism" to describe his philosophy of government. By using this term, he meant that the New Deal and the modern presidency were to be a liberal as well as a democratic phenomenon, "supplementing," as he put it, the traditional American understanding of rights with a new one (see Chapter 4). FDR was astute enough to recognize that if the Court became sympathetic to the new idea of rights he championed, it could help protect liberal programs from inevitable future political attack.

FDR differed from his Progressive predecessors, especially Theodore Roosevelt, who had called for formal constitutional changes to weaken the Court's institutional authority. Theodore Roosevelt's Progressive Party campaign in 1912 favored submitting court decisions to voter referenda and making it easier to amend the Constitution and thus override judicial interpretations of it. As FDR foresaw, when the Democrats lost the presidency to Republican Dwight Eisenhower in 1952, liberals became increasingly dependent on the Court. Although Democrats had a majority in both houses of Congress for most of the 1950s, actual control was exercised by a coalition of Republicans and Southern Democrats. With conservatives commanding the presidency and Congress, the judiciary, remade by the constitutional revolution of 1937, became the agent of national political reform. For the next several decades, much of the Court's reform effort focused not on restraining government but on demanding that government secure rights for people that they were unable to secure for themselves. As political scientist R. Shep Melnick says:

> contemporary liberalism promises a broader security against the vagaries of the business cycle; against the multiple unintended hazards created by a dynamic capitalism; against the prejudices of private citizens and the consequences of three centuries of racism; against the risks of congenital handicaps and inevitable old age; and against the consequences of poverty and of family decomposition.

This new understanding of security forms the basis for many of the Court's novel constitutional interpretations, especially with respect to the Fourteenth Amendment. Many of these new claims on government have also been written into law. The judiciary does not hesitate to supervise wide swaths of the economy and society based on these statutory provisions.

Since the New Deal, the Supreme Court has gone through two distinct phases. During the first phase, from 1953 to 1986, the Warren and Burger Courts were in the forefront of what Shep Melnick has deemed "the Rights Revolution." They not only spearheaded the effort to end racial discrimination but also led crusading efforts to end voting inequality and established a right to privacy. The second period that began with the appointment of William Rehnquist as Chief Justice in 1986 and continues today with John Roberts as Chief Justice is more difficult to characterize. The Rehnquist and Roberts Courts have embodied three distinct and at times conflicting themes: a reaffirmation of most critical aspects of the prior rights revolution; a conservative reaction against some aspects of the rights revolution; and a push to establish new rights dearer to the hearts of conservatives than liberals.

School Desegregation

The Fourteenth Amendment's promise that no state could deprive American citizens of the "equal protection of the laws" appeared to offer African Americans full citizenship, but, as of the 1950s, that promise had not been fulfilled. The nineteenth-century court upheld the notorious Jim Crow laws in the Southern states that forcibly separated the races and deprived African Americans of equal treatment.

In *Plessy v. Ferguson* (1896), the Court invoked the doctrine of "separate but equal," meaning that as long as accommodations of the same quality were provided, it was permissible to segregate according to race. Homer Plessy, a Louisiana resident, boarded a train in New Orleans, having bought a first-class ticket, and took a vacant seat after refusing the conductor's order to sit in the "Colored Only" section. He was arrested and convicted for violating Louisiana's segregation statute. The Supreme Court upheld the conviction, denying that racial segregation was discriminatory. It did not choose to address the obvious reality that accommodations for African Americans were almost never of the same quality as those provided to whites. An 8–1 majority insisted that the Louisiana statute did not imply racial inferiority but was a reasonable exercise of state police power to promote the public good.

Justice Harlan's dissent challenged this tortured interpretation of the Fourteenth Amendment. He insisted that the "constitution is color-blind" and that therefore it was unconstitutional for a state to base laws on race. He noted that the purpose of the Louisiana law was not to exclude whites from black railroad cars but solely to exclude blacks from white cars, which made a mockery of the state's claim that the law was not racially discriminatory.

Justice Harlan's solitary protest was finally vindicated in *Brown v. Board of Education of Topeka* (1954). *Brown* revitalized the Fourteenth Amendment equal protection clause as a weapon to uphold civil rather than economic rights. This case, which involved segregated elementary schools in Topeka, Kansas, had come to the Court in 1951. But in recognition of its great historical importance, the justices delayed their decision until after the 1952 presidential election and until they could achieve unanimity. Chief Justice Earl Warren's opinion was crafted less to convince legal scholars than to gain public support for a decision that would inevitably engender resistance. Hoping to see the entire *Brown* decision printed in every newspaper, he insisted that "the opinion should be short, readable by the lay public, non-rhetorical, unemotional, and, above all, not accusatory." In order to avoid accusations, the justices admitted that the historical intent of the Fourteenth Amendment's Framers was inconclusive regarding segregation. Nor did they argue that the amendment justified school desegregation as a remedy for a century of government neglect and oppression. Rather, *Brown* was rendered on sociological and psychological grounds. It claimed that education had become critical to American democracy, "the foundation of good citizenship." No child could be expected to succeed in life if denied an education, and therefore education had to be provided on equal terms.

The Court then moved to consider the deleterious psychological effects that legal separation of the races had on black children's motivation to learn. It found that segregation generated "a feeling of inferiority as to their status in the community that may affect the hearts and minds." Therefore, de jure segregation (segregation enforced by law) was a form of discrimination and therefore, regarding public education at least, "separate but equal has no place." The Court's reliance on sociological and psychological grounds rather than textured constitutional interpretation made it vulnerable to the charge that it was engaged in judicial legislation. Indeed, the *Brown* decision signaled a new era of court activism.

Equal Representation

In the 1960s the Warren Court began to move aggressively beyond racial justice to insist that government protect other neglected rights. Beginning with *Baker v. Carr* (1962), it took up voter apportionment in order to determine whether various sizes and shapes of state, local, and national election districts were ensuring that every voter had an equal right to determine electoral outcomes. The Tennessee legislature had not reapportioned its legislative districts since 1901, even as the state's population shifted from rural to urban and suburban areas. Charles Baker and several other Tennessee residents sued, claiming that as urban dwellers they were being denied equal protection of the laws. In previous cases, the Court had defined the formation of electoral districts as a political question poorly suited to judicial resolution and best solved by the political branches. It recognized that in the American constitutional order representation was a means for moderating majority opinion as well as for articulating it. The very existence of the Senate, said the Court, shows that the Framers of the Constitution considered state boundaries, not simply population, in designing the nation's legislative branch.

Justice William Brennan's majority opinion in the Baker case abandoned this restrained position. He understood the equal protection clause of the Fourteenth Amendment as protecting the right of all voters to have their votes count equally. Justice Felix Frankfurter, a militant New Dealer appointed by FDR, dissented. He warned his progressive colleagues that they were committing the same constitutional crime they had once accused their conservative predecessors of perpetrating. Just as the Court had previously misused the Fourteenth Amendment to uphold the right of contract and usurp policy responsibility best left to political representatives, so it was now improperly using the same amendment to enter a "political thicket." Denial of franchise because of race, color, religion, or sex was an appropriate matter for intervention by the courts, said Frankfurter, but not the relationship between population and legislative representation, which was never a straightforward matter under the Constitution. The judiciary could not reliably adjudicate such disputes impartially because no clear constitutional standard existed. To involve the courts implied that judges were "omnicompetent" and risked "enthroning the judiciary." Appeals for fairer apportionment should be addressed to "an informed, civically minded electorate." Frankfurter wrote: "There is not under our Constitution a judicial remedy for every political mischief. In a democratic society like ours, relief must come through an aroused popular conscience that sears the conscience of people's representatives."

Critics of Frankfurter might argue that malapportioned districts prevent deprived citizens from finding adequate political avenues for registering their grievances. Even some of the Warren Court's critics conceded that malapportionment was severe enough in many states, as well as in some congressional districts, to warrant a federal judiciary remedy. But they would have preferred the Court to rest its opinion on different constitutional grounds. The political scientist Martha Derthick would have chosen Article IV, Section 4 of the Constitution, which guarantees "every State in the Union a Republican Form of Government." That clause, which had not been invoked since the mid nineteenth century, could have been applied to cases in which a state legislature's failure to reapportion violated its state constitution and thereby undermined the federal constitution's guarantee. Derthick argues that relying on the equal protection clause of the Fourteenth Amendment "catapulted the federal judiciary" into a "mathematical quagmire" in which the states would be held to a standard of equality that had no place in American constitutional history.

Two years later, the Court struck down the apportionment system used by most state legislatures for their upper houses. Like the US Senate, they typically represented smaller units of government, usually counties, of unequal population size. In *Reynolds v. Sims* (1964), the Court declared this non-population method of apportionment unconstitutional. It rejected comparison to the Senate because the Senate had merely been a political compromise struck at the Constitutional Convention. It did not explain why the Senate's status as a compromise made it irrelevant as a model for the design of state legislatures. It also pointed out that counties, cities, and other local subdivisions, unlike states, had no claim to being sovereign entities. Chief Justice Warren's majority opinion stated: "Legislators represent people, not trees or acres. Legislators are elected by voters, not farms or cities or economic interests." The only acceptable constitutional standard was "one person, one vote," a principle the Court extended to almost all popularly elected, multimember, state decision-making bodies as well as congressional districts.

Privacy

In addition to defending programmatic rights, the Court also established a new right against government intrusion, a right of privacy. In *Griswold v. Connecticut* (1965), the Warren Court overturned a Connecticut law that made it a crime to sell, use, or counsel the use of contraceptives for birth control. As Justice Potter Stewart put it, this law appeared to be an "uncommonly silly law"; it grated against most Americans' sense of privacy. No language in the Constitution clearly prohibited such a law. Nevertheless, when Planned Parenthood members were charged with breaking it, the Supreme Court struck down their convictions.

In his majority opinion, Justice William Douglas granted that the Constitution did not explicitly provide a right of privacy. But the spirit of such a right pervaded the whole document. Specific Bill of Rights guarantees created "zones of privacy" that prohibited the peacetime quartering of soldiers in private houses, unreasonable searches and seizures, and self-incrimination. These specific privacy guarantees cast a broader shadow that created a penumbra, a shadow's outer reach, and protected additional privacy rights, including marital privacy.

The Burger Court extended the concept of privacy rights to abortion. *Roe v. Wade* (1973) involved an unmarried pregnant woman who sought an abortion in Texas, where abortions were prohibited by law except when the life of the mother was at stake. Justice Harry Blackmun's decision, for a 7–2 majority, found Texas's anti-abortion law unconstitutional because it violated the Fourteenth Amendment, which he claimed, guaranteed that the states cannot restrict "personal liberty" including a right to privacy. Blackmun did not claim that this right was absolute. "A State may properly assert important interests in safeguarding health, in maintaining medical standards, and in protecting potential life," he said. He sought to balance the right to an abortion with the state's legitimate regulatory interests by distinguishing between different stages of pregnancy. Early in pregnancy he denied the states any power to regulate abortion. Later in the pregnancy he found that the states' "interests become sufficiently compelling to sustain regulation of the factors that govern the abortion decision." He set the dividing line between early and late at the end of the first three months of pregnancy (the first trimester) because until that time the mother is under less risk from abortion than from childbirth. After that time "a state may regulate the abortion procedure to the extent that the regulation reasonably relates to the preservation and protection of maternal health." Because the Texas statute did not distinguish between early and late abortions, it violates women's' right to an abortion during the first trimester. The *Roe* decision had profound political and policy consequences. It invalidated abortion statutes in forty-six states and gave rise to a pro-life movement that was animated by intense resentment of the Court's claim that a fetus was not a "person."

Implementing the New Rights

As we note in this chapter, the judiciary controls neither purse nor sword. When it was protecting rights such as liberty of contract, the judiciary had only to restrain government. But so many of the Warren and Burger court rulings were about securing rights that could only be provided by government. Therefore, the Court became increasingly dependent on other agents of government – lower courts, Congress, and the executive – to implement its will.

Chapter 7 shows that Congress's response to the expansion of national administrative power has been to intervene in the details of administration. By doing so, it has become more like the very bureaucracies it seeks to control. Likewise, as the federal judiciary has intruded into the behavior of administrative agencies, it too has come to assume tasks and responsibilities more typical of a federal agency than a court. This transformation began with the *Brown* decision. The Warren Court was left with the practical problem of how to end school segregation. It waited a year before issuing the so-called Brown 2 case, *Brown v. Board of*

Education (1955), which called for "all deliberate speed" to desegregate schools. Because it felt it could not rely on the very local governments that were resisting desegregation to fashion adequate desegregation plans, the Supreme Court gave federal district courts the power to assess local plans and over rule them if the court determined they were inadequate.

In September 1957, the Democratic governor of Arkansas, Orval Faubus, called up the state National Guard to obstruct a federal court order to desegregate all-white Central High School in Little Rock. President Eisenhower, who privately opposed the *Brown* decision and refused to publicly endorse it, now found himself faced with the most serious state challenge to federal authority since the end of Reconstruction. His meeting with Faubus on September 14 only seemed to encourage the Arkansas governor's resistance to desegregation. On September 23, nine African American students were turned away from the school by a howling mob. Eisenhower still did not come out in support of the *Brown* decision. Yet, fearing that to do nothing in the face of Faubus's resistance would encourage every segregationist governor to defy the law, he finally took action to enforce the court order. His delay enabled resistance to grow so great as to require the largest domestic military deployment in decades. On September 24, a contingent of regular army paratroopers was dispatched to Little Rock. The next day Americans saw shocking photographs of troops wielding bayonets in an American city.

The Little Rock incident dramatically underscored the need for presidential and congressional support in order to achieve desegregation. Until 1964, when President Lyndon Johnson and his congressional supporters made that support reliably available, very little actual desegregation took place. Resistant local governments emphasized "deliberate" rather than "speed" in responding to the Court's school desegregation edict. After 1964, when the combined authority of all three federal government branches was deployed against the South and its system of Jim Crow, desegregation progress came quickly. Within four years, more Southern schools desegregated than in the previous fourteen years.

Progress in desegregation was far slower when the objective shifted from simply eliminating legally mandated segregation to remedying the ill effects of past segregation by purposely mixing whites and blacks together. This goal was particularly hard to achieve in locales in which the two races no longer lived in the same neighborhoods. The most controversial remedy that the courts attempted was busing. In *Swann v. Charlotte-Mecklenburg Board of Education* (1971), the Court approved massive busing of students as well as a system of attendance zones that was marked by sometimes drastic redrawing of traditional school boundaries. Acknowledging the difficulties that judges faced in designing practical integration plans, it claimed that the goal was so important that "administratively awkward, inconvenient and even bizarre" solutions could not be avoided.

In a 1974 Denver, Colorado case, the Court determined that unofficial, de facto segregation patterns were unconstitutional if the school board "intended" to separate the races. Such discriminatory intent was shown in other cities including Detroit, Cleveland, and Boston. Remedying de facto segregation in places such as Boston proved very difficult. The Boston metropolitan area encompassed many separate school districts, but the Court could prove discriminatory intent only with regard to the city school district. Therefore, busing was confined to the city, which encouraged whites to flee to adjacent suburbs. African Americans were bused to white poor and working-class Boston neighborhoods. As Martha Derthick notes, "The spectacle of federal judges deciding the most mundane details of local school administration . . . while ethnic neighborhoods turned into battle zones caused even the most ardent liberals to ponder whether the power of national judges was being appropriately employed." Because so many whites transferred their children to suburban or private schools, few whites remained in the Boston school system, making racial integration impossible.

During the 1970s and early 1980s, the courts, Congress, and administrative agencies reinforced each other's activism. The 1964 Civil Rights Act seemed to disallow any form of racial preference, but the courts frequently interpreted it to allow affirmative action, the use of racial classifications to improve access of racial minorities to education, jobs, and other important social goods. In *Griggs v. Duke Power Co.* (1972), the Court struck down certain employment criteria used by the Duke Power Company because those practices excluded a disproportionate number of African Americans from the employment pool. Chief Justice Burger's majority opinion held employers responsible for justifying practices that were seemingly fair but had an "adverse impact" on women and minorities.

Griggs stopped just short of interpreting the civil rights law as requiring quotas. Congress did not endorse quotas, but it made no effort to stop courts and agencies from inferring the existence of discrimination based on "nonproportional outcomes." Faced with the difficult choice between merely punishing overt discrimination and requiring racial quotas, Congress made no choice at all, delegating this difficult decision to the courts and the bureaucracy.

The importance of the civil rights acts lay not just in their extensive reach but also in the model they established for other legislation. Emulating them, Lyndon Johnson's Great Society legislation and many laws enacted during the 1970s embodied "statutory rights," meaning rights proclaimed by Congress in statute with no direct reference to the Constitution. Statutory rights included "procedural rights," in which the Court held administrative agencies to exacting standards for ensuring "fair representation for all affected interests" (especially those representing "discrete and insular minorities") in the exercise of the discretion

Congress had delegated to them. The judiciary's strict scrutiny of administrative procedures and regulations helped convert welfare, consumer protection, and environmental measures into programmatic rights that codified, in many important respects, the New Deal vision of a good society. Once a critical "veto point" that restrained the growth of government, by the end of the 1970s the judiciary had become an unexpected source of political energy for an expansive welfare and regulatory state.

UPSHOT

The Court decisions in the above landmark cases had great practical consequences. Schools throughout the South became racially integrated. The malapportionment of state legislatures, which usually benefited rural areas at the expense of suburbs and cities, came to an end. Abortion was legalized and became an option that was widely exercised. These decisions also had an enormous impact on government, both empowering and constraining it. The federal government acquired unprecedented authority to intervene in the apportionment of state legislative districts, previously the exclusive province of the states, and in determining the racial makeup of school populations, previously an entirely local matter. But government lost the ability to intrude into matters of sexual conduct and reproduction, matters previously within its purview.

Path Dependency and Deviation: Reaffirming the Rights Revolution, Reconsidering Federalism

Reaffirming the Rights Revolution

Over the past thirty years, the Supreme Court, presided over by William Rehnquist and later by John Roberts, has, for the most part, reaffirmed the landmark decisions made by its New Deal and post-New Deal predecessors. The Warren Court had ruled in *Miranda v. Arizona* (1966) that the Fifth Amendment right against self-incrimination requires that a criminal suspect be warned of that right before he is interrogated by the police or prosecutors. Because law enforcers had bitterly complained about this restriction, Congress passed a law overturning *Miranda*. In *Dickerson v. United States* (2000) the Court threw out the law and reaffirmed *Miranda*. Even more surprising was the Court's reaffirmation of the right to an abortion.

Roe v. Wade, the landmark abortion ruling discussed above, was perhaps the single greatest cause for conservative condemnation of the Burger Court.

The 1980 Republican platform singled it out for criticism and promised to appoint justices who would overturn it. The Reagan and Bush administrations tried five times to overturn it and failed. A sixth, more promising opportunity came in 1992 when the Supreme Court heard *Planned Parenthood of Southeastern Pennsylvania v. Casey*. Only one justice who had endorsed *Roe* – Harry Blackmun, author of the original decision – remained on the bench. He had the firm support of one other justice, John Stevens. It seemed that Reagan and Bush had made enough conservative appointments to overrule the controversial abortion decision.

Planned Parenthood concerned a state law that limited the free exercise of abortion by requiring the informed consent of the woman, waiting twenty-four hours after obtaining consent, notifying the husband in advance, and requiring minors to gain consent from at least one parent. The plaintiff argued that upholding the Pennsylvania restrictions amounted to overturning *Roe*.

The Court upheld the Pennsylvania law, except for the part requiring notification of the husband, but did so on the grounds that the law did not unduly interfere with the right to an abortion. A five-member majority, including Reagan appointees Sandra Day O'Connor and Anthony Kennedy and Bush appointee David Souter, reaffirmed *Roe*'s guarantee of "the right of women to choose to have an abortion before viability and to obtain it without undue interference from the state." Justice O'Connor's opinion, joined by Justices Kennedy and Souter, provided an alternative to the polarized positions on abortion and has since been the controlling view of the Court. It did not confirm that Roe had been correctly decided, but it upheld the right to choose on the basis that Roe had become settled, standing law, which must be respected by the Supreme Court. The right to privacy, Justice O'Connor argued, should be upheld under the principle of stare decisis, meaning, "let the decision stand."

The Rehnquist and Roberts Courts also emulated their predecessors in their expansive reading of the Bill of Rights and of the wide degree of protection it grants individuals against government intrusion. The Court's expansion of the meaning of free speech arose in a series of cases involving whether private groups could express religious views on public school grounds. Stephen and Darleen Fournier lived in Milford, New York and were the adult leaders of the local Good News Club, a private Christian organization for children ages 6 to 12. In September of 1996 the Fourniers asked Dr. Robert McGruder, interim superintendent of the district, for permission to use a school cafeteria, after school, for the club's weekly meetings. McGruder said no because the club's meetings involved Bible readings, religious lessons, and hymn singing and therefore amounted to religious worship. Such worship violated the school district's policy prohibiting use "by any individual or organization for religious purposes." The Fourniers sued claiming that the school district's action violated their First Amendment rights of free speech and free exercise of religion. A New York district court ruled for the district on the grounds that since the district excluded all religious activities it was not discriminating against the Good News Club. A federal court of appeals upheld the lower court ruling.

The Supreme Court agreed to hear the case of *Good News Club v. Milford Central School* because "there is a conflict among the Courts of Appeals on the question whether speech can be excluded from a limited public forum on the basis of the religious nature of the speech." The Milford district had interpreted the establishment clause to mean that it had the right, indeed the duty, to exclude all religious activity from school property. However, in two prior decisions the Rehnquist Court had resolved this tension between free speech and the establishment of religion in favor of free speech. In *Lamb's Chapel,* it ruled that a school district could not exclude a private group from presenting films in school solely because the films defended family values on religious grounds. Likewise, in *Rosenberger,* it held that a university that funded student publications could not refuse to fund one that adopted a religious perspective.

Justice Clarence Thomas's majority opinion in *Good News Club* noted the Milford ban did not extend to all efforts to encourage morality and character development: "For example, this policy would allow someone to use Aesop's Fables to teach children moral values." The sole reason for banning the Good News Club was because its efforts to develop morality and character adopted a Christian approach and as such a basis for discrimination was unconstitutional: "What matters for purposes of the Free Speech Clause is that we can see no logical difference in kind between the invocation of Christianity by the Club and the invocation of teamwork, loyalty, or patriotism by other associations to provide a foundation for their lessons." The protection against an establishment of religion should not be understood as a reason for prohibiting religious speech as long as other points of view, both religious and secular, also had an equal opportunity to be heard.

Justice David Souter's dissenting opinion denied that the Good News Club was merely engaged in moral and character development from a religious perspective. He likened its activity more to a religious worship service in which children as young as 6 were "to commit themselves in an act of Christian conversion." If the Good News Club could hold religious services then "any public school opened for civic meetings must be opened for use as a church, synagogue, or mosque." Therefore, he concluded that the school district was within its rights to discriminate between an act of religious indoctrination, which it could exclude, and other types of activities and discussion, which it could not. He did not, however, provide standards by which to distinguish indoctrination from more benign activities, nor did he consider how school districts should evaluate whether or not secular groups were engaging in indoctrination and should likewise be excluded.

This chapter has already discussed the other key example of the Rehnquist and Roberts Courts' extension of its power to protect rights, its overruling of

Chicago's ban on handguns in the home in *McDonald v. Chicago*. Neither the Burger Court nor the Warren Court had seen fit to incorporate the Second Amendment into the rights protections the Supreme Court would guard against state and local invasion. As was the case with the broad protection offered to religious expression, the Court chose to protect a right beloved of many conservatives, the right to bear arms.

Reconsidering Federalism

The only major reversal by the Rehnquist and Roberts Courts of previous rulings has come in the area of federalism. Chapter 5 began with a discussion of the conflict between Texas and the federal government regarding whether the federal government had a right to ban handguns near schools. Texas claimed that handgun regulation was a local matter and the federal government claimed that the commerce clause of the Constitution enabled it to intervene because school violence threatened interstate commerce. In *United States v. Lopez*, the Rehnquist Court sided with Texas on the grounds that the commerce clause should not be read so broadly as to encompass issues that were essentially local in character. This decision represented the first effort by the Supreme Court to place limits on the commerce clause since the New Deal. In *United States v. Morrison* (2000) it reinforced its earlier decision ruling that the commerce clause did not give the federal government the latitude to make violence against women a federal crime when other forms of violence remained the province of state criminal law. The message of these two decisions was that the federal government could no longer expect the Court to allow it to use the commerce clause as an all-purpose rationale justifying legislation. The relationship between the matter being legislated and commerce had to be reasonably clear and direct. Otherwise, the matter at hand remained the province of the states and localities.

In *Printz v. United States* (1997) the Court provided additional rationales for defending the states against government intrusion: the principle of dual sovereignty and the Tenth Amendment. The Brady Handgun Violence Prevention Act (1993), popularly known as the Brady Bill, required local law enforcement officials to conduct background checks on would-be handgun purchasers. Two county sheriffs, from Montana and Arizona, challenged the constitutionality of this provision. In overturning this aspect of the law, the majority declared that "It is incontestable that the Constitution established a system of 'dual sovereignty'." Although the states surrendered many of their powers to the new federal government, they retained "a residuary and inviolable sovereignty" reflected throughout the Constitution's text. Among the examples it cited were: the prohibition on any involuntary reduction or combination of a state's territory; the judicial power clause, which speaks of the "Citizens" of the states;

the amendment provision, which requires the votes of three-fourths of the states to amend the Constitution; and the guarantee clause, Article IV, Section 4, which "presupposes the continued existence of the states and ... those means and instrumentalities which are the creation of their sovereign and reserved rights." It also cited the Tenth Amendment's assertion that "[t]he powers not delegated to the United States by the Constitution, nor prohibited by it to the States, are reserved to the States respectively, or to the people." Despite the powerful language of the Tenth Amendment, the Court had rarely made reference to it. The majority opinion's assertion of its importance might well give the Court a powerful new weapon for overturning federal efforts to coerce the states. In the same vein, refer back to Chapter 5 for a discussion of the Supreme Court's decision to overrule the Medicaid provision of President Obama's healthcare reform.

CRITICAL THINKING QUESTION: ANALYZE A COURT CASE

Pick one of the Supreme Court cases discussed in the chapter. Do you agree with the outcome. If so explain why. If not explain why not. Go online to read the case summaries provided.

Looking Forward

As Chapter 11 will show, the public holds the national government in low regard. Until quite recently, its view of the Supreme Court was an exception. Remarkably, the Court's favorability survived its intervention in the 2000 presidential election. Although Gore supporters howled in protest, the Court's prestige did not suffer. However, as Figure 9.4 shows, since 2006 the Court's favorability rating has declined precipitously.

This decline coincided with a series of controversial decisions supporting gay marriage and the Affordable Care Act. Previously, the Court's popularity was overwhelming; now only a relatively small majority retain a positive impression of it. As we have seen, over the past half-century the Court issued many controversial rulings but it was still able to maintain its image as the one national institution capable of rising above partisan politics. However, as politics becomes ever more polarized, it has become less able to sustain that image. The public is less willing to look upon the justices as dispassionate judges and rather views them as partisan conservatives or liberals. The distinction between judging and legislating has been blurred, and therefore the Court risks becoming tarred with the same disdain that the public accords to Congress. The key question looking forward is whether the justices can demonstrate a sufficient level of judicial impartiality to keep the public's trust.

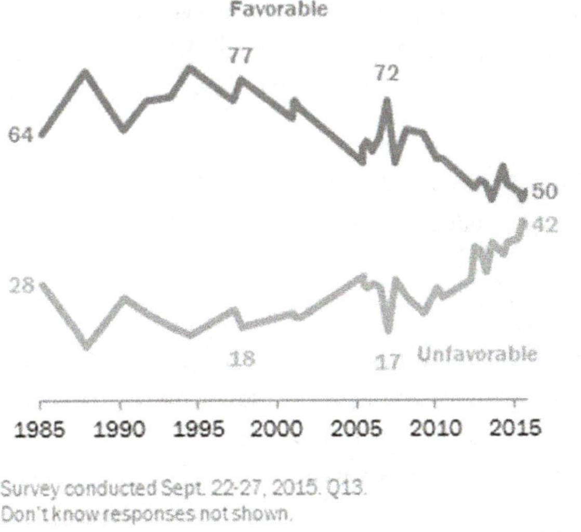

Figure 9.4. Views of the Supreme Court.
Source: People-press.org

CHAPTER SUMMARY

Contemporary portrait:

* The Judiciary deals with three different kinds of law: civil, criminal, and public.
* The American judicial system is made up of two parallel systems: federal courts and state courts.
* The federal judicial system is composed of three tiers: district courts, appeals courts, and the Supreme Court.
* In the most recent major case involving judicial review of a congressional statute, the Supreme Court upheld the constitutionality of the Affordable Care Act.
* The most recent Supreme Court cases dealing with constitutional rights have: confirmed the right of self-defense; overturned a section of the campaign finance law that limited free speech; ruled that an attempt by the government to enforce federal employment discrimination law against a religious body is a violation of religious freedom; and declared that gays have a right to marry.

Critical choice: judicial review and guardianship of national supremacy:

* The Court established the principle of judicial review in *Marbury v. Madison.*
* The Court declared itself in favor of national supremacy in *McCulloch v. Maryland.*
* By means of skillful leadership and carefully reasoned and worded opinions, John Marshall enabled the Supreme Court to provide a centralizing, restraining counterweight to the decentralist and democratic tendencies of the Jefferson and Jackson presidencies.

A false path: *Dred Scott* and the reinforcement of slavery:

* The *Dred Scott* decision temporarily placed the Supreme Court in support of the expansion of slavery.

The Supreme Court and the regulation of commerce:

* In the late nineteenth and throughout the first third of the twentieth century the Court was concerned to brake the government's efforts to curb and regulate economic power. It adopted a very narrow reading of the Constitution's commerce clause and interpreted the Fourteenth Amendment as offering very strict protection of the right of contract.
* After 1936, the Supreme Court retreated from its efforts to prevent meaningful government regulation of the economy and became highly supportive of such efforts. It interpreted the commerce clause as giving the government very wide latitude in regulating the private sector.

Critical choice: redefining rights:

* The Supreme Court's decision in *Brown v. Board of Education of Topeka* (1954) revitalized the Fourteenth Amendment's equal protection clause as a weapon to uphold civil rather than economic rights.
* In the 1960s the Warren Court began to move aggressively beyond racial justice to insist that government protect other neglected rights including: the right of each vote to count equally and the right to privacy.
* Because many Warren and Burger court rulings were about securing rights that could only be provided by government, the Court became increasingly dependent on other agents of government – lower courts, Congress, and the executive – to implement its will. As it involved itself ever more in the detailed behavior of administrative agencies, it too came to assume tasks and responsibilities more typical of a federal agency than of a court.

Path dependency and deviation: reaffirming the rights revolution, reconsidering federalism:

* The Rehnquist and Roberts Courts reaffirmed earlier courts' broad interpretation of the right against self-incrimination and the right to an abortion. They issued broad interpretations of the right to free expression of religion and the right to own guns.
* The Rehnquist and Roberts Courts reversed a fifty-year trend by issuing a series of decisions that restricted the ability of the national government to impose its will on the states.

SUGGESTED READINGS

Abraham, Henry. *The Judicial Process*, 7th edn. New York: Oxford University Press, 1998.

Ackerman, Bruce. *We the People: Volume I, Foundations*. Cambridge, MA: Harvard University Press, 1991.

Bickel, Alexander. *The Least Dangerous Branch: The Supreme Court and the Bar of Politics*. New York: Bobbs-Merrill, 1963.

Burke, Thomas F. *Lawyers, Lawsuits, and Legal Rights: The Battle over Litigation in American Society*: Berkeley, CA: University of California Press, 2004

Fallon, Richard. *The Dynamic Constitution: An Introduction to American Constitutional Law*. New York. Cambridge University Press, 2004.

Ginsberg, Benjamin, and Martin Shefter. *Politics by Other Means*, 3rd edn. New York: W. W. Norton, 2003.

Jacobsohn, Gary Jeffrey. *Constitutional Identity*, Cambridge MA: Harvard University Press, 2010.

Kahn, Ronald, and Kersch, Ken I. *The Supreme Court and American Political Development*. Lawrence: University Press of Kansas, 2006.

Kersch, Ken I. *Constructing Civil Liberties: Discontinuities in the Development of American Constitutional Law*. New York: Cambridge University Press, 2004.

Melnick, R. *Between the Lines*. Washington, DC: Brookings Institution Press, 1994.

O'Brien, David. *Storm Center: The Supreme Court in American Politics*, 9th edn. New York: W. W. Norton, 2011.

Perry, H. W., Jr. *Deciding to Decide: Agenda Setting in the United States Supreme Court*. Cambridge, MA: Harvard University Press, 1991

Powe, Lucas, Jr. *The Warren Court and American Politics*. Cambridge, MA: Harvard University Press. 2002

Shapiro, Martin. *Who Guards the Guardians?* Athens: University of Georgia Press, 1988.

10 Bureaucracy

CHAPTER OVERVIEW

This chapter focuses on:

- **A contemporary portrait of the federal bureaucracy.**
- **The impact of the American tradition of hating bureaucracy.**
- **The critical choice to grant the president removal power.**
- **Warring principles about how best to staff the federal bureaucracy.**
- **The implementation of big government as pioneered by Progressivism and established by the New Deal.**
- **The post-World War II expansion of the federal bureaucracy.**

In 2014 Gavin Grimm, a student at Gloucester High School in North Carolina, needed to go to the bathroom and went to the boy's room. Gavin's birth certificate lists Gavin as a female. However, Gavin considers himself a male and legally acquired a man's first name. Initially, the school did not object, but after parents raised objections, the Gloucester School Board changed its policy and said that Gavin had to use the girl's room because Gavin was officially a girl. Eventually, Gavin brought a suit against the school board demanding to use the bathroom that corresponded to Gavin's chosen gender identity. The suit was based on a set of guidelines issued by the US Department of Education (DOE)'s Office of Civil Rights that interpreted a 1972 federal law known as Title Nine, as requiring all schools that receive federal funding, which means all public schools, to allow people to use the public facility – locker room, bathroom, etc. – that corresponded with their gender identity. A federal court sided with Gavin, upholding the DOE interpretation of Title Nine.

Title Nine makes no mention of the transgendered nor of gender identity. It simply says that no school may discriminate on the basis of sex. Thus, the judge upheld the right of the DOE to determine that sex is not a strictly biological concept but also a matter of identity. Congress has not chosen to revisit Title Nine to clarify this question. Rather, it was left to a federal department to answer it. Whether or not one agrees with the DOE's decision, it is noteworthy that it was made by federal bureaucrats, not elected representatives. As the number and complexity of matters that government undertakes has grown, such bureaucratic discretion has grown apace. First, this chapter provides a portrait of the contemporary bureaucracy. Next, it describes the severe limits place upon it in the nineteenth century. Then it depicts the great twentieth-century transformation of the American bureaucracy that spawned the vast expansion of bureaucratic discretion the DOE guidelines exemplify.

A Contemporary Portrait of the Federal Bureaucracy

This section provides a portrait of the current federal bureaucracy. It examines what it does, how it is organized, and what tools are available to the president to coordinate its activities and exercise control (a list of cabinet departments appears in Chapter 8).

What the Federal Bureaucracy Does

Members of the public have direct contact with the federal bureaucracy in many different ways. The national parks they visit are run by the National Park Service. The US Postal Service delivers their mail. The elderly and the disabled receive monthly checks from the Social Security Administration. Taxpayers file their federal income tax returns with the Internal Revenue Service (IRS). The person at airport security telling people to take off their shoes and put their laptops in a separate bin works for the federal Transportation Security Agency.

The bureaucracy does far more than provide services. The Constitution requires the president to "faithfully execute the laws," and the bureaucracy is the means available to him for fulfilling that responsibility. It is impossible for Congress to write laws that are sufficiently detailed to provide sufficient guidance about how those laws are to be obeyed. Therefore to execute the law, federal agencies write rules and regulations that enable those subject to a given law to obey it. For example, Congress sets standards for clean air but the Environmental Protection Agency issues specific regulations that tell industry what it has to do to meet those standards. Agencies enjoy a great deal of discretion in writing rules but they cannot simply do anything they like. Courts insist that those rules may not be "arbitrary or capricious," meaning that they must be faithful to the intent of the law they implement and they must not impose unnecessary burdens on those who must comply with them. In 1946, Congress passed the Administrative Procedures Act (APA), which codifies the procedures that agencies must follow when devising and issuing regulations. One of its most important goals is to ensure that the public has sufficient opportunity to participate in rule making. It requires an agency to invite the public to comment on a rule it is proposing and then to demonstrate that it seriously considered such comments before it issues the rule.

However, as the opening vignette shows, agencies exercise a great deal of discretion in the interpretation of statutes. Legislation is often the product of a great deal of compromise and is completed in great haste. As a result, key portions of a law remain vague and errors are made. Therefore, it is left to the bureaucrats to determine the actual meaning of the vague language and to use their own judgement about how to correct mistakes. The Affordable Care Act passed in 2009 is an especially complex law. It required a great deal of interpretation by the Department of Health and Human Services (HHS) to make it operative. The situation became especially difficult because the Republicans regained control of the House of Representatives the same year. Since they opposed the law in principle they were not willing to consider statutory changes to fix mistakes that had been made. Thus, the HHS attempted to fix those mistakes on its own, even when the fixes violated the letter of the law. The ACA encourages states to establish marketplaces from which people can purchase health insurance. It also sought to subsidize poorer people who bought policies from those marketplaces. If a state failed to set up an exchange, then the federal government would step in to create one. Some states did not set up exchanges. The language of the law provided that the federal government could subsidize insurance for people who purchase it in a marketplace "established by the state." It did not mention subsidies for those who purchased insurance from the federal marketplace. Nonetheless, the HHS proceeded to set up rules for providing subsidies for federal marketplace purchases. It reasoned that the exclusion of federal marketplaces was just a mistake. Therefore, it could ignore the letter of the law and offer subsidies for insurance purchased from a federal exchange. In a 6–3 decision, the Supreme Court supported the HHS. The dissenters argued that the HHS had violated the rule of law by substituting its own preference for what the law actually said.

The federal government employs roughly 4 million people. More than a quarter of that total is accounted for by the military. Of the 3 million civilian employees, a quarter of that total is accounted for by the postal service.

Three million workers may sound like a big number until one realizes that Walmart, the US's largest private employer, has more than 2 million. The US population exceeds 300 million. Therefore, there is less than one civilian federal employee per 100 persons. The size of the federal government workforce remains relatively small because most federal agencies and departments supervise the work of others. They work indirectly by issuing grants and negotiating contracts with state and local governments, universities, nonprofit social service agencies, and private companies to do a whole host of things that Congress wants done. They write guidelines that grantees, contractors, and state regulatory agencies must follow. They monitor the performance of those nonfederal entities to make sure that those guidelines are being followed. The total state government workforce exceeds the federal workforce by more than 800,000. The local government workforce, which exceeds 10 million, is more than three times the size of the federal workforce. Therefore, the federal civilian bureaucracy is not nearly as big as those of other rich nations, adjusting for population size. But when one includes state and local government workers, many of whom are doing work contracted for by the federal government, the gap between the total government US workforce and that of other rich countries narrows substantially.

Defense is the largest component of the federal government workforce. The US has approximately 1.5 million persons in uniform. Only China has a larger military. As we discussed in the first chapter, the US is the reigning superpower. That role requires it to devote a great deal of effort to maintaining its power and prestige worldwide. US troops and aircraft are stationed on almost every continent as well in bases on US soil. The US Navy patrols sea-lanes around the globe. To maintain such a huge military effort requires an enormous amount of resources and a complex bureaucracy to manage it. The military has its own bureaucratic structure with the Joint Chiefs of Staff at the top. And, as one would expect from a nation born with a fear of standing armies, the military command must answer to civilians. Although military personnel work at the Pentagon, the headquarters of the Department of Defense (DOD), the Secretary of Defense, the DOD senior management team, and many DOD employees are civilians. The Joint Chiefs of Staff are accountable to the Secretary of Defense.

The US maintains embassies and consulates in almost every country. Their employees belong to the Foreign Service, a division of the State Department. Those outposts of the US government overseas issue visas to foreigners who want to visit the US, assist American nationals living or traveling abroad, and facilitates business deals to export to or import from the US. In addition to performing these services, the embassy houses the ambassador, the official representative of the US government in that particular nation. But the most important function of the State Department is to generate and analyze information. Its Washington headquarters houses bureaus devoted to monitoring and interpreting the political, economic, diplomatic, and military activities of every foreign nation. The reports these bureaus produce are read and distilled by the higher levels of the State Department bureaucracy and serve to inform the critical foreign policy decisions that the president and his chief diplomat, the secretary of state, must make. They are also the basis for the extensive briefings that the State Department provides to members of Congress.

Information that is directly related to American national security and that may well be obtained secretly is called intelligence. Each branch of the military also maintains its own intelligence agency, as does the Department of Defense. There is also a CIA (Civilian Intelligence Agency) that is not part of either state or defense. The National Security Agency (NSA), unlike the other intelligence services, does not make use of undercover operatives or informants, but relies on information technology to analyze huge amounts of raw data from foreign nations and to break the codes that seek to render much of that data unintelligible to eavesdroppers. In 2004, Congress gave the president the authority to appoint a Director of National Intelligence (DNI) to serve as his principal advisor on intelligence matters and to coordinate the activities of all the other intelligence agencies. However, the DNI was not actually given authority to manage any of the existing intelligence agencies and so it is not clear how and to what extent the DNI is actually able to coordinate those activities.

Information is also a critical component of the work of the domestic bureaucracy. The Census Bureau counts the number of Americans and provides critical data about where and how they live. The Bureau of Labor Statistics tracks changes in prices and employment. The Environmental Protection Agency (EPA) keeps track of changes in air and water pollution levels. The National Oceanic and Atmospheric Administration (NOAA) monitors changes in ocean currents and patterns of fish migrations. These mounds of information are vital to scientific research, business decision making, and philanthropic activity as well as to informed public policy deliberation. Indeed, the federal bureaucracy comprises the single most important source of information about who Americans are, how they live, and how their economy functions.

The Organization of the Federal Bureaucracy

For the most part, the federal government bureaucracy is organized into departments, each of which is headed by a secretary appointed by the president and confirmed by the Senate. Each department has a specific function – the Labor Department deals with issues relating to workers, the Agriculture Department deal with farming, and so on. But this is not the entire story. Many functions overlap. For example, the Environmental Protection Agency has responsibility for managing the nation's wetlands, but so does the Army Corps of Engineers. And, some agencies are not in the department whose function they share. For example, the National Forest Service manages public lands, a function that is mostly assigned to the Interior Department. Yet the Forest Service is in the Agriculture Department. NOAA is primarily an environmental agency and yet it is in the Department of Commerce, not in the EPA. Also, many important agencies, such as the EPA, National Aeronautics and Space Administration (NASA), and the Peace Corps, are not housed in departments at all. They report directly to the president.

These exceptions cannot be explained logically. Each one is the result of a specific set of political circumstances. For example, when President Nixon had to decide to whom to give the authority to implement the major air and water laws that Congress had passed in the early years of his presidency, the obvious choice was the Department of the Interior (DOI). The DOI already had jurisdiction over most of the environmental issues the government dealt with. But Secretary of the Interior Walter Hickel had become unpopular both within the administration and with a large portion of Congress and the media. Nixon did not want to tarnish his great accomplishment by putting Hickel in charge. Rather, he hoped to gain a great deal of good publicity from signing these powerful laws and so he choose to create a new agency, the EPA, to implement those laws. To maximize his identification with this popular cause, he had the new agency report directly to him. Likewise, John F. Kennedy sought to maximize his identification with the Peace Corps by establishing it as an independent agency reporting to the president.

When the Forest Service (then known as the Forestry Bureau) was created, it was put in the Department of Agriculture because its original function was to give technical advice to commercial tree farmers. When it acquired its land management responsibilities, the chief forester, Gifford Pinchot, resisted efforts to move it to the Department of the Interior, which already housed the Bureau of Land Management and would soon acquire the Park Service, because he was a foe of the Interior Department secretary. Since the Forest Service was the only land management agency in the Agriculture Department, the department hierarchy tended to leave it alone and to trust the judgment of the chief forester. Therefore, Pinchot's successors staved off attempts to move it to the Interior Department, even though they had no personal animosity toward later secretaries of the Interior. As these examples indicate, the haphazardness of federal bureaucratic organization is a very important clue regarding the nature of bureaucratic politics. Where an agency rests in the organization chart will inevitably benefit those political interests whose access to and power over the agency is advantaged by that placement. Conversely, handicaps are created for those for whom the organization chart placement restricts access and denies levers of power.

The terms used to designate the different organs of the federal government obey no clear logic. As the examples discussed above illustrate, there is no clear difference between an agency, as in the Environmental Protection Agency, an administration, as in the Food and Drug Administration, a service, as in the Forest Service, and a bureau, as in the Federal Bureau of Investigation. Therefore, when discussing the functioning of government organizations in general terms, this book uses the generic term "agency."

The agencies we have discussed so far have one very important thing in common: their leaders either report directly to the president, as in the case of cabinet secretaries and the heads of agencies like the EPA and the Peace Corps, or indirectly to the president via a chain of command that leads up to a cabinet secretary. However, as their name implies, the independent regulatory commissions are not fully under presidential control. The most important of these are the Federal Communications Commission (FCC), the National Labor Relations Board

Table 10.1. Independent regulatory agencies.

Agency	Year established
Consumer Financial Protection Bureau	2011
Consumer Product Safety Commission	1972
Commodity Futures Trading Commission	1975
Equal Employment Opportunity Commission	1965
Federal Communications Commission	1934
Federal Deposit Insurance Corporation	1933
Federal Election Commission	1975
Federal Energy Regulatory Commission	1977
Federal Housing Finance Agency	2008
Federal Maritime Commission	1961
Federal Mine Safety and Health Review Commission	1977
Federal Reserve Board	1913
Federal Trade Commission	1914
US International Trade Commission	1916
Merit Systems Protection Board	1978
National Labor Relations Board	1935
Nuclear Regulatory Commission	1975
Occupational Safety and Health Review Commission	1970
Postal Regulatory Commission	1970
Securities and Exchange Commission	1934
Surface Transportation Board	1996

Source: Administrative Conference of the United States.

(NLRB), the Federal Trade Commission (FTC), and the Securities and Exchange Commission (SEC). Each has five commissioners who make their decisions by majority vote. The president can appoint no more than three commissioners from the same political party. The NLRB and SEC commissioners serve five-year terms with one board member retiring each year. This means that a president has to wait until the third year of his term to appoint a majority of the members. FTC commissioners enjoy seven-year terms, thus a president has to be elected to a second four-year term before he can appoint the commission majority. Perhaps the greatest of all the barriers to presidential control of the independent regulatory commissions is that the Supreme Court has ruled that he cannot remove a commission member.

These limits on presidential authority have been imposed by Congress because it did not intend these commissions to operate as normal executive agencies. Congress did not want to politicize such sensitive and technically complex issues as awarding of radio and TV broadcasting licenses, scrutinizing corporate financial disclosure reports, and investigating charges of anticompetitive business activities. It wanted the government bodies making such determinations to be governed by experts. Congress did not fully trust the president to place a concern for expertise above political concerns in making such appointments, and even more importantly, in deciding whom to remove. Congress favored the commission form for the same reason. Any one commissioner might misunderstand the technical merits, or be swayed by partisan bias or personal feelings. Sound technical decisions were more likely to occur if five experts were involved and the decision was made by the majority of them.

As Chapter 4 discussed, the effort to place expertise above politics dates back to the Progressives, who displayed a deep distrust of partisan politics. Progressives believed that many public policy questions had scientifically derivable right answers and that those questions should be settled by experts whose training would enable them to come up with those right answers. Because they were experts, the Progessives did not think that granting them so much discretion posed a threat to democracy. The continuing role of independent commissions in the operations of the federal government, and state governments as well, shows how dependent on Progressivism the path of American government continues to be.

Presidential Control of the Bureaucracy

The federal bureaucracy is so unwieldy and sprawling that the president has enormous difficulty in controlling it. To assist the president in coordinating the efforts of the disparate agencies and in rendering them accountable to the president, the Executive Office of the President (EOP) was created (see Chapter 8).

The two most important arms of the EOP are the Office of Management and Budget (OMB) and the National Security Council (NSC). The OMB is the biggest component of the executive office of the president. It is the critical tool the president uses to coordinate the disparate parts of the federal bureaucracy. It performs specific functions: budget planning and development, management improvement, regulatory analysis, and legislative clearance. Its single most important function is to assist the president to develop the annual budget he submits to Congress. Since the budget provides specific requests for funds for every federal government activity, it is the concrete embodiment of what the president plans to have the government actually do in the upcoming year. In order to make specific funding recommendations, the OMB evaluates agency programs, policies, and procedures and judges amongst competing funding demands within and among agencies in order to establish funding priorities. This budgetary authority also provides it with a powerful tool to influence agency behavior. In the course of its budgetary reviews it makes recommendations to agencies about how they should adjust their policies to bring them closer into line with the president's priorities. Agencies have no legal obligation to bow to OMB pressure, but if they do not, they know that it might well retaliate by cutting their future budget requests.

Congress has the final say in determining the federal budget. The Congressional Budget Office does its own analyses of agency performance and spending priorities (see Chapter 7). But the CBO is no match for the OMB in terms of the comprehensiveness and depth of its investigations. Indeed, the CBO depends to a large extent on the data and analysis the OMB provides. Therefore, even though the budget Congress passes may differ in significant respects from what the president asked for, the OMB's fingerprints will be found all over the final budget document. Once Congress passes a budget, the OMB is responsible for making sure that federal agency spending conforms to the budgetary blueprint.

The OMB serves as an arm of the president in other important ways. To make sure that the legislative proposals drafted by individual agencies conform to the president's wishes and complement one another, it circulates them to other affected agencies and reviews them itself. If it has objections, or objections are voice by other agencies, it oversees a process of interagency consultation to reconcile the divergent points of view. Only when it is satisfied that the key points of controversy have been resolved does it transmit the bill to Congress. It also reviews drafts of all regulations that agencies as diverse as the EPA, the HHS and the Department of Agriculture propose. It does so in an effort to ensure that the proposal is superior to alternative ways of accomplishing the same purpose, that it is cost effective, and that it does not conflict with other regulations already on the books. This process is undertaken by an arm of the executive and is therefore done to ensure fidelity to the president's interests. It does not necessarily do away with the tension between the preferences of bureaucrats and the intent of Congress, as evidenced by the controversial examples of bureaucratic discretion this chapter has already discussed.

As Chapter 7 pointed out, Congress does have means for influencing the behavior of federal agencies. It can threaten to cut their budgets. Legislative oversight committees can grill agency officials about their activities. Congress can prevent the president from reorganizing federal agencies. Executive discretion is far from absolute. Sometimes agencies can ignore congressional pressure and sometimes not. Sometimes the courts will support an agency and sometimes not. Even as the executive increases its power, the path of constitutionally imposed checks and balances has not been entirely abandoned.

Historically, the federal government has lagged far behind the corporate world in developing effective management tools. It has been slow to adopt state-of-the-art techniques for analyzing data, buying supplies, improving the skills of its workforce, and communicating with the public. The OMB is the leading force within the federal government for modernizing management. It mounts government-wide efforts to encourage agencies to improve their information systems, strategic planning, financial management, procurement procedures, and personnel training. It's Office of E-government and Information Technology is in charge of a government-wide initiative geared to making more and better use

Table 10.2. Functions of the Office of Management and Budget

Develop the president's budget proposal to Congress.
Pressure agencies to make their activities more in line with presidential priorities.
Review legislative proposals drafted by individual agencies to ensure that they reflect the president's priorities and that they complement one another.
Review regulations proposed by the various agencies and submit them to cost benefit analysis.
Promote efforts throughout the government to modernize management.

of web-based technologies. Its Office of Federal Procurement Policy devises methods to enable government agencies to lower the cost and improve the quality of the goods and services they buy. The Office of Performance and Personnel Policy devises better methods by which agencies can evaluate their workers and plan for their future staffing needs. These efforts become ever more important as the federal bureaucracy continues to grow in size and complexity providing bureaucrats with ever increasing opportunities to exercise discretion.

The NSC is chaired by the vice president. Its members include the Secretary of State, Secretary of the Treasury, Secretary of Defense, Secretary of Energy, and Assistant to the President for National Security Affairs. Because the members often supply differing and even contradictory information and advice, the president relies on the Assistant for National Security Affairs to sift through the ideas and information those departments provide to help him understand the nature of the disagreements and to assess them. In support of this effort, the NSC has a staff of its own who report to the Assistant to the President for National Security Affairs.

In order to penetrate the actual workings of the other federal agencies, both the OMB and the NSC have had to create bureaucracies of their own. The staffers of both agencies pride themselves on being as knowledgeable about the policy issues at hand as the bureaucrats they are scrutinizing. They do not limit themselves to coordinating and elucidating information from the other departments, but offer information and ideas of their own. Therefore, the NSC and OMB serve both to help the president control the bureaucracy and as additional bureaucratic competitors for his attention and his favor.

Path Dependency: Hating Bureaucracy

The United States was born hating bureaucrats. In theory, the American Revolution was fought against the British king. But it was the agents of the king, British soldiers and tax collectors, whose offenses drove the colonists to rebel. From the beginning, less effort was expended to create an efficient and forceful government apparatus than to establish strict methods for limiting bureaucratic license. By European standards, the American bureaucracy has always seemed incompetent. But it is also less intrusive and despotic. In bureaucracy, as in so many other aspects of political life, Americans opted for liberty even at the price of effective government.

For most of America's history, this liberty was obtained less by wrapping the bureaucracy in red tape than by simply having less of it. Minimizing bureaucracy was part and parcel of the broader commitment to limiting government that the Declaration of Independence and the Constitution proclaim. Because the Constitution limited the powers of government, those tasked with implementing public policies had relatively little to do, at least in peacetime. Their numbers were small; their tasks were few and simple. As we have seen in previous chapters, the twentieth century witnessed a great expansion in the tasks assumed by government. As those ambitions grew, the size of the government bureaucracy grew with it. But the antipathy to bureaucracy evident at the birth of the Republic did not change, even as its role expanded.

Effectiveness versus Liberty: Citizens versus Soldiers

The earliest point of tension between hatred of government agents and the need for public action occurred with regard to national security. The colonies had been forced to abide garrisons of British troops and suffer their swaggering arrogance. This dreadful experience reinforced the deep antipathy that the colonist's already felt toward professional armies. The Bill of Rights forbids the quartering of troops in people's homes during peacetime without their permission and allows it during wartime "only in a lawful manner." However, this antipathy had to be reconciled with the recognition that the new nation faced grave security threats. Despite signing a peace treaty, the British retained strategically located military installations in North America from which they could very plausibly stage a new invasion. The United States had hostile relations with several Indian nations, and many frontier settlers faced great risks from Indian raids.

The first impulse of the new nation was to rely on local and state militia to provide national security. A militia is composed of ordinary citizens prepared to fight in the event of a military emergency. They train and drill on a part-time basis. Unlike soldiers, they are not agents of the government. To the contrary, they stand armed and ready to defend against any threat to their local liberty and security, whether posed by marauding Indians, foreign armies, or the national government itself. Support for the militia and hatred of standing armies is at the core of the Bill of Rights. The Second Amendment states that "a well-regulated militia being necessary to the security of a free State, citizens must retain the right to bear arms."

Although militias did participate in the American Revolution, the bulk of the fighting was done by the Continental Army. At war's end, public sentiment was strongly behind disbanding the army. However, it soon became clear that as currently organized, the militias were inadequate for responding to the growing threat of attack by hostile Indians. In 1791, a 1,400-person force composed of militia and some hastily recruited volunteers, commanded by General Arthur St. Clair, was annihilated by a smaller army of Miami Indians. In the wake of this catastrophic defeat, Congress endorsed President Washington's request for a 5,000-man army composed of regular soldiers to fight the Indians. That new army, under the brilliant leadership of Anthony Wayne, succeeded where St. Clair's poorly organized and poorly trained army had failed.

Wayne's victories convinced Congress to maintain a permanent professional frontier patrol to ward off Indian attack. But it refused to create a permanent standing army comparable in size to the massive European ones. As this initial effort to keep the nation safe illustrates, America would adopt key trappings of a modern bureaucratic state but only in a reluctant, minimal fashion. The people clung to their constitutional right to bear arms. They sought to keep the independent power of that most powerful of all bureaucracies, a standing army, to a minimum.

The Constitution provides only a sketchy account of administration. The "executive power" vested in the president is not defined. The Constitution does not explicitly grant the president control over the heads of executive departments. Rather, it authorizes the president to require their opinion, in writing, on subjects pertaining to their departments. (see Table 10.1 for a display of current executive departments.) The president is instructed to appoint heads of departments, subject to Senate confirmation.

But the power to appoint lesser officials is left unsettled. Congress may choose to let the president make such designations, vest them in the courts, or grant them directly to department heads. The first Congress had to sort out the meaning of these ambiguous constitutional provisions.

CRITICAL CHOICE: THE PRESIDENT'S REMOVAL POWER

In its very first session, Congress made a critical choice about the relationship of the bureaucracy to the president. It granted the president the power to remove executive officials. During its first session, Congress took up the problem of establishing executive departments, beginning with Foreign Affairs (later, the Department of State). The key question was whether departmental control would be shared with the president. Some members of Congress argued that the constitutional requirement that the Senate approve department heads implied it should also approve a presidential decision to remove them. Depriving the president of the removal power would have greatly increased bureaucratic independence. To resist removal, a bureaucrat could cultivate strong ties to Congress. Thus, the bureaucrat could maintain a great deal of personal discretion by skillfully playing the president and Congress against one another.

James Madison supported giving the president exclusive removal power on democratic grounds. Citizens did not vote for department heads, but they did vote for the president. If the president could not fire executive officials, those officials would feel free to ignore the president's instructions. It would be impossible to hold them publicly accountable for their actions. Congress eventually accepted this argument.

UPSHOT

Although it would later try to challenge the president's administrative preeminence, Congress never regained the administrative power that it gave away at the outset. As a result of granting the president removal authority, the heads of executive departments were considered assistants to the president and a chain of command was established within the executive branch with the president at the top.

Warring Principles: Spoils versus Merit

In the course of the nineteenth century two principles for determining how public officials should be appointed and removed warred with one another. One principle stressed party loyalty while the other stressed the use of objective examinations. The first is commonly referred to as the "spoils system," the latter as the "merit system."

Rotation in Office

In Chapters 4 and 8 we discussed the crucial democratic changes that occurred during the Jacksonian era, including the expansion of voting rights, the development of a political party system, and the withdrawal of government from previous efforts to place control of the economy in the hands of a privileged few. Nowhere was the impact of this democratic transformation felt with greater force than within the government bureaucracy itself. The creation of a mass electorate challenged the principle of the "rule of gentlemen." The greater political influence of ordinary citizens made them less tolerant of rule by people they no longer considered their betters. They demanded to be governed by people more like themselves. And many of them looked forward to improving their lot by going to work for the government.

Washington made his bureaucratic appointments on the basis of character. He recognized that local post offices and land offices were the only points of federal government contact that most citizens would ever have. Therefore, he took pains to appoint to these offices people of superior moral character who enjoyed the respect and affection of their neighbors. Thus, he could ensure the reliability of the federal service and also enhance the reputation of the federal government as a whole among the citizenry at large.

Despite the lack of an extensive administrative apparatus, the small size of the federal bureaucracy enabled the president to keep track of administrative performance. Traditional social arrangements were still strong. Most communities had an upper class to whom the rest of the people paid deference and respect. It was from this stratum of "gentlemen" that Washington recruited his administrators, and he relied on them to serve as effective ambassadors of the federal government to their hometowns. Because he was so confident of their character , he did not feel the need to construct regulations and other control mechanisms to limit their discretion.

As the leader of the first real political party (see Chapter 11), Jefferson chose to replace many of Washington and Adams' appointments with Republican loyalists. But he did not deviate from his predecessors' preference for appointing gentlemen. Although Jefferson invented the so-called spoils system, it was Jackson who made use of it to transform the character of American public administration by insisting that federal bureaucracy could and should be staffed by ordinary people.

Andrew Jackson's first annual message to Congress in 1833 highlighted the threat to democracy that was posed by allowing public officials to remain too long in office:

> Office is considered as a species of property and government, rather as a means of promoting individual interests than as an instrument created solely for the service of the people. Corruption in some and, in others, a perversion of correct feelings and principles, diverts government from its legitimate ends and makes it an engine for the support of the few at the expense of the many.

In other words, if bureaucrats were not closely subject to presidential control they would treat their office as their own property and do as they pleased. In order for them to be true public servants, they should serve at the pleasure of the public, and therefore of the public's tribune, the president. The best way to preserve this spirit of democratic subservience was through rotation in office. A new president should be free to appoint a new team of public officials who reflected the new president's point of view and who would therefore be more responsive to the majority of voters who put that president in office.

This approach was nicknamed the "spoils system," but that term is misleading. "Spoils" places the emphasis on the opportunity for enrichment that public office provides. But Jackson's chief concern was party loyalty, not spoils. By appointing only those who shared the outlook of the electoral majority and firing those who did not, he would make the government obey the will of the people. He would appoint only Democrats, recognizing that if he were defeated for reelection, his opponents would, and should, appoint only Whigs.

Jackson did not, and could not, wield the spoils system to centralize power in his own hands. As we discuss in Chapter 11, Jackson was beholden to state and local Democratic Party leaders. They dictated who was appointed to federal posts in their own bailiwicks. Thus, rotation became a valuable tool for strengthening bonds between citizens and their government. As the tradition of deference to one's social superiors waned, the government needed new means of solidifying its hold on the loyalties and energies of the citizenry. This problem was greatly aggravated by the rapid westward expansion of the country, which increased the emotional as well as the physical distance that separated citizens from the nation's capital. It became even more important to improve the levels of trust and respect for the government that were accorded by the increasingly far-flung citizenry. Ceding control of federal appointments to local Democratic political organizations decreased the psychic distance between Washington and the hinterlands. It gave the national government a friendly, recognizable local face.

Jackson understood that the success of the rotation system required limited government: "The duties of all public officers are, or at least admit of being made, so plain and simple that men of intelligence may readily qualify themselves for their performance." Delivering the mail, collecting tariffs, and selling off public lands were all tasks that ordinary persons could perform. Because government did not do many ambitious and complicated things, it did not need a highly skilled and experienced workforce and therefore its employees could be easily and painlessly replaced. In later years, as government expanded and the demands placed on the bureaucracy grew ever more complex, this basic assumption on which the principle of rotation rested became less and less plausible.

The spoils system ended the era of government by the elite and initiated the full democratization of American public life. Now, in addition to juries and other purely local activities, the bureaucracy itself would become a schoolroom for democracy, educating hundreds of thousands of Americans in the mundane realities of politics. The greatest compliment paid to this system came with the defeat of Jackson's protégé, Martin Van Buren, for reelection as president in 1840. The new Whig president, William Henry Harrison, while opposing most of Jackson's policies, openly endorsed the principle of rotation in office; he removed thousands of Jacksonians and replaced them with Whig loyalists. At this next stage of the development of American public administration, party discipline replaced good character as the solution to the problem of bureaucratic license.

The spoils system flourished throughout most of the rest of the nineteenth century. As the number of federal jobs expanded, dispensing them in return for political support became an ever more important aspect of party politics. The late nineteenth century was the heyday of congressional dominance of American government (see Chapter 7). Congress, not the president, became the de facto ruler of the public service. Administrative personnel and budget decisions were determined in congressional committee and in coordination with the congressional leadership.

But even as the spoils system was growing in prominence, its democratic luster began to fade. Because Congress was seen less as the voice of public opinion than as the errand boy for powerful business interests, its servant, the bureaucracy, acquired a similarly sinister reputation. Patronage appointees – postal workers, customs collectors, and land agents – were viewed not as public servants but simply as hacks, people who were concerned only with personal gain. The prestige of the federal government faded as it came to be seen as a hotbed of incompetence and favoritism.

Despite its tarnished image, the federal government grew rapidly. Between 1870 and 1880, the number of federal employees doubled, from 53,000 to 107,000. By 1890, it grew an additional 50 percent, to 166,000, and by 1901 it reached 256,000, almost a fivefold increase in thirty years. European immigration, the populating of the western territories, economic growth, and technical change all conspired to accelerate demands on the public sector. The federal government did not add many new functions during this period. Rather, this explosion of personnel resulted from expansion in the volume of existing types of federal business and from the growing pressure on the political parties and their representatives in Congress to produce more jobs for partisan loyalists.

Figure 10.1. For Their Own Good: an 1895 cartoon depicting President Grover Cleveland reforming the US civil service.
Source: Granger Collection, NYC –

The government in Washington was in the happy position of being able to respond to these demands without imposing greater tax burdens. The bulk of federal revenue came from tariffs on imported goods, which grew as the economy grew, providing ample funds to hire more federal workers. Although the post-Civil War Republicans were not big government advocates in the modern sense, they did not adopt Jackson's strict construction of the limits on federal power. As a result, the size of the federal government grew dramatically, and with it grew the opportunities for poorly trained and inexperienced workers to abuse their discretion. The spoils system degenerated because subsequent presidents violated the system's original basis on limited government. Party discipline proved inadequate to the task of checking bureaucratic license, setting the stage for a more rule-oriented form of control and the inevitable red tape that reliance on rules and regulations brings about.

Civil Service Reform

The beginning of the end of the spoils system came with the passage of the 1883 Civil Service Act. The act extended only to employees of the executive branch in Washington or in major customhouses and post offices around the country. The vast majority – all but 14,000 of 131,000 federal officeholders, including many postal workers – were not covered. Nonetheless, the act set a critical precedent by expanding the existing but rarely used system of competitive examinations for public posts. It stipulated that appointees would have to be chosen from among those with the highest exam grades. To oversee the examination system and investigate abuses of it, the act created a three-member, bipartisan Civil Service Commission consisting of one Democrat, one Republican, and one independent; these members were appointed by the president, subject to Senate confirmation.

The catalyst for dissolving congressional resistance to civil service reform was the 1881 assassination of President James A. Garfield by an unsuccessful office seeker. The direct connection between the patronage system and such a heinous crime, the second presidential assassination in less than twenty years, galvanized public outrage and forced a reluctant Congress to commit itself to civil service reform.

CRITICAL THINKING QUESTION

The spoils system distributes government jobs on the basis of party loyalty. The civil service system relies on competitive examination for that purpose. Discuss the strengths and weaknesses of each approach. Which one do you favor?

CRITICAL CHOICE: IMPLEMENTING BIG GOVERNMENT

During the Progressive Era and the New Deal, reform efforts widened beyond the appointments process to encompass the very mission of public service and the role of public administrators in pursuing it. This expansion was a direct result of the rethinking of the relationship between government and society undertaken by Progressivism (see Chapter 4 for a fuller discussion of Progressivism) and the vast expansion of federal responsibilities undertaken during the New Deal.

Woodrow Wilson: the Political Scientist President

Woodrow Wilson was the first and only political science professor ever elected president of the United States. He, more than anyone else, framed the Progressive understanding of public administration. In his classic essay "The Study of Administration," published in 1887, Wilson explained that the role of public administration had to greatly expand in order to respond adequately to the economic transformation that had begun in the aftermath of the Civil War.

As we discussed in Chapter 5, the economy was no longer the domain of small farmers and family businesses. It was now dominated by giant monopolies whose new production methods threatened to cause class warfare. According to Wilson, the federal government was the only institution capable of taming these despotic economic powers and diffusing the conflict between management and labor. Because these new responsibilities were so weighty and difficult, Jackson's axiom that administrative tasks could be kept simple enough to be performed by inexperienced amateurs no longer held true. "To straighten the paths of government, to make its business less unbusinesslike, to strengthen and purify its organization and to crown its dutifulness," wrote Wilson, would require a whole new science, the science of administration.

Underlying this new science was the separation of politics and administration. A more active and expert administrative corps would not threaten liberty and democracy because political control would remain the exclusive domain of popularly elected officials. These politicians would set the broad course of public policy and leave it to expert administrators to implement those policies efficiently and effectively.

Wilson likened the distinction between politics and administration to that between the head of a household and the kitchen staff: "Self-government does not consist in having a hand in everything any more than housekeeping consists necessarily in cooking dinner with one's own hands. The cook must be trusted with a large discretion as to the management of the fires and the ovens." The head of household remains in control because he or she is the one who tells the cooks what sort of food the family likes, provides them with a firm budget for food and kitchen maintenance, and fires them if they make lousy meals. But, having established broad policy principles and performance guidelines, the head of household stays out of the kitchen, enabling the cooks to make full use of their special talents and expertise to put tasty and nutritious food on the table.

Progressive Reform

During the Progressive Era, both the study and practice of public administration changed along the lines proposed by Wilson. In 1914, the University of Michigan established the first graduate program in municipal administration. Soon, other state and private universities began to offer degrees in public administration for the purpose of training students for public service careers. The faculties of such programs also did research aimed at establishing a scientific basis for such critical administrative tasks as budgeting, contract compliance, financial auditing, and personnel management. In 1916, the Institute for Government Research, later renamed the Brookings Institution, was created as the first private research institute devoted to the systematic analysis of issues relating to governmental performance and public policy.

Progressive reform of administration was particularly noteworthy in the area of natural resource management. The federal government was the nation's biggest landlord. It owned vast tracts of forest and grazing land, particularly in the West. In 1898, Gifford Pinchot was appointed to head a new Bureau of Forestry placed in the Department of Agriculture that was dedicated to improving forest conservation. This bureau would manage the nation's timber and mineral resources to maximize the benefits they would provide over the long term. Because the United States had no forestry school, Pinchot had gone to Germany for his professional training. He would later found the Yale School of Forestry. In 1905, authority for managing 60 million acres of western federal forests was transferred from the Department of the Interior to the Bureau of Forestry, renamed the Forest Service. In 1911, the Forest Service was granted authority over all federal forests.

Pinchot was determined that the Forest Service break the mold of corruption and ineptitude that had enveloped federal public administration. He sought to establish an organization in which personnel at all levels were committed to its goals and were competent, energetic, and skillful enough to attain them. Forest rangers received special training and were encouraged to think of themselves as professionals. They were expected to respond to orders from regional and national service headquarters, not to demands of local citizens or politicians living near the forests they were managing. This quasi-military mode of organization was in stark contrast to the Jacksonian model in which public servants were expected to identify closely with their local community, have no strong sense of professional identity, and remain loyal to their political party leaders, not their bureaucratic superiors. As their distinctive uniforms proudly proclaimed, the forest rangers were an elite corps. The democratic threat posed by such elites within the public service was presumably outweighed by their expertise and dedication.

Wilson's principle of separating politics and administration required that elected officials provide broad policy direction for the bureaucracy. Congress was simply too large and unwieldy to provide such guidance, and so, increasingly, that responsibility was borne by the president. The Budget Act of 1921 provided the president with a powerful tool for performing that task. It created the Bureau of the Budget (BOB), which was later renamed the Office of Management and Budget (OMB), housed in the Treasury Department. The chief task of this new agency was to prepare a budget for the entire federal government. It would review the requests of all federal programs and agencies, assemble those requests, and then suggest to the president how the requests should be pared down to keep overall federal spending in balance with expected revenues.

This notion of an executive budget has become so deeply embedded in the operations of the federal government that it is hard to believe that no such organizing principle for federal spending existed for the first 130 years of the republic. Spending decisions had been a haphazard affair in which, for the most part, individual federal departments made up their own budget proposals and took them directly to Congress. Creation of a budget bureau enabled the president to establish spending priorities and maintain some degree of financial control over his administrative subordinates.

Congress still preserved its constitutionally mandated power of the purse. It could choose to modify the president's budgetary proposals or even to ignore them altogether. But the sheer existence of an overall budgetary plan gave the president the initiative in policy planning and enabled him to appear fiscally responsible. Congress was put on the defensive. If it chose to deviate from this comprehensive blueprint, it bore the onus of demonstrating that its alternative was not a "budget breaker."

The New Deal Administrative Transformation

President Wilson had only limited opportunity to put his vision of a new science of administration into practice. The Great Depression opened far greater possibilities for Wilson's disciple, Franklin Roosevelt (FDR). The Depression ushered in the modern era of big government and thus gave FDR a larger canvas on which to impose Progressive notions of administration.

FDR had considerable administrative experience; he had served as Wilson's assistant secretary of the Navy, and then succeeded one of the greatest of all

Progressive executives, Al Smith, as governor of New York. To implement New Deal innovations in banking, labor relations, social insurance, and many other fields, FDR relied heavily on seasoned administrators who had pioneered similar programs in progressive-minded states such as Wisconsin and New York. The depth of the crisis and the verve of FDR's response to it greatly increased the attractiveness of government service to students and graduates of the most prestigious professional and graduate schools. Not since the early days of the republic had the government been so successful in attracting members of the elite to serve the government in peacetime.

Graduates of Yale, Columbia, and Harvard law schools and departments of economics flocked to Washington to work for new agencies such as the Securities and Exchange Commission (SEC), the Federal Deposit Insurance Corporation (FDIC), the National Labor Relations Board (NLRB), and the Agricultural Adjustment Agency (AAA), as well as expanded and reinvigorated organizations such as the Antitrust Division of the Justice Department and the Department of the Interior. Their bosses were often their own former professors. These highly trained professionals were able to apply their knowledge of such arcane subjects as securities and banking law or labor and resource economics to the daunting task of restoring prosperity.

As we discussed in Chapter 8, FDR's effort to reorganize the executive branch failed. However, Congress did significantly expand his ability to manage the increasingly massive and specialized federal bureaucracy. It created the EOP, which provided him with a well-staffed nerve center for obtaining information about the activities of the various executive departments and for planning and coordinating them. At the EOP's core was the Bureau of the Budget, which was transferred to the EOP from the Treasury Department. The purpose of this reorganization was to fulfill the democratic as well as the scientific promise of Progressive administration. An expert bureaucracy would be rendered accountable to public opinion by providing the representative of public opinion, the president, with sufficient political and managerial tools to control and direct it. FDR declared, "The day of enlightened administration has come."

Table 10.3. Key Progressive and New Deal public administration innovations

- Create institutions, such as Brookings, for the systematic study of public administration
- Establish an agency, the Forest Service, dedicated to the conservation and scientific management of natural resources
- Establish the Bureau of the Budget to prepare a comprehensive federal budget
- Improve the president's ability to manage the bureaucracy through the creation of the Executive Office of the President (EOP)
- Vastly expand civil service protection for federal employees

However, the New Deal was not simply Progressivism writ large. FDR's approach to putting the unemployed back to work had more in common with the older spoils system. Although it might have been more efficient to simply give money to the unemployed to alleviate their misery and encourage consumer spending, FDR rejected this approach. He was as concerned about the self-respect of the unemployed as he was about their economic condition. Therefore, he determined that the bulk of New Deal relief for the poor would come in the form of jobs. He established a series of job-creating relief agencies. The largest and most successful was the Works Progress Administration (WPA), which put millions of people to work in a remarkably short span of time.

Harry Hopkins, head of the WPA, insisted that the WPA create simple jobs that any able-bodied person could do. Skill and expertise were sacrificed to the greater cause of putting Americans back to work. This approach resulted in a lot of wasted effort and misallocation of resources, but it also enabled millions of Americans to hold their heads high. They were not paupers seeking handouts. They were full-fledged Depression fighters, working hard to build a better country. The WPA and its sister agency, the Civilian Conservation Corps (CCC), left a brilliant legacy of accomplishment. Cultural and recreational opportunities for ordinary people were greatly expanded. Parks were built; hiking trails blazed; murals painted; concerts performed. By creating simple jobs on a massive scale, the New Deal relief programs were more in keeping with Jackson's view of democratic administration than with Wilson's view of administration as a science.

FDR distinguished between the permanent bureaucracies he was establishing, which would function along Progressive lines, and the emergency relief agencies, which would be terminated when the economic crisis had passed. The massive spoils system instituted by the WPA and the CCC did not survive the Depression, but they did leave an indelible mark. Before the New Deal, people did not expect the government to help them if they lost their jobs. The success of the WPA and the other relief agencies altered those expectations. Congress acknowledged this new understanding of the responsibility of government when it enacted the Full Employment Act in 1946. This act charges the federal government with the specific responsibility of maintaining prosperity.

As we explained in Chapter 8, FDR insulated his most important New Deal reforms from repeal. Even as he increased presidential power by creating the EOP, he tied the hands of future presidents by transforming his policy goals into a new set of rights. By virtue of being "unalienable," these rights-based programs would be buffered from temporary shifts in public opinion and political power. FDR further constrained his successors by extending civil service protections to his federal appointees. As long as they lived, the committed, youthful New Dealers that he appointed to implement these new programmatic rights would remain in charge of the federal bureaucracy.

UPSHOT

FDR's effort to create an administrative state in service to the new programmatic rights was in tension with his desire to strengthen the presidency. This conflict has permeated American government and politics ever since. The democratic principle that policy should bend to the popular will as championed by the president has coexisted uneasily with the liberal principle that rights are immune from revision.

The Postwar Expansion of the Federal Bureaucracy

The modern federal bureaucracy is vastly bigger and engages in a much wider set of activities than its pre-WWII counterpart. Before the war there were only eleven cabinet departments; today there are eighteen. The creation of new agencies, commissions, and other forms of federal bureaucratic activity has occurred at a still more rapid clip. And, previously existing agencies like Agriculture and Labor have taken on a whole host of new responsibilities. It may still be true that Americans harbor negative views about bureaucracy, but it is no longer true that those sentiments translate into a successful effort to minimize bureaucratic intrusion.

Lowering the Legitimacy Barrier

The most important causes of this expansion have been war, both hot and cold, and the decline of the legitimacy barrier as an obstacle to new statutory initiatives. The legitimacy barrier refers to the constitutional insistence on limited government. In the original understanding of the Constitution, a policy was not legitimate if it did not have a clear basis in the Constitution's enumerated powers. A policy did not just have to serve a legitimate public purpose; it had to be constitutionally legitimate. The success of the Progressive movement and the New Deal served to greatly diminish the principle of enumerated powers as a barrier to legislation. As we have seen in Chapter 9, a vast number of Progressive, New Deal and post-New Deal laws were justified under the commerce clause. And, the Supreme Court did not overturn a single one of those between 1936 and 1995. The older interpretation of the commerce clause would not have countenanced such major and expensive programs as healthcare reform, No Child Left Behind, or the Americans with Disabilities Act (ADA).

The ADA requires that all public buildings provide easy access for the disabled. Each of these, and a multitude of other statutory initiatives, require a great deal of implementation. Someone has to write the specific guidelines that determine what does and does not constitute a disability, and what does and does not constitute easy access. For example, if a member-owned sports club allows guests to play, does it have to put in an elevator and a handicapped toilet even if none of the members of the club are disabled? Does the fact that it invites non-member guests make it a public building and therefore subject to the easy access provision of ADA, or is it a private club and therefore exempt? This and thousands of other equally thorny questions must be addressed to make the ADA effective and workable. Although the question may ultimately be settled in court, the task of interpreting the law and translating it into specific guidelines to address this sort of question falls first to bureaucrats.

The vast expansion of government activity also changed the environment in which bureaucrats operated. Congress, the courts, and interest groups have all become much more active and influential in bureaucratic affairs. Normally one thinks of politics as creating policies. Interest groups lobby Congress to obtain new forms of aid or otherwise further their objectives. But it is equally true that policies create politics. Once the legitimacy barrier was lowered, Congress frequently created programs even in the absence of strong lobbying from interest groups. It passed strong environmental laws and major new science and educational funding programs before lobbying groups for such programs had become politically powerful. Once those programs were in place, however, the beneficiaries quickly organized themselves to lobby Congress to protect and expand the programs themselves and the agencies that implement them. Superficially these support efforts may sound like harsh criticism: environmental groups will criticize EPA for not meeting deadlines or the Department of Education for not doing enough to support Special Education. But the purpose of the criticism is actually to assist the agencies; to obtain more personnel for EPA so that it can act more quickly or to gain more funding for the DOE so it can more amply support Special Ed.

The Military-Industrial Complex

World War II, the Cold War, and the War on Terror each made major contributions to the expansion of the federal bureaucracy. World War II's daunting logistical challenges led to an intimate partnership between government and the private sector. Confronted with the massive challenge of providing supplies, munitions, and transportation to fight a war on two separate fronts, FDR briefly considered nationalizing the war-related sectors of American industry. But he quickly realized that the government lacked sufficient knowledge and the management skill to run those industries. Instead, he relied primarily on voluntary cooperation from private suppliers. Government restricted its involvement mostly to stimulating such cooperation by paying high prices. Even so, a great deal of direct interaction between government and suppliers was necessary to ensure that the right things were being produced in a timely fashion. To facilitate such coordination, suppliers loaned experienced managers to government for the token price of a dollar a year. These "dollar-a-year men" became vital cogs in the war machine, helping to achieve rates of ship, plane, tank, and munitions production that America's enemies had not thought possible.

To hasten production, government contracts were often written on a cost-plus basis, which meant that suppliers could recover their full costs plus a specified percentage of profit. Therefore, war industries had no material incentive to keep costs down. Indeed, the greater their costs, the greater the absolute amount of profit they would obtain. Working for the government for a dollar a year did not cause managers to forget who really paid their salary. Throughout their government service, they retained a strong loyalty to the companies from which they came and to which they would return.

With the onset of the Cold War, these-dollar-a-year men became valued intermediaries between the government and the industries whose ability to produce armaments and related supplies and equipment were vital to the US's ability to compete militarily with the Soviet Union. For the first time in American history, the high levels of war-related industrial production continued during peacetime. As the technology of warfare grew in complexity, government came to depend on science. Grants from the federal government to university physics, chemistry, and engineering departments became a crucial supplement to corporate research and development as a means for stimulating militarily useful scientific discoveries and technological advances. Figure 10.2 charts the growth in federal funding for research and development from the mid 1950s through 2011.

The executive branch was ill-equipped to handle the strategic, scientific, and management complexities created by the Cold War. The Army and the Navy each reported to the president via separate cabinet departments. The Army was part of the War Department headed by the Secretary of War while the Navy had its own department headed by the Secretary of the Navy. Nor was there any mechanism for integrating planning and force deployments involving both the Army and the Navy. Such efforts took place on an ad hoc basis. To give the president a better tool for protecting national security, Congress, in 1947, passed legislation merging the Navy and the War Department into a single Department of Defense (DOD). The Secretary of Defense was given authority over all branches of the military including the newly established US Air Force (previously part of the Army). The Marine Corps remained part of the Navy. The DOD is also in charge of two intelligence agencies, the National Security Agency created in 1952 and the Defense Intelligence Agency, established in 1961.

The increasingly close relationship between the DOD, corporations, and universities led to the creation of a revolving door by which the military and civilian

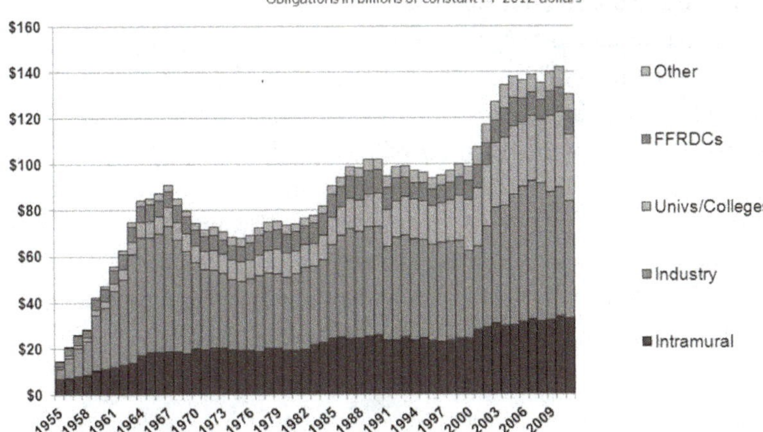

Figure 10.2. R&D funding.
Source: NSF, National Center for Science and Engineering Statistics, *Federal Funds for R&D* series, based on national survey data. FY 2010 and FY 2011 data are preliminary.
© 2013 AAAS

bureaucrats who issued defense contracts and grants would leave to work for the very companies or universities who had won those awards. In his farewell address, President Dwight Eisenhower, the great American hero of World War II and himself an architect of the Cold War, warned of the dangers posed by this new, increasingly unaccountable "military-industrial complex." Eisenhower recognized that government dependence on outside expertise and the increasing interpenetration between government and profit-making corporations was undermining the Wilsonian notion of a scientific administration subservient to executive authority.

The 9/11 attacks on New York and Washington DC destroyed the comforting illusion that war was something that only happened on foreign soil. Before September 11, 2001, the nation's antiterrorism effort resembled the early republic's effort to provide military security through militias. Airport security was supervised by state and local governments and was performed by the airlines themselves. Investigation of biological threats was largely in the hands of local public health departments. In the wake of the attack on the World Trade Center and the Pentagon and the anthrax attacks that took place in the months that followed, the demand for federal intervention drastically increased. The militia phase was over. The federal government would create a standing force to provide homeland security.

The new Department of Homeland Security (DHS) created in response to 9/11, which we discussed briefly in Chapter 1, was the most ambitious reorganization of the federal government since the creation of the DOD half a century earlier. As noted in Chapter 8, President Bush had initially resisted forming another government department. After considerable prodding from Congress, however, the Bush administration agreed to support legislation creating a vast new department to cope with the domestic threat of terror. The DHS, established in 2003, is the third largest cabinet department in the US federal government after the DOD and Department of Veterans Affairs (DVA). As of 2010, it had more than 180,000 employees and an additional 200,000 private contractors. Most of those employees are not new; they were transferred to the new department from existing departments including treasury, agriculture, energy, transportation, state, commerce, and health and human services as well as such previously independent agencies as the Federal Emergency Management Agency (FEMA).

Congress and the Courts

As we saw in Chapter 7, Congress has sought to compensate for its loss of legislative initiative to the executive by becoming more active in its oversight of executive agencies. By threatening to reduce agency appropriations or by exposing agency failures to the glare of publicity, Congress has used its powers to conduct investigations, hold hearings, and appropriate funds to exert substantial influence on the day-to-day conduct of the bureaucracy.

The shift away from centralized leadership control and toward the standing committees and their chairs facilitated these expanded congressional oversight activities. Legislators became careerists, solidifying their hold on their districts by using their committee assignments to oversee executive activities of special concern to their constituents. The Legislative Reorganization Act of 1946 provided members of Congress with expanded staffs to aid their bureaucratic probes. As members' terms of service lengthened, their own policy expertise and knowledge of departmental folklore often matched, or even exceeded, that of the administrators they were scrutinizing.

The diffusion of authority in Congress that began in the 1970s further dispersed political control of the bureaucracy. Bureau chiefs and agency heads found that their budgets, their lifeblood, were controlled as much by congressional committee and subcommittee chairs as by their department heads or the OMB. This dual control opened new doors to the interest-group constituencies of federal agencies. If they lacked influence with the president, they could still obtain favored treatment from the bureaucracy by persuading the relevant congressional committee chair to be their champion.

In the 1970s the federal courts also expanded their influence over the bureaucracy. Previously, the courts had shown great deference toward bureaucratic judgments in recognition of the bureaucrat's claim to expertise and impartiality. But in a series of important cases, courts substituted their own judgment for that of a government agency and ruled that the agency had been insufficiently scrupulous in its implementation of the law. For example, in *Calvert Cliffs Coordinating Committee v. Atomic Energy Commission* (AEC), a federal appeals court ruled that the AEC had not performed a sufficiently thorough environmental impact analysis of the proposal to build a nuclear power plant at Calvert Cliffs, Maryland. The AEC was the very model of a Progressive regulatory agency. It was established in 1947 to oversee the development of atomic energy for peaceful purposes. In order to give it maximum flexibility to hire the best nuclear scientists and engineers, Congress exempted it from many federal civil service requirements. Among its responsibilities was the licensing of nuclear power plants in order to ensure that they would operate safely.

In 1969, Congress passed the National Enivironmental Protection Act that required all federal agencies to conduct an Environmental Impact Statement (EIS) for each project they were conducting, sponsoring, or licensing. It does not specifically instruct the agencies about what they are supposed to do with the statements once they have been conducted. The AEC did commission an EIS of the Calvert Cliffs project, but it did not make substantial use of it during the license approval process. The federal appeals court ruled that the AEC's perfunctory treatment of the EIS violated the act's intent and commanded it to reconsider granting the license in the light of a full consideration of the project's environmental impact. In the end, the AEC did approve the plant. But the court had made its point. It would feel free to intervene in agency decision making even if the agency involved was composed of physicists, nuclear engineers, and other highly trained experts.

The courts often worked in tandem with constituency groups to press agencies to act more quickly. Public interest groups (see Chapter 14) would file suit against a regulatory agency such as the OSHA or EPA, claiming that the agency was not living up to its statutory responsibility to speedily issue a particular set of regulations. The courts would then order the agency to move faster, imposing specific guidelines and timetables. Sometimes the agencies themselves actually welcomed a court order, because it enabled them to demand more cooperation from their reluctant political superiors. But just as often the judicial mandates wreaked havoc inside the agency, because they forced it to reorder its own priorities and reassign funds and personnel away from projects it thought more important to the one the court had ordered it to accomplish at a more rapid clip.

Looking Forward

This chapter has chronicled the difficulties of making the bureaucracy effective and respectful of American liberties. It has shown how at different eras in American political development different methods for accomplishing these goals have been relied upon including: choosing people of good character, rotation in office, civil service examinations, professionalism, executive oversight, congressional oversight, and judicial review. It has also emphasized that the expansion of the bureaucracy that has taken place has been accomplished grudgingly. One has only to travel to France or Germany, or even Canada, to realize that not all peoples are as resentful of bureaucratic intrusion and bureaucratic authority as Americans are.

The American disaste for bureaucracy has not prevented major bureaucratic expansion. But the antipathy toward government continues to give the American bureaucracy a distinctive caste. Instead of establishing a federal bureaucracy large enough to implement the myriad responsibilities now assigned to it by Congress, the president, and the courts, many federal agencies function mostly as supervisors overseeing the work done by state and local officials, nongovernmental agencies, and private companies. This complex set of relationships makes it extremely difficult to hold the bureaucracy acountable.

The dual impact of the decline of the legitimacy barrier and the relentless pressure of national security has pushed the US off the path of limited government. The larger and more complex the task of implementing policy becomes, the more discretion devolves to nonelected officials. No matter how much the public may complain about the bureaucracy, it can only reduce that heavy hand by checking its own appetite for ever more ambitious government programs.

CHAPTER SUMMARY

Contemporary portrait:

* Bureaucrats exercise considerable discretion because it is impossible to write laws that are so clear and comprehensive that they do not require further interpretation and elaboration.
* The civilian component of the federal bureaucracy is surprisingly small. Most of what it does affects the public only indirectly. Much of the actual work the federal government inspires is done by others either in response to grants and contracts issued by the federal bureaucracy or in response to regulatory demands issued by federal agencies.
* The Congress exerts very significant controls over the federal bureaucracy, sometimes thwarting the president's effort to coordinate the efforts of various parts of the bureaucracy.
* The haphazardness of federal bureaucratic organization is a very important clue regarding the nature of bureaucratic politics. Where an agency rests in the organization chart will inevitably give advantages to those political interests whose access to and power over the agency is advantaged by that placement.

Conversely, handicaps are created for those whom the placement restricts access and denies levers of power.

* The Executive Office of the President (EOP) was created to help the president manage the bureaucracy. Its two most important components are the Office of Management and Budget and the National Security Council.

Path dependency: hating the bureaucracy:

* Antipathy to the intrusion of British governors and the British army set the US on a path designed to limit the scope and ambition of the new federal bureaucracy.
* The people clung to their constitutional right to bear arms and created a small weak standing army.

Critical choice: removal:

* The First Congress made the critical choice to grant the president power to remove federal officials.

Warring principles: spoils versus merit:

* The spoils system awarded government jobs on the basis of party loyalty.
* The civil service system awarded jobs on the basis of competitive examinations introducing a greater emphasis on expertise, professionalism, and impartiality into the staffing and management of the federal bureaucracy.

Critical choice: implementing big government:

* The vast expansion in the size of the federal bureaucracy was a result of the greater role the Progressives assigned to government and the fleshing out of that role during the New Deal.
* The Progressives sought to place public administration on a scientific basis, separating politics from administration.
* The creation of the Executive Office of the President strengthened the president's ability to manage the federal bureaucracy.
* The programmatic rights created by the New Deal serve to insulate the agencies that implemented them from political control.

The post-WWII expansion of the federal bureaucracy:

* The most important causes of the postwar expansion of the federal bureaucracy have been war, both hot and cold, and the decline of the "legitimacy barrier" as an obstacle to new statutory initiatives.
* Congress and the courts have both substantially increased their involvement in the activities of government agencies.

SUGGESTED READINGS

Arnold, Peri. *Making the Managerial Presidency: Comprehensive Organization Planning, 1905–1996*, 2nd edn. Lawrence: University Press of Kansas, 1998.

Cook, Brian. *Bureaucracy and Self-Government: Reconsidering the Role of Public Administration in American Politics*. Baltimore, MD: Johns Hopkins University Press, 1996.

Derthick, Martha. *Agency under Stress: The Social Security Administration in American Government*. Washington, DC: Brookings Institution Press, 1990.

Policymaking for Social Security. Washington, DC: Brookings Institution Press, 1979.

Goldsmith, Stephhen, and Eggars, William. *Governing by Network: The New Shape of the Public Sector*. Washington, DC: Brookings Institution Press, 2004.

Goodsell, Charles. *Mission Mystique: Belief Systems in Public Agencies*. Washington, DC: CQ Press, 2011.

Hoffer, Williamjames Hull. *To Enlarge the Machinery of Government: Congressional Debates and the Growth of the American State, 1858–1891*. Baltimore, MD: Johns Hopkins University Press, 2007.

Kaufman, Herbert. *The Forest Ranger: A Study in Administrative Behavior*. Baltimore, MD: Johns Hopkins University Press, 1960.

Kettl, Don. *The Transformation of Governance: Public Administration for Twenty-first Century America*. Baltimore, MD: Johns Hopkins University Press 2002.

Landy, Marc K., Marc J. Roberts, and Stephen R. Thomas. *The Environmental Protection Agency: Asking the Wrong Questions from Nixon to Clinton*, 2nd exp. edn. New York: Oxford University Press, 1994.

Moynihan, Daniel P. *Maximum Feasible Misunderstanding: Community Action in the War on Poverty*. New York: Free Press, 1970.

Rosenbloom, David. *Building a Legislative-Centered Public Administration: Congress and the Administrative State, 1946–1999*. Tuscaloosa, AL: University of Alabama Press, 2002.

Selznick, Philip. *TVA and the Grass Roots: A Study in Politics and Organization*. Berkeley: University of California Press, 1984.

Skowronek, Stephen. *Building a New American State: The Expansion of National Administrative Capacities, 1877–1920*. New York: Cambridge University Press, 1982.

White, Leonard. *The Federalists: A Study in Administrative History*. New York: Macmillan, 1948.

The Jacksonians: A Study in Administrative History. New York: Macmillan, 1954.

The Jeffersonians: A Study in Administrative History, 1801–1829. New York: Macmillan, 1951.

The Republican Era: A Study in Administrative History, 1869–1901. New York: Macmillan, 1958.

Wildavsky, Aaron. *The New Politics of the Budget Process*, 2nd edn. New York: HarperCollins, 1999.

Wilson, James Q. *Bureaucracy: What Government Agencies Do and Why They Do It*. New York: Basic Books, 1989.

Part IV
Political Life

11 Public Opinion

CHAPTER OVERVIEW

This chapter focuses on:

- **A contemporary portrait of public opinion and its relationship to political culture.**
- **The sources of the political memories that underlie political attitudes.**
- **Key shifts in public opinion.**

> You can fool some of the people all of the time, and all of the people some of the time, but you can not fool all of the people all of the time.

This quote has long been attributed to Abraham Lincoln. Scholars continued to debate whether he actually said it, but it certainly represents his way of thinking. It is a powerful defense of American public opinion. Yes, some people are very gullible. Yes, the public can sometimes be misled. However, the common sense of the mass of the people will ultimately prevail. This chapter examines what people think about politics and the opinions they hold. Readers can decide for themselves whether Lincoln was right.

In Chapter 2 we examined American political culture, the core beliefs that form the intellectual, moral, and emotional foundation of the American political order. The relationship between public opinion and political culture is similar to that between the weather and the climate. Like the weather in many parts of the country, public opinion is quite changeable. Political culture, like the climate, remains stable for long periods of time. Deserts do not suddenly become rain forests. Likewise, the fundamental aspects of American political belief tend to remain stable. However, climate does change, but slowly, often imperceptibly. Similarly, political culture is not immutable. But it is highly resistant to change and its alterations happen gradually. If a change in public opinion persists over time, it indicates that the political weather has shifted sufficiently to constitute climate change. This chapter looks both at how public opinion fits in to American political culture and reflects on the tensions between Liberalism, Communitarianism and Egalitarian Democracy that culture embodies. It also examines shifts in opinion that may indicate that political cultural climatic change is taking place.

Chapter 1 explained that a crucial reason for adopting a political development approach to the study of American politics lies in the importance of political memory. The past shapes people's ideas and sentiments, endowing the present with meaning. Stories from the past pervade our imaginations. People form their opinion about the present and even the future largely on the basis of perceptions and understandings they glean from the past. Political scientist Sam Beer described how opinions are formed by a "restless psyche, striving, complex, acting and reacting at different levels, often in conflict with itself, moved by symbols that unite both thought and feeling, its clarities of idea and norm surrounded, supported and transformed by metaphor." Of course, that is not the whole story. People also make use of facts and information gleaned from contemporary sources when they make up their minds. However, as the Beer quote shows, the mind is not simply an information processor. To understand contemporary public opinion it is therefore necessary to look at the past to see how powerful stories, symbols, and metaphors became embedded in political memory and worked to shape political imagination.

A Contemporary Portrait

Contemporary American public opinion is a complex mix of continuity and change. Opinions that fit squarely within the American political cultural climate have persisted. There is a strong consensus among the public with regard to them. Americans continue to cherish free markets, hard work, local government, and limits on the reach of the national government. They are willing to pay to support the government. On the other hand, issues have emerged that polarize public opinion. Supporters of homosexual marriage and abortion place them squarely in the American grain, whereas opponents see them as profound threats to the American way of life. Supporters appeal to hallowed principles of rights and equality while opponents deny that rights should be extended to those they consider socially deviant and to practices they view as immoral and anti-Christian. A look at the polarized attitudes on such issues as abortion, gay rights, and immigration gives substantive meaning to the otherwise amorphous terms "liberal" and "conservative."

Continuities

Previous chapters showed how a variety of different political principles, attitudes, and institutional arrangements embedded themselves in American political life.

In crucial ways, public opinion continues to support those principles, attitudes, and arrangements.

Chapter 2 described the high level of patriotism that exists among Americans. Eighty-five percent of Americans think the US is either the greatest or among the greatest countries in the world (www.pewresearch.org/fact-tank/2017/06/30/most-americans-say-the-u-s-is-among-the-greatest-countries-in-the-world/). The public specifically links American greatness to its history and constitution. Chapter 4 examined the origins and development of constitutional veneration. It is easy to sound like a patriot, but much more difficult to act like one. Real patriots are willing to defend their country and pay the taxes needed to support it. The United States no longer has a draft army so citizens are no longer called upon to serve in the military. But they are called upon to pay taxes. To a remarkable extent they do indeed pay their taxes. Their level of tax compliance is among the very highest in the world. Of course, taxpaying is not entirely voluntary. The Internal Revenue Service audits tax returns and penalizes those who cheat. But the chances of being audited are very low. On the whole, Americans pay their taxes because they believe that is the right thing to do. Political scientist Vanessa Williamson reviewed surveys of American attitudes toward taxpaying and reports that "Around four in five Americans ... see taxpaying as a moral responsibility and tax evasion as morally wrong" (quoted in Robert Samuelson, "Taxes – The Great Uniter?," *Washington Post*, April 10, 2017).

The second chapter also stressed Classic Liberalism's commitment to rights. Although it took far too long, Americans now fully approve of extending full civil rights to African Americans (see Figure 11.1). Although specific issues

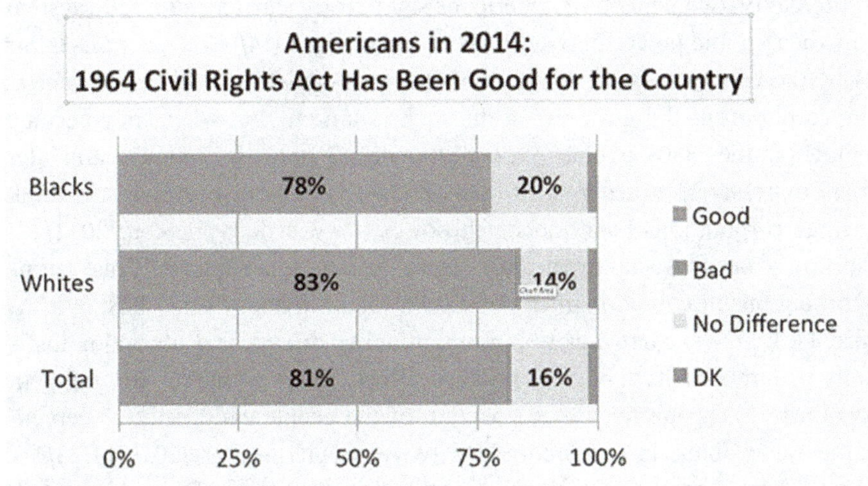

Figure 11.1. Views of the Civil Rights Act.
Source: Roper Center.

that have a strong racial component such as policing and affirmative action remain highly controversial, only a very small minority holds the view that the 1964 Civil Rights Act has not been good for the country.

Chapter 6 linked the strong American commitment to a free enterprise economy to the enduring impact of Classic Liberalism on American political culture. Public opinion continues to support free enterprise. Figure 11.2 shows that, internationally, only South Koreans and Germans are more likely than Americans to agree with the statement that "most people are better off in a free market economy even though some are rich and some are poor."

As the previous question indicated, Americans acknowledge the existence of the poor, but they do so while still insisting that the egalitarian principles proclaimed most eloquently in the Declaration of Independence and the Gettysburg Address remain in force. By a decisive majority they reject the claim that "society is divided into the haves and have 'nots'" (www.people-press.org/2011/12/15/section-2-occupy-wall-street-and-inequality/?src=prc-number).

Chapter 4 described the importance of the commitment to earning one's living by the sweat of one's brow in mobilizing opposition to slavery. The slogan was "Free Labor." Most Americans still view hard work as the road to success. Although the percentage has diminished in recent years, the majority agrees that "most people who want to get ahead can make it if they are willing to work hard" (www.people-press.org/2011/12/15/section-2-occupy-wall-street-and-inequality/?src=prc-number). However these commitments to free markets and hard work coexist with grave doubts about how the economic order functions. As Chapter 6 showed, the Jacksonians combined a belief in free markets with the democratic fear that the existing political economic system favored the elite. Sixty-two percent of Americans say that the current economic system favors the rich and powerful (www.people-press.org/2014/06/26/section-3-fairness-of-the-economic-system-views-of-the-poor-and-the-social-safety-net/). Large corporations did not exist in the Jacksonian era, but when they became prominent in the 1880s, public opinion, influenced first by the Populists and later by the Progressives, turned against them. Today, 77 percent of Americans think that large corporations have too much power (www.people-press.org/2011/12/15/section-2-occupy-wall-street-and-inequality/?src=prc-number). This antipathy to big business is in marked contrast to opinion about small business. As Figure 11.3 shows, small business ranks number one among all major institutions in terms of its having a positive effect "on how things are going in this country." It is approved by 82 percent of the people while only 33 percent say the same about large corporations (www.people-press.org/2015/11/23/11-how-government-compares-with-other-national-institutions/). Technology companies ranked second only to small business and were far ahead of the

Support for Free Market System

Most people are better off in a free market economy, even though some people are rich and some are poor.

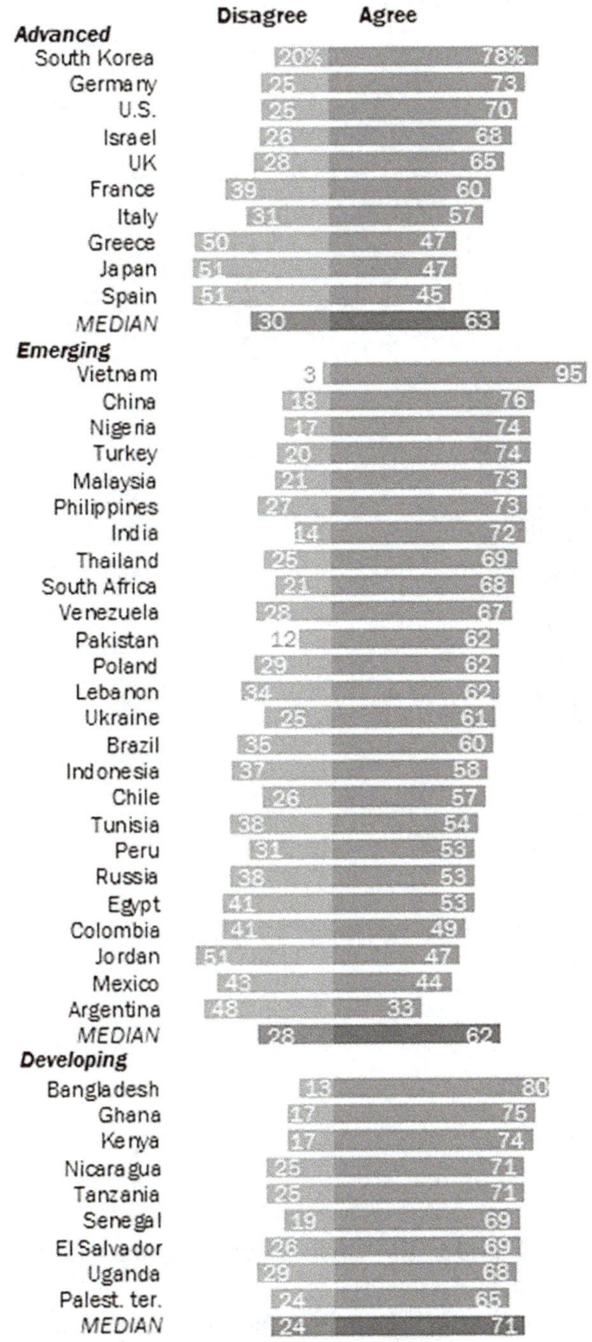

Source: Spring 2014 Global Attitudes survey. Q13a.

Figure 11.2. Support for the free market.
Source: Pew Research Center.

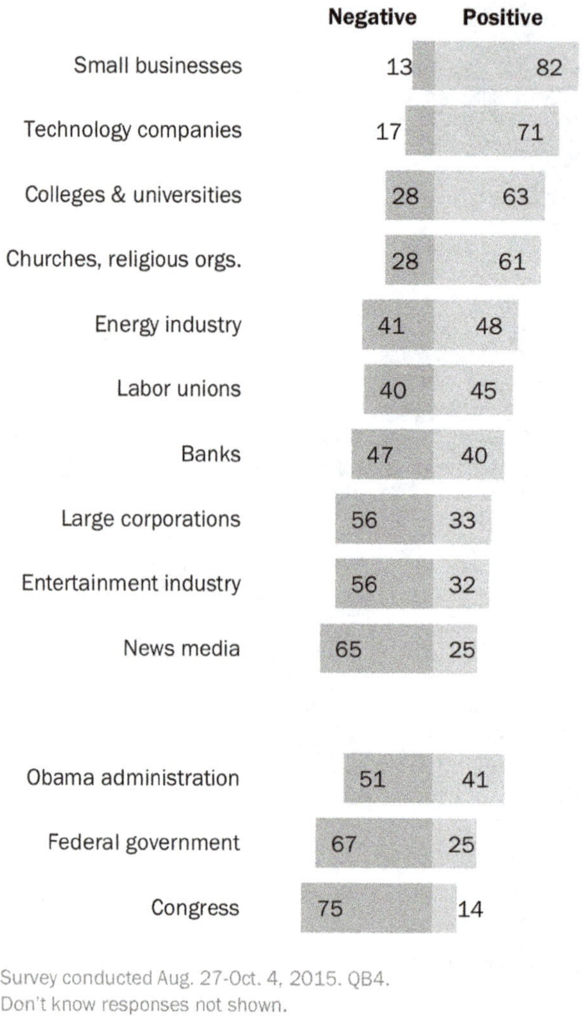

Figure 11.3. Government and other institutions.
Source: Pew Research Center.

third-place finishers, religious institutions. The origin of this abiding faith in technology is discussed in Chapter 4.

The communitarian preference for the small over the large also relates to government. Chapters 2 and 5 showed how attached Americans are to

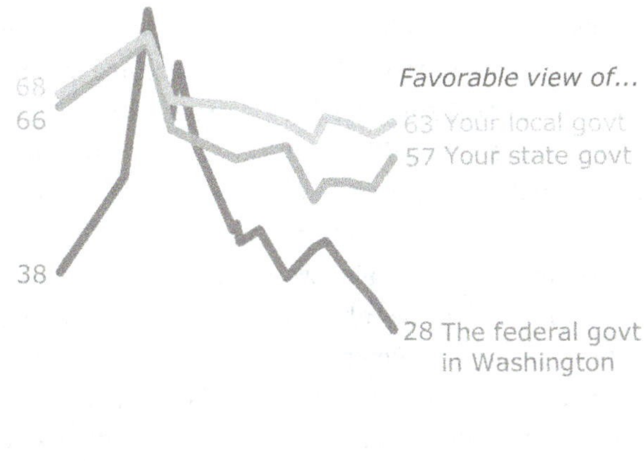

Figure 11.4. Widening gap in views of federal, state and local governments.
Source: Pew Research Center.

their local communities. Figure 11.4 shows that most Americans have a favorable view of their local government and vastly prefer it to the national government.

Americans remain skeptical about the scope as well as the size of government, evincing a commitment to Classic Liberal rather than democratic/egalitarian norms. While the government now provides a great deal of assistance to low-income people, it is less generous in providing such assistance than most other rich countries. Public opinion displays skepticism about the value of providing too much help to the needy. Half of those polled say that "government aid to the poor does more harm than good," and a clear majority say that "government can't afford to do more to help the needy."

Despite concern about domestic terrorism, three-quarters of Americans say that their privacy should not be sacrificed in order to make them safe from it. A decisive majority oppose government collection of data from phone calls and the internet (www.people-press.org/2014/06/26/section-6-foreign-affairs-terrorism-and-privacy/).

Polarizing Issues

With regard to a set of other very prominent issues, especially abortion and same-sex marriage, the public remains highly polarized. What these questions have in common is that until fairly recently they were not issues at all. The public was against them. They were illegal and socially stigmatized. The public is not evenly divided on these issues. Majorities favor legalizing abortion and same-sex marriage. They are polarizing because a sizeable minority that the Pew Center labels "steadfast conservatives" vehemently opposes both while a sizeable minority that the Pew Center labels "solid liberals" supports both with a similar level of vehemence (www.people-press.org/2014/06/26/the-political-typology-beyond-red-vs-blue/). Thus, the staunch opponents of abortion speak of a right to life, a right of fetuses to be born. In their mind, abortion is not just a bad policy, it is murder. By contrast, abortion advocates speak of a woman's right to choose. Interfering with her decision to abort deprives her of her right to control her own body. Although each represents a minority of voters, each of these positions is growing, meaning that an increasing segment of the American public holds views about profound issues that do not just differ from those on the other side but do so on the basis of appeals to fundamental principles.

Until the Supreme Court legalized abortion in 1973, most states banned it except to protect the health and life of the mother. Ever since, public opinion has been divided. As of 2016, 47 percent call themselves pro choice while an almost equal number, 46 percent, call themselves pro life. By contrast, attitudes toward same-sex marriage have changed dramatically in the past twenty years. Support for it has more than doubled in that timespan, and it is now approved of by a majority of almost two to one. As with abortion, neither side in the dispute sees it as representing a mere difference of opinion. Both sides believe that fundamental principles are at stake. Each side appeals to one of the two cornerstones of American political culture described in Chapter 2. Advocates appeal to Classic Liberalism by defining the issue in terms of rights. They claim there is a right to marry. Since rights are inalienable, homosexuals cannot be deprived of them. Opponents ground their opposition to homosexual marriage in their understanding of Christianity. They use the language of the Bible to show that Christianity only approves of marriage between a man and a woman.

Public attitudes only become politically relevant when they become salient, in other words, when those holding them consider them to be very important. For example, a Gallup poll showed that ever since the 1970s there was a great deal of public support for decreasing the number of immigrants allowed to enter the United States (www.gallup.com/poll/1660/immigration.aspx). Yet this issue played a very small role in national elections. It lacked salience. The number of people favoring immigration restriction did not grow appreciably in 2016, and yet Donald Trump highlighted it in his successful presidential campaign. Seventy percent of registered voters said that the immigration issue was very important to them (www.people-press.org/2016/07/07/4-top-voting-issues-in-2016-election). As a result of its increased salience, immigration joined abortion and gay rights as an important source of political polarization.

A Loss of Trust, Faith, and Confidence

Americans no longer display the trust, faith, and confidence in their government and in other critical national institutions that they once did. Above, we looked at favorability comparisons between different levels of government to call attention to the favorable view Americans hold of local government. But the flipside of those comparisons is the extraordinarily low esteem in which Americans hold the national government. As Figure 11.4 shows, a mere 28 percent views it favorably; only Congress scores lower, with a mere 19 percent, and it is, after all, a part of the national government (www.gallup.com/poll/201974/congress-job-approval-start-new-session.aspx).

Figure 11.5 also shows that the decline in trust is mirrored by a decline in the belief that the government operates fairly. By the same overwhelming percentage, people reject the notion that the government operates to benefit all. Not only does government only benefit a select few, it is run by the few as well. Figure 11.6 shows that 76 percent believe that "government is run by big interests." Here again, these negative views only emerged in the late 1960s.

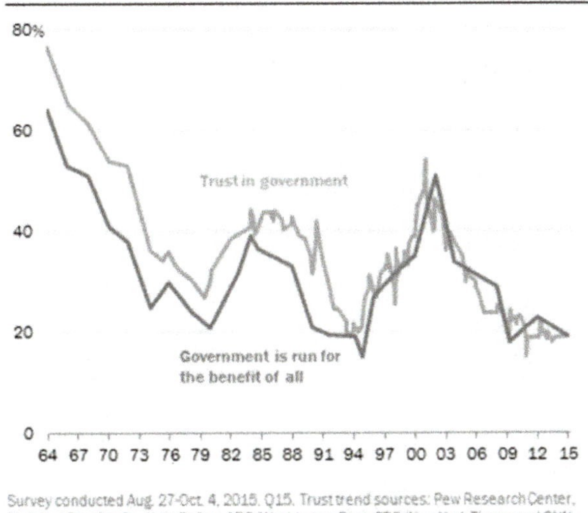

Figure 11.5. Trust in government and perceptions of government fairness.
Source: Pew Research Center.

Since they believe that big interests run the government, it is not surprising that Americans do not trust elected officials. Seventy-four percent say that "most elected officials don't care what people like me think" (www.people-press.org/2015/11/23/1-trust-in-government-1958-2015/ p. 7). This lack of respect

Table 11.1. Summary of attitudes.

The public supports:	The public is unfavorable toward:	The public is especially polarized regarding:
• National pride • Civil rights • Free markets • Hard work • Small business • Technology • Local government	• Big business • Big government (especially Congress) • Elected officials • Intrusions on privacy	• Gay marriage • Abortion • Immigration

About three-quarters of Americans say the government is run by big interests

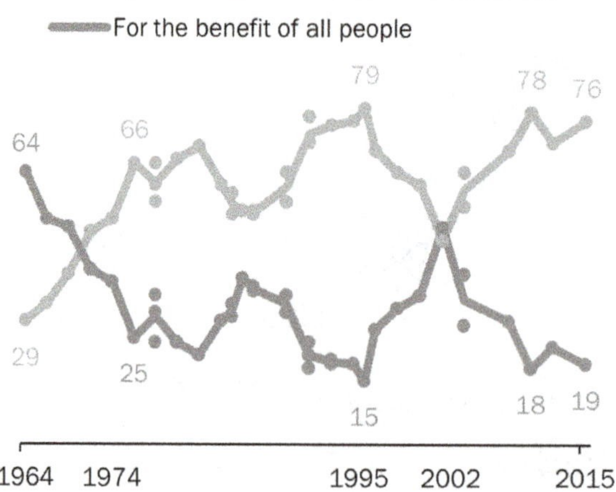

Survey conducted Aug. 27-Oct. 4, 2015. Q43. Data points indicate individual surveys, line shows yearly averages. Trend includes data from other organizations. See topline for full details.
Don't know responses not shown.

Figure 11.6. Big interests.
Source: Pew Research Center.

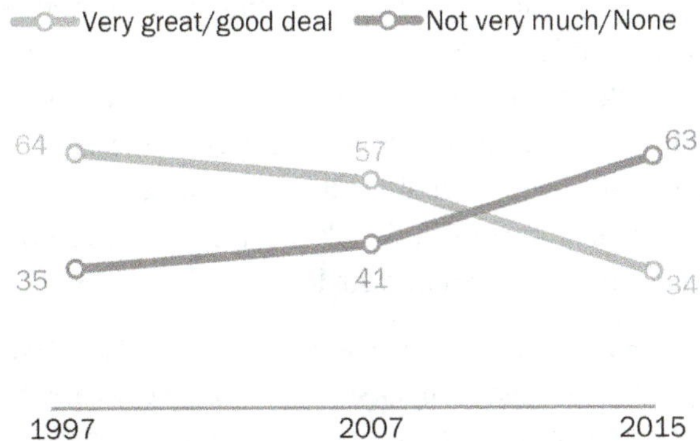

Figure 11.7. Public political wisdom.
Source: Pew Research Center.

that Americans have for elected officials is mirrored by a lack of faith in their own political wisdom. Figure 11.7 shows only about a third places very much "trust confidence in the wisdom of the American people when it comes to making political decisions," while almost two-thirds places not very much or none.

The Sources of Political Memory

A look at key episodes in American political development shows the roots of the attitudes painted in this chapter's contemporary political portrait. They provide the sources of the political memories that exert such influence on contemporary attitudes. These critical moments also reveal that polarization and loss of respect and trust in the government and its leaders are not new to American political life but have permeated much of American history. In certain periods, issue differences have become accentuated while at other times they have diminished. Likewise, certain periods exemplify high levels of confidence and faith in national institutions and their leaders while others exhibit the loss of such faith and confidence.

Nationalism

The United States came into being with no strong accompanying sense of American nationhood. Chapter 2 discussed the important contributions that Noah Webster, Benjamin Franklin, and General Washington made toward establishing such a sense before, during and after the revolution. However, these efforts were merely preliminary. During the Federalist period, nationalist sentiment grew, thanks largely to Washington's presidential leadership. The prestige with which he endowed the office of president, the only aspect of the national government chosen by the nation as a whole, enabled it to serve as a focal point for national attention and as a vital source of national inspiration. His farewell address gave eloquent expression to his nationalist credo:

> it is of infinite moment, that you should properly estimate the immense value of your national Union to your collective & individual happiness; that you should cherish a cordial, habitual & immoveable attachment to it; accustoming yourselves to think and speak of it as of the Palladium of your political safety and prosperity . . .

Reverence for Rights

As Chapter 3 discussed, the original Constitution did not contain a Bill of Rights. Proponents of ratification promised to support adding one as a means for obtaining the backing of those undecideds who were troubled by its absence. The Bill of Rights was passed by the first Congress elected in 1788 and swiftly ratified by the states. Those who fought for its inclusion viewed it as a critical piece of civic education for future generations. In the absence of a clear delineation of their rights, future generations of Americans might forget that the very purpose of the Constitution was to protect individual rights. Today, when Americans are asked about the Constitution they invariably point to the rights enumerated in the first ten amendments as forming its most crucial aspect. They have learned the lesson that the Bill of Rights advocates sought to teach.

As earlier chapters have described, the Washington administration came to power against a backdrop of democratic/egalitarian, antielitist sentiment. The American Revolution had been fought against a king. The state governments established afterwards minimized executive power. And yet for the first twelve years of the nation's history it was governed by an avowedly elitist political faction. The Federalists made no secret of their disdain for popular rule. They felt it their duty to govern for the people and they were honor bound to abide by election results. But they fully expected the people to vote for them in recognition of their intellectual and moral superiority not because they would do the people's bidding. Washington's executive appointments reflected his conviction that such jobs should go to individuals of distinction. A few decades later the pendulum of public opinion would swing in a decidedly antielitist direction. Nonetheless, a crucial precedent for the principle that authority should be placed in the hands of those with superior talents was established, a principle that would episodically reemerge throughout the course of American political development.

An Empire of Liberty

The contemporary portrait above showed that Americans combine strong nationalist sentiment with a preference for local government. Jefferson taught that these seemingly contradictory attitudes were indeed compatible with one another. As Chapter 4 discussed, he defended the Louisiana Purchase as a means for establishing "an Empire of Liberty." The vast territorial expansion the purchase brought about would encourage Americans to see themselves as part of a monumental enterprise. But this "empire" would not be dominated by the national government. Instead, it would be carved up into individual states which would largely govern themselves. The liberty that flowed from a lack of centralized control would flourish.

Jackson reinforced the Jeffersonian communitarian commitment to locality. As Chapter 4 described, he drastically cut national government spending and declared that it was unconstitutional to subsidize building a road that did not cross state lines. But he also deepened the commitment to American nationhood through his unwavering support for national supremacy by crushing South Carolina's effort to nullify the tariff.

The controversy that broke out in the 1840s regarding the annexation of Texas gave birth to a new nationalistic rallying cry, "Manifest Destiny." Coined by the journalist and fervent Jacksonian Jeremiah O'Sullivan, it promoted the idea that since the United States embodied such virtuous political principles it was the country's right and duty to spread those principles to the entire continent. The view that America possessed exceptional virtues was not new; as Chapter 2 described, it was grounded in John Winthrop's conception of the Puritan settlement as a "a city on a hill" radiating its moral and religious superiority back to England. But the Puritan view was not connected to territorial expansion. O'Sullivan's formulation opened the door to the use of American diplomatic and military power to impose American ideals far and wide. Although public opinion has not always supported efforts to exert American power internationally, when it has shown such support it has always sought to justify such incursions on the grounds that they serve the cause of liberty and democracy. Figure 11.8 illustrates exploration and settlement from 1835 to 1850, including cities, roads, canals, and railroads.

Mistrust of Centralized Government

Jefferson's dismantling of Alexander Hamilton's ambitious national programs was the first clear manifestation of public mistrust of the national government and its leaders. Jackson and his Democratic Party followers fanned the flames of

Figure 11.8. Westward expansion.
Source: public domain.

this discontent. Jackson blamed his defeat in 1824 on a "corrupt bargain" between two of the nation's most important leaders, Speaker of the House Henry Clay and Secretary of State John Adams, Jackson's main rival for the presidency. In his mind, Jackson had been the democratic choice since he garnered the most popular votes and the most electoral votes. Nonetheless, because he lacked an Electoral College majority, the final decision rested with the House of Representatives. Clay delivered a congressional majority to Adams. Adams named him Secretary of State. Jackson assumed that Adams had promised this coveted appointment to Clay in exchange for Clay's delivering the election to him. While not corrupt in a legal sense, Jackson portrayed Clay and Adams as devious manipulators who succeeded in flouting the will of the people.

Jackson fomented further public anger against national institutions and the persons who led them by his ferocious attack on the Second National Bank of the United States, which he labeled the "Monster Bank," and on the bank's president, Nicholas Biddle. His critique of national institutions extended beyond the bank to encompass the entire federal bureaucracy. He characterized it as being largely composed of individuals who viewed their positions as their own personal property, and who used those positions to serve their selfish interests rather than the public good. Thus, he rejected Washington's view of government service as the province of superior individuals and encouraged the public to mistrust public officials. Through what came to be called the "spoils system" (see Chapter 10), he sought to place federal officeholders under political party control, removing them if they were insufficiently loyal to the party. Only by keeping them on such a tight leash could they be prevented from subverting the common good. Party, not government, became the focal point of public loyalty and trust.

War

War is so disruptive that it can push political positions and public sentiment in unforeseen directions. By ending slavery, the Civil War witnessed the first great rights expansion since the passage of the Constitution and the Bill of Rights. Prior to the war, only a small fraction of the public supported the abolition of slavery. As Chapter 4 explained, the Republican Party and Lincoln himself only opposed its spread to the territories because the Constitution guaranteed the slave states the right to perpetuate it. The unexpected difficulty the Union experienced in defeating the South pressed Lincoln to redefine the war aims in order to improve the Union's military position. He freed the slaves in order to weaken the South. To do so without violating the Constitution, he justified abolition not on human rights grounds but rather on the right of a nation at war to confiscate the property of its enemy. But regardless of the rationale, the Union was now fully committed to emancipation and the public was in full support. War had accomplished what the political process on its own had failed to do.

Another great contribution the Civil War-era Republican Party made to public opinion was the doctrine of Free Labor. As we discussed in Chapter 6, this doctrine stressed that Americans succeed in life by working hard. Classic Liberalism declared that each person is entitled to the fruits of their labor. The free labor doctrine declared that the heavy toil such efforts required was both noble and dignified. Other societies might look down on hard work, but Americans should exalt it. In a speech to the Wisconsin State Agricultural Society in 1859, Abraham Lincoln described free labor as "the just, and generous, and prosperous system, which opens the way for all, gives hope to all, and energy, and progress, and improvement of condition to all." Lincoln considered that the opportunity to improve one's lot by working hard was so readily available that only those who chose not to avail themselves of that opportunity would fail to succeed in becoming their own boss: "If any continue through life in the condition of the hired laborer, it is not the fault of the system, but because of either a dependent nature which prefers it, or improvidence, folly, or singular misfortune." He recognized that this reverence for hard work marked a crucial change in public opinion. From now on the privileged would revere it as much as those lower down the socioeconomic scale, and they too would have to work hard:

> The old general rule was that educated people did not perform manual labor. They managed to eat their bread, leaving the toil of producing it to the uneducated. But now, especially in these free States, nearly all are educated – quite too nearly all to leave the labor of the uneducated in any wise adequate to the support of the whole. It follows from this that hence forth educated people must labor.

Classic Liberalism declared that each person was entitled to keep the fruits of their labor. The Free Labor doctrine added a critical democratic/egalitarian dimension to the American embrace of free enterprise.

The Curse of Bigness

Chapter 6 described the rise and dominance of large corporations that took place in the late nineteenth century, and the strong political opposition that arose against them. It quoted the Populist leader and three-time Democratic Party presidential candidate William Jennings Bryan's moving attack on corporate dominance and his eloquent defense of the virtues of small businessmen. Although large corporations remain a major force in the American economy, as this chapter's contemporary portrait showed, they remain very unpopular. By contrast, small business is held in high esteem. Bryan couched both his attack on the big and his defense of the small in biblical terms. Current arguments about the relative merits of large versus small business are no long expressed in such terms, and yet the moralistic residue of Bryan's argument is still in evidence. In the minds of Americans, small businessmen display virtues that the leaders of large corporations lack. They are the hard workers that Lincoln so esteemed and provide a bulwark for the sustenance of local communities.

The revulsion against big business that the Populists spearheaded had broader political implications. It was widely perceived that leading politicians were being bribed to do the bidding of the so-called "robber barons" who led the biggest and most aggressive large corporations. This perception was fed by investigative journalists such as Lincoln Steffens and Ida Tarbell, who unearthed ample evidence of collusion between prominent businessmen and key state and federal public officials. Once again, trust in government and its leaders went into decline. This time, in contrast to the age of Jackson, faith in parties did not counterbalance distrust of government. Rather, parties themselves came to be seen as part of the problem.

Table 11.2. Summary of crucial episodes in the construction of political memory.

- The leadership of George Washington mobilizes public support for American nationalism and respect for the national government
- Congress adopts a Bill of Rights
- The "Empire of Liberty" weds a belief in American greatness with a commitment to decentralized government
- Jackson vetoes the "monster" bank
- Victory in the Civil War commits the nation to emancipation of the slaves and reinforces commitment to the doctrine of free labor the Republicans promoted
- The rise and dominance of large corporations that took place in the late nineteenth century provoked public anger and mistrust

Key Shifts in Public Opinion

As we said at the beginning of the chapter, deeply held political beliefs can change in the face of transformative events. In the twentieth century such events led to an enhanced respect for and trust in the national government, acceptance of civil rights for racial minorities, and then to a loss of the newly acquired positive attitudes toward government.

Embracing the National Government

Progressivism instigated a great improvement in faith and trust in the national government. As Chapter 6 showed, the Theodore Roosevelt and Woodrow Wilson administrations undertook ambitious efforts to reign in big business and reduce political corruption. As Chapters 4 and 10 showed, a key ingredient of Progressive reform was its emphasis on expertise. No longer would key decisions about the economy be made by corrupt politicians. Instead, regulatory efforts would rest with highly trained experts who operated free of political pressure. These experts could and would rise above mere party loyalty. As Chapters 4 showed, the Progressive faith in expertise had some antidemocratic political consequences. But for a period of time it did succeed in restoring public respect for and trust in government. The belief in expertise it promoted remains a key component of American political culture.

The positive impressions of government and expertise established during the Progressive Era were powerfully reinforced during the New Deal. Americans credited the New Deal programs and the experts who administered many of them with successfully combatting the Great Depression. From that time onward, the Democratic Party would identify itself with an ambitious national government. As Figure 11.7 showed, through the mid 1960s public opinion displayed faith and trust in the national government and support for the policies championed by FDR and his successor, Harry Truman.

As Chapter 4 discussed, FDR expanded the definition of rights to include what the chapter calls "programmatic rights." Unlike the rights specified in the Bill of Rights, these are not protections against government intrusion but rather entitlements that require positive action by government. Thus, a right to social security can only exist if the government provides pensions to the elderly. This right is not official because a right to social security has never been incorporated into the Constitution, but it is a right just the same because the public so firmly believes it to be one. Any effort to modify Social Security has met with the sort of unified public opposition that one would expect to see when the people's rights are being violated.

In 1981, President Reagan proposed cuts in Social Security. The public reacted with outrage and he soon withdrew the proposal. After winning reelection in

2004, President George W. Bush put forth a plan to change Social Security by allowing people to divert part of their social security tax into personal retirement accounts. He argued that this would enable younger workers to take advantage of gains in the stock market to build bigger retirement nest eggs than would occur if all their contributions continued to go to the US Treasury. Of course, the stock market does not always go up. One could not say for sure that investing in a personal retirement account would produce results that were as good as the guaranteed amount that the current scheme provided. Because they had come to see that specified sum as a right, the public stoutly rejected any plan that created uncertainty about what that sum would be. Bush's appeals fell on deaf ears, and even though his party controlled both Houses, Congress took no action on his proposal.

Respecting Minority Rights

The outstanding accomplishment of American politics and government since the New Deal has been the provision of full civil and voting rights to African Americans. The Thirteenth, Fourteenth, and Fifteenth Amendments to the Constitution passed soon after the end of the Civil War were intended not only to end slavery but to protect such rights. However, for almost a century the government failed to enforce the rights those amendments proclaimed. The Social Security example showed that public opinion can establish a right even when the Constitution does not mention it. The government's failure to fulfill the promise those amendments made makes the opposite point. The Constitution can declare a right, but if the public does not demand that the right be protected it does not really exist. For decades, African Americans were denied their rights because Southern states suppressed those rights and the rest of the American public remained, for the most part, indifferent to their plight.

Public indifference did not simply disappear. Public opinion was led. Opinion leadership took a variety of forms. The Supreme Court, the civil rights movement, and the president all played vital roles in the process of opinion change (Chapter 14 charts the development of the civil rights movement in greater detail). As Chapter 5 discussed, in 1954 *Brown v. Board of Education* declared racial segregation of schools to be unconstitutional. Although President Eisenhower did not agree with the Supreme Court's decision, having sworn to faithfully execute the law, he felt he had no choice but to ensure that it was obeyed. Therefore, when the governor of Arkansas forbade African-American students from attending Little Rock High School, he ordered federal troops to escort them in. Television conspired with this aggressive use of federal power to overcome public indifference to the plight of African Americans in the South. Millions watched as the television cameras graphically depicted brave and dignified young African Americans being harassed by mobs of angry, often violent white adults trying to keep them out. Sensing that it was now possible to mobilize public support for their cause, African Americans launched lunch counter sit-ins, bus boycotts, and marches that burgeoned into a full-fledged movement for civil rights. The media once again proved helpful in rallying such support by depicting the stark contrast between the peaceful and dignified behavior of the demonstrators and the violence wreaked upon them by Southern sheriffs, policemen, and gangs of thugs.

Presidential leadership and electoral shifts also played their part. President Kennedy had tried to pass a civil rights bill before his death but had not succeeded. In the wake of his assassination President Johnson demanded that Congress pay homage to JFK's legacy by passing a civil rights bill. In truth, the bill the president was pushing was much tougher than the one Kennedy had proposed. But Johnson's rhetorical success in linking veneration for the late president to passage of his bill won over enough previous opponents to enable its passage. His landslide victory in 1964 was coupled with the election of so many pro-civil rights Northern Democratic congressional candidates that the anti-civil rights stranglehold exercised by Southern Democrats was decisively broken. Thus, in 1965 Congress easily passed the Voting Rights Act, which gave the federal government the tools to make the Fifteenth Amendment's promise of full voting rights for African Americans a reality.

The existence of these powerful laws was itself a crucial source of change in public opinion. The combined impact of the Supreme Court's decision and the civil rights protests did much to overcome public indifference. Nonetheless, a month after the 1964 act was passed roughly half the public still opposed it (www.ropercenter.cornell.edu/public-opinion-on-civil-rights-reflections-on-the-civil-rights-act-of-1964/). However, as the public came to recognize that these civil rights statutes were indeed the law of the land, acceptance of them grew. As the contemporary portrait section of this chapter showed, by the 1980s the principle that African Americans were entitled to full civil and voting rights was no longer controversial.

The courts have also played a key leadership role with regard to the other significant new rights claims, those involving abortion and homosexuals. This chapter's contemporary portrait shows that these claims remain controversial. Nonetheless, they are both now supported by a majority of Americans. Prior to the Court's affirmation of a right to have an abortion, it was a criminal act in most states. Likewise, homosexual marriage did not have a great deal of public support until the Massachusetts Supreme Court declared that gays had a right to marry in 2003 and a number of other state courts followed suit in ensuing years.

Since opinions form largely on the basis of stories, metaphors, and symbols, they are highly dependent on what is perhaps the leading source of such material, the mass media. Television played a key role in constructing a narrative about the civil rights struggle and more recently it has done so with regard to homosexuality. In earlier decades, it was quite common to treat homosexuals as objects of ridicule and caricature. Beginning in the 1980s it became more common for them to be depicted with sensitivity and respect. In 1998 a major network situation comedy, *Will and Grace*, had an openly gay character as one of its two leads. The show lasted for eight seasons and was consistently among the twenty most widely viewed network programs, reaching in the neighborhood of 18 million viewers. In 2009 another popular network situation comedy, *Modern Family*, debuted featured a gay couple that was raising an adopted daughter. These shows and others like them have served to change the popular narrative regarding homosexuals, treating them as ordinary people leading conventional lives rather than as deviants.

A Loss of Faith in Government

The contemporary portrait depicted the low level of trust and respect for the national government. As Figure 11.5 showed, trust and respect were quite high as late as 1964 and then went through a precipitous decline beginning in the mid 1960s and continuing, with only a brief upward blip, through the late 1970s. This decline is largely attributable to three seminal events: the war in Vietnam, Watergate, and the Iranian hostage crisis. The war in Vietnam shattered the belief in American invincibility nurtured by the nation's victories in the two world wars. In Vietnam, despite the massive commitment of troops and the large number of casualties American forces sustained, the war was lost. The war was also a blow to Americans' belief in manifest destiny. Many felt that not only had the US lost, it had backed the wrong side. It had joined forces with a series of corrupt dictators to oppose a movement of national liberation. Therefore, it could no longer claim that its military might was being used to promote freedom and democracy. Thus the government stood accused of being both ineffectual *and* hypocritical.

The mistrust engendered by the war was deepened by the Watergate scandal. As Chapter 7 described, President Nixon was accused of trying to cover up a crime, the Watergate break-in, and of lying to Congress and to the public. The congressional investigation of Watergate also unearthed a whole series of other dirty tricks performed by Nixon's campaign team during the 1972 election campaign. Also, the huge volume of taped Oval Office conversations made public during the course of the investigation contained numerous examples of the president engaging in vulgar remarks and ethnic slurs. In the public mind, the president was revealed to be a criminal and an undignified one at that.

The Iranian hostage crisis compounded the loss of confidence in government engendered by the war in Vietnam and Watergate. In November 1979, in the midst of the overthrow of the Shah of Iran, fifty-two American embassy workers and other American nationals were captured and held hostage. They remained hostage for 444 days, the remainder of President Carter's term in office. Carter's diplomatic efforts to obtain their release failed, as did an attempt to launch a helicopter strike to free them. Public anger was heightened by the intense media scrutiny the hostage crisis enjoyed. At that time, there were only three national television networks, and their nightly news programs were the nation's major source of news information. *CBS Nightly News* was the most popular of the three and its anchor, Walter Cronkite, was the most revered of all news broadcasters. It therefore made an indelible impression on the public when he ended every one of his broadcasts by reminding his listeners how many days it had been since the hostages had been seized. The journalist Ellen Goodman said of Cronkite's relentless reminder: "[it] has become a flag at half-mast, a daily probe of a wound . . . a dramatic epitaph to the news" (www.washingtonpost.com/wp-dyn/content/article/2009/05/14/AR2009051403597.html).

Looking Forward

Public trust and confidence rebounded during the Reagan presidency and again in the aftermath of 9/11. But these improvements remained far below the peaks of trust and confidence reached in the early 1960s and, as Figure 11.7 shows, they were short-lived. Americans now display a much diminished respect for and trust in the large institutions that dominate political and economic life. They have developed decidedly low opinions of the three branches of the national government, political leaders, large corporations, and the media. Chapter 9 showed that even the Supreme Court, long the most exalted branch of government, is experiencing a decline in public esteem. Such a withdrawal of allegiance threatens to undermine the coherence and stability of the political system. If those trends worsen, this outbreak of foul weather could wreak lasting damage on the American political cultural climate.

CRITICAL THINKING QUESTION

This chapter has traced the sources of the current opinions expressed in its contemporary portrait section. The contemporary portrait of public opinion is selective with regard to the issues it discusses. Pick an issue that it does not discuss, find polls that show how the public stands on the issue, and then show how a look at the past helps you to understand the sources of current opinions about it.

Here is a list of some suggested issues, but you are free to choose another:

- Should marijuana be legalized?
- Should trade with other nations be made freer or more subject to restriction?
- Should the minimum wage be raised?
- Should transgendered people be free to use either the men's or women's bathroom?
- Should guns be more strictly regulated?

CHAPTER SUMMARY

Contemporary portrait:

* Opinions that fit squarely within the American political cultural climate include support of: free markets, hard work, local government, patriotism, limits on the reach of the national government, privacy, suspicion of big business, and a strong commitment to rights (although some rights claims remain highly contested).
* Public opinion is highly polarized with respect to gay rights and abortion.
* Americans no longer display the trust, faith, and confidence in their government and in other critical national institutions that they once did.

Political memory:

* The prestige with which Washingon endowed the office of president enabled it to serve as focal point for national attention and a a vital source of national inspiration.
* Jefferson's idea of an "Empire of Liberty" fostered both nationalist sentiment and public support for decentralized government.
* Jackson's contention that he had been deprived of victory in 1824 by a "corrupt bargain" fueled public mistrust of the national government and its leaders.
* Antislavery sentiment was fueled by the civil war and enshrined in the Thirteenth, Fourteenth, and Fifteenth Amendments to the Constitution.
* The Populists and the Progressives fueled public distrust of big business.
* The New Deal's success in coping with the Great Depression restored public trust in government and instilled a greater willingness to support a much larger and more intrusive government.

Key shifts in public opinion:

* The combination of Supreme Court decisions, presidential leadership, and the inspired activism of the civil rights movement led to a vast shift in attitudes toward African Americans.

* Television played a key role in constructing a positive narrative about the civil rights struggle and more recently it has done so with regard to homosexuality.
* The decline in trust and respect for government that began in the late 1960s was largely attributable to three seminal events: the war in Vietnam, Watergate, and the Iranian hostage crisis.

SUGGESTED READINGS

Ellis, Christopher, and James Stimson. *Ideology in America*. Cambridge, MA: Harvard University Press, 2012.

Gilens, Martin. *Affluence and Influence: Economic Inequality and Political Power in America*. Princeton, NJ: Princeton University Press, 2014.

Levendusky, Matthew. *How Partisan Media Polarize America*. University of Chicago Press, 2013.

Lewis-Beck, Michael, et al. *The American Voter Revisited*. Ann Arbor: University of Michigan Press, 2008.

Lodge, Milton, and Charles S. Taber. *The Rationalizing Voter*. Cambridge, MA: Harvard University Press, 2013.

Taylor, Paul. *The Next America*. New York: Public Affairs, 2014.

Tesler, Michael. *Post-Racial or Most-Racial? Race and Politics in the Obama Era*. University of Chicago Press, 2016.

12 Political Parties

CHAPTER OVERVIEW

This chapter focuses on:

- **A contemporary portrait of the two political parties and the coalitions that form them.**
- **The critical choice to found the first political party and then to create a two-party system.**
- **The party system's ability to absorb the shocks of conflict over slavery, mass immigration, and the rise of corporate economic power.**
- **The Progressive attack on party.**
- **The creation of the New Deal Democratic Party coalition.**
- **The post-WWII reestablishment of a competitive two-party system.**

> I am not a member of any organized political party. I am a Democrat.
>
> Will Rogers

Of course, this great humorist knew that the Democrats, like the Republicans, were organized into local and state bodies as well as a national committee. What Will Rogers was expressing was a sense that although he was a loyal party man, being a Democrat was confusing. In his day, both the supporters of banning alcohol and the most vigorous opponents of prohibition were Democrats. Later, the party would contain African Americans as well as Southern supporters of racial segregation. While the Republicans were perhaps somewhat less "disorganized," they still included in their midst such disparate types as big city financiers and Midwestern farmers in addition to Progressives and stalwart opponents of Progressivism. And yet, despite these confusions, party identification was and is the most powerful predictor of how a person will vote. In 2016, ninety percent of Republicans voted for the Republican Party presidential candidate, Donald Trump. Eighty-nine percent of Democrats voted for the Democratic Party candidate, Hillary Clinton.

Ironically, the great influence of partisan identification on voting coincides with the fact that most Americans have a negative opinion of political parties. This chapter will explore the roots both of party identification and of the unfavorable light in which parties are held. The previous chapter stressed the relationship between political opinion and political memory. Political memory is especially influential in determining party identification. Rather than becoming Democrats or Republicans, a great many people inherit their party loyalty. They grow up being exposed to stories and symbols that establish powerful partisan attachments. They learn to treat great party leaders as heroes. Decades after his death, many Republicans still talk about their party as the party of Reagan. Democrats dig even deeper into past history to depict their party as the party of FDR and JFK. Therefore, an understanding of the historic development of the parties is crucial for understanding how people define their party ties. This connection is explored in the political development section of this chapter.

A Contemporary Portrait

Party Coalitions: Enduring Elements and Defections

Unlike parties in western Europe, many Americans who consider themselves to be very loyal party members do not officially join a party. They do not carry membership cards. In many states voters can vote in whichever party primary they choose. Nonetheless, there are identifiable segments of the population who do continue to support one or the other parties by large margins. They form the party's coalition, which constitutes its reliable base of support.

Later in the chapter we shall discuss the formation of the most enduring majority party coalition ever assembled, forged in the 1930s, the New Deal Democrats. Key voting segments of that coalition still remain staunchly loyal to the Democrats. In 2016, 88 percent of African Americans voted for the Democrats, 71 percent of Jews voted Democratic, and while support for the Democrats by labor union members has declined over recent decades, Clinton still received 51 percent of union votes compared to 43 percent for Trump.

The most severe defection from the New Deal Democratic coalition has taken place in the South. Before the 1965 Voting Rights Act, Southern whites voted overwhelmingly for the Democrats while Southern African Americans were precluded from voting. Since 1965, Southern African Americans have adopted the Democratic Party loyalty of their Northern brethren while Southern whites have departed the Democrats. In 2016, Donald Trump carried every Southern state except Virginia. The Republicans now hold almost all the US Senate seats in the Southern states and the vast majority of House seats and governorships and a continually expanding number of state legislative seats. The South is still "solid," but now it is solidly Republican. The other large voting bloc comprising the New Deal coalition were Catholics. They are no longer reliable Democratic supporters. Indeed, in 2016 white Catholics voted for Trump by a margin of 60 percent to 37 percent.

The Republican coalition is, to some extent, a mirror image of the contemporary Democratic one. Democrats do well in big cities – Republicans in small towns and rural areas. In 2016, 58 percent of whites supported Trump while only 37 percent supported Clinton. Each party does well in different sectors of the business community. The Democrats dominate Hollywood and high tech; Republicans dominate the energy sector, manufacturing, and small business.

New Additions to the Party Coalitions

Some of the greatest changes in the make-up of the party coalitions have taken place as a result of the increasingly political importance of matters that previously were not highly politicized – marriage, sexual orientation, guns, and religion.

Religion has often been a divisive element in American party politics. But, with the exception of African Americans, the electorate now divides less over which religion one belongs to than whether one is religious at all. Because most Americans continue to claim to be religious, the Democratic Party leadership has sought to erase its image as the secular party. Nonetheless, Republicans are much more united in their support of proposals to give federal grants to religious schools and to religious social service providers and less reticent in identifying with religious causes. Thus, they retain the allegiance of non-African American religious voters. Frequent church attendance is among the most accurate predictors of partisanship among whites. Whites who say they attend church frequently vote overwhelmingly for the Republicans. The Republican religious edge is greatest among those who identify themselves as Evangelical Christian. They supported Trump by a margin of 81 to 16. Just as the Republicans have become the party of churchgoers, the Democrats have solidified their hold among non-churchgoers. Those who say they do not go to church supported Clinton by a margin of 62 to 31.

For the first fifty years that women had the right to vote, they voted for the two parties in the same proportion as men. But, for the last thirty years, women have tended to vote for the Democrats more than men do. In 2016, 54 percent of women voted for Clinton whereas only 41 percent of men did. On closer examination, however, the "gender gap" is dwarfed by the "marriage gap." In 2016, Clinton received only 43 percent of the votes of married people while Trump obtained 53 percent. Among unmarrieds, Clinton was the choice of 55 percent while Trump received 38 percent. The precise nature of the gap becomes much clearer when gender and marriage are combined. Married men are staunch Republicans while unmarried women are steadfastly Democratic. Clinton

Gender gap in vote choice: 1972–2016

Presidential candidate preference, by gender

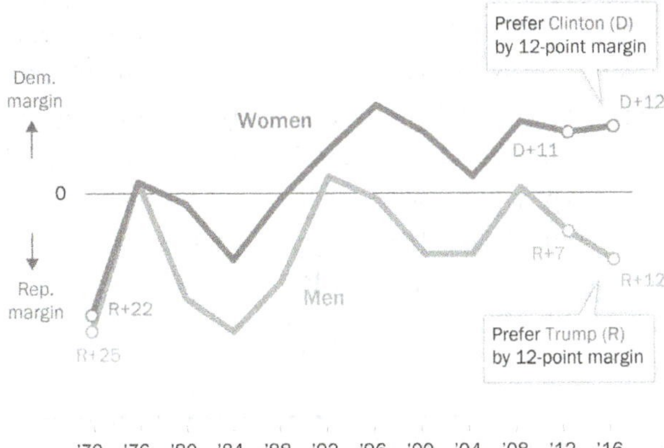

Source: Based on exit polls conducted by Edison Research for the National Election Pool, as reported by CNN. Data from prior years from national exit polls.

Figure 12.1. Gender gap.
Source: Pew Research Center.

received only 37 percent of the vote of married men while Trump won 58 percent. Sixty-two percent of unmarried women supported Clinton and only 33 percent supported Trump. By contrast, unmarried men and married women split almost evenly between the two candidates. Unmarried men supported Clinton by a vote of 46 to 45. Married women voted 49 percent for Clinton and 47 percent for Trump. The very different voting behaviors of married and unmarried people suggest that either conservatives are more likely to marry or marriage exerts a conservative influence on those who marry, or some combination of both. Figure 12.1 shows how much the gender gap has widened since 1972.

There are no reliable historical data about the electoral behavior of homosexuals. Until recently, being gay was not respectable and so their political behavior went largely unexplored. Now that gays have attained full civil rights, some surveys, including the 2016 National Exit Poll, do inquire about their voting choice. They have become a staunch component of the Democratic Party coalition. In 2016, 78 percent of those who identified as gay, lesbian, bisexual, or transgendered voted for Clinton.

Forty percent of American voters own guns. Only 32 percent of Democrats own them whereas 55 percent of Republicans do (www.gallup.com/poll/21496/gun-ownership-higher-among-republicans-than-democrats.aspx). In 2016, Trump repeatedly proclaimed his support of the Second Amendment, which declares a right to gun ownership. He claimed that his opponent would "essentially abolish" it. As a result, he gained the endorsement of many organizations of gun owners, most especially the National Rifle Association. On the other hand, Clinton gained the endorsement of seventeen gun control groups including the most prominent ones. Because gun owners are mostly white, often religiously evangelical and come disproportionately from rural areas, small towns, or less densely settled suburbs, one cannot say for sure that they support the Republicans solely because they are gun owners. It is safer to say that concern about excessive gun control meshed with the other characteristics that typify gun owners to establish an increasingly powerful identification with the Republicans (see the next chapter for further discussion of the rural and small town white vote in 2016).

Income and Education

During the New Deal the Democrats solidified their hold on voters of modest means and lower levels of education. Income was a reliable indicator of which party a person belonged to. In 2016 this was only true at the low end of the income ladder. The poorest Americans, the 17 percent of the population making $30,000 or less, supported Clinton by a margin of 53 percent to 41 percent. At all the higher income rungs the margin between the two candidates was slim.

In 2016 the Republicans reversed the historic tie between lack of education and allegiance to the Democrats. Trump gained 51 percent of those with a high school education or less while Clinton gained 45 percent. Among those with some college education, Trump won 52 percent to 43 percent. Clinton won among college graduates by 49 percent to 45 percent. Her greatest education margin was among those with postgraduate education, among whom she won by a margin of 58 percent to 37 percent. The correlation between relatively low educational attainment and support for the Republicans becomes much stronger if one controls for race. Among whites with no college degree, Trump led 67 percent to 28 percent for Clinton. Figure 12.2 charts the voting preferences based on education level of all voters and of only white voters.

"Swing" Voters

In order to gain political strength, both parties seek to recruit new blocs of voters. Hispanics is the fastest-growing ethnically identifiable segment of the population. As of 2015, there were approximately 56.6 million Hispanics making up roughly 17.6 percent of the US population. Therefore, the parties have been particularly active in pursuing them. However, many Hispanics are not citizens, and even those who are register to vote in lesser numbers than other groups do. Hispanic Americans currently constitute about 12 percent of the electorate. But as their number grows and they assimilate to life in the United States, this

Table 12.1. Trump and Clinton supporters.

Trump supporters	Clinton supporters
Rural and small town dwellers	Urban dwellers
Churchgoers (white)	Non-churchgoers
Catholics (white)	Catholics (Hispanic)
Gun owners	Gun control advocates
Married men	Unmarried women
Southerners (white)	Holders of advanced degrees
No college degree (white)	The poor
	African Americans
	Gays
	Jews

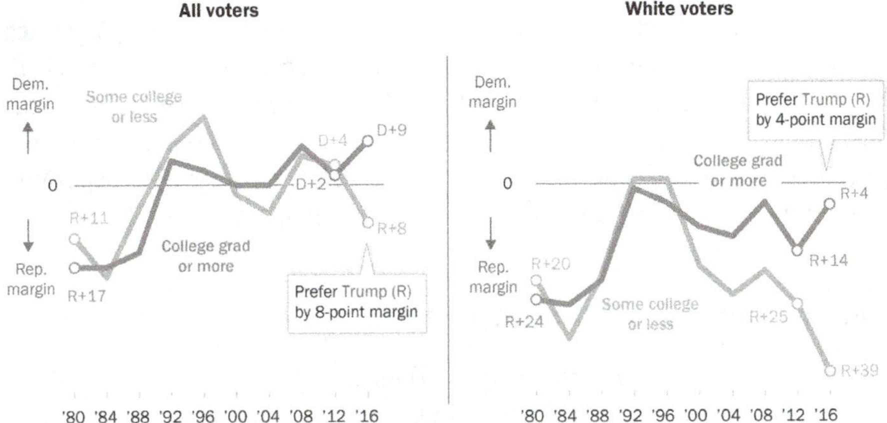

Figure 12.2. Education gap.
Source: Pew Research Center.

percentage is expected to grow substantially. It is already much higher in several of the most populated states, including the three largest – California, New York, and Texas – as well as "battleground" states (see next chapter) such as Arizona, Colorado, and Nevada. Republicans believe that the strong religious and family ties and work ethic of Hispanics make them very susceptible to Republican appeals. But, so far, those hopes have not been realized. In 2016 Hillary Clinton won 65 percent of the Hispanic vote while Trump only garnered 29 percent.

Political Party Organization

Political parties are organized at local, state, and national levels. State and local political parties vary enormously in their level of ambition and effectiveness. In some states, they may be very active. They may engage in voter registration drives and seek to mobilize volunteers for national as well as local and statewide candidates. They may also try to maintain and instill party loyalty by hosting speeches by public officials of their party and by celebrating party holidays – Jefferson–Jackson Day (Democrats) and Lincoln's birthday (Republicans). In others, they may exist in name only.

Each party has a national committee and also a House and a Senate campaign committee.The national committees raise funds to spend to help party candidates and to suppport registration drives and other marketing activities aimed at promoting the party's electoral prospects. They also organize and stage their respective presidential nominating conventions (see the next chapter for a discussion of party conventions, including the 2016 party conventions).

The House and Senate campaign committees are organizationally separate from the national committees. Each campaign committee is chaired by a member of its respective branch, who is elected by a caucus of all the party's elected members. In addition to providing funds and logistical support to incumbent party members, the campaign committees aid challengers to incumbents of the other party and to those nominated to seek open seats. Also, the committees work actively to recruit candidates particularly in districts where the opposition incumbent appears vulnerable or where an open seat appears winnable.

CRITICAL CHOICE: FOUNDING A PARTY AND A PARTY SYSTEM

Despite the founders' opposition to party, Thomas Jefferson and James Madison created the first American political party, the Republicans. The party's very success led to its decline. After an interval of no party politics, Martin Van Buren and Andrew Jackson revived the Republicans, renaming them the Democrats. The political opponents of Jackson and Van Buren formed an opposition party, the Whigs, and thus a two-party system came into being.

The United States prides itself on being a constitutional republic. All the other key components of the political order – Congress, the executive, the judiciary, and the states – are described in the Constitution, but political parties are not. This omission is no accident. The drafters of the Constitution disagreed about many things, but they shared an antipathy to parties. The Framers tried their best to produce a governing blueprint that would make parties unnecessary and difficult to form.

The root of the word "party" is "part." The Founders were concerned about the "whole." They saw parties as efforts to form majority *factions* that would substitute partial interests for the common good. The elaborate structure of separation of powers and checks and balances in the Constitution was designed to keep such a majority faction from forming. The very idea of the large republic described in *Federalist* 10 was conceived as a defense against party. The republic's size would encourage factions to proliferate and thus would keep any single one from growing large and strong enough to dominate. Both those in favor of democracy and those wary of democracy found reasons to oppose party. The Framers who most feared tyranny of the majority believed that party would enable the untutored masses to deprive others of their liberty. The Framers who feared elitism expected defenders of privilege to cunningly manipulate party to deprive the people of their liberty and their democratic powers. The Framers' anti-party sentiments have never been absent from the political scene. They provide a narrative that later anti-party crusaders have adopted, an attitude that has never died away. This narrative proved especially potent during the Progressive Era and led to changes that greatly decreased the strength and cohesiveness of parties. And, as demonstrated in the beginning of this chapter, antipartisan sentiment dominates current attitudes toward the parties.

Yet, unwittingly, the founding generation created electoral laws that favored the very thing they so desperately opposed. The Constitution itself does little to specify how national elections are to be conducted. Presidential electors were to be chosen by the states, but state legislatures were free to choose them as they wished as well as determining the "time, place and manner" of holding elections for senators and members of the House. Likewise, they had complete discretion about how to choose their state legislators and governors. They could have adopted a proportional method for choosing state legislative and congressional representatives. A proportional system allocates votes among parties based upon the percentage of the vote each party receives. Instead, they created legislative and congressional districts in which a single representative was chosen on a plurality basis.

Proportional representation encourages the growth of several political parties since it does not require a large fraction of the vote to elect at least one representative to office. Single member districts favor two parties because only one candidate can win. Therefore, the "outs" have a strong incentive to band together in support of a single challenger to defeat the incumbent. Awarding victory to the candidate with the most votes, even if the candidate lacks a majority, avoids the need for a run-off election between the two top finishers. Therefore, it deprives smaller parties whose candidates came in third or worse of the political leverage they would have had if one or the other of the top finishers needed their support to gain a majority in the run-off. The decision of almost all states to also award presidential electors on a winner-take-all plurality basis played precisely the same role in discouraging multiple parties that single member districts and plurality election played in legislative races. These three choices regarding the ground rules for conducting elections are a large part of the reason that with only a few brief exceptions the United States has always had a two-party political system. As the next chapter describes, the Twelfth Amendment to the Constitution also served to improve party prospects.

Founding a Party

James Madison changed his mind about political parties as he watched Secretary of the Treasury Alexander Hamilton – his former partner in the writing of the Federalist Papers – strive to amass greater power for the national executive. Madison decided that this centralization of power in the hands of the few was an even greater threat to liberty than a tyranny of the majority. The only way to combat this evil was to organize the many to take power away from Hamilton and his cronies, and so Madison and Jefferson undertook to create a political force capable of defeating Hamilton and thus the Republican Party was born. That party was the direct ancestor of the modern-day Democratic Party; today's Republican Party has other roots.

Because prevailing opinion was so hostile, Madison and Jefferson's party-building efforts were very circumspect. In May of 1791, these two Virginians went on a "botanizing" expedition to the Northeast. Why would Secretary of State Jefferson and Congressman Madison take time out from their important governing responsibilities to look at northern plants unless those flowers and shrubs happened to reside in the backyards of important political personages whose support the two Virginians sought to cultivate? By August of 1791, Jefferson was writing letters to men he had identified as opponents of the Washington administration, urging them to run for Congress. He convinced Madison's friend, Philip Freneau, to start an opposition newspaper in Philadelphia, funded in part through printing contracts award by the State Department, of which he was the head. To create a truly national party, these two Southerners needed to cement alliances with budding Northern political organizations such as the one Aaron Burr was creating in New York. The bond that these men established between New York and Virginia was critical to the growth of the infant Republican Party.

At the same time that an opposition was forming among prominent politicians, ordinary citizens were protesting the pro-British tilt of the Washington administration. In more than thirty cities, Democratic-Republican societies arose to support America's sister republic and Revolutionary War ally, France (see Chapter 12). These societies soon died out, but their members gravitated to the Republicans, providing the party with new members and leaders. Schooled in the societies' lively debates and discussions, they transferred this same democratic spirit to their party activities.

These different strands of opposition were woven together into the durable thread of party by a single catalytic event – the Jay Treaty. The treaty was designed to solve outstanding disputes with the British regarding prewar debts,

Table 12.2. Senate vote on the Jay Treaty, June 1795.

Supported		Opposed
William Bingham (F–PA)	Samuel Livermore (F–NH)	Timothy Bloodworth (R–NC)
William Bradford (F–RI)	Humphrey Marshall (F–KY)	John Brown (R–KY)
George Cabot (F–MA)	Elijah Paine (F–VT)	Aaron Burr (R–NY)
Oliver Ellsworth (F–CT)	Richard Potts (F–MD)	Pierce Butler (R–SC)
Theodore Foster (F–RI)	Jacob Read (F–SC)	James Jackson (R–GA)
Frederick Frelinghuysen (F–NJ)	James Ross (F–PA)	John Langdon (R–NH)
James Gunn (F–GA)	John Rutherfurd (F–NJ)	Alexander Martin (R–NC)
John Henry (F–MD)	Caleb Strong (F–MA)	Stevens Mason (R–VA)
Rufus King (F–NY)	Jonathan Trumbull, Jr. (F–CT)	Moses Robinson (R–VT)
Henry Latimer (F–DE)	John Vining (F–DE)	Henry Tazewell (R–VA)

Source: Library of Congress.

British occupation of forts on the Northwest frontier, and the British Navy's seizing of sailors aboard American ships. But it failed to settle most of these outstanding issues. Madison, Jefferson, and their supporters saw it as a virtual capitulation to the British and a sellout of the French.

In the temporary national capital, Philadelphia, an informal committee formed to coordinate opposition to the treaty. For the first time, a major constitutional debate was organized on a party basis. The Constitution grants the power to ratify a treaty exclusively to the Senate. But the power to provide or withhold the funds necessary for implementing the terms of the treaty rested largely with the House of Representatives. A caucus of all Republican congressmen was convened to oppose the appropriation to implement the treaty. Nonetheless, the appropriation passed and the intent of the Constitution was preserved. Table 12.2 shows the degree to which partisan voting had developed even at this early date.

In the election of 1796, a coordinated effort was made to defeat members of Congress who supported the treaty. Of the seven legislators targeted, four were defeated and two reversed their positions. Only one unrepentant incumbent was reelected. This success in punishing disloyalty shows that less than a decade after passage of the Constitution, a political organization had come into being that possessed all the crucial attributes of a political party – a mass membership, an ability to coordinate its activities, and mechanisms for imposing party discipline.

In the Jay Treaty debate, party mechanisms were used to undermine constitutional intent, but Jefferson's presidential party leadership showed that party could also be used to protect the Constitution. He sought to democratize the government, but not at the expense of the rights he himself had declared inalienable in the Declaration of Independence. To accomplish this tricky task, he needed to amass political support to push his democratizing initiatives and to impose discipline on his supporters to keep them from pushing those reforms too far. He accomplished both these tasks and thus he enabled his party allies in

Congress to greatly curtail government but to do so without undermining the constitutional checks and balances that protected liberty. Jefferson's Revolution of 1800 abolished all taxes except the tariff, provided for a swift repayment of the national debt, and greatly reduced federal expenditures, but it also left the constitutional governing structure untouched.

Although the term "spoils system" is associated with Andrew Jackson, this means of imposing party discipline was first instituted by Jefferson. During his first two years in office, Jefferson replaced more than half the federal office-holders with Republican appointees. By the end of his second term, only one-third of the remaining holdovers were still there. Jefferson's ruthlessness in hiring and firing on the basis of party loyalty gave his supporters second thoughts about opposing his plans and policies. When the Republican leader of the House of Representatives, John Randolph, rallied radical Republicans to oppose some of his policies, Jefferson denied favors to Randolph's allies and awarded them to defectors from Randolph. The rebellion was crushed.

Although Madison and Jefferson created a political party, they did not believe in the virtues of party; they viewed their party as the "party to end party." By triumphing over Hamilton and his allies, the Republicans hoped to restore the power of the Constitution to direct and control American government. Once proper constitutional government was in place, the need for, and usefulness of, political party would disappear. Jefferson said as much in his first inaugural address when he declared, "We are all republicans; we are all federalists."

By the end of Jefferson's two terms, he had converted moderate Federalists into Republicans and destroyed the Hamiltonians. During the administrations of Madison, Monroe, and John Quincy Adams, the country experienced one-party government. In 1820, Monroe was unopposed for reelection. In homage to the lack of partisan rancor, this period, which lasted until the election of 1828, was called the "Era of Good Feelings."

Regardless of his own qualms about party, Jefferson's success in vanquishing the Federalists made him the first great party hero and over the ensuing decades his name continued to be revered by Democrats. Even FDR, an apostle of big government, associated himself with Jefferson. To this day, Democrats continue to celebrate Jefferson, and his loyal successor Jackson by holding festive dinners in their honor.

The Price of Nonpartisanship

The Era of Good Feelings was hardly that. It sparked a variety of bad political feelings that is all too likely to arise in the absence of vigorous party life and discipline. In the face of weak central leadership and attachment, sectional differences grew. The West became increasingly disgruntled at the financial dominance of the East and the seeming unconcern of the national government toward the threat posed by the Indians. The South shared the West's resentment of Eastern bankers and was becoming increasingly defensive about mounting Northern opposition to slavery. A division of the country into three or four separate nations seemed a real possibility as public interest in and concern for the idea of American nationhood seemed to ebb.

Within the government itself, the principle of separation of powers was in decline as executives and legislators intermingled their functions, rendering neither accountable. Congress increasingly involved itself in the details of administration. Cabinet officials paid less and less attention to presidential dictates and pursued their own departmental agendas through direct contact with congressional committees. Thus, both the authority of the president and the authority of the leadership of Congress were undermined.

This political decline was accelerated by the presidential election of 1824, which cast doubt on the legitimacy of the presidential office itself. No candidate received a majority of the electoral vote. As specified by the Twelfth Amendment to the Constitution, the House of Representatives chose the winner from among the top three finishers – Andrew Jackson, John Adams, and William Crawford. In addition to having the most electoral votes, Jackson was also far ahead in the popular vote. He tallied 153,000 votes, almost 50,000 more than the second place finisher, Adams. Nonetheless, the House voted to make Adams president. Clay, eliminated as a presidential contender, served as president maker. He used his authority as Speaker of the House to obtain votes for Adams. Adams then named Clay secretary of state. Because this position had been the traditional stepping-stone to the presidency since Madison assumed the office in 1809, Clay was virtually anointed as Adams's successor. No evidence existed that Adams had bribed Clay with the offer of secretary of state. But the result inspired widespread public outrage because, in contrast to all previous presidential elections, the most popular candidate did not win. Jackson accused Clay and Adams of making a "corrupt bargain."

The First Party Insurgency

The 1824 election witnessed the first example of the intra-party insurgencies that periodically erupt in American politics, most recently in 2016 as exemplified by Bernie Sanders and Donald Trump (see Chapter 13). Andrew Jackson was a war hero and creature of the frontier. He had no real standing within the Republican Party. He did not enjoy the backing of the Republican congressional caucus as every president since Jefferson had. Thus, he was the first candidate to claim popular support in opposition to the party establishment. His decision to run again in 1828 signaled the demise of the Republican Party. Those Republicans who decided to back Jackson reconstituted themselves as the Democrats. Thus, the first party insurgency resulted in the birth of a new political party. Those who backed Adams for reelection would soon emerge as a rival party, the Whigs.

As the "victim" of antidemocratic forces, Jackson, already a military hero, became the foremost spokesman for the rapidly expanding popular discontent. Although many hoped that he would serve as the voice of the people, others feared that he would prove to be a demagogue, exploiting his popularity to assume dictatorial powers. Martin Van Buren, a senator from New York and the leader of a powerful New York political faction, sought to take advantage of Jackson's popularity and curb his demagogic tendencies by making him the candidate of a reinvigorated Jeffersonian party.

After meeting with like-minded politicians from Virginia, Van Buren was able to resurrect the powerful New York–Virginia alliance that had proven so valuable in electing Jefferson. It would support Jackson in exchange for his promise to accept party discipline. Jackson agreed. Although he might well have won anyway, the solid support of New York and Virginia, added to his strength in the South and West, ensured his victory. Of course, Jackson could easily have reneged on his bargain with Van Buren after the New Yorker had delivered on his part of the deal. But Jackson was a man of honor. And, he admired the discipline and sense of purpose embodied by the victorious party, renamed the Democratic Party. He authorized the first national major party convention, held in 1832 for the express purpose of lining up support for Van Buren's nomination as vice president, thus ensuring that Van Buren would be his successor.

Jackson made vigorous use of the Democratic Party to decentralize and democratize political and economic power. He vetoed the Second National Bank of the United States, ending the cozy relationship between government and the Eastern economic establishment that the bank had cemented. He reintroduced, indeed championed, the spoils system, using it to enable ordinary people to serve in government (see Chapter 10). Although his enemies decried his aggressive use of presidential power, that power was employed for the purpose of limiting and reducing governmental intrusion. Therefore, on the whole, the democratizing impact of this reborn political party was compatible with the preservation and even the expansion of liberty.

Creating a Party System

As the Jefferson–Jackson celebrations demonstrate, Jackson became the next great party hero. But party lore is not limited to heroes. It also revels in anti-heroes. Hatred of Jackson was one of the most important impulses driving the creation of the Whigs. Indeed, the very name"Whig" was chosen so as to identify this new party with the English party of the same name that had deposed the autocratic English King James II in the late seventeenth century. Like their namesakes, the new Whigs promised to vanquish the heirs of "King Andrew the First" and remove any trace of the monarchism with which he had endowed the presidency.

Van Buren, unlike Jefferson, did not believe that threats to the Constitution would disappear once his party came to power. The danger of despotism was a perennial one. The Constitution might provide for the indirect election of the president, but the events of 1824 revealed that the people expected to make the real decision. Nothing could prevent would-be demagogues from making direct appeals to the people and exploiting their own popularity for tyrannical ends. Taming presidential ambition would require buttressing the Constitution with the collective restraint and discipline that only party could impose.

Having witnessed the demise of Jefferson's party, Van Buren recognized that one-party rule would eventually turn into no-party rule. The long-term health of a party depended on the existence of a strong and healthy opposition party. Only the continual threat of defeat, and its occasional reality, could keep a party vigorous and cohesive. For a system to endure, it must have rules. Each side must be willing to accept defeat, grudgingly if not gracefully. Neither side must fear that, if they lose, their most cherished values and interests will be destroyed, because under those circumstances neither side will graciously and peacefully accept defeat.

Van Buren as the prophet of the party system triumphed at the expense of Van Buren the politician. Having won the presidency in 1836, Van Buren was defeated by William Henry Harrison in 1840. Harrison ran as a candidate of the Whig Party, which, as Van Buren had predicted, grew up in opposition to Jackson and the Democrats. To defeat Van Buren, the Whigs used the same partisan techniques that had proven so successful for the Democrats. They staged rallies, published party newspapers, and wielded symbols in an effort to excite and mobilize masses of voters. In this election, the modern notion of an election "campaign" was born. "Campaign" was a military term, and its application to elections implied that they would now acquire the hard-fought, tactical, and disciplined character associated with warfare. Parties would provide the troops and the logistical support for these political wars.

"All Liberals, All Democrats"

Although the Democrats identified more closely with "the common man" and the Whigs had more support among the wealthy, they were not "liberal" and "conservative" parties in the modern sense. They were both liberal in that they both favored free enterprise and protection of private property and adhered to the basic principles of the Constitution and the Declaration of Independence – natural rights and limited government. And they were both democratic. The Whigs had abandoned the Federalists' efforts to promote elitist rule. Indeed, by attacking the "monarchic" presidency of Jackson, they claimed to be more democratic than the Democrats.

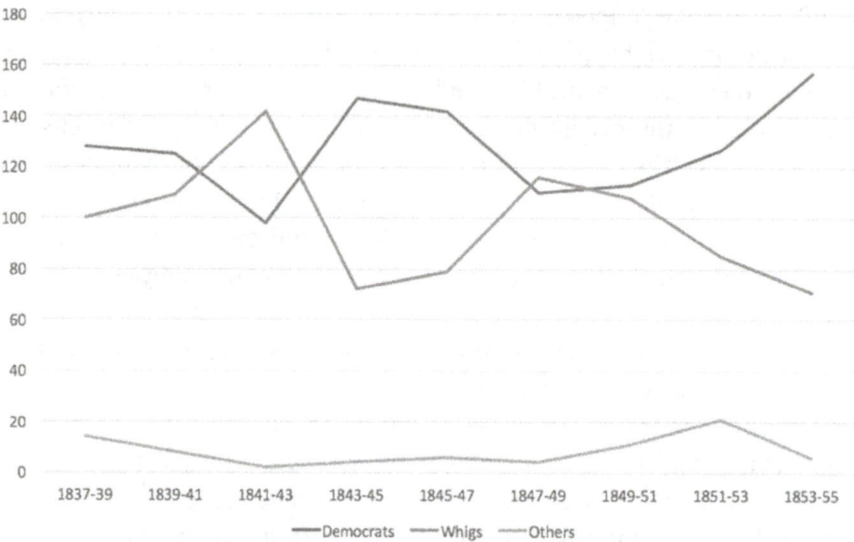

Figure 12.3. Party strength in House, 1837–55.
Source: US House of Representatives.

The Whigs favored using government to build canals, roads, and other physical improvements that benefited interstate commerce. And they wanted to raise the tariff on imported products to fund those projects and to protect domestic manufacturers. They also favored the establishment of a national banking and financial system that would provide greater availability and security of credit and facilitate all manner of commercial transactions. In modern terms, such enthusiasm for activist government would be called "liberal." But the Democrats claimed that these activities were inevitably "illiberal" because they were designed to benefit a select few. Government insiders and their friends would always be better positioned to enjoy the fruits of government-funded projects and to obtain governmentally sponsored bank credit. Democrats believed that the ordinary person had a better chance for equal opportunity in a competitive marketplace than in one dominated by government subsidies and favoritism.

Both parties were truly national in scope. Two of the four Whig presidents were Southerners: John Tyler and Zachary Taylor. Two of the three Democratic presidents during this same period were from the North. In states such as New York, Illinois, and Pennsylvania, the two parties were intensely competitive, with frequent alternations in power occurring between them. This national focus born of the parties' ambition to win the presidency suppressed regional rivalries and helped foster a sense of American nationhood. Figures 12.3 and 12.4 show the relative strength of the two parties in the House and Senate between 1837 and 1855.

Table 12.3. Whigs versus Democrats.

Whigs	Democrats
Pro tariff	Anti tariff
Build infrastucture	Leave infrastructure to the states
Pro Congress	Pro presidency
Active government	Limited government

Figure 12.4. Party strength in Senate, 1837–55.
Source: US Senate.

UPSHOT

The party system that developed in the 1830s served to promote political and governmental decentralization as well as a sense of American nationhood. Because electoral votes were allocated state by state, the partisan apparatus created to win presidential elections also had to be constructed state by state. In order to maintain the support of the state parties that had brought a president to power, that president had to reward them and be disciplined by them. The spoils system thrived during this period, as state parties demanded what they deemed their fair share of federal jobs.

The dependence of national officeholders on state parties was duplicated by the dependence of state party leaders on local ones. To win statewide elections, party leaders had to rely on local party organizations in cities, towns, and counties to turn out the vote. Therefore, localities held the key to both statewide and national political success and could make powerful demands on higher political authorities. Because the two parties were so evenly matched, they could not afford to ignore even small localities because such seemingly insignificant places might well provide the margin of victory in a close election. This localizing political pressure served as a brake on national political power and a powerful protection of the individuality and diversity of states and localities. Although both parties strongly supported the Constitution, their decentralized character embued them with principles and outlooks that echoed the Anti-Federalists (see Chapter 3).

In an era before mass media, local party life was not only a source of spoils but of entertainment as well. Political parties held picnics, rallies, parades, and other public spectacles. These occasions were intended to be lighthearted, even frivolous, but they also served a crucial democratic function. As Tocqueville had remarked, large republics increased an individual's sense of isolation, weakness, and vulnerability. The instinctive reaction to such threatening feelings was to withdraw from public life into the relatively safe private world of self and family. Local party life was sufficiently unthreatening and pleasurable to encourage tentative steps out of the private and into the public realm. Parties provided a link to the wider world of politics that more impersonal and drab governmental entities could not provide, and parties were therefore a critical stimulus for democratic citizenship.

Absorbing Shocks to the Party System

The two-party system established in the 1830s continues to this day. Its resilience is attested to by the severe shocks it has successfully absorbed. In the nineteenth century it survived the crisis over slavery that reached a fever pitch in the 1850s; the wave of immigration that began in the 1880s; and the conflict over the rise of concentrated economic power of the 1880s and 1890s.

The Birth of the Republicans

The party system could not resolve the slavery conflict – that required a war. But the replacement of one of the two party contenders with a new party enabled the system to survive the crisis. The Whigs were destroyed but their sucessor the Republicans entered into a competition with the Democrats that still continues.

Both the Whigs and the Democrats contained pro- and antislavery factions. Their desire to survive as national entities, and therefore to paper over their internal differences about slavery, was one of the most important factors that delayed the onset of civil war. Ultimately, however, the controversy about whether to admit new states as slave or free became so fierce that it overwhelmed the possibility of compromise. From the mid 1840s onward, regional loyalty came increasingly to outweigh party loyalty. The Democrats became the party of the South, shedding their democratic and egalitarian concerns to focus on protecting slavery. The Whigs could not resolve their differences over slavery and the party died, to be replaced by the antislavery Republicans, who also included antislavery Democrats in their ranks.

Abraham Lincoln, the first Republican president, had been an ardent Whig. He joined the new party only when it became clear to him that the Whigs were not prepared to lead the attack on slavery's expansion. As we discuss in Chapters 5 and 12, during the 1860 presidential election and during his presidency, Lincoln gave effective voice to the key Republican principle: incorporation of the ideas of liberty contained in the Declaration of Independence into the principle of union contained in the Constitution. In town squares and community halls throughout the North, a constitutional debate took place along party lines. The 1860 election pitted Lincoln against the Democrat who defeated him for the Senate – Stephen Douglas. Douglas sought to hold the pro- and antislavery factions of his party together by advocating the principle of popular sovereignty, which allowed each new territory to decide for itself whether to adopt a pro- or antislavery state constitution. Lincoln opposed popular sovereignty. He grounded his unalterable opposition to slavery's expansion on the principle of "unalienable rights" enumerated in the Declaration of Independence. The voter realignment that followed, which granted the Republican Party majority status in most parts of the country except the South, was the political outcome of this party-sponsored constitutional reconsideration that gave deeper import to the noble phrase that "all men are created equal."

Lincoln did not succeed through rhetoric alone. He relied on his party to mobilize campaign support for him and to stand behind his program in Congress. He adroitly manipulated patronage and cabinet appointments to reinforce party cohesion. Most important, during the critical election of 1860 and after, he depended on Republicans to carry on spirited and probing discussions at the state and local level, pressing their constituents to understand and accept the profound principles on which Lincoln was basing his effort to refound the Union. Lincoln emerged as the first great hero of the Republicans. To this day their Lincoln Day dinners serve as their primary annual celebration and fundraising event.

In the decades after the Civil War, the Republicans enjoyed great success by portraying themselves as the party of victory. To remind voters of the sacrifices endured during the Civil War, their candidates would “wave the bloody shirt,” dusting off their bloodstained uniforms to provide tangible testimony of their service to the Union. As the decades wore on, those same uniforms were displayed by their children and grandchildren to reinforce their constituents' devotion to that great cause and to the “Grand Old Party” that embodied it. In the former Confederacy, the Democrats did likewise. Party candidates and their descendants waved “the bloody gray shirt” to identify themselves with those who had died bravely in the losing cause.

After the Civil War, the two-party system that had been created in the Jacksonian era solidified itself. Although both parties have undergone vast transformations, and important third-party challenges have occurred, since 1852 one or the other of the two major parties has won all the presidential elections and controlled the two houses of Congress. No other nation has demonstrated this degree of political party stability and endurance. Between 1876 and 1896, the Republicans held the upper hand, but not by much. They won the presidency five times and the Democrats won twice. For most of this period they controlled the Senate but the Democrats usually controlled the House of Representatives.

Coopting the Immigrants

The Democrats' postwar resurgence was due in large measure to their ability to take advantage of the great population change that took place in the latter part of the nineteenth century, the explosive growth of the big cities. Thus they extended their reach beyond their Southern bastion. Starting in the 1880s, one of the greatest mass migrations in human history took place, bringing millions of immigrants from southern and eastern Europe and from Ireland to America. The overwhelming bulk of these newcomers settled in the big cities of the North and Midwest. The Republicans were so dominant in these areas that they showed less energy and enthusiasm in recruiting these new voters than the out party, the Democrats, did. Local Democratic leaders, most famously William Marcy “Boss” Tweed, head of the New York Democratic Party organization known as Tammany Hall, met the newcomers as they arrived at the dock. He and his associates promised them food and shelter and jobs. In exchange, the immigrants were expected to become loyal Tammany Hall supporters. Some cities permitted resident aliens to vote, and so the immigrants could make good on their promise quickly. Other cities restricted voting to citizens. But even there, the Democratic leaders often enlisted sympathetic federal magistrates to ignore the residency requirements and add the newcomers to the voting rolls. As this chapter has already discussed, the spoils system was the invention of Jefferson, Jackson and Van Buren. However, the urban political organizations took it to a whole new level.

To provide jobs for the immigrants was a massive undertaking. To keep them employed, party organizations undertook massive building projects: trolley tracks were laid, streets and roads were expanded, new courthouses and municipal buildings were built. New York's Central Park was designed by a Republican, Fredrick Law Olmsted. But to get it built, Olmsted employed hordes of Irish immigrant laborers supplied by Tammany Hall. These laborers were not only expected to vote for Tammany candidates, in order to pay the organization's expenses and enrich its leaders they had to hand over a percentage of their wages to it. This practice came to be known as a "kickback". Because so much money was involved in these great undertakings, there were great opportunities for corruption. Tweed himself went to jail, convicted of fraud.

These urban political organizations, often called "machines," were not just glorified employment agencies. Although often engaged in corrupt practices, their leaders were also committed Democrats. They sought to instill party loyalty that went beyond mere self-interest. At rallies and meetings they impressed the newcomers with the great traditions, symbols, and heroes of their party, and the key principles that distinguished them from the Republicans. They welcomed the immigrants to picnics and dinners. Indeed, the party organization was the only American institution, apart from the Catholic Church, to fully make immigrants feel at home. The strong attachments with the party organizations that immigrant families developed lasted for generations.

Preempting the Populists

As of the late nineteenth century, both major parties were, by contemporary standards, conservative. The Democrats remained true to their Jeffersonian roots by advocating limited federal government and opposing efforts to regulate free markets. The Republicans were less committed to states' rights, but they opposed using government to curb corporate power or reduce income disparities. It took the creation of a third party - the People's Party, known as the Populists - to disturb the bipartisan conservative consensus and advocate policies that would today be called liberal. The two-party system survived the Populist insurgency because one party, the Democrats, shifted in a populist direction winning over Populist supporters and thereby destroying the insurgent third party.

The Populists arose in the economically depressed grain-growing areas of the Midwest. They sought federal laws to protect farmers from the monopoly power of railroads and to reduce the gap between rich and poor. As the agricultural recession worsened, Populist support grew. By the mid 1880s, the Populists had elected governors, senators, and representatives in several Midwestern states, and were also gaining strength among Southern farmers. The 1892 People's Party platform was a remarkably progressive document. It called for an expanded

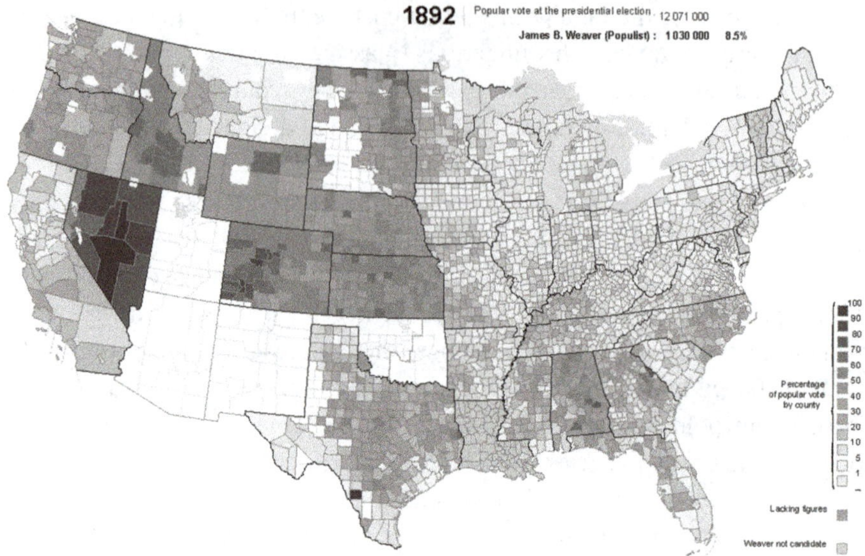

Figure 12.5. Populist vote strength.
Source: Geographie Electorale.

coinage of silver to inflate the currency, a graduated income tax, a constitutional amendment that mandated civil service reform, and government ownership of railroad, telegraph, and telephone companies. The People's Party ticket garnered more than a million popular votes and twenty-two electoral votes. Figure 12.5 is a map of the 1892 Populist vote for president. It shows the large regional disparities in Populist support.

In 1896, the Democratic Party was at a crossroads. It was led by President Grover Cleveland, who had been elected in 1884, lost in 1888, and was then reelected in 1892. Cleveland was a devout believer in limited government. When farmers in Texas, who had been forced to eat their seed corn because their crops had been destroyed by drought, asked the president to give them some of the surplus seed corn being kept in government granaries, he refused, saying, "It is the job of the people to support the government, not the job of the government to support the people."

But Cleveland's views were challenged by Democrats who wanted to come to the aid of economically distressed farmers in Texas and elsewhere. Cleveland's victories had been something of a fluke, due largely to factional feuding among Republicans. Although competitive at the congressional level, the Democrats were still the out party when it came to presidential elections and therefore more open to new political trends and ideas. Populist ideas were making greater inroads among Democrats than among Republicans. Some Democratic politicians, most notably Congressman William Jennings Bryan of Nebraska, were openly courting Populist support.

The 1896 Democratic convention turned into a pitched battle between pro- and anti-Populists. William Jennings Bryan's Cross of Gold speech tipped the balance toward the Populists. In his speech, he depicted the struggle between rich and poor, creditor and debtor, in biblical terms, appealing to the strong religious feeling of many delegates (see Chapter 6 for further discussion). His words electrified the crowd, and Bryan himself was chosen as the Democratic Party candidate for president. He would later obtain the endorsement of the Populists as well.

Bryan's campaign moved the Democrats in a new direction. Ever since the debate between Jefferson and Hamilton, the party that presumed to speak for the people had been the party most resistant to national power, which it associated with privilege, and most committed to the virtues of local self-government. Preempting the Populists, the Democrats now sought to invoke national power for democratic purposes. In response to the challenge posed by the fusion of Populists and Democrats, the Republicans rallied behind the theme of stability. Their support of the Gold Standard was put in the context of a more general defense of the essential soundness of the American economy and the way of life it represented. The two pillars of the Republican platform were sound money and protectionism. Defense of the Gold Standard resonated not only with the wealthy but also with many industrial workers, who feared that silver-generated inflation would lessen the value of their wages. High tariffs also appealed to employer and employee alike. Taxing imported manufacturing products was viewed as the best way to defend American workers and manufacturers against the threat of cheap foreign imports produced by oppressed foreign labor. As consumers of foodstuffs, workers opposed farmers' efforts to raise food prices. The Republicans won the 1896 election decisively and remained the dominant party for the next thirty-four years. But the 1896 campaign also had a long-term impact on the Democrats. Ever since, they have claimed to be the party that is more dedicated to the wellbeing of the dispossessed and more energetic in using government to help those least able to help themselves.

The Republican 1896 victory ushered in a period of Republican electoral dominance that lasted until 1932. The only Democrat elected president during this thirty-six-year period, Woodrow Wilson, won only because of the independent candidacy of Theodore Roosevelt that sapped Republican strength. The Democrats did somewhat better in congressional elections, but the Republicans controlled both houses most of the time. This decline in party competition appears to be the most important cause of the decline in voter turnout rates that one observes after 1896 – even the return of more competitive parties after the New Deal has not managed to restore the pre-1896 turnout rates. It would seem that the nineteenth-century parties were not only more competitive; because they were so decentralized, they were able to exert a stronger hold on the loyalty and energy of voters.

The Progressive Attack on Party

As we discussed in Chapter 4, Populism was soon followed by another, more broadly based, reform movement: Progressivism. Progressivism's impact on party politics was greatly hastened and expanded by the assassination of President McKinley shortly after his reelection in 1900, which propelled Vice President Theodore Roosevelt (TR) to the presidency. TR, former governor of New York, was among the most prominent Progressive politicians. Anti-Progressive New York Republicans helped him secure the vice presidential nomination to get him out of the state. They expected him to do little harm in that largely ceremonial role. To their considerable chagrin, fate placed TR in the most powerful political post in the land.

Because he could not control his party in Congress, TR was not able to implement the full Progressive agenda, but he did greatly increase the visibility and popularity of Progressive ideas. When he retired from office, in 1909, he manipulated the nomination of his chosen successor, William Howard Taft. Taft won the general election easily, but TR considered Taft's approach too conservative. In 1912, TR tried and failed to win back from Taft the Republican presidential nomination. His 1912 Bull Moose campaign would prove to be the most successful third-party challenge in the twentieth century.

Rather than support the Republican nominee, TR formed a third party, the Progressive Party, nicknamed the "Bull Moose," and continued his presidential bid under that label. Free from the need to mollify anti-Progressive Republicans, TR and his new party adopted a much more radical reform agenda. TR did not win. But by depriving Taft of the votes of Progressive-minded Republicans, he ensured the victory of the Democrat, Woodrow Wilson, whom he considered to be the more progressive of the major party candidates. Indeed, Wilson borrowed heavily from the Progressive Party platform. For the second time in a generation, a third party had proven to be highly influential in altering the course of American politics. In 1896, the Populists had furthered their cause by joining with the Democrats. In 1912, the Progressives did so by splitting from the Republicans. Ironically, Taft was the first sitting president to emulate Bryan and campaign actively on his own behalf, but this did not prevent him from coming in third. Both TR and Wilson also campaigned actively, making 1912 the first campaign in which all candidates, including the winner, did so.

The Progressives sought to destroy the power of party organizations by ending leadership control of candidate selection and draining them of their lifeblood, patronage. Existing civil service legislation only applied to federal jobs. Progressives imposed the merit system on many state and local governments, which were a much greater source of employment than was the federal government. At the municipal level, Progressives sought to eliminate parties altogether, claiming that there was no "Republican" or "Democratic" way to clean streets or remove garbage, there was only the right way. They prodded many cities to elect local officials on a nonpartisan basis.

To deprive state and local party leaders of control over candidate selection, Progressives supported primary elections. Voters, not bosses, would decide who would represent their party in the general election. Primaries undermine party loyalty and cohesion because they encourage would-be candidates to further their own cause by publically criticizing and attacking their opponents. Thus, competition within the party becomes as vicious and divisive as that between the parties. Supposedly grounded in harmony and friendship, primaries prod parties to shed those qualities and, instead, become arenas for discord and strife. Florida was the first to establish a presidential primary, in 1901. Wisconsin followed in 1905. By 1920, twenty states had established them. There ensued a long period of declining use of them. Nonetheless, the Progressives had set a crucial precedent for wrenching control of candidate selection away from the party leadership, one that would not fully take hold until the late 1960s, as will be discussed later in the chapter.

Forging the New Deal Coalition

The Repubicans enjoyed control of both the presidency and Congress from 1920 to 1930. The opportunity to reverse the Democrats' fortunes was provided by the Great Depression, which began with the collapse of the stock market in 1929 (see Chapter 4). Voters responded to this catastrophe by punishing the party in power, giving the Democrats a majority in the House of Representatives in the 1930 election and electing Franklin Delano Roosevelt (FDR) president in 1932.

FDR exploited his victory to create the enduring majority coalition for the Democrats that we discussed at the beginning of this chapter. It provided the political power to fuel the New Deal Conservative Revolution (see Chapter 4). FDR's1936 landslide set the Democrats on the road to long-term political dominance. From 1936 to 1964, the Democrats won six of eight presidential elections, and they controlled the House and Senate for thirty-two years of a thirty-six-year span. This winning record, unparalleled in the history of American two-party politics, reflected widespread popular acceptance of and support for the essential features of the New Deal and the important changes in constitutional understanding that it represented. As we discuss in several chapters, the New Deal redefined the meaning of rights to include a right to economic security. This newfound government obligation to provide such security was the glue that held the New Deal coalition together. Like the election in 1860, the 1936 election was one in which a political party, this time the Democrats, provoked a debate about the meaning of the rights enumerated in the Declaration of Independence and recast the meaning of those rights in a manner that strengthened the ties between liberty and democracy.

FDR succeeded by retaining traditional Democratic adherents, especially Southern whites, while adding large numbers of new recruits. His greatest weapon was his willingness to spend federal money to help people in need. Even conservative Southerners did not desert him, because they were too dependent on the jobs and other benefits that the New Deal provided. FDR, for his part, refrained from the one provocation that would have caused Southern representatives to bolt: a direct assault on racial segregation.

FDR was one of very few influential Protestant Democrats to support the presidential candidacy of his predecessor as New York governor, Al Smith, a Catholic. FDR did so in 1924, when Smith failed to receive the nomination, and in 1928, when Smith succeeded. Going out on a limb in 1924 to identify with Catholic political aspirations, coupled with his pro-Catholic reputation as governor of New York (1928–32), enabled FDR to retain the support of Catholic voters, even after Al Smith angrily broke with FDR in 1934. Jews were similarly drawn into the Democratic orbit. FDR's administration was the first to appoint many Jews to important posts, most prominently Henry Morgenthau as secretary of the treasury.

FDR also won over the support of organized labor. Before 1932, labor unions had mostly remained politically neutral in national elections. In the 1932 election, prominent labor leaders such as John L. Lewis, president of the United Mine Workers of America, endorsed Herbert Hoover. But between 1932 and 1936, the labor movement mushroomed in size. It made inroads in many of America's largest industries, such as steel, mining, and automobile manufacture. Although FDR did not openly support these organizing efforts, he did support section 7a of the National Industrial Recovery Act (NIRA), which unambiguously gave labor unions the right to organize. After the NIRA, including section 7a, became law, Lewis and other labor leaders told workers "FDR wants you to join our union." Although these statements were not literally true, FDR did not repudiate them. As a result, he came to be viewed by labor leaders and members alike as a friend of labor, the first president of the industrial age to enjoy such a status (see Chapter 6). In 1936, the labor movement strongly endorsed FDR and provided him with the largest source of his presidential campaign funds.

In the 1930s, African Americans were a small but strategically important segment of the electorate. Their voting strength was concentrated in the biggest cities in such large and politically competitive states as New York, Pennsylvania, and Illinois. A strong turnout of African Americans in a close presidential election could swing a large number of electoral votes from one party column to the other. African Americans had been among the most loyal supporters of the Republican Party, the party of Lincoln. FDR pursued cautious racial policies. African Americans participated in New Deal jobs and welfare programs, but not on an equal footing with whites. However, for the first time since Reconstruction,

African Americans actually received some help from the federal government. They showed their gratitude by reversing their seventy-year partisan tradition and voting overwhelmingly for FDR in 1936.

In summary, the New Deal Democratic coalition comprised the following:

- Labor unions
- Catholics
- Jews
- Southerners
- African Americans

In order to ensure an enduring Democratic majority, FDR knew that he had to end the South's ability to veto presidential nominees. Otherwise, Southern conservatism would undermine the party's newfound strength among labor union members and African Americans. At the 1936 convention, when his popularity was at its zenith, FDR stacked the Rules Committee with loyal supporters, and it voted to have nominations determined by a simple majority rather than a two-thirds majority. By effecting this rule change, FDR ensured that future Democratic presidential candidates would be in tune with majority party sentiment and would not have to bend to the wishes of a single bloc of delegates. Although it would be another generation before the Democratic Party would take up the cause of civil rights, the seeds of that undertaking were sown in the fight over the two-thirds rule that destroyed the South's veto power over the choice of the Democratic Party presidential nominee.

Thus, the Democratic Party became the majority party for the first time since the Civil War. It was capable of winning statewide elections in the Northeast, the industrial Midwest, and parts of the Pacific Coast as well as in the "solid" South. The only regions where it did not have a decent chance to win statewide were New England, the nonindustrial Midwest, and the Great Plains. Figures 12.6 and 12.7 show the relative party strength in both houses of Congress from 1932 to 1968 revealing the great dominance that the Democratic Party enjoyed.

FDR did not seek victory for its own sake. Heir to the Progressive legacy, he sought to exploit the Democrats' large congressional majority to erect a strong and resilient national administrative state. This state would provide on a routine and impartial basis what parties had provided on a discretionary basis. Instead of depending on party patronage, people could rely on a social security pension when they got old; unemployment insurance if they were laid off; and welfare payments if they were poor or disabled. FDR recognized that the new administrative state would weaken political parties, including the powerful one he built and led. For all his skill as a party builder, his attitude toward party was strikingly similar to Jefferson's. The New Deal Democratic Party would be a party to end party. Once the welfare state he sought to construct was fully in place, FDR believed, parties would become far less important, if not wither away.

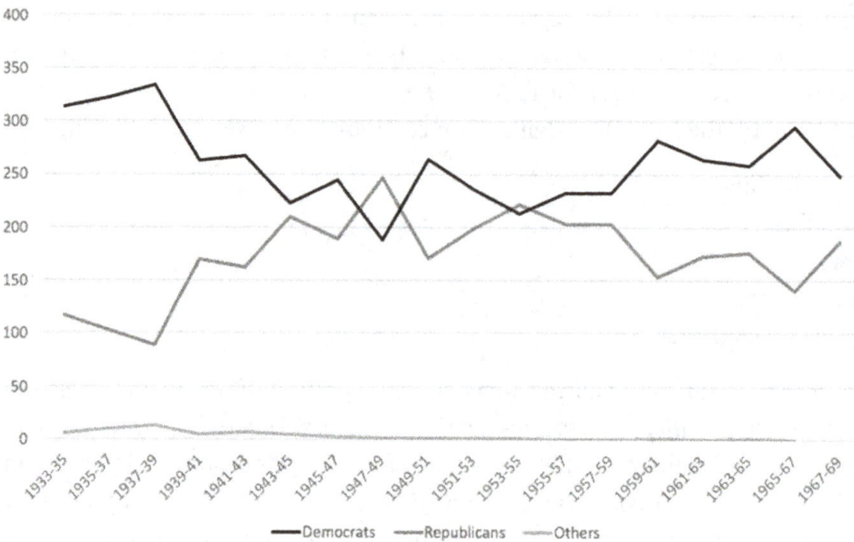

Figure 12.6. Party strength in the House, 1933–69.
Source: US House of Representatives.

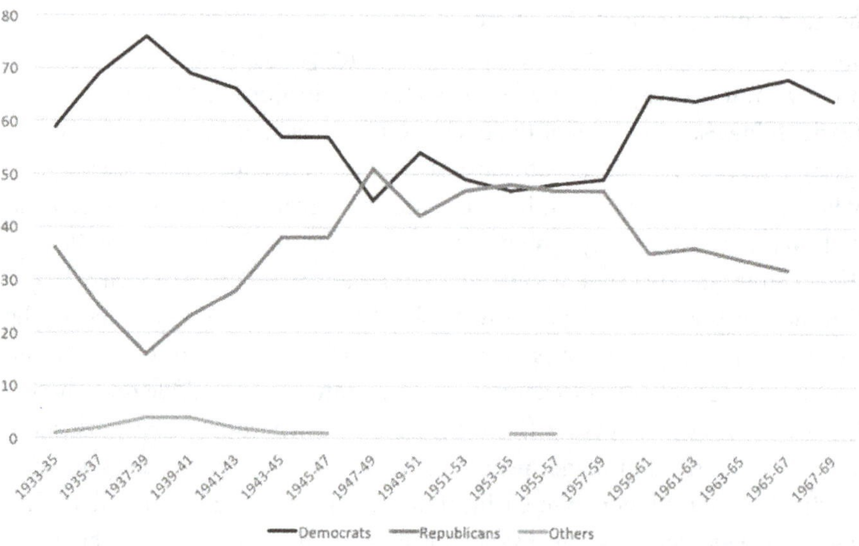

Figure 12.7. Party strength in the Senate, 1933–69.
Source: US Senate.

Postwar Reestablishment of a Competitive Party System

After World War II the party system once again became highly competitive. Both parties enjoyed great successes, staggering defeats, and internal dissension. Presidential elections swung back and forth. Since 1980 parties have frequently exchanged control of the Senate, and since 1994 this has been true of the House of Representatives as well. However, even as the parties became more competitive with one another, party patronage became less important, elections became more candidate-centered, and party loyalty declined.

Republican Resurgence

As of 1952, the Republicans had not won a presidential election in twenty-four years. They seemed on the verge of suffering the same fate as the Whigs and the Federalists. Instead, they demonstrated a resilience even more impressive than that shown by the Democratic Party in the wake of the Civil War. Since 1952, Republicans have won eight presidential elections, the Democrats six. The Republicans have never been out of the presidential office for more than eight years. The Democrats were out of office for twelve years, from 1980 until 1992. The Democrats controlled both houses of Congress from 1954 until 1980. Since 1980, Republicans have held the Senate for most of the period between 1980 and the present, and they controlled the House of Representatives from 1994 until 2006 and won it back in 2010.

Like the Democrats in 1828 and the Whigs in 1849, the Republicans revived their fortunes by running a military hero, General Dwight David Eisenhower, for president. In World War II, Eisenhower had led the greatest amphibious landing in history, D-Day. He was so popular that a group of prominent Democrats, including FDR's son James, had tried to recruit him in 1948 to replace Truman, whom they, mistakenly, deemed to be unelectable.

Eisenhower won easily in 1952 and again in 1956. He did not oppose, and thereby tacitly accepted, the key programs of the New Deal, most especially Social Security and the legitimacy of labor unions. And, he embraced Truman's cautious but firm internationalist foreign policy based on the alliance of the Western powers and resistance to Soviet expansionism. As a result, many independent-minded voters were now willing to consider voting Republican because to do so no longer threatened their economic security, protected by the welfare state, and their security against foreign threat, protected by the Atlantic Alliance. The Republican Party suffered its worst post-World War II defeat in 1964 when these moderate Eisenhower Republicans deserted the Republican candidate, Senator Barry Goldwater of Arizona, because they viewed him as an opponent of the New Deal and a foreign policy radical. However, in the very next election the Republican, Richard Nixon, recaptured the White House.

Suburbs and Sun Belt

In the first half of the twentieth century, population changes, especially increased immigration and the growth of big cities, favored the Democrats. In the second half, the two most important population trends – migration from the Northeast and Midwest to the Southeast and Southwest, and from rural and urban areas to suburbs – favored the Republicans. Most of those moving to the Sun Belt were small-town and suburban Northern Republicans. They turned states such as Utah, Colorado, and Arizona solidly Republican and gave them added congressional districts and electoral votes. Florida, Georgia, and Texas, previously solidly Democratic, became competitive two-party states. California became the largest state in the Union and therefore the greatest electoral prize. Four of the five Republicans elected president since Eisenhower – Richard Nixon, Ronald Reagan, George H. W. Bush, and George W. Bush – came from the Sun Belt states of California and Texas.

Feuding Democrats

Republican fortunes were also greatly aided by the feuding among Democrats in 1968 over Lyndon Johnson's conduct of the Vietnam War. Not since the annexation of Texas in 1844 had a foreign policy disagreement proven so divisive. For the first time, an incumbent president faced a serious challenge in presidential primaries. Senator Eugene McCarthy (D–Minnesota), ran against Johnson in the New Hampshire primary. Although Johnson narrowly prevailed, the media interpreted McCarthy's impressive showing as a serious setback for Johnson.

In the wake of this "defeat," Johnson withdrew from the race. A three-way contest ensued between Vice President Hubert Humphrey, who defended Johnson's Vietnam policy, Senator McCarthy and Senator Robert Kennedy (D–NY), who also opposed the war. McCarthy and Kennedy each won several primaries. The night he won the California primary, Kennedy was assassinated. Although Humphrey had enough delegates to ensure his nomination, many antiwar Democrats refused to endorse him or did so tepidly. Tensions were heightened by the antiwar riots during the Democratic National Convention in Chicago. The Republican candidate, Richard Nixon, profited from the image of Democratic disarray that emerged from Chicago.

In 1972, the feud among Democrats rekindled. The presidential nomination was won by a passionately antiwar candidate, Senator George McGovern of South Dakota. McGovern had chaired a commission created at the 1968 convention to rewrite the party's nominating rules to make them more democratic. The commission did so by establishing complex formulas by which state parties chose convention delegates, including requirements that the delegate slate embody the full racial and gender diversity of the party's membership. The rules also contained devices to ensure that state and local leaders could not exert the same level of influence over candidate selection that they had in the past. The rules permitted states to avoid these burdensome procedures by conducting primaries instead. A primary is an election devoted to choosing party candidates. States differed as to whether they only allowed party members to participate in the primaries or whether they allowed non-party members to participate. Some states have chosen to allow any voter, even those registered with the opposition party, to vote in the primary. McGovern's bid for the nomination was greatly assisted by the fact that he and his staff understood the rules and his rivals did not.

The rules designed to make the nominating process more open and democratic resulted in the choice of a candidate who could not obtain the support of key party leaders and coalition members. Organized labor was so offended by McGovern's antiwar stand that the American Federation of Labor – Congress of Industrial Organizations (AFL-CIO), for the first and only time since it was created, refused to endorse the Democratic nominee. Chicago mayor Richard Daley and many other party leaders extended only pro forma support. McGovern suffered the worst defeat of any modern Democratic presidential candidate. He was the first Democratic presidential candidate since the Civil War not to carry the South. Indeed, he did not win a single Southern state. In every presidential election since 1976, Republicans have won the South. In both 2000 and 2004, George W. Bush carried every Southern state.

Partisan Foreign Policy

The 1972 election proved to be a historic turning point in the relationship between party and foreign policy. Since FDR, the Democrats had been the more aggressively internationalist of the two parties. A favorite Republican slogan was "the Democrats are the party of war!" Eisenhower and Nixon fought bitter intra-party battles against isolationism. But ever since 1972, it is the Republicans who have been consistently more aggressive in prosecuting the Cold War, the First Gulf War and the War in Iraq, while the Democrats have fought bitter internal battles over freezing nuclear weapons production, the Gulf War, and the Iraq War. A majority of Democratic senators voted against the 1991 resolution endorsing the Gulf War. Although a majority of them supported the 2002 resolution endorsing the invasion of Iraq, the 2004 Democratic presidential candidate John Kerry, made opposition to the war his major campaign theme. As we discussed early in the chapter, party polarization over foreign policy continues.

Reagan

In the wake of Nixon's resignation, brought on by the revelations concerning illegal activities related to the 1972 election, the Democratic candidate, Jimmy

Carter, was victorious in 1976. But he was defeated by Ronald Reagan in 1980, the first elected president to lose reelection since Herbert Hoover in 1932. Reagan's initial victory was mainly due to Carter's unpopularity. But during his first term, he greatly improved Republican fortunes by devising a new, politically popular approach to taxing and spending. Ever since FDR, the Republicans had been divided into two economic policy factions. Moderate Republicans accepted the Keynesian economic doctrines deployed by the Democrats, meaning that they were willing to live with federal budgetary deficits in times of recession as a means of promoting economic expansion (see Chapter 5). They preferred to criticize individual Democratic spending programs rather than to attack "big government" in general. Conservative Republicans objected to deficit spending. They wanted large cuts in the federal income tax but demanded equally large cuts in the budget in order to avoid deficit.

Both Republican positions were politically problematic. The moderate approach was virtually indistinguishable from that of the Democrats, whereas the conservative formula required politically popular programs to be cut. Ronald Reagan departed from both strategies. He accepted the use of deficit spending, but only to enable tax cuts. He turned traditional conservatism on its head by first proposing tax cuts and only then asking Congress for the budget cuts to pay for them. Thus, he was able to do the politically popular thing, cut taxes, first. Although some representatives in both parties doubted the prudence of this approach, few were willing to vote against giving money back to the people. Reagan's tax cut plan of 1981 passed Congress overwhelmingly.

Reagan's subsequent proposals to cut programs did not receive the same enthusiastic reception. Although some reductions were passed, spending and revenue remained out of balance. Nonetheless, by putting tax cuts ahead of spending cuts, Reagan had found a successful formula for gaining political popularity while halting the expansion of federal domestic spending. Deficit pressure was insufficient to reduce the budget, but for the next decade it did restrain additional domestic spending.

The Republicans also gained public support by attacking the Democrats for being soft on crime and welfare. Until the 1960s, crime was considered to be primarily a local problem. But President Johnson and many Democratic mayors and governors responded to the mid-1960s urban riots with what voters perceived as appeasement. This perception enabled Republicans to turn the crime issue into a national, partisan one, identifying themselves as the law-and-order party.

Federal welfare payments to single parent families with dependent children had been relatively uncontroversial since their inception during the New Deal. But during the 1960s and 1970s, skyrocketing levels of illegitimate births and crime waves in welfare-dependent neighborhoods made welfare policy unpopular. Because this policy was identified with the Democrats, it provided an inviting target for the Republicans. Strong opposition to crime and to generous welfare benefits enabled the Republicans to regain the status they had enjoyed in the mid and late nineteenth century as the party of hard work, piety, and middle-class virtue.

In summary, the factors contributing to the Republican resurgence are as follows:

- Popularity of Eisenhower
- Divisiveness of Vietnam War
- McGovern candidacy
- Reagan tax cuts
- Growing salience of crime and welfare

Sources of Party Decline

Republican electoral successes stretching from the 1950s to the 1980s did not restore parties to their previous position of power and strength. As the chapter has already noted, the advent of party primaries weakened party unity. Also, civil service reform greatly diminished the number of jobs that victorious parties could dispense. Patronage powers did not entirely disappear. Local probate judges, for example, retained the discretion to choose which lawyers to assign to lucrative cases. Highway officials kept considerable freedom in choosing companies to perform profitable highway construction jobs. But the decline in the quantity of patronage sapped party leaders of a critical tool for maintaining party discipline and cohesion.

Television diminished the importance of traditional methods of political campaigning that had been the province of local parties – door-to-door canvassing, rallies, and get-out-the-vote drives. The direct communication between politicians and the public that mass media enabled meant that party was no longer a mediator between the two. FDR proved a master at using radio to speak intimately to voters; he encouraged them to think of these one-way discussions as "fireside chats." Television connected a face to the candidate's voice and increased the feeling of connectedness between candidate and citizen. The televised presidential debates between John F. Kennedy and Richard Nixon in 1960 demonstrated the power of this new medium. Voters were struck by the contrast between his grizzled, harsh face and Kennedy's handsome and serene visage. Kennedy was a Democrat, but the capacity to look good on television and speak with warmth and conviction would benefit candidates from both parties, especially the former movie actor Ronald Reagan, the magnetic, empathetic Bill Clinton, and the dignified Barack Obama.

Changes in campaign organizations further weakened the connection between candidates and voters. Since FDR, presidential candidates had increasingly come to rely on their own personal campaign organizations, which made them less dependent on their parties. This trend culminated in 1972, when Richard Nixon staked his campaign fortunes almost completely on his personal organization – the Committee to Re-elect the President (CREEP) – rather than relying on the existing Republican Party organization. CREEP raised unprecedented sums of money, making the 1972 Nixon campaign by far the most expensive up to that time. As we discussed earlier, CREEP was also deeply implicated in the Watergate scandal. The Democratic Party that Van Buren created in the late 1820s demonstrated how party could tame presidential ambition. The unscrupulous behavior of CREEP showed that displacing party with a candidate-dominated campaign organization could give full vent to overweening presidential ambition.

"New Democrats"

In 1992, as in 1912, the Democrats were able to regain the presidency after a period of Republican dominance in an election that featured a third-party candidate. Like TR, Ross Perot concentrated his attacks on the Republican incumbent. Perot promised to eliminate the deficit Reagan had created and George H. W. Bush had perpetuated. He garnered 19 percent of the vote, the best showing by a third-party candidate since 1912.

Like Woodrow Wilson, Clinton took heed of the third candidate's strong showing and shifted his rhetoric and policy proposals accordingly. He pledged to reduce the budget deficit. He refused to support expensive programs despite their strong appeal to key Democratic Party constituents. The crucial exception to this policy – healthcare reform – was defeated in Congress, followed by the Republican sweep of the 1994 elections (see Chapter 7), giving them control of both House and Senate for the first time since 1954. Then Clinton returned to the centrist themes and policies he touted in his run for the presidency. The combination of spending restraint and a strong economy enabled a steady decline in the deficit. By late in Clinton's second term, there was actually a budgetary surplus.

Clinton declared himself to be a "New Democrat." Like Reagan, he recognized that his party could not thrive without changing its approach. Not only did he strive for a balanced budget, he also aggressively altered his party's posture on welfare and crime. As governor of Arkansas, he rejected clemency appeals from prisoners condemned to die. As president, he sponsored legislation providing federal subsidies to cities and towns to hire additional police. He promised to "end welfare as we know it" and signed the Republican-sponsored welfare reform bill, even though it was much harsher to recipients than his proposal.

Clinton's reversal of Democratic positions on budget balancing, crime, and welfare enabled him to recover from the 1994 congressional election debacle and win reelection in 1996. Deprived of their most popular issues, Republicans made no gains in the 1998 and 2000 elections despite the scandals that plagued

Clinton's second term. As of 2000, the partisan balance was the most even in all of American history.

Polarization and Pendulum Swings

The 2000 election ushered in a period of greater partisan polarization and pendulum swings in the fortunes of the two parties. Between 2000 and 2016 each party held the presidency for eight years. Each enjoyed control of both the presidency and both houses of Congress for only brief periods: the Republicans for four years and the Democrats for only two. Thus, most of the time during this sixteen-year period the government was divided. During the Clinton years divided government had resulted in a good deal of compromise. But during this later period, divided government accentuated party polarization. The Republicans lost control of both houses of Congress in 2006 largely on the basis of opposition to the War in Iraq. Nonetheless, in 2007 President Bush embarked upon a significant escalation of that war. For the last six years of the Obama presidency, the two parties could not find common ground on any major policy issue, the most rancorous of all involving failure to reform the immigration system and to provide remedies to problems facing the healthcare reform program that the original Affordable Care Act had overlooked. As we discussed in the presidency chapter, once having lost control of Congress, Obama issued executive orders to obtain policy changes that Congress would not approve. This aggressive assertion of executive power served to further heighten the level of partisan rancor present as the 2016 presidential election season approached.

Looking Forward

Despite the inroads of civil service reform, mass media, and campaign finance limits, the current party system still performs some of the critical political functions that Martin Van Buren expected it to perform when he championed parties in the 1830s. It encourages political accountability. Because there are only two major parties, voters can readily replace the "in" party with a coherent organization of "outs". The two-party system also simplifies and structures voter choice. The typical Republican candidate has very different opinions about a whole host of issues including abortion, guns, taxes, environmental regulation, relations between church and state, and education than does the Democratic counterpart. Therefore, voters can rather easily distinguish between candidates based on their party label.

But, parties no longer perform other critical functions that Van Buren claimed for them. He saw party as a device for restraining presidential ambition. But party leaders do not now exert much influence on the actual choice of presidential candidates. Therefore, after the election, the winner is not much beholden to party chieftains. Indeed, the roles are reversed; it is the president who anoints the national party chair and dominates the life of the national party. The two parties are no longer primarily state and local organizations who come together in convention once every four years to choose a president. Now, the national organization of the president's party is mostly just another tool for raising money and promoting the president's agenda and his prestige with the voters.

Van Buren conceived of parties as a means for overcoming sectionalism. Ever since the Virginian Thomas Jefferson chose the New Yorker Aaron Burr as his running mate, parties sought to encourage national ties and feelings. When they failed to do so in the 1850s, there was civil war. As this chapter mentions, each party is becoming more dominant in particular regions; the Republicans in the South and West, and the Democrats in the Northeast and along the Pacific coast. Fewer states remain competitive between them. The national parties are no longer effective agents for encouraging national unity.

In Van Buren's day parties were essentially local in nature. The association of local parties at the state level and the association of state parties at the national level mirrored the Constitution's federal structure providing a second important bulwark against oppressive central authority. Parties are no longer deeply grounded locally, so they cannot play this important role. Equally troubling, they no longer command the loyalty of a very large fraction of the people, and the nonparty fraction is growing. Party once provided a means for people to escape the chains of private self-absorption and reach out into the public realm, but it is less and less able to do so.

Parties arose to redress key threats to democracy and liberty that the Constitution could not cope with by itself. Restraining presidential ambition, reducing regional tensions and combating privatism remain as critical as ever to the wellbeing of the republic. Looking forward, the great challenge for the parties is to recapture the capacity to perform those vital tasks.

CRITICAL THINKING QUESTION

Do you identify with a political party? If so, why? If not, why not?

CHAPTER SUMMARY

Contemporary portrait:

* The Republican coalition is, to a large extent, a mirror image of the contemporary Democratic one.
* The greatest shift in political support for the two parties in recent decades is that of whites in the South from the Democrats to the Republicans.

* Major changes in the make-up of the party coalitions have taken place as a result of the increasingly political importance of matters that previously were not highly politicized – marriage, sexual orientation, guns, and religiosity.
* The regulations and procedures that govern elections embody the full complexity inherent in Federalism. All levels of government are involved in a manner that continually causes them to intersect and intermingle.
* Statewide primaries and caucuses have replaced the party nominating conventions as the key venues for choosing presidential candidates.

Critical choice: founding a party and a party system:

* The Framers of the Constitution were staunch opponents of political parties.
* The early adoption of winner-take-all elections for Congress and for presidential electors greatly favored the rise of a two-party system.
* The first political party, the Republican Party, was launched by Jefferson and Madison to oppose Alexander Hamilton's ambitious national government program.
* The total dominance of a single party, the Republicans, led to a serious decline in the quality of national government and the rise of regional political differences.
* The party system arose from the effort to elect Andrew Jackson in 1828 and the effort in 1836 to defeat him. It also served to tame presidential ambition, develop national identity, reinforce the decentralized nature of government, and foster attachment to political life.

Absorbing shocks to the party system:

* The slavery issue destroyed the Whigs and provided the focal point for the creation of the Republican Party.
* The post-Civil War resurgence of the Democrats owed much to their ability to obtain the support of immigrants who were arriving in the big cities in great numbers. In return, the urban Democratic organizations improved the immigrants' economic lot and fostered immigrant assimilation.
* In order to preempt the Populists, the Democrats began to advocate the use of national power for democratic purposes.

The Progressive attack on parties:

* The Progressives sought to undermine the strength of political parties by replacing patronage based hiring with merit based hiring, switching from partisan to nonpartisan elections and using primary elections to choose candidates.

Forging the New Deal coalition:

* The party coalition assembled by FDR provided the political energy that fueled the New Deal and ushered in the longest period of one-party dominance in American history.

The postwar reestablishment of a competitive party system:

* The resurgence of the Republicans began with Eisenhower's election as president in 1952.
* The two most important population trends of the second half of the twentieth century – migration from the Northeast and Midwest to the Southeast and Southwest, and from rural and urban areas to suburbs – favored the Republicans.
* Republican fortunes were also greatly aided by the feuding among Democrats in 1968 over Lyndon Johnson's conduct of the Vietnam War and the unpopularity of George McGovern's insurgent candidacy in 1972.
* In addition to the loss of patronage, the other key contributors to the decline of political parties were the direct access of candidates to voters via television and the rise of candidate controlled campaign organizations.
* Ronald Reagan greatly improved Republican fortunes by devising a new, politically popular approach to taxing and spending. He turned traditional conservatism on its head by first proposing tax cuts and only then asking Congress for the budget cuts to pay for them.
* Bill Clinton's reversal of unpopular Democratic positions on budget balancing, crime, and welfare enabled him to recover from the 1994 congressional election debacle and win reelection in 1996.
* The 2000 election ushered in a period of greater partisan polarization and pendulum swings in the fortunes of the two parties. Between 2000 and 2016 each party held the presidency for eight years. Each enjoyed control of both the presidency and both houses of Congress for only brief periods, the Republicans for four years and the Democrats for only two.

SUGGESTED READINGS

Aldrich, John. *Why Parties?* University of Chicago Press, 1995.

Burnham, Walter Dean. *Critical Elections and the Mainsprings of American Politics.* New York: W. W. Norton, 1971.

Chambers, William Nisbet, and Walter Dean Burnham. *The American Party Systems: Stages of Political Development.* New York: Oxford University Press, 1975.

Epstein, Leon. *Parties in the American Mold.* Madison: University of Wisconsin Press, 1986.

Fiorina, Morris. *Divided Government.* Boston: Allyn & Bacon, 1996.

Green, Donald, Bradley Palmquist, and Eric Schickler. *Partisan Hearts and Minds: Political Parties and the Social Identities of Voters.* New Haven, CT: Yale University Press, 2002.

Hershey, Marjorie Random, and Paul Allen Beck. *Party Politics in America*, 10th edn. New York: Longman, 2002.

Key, V. O. *Politics, Parties, and Pressure Groups*, 5th edn. New York: Thomas Y. Crowell, 1964.

Reichley, A. James. *The Life of the Parties*. Lanham, MD: Rowman & Littlefield, 2000.

Schattschneider, E. E. *Party Government*. New York: Holt, Rinehart & Winston, 1995.

Wattenberg, Martin P. *The Decline of American Political Parties, 1952–1996*. Cambridge, MA: Harvard University Press, 1998.

13 Campaigns, Elections, and Media

CHAPTER OVERVIEW

This chapter focuses on:

- **A contemporary portrait of primary and general election campaigns that focuses on the 2016 presidential election. It explores its similarities to and differences from previous campaigns and elections.**
- **The democratization of the electorate that has taken place over time.**
- **The impact of radio and television.**
- **The critical choice to pass the 1965 Voting Rights Act.**
- **The crises of legitimacy posed by contested presidential elections and the end of the two-term tradition.**
- **The change from party-centered to candidate-centered campaigns.**

On September 26, 1960, John F. Kennedy and Richard M. Nixon took part in the first televised debate between rival presidential candidates. It was watched by as many as 70 million viewers. Nixon, who had already had a successful career as a congressman, senator and vice president, was known to be a skilled debater. Kennedy was younger and less experienced. However, a campaign debate is not really a debate at all. It is not about scoring points but rather about who makes the better impression on the voters. Here Nixon was at a disadvantage. A month before, he had banged his knee against a car door. The knee became infected and he had to be hospitalized. When he came out of the hospital two weeks later, having lost twenty pounds, he looked pale and sickly. On the day of the debate he banged his knee again and was in pain during the event. Although he was very articulate in the debate, he looked tired and drained. Although he had shaved before the event, his beard grew back so quickly that he looked unshaven. By contrast, Kennedy was well tanned, buoyant, and healthy looking. Throughout the debate he faced straight into the camera, giving the impression that he was speaking directly to each individual viewer. His steady gaze exuded calm and serenity. Nixon made the mistake of looking away from the camera at whichever reporter was asking him a question. Thus, he gave the impression that he was avoiding eye contact with the viewers. The TV audience declared Kennedy the victor. Shortly after winning the election, Kennedy acknowledged the crucial role the debate had played in his victory. "It was the TV more than anything else that turned the tide" (www.time.com/time/nation/article/0,8599,2021078,00.html).

As the Kennedy–Nixon debate illustrates, events that occur during the presidential campaign matter. They may even prove decisive. The previous chapter stressed the role of party identification as the primary means by which people orient themselves in politics. And, as Chapter 11 showed, those who identify with a party consistently vote for the candidate of that party. This trend has become even more pronounced in recent presidential elections. But party identification alone cannot account for election outcomes. Since 1950, the Democrats have held a consistent advantage in party identification and yet they have lost more presidential elections than they have won (www.people-press.org/interactives/party-id-trend/). Only once during that period, in 1990, did the Republicans even succeed in tying the Democrats in terms of party identification. As Figure 13.1 shows, a very large fraction of the electorate does not choose to identify with any party. Almost as many call themselves independents as call themselves Republicans. Thus, campaigns matter even if the majority of voters have made up their minds beforehand.

This chapter examines presidential campaigns and elections. The contemporary portrait describes the rules by which elections are carried out and the events that dominated both the 2016 presidential general election and the candidate selection process that preceded it. It also analyzes the results of the election, including a consideration of voter turnout. It provides critical background for understanding contemporary elections by tracing the democratization of the electorate and the resolution of challenges to the legitimacy of the result that presidential elections have encountered.

A Contemporary Portrait

Candidate Selection

The presidential candidate selection process looks very different when it is focused on defeating the opposition than when it is dominated by internal feuds. In ordinary times, a very strong consideration in the selection process is determining who has the best chance of winning in the fall. However, every so often the deepest divisions take place within, not between, the two parties. An insurgency arises that seeks to radically change what the party stands for. If the insurgency is successful, key segments of the party may either take the radical

Trends in Party Identification, 1939-2014

For more than 70 years, with few exceptions, more Americans have identified as Democrats than Republicans. But the share of independents, which surpassed the percentages of either Democrats or Republicans several years ago, continues to increase. Currently, 39% Americans identify as independents, 32% as Democrats and 23% as Republicans. This is the highest percentage of independents in more than 75 years of public opinion polling. **Report:** A Deep Dive Into Party Affiliation

% of Americans who say they are ...

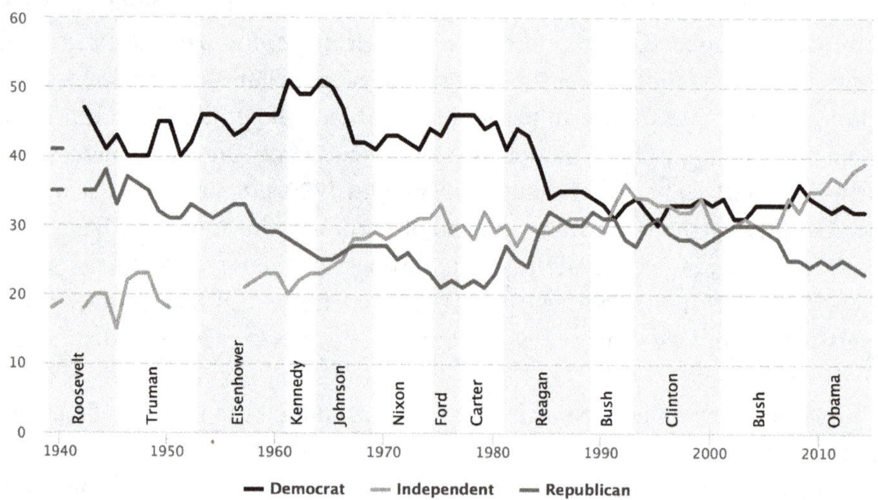

Note: 1939-1989 yearly averages from the Gallup Organization interactive website. 1990-2014 yearly totals from Pew Research Center aggregate files. Based on the general public. Data unavailable for 1941. Independent data unavailable for 1951-1956.

Figure 13.1. Party ID chart.
Source: Pew Research Center.

step of openly opposing the candidate selected or, at best, provide only perfunctory support for that person. Chapter 11 discussed the previous party insurgencies that took place in 1824, 1896, 1912, 1964, and 1972.

The 2016 presidential candidate selection process was unique in that *both* parties experienced significant insurgencies and the Republican insurgent, Donald Trump, won both the nomination and the general election. The Democratic insurgent, Bernie Sanders, lost but his unexpectedly strong showing and the great loyalty he inspired enabled him to exert a significant influence on the party platform and pushed the nominee, Hillary Clinton, to back away from positions she had previously held in favor of the issue positions he was advocating. Insurgents take a very different approach to securing the nomination than their opponents do. Therefore a contemporary portrait of presidential candidate selection, focused on 2016, must pay attention both to the strategies and tactics employed by the noninsurgents, approaches that mirrored what their predecessors had done in previous elections, and those novel approaches taken by the two insurgents.

The Invisible Primary

The selection process has distinct two phases. The first phase, often called the invisible primary, has no official beginning. In reality, it starts as soon as the previous presidential election is over. During this phase, would-be candidates seek to rally sufficient support to enable them to mount a viable primary campaign. Those hopefuls who already enjoy a good deal of name recognition and support seek to raise it to such a high level as to project an aura of invincibility sufficient to discourage others from entering the race. In 2016, Hillary Clinton so dominated the invisible primary that she was able to keep Vice President Joseph Biden, perceived to be her strongest rival, from running against her. According to the political analyst Nathan Silver, she was far more successful in obtaining the endorsements of prominent elected officials than any of her predecessors dating back to 1984. Indeed, she was four times more successful than her husband, Bill (http://projects.fivethirtyeight.com/2016-endorsement-primary). Clinton's great success was not sufficient to prevent Bernie Sanders from running. Sanders did not need to "win" the invisible primary because he was planning to run an insurgent campaign in which he would criticize the very "fat cats" who were contributing mightily to Hillary Clinton. Despite his lack of press coverage, he was able to garner sufficient support among small donors and among highly educated and energetic young people to enable him to mount a credible primary campaign.

During the invisible primary, would-be candidates seek to burnish their public image. They give speeches and appear on TV talkshows in order to demonstrate that they have the talent and the knowledge worthy of a successful candidate. These efforts are aimed less at the general public than at influential opinion makers. The goal is to win the backing of party leaders and elected officials, prominent media figures, and, perhaps most importantly, potential donors. The hopefuls appear at endless rounds of receptions, cocktail parties, and other events at which they meet with this same array of politically powerful people in an effort to curry favor. They strive to provide a convincing answer to the question, why me?

The 2016 Republican invisible primary proved indecisive. No single hopeful emerged as the consensus choice of party insiders. Rather, a number of candidates acquired enough in the way of endorsements by important Republicans, favorable media commentary, and sufficient pledges of financial support to encourage them to enter the primaries.

Table 13.1. 2016 presidential election results.

Presidential candidate	Vice presidential candidate	Political party	Popular vote	Percentage
Donald J. Trump	Michael Pence	Republican	62,979,879	45.95
Hillary Clinton	Tim Kaine	Democratic	65,844,954	48.04
Gary Johnson	William F. Weld	Libertarian	4,488,919	3.28
Jill Stein	Ajamu Baraka	Green	1,457,044	1.06

Source: Brookings Institute.

Two aspiring candidates, Ted Cruz and Donald Trump, did not follow the conventional invisible primary script. Although Cruz was a US senator from the second-largest state, Texas, dating back to his first days in office he had adopted the posture of an insurgent. He identified himself with an insurgent movement, the Tea Party (see Chapter 14) that viewed the Republican congressional leadership as insufficiently conservative on matters of policy and insufficiently bold and steadfast in its opposition to the Obama administration. His filibuster obstructing the confirmation of CIA Director John Brennan provoked Senator John McCain (R–Arizona) the Republican Party's 2008 presidential candidate, to call him "a wacko bird." He further alienated his fellow Republican senators by fomenting a sixteen-day shutdown of funding for the federal government. They felt that his effort to force the Obama administration to defund its healthcare reform as the price of restoring funding was mere "grandstanding." They resented his effort to curry favor with Tea Party supporters at the cost of bringing the government to a halt and making the Republican Party appear irresponsible in the eyes of the general public. When he embarked on his candidacy he made no effort to curry favor with established Republican leaders or with the type of donor who had contributed to recent past Republican nominees John McCain and Mitt Romney. Instead, he reveled in his reputation as a rebel and sought support among influential commentators and donors who shared his rebellious attitude. Cruz was especially successful in winning the support of leaders of many of the most important evangelical Christian organizations.

Cruz's insurgency was in the tradition of the two previous major Republican insurgencies, Barry Goldwater's in 1964 and Ronald Reagan's in 1976 and 1980. Like them, he claimed that the party establishment was not conservative enough in its principles and was too ready to make deals with the Democrats. But Cruz failed. The nomination was won by a much more unconventional insurgent, Donald Trump. Trump's campaign slogan "Make American Great Again" echoed Ronald Reagan's patriotic message. But Trump's proposals for bringing about such a restoration were radically different. Reagan was a proponent of free trade. Trump opposed the free-trade agreement known as the Trans-Pacific Parternship (TPP) signed by the Obama administration as well as the 1994 free-trade agreement with Mexico and Canada called the North American Free Trade Agreement (NAFTA), which Republicans had overwhelmingly supported. Reagan had liberalized immigration policy; Trump proposed severely curtailing immigration of Muslims and building a wall on the Mexican border to keep illegal immigrants from entering the United States.

All previous party insurgents had been seasoned politicians. Trump had never run for public office or held a government post, and he boasted of not being a politician. Central to his campaign was his status as a businessman. He claimed that the skills he had acquired in business were actually more important for success as president than those one learned during a political career. He especially stressed his deal-making abilities. He did not apologize for engaging in cutthroat practices such as paying suppliers less than they were due or laying off workers. Rather, he bragged that these examples demonstrated his toughness.

Trump's unique attributes coupled with his unconventional strategy for winning the primaries enabled him to ignore key aspects of the invisible primary. Because, like Cruz, he was greeted with hostility by party leaders and elected officials, he made no effort to court them. He received virtually no endorsements from them. Rather, he treated their contempt as a mark in his favor because it showed that he was not beholden to them. Because his plan for the primaries depended on access to free media, his campaign expenses would be small. He would pay those costs himself and thus he did not need to court campaign donors. As of December 2015, Trump had spent a meager $217,000 on television advertising, whereas Jeb Bush had spent 29 million; Rubio 10.6 million, and John Kasich 8 million. Nonetheless, Trump had already developed a sizeable lead in the polls.

Trump made extensive use of social media to reach out to voters. His Twitter account had 16 million followers (www.weeklystandard.com/tweeter-in-chief/article/2005544). That number vastly underestimates the impact of his tweets since so many of the most controversial were picked up and reported in the mass media. He was not the first presidential candidate to post on Facebook and Twitter, but he exploited these media in a new and apparently successful way. Whereas other candidates, including Hillary Clinton, used social media to convey information about their candidacies and policies, Trump used it to show his unconventionality. His tweets attacked his opponents, celebrated his accomplishments, and offered his personal opinions about whatever subjects interested him at that moment. Although some voters were undoubtedly put off by the venom and vulgarity of some of the tweets, to others they showed that he would say what was really on his mind, unhampered by "political correctness." Political correctness referred to the unwillingness of politicians to tell the truth about matters they considered to be too sensitive to be discussed honestly. For example, Trump attacked the Obama administration for refusing to admit that terrorism was linked to radical Islam.

The Campaign Team

Another crucial aspect of the invisible primary is the assembling of a team to perform all the diverse activities a campaign requires: preparing and adjusting campaign strategy, developing issue positions, polling, managing the candidate's schedule, raising funds, creating advertisements and other marketing tools, communicating with the media, and coordinating all these various functions. The team also consists of operatives put in charge of the key primary battlegrounds. Here again, the conventional candidates operated very differently from the insurgents. Hillary Clinton's team was dominated by seasoned professionals, most of whom had either worked in her husband's administration, worked in her previous campaigns, served in high posts in the Obama administration, or in two or even all three of these roles. Jeb Bush, former Republican governor of Florida, son of president George H. W. Bush and brother of president George W. Bush, put together a similar sort of campaign team. His senior staff included a number of veterans of his father's and/or brother's presidential campaigns and administrations. By contrast, the Democratic insurgent Bernie Sanders's senior staff was composed of operatives who had never taken part in a presidential campaign. Only the senior advisor, Tad Devine, had extensive experience at the presidential level. Donald Trump's approach to campaign staffing was far more unusual. Prior to the primaries he did not bother to put together a full-fledged campaign team. He did not need to hire experts in media, advertising, policy research, or grassroots organizing because he was not going to invest heavily in the areas in which they specialized.

The failure of the invisible primary to reduce the number of Republican candidates meant that it was extremely difficult for them to distinguish themselves from one another no matter how many speeches they gave and how many ads they placed on TV. The same difficulty afflicted them in the debates that preceded the primaries. Only Trump succeeded in setting himself apart by unleashing a continual barrage of brash and inflammatory statements during the debates and on the campaign trail. These pronouncements were widely condemned. However, precisely because they were so colorful and controversial they enabled him to dominate media coverage and thus acquire a stature the others lacked. For example, in June 2015 he said that Mexican illegal immigrants were "bringing drugs, they're bringing crime, they're rapists, and some, I assume, are good people." In July, he declared that the 2012 Republican candidate John McCain, who had spent more than five years in a Vietnamese prison camp, was "not a war hero." In December, in the aftermath of a terrorist attack in San Bernadino, California, that killed fourteen people, he called for a complete ban on Muslims entering the United States. Having succeeded in dominating the news cycle, he would occasionally back off from some of his extreme statements. But they were so evocative and passionate that they seemed to convince a large number of Republicans that only he had the strength and audacity to defeat Hillary Clinton and undo the damage done by the Obama administration.

The Democratic candidate debates likewise worked to the advantage of the insurgent. Despite his relative obscurity, the debate stage accorded Sanders an opportunity to confront the front runner as an equal. It also provided him with a wide audience for the issue stands he took on such matters as foreign trade, energy, and healthcare that were popular with hardcore Democrats. Clinton's positions on these questions were more moderate. Such stands might prove more popular to the general election electorate but were less pleasing to those most likely to vote in a Democratic primary or attend a caucus. Thus, despite her far greater success in gaining endorsements, raising money, and assembling a seasoned campaign team, Clinton did not emerge from the invisible primary with a decisive edge over Sanders.

Primaries, Caucuses, and Super Delegates

The next phase of the campaign consisted of the actual contests, primaries, and caucuses that would determine the nomination. Both parties had adopted rules that allowed states to choose among those two alternatives. A primary resembles a general election but with two important differences. States can decide whether to have closed primaries in which only voters registered with a given party can vote. Or, they can have open primaries, which allow registered voters to choose which party primary to participate in. A third option is a semi-closed primary, which limits voters registered with a party to vote only in that party's primary but also allows voters to register as unaffiliated. Unaffiliated voters may vote in the primary of their choice. Figures 13.2 and 13.3 show for each party which states adopt closed, semi-closed, and open rules for participation in primary voting.

The two parties differ regarding how delegates to the national convention are to be apportioned. The Republicans allow states to choose between a winner-take-all system that awards all the state's delegates to the candidate with the most votes or to award delegates in proportion to the votes received. States can also create a mix of the two approaches by apportioning some delegates to the candidate with the most votes statewide and some delegates to the winner of each congressional district or by supplementing the proportional allocation with a bonus to those candidates who get above a certain threshold of votes. Figure 13.4 provides a map showing how different states allocate delegates in Republican primaries.

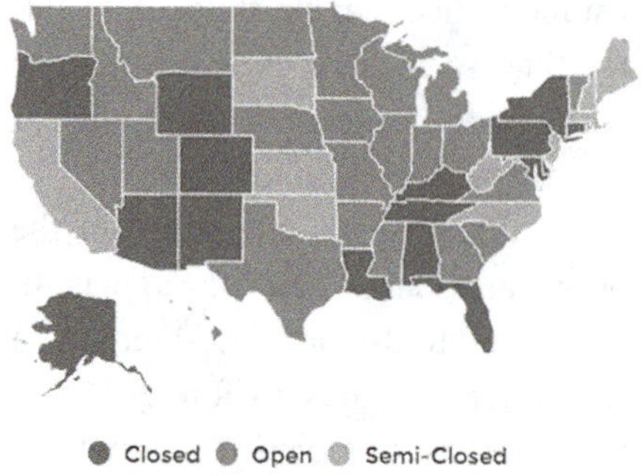

Figure 13.2. Who can vote in presidential primaries (Democratic)?
Source: FairVote.

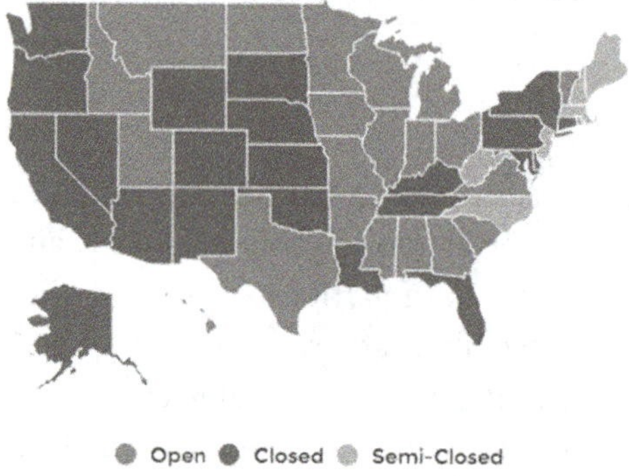

Figure 13.3. Who can vote in presidential primaries (Republican)?
Source: FairVote.

The Democrats require delegates to be awarded proportionally. In addition to the delegates chosen by voters, the Democrats, but not the Republicans, have created another delegate category, so-called "super delegates." Super delegates are not required to pledge themselves to any particular candidate. They consist of Democratic governors, House members, and senators; current and former Democratic presidents, vice presidents, and congressional leaders and designated members of the Democratic National Committee. Of the 4,763 delegates who chose the candidate, 712 were super delegates, approximately 30 percent of the number needed to win the nomination (www.pewresearch.org/fact-tank/2016/05/05/who-are-the-democratic-superdelegates/).

The super delegate category was put into effect in 1984. Its purpose was to give more power to party professionals and elected officials to counterbalance what many in the party had come to consider the excessive weight given to the party grassroots. Later, this chapter will discuss the intense party faction fights that arose during the 1968 election and carried over into the disastrous defeat of the

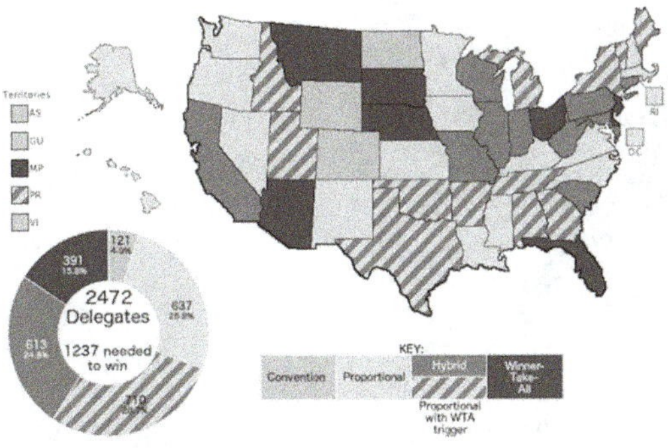

Figure 13.4. 2016 Republican delegate allocation rules by state.
Source: Frontloading HQ.

Democratic presidential candidate, George McGovern in 1972. The creation of super delegates was a delayed response to those events.

Both parties allow states to adopt a caucus rather than a primary as the way to choose delegates. A primary resembles an election in that voters go to designated precincts and cast ballots for their preferred candidate. A caucus consists of meetings held throughout the state in which local people sit down in a room and first discuss the candidates before choosing delegates from among themselves. Those chosen then attend a state convention to choose delegates to the national convention. The rival candidates contest the caucus states just as they do the primary states striving to mobilize their supporters to attend the caucuses. Because attending a caucus is so much more trouble than voting in a primary, the caucus system benefits candidates who have very committed followers. For example, in 2008, Hillary Clinton won most of the primaries but Barack Obama defeated her so resoundingly in the caucus states that he prevailed. He was able to arouse an intensity of support that she could not match despite her greater overall popularity. In 2016, Sanders likewise performed far better in caucus than in primary states.

States set the dates for their primaries and caucuses but in an attempt to spread the primaries over several months the national party committee penalizes those states that try to move up their primary dates if the committee deems that such a move damages the selection process. In 2016, those states that moved up their primary dates without the party's permission suffered a reduction in the number of votes they cast at the convention.

The early primaries are held in relatively small states. These smaller arenas are supposed to give lesser-known, less well-funded candidates a chance to establish themselves. Most states hold their primaries and caucuses in March. A key event known as Super Tuesday is the date on which the greatest number of states conduct their primaries or caucuses. A candidate who does poorly on Super Tuesday has great difficultly continuing to compete. On Super Tuesday

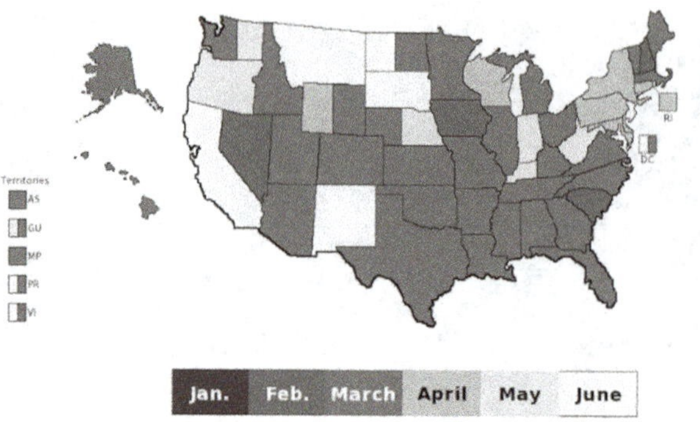

Figure 13.5. 2016 primary calendar map.
Source: Frontloading HQ.

2016, both Republicans and Democrats held primaries or caucuses in Alabama, Arkansas, Georgia, Massachusetts, Minnesota, Oklahoma, Tennessee, Texas, Vermont, and Virginia. Figure 13.5 provides a map of the 2016 presidential primary calendar.

The Primary and Caucus Results

The sequence of primaries and caucuses benefited the Democratic insurgent, Bernie Sanders. The very first, in Iowa, was a caucus. The intensity of support for his insurgency enabled him to score a virtual tie with Clinton, garnering 21 of the 44 delegates at stake. The next contest was a primary but it was held in another small state, New Hampshire, which has a history of strong showing by insurgents dating back to Eugene McCarthy's 1968 challenge to the incumbent president, Lyndon Johnson. Sanders won it by a resounding margin, garnering 60.4 percent of the vote to Clinton's mere 38 percent. These results demonstrated that the Sanders insurgency had real support and would have to be taken seriously. Clinton began to develop a decisive lead on Super Tuesday when she won eight of the twelve contests at stake. Sanders went on to win many caucuses and some primaries. But Clinton won in most of the heavily populated states including the nine largest. Nonetheless, Sanders carried on his campaign until after Clinton had won a majority of delegates. He did not concede until July 12, 2016, two weeks before the Democratic National Convention.

On the Republican side, Trump was able to generate both the intensity of support needed to do well in caucuses and the breadth of support needed to prevail in primaries. The only large state primaries he lost were Texas and Ohio, each of which was the home state of a rival. Texas Senator Ted Cruz won Texas and Ohio Governor John Kasich won Ohio. In the early going Trump did not win many of the contests decisively. For example, in New Hampshire he only got 35.3 percent of the vote. But the opposition vote was scattered among his numerous rivals. The second place finisher, John Kasich, won only 15.3 percent of the vote. In the third contest, South Carolina, Trump likewise obtained only about a third of the vote but the second place finisher, Mario Rubio, garnered less than a quarter of the vote. The same trend continued on Super Tuesday, when Trump won most of the primaries but only came close to winning a majority of the vote in Massachusetts. It is conceivable that if his four leading opponents – Kasich, Rubio, Bush, and Cruz – could have agreed to coalesce around a single anti-Trump candidate, Trump might have been defeated. But each of them proved far more committed to winning themselves than in forging an anti-Trump coalition. Only Jeb Bush pulled out before Super Tuesday. Marco Rubio withdrew in mid-March after losing his home state, Florida, to Trump. By that time Trump had developed sufficient momentum that he was able to defeat both Cruz and Kasich in most primaries and caucuses. By April, he was winning absolute majorities in many of the remaining contests, and despite continued efforts by prominent Republicans who were unyielding in their opposition to him, he was so far ahead in the delegate count that he could not be stopped.

Both candidates announced their choice of vice presidential running mate prior to the party convention. The Clinton campaign chose Tim Kaine, a senator from Virginia. The Trump campaign chose Michael Pence, governor of Indiana. Each had strategic reasons for making their choice. Virginia was a key battleground state and therefore the choice of a popular senator from there might well enhance Clinton's chances of carrying it. Trump had no governmental experience and therefore Pence's background as both a governor and a former congressmen was especially valuable to him. In addition, Pence had close ties Christian evangelicals and could serve as a valuable link between Trump and that vital element of the Republican coalition.

The Party Conventions

The party conventions were both held in July 2016. In the past, so many delegates came to the convention uncommitted to a particular candidate that the choice of candidate was actually made at that time. But in more recent times the overwhelming number of delegates have been chosen in primaries. It became possible for a candidate to amass a majority of delegates before the convention took place. Indeed, the Republicans have not experienced a contested convention since 1976. The year 1984 was the last time the leading Democrat came to the convention with less than a majority of delegates. Since both Clinton and Trump

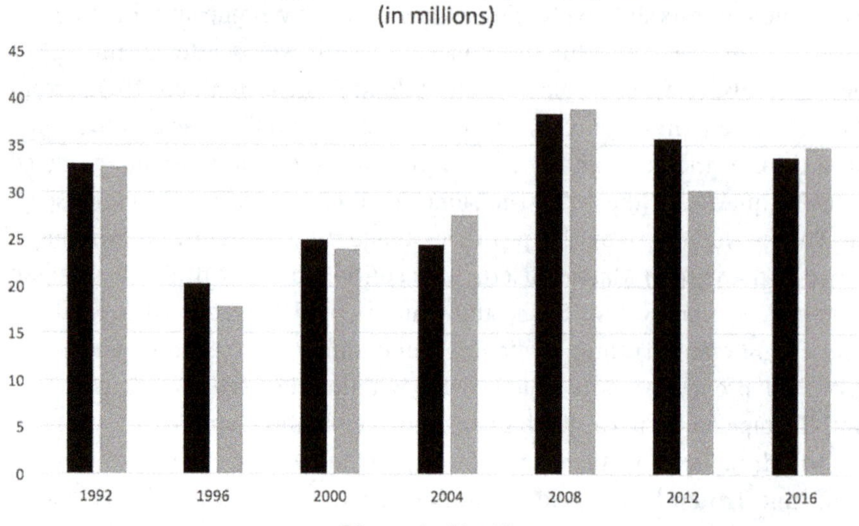

Figure 13.6. Convention ratings. Various news sources.

came to their respective conventions having already amassed a clear majority, the convention roll call was a mere formality.

Even though the conventions no longer have an active role in choosing the presidential nominee, they retain considerable political importance. They are one of the few occasions during the campaign that attract millions of television viewers. In an age of ten-second soundbites and thirty-second ads, the conventions are an opportunity for the public to have a more lengthy opportunity to hear why each party and its nominee claim that they should be entrusted with the presidency. Figure 13.6 is a graph of the viewership of each candidate's acceptance speech (the final night of their conventions) from 1992 to 2016.

The most important convention event is the candidate's acceptance speech, which candidates give after the roll call of the states and before they have been officially nominated. The speech provides a relatively lengthy occasion for candidates to define themselves to the voters and to explain why each is the superior choice. Clinton's acceptance speech was viewed by 27.2 million people and Trump's by 25.2 million. Second in importance are the speeches that nominate the candidate. The nominators are carefully chosen by the candidates and their staffs (not the party leadership) to display the wide range of their support and to ensure that important reasons for supporting them are publicized, reasons that it would be impolitic for the candidate to mention in their own speech. These speeches expand upon the themes that the candidates will later take up in their acceptance speech and also visibly demonstrate that key leaders, representing various elements and factions of the party, are giving their enthusiastic support. The other speeches given in prime time are also politically significant because they are an opportunity for less well-known, up-and-coming politicians to make an impact on a mass public. These other speeches also provide an opportunity to show that the party is concerned about the various causes and constituencies that these speakers represent.

Speakers at the Republican Convention harped on Trump's central campaign theme of making America great again. His own speech, given a little more than a week after the killing of five policemen in Dallas, stressed law and order. The Democratic Convention stressed unity. The themes announced for three of the four days of the convention each included the word "together" – United Together, Working Together, Stronger Together. "Together" imparted the dual message of healing wounds in the nation at large and also of healing the wounds created by the Sanders insurgency.

Off camera, the business of the convention includes determining the party platform and listening to many nonbroadcast speeches. These activities are often of great importance to delegates and speakers themselves. They are a vital part of the secondary function of the convention, which is to stir up enthusiasm and improve the morale of party loyalists whose help is desperately needed by the candidate during the campaign. The platforms are a catalog of the various stances on public policy questions that a majority of the party delegates choose to endorse. Candidates are not necessarily bound to support every plank of the platform. As the two parties have come to be more ideologically distinct from one another and more internally cohesive, the platforms have become less politically relevant because the public already has a pretty clear idea regarding what the parties differ about.

Conventions often produce a strong "bounce," meaning that voters react to the positive image of the candidate the convention creates by providing the candidate with increased support. The Republican convention provided Trump with at best a small bounce. By contrast, Clinton garnered a sizeable one, enabling her to vault into the lead. However, her bounce did not last. By the time the first candidate debate was held in late September, most polls considered the race to be virtually tied.

The Battleground

Chapter 3 explained how the Constitution defines the system for electing presidents. The Electoral College determines that in fact there is not a single national presidential election but rather fifty state elections. Thus, candidates must concentrate on winning those individual state elections in order to garner the necessary electoral vote majority rather than maximizing their national vote totals. In 2016, Trump won the majority of electoral votes even though he lost the popular vote. This was because he carried a number of states by razor-thin margins, thus winning their electoral votes, even as he lost in a number of other states by huge margins. (Compare the results in Wisconsin, Michigan, and Pennsylvania with those in California, New York, and Massachusetts.) Yet it is impossible to say who would have won if the election were decided by the national popular vote, because each candidate would have adopted a very different campaign strategy, one geared to maximize votes rather than electoral votes. For example, Trump spent virtually no time campaigning in California because he knew he had no chance of winning the state. But if he was simply trying to gain the most votes nationwide, he might well have spent a good deal of time in this state containing the most voters. Likewise, Clinton ignored the solid red states in the deep South. Instead, the candidates devote themselves to campaigning in what have come to be called "battleground states." the relatively small number of states in which the balance of partisan loyalties is sufficiently even that candidates can only win by fully mobilizing their party supporters and by appealing to the majority of those who do not identify with a party or have only the weakest of ties to the opposition. According to the website Politico, there were thirteen battleground states in 2016 – Virginia, Colorado, Iowa, New Hampshire, Florida, Nevada, Ohio, Arizona, Pennsylvania, Georgia, North Carolina, Michigan, and Wisconsin. This total represents an increase of two states from 2012, Arizona and Georgia, both of which were won by the Republican candidate, Mitt Romney. Thus, more than three-quarters of the states, including three of the four most populous, were largely ignored by the Clinton and Trump campaigns. Not a single Northeastern or Pacific coast state made the battleground list. Table 13.2 shows the 2016 election results state by state.

Presidential Debates

No presidential debates were held in 1964, 1968, and 1972, but they have been a fixture of presidential elections ever since. In 2016, there were three debates, on September 26, October 9, and October 19. Although a wide range of domestic and foreign policy issues were covered, each was dominated by the personal attacks that characterized the rest of the campaign. Commentators praised Clinton for her poise and command of the issues while criticizing Trump for his lack of knowledge about the issues and his sometimes rambling delivery. Polls taken after each debate gave Clinton a decisive edge, and yet she lost the election. It appears that a sufficient number of voters in the battleground states chose Trump despite

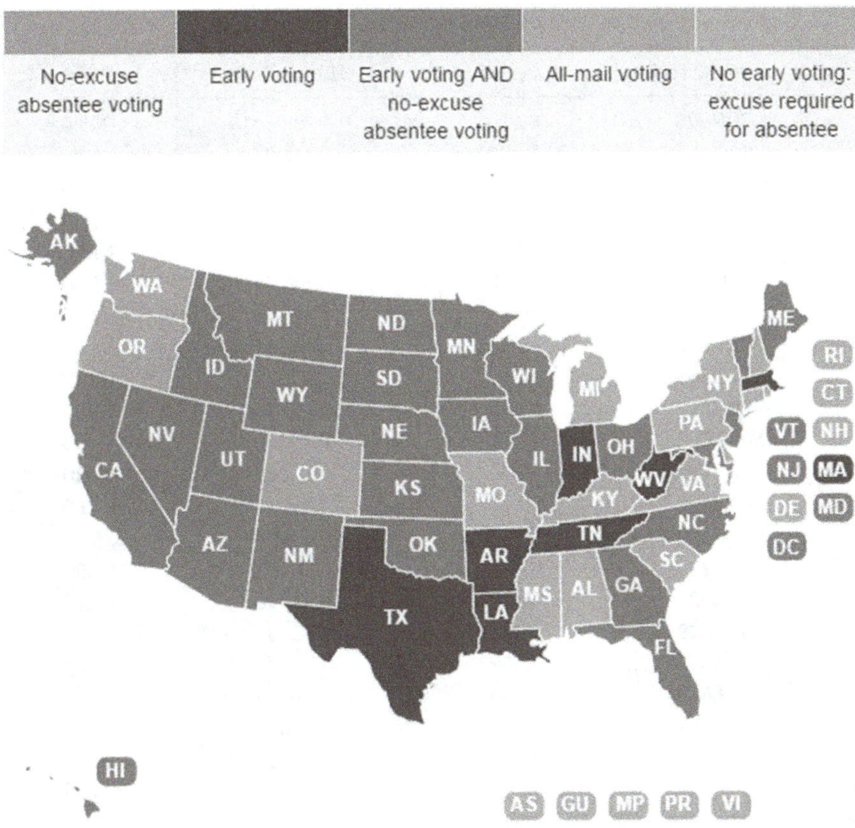

Figure 13.7. Mail voting, early voting, and no excuse absentee voting.
Source: NCSL.

his debate performance. Campaign events matter but each campaign may be affected by different events. The debates, which may have been decisive in 1960, do not appear to have mattered much in 2016.

Elections: A Study in Federalism

The regulations and procedures that govern elections embody the full complexity inherent in federalism (see Chapter 5). All levels of government are involved in a manner that continually causes them to intersect and intermingle. The US Constitution sets eligibility rules for voting. The Twenty-sixth Amendment declares all US citizens over the age of 18 to be eligible to vote. The Fifteenth Amendment prohibits denial of the suffrage on the basis of race and the Nineteenth Amendment guarantees voting rights to women. But these guarantees are not absolute. Many states bar convicted felons from voting. Some states bar felons only while they are in prison; others until they have completed their parole or probation, and still others bar them for their entire lifetime.

Table 13.2. 2016 presidential election state results.

State	Donald Trump	Percentage	Hillary Clinton	Percentage
AL	1,306,925	62.90	718,084	34.60
AK	130,415	52.90	93,007	37.70
AZ	1,021,154	49.50	936,250	45.40
AR	677,904	60.40	378,729	33.80
CA	3,916,209	32.80	7,362,490	61.60
CO	1,136,354	44.40	1,208,95	47.20
CT	668,266	41.20	884,432	54.50
DE	185,103	41.90	235,581	53.40
DC	11,553	4.10	260,223	92.8
FL	4,605,515	49.10	4,485,745	47.80
GA	2,068,623	51.30	1,837,300	45.60
HI	121,648	30.10	251,853	62.30
ID	407,199	59.20	189,677	27.60
IL	2,118,179	39.40	2,977,498	55.40
IN	1,556,220	57.20	1,031,953	37.90
IA	798,923	51.80	650,790	42.20
KS	656,009	57.20	414,788	36.20
KY	1,202,942	62.50	628,834	32.70
LA	1,178,004	58.10	779,535	38.40
ME	334,838	45.20	343,873	47.90
MD	873,646	35.50	1,497,951	60.50
MA	1,083,069	33.50	1,964,768	60.80
MI	2,279,805	47.60	2,268,193	47.30
MN	1,322,891	45.40	1,366,676	46.90
MS	678,457	58.30	462,001	39.70
MO	1,585,753	57.10	1,054,889	38
MT	274,120	56.50	174,521	36
NE	485,819	60.30	273,858	34
NV	511,319	45.50	537,753	47.90
NH	345,789	47.20	348,521	47.60
NJ	1,535,513	41.80	2,021,756	55
NM	315,875	40	380,724	48.30
NY	2,640,570	37.50	4,143,874	58.80
NC	2,339,603	50.50	2,162,074	46.70
ND	216,133	64.10	93,526	27.80
OH	2,771,984	52.10	2,317,001	43.50
OK	947,934	63.50	419,788	28.90
OR	742,506	41.10	934,631	51.70
PA	2,912,941	48.80	2,844,705	47.60
RI	179,421	39.80	249,902	55.40
SC	1,143,611	54.90	848,469	40.80
SD	227,701	61.50	117,442	31.70
TN	1,517,402	61.10	867,110	34.90
TX	4,681,590	52.60	3,867,816	43.40
UT	452,086	45.90	274,188	27,80
VT	95,053	32.60	178,179	61.10

Table 13.2. *(cont.)*

State	Donald Trump	Percentage	Hillary Clinton	Percentage
VA	1,731,156	45	1,916,845	49.90
WA	1,129,120	38.20	1,610,524	54.40
WV	486,198	68.70	187,457	26.50
WI	1,409,467	47.90	1,382,210	46.90
WY	174,248	70.10	55,949	22.50

State governments regulate the voter registration and voting process within bounds established by federal law. They regulate party primaries and state elections as well. They also determine the shape of congressional and state legislative districts. States determine how long the polls will remain open. But individual localities provide and manage the locations where people vote and, in some states, decide what sort of ballot is used. Some localities use paper ballots while others use one or another variety of voting machine. In 2000, Palm Beach County, Florida became notorious because the ballot design it used, the so-called "butterfly" ballot, so confused elderly voters that many voted for candidates other than the one they intended to vote for.

Citizens are not automatically registered to vote. Every state except North Dakota requires them to register. The American political development section of this chapter examines the implications of changes in the registration process. Most states insist that one register at least thirty days before an election, but a few allow registration on election day.

However, registration is no longer entirely a state and local function. The US Justice Department monitors the process to ensure that no racial discrimination occurs. And, as discussed later in the chapter, since 1993 the federal government has also intervened in order make registration easier and encourage more people to do so. Federal law now requires states to increase the number and variety of voter registration opportunities. Because registration is now available at motor vehicle bureaus, disabled centers, and welfare offices, people do not have to make a separate trip to register. They can do so when they apply for a driver's license or have an interview about their welfare status.

In order to make voting easier and to reduce crowding on election day, thirty-four states provide for early voting. In Texas, for example, early voting starts seventeen days before election day and ends four days before. Absentee voting is permitted in twenty-eight states. In twenty-two of them one needs an excuse to do so. Valid excuses usually involve being out of town on election day because one is attending school elsewhere, serving in the military, living abroad, or for some other acceptable reason.

Oregon uses mailed ballots as its primary voting method. A pamphlet with information about each measure and candidate in the upcoming election is mailed to every Oregon household three weeks before each statewide election. Ballots are mailed to every registered voter fourteen to eighteen days before the election. Voters fill out the ballot, sign it, and mail it back. Mailed ballots are accepted anytime until 8 p.m. of election day. Figure 13.7 above shows which states allow for mail voting, early voting, and no excuse absentee voting.

The General Election Campaign

The two campaigns differed greatly in their fundraising. As of ten days before the election, Clinton had raised over $1 billion while Trump raised only half a billion (www.bloomberg.com/politics/graphics/2016-presidential-campaign-fundraising/). This discrepancy was grounded in the different strategies of the two campaigns. Hillary Clinton spent vastly more on paid television advertising whereas Trump relied on his ability to generate headlines to garner free air time (www.bloomberg.com/politics/graphics/2016-presidential-campaign-tv-ads/). Both candidates appeared at many rallies, mostly in battleground states. However Trump attracted far larger and more enthusiastic crowds.

Clinton also invested much more heavily in what is referred to as the "ground game." This is the grassroots effort, organized by local field offices, to knock on voters' doors, identify those who will vote for one's candidate, and then ply them with phone calls on election day to prod them to vote. An effective ground game operation even offers rides to the polls and free baby-sitting to make it easy for one's voters to vote. Clinton had 489 field offices. Trump had only 178. A Politico/Morning Consult exit poll found that more than twice as many people who were voting on election day were contacted by the Hillary Clinton campaign than the Donald Trump campaign (www.politicususa.com/2016/11/08/hillary-clinton-trouncing-trump-ground-game-exit-poll.html).

The general election campaign was dominated by bitter personal invective and accusations of malfeasance and even illegality hurled by each candidate at the other. Trump claimed that Hillary Clinton's use of a personal email server to conduct official State Department business, including the sending and receiving of classified information on that server, was a crime for which she deserved to be indicted. Among other personal attacks, he called her a "nasty woman." Clinton demanded that Trump release his tax returns, which he steadfastly refused to do. Campaigning for Clinton the day before election day, President Obama charged that "Donald Trump is temperamentally unfit to be commander in chief." "He's unqualified to be America's chief executive," he continued. The tenor of the campaign was further lowered by damaging information released to the media. In early October the *Washington Post* obtained a video of Donald Trump bragging about groping and attempting to have sex with women. The video was made in 2005 on a bus carrying him to a studio to tape a segment of the soap opera *Days of Our Lives*. Many prominent Republicans found his remarks so disgraceful that they withdrew their support for him and some even called for him to resign his candidacy.

All through the campaign, Hillary Clinton had been dogged by leaks of emails relating to official state department business that appeared on her private email server. In July 2016, FBI Director James Comey announced that he would not seek an indictment although he did criticize her for being "extremely careless." However, only ten days before election day, Comey announced that the FBI was reopening the email investigation because of possibly damning information found on a computer that a top aide, Huma Abedin, had shared with her then husband Anthony Weiner. The day before the election, Comey revealed that these new tapes did not in fact contain any damaging information, but this news arrived so late that it is probable that many voters were not aware that she was once again no longer under active investigation.

The tenor of the campaign both reflected and contributed to the very low esteem in which the public held both candidates. As of election day 2016, Clinton was viewed unfavorably by 55 percent of the public and favorably by only 42 percent. Trump was viewed unfavorably by 59 percent and favorably by 38 percent (www.realclearpolitics.com/epolls/other/president/clintontrump favorability.html). According to election analyst Nate Silver, "they were the two most disliked presidential candidates in modern American history." (www .fivethirtyeight.com/features/trump-is-more-unpopular-than-clinton-is-and-that-matters/).

Chapter 11 discussed the two coalitions that formed the base of support for Clinton and Trump. Self-identified Democrats, African Americans, Hispanics, big city dwellers, non-churchgoers, single women, and the highly educated were the core of the Clinton vote. Self-identified Republicans, married people, white men (especially those of modest income and less education), churchgoers, gun owners, and rural and small town residents were the heart of the Trump vote. These were the same categories of voters who had provided the core of each party's vote in the last few presidential elections. The 2016 outcome was decided by the increased margins Trump enjoyed among groups that were already solidly Republican, most especially non-college-educated whites, and by reduced turn-out among a key component of the Democratic coalition, African Americans. These factors accounted for Trump's victories in the key battleground states of Wisconsin, Michigan, and Pennsylvania. Preelection polls had given those states to Clinton. If she had won them, she would have won the election. In 2012, Republican Mitt Romney carried the votes of non-college-educated whites by a 25 percent margin. Trump increased that margin to 39 percent. Clinton suffered from serious reductions in turnout in heavily African-American areas. In Mil-waukee, turnout declines by 41,000 votes (www.jsonline.com/story/news/local/milwaukee/2016/11/10/milwaukee-elections-head-says-voter-id-law-hurt-citys-turnout/93607154/). Clinton lost Wisconsin by roughly 27,000 votes. In Wayne

County, which includes Detroit, turnout declined by 37, 000 votes (www.mlive.com/news/index.ssf/2016/11/see_how_every_michigan_county.html?appSession=974840179727449850756304830031 9). Clinton lost Michigan by approximately 9,500 votes.

Democratization

During the course of American political development significant changes have taken place in the rules and methods governing presidential elections. The most important impact of those changes has been to democratize the process. Direct election of the president replaced indirect election. Property and other qualifications were eliminated, enabling virtually all white males to vote. The Fifteenth Amendment, finally given teeth by the 1965 Voting Rights Act, provided African Americans with the right to vote. The Nineteenth Amendment gave women the right to vote.

Candidate selection was also democratized. First, party conventions replaced the congressional party caucus, expanding the selection process from the small number of congressional party members to the much larger number of party identifiers who elected delegates to state party conventions where delegates were then elected to the national one. Then party primaries opened the selection process directly to the voters. Campaigns likewise acquired a more popular character. After many decades candidates broke with tradition and began to campaign actively, crisscrossing the country appearing before crowds of voters. Later, they were able to use radio and television, and, most recently, social media to reach a far wider segment of the public.

However, this process of democratization encountered significant setbacks and challenges. During the latter part of the nineteenth century, in an effort to curtail the growing political power of big city political machines, new obstacles were created to make it more difficult for their supporters to vote. Most egregiously, Southern states systematically deprived African Americans of their voting rights. Only with the passage of the 1965 Voting Rights Act did African Americans in Southern states finally come to enjoy the voting rights the Fifteenth Amendment had promised them a century before.

1800 and the Twelfth Amendment

The election of 1800 marked the first stage in the democratization of the presidential electoral process by involving voters directly in choosing the winner. The Constitution's original method for electing presidents was profoundly and permanently changed. The Framers had intended the electors to be independent, exercising their own individual judgment about who would make the best president. Thus, the ordinary voter was only indirectly involved in the election, choosing the people who would make the choice. But in 1800, the Republican leaders in the capital coordinated with party organizations in the various states so that electors were selected as instructed agents of the party, pledged to vote for Jefferson. Thus, when voters cast their ballots for the Republican slate of electors they were indeed voting for the Republican candidate.

Expanding the Electorate and Presidential Selection

The 1820s witnessed further democratization of the electoral process resulting from a vast expansion of the electorate. Most states abolished property qualifications for voting. By the 1830s virtually all white male citizens, and many resident aliens, were able to vote. These changes greatly aided the election of Andrew Jackson, who appealed especially to those of modest means. Several factors contributed to these changes. Many poor men were recruited to fight in the War of 1812. They naturally wondered why they were good enough Americans to fight for their country but not good enough to qualify to vote. In the newly admitted, underpopulated states, reducing the obstacles to voting was seen as a useful tool for attracting people to move there. Most importantly, even those who met the property qualifications became increasingly convinced that such restrictions were improper. They were becoming ever more devoted to the democratic principles inherent in the Declaration of Independence and championed by the Jeffersonians.

The election of 1828 further democratized the election process. For the first time a party's candidate was not chosen by the party's congressional caucus; instead, most states held nominating conventions and thus a large number of party loyalists replaced the small group of congressional party members as the determiners of who would secure the party's nomination. In 1832, the Democrats held a national nominating convention to which each state party sent delegates. The nominating convention would remain the key arena for determining presidential candidate selection until the late 1960s (Democrats) and late 1970s (Republicans). Figure 13.8 shows the expansion of the suffrage that took place between 1800 and 1860.

Restricting the Electorate

In 1870, the Fifteenth Amendment was ratified granting African Americans the right to vote. However, the end of Reconstruction enabled the Southern states to keep African Americans from voting. In the late nineteenth century, those states went beyond simple intimidation to establish formal legal barriers to deprive African Americans of the vote. Because these barriers were not specifically directed at African Americans, the Southern states could claim that they did

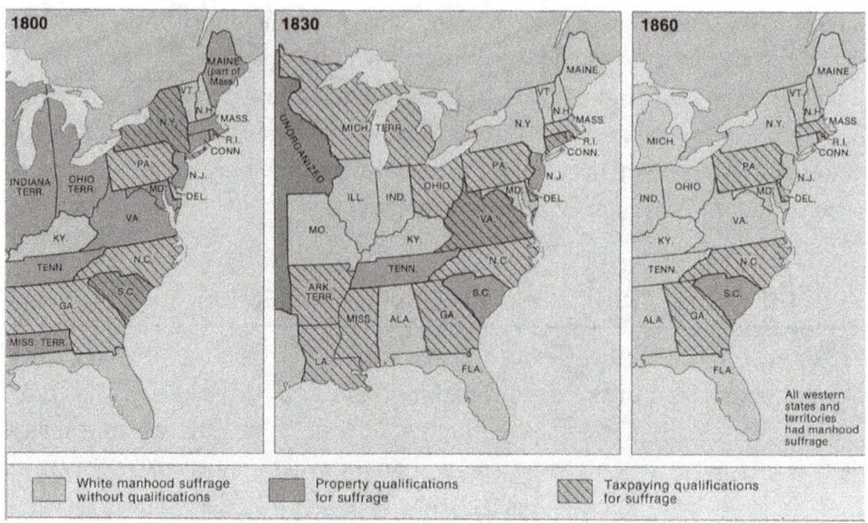

Figure 13.8. Expansion of suffrage.
Source: American Geographical Society of New York.

not violate the Fifteenth Amendment. The most important barriers consisted of poll taxes that African Americans could not afford, literacy tests that were purposely made so difficult that poorly educated peope could not pass them, and residency requirements that were so complex that often African Americans could not meet them. In principle, these restrictions applied to white voters as well. But, in practice, election officials applied them selectively, often exempting whites while enforcing them against blacks. Party primaries were not subject to federal law and were thus not governed by the Fifteenth Amendment. Therefore, the Democratic Party in the Southern states restricted participation in primaries to whites only. Winning the Democratic nomination was tantamount to election in the one-party South. Thus, preventing African American participation in the primary was tantamount to depriving them of the right to vote.

In the latter part of the nineteenth century the North too experienced efforts to restrict the franchise, although on a lesser scale. The massive influx of immigrants and the rise of urban political organizations that were succeeding in winning over and manipulating the immigrant vote led the political establishments in many Northern states to try to stem this rising political tide. Various states passed laws prohibiting noncitizens from voting, establishing strict residency rules and creating cumbersome registration requirements. These restrictive efforts were defended as necessary means for combatting voter fraud. Indeed, the immigrant-based political organizations were guilty of taking advantage of ineffective registration and voter identification procedures to commit fraud, urging their supporters to vote "early and often." But these restrictions also placed onerous burdens on honest voters. For example, the registration requirement meant that a worker had to take time off and lose pay to register and then do so again on election day. This posed a severe economic hardship on those who could barely survive on their low wages.

The imposition of the secret ballot, known as the Australian ballot, was simultaneously an effort to protect the privacy of voters and a means for limiting the power of the urban political organizations. Previously, voters would receive fully marked ballots from party workers and simply deposit them in the ballot box. Now, voters had to mark their ballots in a private voting booth, which meant that even in the absence of literacy tests, those who could not read could not meaningfully participate.

Women's Voting Advances

In the midst of these restrictive efforts, an important democratic advance was taking place. Even before the ratification of the Nineteenth Amendment in 1920, a number of states had granted voting rights to women. As early as 1869, the Wyoming Territory allowed women to vote and women's suffrage was written into the state constitution passed in 1889. Colorado did so in 1893. Utah and Idaho followed suit in 1896. All of these states were in the Far West. Scholars offer various explanations for why these Western states took the lead. Some attribute it to the strength of the Populist movement there (see Chapter 11). The Populists advocated for women's suffrage. Others stress the desire of the under-populated Western states to entice more women to move there.

The 1896 Campaign

In crucial ways, 1896 was the first modern presidential campaign. Both sides introduced political innovations that are now fundamental features of the electoral contest. Prior to 1896, no party nominee had actually campaigned for office. It was considered to be undignified. Personal participation in the hurly burly of rallies and parades would make the candidate seem too common and partisan to be worthy of the nation's highest office. But, because Bryan was so little known nationally and his views were so unconventional, he determined that he had to take his message directly to the people. He travelled across the country addressing crowds of voters in an effort to personally win them over. Bryan was not literally the first presidential candidate to take his message to the people. William Henry Harrison had done so in 1840. Subsequently, however, the tradition had developed that it was unseemly for a candidate to personally toot his own horn and that task was relegated to party leaders. In 1908, both Bryan, again the Democratic nominee, and the winner, Republican William Howard Taft, campaigned actively and the tradition of candidate aloofness came to an end.

To counter Bryan's aggressive 1896 campaign effort, McKinley's campaign manager made an equally significant change in campaign strategy and tactics. Previously state and local parties had run the presidential campaign within their borders pretty much on their own. Hanna organized and directed a vigorous national effort. The national campaign headquarters produced massive amounts of campaign literature and introduced a key emblem of subsequent campaigns, the campaign button. More importantly, Hanna put pressure on the factory owners and other large employers who benefited from Republican tariff and subsidy policies to contribute generously to this more ambitious campaign effort and to pressure their workers to support McKinley. Although McKinley himself remained aloof from the campaign, Hanna's effort to centralize fundraising and publicity and to pressure business to more actively support its patron was crucial to McKinley's victory.

The Nineteenth Amendment

In 1919, Congress passed the Nineteenth Amendment granting women the right to vote. Support for women's suffrage had been growing during the Progressive Era. In 1910, President Taft endorsed it. In 1912, the Progressive Party led by former president Theodore Roosevelt supported it. By 1918, six additional states had granted voting rights to women, including New York and Michigan.

The effort to pass a constitutional amendment was accelerated by WWI. Women contributed mightily to the war effort. The 2-million-strong National American Women's Suffrage Association (NAWSA) suspended its lobbying efforts to concentrate on supporting the Wilson administration. This valuable assistance caused President Wilson to overcome his previous ambivalence and to come out forcefully in favor of a constitutional amendment. These same factors, combined with NAWSA's vigorous and well-organized lobbying efforts in state legislatures, succeeded in winning over the necessary support of three-quarters of the states and ratification of the amendment was achieved by 1920.

The Impact of Media: Radio and Television

Chapter 8 described the seminal importance of radio and television in personalizing the presidency. These revolutions in mass communications had a similarly revolutionizing impact on presidential campaigns. They created a far more intimate relationship between the candidate and the public. Radio extended the range of those who could hear the candidate's message delivered in his own voice far beyond those who attended his rallies in person. FDR, in particular, took advantage of his graceful and charming speaking style to ingratiate himself with the voters.

The first presidential campaign to make extensive use of television was 1952, by which time television sets had become widely available. The Democratic candidate, Adlai Stevenson, confined himself to thirty-minute informational broadcasts that appeared late at night and were not widely watched. The Eisenhower campaign, on the other hand, broadcast a number of brief lively and witty commercials. It took advantage of Eisenhower's pleasant demeanor to make effective use of his image in TV ads as well. As the opening vignette showed, 1960 marked the first time that television may have been decisive in determining the election outcome. Kennedy understood what Nixon did not, that the television screen magnifies and distorts hand and face gestures. Arm movements that might appear perfectly natural in front of a live crowd may look wild and grotesque on television. Kennedy kept his face steadily looking into the camera and avoided all motion. As a result, he came across as calm and self-confident while Nixon's gesticulations made him appear unnerved and insecure. Over time, television advertising and televised candidate appearances came to dominate presidential campaigns.

CRITICAL CHOICE: THE 1965 VOTING RIGHTS ACT

The landslide Democratic Party victory in the 1964 election removed the ability of Southern Democrats to block or stall voting rights legislation. Almost a hundred years after passage of the Fifteenth Amendment, African Americans in the South were actually able to vote.

The civil rights agitation of the 1950s put great pressure on the federal government to address voting rights discrimination in the South. In 1957, despite Southern opposition, Congress passed the first civil rights law since Reconstruction. Its voting rights provisions established a civil rights division within the Justice Department to enforce the new powers the law gave to the attorney general to pursue voting rights cases in court. Although the law proved difficult to enforce, it did result in a significant rise in African American voter registration in some Southern states.

Recognizing that citizens of the District of Columbia, which had a very large African American population, were disenfranchised in presidential elections, in 1960 Congress passed the Twenty-third Amendment awarding electoral votes to the District. The amendment was ratified by the states in 1961. In 1962 Congress passed the Twenty-fourth Amendment abolishing the poll tax in federal elections. It was ratified by the states in 1964. Despite these measures, most African Americans in the South remained disenfranchised. This situation was finally remedied by the passage of the 1965 Voting Rights Act. It provided the teeth needed to enforce the voting guarantees the Constitution afforded. In districts where fewer than 50 percent of adults had voted in 1964 (a measure of the extent of voting discrimination against African Americans), the act suspended literacy tests as well as any other devices intended to suppress voting. To keep Southern states from putting new obstructive devices in place, it required them to obtain prior approval from the Justice Department for any proposed changes in how elections were carried out. Most important of all, the act provided for direct federal involvement in Southern voter registration operations. It allowed the attorney general to appoint federal examiners to oversee those operations and to enroll voters when the local registrars were found to be obstructing African Americans from registering.

UPSHOT

The results of the act were startling. In 1965 alone, almost 250,000 African Americans registered to vote, one-third of them by federal examiners (www.ourdocuments.gov/doc.php?flash=true&doc=100). *By the end of the decade, African American voter registration in the South exceeded 62 percent. In the 2012 presidential election, African American turnout nationwide actually exceeded white turnout.*

Motor Voter

As noted, strict voter registration laws were put into place in the late nineteenth century ostensibly to combat voter fraud. However, such requirements often placed great burdens on working people if the hours were too limited; if the requirements were confusing; or, if the places of registration were few in number or were constantly shifting in location. Starting in the 1970s, many states chose to make registration easier. Some passed laws permitting registration by mail. Others enabled a variety of different state offices to conduct registration. A few allowed voters to register on election day. As mentioned earlier in the chapter, in 1993 Congress passed the National Voter Registration Act, which greatly facilitated voter registration. It enabled voters to register at the same state offices that issued driver's licenses and thus it acquired the nickname of the "motor voter" law. It also allowed voters to register at state welfare offices and offices serving the disabled. Although Congress only has the power to set requirements for federal elections, all states have chosen to unify their state and federal registration practices and therefore abide by the federal law. The new law resulted in a large increase in voter registration. In 1995, two years after Motor Voter went into effect, 9 million new voters signed up. However, this increase has not translated into gains in voter turnout in either presidential or congressional elections. In 1996, turnout was the lowest in a presidential year since 1994. The 2016 turnout was the lowest since 1996.

Table 13.3. Democratization timeline.

1800	Republican Party mobilizes voters to support a specific presidential candidate.
1820s	Universal white male suffrage in most states.
1870	Fifteenth Amendment to the Constitution ratified prohibiting federal and state gov ernments from denying African American males the right to vote.
1920	Nineteenth Amendment ratified prohibiting federal and state governments from denying the right to vote on the basis of sex.
1965	Passage of Voting Rights Act that provided the Justice Department with the tools to enforce the Fifteenth Amendment.
1993	National Voter Registration Act facilitates voter registration by enabling voters to register at state welfare offices, offices serving the disabled and those that issue drivers licenses.

Crises of Legitimacy

Whether or not an election outcome truly represents the populace requires that the losers believe that the election was decided fairly: in other words, both sides acknowledge its legitimacy. As the contemporary portrait discussed, Donald Trump said that if he lost in 2016 it would be because the election was rigged. Some Clinton backers blamed her loss on efforts to prevent her supporters from voting. Several times in American electoral history, doubts have been raised about the fairness of the election. This happened in 1800 and 1824, when neither candidate amassed an electoral majority and the presidential choice was made by the House of Representatives. It also occurred in 1876 and 2000, when the outcome was disputed on the grounds that votes were not properly counted. In each of these cases, means were found for resolving the dispute such that the legitimacy of the electoral process was sustained.

The Twelfth Amendment

In the original Constitution, the electors were to vote for two candidates for president. The candidate who received the most electoral support, provided it was a majority, became president, and the second place finisher became vice president. Such a mechanism introduced an element of unreliability into the creation of a party ticket as demonstrated by the 1800 election.

The Republicans' choice for president (Jefferson) and vice president (Aaron Burr) received the same number of electoral votes, thus throwing the contest to the House of the Representatives. The Federalist-controlled House flirted with selecting Burr rather than Jefferson as president. Ironically, it was Alexander Hamilton, Jefferson's sworn enemy, who led the fight for Jefferson. As he said in a letter to Congressman Harrison Gray Otis of Massachusetts,

> In a choice of Evils let them take the least – Jefferson is in every view less dangerous than Burr . . . Mr. Jefferson, though too revolutionary in his notions, is yet a lover of liberty and will be desirous of something like orderly Government – Mr. Burr loves nothing but himself – thinks of nothing but his own aggrandizement – and will be content with nothing short of permanent power in his own hands.

To ensure against a repetition of such a crisis, the Republicans successfully pressed for enactment of the Twelfth Amendment to the Constitution, ratified in 1804. It required electors to cast separate ballots for president and vice president. This change further empowered voters because it removed any ambiguity about whom their vote was intended to support. It strengthened the Republican Party by enabling it to put together a slate of candidates – one presidential and one vice presidential. The 1800 election showed the virtue of slate making – allowing the party to strengthen its national appeal by promoting candidates from two different regions – the Northeast and South – and from two of the most populous states – New York and Virginia. But the inability to designate one as the presidential and the other as the vice presidential candidate opened the door to chaos and divisiveness. The Twelfth Amendment solved that problem. In addition, in the event that no candidate received an electoral college majority, the House would choose among the three leading candidates rather than among five as the original Constitution specified.

The Election of 1876

Chapter 11 discussed the 1824 election in which Andrew Jackson, who had amassed large leads in both the popular and the electoral vote but had fallen short of a majority, was defeated in the House of Representatives. His claim that the loss was due to a corrupt bargain between John Quincy Adams and Henry Clay might well have done lasting damage to the legitimacy of the electoral system had he not triumphed decisively four years later. In 1876, the challenge to the legitimacy of the electoral process resulted from charges of voter fraud and intimidation. The Republicans challenged the election results in three former Confederate states – Louisiana, Florida, and South Carolina – claiming that Republican supporters, primarily African Americans, had either been denied access to the polls or had not had their votes fairly counted. The Democrats also challenged the credentials of one elector in Oregon, claiming that as a federal employee he was ineligible. The number of electoral votes under dispute was enough to deprive either candidate of a majority. Because the issue was the vote count itself, not the lack of a majority of electoral votes, the Constitution offered no means for deciding the matter.

Congress chose to resolve the impasse by appointing a Commission composed of five congressmen from each party, two Supreme Court Justices loyal to each party, and one Independent, Justice David Davis. Because Davis was then elected to the

Senate, he withdrew from the commission and was replaced by Joseph Bradley, a Republican but one acceptable to the Democrats. Bradley sided with the Republicans in a series of 8–7 votes that gave Hayes an electoral majority. Democrats threatened to filibuster, but ultimately the commission report was accepted because of a compromised worked out by the leadership of both parties. In exchange for accepting the commission's findings, the Republicans agreed to accelerate and complete the withdrawal of federal troops from the South, putting an end to Reconstruction. One party gained the presidency and the other gained a critical policy objective. Thus, the party system proved itself sufficiently resilient to deal with this threat to the legitimacy of the election results. The opening vignette of Chapter 9 described the dispute over election results that occurred in 2000. In that instance, the Supreme Court made the final determination. Despite the partisan uproar resulting from the decision, no serious challenge to its legitimacy occurred.

The Twenty-second Amendment

In 1940, the United States experienced another legitimacy controversy when FDR became the first president to be elected to a third term in office. In 1944, he was elected to a fourth term. The Constitution did not limit the president's reelectability, but in fact no previous president had served more than two terms and there was widespread feeling that this two-term limit tradition should be honored. In 1946, when Republicans gained control of the House and Senate for the first time since 1928, they determined to make the two-term limit official, via constitutional amendment. They were able to garner sufficient Democratic support to muster the two-thirds vote in both houses needed to pass it in 1947. By 1951, three-quarters of the states had ratified it and it went into effect. In addition to limiting a newly elected president to only one more term, it also states that a president who succeeds to the office due to the death or resignation

Table 13.4. Constitutional amendments.

Twelfth Amendment	• Required electors to cast separate ballots for president and vice president • House decides among top three leading contenders in event an electoral majority is not achieved • Ratified June 15, 1804
Fifteenth Amendment	• Granted right to vote to African Americans • Ratified February 3, 1870
Nineteenth Amendment	• Granted right to vote to women • Ratified August 18, 1920
Twenty-second Amendment	• Limited president to two terms • Ratified February 27, 1951

Source: USConstitution.net

Table 13.5. Crises of legitimacy timeline.

1800	The two Republican candidates, Thomas Jefferson and Aaron Burr, receive the same number of electoral votes.
1804	The Twelfth Amendment to the Constitution is ratified requiring electors to cast separate ballots for president and vice president.
1824	No candidate obtains a majority of the electoral vote. Despite the fact that Andrew Jackson had garnered the most popular and electoral votes, the House of Representatives elects John Adams. Jackson calls the legitimacy of the process into question, declaring that the Speaker of the House, Henry Clay, and Adams have struck a "corrupt bargain."
1876	The election results in several states are challenged. A commission is appointed to investigate the charges and decide the outcome. A bargain is struck between the two parties electing the Republican, Rutherford B. Hayes, in exchange for the end of Reconstruction.
1940	FDR breaks with tradition and runs, successfully for a third term.
1951	The Twenty-second Amendment is ratified limiting the president to two terms.

of a sitting president can only run for two additional terms if that person has served less than two years of the prior president's term.

From Party- to Candidate-Controlled Presidential Campaigns

The advent of television combined with the increased role of primaries and changes in campaign finance laws to diminish the role of political parties in the selection of presidential candidates and the conduct of presidential campaigns. The direct visual exposure of candidates to the voting public increased the importance of candidates' personal attributes – their appearance and demeanor – in influencing voter choice. As primaries became the main source for choosing national convention delegates, party leaders lost their ability to dictate the choice of candidates. Because candidates were not beholden to party leaders, they chose not to hand their electoral fate over to the party organization. Instead, they organized their own campaigns. Although changes in campaign finance law initially favored the parties, more recent changes have undercut them.

Primaries and Personal Campaign Teams

In addition to the increased importance of television, the 1960 campaign had two other critical impacts on presidential campaigns. Although primaries had played a role in presidential selection since the Progressive Era, they had never proven decisive in the choice of candidate. Even in 1960, not enough delegates were at stake to enable a candidate to win the nomination solely by winning primaries. However, Kennedy was a decided underdog. He had served little more than one term in the Senate. More importantly, he was a Catholic. The only previous Catholic candidate, Al Smith, had been badly beaten and there remained considerable anti-Catholic prejudice among Democrats as well as the public at large. Party leaders were skeptical about his ability to win. To prove he was electable, he had to win the bulk of the primaries. Indeed of the sixteen primaries held that year, he won ten. His principle rival Hubert Humphrey only won two. No other candidate gained more than one. Because many of his victories came in heavily Catholic states, it was his victory in West Virginia, a state with very few Catholics, that served to fully convince party leaders that he could indeed prevail in the general election.

Ensuing elections served to reinforce the importance of primaries. President Johnson's disappointingly narrow victory in the 1968 New Hampshire primary caused him to withdraw from the race. In 1972, insurgent Democrat George McGovern defeated the party establishment choice Edmund Muskie by defeating him in the primaries. Ever since, primaries have determined the Democratic Party's presidential selection. They have also been decisive in determining the Republican outcome since 1980.

Party leaders also suffered in 1960, and subsequently, because they lost control of the presidential campaign itself. Kennedy was the first candidate not to place it in their hands. Instead, he and his brother Robert chose a team of advisors, pollsters, media specialists, and organizers whose loyalty was primarily to them and not to the party. Richard Nixon emulated this approach in 1972 when he placed his reelection effort in the hands of a committee separate from the Republican Party and comprised of personal loyalists. Ever since, the official party apparatus has played only a minor role in presidential campaigns.

Campaign Finance

The growing importance of television in political campaigns greatly increased the amount of money campaigns spent on television advertising and so campaigns became vastly more expensive. Despite these increases, government made very little effort to establish rules regarding how money was raised and spent. The Watergate scandal sparked public outrage about the conduct of campaigns, prodding Congress to take action to restore public confidence in the election process. The result was the first serious effort to regulate how campaigns were paid for. The1974 amendments to the Federal Elections Campaign Act sought to limit the resources and the spending opportunities available to personal campaign organizations like CREEP. They established strict disclosure requirements for campaign donations; limited the size of those donations; expanded public financing of presidential elections to include primaries and nominating

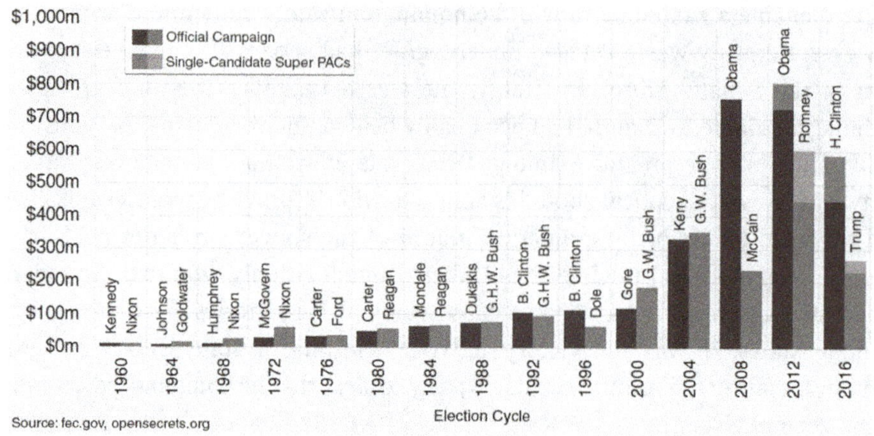

Figure 13.9. Presidential campaign spending, 1960–2016.
Source: Metrocosm.

conventions as well as the general election; set limits on campaign expenditures; and established the Federal Election Commission (FEC) to oversee compliance with the law.

Fueled by the voluntary check-off on tax forms (now $3), the Presidential Election Campaign Fund matched up to $250 of each contribution made to eligible primary candidates. In return, the candidates had to promise that they would limit spending to a specified amount. Then, in the general election season, the presidential candidates received a lump sum in return for not accepting any further private donations. Because that limit is now perceived to be too low to conduct a successful campaign, presidential candidates no longer accept money from the fund, preferring to fund the entire campaign with private donations. Figure 13.9 charts campaign spending in every election from 1960 to 2016.

The 1974 law set contribution limits differently for individuals and for Political Action Committees (PACs). PACs were entities that corporations, labor unions, and other types of organizations were required to establish in order to legally contribute to campaigns. An individual was allowed to donate $1,000 to a candidate per primary or general election; $20,000 to any other political committee per year; $5,000 to a national party committee per year but no more than $25,000 in total. PAC contributions were limited to $5,000 to a candidate per primary or general election; $15,000 to any other political committee per year; and $5,000 to a national party committee. No limit was placed on its total contributions per year.

In *Buckley v. Valeo* (1976), the Supreme Court struck down the expenditure limits contained in the 1974 law. It ruled that because advertising is a form of speech, it was unconstitutional to place limits on how much money a candidate could spend to purchase advertising. This ruling made it impossible to place meaningful limits on television advertising, which increased its centrality in the presidential and congressional campaign process and decreased the relative importance of such campaign devices as leafleting, signposting, rallies, and other techniques in which parties specialize. The Court also struck down a provision that would have limited how much money a candidate could contribute to his or her own campaign, thus opening the way for very rich individuals to self-finance their campaigns.

The 1974 law did not seek to regulate donations to political parties that were used to support state and local party building efforts, voter registration, and get out the vote drives. Such funds came to be known as "soft money" to distinguish them from the "hard money" donated in support of candidates. Both parties raised huge sums of soft money, which – according to advocates of campaign finance reform – were used to evade the spirit, but not the letter, of the law. In the most controversial action, national parties funneled large sums of soft money to state parties for TV and radio advertising praising party candidates and attacking their opponents. These ads were not subject to campaign donation limits as long as they did not specifically ask voters to vote for or against a particular candidate. Interest groups evaded donation limits by doing the same thing.

Seeking to close the soft money loophole, Congress further weakened parties. The 2002 Bipartisan Campaign Finance Reform Act (BCRA), commonly known as McCain–Feingold in honor of its senatorial sponsors, limited donations to political parties to $25,000 per donor. Recognizing that these restrictions would reduce the money available to carry out campaigns, the act raised the limit on candidate donations from $1,000 to $2,000. It also banned corporations, trade associations, public interest groups, and labor unions from financing "electioneering communications" within sixty days of a general election or thirty days of a primary. An electioneering communication was defined as an ad that clearly identified a candidate and targeted his or her state or district, whether or not the ad explicitly asked voters to support or oppose the candidate.

Not only did the soft money ban reduce the financial clout of the parties, it created a new loophole that advantaged organizational rivals to the parties. McCain–Feingold's limit on donations applied only to political parties, not to other types of political advocacy organizations. Thus, groups such as NARAL Pro-Choice America (formerly the National Abortion and Reproductive Rights Action League), the National Rifle Association, and other single-issue lobbying groups can spend as much as 50 percent of their resources on election-related activities. A tax-exempt group organized under section 527 of the Internal Revenue Code can spend unlimited amounts for political activities such as voter registration and mobilization efforts and issue advocacy. The only limitation is that this money cannot be spent for the express purpose of telling people to vote

one of the few occasions during the campaign that attracts millions of television viewers.

* Because most states are perceived to be either solidly Democratic or solidly Republican, presidential campaigns devote most of their efforts to a small number of states in which the balance of partisan loyalties is relatively even.
* The 2016 outcome was decided by the increased margins Trump enjoyed among groups that were already solidly Republican, most especially non-college-educated whites, and by reduced turnout among a key component of the Democratic coalition, African Americans. These factors accounted for Trump's victories in the key battleground states of Wisconsin, Michigan, and Pennsylvania.
* All levels of government are involved in defining and regulating the rules and procedures that govern national elections.

The democratization of the electorate:

* The election of 1800 marked the first stage in the democratization of the presidential electoral process because a political party was used as a vehicle for mobilizing voters.
* During the 1820s most states abolished property qualifications for voting. By the 1830s virtually all white male citizens, and many resident aliens, were able to vote.
* Despite the Fifteenth Amendment, African Americans were denied the vote either through direct intimidation or the use of such tactics as the poll tax, literacy tests, and the White Primary.
* The 1896 presidential campaign was the first one in which a major party candidate campaigned actively and in which a party organization mounted a truly national campaign.
* In 1919, Congress passed the Nineteenth Amendment granting women the right to vote. A number of states had granted women the vote prior to the amendment's passage.

The impact of radio and television:

* Radio extended the range of those who could hear the candidate's message delivered in his own voice far beyond those who attended his rallies in person.
* Television advertising and televised candidate appearances came to dominate presidential campaigns.

Critical choice: the 1965 Voting Rights Act:

* The 1965 Voting Rights Act suspended literacy tests and other devices intended to suppress African American voting; required Southern states to obtain prior approval from the Justice Department for any proposed changes in how

elections were carried out; and provided for direct federal involvement in Southern voter registration operations.

* The 1993 National Voter Registration Act enables voters to register at state welfare offices, offices serving the disabled and those that issue drivers' licenses.

Crises of legitimacy:

* In 1800 Congress had to settle the election because the two candidates on the Republican ticket were tied. The Twelfth Amendment to the Constitution, ratified in 1804, ensured this would not happen again because it required electors to cast separate ballots for president and vice president.
* In 1876 and 2000 the results of the presidential election were contested. The first was settled through a political compromise, the second by the Supreme Court.
* In 1940, FDR broke with tradition and ran for a third term. The Twenty-second Amendment later limited the president to two terms.

From party-centered to candidate-centered campaigns:

* 1960 was also the first time that primaries proved decisive in determining a party's candidate selection and that the candidate rather than the party took control of the presidential campaign.
* Since 1972, primaries have determined the Democratic Party's presidential selection. They have also been decisive in determining the Republican outcome since 1980.
* Changes in campaign finance law diminished political party importance in presidential campaigns.

SUGGESTED READINGS

Aldrich, John. *Why Parties?* University of Chicago Press, 1995.

Burnham, Walter Dean. *Critical Elections and the Mainsprings of American Politics.* New York: W. W. Norton, 1971.

Cohen, Marty, David Karol, Hans Noel, and John Zaller. *The Party Decides: Presidential Nominations Before and After Reform.* University of Chicago Press, 2008.

Epstein, Leon. *Parties in the American Mold.* Madison: University of Wisconsin Press, 1986.

Galvin, Daniel. *Presidential Party Building: Dwight D. Eisenhower to George W. Bush.* Princeton University Press, 2009.

Key, V. O. *Politics, Parties, and Pressure Groups*, 5th edn. New York: Thomas Y. Crowell, 1964.

Muirhead, Russell. *The Promise of Party in a Polarized Age.* Cambridge, MA: Harvard University Press, 2014.

Reichley, A. James. *The Life of the Parties.* Lanham, MD: Rowman & Littlefield, 2000.

Rosenblum, Nancy L. *On the Side of the Angels: An Appreciation of Parties and Partisanship.* Princeton University Press, 2010.

Rosenfeld, Sam. *The Polarizers: Postwar Architects of Our Partisan Era*. University of Chicago Press, 2017.

Schickler, Eric. *Racial Realignment: The Transformation of American Liberalism, 1932–1965*. Princeton University Press, 2016.

Schlozman, Daniel. *When Movements Anchor Parties: Electoral Alignments in American History*. Princeton University Press, 2015.

14 Political and Civic Participation: Movements, Lobbies, Voluntary Associations, and the Role of Media

CHAPTER OVERVIEW

This chapter focuses on:

- A contemporary portrait of movements, lobbies, and voluntary associations and the seminal role that social media now plays in stimulating and sustaining new social movements.
- The origins and development of the three forms of participation, and the critical role of the telegraph and the railroad in that development.
- The development and influence of the labor and civil rights movements, and the impact that television had on the success of the civil rights cause.
- The critical choice that modern social movements made to adopt the language of rights.
- A new form of political participation: the public interest movement.
- The decline of voluntary associations.

In April of 2012 George Zimmerman shot and killed Trayvon Martin, an African American teenager. Zimmerman was a member of the Sanford Florida Neighborhood Watch, a volunteer group that organizes civilian patrols of neighborhoods for the purpose of preventing crime. He was on patrol when he spotted Martin, whom he believed was acting suspiciously. He gave chase. Zimmerman claimed that Martin then attacked him and that he shot Martin in self-defense. The prosecution claimed the opposite, that Zimmerman had been the attacker and the shooting was unprovoked. Martin was unarmed. There were no witnesses to the shooting. Many African American commentators considered Martin's death to be racially motivated, an armed man (Zimmerman was of white and Hispanic descent) killing an unarmed African American teen who had committed no crime.

In April of 2013 Zimmerman was acquitted. When Alicia Garza, a young writer living in California, heard the news she posted the following message on Facebook, "Black people. I love you. I love us. Our lives matter." In response, Garza's friend

Table 14.1. Mass media timeline.

1830s	Railroads enable national spread of pamphlets
1840s	Telegraph
	Mass circulation
1890s	National magazines
1920s	Radio
1950s	Television
1980s	Cable TV
2000s	Facebook
2000s	Twitter

Patrisse Cullors replied, ending with the hashtag #blacklivesmatter. The hashtag was picked up on Twitter and attracted thousands of followers. Then in August 2014 an unarmed young black man was killed by a white policeman in Ferguson, Missouri. Over the next three weeks the hashtag's use exploded attracting an average of 58,747 appearances per day. In November 2014, a grand jury decided not to indict the policeman. Over the next three weeks the hashtag attracted 1.7 million appearances, almost all of which were expressions of outrage (www.pewinternet.org/2016/08/15/the-hashtag-blacklivesmatter-emerges-social-activism-on-twitter/). Twitter following became the focal point of efforts to mount organized protests. During the weeks that followed people from around the country, many recruited via Twitter, converged on Ferguson and launched a series of demonstrations. In the course of these protests, Black Lives Matter emerged as more than an online community, it became a movement. Table 14.1 shows the most important innovations in mass media that have occurred in the course of American political development and that will be discussed in this chapter.

Three Types of Participation

This chapter examines three critical dimensions of *political* and *civic participation* in America. Black Lives Matter exemplifies political participation "out of doors." Out-of-doors politics originates and flourishes beyond the halls of power. It mobilizes ordinary people to take part in rallies, demonstrations, strikes, and other forms of protest. It is often noisy, chaotic, passionate, and motivated by a sense of injustice and injury. If an out-of-doors participatory effort gains lots of members and national prominence, it becomes a movement. The very word "movement" evokes the surging energy and intense commitment Black Lives Matter's predecessors – the temperance, labor, civil rights, and feminist causes – embodied.

Black Lives Matter resembles earlier political movements in several critical ways. As we have seen, it was born on Facebook and grew on Twitter. As we shall see, the Progressive and the civil rights movements, among others, also successfully exploited new forms of mass communications to arouse supporters and increase visibility. Although it is spoken of as a single entity, Black Lives Matter is, in reality, a decentralized and diverse array of independent local groups. There is no national hierarchy. Instead, those who identify with Black Lives Matter – like the abolitionists, Temperance Society members, and environmentalists who preceded them – derive their sense of solidarity and coherence from the outrage they share. Its leaders are not well known. Movements tend to be suspicious of authority. However, if the movement continues to grow, its leaders will become better known and may even become famous, likes such great movement figures of the past as William Lloyd Garrison, John L. Lewis, and Martin Luther King.

This chapter examines these and other characteristics of political movements in order to understand how and why they form and grow; the complex ties they forge with public opinion and the mass media; the challenges they face; and how they influence and are influenced by the broader world of politics and government. It describes how political movements learn from their predecessors. For example, it looks at how and why the Anti-Vietnam War movement borrowed strategies and tactics from the civil rights movement just as the civil rights movement had adopted organizing principles and techniques from the labor movement.

Compared to the out-of-doors drama of protests, rallies, and demonstrations, "indoor" political participation is calm, even dull. The term most often used to describe such activity, "lobbying," conveys an atmosphere of low-key, casual encounters in the halls outside of legislative chambers, government offices, and hotel rooms. Of course, the large trade associations, public interest organizations, and law firms that are the most powerful lobbyists do not confine themselves to such venues and occasions. For the most part, indoor politics plays out in law offices, judges' chambers, and regulatory hearing rooms.

Because they want to demonstrate to their targets that the public is on their side, lobbying organizations intentionally blur the distinction between indoor and outdoor politics. They launch extensive media campaigns aimed at influencing public opinion. They also stimulate and assist their local affiliates to send delegations to Washington and choke the inboxes of their congressmen with supportive emails. Likewise, out-of-doors organizations establish offices in Washington and in the state capitals staffed with lobbyists, lawyers, and researchers. They recognize the need to convert the political energies of their members into favorable policy outcomes. And yet these encroachments on one another's turf do not undermine the essential difference between a movement, whose strength lies in its ability to excite the passions of large numbers of loyal adherents, and a lobby that relies primarily on expertise, discretion, and the quiet exertion of influence. Table 14.2 shows the most important political movements that have occurred in the course of American political development and which will be discussed in this chapter.

Table 14.2. Important political movements.

Origination date	Key political movement
1790s	Democratic–Republican societies
1820s	Temperance
1830s	Abolitionism
1880s	Populism (see Chapter 12)
1900s	Progressivism
1930s	Labor movement
1950s	Civil rights movement
1960s	Anti-war movement (Vietnam)
1960s	Women's movement
1970s	Environmental movement
1970s	Gay rights movement
1970s	Christian right

Despite the dramatic difference between protest movements and lobbying organizations, they share a critical similarity. Both devote themselves to changing governmental policies and practices. Dating from long before the American Revolution, America has also been home to a different form of participation, civic participation, which seeks not to influence government but to substitute for it. Even today, many towns rely on voluntary associations to accomplish tasks that would otherwise be performed by government or not performed at all. Instead of employing firefighters, many towns depend on ordinary citizens to organize and staff a volunteer fire brigade. Neighborhoods establish citizen crime patrols to provide a level of surveillance that the city police force cannot provide. Local garden clubs prune trees, plant and tend flowers and shrubs in parks and plazas, tasks that would otherwise be done by municipal public works employees. These activities tap into wellsprings of individual initiative and optimism deeply embedded in American political culture, and they replenish the supply. They are the prime embodiments of the communitarian cornerstone of American political culture at work. Because they directly involve people in the public life of the community, they cultivate the skills and attitudes necessary for effective and responsible citizenship.

A Contemporary Portrait

Social Movements

Black Lives Matter is the newest of the four major protest movements to emerge in the twenty-first century. The other three have been the antiwar movement that galvanized in opposition to the Iraq War, the Tea Party, and Occupy Wall Street.

The months leading up to the US invasion of Iraq witnessed a wave of demonstrations across the United States, the largest of which took place on February 15, 2003. Estimates of crowd size varied widely, but it is safe to say that many hundreds of thousands, and perhaps as many as a few million, of people rallied in 150 US cities. The largest, somewhere between 300,000 and a million, took place in front of the United Nation's headquarters in New York City. Demonstrations continued over the next several years as the war continued. Many prominent political and media figures participated in the protests, but there was no clear leader. The actual organizing was done by a coalition of existing peace organizations, none of which had a mass membership. It was the cause, not the leadership, that produced the massive outpouring of protest.

The birth of the Tea Party resembled that of Black Lives Matter in that both were born on mass media. Black Lives Matter was sparked by Facebook and Twitter; the Tea Party on cable TV. Business news is normally reported in a calm, noncommittal manner. But in February 2009, when CNBC Business News editor Rick Santelli commented over the air on the government plan to refinance mortgages, his remarks sounded more like a diatribe than a news report. From the floor of the Chicago Mercantile Exchange, he hotly accused the government of "promoting bad behavior" by "subsidizing losers' mortgages" (www.youtube.com/watch?v=zp-Jw-5Kx8k). He urged the president to use the internet to ask ordinary people what they thought of the bailout:

> Why don't you put up a website to have people vote on the Internet as a referendum to see if we really want to subsidize the losers' mortgages; or would we like to at least buy cars and buy houses in foreclosure and give them to people that might have a chance to actually prosper down the road, and reward people that could carry the water instead of drink the water? This is America! How many of you people want to pay for your neighbor's mortgage that has an extra bathroom and can't pay their bills? Raise their hand.

Harking back to the Sons of Liberty who dumped British Tea in Boston Harbor to protest British imposed taxes, Santelli proposed that the Mercantile Exchange traders stage a tea party to gather and dump the mortgage-related securities they were trading into the Chicago River. Instead of displaying contempt for this breach of journalistic protocol, many of the traders cheered. Within hours of the broadcast, two websites had been created promoting protest activities under the "tea party" banner. The next day, a Facebook page was created to enable tea partiers to communicate with one another and plan rallies and demonstrations not only against the mortgage bailout, but also against the stimulus plan, the healthcare reform, and a host of other Obama administration "big government" programs. After a video of the occasion was posted on the Drudge Report, it became one of the most popular of all the postings on that very popular site that was receiving approximately 18 million hits daily. That week, protests against the expanding reach of federal government broke out all over the country. The Tea Party was dramatically transformed from a semiserious remark into a political movement involving thousands of people.

As the Tea Party movement grew in size and strength, it moved from simply voicing its dissatisfaction with increased government spending and bailouts to trying to change the direction of American politics, to shrink the size and scope of government. Its first great political success came in the January special election called in Massachusetts to fill the empty seat caused by the death of Senator Edward Kennedy. Self-identified Tea Partiers were very active and vocal in their support of the surprise winner, Republican Scott Brown, an opponent of Obamacare. But the Tea Party was not content to serve as an instrument of the Republicans. In several states, its members actively supported challengers to Republican incumbents who had supported some of Obama's programs – the stimulus, the healthcare reform, and/or the bank bailout. In Utah, it succeeded in defeating longtime incumbent Robert Bennett. In Nevada, it succeeded in nominating the most antigovernment of the Republican challengers, Sharon Angle, to oppose incumbent Democrat, Senate Majority Leader Harry Reid. In Delaware, it rallied support for the more radical Republican senatorial aspirant, Christine O'Donnell, who defeated her more moderate opponent. The results of the Tea Party intervention were mixed. Republicans easily held the Utah seat, but both Angle and O'Donnell lost to highly vulnerable Democrats. However, the Tea Party also helped energize the campaigns of scores of Republican House and Senate nominees. Their hard work campaigning door to door and mobilizing their friends, neighbors, and family undoubtedly contributed to the ensuing Republican landslide.

The Tea Party is not an organization. Several different national organizations and websites include those two words in their titles, but none can claim to speak for the movement. In reality, Tea Partiers are whoever show up at meetings of the local and county organizations that have sprung up around the country and have "Tea Party" in their title, as well as those who simply show up at the demonstrations and rallies these groups sponsor or who volunteer to campaign for Tea Party-endorsed candidates.

Like Black Lives Matter, the Tea Party has no individual leader. Many nationally prominent conservatives, most famously Sarah Palin, praised the Tea Party and speak at its rallies, but they do not speak *for* the Tea Party. The most important leadership is exercised at the local level by ordinary people who rent the meeting halls, manage the websites, and organize the phone banks.

Like Black Lives Matter, Occupy Wall Street began with a hashtag, #occupywallstreet. In 2011, Kalle Lasn, a Canadian and founder of the anticommercialism magazine *Adbusters*, started a website devoted to launching a demonstration on Wall Street to protest the exploitation of humans and the environment by the forces of global capitalism. In September 2011, the demonstration took place and several hundred protestors encamped in nearby Zuccotti Park, where they remained for many weeks – erecting tents and cooking communally. One of the movement's manifestos declared that it was "fighting back against the corrosive power of major banks and multinational corporations over the democratic process, and the role of Wall Street in creating an economic collapse that has caused the greatest recession in generations." Soon, similar protests and encampments appeared in many other cities including Los Angeles, Boston, San Francisco, Denver, and Chicago. The protests gained the support of the national labor union federation, the AFL–CIO, and one of its largest affiliates, the Service Employees International Union. President Obama praised the Occupy movement's objectives. Many celebrities visited the encampments to demonstrate their support. Figure 14.1 shows support for the Tea Party and Occupy Wall Street by partisan affiliation in 2011, when both were still quite active and prominent.

Neither the antiwar movement nor the Tea Party nor Occupy Wall Street is as visible and politically important as it used to be. The reasons for the decline provide insight into how politics functions out of doors. The antiwar movement was the victim of its own success. It was instrumental in creating the political climate in which an antiwar candidate, Barack Obama, was elected president. He fulfilled his pledge to withdraw American troops. Therefore, the movement lost its primary object of protest and withered away. However, given the experience of the anti-Vietnam and anti-Iraq movements, should the US commit troops to another war, a new antiwar movement will arise.

The decline of the Tea Party and Occupy Wall Street was tied to the 2016 presidential election campaign. As we discussed in Chapter 13, that election campaign

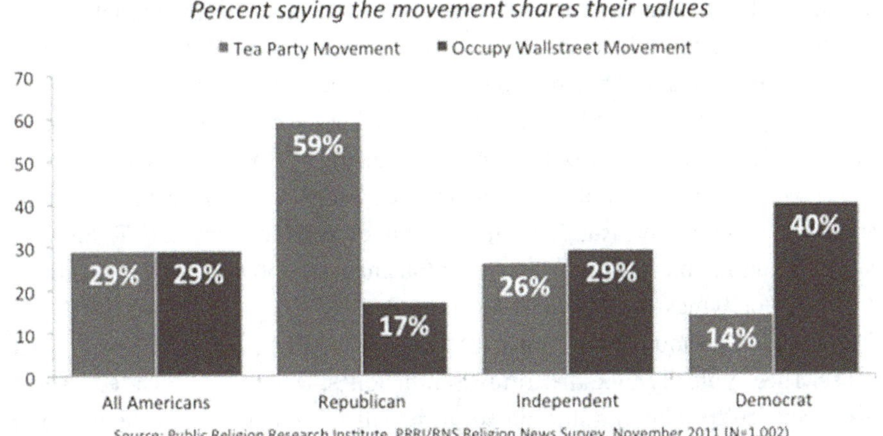

Figure 14.1. The Tea Party versus Occupy Wall Street by political affiliation.
Source: PRRI.

produced two insurgencies: the Trump and Sanders campaigns. Many adherents of the two movements abandoned protest in favor of the hope of gaining power, or at least of radically transforming a major political party, that the Trump and Sanders campaigns offered. Sanders's attacks on Wall Street impressed many occupiers and they flocked to his campaign. Unlike Occupy, the Tea Party had previously engaged in electoral politics without losing its identity as a movement. But the prospect of electing a president was sufficiently enticing to cause its adherents to more completely shift their energies from protest to politics. Although Trump's focus on immigration and trade did not mesh with the Tea Party's emphasis on limiting government, Tea Partiers resonated with his attacks on political correctness, his mockery of the liberal establishment, and his promise to cut taxes. Thus, these movements were subsumed by the two insurgencies. Each of these experiences echoes the past. The abolitionist movement did not survive the accomplishment of its greatest goal, freeing the slaves. The Progressive movement became attached to Teddy Roosevelt's 1912 insurgent political campaign and was then, over time, absorbed by the Democratic Party.

Lobbying

A good way to appreciate the diversity and abundance of Washington lobbies is to walk the streets of the nation's capital and read the names on brass plaques mounted at the entrances to the office buildings. One gets the impression that no imaginable activity is too obscure or specialized to be denied representation in Washington. In addition to such large long-established associations as the National Association of Manufacturers, the National Association for the Advancement of Colored People (NAACP), the US Chamber of Commerce, the National Rifle Association, and the National Education Association one finds the Canoe Cruisers Association, the National Cannabis Industry Association, the International Society of Crytpozoology, and thousands more. In 2016, more than $1.36 billion was spent on lobbying Congress and federal agencies (www.opensecrets.org/lobby/). The ten biggest lobbying firms were the US Chamber of Commerce, the National Association of Realtors, Blue Cross Blue Shield, the American Hospital Association, the Pharmaceutical Research and Manufacturers of America, the American Medical Association, Boeing, the National Association of Broadcasters, AT&T, and the Business Roundtable (http://thehill.com/business-a-lobbying/business-a-lobbying/318177-lobbyings-top-50-whos-spending-big).

Plaques also announce the name of firms whose titles do not reveal their purpose. They typically take the form "Smith, Jones, Doe and Associates." These firms specialize in lobbying and do so on behalf of whoever hires them. Major Washington law firms typically include a department similarly devoted to lobbying for clients. The principals of such lobbying firms, as well as leading trade associations are usually people who have extensive high-level government experience. Many are former congresspersons, cabinet secretaries, and heads of government agencies. Their key subordinates are typically former congressional staffers and executive branch personnel. They bring their extensive knowledge of how the government operates as well as their extensive friendship network of former colleagues, people who are likely to return their calls and who may owe them a favor. Major profit-making and not-for-profit institutions such as large corporations, hospitals, and universities do not rely solely on their trade associations. They have such a heavy reliance on and complex relationships with government that they have their own lobbying staffs, usually headed by a Vice President for Public Affairs.

State, county, and local governments are major recipients of federal spending. Therefore, these governments are concerned both in the spending levels Congress sets for programs that subsidize them and also the formulas that Congress establishes for the distribution of such monies. Formulas are never entirely neutral in their impact. For example, a heavily populated state like New York will want spending formulas based on population. A lightly populated state like Wyoming will seek to ensure that a minimum amount of the grant in question be reserved for each state, regardless of size. Because they have so much at stake, state, county, and local governments maintain their own lobbying organizations. Many cities belong to the National League of Cities. Because big cities have concerns that often differ from their smaller counterparts, big city mayors have their own organization, the National Conference of Mayors. The National Governors' Association and the National Council of State Legislatures lobby on behalf of the states collectively. Specific types of state agencies also form national associations. For example, the Association of State and Interstate Water Pollution Control Administrators lobbies the federal government on behalf of the state and interstate agencies that regulate water quality and water pollution.

Later in the chapter we discuss the rise of the public interest movement. It is not a movement in the sense that this chapter has used the term, since it relies less on mass demonstrations than on publishing exposés and on such indoor tactics as bringing suit and lobbying. But it ressembles a movement in that it both stimulates and feeds on public outrage and has a profound effect on public opinion. As the term implies, public interest organizations differentiate themselves from the other groups seeking to influence public policy on the grounds that they are not self-interested but rather work for the good of all. As we shall see, the early public interest groups were on the political left. They fought for such objectives as car safety, clean air, and clean water. They were so successful that they were soon emulated by forces on the right that also claimed to operate in the public interest as they fought against abortion and gay marriage and in defense of what they called "family values." Among today's most influential liberal public interest groups are: the National Resources Defense Council, which lobbies for a variety of environmental objectives most notably clean air; NARAL:

Pro-Choice America, which lobbies against abortion restrictions; and the Human Rights Campaign, which advocates on behalf of gays, lesbians, bisexuals, and the transgendered. Among the important conservative public interest groups are: the Competitive Enterprise Institute, which works to encourage economic competition by opposing excessive government regulation; the Family Research Council, which devotes itself to preserving a traditional understanding of marriage; and Citizens United, which seeks to restore limited government.

Regardless of whom they work for, lobbyists perform three related tasks: they inform, they influence, and they seek financial and political support for their legislative and executive branch allies. The quest for information and the contest between conflicting information is at the heart of the legislative process. Facts do not speak for themselves. Lobbying organizations devote considerable time and effort to assembling data and packaging it in a manner that is most supportive of their legislative objectives. This information is vital even to those legislators who are most supportive of those objectives, because they need to understand an issue if they are to make a persuasive case on its behalf. Information is also crucial as a means for shaping the broader public debate on the issue at hand, since those legislators not so closely allied with the lobby will resist supporting the objective if they do not believe it is publically defensible.

Information also drives much of executive branch decision making. Regulatory agencies depend on scientific and economic information to provide the basis for their decisions. They do not have the resources to conduct all the research and assemble all the data they need. Some of it is provided by research agencies within the government, but a great deal is also provided both by the affected firms and often by public interest groups on the right, who try to make the case for less costly and intrusive regulation, and public interest groups on the left, who seek more stringent regulation. Lobbying organizations make extensive use of the public comment period that follows an agency's issuance of a proposed regulation as described in Chapter 10.

Lobbyists exert influence in many different ways. Influence may reside in the lobbyists themselves. The author of this book was told an unverifiable story about a Japanese company who badly needed a prompt favorable decision on a trade regulation matter. It had tried to make its case to the regulatory authorities and had been unable to obtain a final decision. Finally, its own lobbyist advised it to ask a former secretary of state to intervene. That person demanded several thousand dollars to make a phone call to the relevant decision maker. The call lasted only a few minutes, but the company obtained the ruling it needed.

Influence also comes through mobilizing an association's membership. Almost every medium-sized town in America has at least one auto dealership. If the National Automobile Dealers Association is seeking to influence a particular congressperson, perhaps the best weapon at its disposal is to urge all the auto dealers and their employees in the district to show up at the district office when the representative is there and remind the member just how numerous and locally well connected they are.

Because the public, the media, and the Congress are impressed by the large impassioned shows of support for a cause that political movements mobilize, public relations firms try to help their clients exert political influence by putting together organizations that simulate such movements but whose expenses, and perhaps its participants, are paid by the firm. This phenomenon has been labeled "astro turf," because it offers the appearance but not the reality of the grassroots. Cable companies are known to have organized and sponsored "concerned citizens" movements when states threaten to change the laws granting them local monopolies. Likewise, tobacco and coal companies have funded citizens' groups that have protested what they consider to be the excessive health and environmental regulations affecting those industries. Public interest groups have also been accused of "astro turfing" when the "volunteers" they send door to door with petitions calling for tougher environmental laws are not volunteers at all but paid laborers.

In order to maintain good relations with elected officials whom they hope to influence, lobbyists encourage their clients to make campaign contributions. Such contributions enable lobbyists to have ready access to those officials but they rarely allow the lobbyists to bully them into taking positions with which they are uncomfortable. Threatening to withhold contributions is dangerous because to do so is to lose access to someone whose help will be needed in the future, regarding other issues. Also, those on the other side of the question will see this threatened withdrawal of support as an opportunity to offer the embattled politician more support, thereby ingratiating themselves with that person. The funding of elections was discussed in the previous chapter.

Voluntary Associations

Voluntary associations exist in many different forms and perform many diverse functions. From the standpoint of promoting community wellbeing and cultivating citizenship, the most important are the ones that are organized and operate locally. These include service clubs such as the Kiwanis, Knights of Columbus, Rotary, and Lions clubs. The local chapters of these clubs are members of a national, and even international body, but they perform their greatest services in their home communities from sponsoring Little League teams to organizing community service projects to providing funds to local hospitals and cultural organizations. The Boy Scouts, Girl Scouts, YMCAs, YMHAs, and Jewish Community Centers provide a wide range of recreational, fitness, and cultural activities. The League of Women Voters does valuable research on a whole host of public issues, including but not limited to local matters.

In some instances, voluntary associations substitute almost entirely for government. Volunteer fire brigades and neighborhood crime watches may receive training and consultations from fire and police departments but they organize themselves and perform their fire fighting and surveillance activities on their own. Of the more than 1 million firefighters in the US, roughly 70 percent are volunteers (www.nfpa.org/news-and-research/fire.../us-fire-department-profile). Various types of volunteer crime prevention programs operate in many cities and towns throughout the nation.

In Maine, lobstermen substitute for government agents as regulators of the lobster supply. In order to prevent lobsters from becoming scarce, it is necessary to control the lobster harvest. The trouble is that no individual lobsterman has an incentive to limit his catch if he fears that at least some of the others are failing to do so. Normally this sort of problem, known as the Tragedy of the Commons, is solved by government-imposed limits on how much each boat can catch and government inspection of the lobster boats to make sure they are not exceeding their quota. But in 1995, Maine lobstermen won the authority, through local councils, to develop local fishing rules. Limits on the number of traps per lobsterman and the frequency with which the lobsterman may check them are ratified by the district council of lobstermen, who must approve these restrictions by a 2 to 3 vote. The lobstermen are more effective enforcers than government agents because they have participated in creating rules that reflect their intimate knowledge of local conditions.

A second category of civic participation involves partnerships between voluntary associations and government, for example the Central Park Conservancy. New York's Central Park attracts more than 20 million visitors a year. Until 1995, it was maintained by a government agency, the New York City Parks Department. Because of deep dissatisfaction with the appearance of the park and the lack of security provided its users, a group of private citizens established the Central Park Conservancy. The conservancy negotiated an agreement with the City of New York to take over the park's management. It provides more than 85 percent of Central Park's annual $20 million operating budget and is responsible for all basic care of the park. Approximately three out of every four Central Park employees are funded by the conservancy. Conservancy staff nurture the lawns, ponds, lakes, shrubs, trees, and flowers; they protect wildlife, control drainage, erosion, and pollution, and maintain the ball fields, bridle paths, and playgrounds. Staff have renovated many of the park's most important landmarks and built and staffed new visitors' centers.

Charter schools are another example of public–private partnership. Because parents and teachers in many school districts became deeply dissatisfied with the public schools, states have established an alternative. Educators may apply to establish and run their own schools paid for by the taxpayers. Charter schools must meet government-established standards and choose their students randomly among those who apply, but they are not subject to the specific curriculum guidelines nor the hiring, firing, and promotion practices of the public schools.

Voluntary associations also work for government as contractors. Government specifies the purposes and terms of the contract and pays the voluntary association to do the work. Many publically funded mental health, nutrition, emergency relief, drug treatment, and family planning programs are actually performed by such prominent private organizations as Catholic Charities, Planned Parenthood, and the Red Cross.

The Origins and Development of the Three Forms of Participation

Democratic Protest: The Democratic-Republican Societies

The earliest mass protest movement after the American Revolution erupted during the 1790s. The *Democratic-Republican societies* considered themselves extraconstitutional agents of the people. As one proponent argued, "the security of the people against any unwarrantable stretch of power" should not be "confined to the check which a constitution affords nor to the periodical return of elections; but rests also on the jealous examination of all the proceedings of the administration." The Democratic-Republican societies saw themselves as the philosophical and political heirs of the Sons of Liberty and Committees of Correspondence that acted as enforcers of republican orthodoxy during the revolution. Like their predecessors, they too held their meetings without asking for government permission, and used those occasions to vigorously proclaim their political grievances and their demands that government pay more heed to the concerns of ordinary people.

The controversies stirred by the Democratic-Republican societies came to a head with the Whiskey Rebellion in 1794. Secretary of the Treasury Alexander Hamilton's 1791 financial plan included a tax on whiskey. The democratic climate of opinion the societies fostered emboldened those farmers most aggrieved by the tax to take direct action against it. The rebellion was centered in the four westernmost counties of Pennsylvania, where whiskey was so important to the local economy that it was used, like money, as a medium of exchange. The tax was especially detested because it was levied and enforced by what seemed a distant, indifferent federal government.

With support from Democratic-Republican societies in western Pennsylvania, farmers sent petitions to Congress and resisted efforts to collect revenues. A federal marshal and an excise inspector were forced to flee the area, and for two weeks western Pennsylvania was agitated by impassioned meetings, radical oratory, threats to oust all federal authority from Pittsburgh by force, and occasional acts of violence. President George Washington called out the militia of four states and, with Secretary Hamilton and Pennsylvania governor Thomas

Mifflin at his side, led an army of 13,000 to confront the rebels. In the face of this massive show of force, the rebellion quickly dissolved.

The Constitution does not discuss whether direct protest in the name of rights against government is legitimate. Washington and the Federalists feared that organizations like the Democratic-Republican societies were a threat to representative government. Washington denounced them as threats to the wellbeing of a stable constitutional order. This opposition to the very idea of voluntary political association sparked a heated debate on the nature of democracy and representation. The Democratic Society of Philadelphia, which had condemned the Whiskey Rebellion, now championed vigorous public debate: "If the laws of our Country are the echo of the sentiment of the people is it not of importance that those sentiments should be generally known? How can they be better understood than by a free discussion, publication and communication of them by means of political societies?"

The Democratic-Republican societies wilted in the face of Washington's denunciation. But, as happened with later protest movements most recently the Tea Party and Occupy Wall Street, many members became prominent party activists and taught the Republicans valuable lessons gleaned from their previous experience. Schooled in the societies' freewheeling activities, they invigorated the party's commitment to popular, mass-based politics. Figure 14.2 shows the rapid growth and decline of the societies.

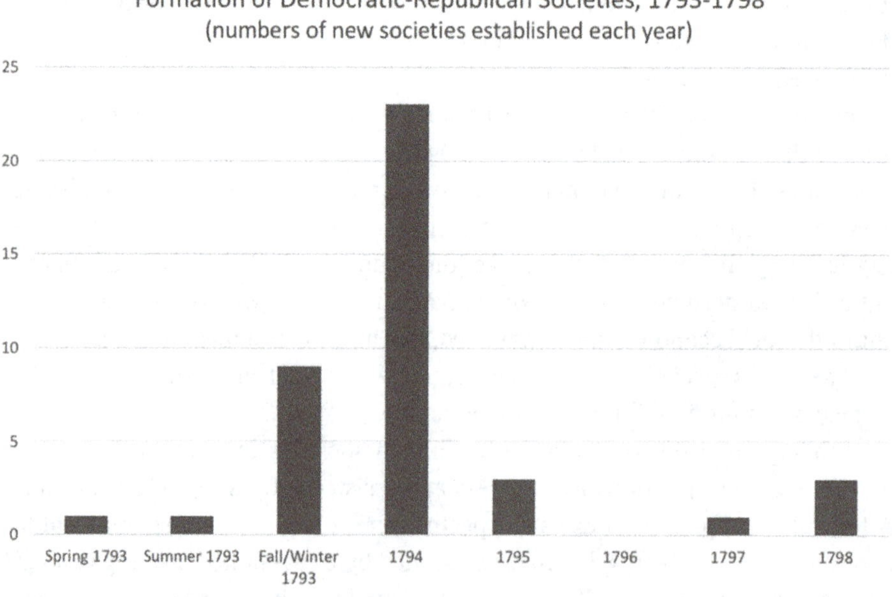

Figure 14.2. Democratic-Republican societies.
Source: Encyclopedia of Greater Philadelphia.

Early Voluntary Associations

As we discussed in Chapter 2, voluntary associations are a critical expression of the communitarian "habits of the heart" that form a vital aspect of American political culture. From the beginning, Americans were actively engaged in governing themselves. In New England, self-government took the form of town meeting in which all town residents were entitled to take part in critical decisions regarding town governance. Throughout the nation it involved widespread active participation in voluntary associations that served as alternatives to formal, representative government. These associations were formed to fight fires, protect public safety, maintain roads and public buildings, sustain the indigent, and provide many other services that in Europe were performed by government officials and paid for by tax revenue.

As Alexis de Tocqueville noted, voluntary associations strengthened political life by correcting for the Constitution's greatest weakness, its insufficient attention to the conditions nurturing an active and competent citizenry:

> Americans combine to give fetes, found seminaries, build churches, distribute books, and send missionaries to the antipodes. Hospitals, prisons, and schools take shape in that way. Finally, if they want to proclaim a truth or propagate some feeling by the encouragement of a great example, they form an association. In every case, at the head of a new undertaking, where in France you would find the government or in England some territorial magnate, in the United States you are sure to find an association.

Echoing Anti-Federalist concerns, Tocqueville warned that "if they did not learn to help each other voluntarily," individuals who were obsessed with their privacy and rights would become helpless, expecting government to do everything for them. By participating in voluntary associations, the democratic individual would become part of a vital community that would counter the "danger that he would be shut up in the solitude of his own heart."

Temperance, Abolition, and Parties

The Democratic Republican societies of the 1790s represented the beginning of one sort of protest movement that has survived until the present, a movement dedicated to giving the public a wider and louder voice in political decision making. In the 1830s, two other types of movements were born that also remain a part of modern American politics. One involved moral reform and the other civil rights. Both the temperance and abolitionist movements grew out of a powerful religious movement that swept the country in the 1820s and 1830s. Known as the Second Great Awakening, the movement was characterized by mass meetings, often held out of doors, known as revivals. These meetings offered individuals the opportunity to personally accept Jesus Christ as their savior. The theology of the Great Awakening deemphasized the Calvinist notion that God alone determined who would and would not be saved. Instead, each individual was free to choose between sin and salvation. This emphasis on individual responsibility sparked a desire to eradicate evil from the world. In the view of many Americans of that era, two of the worst evils were drunkenness and slavery.

The American Temperance Society, founded in 1826, devoted itself to reducing alcohol consumption. It grew rapidly. In a single year, the New York branch gained 50,000 members. It benefited greatly from the vast expansion in the speed and reach of the US Postal Service made possible by the extensive railroad network the US had developed by the late 1830s. No longer did the mail have to travel at the speed of a coach horse. Thanks to this communications revolution, it was able to distribute hundreds of thousands of pamphlets that advocated for its cause. Later, during the Progressive Era, a vastly expanded rail network would combine with new inexpensive printing techniques to bring about the mass circulation of national magazines. Readers were especially drawn to the exposés that appeared in *Arena, McClures*, and others written by a new breed of investigative reporters whom TR nicknamed "muckrakers." These widely publicized exposés were critical to the political success of Progressivism (see Chapters 4 and 12).

Although the temperance movement had religious origins and stressed voluntary action, it sought state and national government support. It besieged Congress with petitions asking representatives to promote abstinence. In 1833, Secretary of War Lewis Cass presided over a congressional temperance meeting that adopted a resolution proclaiming Congress's responsibility to aid in protecting public morals. By 1833, the society had 2 million members, out of a national non-slave population of only 13 million. Alcohol consumption had soared after the Revolution and reached a high of four gallons a year per person by 1830, nearly triple present-day levels. By 1845, as the temperance movement gained momentum, consumption dropped to below two gallons a year per person. This success shows how local communities and religion revitalized the American democratic tradition. Although social movements operated outside the formal institutions and practices of the Constitution, they helped galvanize political participation that significantly reduced the space between government representatives and public opinion. Figure 14.3 charts per capita alcohol consumption from 1720 to 1970.

Abolitionism devoted itself to ending slavery and granting civil rights to African Americans. The movement's militancy was exemplified by William Lloyd Garrison. He had once been a supporter of the American Colonization Society, which favored gradual abolition and returning former slaves to Africa. However, by the early 1830s his newspaper, *The Liberator*, was advocating immediate, uncompensated emancipation. In what is perhaps the most famous editorial in American history, Garrison told his readers, 60 percent of whom were black,

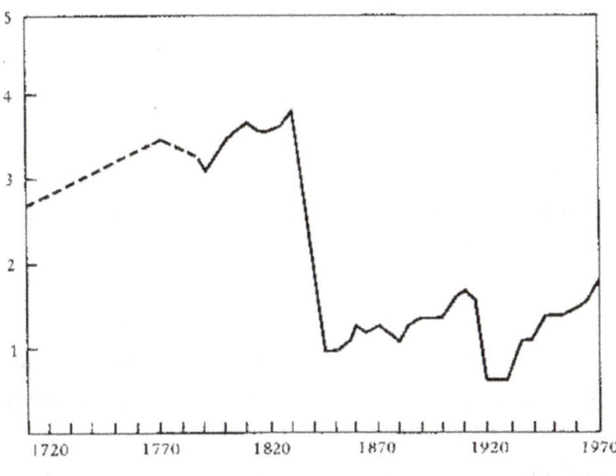

Figure 14.3. Consumption of alcohol.
Source: Oxford University Press.

"Urge me not to use moderation in a cause like the present. I am in earnest – I will not equivocate – I will not excuse – I will not retreat a single inch – AND I WILL BE HEARD."

Garrison revolutionized the antislavery movement by linking immediate abolition to African Americans' claim to equal rights. Slavery, he wrote, violated the "self-evident truth ... that all men are created equal." Calling the Constitution "a covenant with death and an agreement with hell," he burned a copy of it on July 4. No person of conscience, he argued, should participate in the corrupt political system it formed.

Garrison led the American Anti-Slavery Society, whose determined organizers spread antislavery sentiment in the North and challenged slavery's existence in the South. Before the Civil War, roughly 200,000 people, mostly from New England and the parts of western New York and northern Ohio settled by New Englanders, belonged to abolitionist societies.

As vital as the American Anti-Slavery Society was in stirring antislavery sentiment, its impact was limited by its extremism. Americans were repelled by Garrison's burning of the document so many of them held sacred. And they were frightened by its openness to the use of violence to achieve its ends. Although the society's Declaration of Sentiments opposed "physical resistance," it also acknowledged that sometimes it was necessary to "wage war against oppressors."

But not all abolitionists rejected conventional politics. Other antislavery militants formed the Liberty Party, which garnered 7,000 votes in the 1840 presidential election. In 1848, many of them supported the Free Soil Party candidate, former president Martin Van Buren, who received over 300,000 votes, about 10 percent of the total. Abolitionists formed a key part of the new Republican Party that replaced the Whigs as the Democrats' major rival in a realigned two-party system (see Chapter 11) and that succeeded in electing its presidential candidate, Abraham Lincoln, in 1860. Thus, the abolitionists helped forge the political transformation that led to the critical choice to emancipate the slaves.

Local temperance and other voluntary associations wrote constitutions and bylaws, elected officers, and formed statewide federations governed by annual conventions of locally elected delegates. These practices became models for political parties, which by the 1830s were governed by local, state, and national conventions that nominated candidates, published platforms, and enacted rules for election campaigns.

Political parties reciprocated, helping to sustain the vitality of civic associations by drawing people into political life and cultivating a habit and taste for collective action. "A whole crowd of people who might otherwise have lived on their own," Tocqueville noticed, "are taught both to want to combine and how to do so." So, one may think of political parties as "great free schools to which all citizens came to be taught the general theory of association."

Participation in elections became a form of self-expression, an assertion of one's understanding of one's rights, but one that took place in concert with other citizens in the collective act of self-government. Voting was not just an opportunity to select public officials. As Philip Nicholas argued on the floor of the Virginia Constitutional Convention of 1829, "it was the right by which man first signifies his will to become a member of Government of the social compact ... Suffrage, is the substratum, the paramount right" on which rested the rights stated in the Declaration of Independence: "the right to life, liberty, and the pursuit of happiness."

By the 1830s, this strong bond between voting and natural rights encompassed virtually every aspect of American life. Club officers, schoolteachers, and team captains were all elected. Democratic principles even penetrated military affairs. Rejecting a standing army as an affront to their egalitarian sensibilities, Americans until the Civil War fought mainly in state militia that selected their own leaders. Foreign visitors, accustomed to the deference accorded to public officials in Europe and Great Britain, were startled by the constraints that elections placed on officeholders. State legislators, and even members of Congress, were expected to return home after every legislative session to talk with constituents about what they had done and what they would do in the future. "Christ how I hate democracy," moaned a weary North Carolina congressman suffering from the ceaseless chase for public approval.

Andrew Jackson was one of the first political leaders to grasp the new politics that celebrated the ordinary citizen; indeed, his presidency signified its ascendance. For the first time, an inauguration was held outdoors, and ordinary citizens gathered in Washington to celebrate their hero's rise to power. Jackson's opponents claimed that crowds rushed the new president as soon as he took his oath and that Jackson was forced to escape from the back of the Capitol, only to fight past a wall of people to reach the White House. They claimed the executive mansion was swamped by a mob of 20,000 supporters who "spread filth, smashed glassware, vaulted through windows to get at tubs of whiskey on the lawn, and even obliged a makeshift ring of guards to escort the president to safety." In fact, the large crowd that welcomed Jackson to the presidency was mostly well behaved. Jackson himself thought things went quite well that day. The excitement aroused by his election, he sensed, would encourage him to use his office aggressively. Democratic elections not only empowered voters, they gave influence to a new breed of politician who appeared to embody the will of the people. As of November 7, 1848, the United States established a standard presidential election day, and nearly 80 percent of all male citizens voted. European nations relied on ancient traditions and folk spirits to unite them; Americans called on democracy. Walt Whitman, the great poet, declared the rite of selecting presidents "America's choosing day," the Western world's "powerfulest scene and show."

The Telegraph

The capacity to organize and act politically was greatly enhanced by what was perhaps the single greatest transformation in mass media since the printing press, the invention of the telegraph. The telegraph enabled news to be transmitted instantaneously. As important as the advent of radio, television, and the internet have proven to be, none of them has achieved as dramatic increase in the speed of communication as did the telegraph. Although various telegraph schemes had existed since the 1790s, the first real use of the device as a medium of mass communications did not take place until 1844 when news of the Whig Party's nomination of Henry Clay for president was transmitted over the first long-distance telegraph line, extending from Baltimore to Washington DC, built the previous year.

The telegraph transformed the Lincoln–Douglas debates of 1858 from a series of local occasions into a great national political event. Reporters used shorthand to copy the speeches even as they were being spoken. As soon as each debate was over, they sped to the nearest telegraph office where telegraphers translated the text into Morse code and transmitted it to newspaper offices nationwide. The next morning, newspaper readers around the country were able to read the debate in its entirety. Although he lost the Senate election to Douglas, the enthusiastic national reception of his speeches made Lincoln a national political celebrity and a plausible candidate for the 1860 Republican presidential nomination. Lincoln was quick to recognize the political potential of the telegraph. It is no accident that his two greatest public utterances – the Gettysburg Address and the Second Inaugural – were remarkably brief. He intentionally made them short so that they could easily be printed and read in the nation's newspapers which would have quick and ready access to them via the telegraph.

The Civic Dimension of Progressivism

As we discussed in Chapter 6, the late nineteenth century witnessed the birth of another form of protest movement aimed at ending the abuses and curbing the power of "monster" corporations. First the Populists and then the Progressives (see Chapters 4, 12, and 13) arose to fight the private economic powers that they believed were oppressing farmers and workers and threatening to undermine individual freedom and democratic accountability. However, the Progressives also added a vital civic dimension to their activities in the form of the social centers movement dedicated to recreating "the neighborly spirit" that Americans knew before they moved to live in large, socially fragmented cities. This movement started in Rochester, New York, where a former Presbyterian minister, Edward Ward, envisioned public schools as "the instrument of that deepest and most fundamental education upon which the very existence of democracy depends." In Rochester, public schools were used as public baths, libraries, theaters, and forums for debate. In 1912, Ward founded the National Community Center Association to help proliferate community centers nationwide. During the 1912 election, both Theodore Roosevelt and Woodrow Wilson celebrated the use of schoolhouses as neighborhood headquarters for political discussion.

Participation Moves Indoors

Political scientists Richard Harris and Daniel Tichenor have documented the rising influence of lobbying organizations during the Progressive Era. Between 1889 and 1899, 216 groups appeared for the first time ever at a congressional hearing. Nearly three times that many, 622, testified for the first time in the first decade of the twentieth century. During the following eight years, more than a thousand new groups testified before congressional committees. Nearly every form of lobby increased during the Progressive Era. Growth was especially rapid among trade associations and citizens' groups, reflecting the intensity of the struggles between corporations and insurgents over the shape of the American economy during this period.

The Seminal Role of the Labor and Civil Rights Movements

In the wake of the Great Depression, American workers mobilized themselves to create a powerful political movement. Not only did the labor movement greatly improve the lives of industrial workers and transform party politics, it set an example for the next great political movement of the twentieth century, the civil rights movement.

The New Deal and the Labor Movement

Just as it transformed the size and scope of American government, the New Deal radically altered and expanded political participation, both indoors and out. Prior to the New Deal, America remained the only rich industrial nation without a strong labor movement. Unionism was mostly confined to the building trades – carpenters, plumbers, brick-masons – and a few other highly skilled but relatively small industries such as cigar making. The one exception was coal mining, much of whose workforce belonged to the United Mine Workers of America (UMWA).

The 1920s had witnessed a huge boom in manufacturing resulting in the proliferation of factories across the Northeast and Midwest and a vast expansion of the industrial workforce. But until the New Deal these millions of factory workers remained unorganized. The condition of workers deteriorated as a result of the Great Depression beginning in 1929. In response to falling consumer demand, workers were asked to work longer hours for less pay under deteriorating working conditions. The National Industrial Recovery Act (NIRA) of 1933 offered half-hearted encouragement to workers' efforts to improve their circumstances. Section 7a of the NIRA proclaimed that "Employees shall have the right to organize and bargain collectively through representatives of their own choosing". But these strong sentiments were not accompanied by any mechanism for enabling this to happen. Nonetheless, the head of the coal miner's union, John L. Lewis, saw 7a as an opportunity to create a new labor movement. He ordered his best organizers to fan out into the auto, steel, aluminium, and glass factories and tell workers that "FDR wants you to organize." This was not strictly true, but Lewis gambled that faced with the prospect of hundreds of thousands of workers joining unions in the expectation of support from the president, FDR would be politically compelled to come to their aid. And FDR did. In 1935, Congress passed the National Labor Relations Act, known as the Wagner Act in honor of its chief sponsor, Senator Robert Wagner of New York. The act created a government agency, the National Labor Relations Board, charged with ensuring fair collective bargaining elections and forcing management to "bargain in good faith" with the unions that won those elections. With government tilting toward their side, Lewis's organizers succeeded beyond their wildest dreams. With their guidance, workers established the United Auto Workers, the United Steel Workers, the United Rubber Workers, and many other successful labor organizations. Overall, union membership jumped from roughly 2 million in 1933 to more than 9 million in 1940.

Although the unions benefited greatly from the labor legislation passed "indoors," winning recognition from management and gaining better wages and working conditions resulted from bloody battles waged "out of doors." Labor's chief weapon in these battles was the strike. If their demands were not met, workers would withdraw their labor and shut the factory down. Strikes turned violent when strikers tried to physically prevent replacements, whom they called "scabs," from entering the workplace and when strikers picketing the factory were attacked by police or by gangs hired by management, whom the unionists called "goons." These labor wars were the most widespread and violent instances of civil unrest since the end of the Civil War.

Because it was so difficult to keep "scabs" from breaking through union picket lines, the auto and rubber unions borrowed a European technique, the sit-down strike. Instead of declaring a strike and setting up picket lines, workers remained at their work stations at the end of a shift and refused to leave. Management was reluctant to forcibly remove them for fear that valuable machinery would be destroyed in the process.

Although its specific objectives were economic – better pay and working conditions – the labor movement was imbued with the religious fervor and the indignation that comes of being denied one's rights that had characterized earlier

Figure 14.4. New Technique: a 1937 cartoon by Harry E. Homan depicting the paralyzing effect of the "sit-down strike" on the American automobile industry.
Source: Granger Collection, NYC –

protest movements. Union rallies embodied the passion and commitment of revival meetings. The labor movement's unofficial anthem, "Solidarity Forever," was the "Battle Hymn of the Republic" with different words. The coal union song "Miner's Lifeguard" was taken from the hymn "Life is Like a Mountain Railway." The original refrain

> Blessed Savior, Thou wilt guide us,
> Til we reached that blissful shore;
> Where the angels wait to join us in thy praise for evermore

Was changed to:

> Union miners stand together,
> Heed no operator's tale,
> Keep your hand upon the dollar, and your eye upon the scale.

Workers did not simply complain about low wages, they claimed that, like slaves, their civil and human rights were being denied. Asked why they were willing to risk their livelihoods, and even their lives, to fight the boss, they often replied, "because he treats me like a dog." Their nickname for the Wagner Act was "Labor's Bill of Rights." This nickname is indicative of the veneration that most American workers paid to American constitutional principles. During the 1930s and 1940s, that veneration was tested as many unions endured vicious internal struggles between the so called "business" unionists who sought to promote worker interests without challenging Classic Liberal principles of private property and a market economy and radical unionists who were committed to the class struggle and to socialist principles. In almost every case, the business unionists triumphed. As a result, the labor movement emerged as a bulwark of support for the American constitutional path of limited government and free enterprise.

By the late 1930s, most major industries had been successfully unionized. For the next several decades, strikes remained numerous. But those strikes rarely took on the violent aspect common in the 1930s. For the most part workers respected company property and management did not try to break the strike with scabs and goons. Most strikes were settled after a relatively short time. "Indoor" negotiations replaced violence as the central aspect of union–management relations.

Because labor union leaders were acutely aware of how much their organizations' wellbeing depended on government policy, the labor movement became increasingly active in party politics. As we discussed in Chapter 12, the major national labor organization, now known as the American Federation of Labor–Congress of Industrial Organizations (AFL–CIO), became one of the most powerful and loyal members of the Democratic Party coalition. It established its headquarters in Washington and devoted considerable staff and money to testifying at committee hearings, lobbying individual congresspersons, and other typical "indoor" Washington political activities.

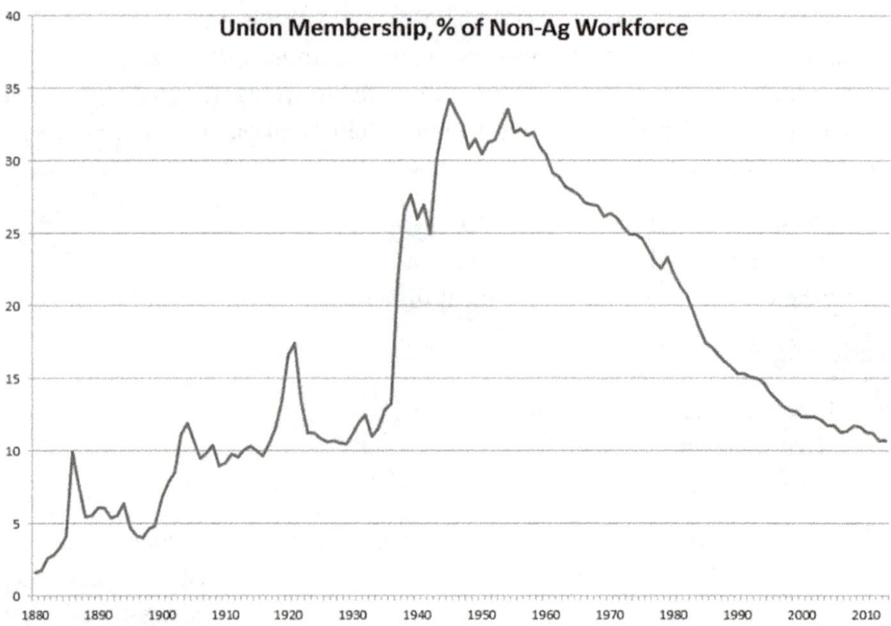

Figure 14.5. Union membership.
Source: New Feudalism, Eric Kades.

The greatest labor movement successes of the postwar era were won in the state capitals. Union lobbyists convinced many state legislatures to pass laws establishing collective bargaining rights for public employees. As a result, unions were able to enlist state and local government workers as members and bargain on their behalf. In recent decades, the number of manufacturing workers, the original base of union membership, has steadily declined while the state and local government workforce has grown very rapidly. The labor movement now has more public than private sector members. The nation's three largest labor organizations are all composed of public employees. The biggest, the National Education Association (NEA), composed of public school teachers, has more than 2.7 million members. The second, the Service Employees International Union, whose members include hospital workers, mental healthcare workers, school bus drivers, and custodians, has more than 1.5 million members. The third, the American Federation of State, County and Municipal Employees (AFSME), has almost 1.5 million. Figure 14.5 charts the rise and decline of union membership as a percentage of the workforce.

The New Deal and Lobbying

Just as the New Deal transformed American government, so it transformed efforts to influence government. The New Deal's reach extended to virtually everyone involved in the economy regardless of whether they were farmers, bankers, truckers, manufacturers, miners, or merchants. Therefore, all of these persons and firms came to recognize the need to organize amongst themselves in order to keep abreast of policy developments, fend off adverse government actions, and encourage favorable ones. Notice that the major policy innovations like the NIRA, the Wagner Act, and the Securities and Exchange Act preceded the establishment of interested private sector organizations. Policy created politics as the interested parties formed in response to actions by government.

As the New Deal wore on, these organizations were often able to hire away the very persons who had written the regulations and guidelines the interest groups were now seeking either to sustain or to alter. This was the birth of the "revolving door" between the bureaucracy, congressional staffs, and interest groups that has dominated the labor market for lobbyists ever since. This growing interpenetration of government and interest organizations was by no means limited to the business and labor sectors. One of the largest and most influential Washington lobbies, the American Association of Retired Persons (AARP), was established to defend the interests of social security recipients. Launched in 1958 with backing from a teachers' retirement group and insurance company, it now has 33 million members, a sufficient base to give it considerable influence over the development of all federal legislation affecting seniors.

The Civil Rights Movement

The civil rights movement that emerged in the 1950s borrowed key tactics and strategies from the labor movement. This was no accident. The coal and auto unions were the first large organizations to racially integrate, and many African Americans participated in the epochal labor battles of the 1930s. One of the pioneers of the civil rights movement, A. Phillips Randolph, was the longtime president of the powerful all-black Union of Sleeping Car Porters. Likewise, several important labor leaders, most prominently Walter Reuther, president of the United Auto Workers, were active supporters of the civil rights cause.

The sit-down strike was the model for the approach that civil rights demonstrators took to integrating public facilities. Indeed, the first major "outdoor" civil rights action, the Montgomery bus boycott, stemmed from Rosa Parks's decision on December 1, 1955 to sit down in the front of a city bus and refuse to move to the back when the bus driver ordered her to do so. Under the leadership of the Reverend Martin Luther King, the black citizens of Montgomery declared that if they could not ride in the front of the bus, they would not ride it at all. Instead, they pledged to either walk to work or ride in the car-pools that King and his colleagues organized. The boycott lasted more than a year. It received worldwide media attention and did much to arouse national public opinion against

Montgomery's racist policy. In November of 1956, the Supreme Court declared Montgomery's city ordinance segregating bus seating to be unconstitutional.

Emulating Rosa Parks, the sit-in was adopted as the tactic for integrating public facilities throughout the South. On February 1, 1960, four students from the blacks only Agricultural and Technical College of North Carolina entered a local Woolworth's department store and sat down at the "whites only" lunch counter and ordered coffee. When they were asked to leave, they refused and remained in their seats until the store closed. The next day, they were joined by sixteen more students. By the end of the next week, black college students were sitting in at lunch counters in other North Carolina cities – Durham, Raleigh, Winston Salem, and Charlotte. The movement soon spread to Virginia, Kentucky, and Tennessee. On July 25, 1960, Woolworth's desegregated its lunch counters.

Starting in 1961, teams of blacks and whites who called themselves "Freedom Riders" boarded buses and rode throughout the South, refusing to leave their seats when the blacks among them were ordered to move to the back of the bus. They would also sit down together in segregated bus terminal lunch counters. The Freedom Riders were often violently removed from their seats and severely beaten by mobs of local citizens and local police. Finally, in the fall of 1961 the Interstate Commerce Commission issued regulations requiring the racial desegregation of all interstate buses and terminals.

Despite the provocations provided by the mobs, which spit and beat them, and the mayors, governors, and sheriffs who abetted such behavior, the leaders of the civil rights movement recognized the need to remain within the bounds of civility and constitutionality set by American political culture. Like the labor movement, they remained committed to nonviolence and continually reiterated their belief in and support for the American constitutional order and the principles it was based on. As we discussed in Chapter 2, the idea of an American dream, as "yet unfulfilled," was a constant theme of King's speeches and writings. It permeated his most famous oration, the "I Have a Dream" address heard by more than 250,000 people gathered at the Lincoln Memorial during the 1963 march on Washington.

The advent of television greatly increased the movement's ability to influence public opinion. As painful as the beatings and the shocks from the cattle prods were, the spectacle of brave men and women submitting to them while remaining peaceful and dignified was critical in turning public opinion in the movement's favor. Thanks to television, these horrific acts were witnessed by tens of millions of viewers nationwide on the nightly network news. Ever since, political movements have orchestrated their out-of-doors activities in order to maximize both the extent and the favorability of TV coverage.

It is no coincidence that so many of the great civil rights leaders – Ralph David Abernathy, Fred Shuttlesworth, Joseph Lowery, and Wyatt Walker, as well as Martin Luther King Jr. – were Christian ministers. As we noted in Chapter 12,

African Americans as a group are deeply religious. Ever since they were slaves they have looked to Christianity as a source of solace and hope. Churches are among the strongest institutions in African American communities, particularly in the South. The Montgomery bus boycott and the thousands of sit-ins and rallies it inspired were planned and organized in church basements. In their Sunday sermons, preachers retold the great biblical stories of struggles for freedom, most especially the exodus of the Jews from Egypt, to inspire and embolden the congregants to emulate those efforts.

The leadership that President Lyndon Johnson, a Democrat, provided for the passage of the 1964 Civil Rights Act and the 1965 Voting Rights Act cemented the loyalty of the civil rights movement and the African American voters it mobilized to the Democratic Party. This gain was especially important in the South, where in a matter of only a few years African American voters went from being disenfranchised to voting in massive numbers. However, the alienation of white Southern voters from the Democrats, caused at least in part by the party's aggressive civil rights policies, resulted in a major party realignment in that region in which whites came increasingly to support the Republicans.

The success of the civil rights movement depended upon the combination of courageous protests and inspiring speeches that took place out of doors and artful "indoor" lawyering. As discussed in Chapters 9 and 11, *Brown v. Board of Education of Topeka* (1954), which declared school segregation unconstitutional, launched the civil rights struggle that would dominate American politics and government for the next twenty-five years. The Warren Court, which rendered this decision, continued the New Deal court's encouragement of citizen groups such as the National Association for the Advancement of Colored People (NAACP), founded in 1909, to turn to the courts to pursue their policy agendas. The NAACP established the Legal Defense and Education Fund in 1939 with a full-time legal staff and eligibility for tax-deductible contributions. NAACP lawsuits against school segregation finally bore fruit in *Brown*.

Like the abolitionists, Progressives, and the labor movement, the civil rights movement had increasing difficulty remaining unified. As the 1960s wore on, many civil rights activists came to question the wisdom of Martin Luther King's adherence to the American creed, a set of principles that they found to be hypocritical in the extreme. They came to believe that freedom for African Americans could best be achieved by separating politically and culturally from the American mainstream and creating their own alternative schools, businesses, and political institutions. They also sought to expel whites from the positions of influence that many had come to occupy in the civil rights movement and they questioned the movement's commitment to nonviolence. They replaced the goal of full integration into American life with the slogan, "Black Power." The ensuing split that took place between those who remained committed to peaceful protest and racial integration and those who embraced "Black Power" sapped the movement's strength. Even as African Americans continued to win crucial legal battles and use their voting power to achieve important public policy victories, the political influence and moral authority of the civil rights movement declined.

CRITICAL CHOICE: MOVEMENTS ADOPT THE LANGUAGE OF RIGHTS

In the 1960s and early 1970s, inspired by the success of the civil rights movement, new protest movements emerged involving college students, war protesters, women, gays, and environmentalists. Many of the leaders of these various causes had been civil rights activists themselves and they brought the energy and idealism they derived from their participation in that movement to their new causes. Most importantly, they chose to emulate the civil rights movment by framing their demands in the language of rights: a right to a decent income; a right to gender equality; a right to choose an abortion; a right to a healthy environment; the right of peoples around the world to self-determination. A bit later, countermovements arose that likewise spoke the civil rights-inspired language of rights: the right of a fetus to live, the right to freely express one's religion. The decision of so many and diverse social movements to adopt the language of rights was a critical choice that radically altered American politics.

Student Protest

What the churches had been to the civil rights movement, college campuses were to the protest movements of the 1960s. Intellectuals, college professors among them, had been active in all the previous protest movements. One of the greatest abolitionists, Charles Grandison Finney, was a professor and later president of Oberlin College. W. E. B. Dubois, an important Progressive and one of the founders of the civil rights movement, was the first African American to earn a Ph.D. at Harvard and spent much of his life as a university professor. But college students had only rarely been active movement members. By contrast, the single most powerful and influential protest movement of the 1960s, the antiwar movement, was born on college campuses and derived much of its support and energy from college students.

In the spring of 1965 the leaders of the antiwar movement decided that the best way to show the size and depth of antiwar feeling was to emulate the epochal march on Washington for civil rights that Martin Luther King had addressed in 1963 with their own march on Washington. On college campuses throughout America antiwar activists chartered buses and enlisted fellow students to attend the march, which ultimately attracted between 15,000 and 25,000 participants. Throughout the 1960s and 1970s antiwar marches on Washington filled by college students became a staple of the antiwar movement. To further dramatize their cause, students also engaged in sit-ins. They occupied university administration buildings on hundreds of college campuses and refused to leave. Videos of war protestors being dragged off by policemen became a regular feature of nightly TV news.

Until the establishment of an all-volunteer army in 1973, male college students were subject to being drafted into the army once they graduated. Much of their motivation for protesting the war came from their strong desire not to serve. However, the antiwar cause was framed in human and civil rights terms, not self-interest. War protestors insisted that the Vietnam War was a civil war and that American support for the South Vietnamese government was depriving South Vietnamese citizens of their right to self-determination. Thus, the protestors claimed the same moral highground, the defense of essential rights, occupied by the labor and civil rights movements before them.

Environmental and Women's Movements

The two other most influential movements that adopted civil rights as their model were the environmental and the women's movements. They also framed their cause in the language of rights and sought to dramatize their grievances in a media friendly manner. Environmentalists demanded clear air and water on the grounds that every person had a right to a safe and healthy environment. They fought to protect endangered plant and animal species, claiming that nonhumans too enjoyed rights against extinction. Women couched their demands for equal pay and equal opporunity for hiring and promotion as the fulfillment of the rights crusade begun by the suffragists, whose first victory had been obtaining the right to vote (see Chapters 2 and 13). The environmentalists were particularly adept in their use of the media. To protest strip mining for coal they sat down in front of massive bulldozers that were poised to gouge the mountainsides to remove the trees and soil that covered the coal seam. They produced videos of the wholesale slaughter of baby seals by fur hunters and of basement walls turning purple and yellow from the toxic chemicals that oozed into them from abandoned toxic waste dumps.

Unlike the Progressives and the civil rights movements to whom they owed so much, these protest movements did not have deep Christian roots. Many clergy joined them, but their most prominent leaders and their most important symbols were either strictly secular or, in the case of environmentalism, rooted in nature worship. It was in this period that religiosity began to acquire partisan meaning. As we discussed in the previous chapter, devout Christians came to see themselves as conservatives. Abortion advocates, feminists, and gays came increasingly to view organized religion as their enemy.

Like their predecessors, these movements were highly successful in shifting public opinion in their favor, forcing government and private industry to improve environmental quality and the status of women. But they too were plagued by extremism. The public recoiled from antilogging activists who hid metal spikes in trees in order to destroy loggers' chainsaws; animal rights activists who broke into mink farms releasing the minks into the wild; and feminist activists burning their bras in public.

The New Right

The civil rights, environmental, and feminist causes were embraced by the political left and adopted by the Democratic Party. It was not until the late 1970s that movements and lobbies arose on the right to be embraced by the Republicans. The Christian Coalition, the National Right to Life Committee, and other organizations copied their opponents' legal, lobbying, and marketing tactics to oppose court and agency decisions that mandated school busing for racial balance, affirmative action to increase the number of minorities and women in higher education and the workplace, and abortion. These conservative organizations resembled their liberal forebears in crucial ways. They too spoke the language of rights: the right of a fetus to live; the right of a child to pray; equal opportunity for all, including white males. They too found ways to exploit the news media, producing compelling images of human fetuses followed by horrifying footage of those fetuses being removed from the mother and destroyed.

The Christian right added a new weapon to the media arsenal of protest movements by producing television programs of their own. Several of their most prominent leaders – Reverends Jerry Falwell, Oral Roberts, and Pat Robertson – hosted weekly television shows. They combined prayer, hymn singing, and sermons on traditional biblical topics with ringing denunciations of abortion, feminism, and other liberal causes. They appealed for funds and volunteers for their efforts to restore religious sanctity and the integrity of the family. Later, conservative spokesmen created vast nationwide audiences for themselves by resuscitating a neglected media vehicle, AM radio. FM had increasingly replaced AM as the preferred medium for music broadcasting. AM stations were becoming increasingly desperate for programs with popular appeal. At the same time, many conservative citizens were becoming increasingly dissatisfied with what they took to be the liberal bias of the mainstream media – network television news, National Public Radio, and major newspapers, especially the *Washington Post* and the *New York Times*. Conservative talk radio filled the needs both of the stations for programming and of conservatives for alternative sources of news and opinion. Rush Limbaugh and Glenn Beck became the most prominent national conservative talk radio spokesmen. Dozens of others attained great popularity in regional and local media markets. Conservatives also copied the left's indoor approaches. The nonprofit public interest law firms and lobbying organizations they founded proved equally adept at winning seminal Supreme Court cases and convincing Congress and the executive branch to adopt their policy proposals.

UPSHOT

Civil rights-inspired movements of the left and right continue to form an important element of the contemporary political landscape. The three movements described in the contemporary portrait are likewise cut from the same rights-focused mold. The dominance of rights talks should come as no surprise in a nation formed on the basis of the inalienable rights to life, liberty, and the pursuit of happiness. However, this rights focus does create political difficulties. Rights are by their very nature absolute. For example, a woman's right to control her own body, and hence to have an abortion, cannot be reconciled with an unborn child's right to life. Thus, the movements dedicated to protecting and opposing abortion have grave difficulty finding common ground. The tendency of contemporary social movements to frame their concerns in terms of rights polarizes American politics. It makes it very difficult for lawmakers to exercise the political art of compromise, which is so crucial for sustaining a stable political order.

A New Form of Political Participation: The Public Interest Movement

The movements of the 1960s operated primarily out of doors, fomenting protests on college campuses, marches on Washington, sit-ins, and demonstrations at City Hall. Beginning in the late 1960s, consumer advocate Ralph Nader became the leading innovator of a new form of indoor politics, known as the public interest movement. Nader and his exposé of the automobile industry, *Unsafe at Any Speed: The Designed-in Dangers of the American Automobile*, energized this new reform movement with revelations of corporate malpractice. When Congress responded by creating the National Highway Traffic Safety Administration (NHTSA) in 1970, Nader and other consumer advocates remained vigilant, constantly criticizing the agency for not regulating the auto industry aggressively enough. This political assault continued even after Jimmy Carter was elected president in 1976 and Nader's protégé, Joan Claybrook, was appointed head of NHTSA.

Many of the founders of the public interest movement were veterans of the protest movement of the 1960s, but they determined that the cause of reform needed a greater indoor dimension. Rather than organize demonstrations, they published reports exposing industry malfeasance and government foot-dragging. They brought lawsuits based on those exposés. They pressed for the appointment of movement loyalists like Claybrook, and vigorously lobbied Congress and government agencies. As the political scientist Jeffrey Berry has written, "Leaders of the new [public interest groups] wanted to transcend 'movement politics' with organizations that could survive periods of intense emotion." Therefore, despite their antiestablishment rhetoric and profound suspicion of centralized power, public interest activists did not try to get rid of bureaucracy. Instead, they made themselves an integral and permanent part of bureaucratic policy making.

In addition to NHTSA, public interest lobbies fought to establish new agencies such as the Environmental Protection Agency (EPA) and the Consumer Product Safety Commission, and to reinvigorate such Progressive Era regulatory bodies as the Federal Trade Commission (FTC) and the Food and Drug Administration (FDA). As Nader urged, regulatory bodies were not to be trusted to act for the public, but were to be directed by administrative procedures to enable public participation, "so that agency lethargy or inefficiency could be checked by interested citizen activity." By the late 1970s, this commitment to citizen involvement became engrained in statutory mandates and agency regulations. For example, Section 101(e) of the Federal Water Pollution Control Act Amendments of 1972 stated that "[p]ublic participation in the development, revision, and enforcement of any regulation, standard, effluent limitation, plan or program established by the Administrator, or any State under this Act shall be provided for, encouraged, and assisted by the Administrator and the states."

Congress also fostered public participation by authorizing direct financial aid to citizen groups who participated in specific regulatory actions of certain agencies, most notably the FTC, EPA, and the Consumer Product Safety Commission. In practice, the citizens best equipped and most interested in availing themselves of these participatory opportunities were the staffs of the public interest groups themselves.

As we have seen, voter turnout declined dramatically in the second half of the twentieth century. If ordinary citizens find it difficult to muster the interest and time to take part in the relatively simple task of voting, they are most unlikely to participate in the far more complex and lengthy process of bureaucratic rule making. Therefore, the new governmental provisions promoted the participation of these self-proclaimed "public interest" representatives, not the public at large. For example, public participation funds that supported citizen access at the FTC were concentrated among a relatively few organizations. Consumer activists claimed that genuine grassroots participation in agency rule making was impossible because of the high level of expertise required. Federal subsidy was necessary to enable these activists to represent the public and to counter the influence of business and trade groups.

Many public interest advocates were lawyers. Therefore, they naturally turned to the courts as allies in their reform efforts. Courts and citizen activists would appear to be strange bedfellows. As we point out in Chapter 9, the Constitution established the judiciary as the guardian of the liberal order, of individual rights against unruly majorities, and gave federal judges life tenure to ensure their independence from public opinion. But the New Deal transformed the meaning of liberalism and the role of the courts. In the 1960s and 1970s, a raft of laws was enacted that couched public policy in terms of entitlements, as statutory rights, thereby inviting the federal judiciary, the arbiter of rights, to become a forceful and consistent presence in administrative politics. Lawsuits and statutory language expanded access to the courts for advocates who claimed to speak for racial minorities, consumers, environmentalists, and the poor. By the 1970s, these citizen suits had become a powerful tool enabling public interest groups to take direct action against lethargic government agencies and unethical corporations.

Joseph Sax, a law professor who educated many public interest lawyers, celebrated citizen suits as "a means of access for ordinary citizens to the process of governmental decision making and a repudiation of our traditional reliance upon professional bureaucrats." Reformers could fight big government and corporations by making innovative legal arguments rather than building political organizations. Of course, "ordinary citizens" could not do this themselves; they had to rely on "public interest" advocates to represent them.

The public interest movement gained substantial influence on the policy process, but it did not solidify into an enduring political coalition. Its reliance on lawsuits, media exposure, and single causes was characteristic of what political scientist James Q. Wilson calls "entrepreneurial politics." The movement was and is dominated by a small number of Washington-based groups. Although it gained numerous supporters through direct mail solicitations, appeals for donations made little demand on the donors' time, energy, and intellect. As one prominent consumer activist, Michael Pertschuck, put it: "We defended ourselves against charges of elitism with strong evidence that the principles we stood for and the causes we enlisted in enjoyed popular, if sometimes passive support. But if we were 'for the people,' for the most part we were not comfortably 'of the people.'" Figure 14.6 charts the growth of various types of interest groups from 1959 to 2004.

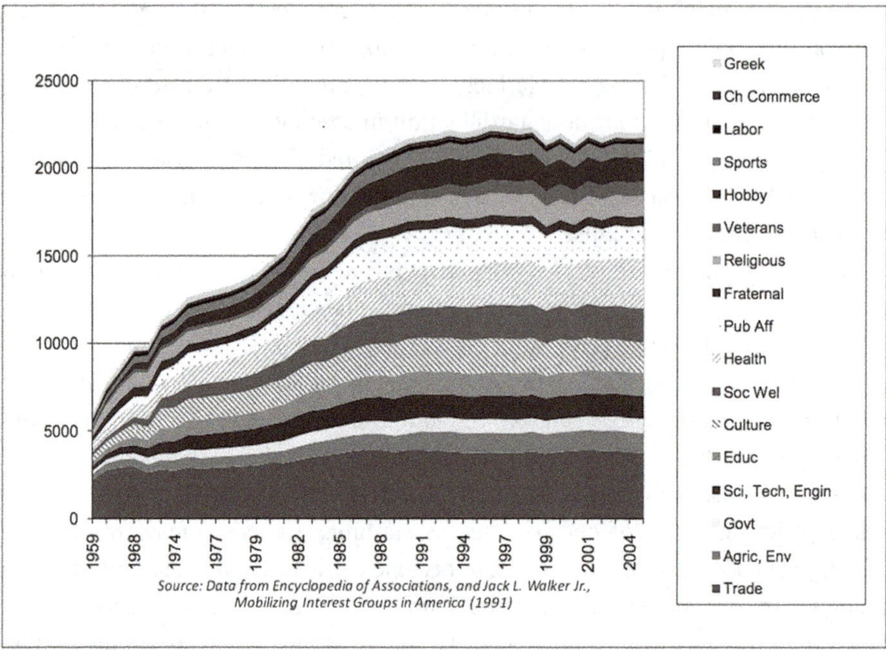

Figure 14.6. Interest groups: growth by sector, 1959–2005.
Source: UNC.

The Decline of Voluntary Associations

This chapter's contemporary portrait showed that voluntary associations still exist in profusion and perform very valuable service. However, over the past several decades they have been in decline. The overall rate of volunteering is down. Kiwanis, Rotary, and the Lions have fewer members as do the Boy Scouts and the League of Women Voters. Local chapters of some of these organizations have closed. Political scientist Robert Putnam began to worry about the loss of community spirit in the 1990s when he noticed that there were fewer bowling leagues and more people were bowling by themselves or with just a few friends. He wrote a book about it called *Bowling Alone*, which drew attention to the decline of organized local activities and the dangers this diminution posed for community cohesion and civic life. He coined the term social capital to describe the critical importance of strong and active social networks that build friendly and cooperative attitudes and relationships among people. As the bowling example shows, those networks are not overtly political. One might call them pre-political in that they develop the cooperative and friendly interpersonal relations that healthy politics requires.

CRITICAL THINKING QUESTION

Why do you think voluntary associations are declining? Is this decline inevitable or can you think of ways to reinvigorate them? Do you belong to a voluntary association? If so, do you think it performs a civic purpose? If so, what is that purpose? If not, do you think it should perform a civic purpose and what purpose should it perform?

Looking Forward

As this chapter reveals, the three different modes of participation have fared very differently over the course of American political development. Protest movements continue to thrive. Although the modern ones have access to modes of communications media beyond the wildest dreams of the earlier ones, their essential character has remained the same. From the Democratic Republican societies to the Tea Party and Black Lives Matter, political movements have all appealed to a mounting sense of resentment and indignation among large sections of the public. They have all sought ways to dramatize their cause, using whatever the most effective forms of media were available to them.

Lobbying has grown enormously in scope and importance. Although people have always sought to influence Congress and the executive branch, it was not until the twentieth century that large numbers of organizations established permanent offices in Washington staffed by professionals devoted to the exertion of political influence on a continual and persistent basis. The extraordinary profusion of lobbies that has taken place since the New Deal is essentially a byproduct of the ever-expanding role of the national government. Once people recognize how dependent they are on the spending and regulatory decisions made by Congress and by executive agencies, they are impelled to organize to protect the policies that benefit them and defeat those that harm them.

Looking forward, the future of outdoor and indoor politics seems assured. While it is impossible to say what future social movements will form around, it is certain that segments of the population who feel ignored or victimized will continue to take their politics out of doors and take advantage of the most advanced forms of communications to spread their message. In all likelihood, they will continue to frame their issues in terms of rights. As long as the national government remains as active as it is currently, those who are affected by its policies will lobby Congress and the executive to minimize the harm such policies might do them and maximize the benefits to be obtained.

The future of voluntary associations is far less certain. As we have noted, many of them are in decline. If this decline continues, it remains to be seen whether other forms of organization and activity will emerge to provide the social capital necessary to sustain strong and vibrant communities.

CHAPTER SUMMARY

Contemporary portrait:

* "Out-of-doors" politics mobilizes ordinary people to take part in rallies, demonstrations, strikes, and other forms of protest. If it gains lots of members and national prominence, it becomes a movement.
* Black Lives Matter is the newest of the four major protest movements to emerge in the twenty-first century. The other three were the antiwar movement that galvanized in opposition to the Iraq War; the Tea Party; and Occupy Wall Street.
* The most common form of "indoor" politics is lobbying. Lobbyists use a variety of tactics to attempt to influence legislators, executive officials and their staffs. These include personal persuasion, providing data and analysis, and organizing delegations of the people they represent to meet with public officials and stimulating campaign contributions.
* Voluntary associations are the prime embodiments of the communitarian cornerstone of American political culture at work. Because they directly involve people in the public life of the community, they cultivate the skills and attitudes necessary for effective and responsible citizenship.

The origins and development of the three forms of participation:

* The Democratic Republican societies arose in protest against what their members considered to be oppressive actions by the Washington administration. They wilted in the face of Washington's denounciation of them. Many of the members joined the Republican Party invigorating its commitment to popular, mass-based politics.
* The two most impressive movements of the nineteenth century, temperance and abolitionism, stemmed from the religious revival called the Great Awakening.
* Perhaps the single greatest transformation in mass media since the printing press was the invention of the telegraph, which enabled news to be transmitted nationwide instantaneously. Later movements too benefited from media innovation: the Progressives from cheaper printing costs and delivery via railroad; the civil rights movement and the movements of the 1960s from television; the Christian right from television and AM radio.
* In the late 1800s, first the Populists and then the Progressives arose to fight the private economic powers that they believed were oppressing farmers and

workers and were threatening to undermine individual freedom and democratic accountability.

* The Progressive Era witnessed a massive increase in lobbying. Growth was especially rapid among trade associations and citizens' groups, reflecting the intensity of the struggles between corporations and insurgents over the shape of the American economy during this period.
* The Progressives did not want merely to empower public opinion, but also to educate it. They added a civic dimension to their activities in the form of the social centers movement dedicated to recreating "the neighborly spirit" that Americans knew before they moved to live in large, socially fragmented cities.

The seminal role of the labor and civil rights movements:

* The labor movement owed the success it achieved during the 1930s both to the aid it received from the federal government and the strikes, sit-ins, and demonstrations it staged "out of doors."
* The greatest labor movement successes of the postwar era were won in the state capitals. Union lobbyists convinced many state legislatures to pass laws establishing collective bargaining rights for public employees. As a result, unions were able to enlist state and local government workers as union members and bargain on their behalf.
* The civil rights movement adopted key strategies from the labor movement. The sit-in was modeled after the sit-down strike.
* Despite immense provocation, the leaders of the civil rights movement remained committed to nonviolence, recognizing the need to remain within the bounds of civility and constitutionality set by American political culture.
* The advent of television greatly increased the movement's ability to influence public opinion. Tens of millions of viewers witnessed brave men and women remaining peaceful and dignified in the face of beatings by mobs and by the police.
* Both the labor and civil rights movements became staunch supporters of the Democratic Party.

Critical choice: movements adopt the language of rights:

* In the 1960s, inspired by the success of the civil rights movement, new protest movements emerged involving college students, war protesters, women, gays, environmentalists, and consumer advocates. They chose to emulate the civil rights movement by framing their demands in the language of rights.
* All the major political movements discussed in this chapter were subject to serious internal battles between the faction that sought to work within the existing political order and uphold key constitutional principles, and those who favored more radical objectives and tactics.
* The Christian right became a key supporter of the Republican Party. It added a new weapon to the media arsenal of protest movements by producing television programs of its own.

A new form of political participation, the public interest movement:

* The public interest movement that emerged in the 1970s shared many of the same objectives as the 1960s movements, but relied more heavily on a mix of "indoor" tactics – especially resort to the courts – and muck-raking.

The decline of voluntary associations:

* Voluntary associations are in decline. The overall rate of volunteering is down. Many prominent voluntary organizations have lost members and have closed a number of local chapters.

SUGGESTED READINGS

Baumgartner, Frank Berry, M. Jeffrey, Marie Hojnacki, David C. Kimball, and Beth L. Leech. *Lobbying and Policy Change: Who Wins, Who Loses, and Why*. University of Chicago Press, 2009.

Burns, Nancy, Kay Lehman Schlozman, and Sidney Verba. *The Private Roots of Public Action*. Cambridge, MA: Harvard University Press, 2001.

Ellis, Richard. *Democratic Delusion: The Initiative Process in America*. Lawrence: University Press of Kansas, 2002.

Gerstle, Gary. *American Crucible: Race and Nation in Twentieth-Century America*. Princeton, NJ: Princeton University Press, 2002.

Key, V. O. *Public Opinion and American Democracy*. New York: Knopf, 1961.

Keyssar, Alexander. *The Right to Vote*. New York: Basic Books, 2000.

Lippmann, Walter. *Public Opinion*. New York: Harcourt Brace, 1922.

Putnam, Robert. *Bowling Alone: The Collapse and Revival of American Community*. New York: Touchstone Books, 2001.

Schudson, Michael. *The Good Citizen: A History of American Civic Life*. Cambridge, MA: Harvard University Press, 1999.

Shklar, Judith N. *American Citizenship: The Quest for Inclusion*. Cambridge, MA: Harvard University Press, 1991.

Skocpol, Theda, and Morris Fiorina, eds. *Civic Engagement in American Democracy*. Washington, DC: Brookings Institution Press, 1999.

Verba, Sidney, Kay Schlozman, and Henry Brady. *Voice and Equality: Civic Volunteerism in America*. Cambridge, MA: Harvard University Press, 1996.

Wiebe, Robert. *Self Rule: A Cultural History of American Democracy*. University of Chicago Press, 1995.

Zukin, Cliff, Scott Keeter, Molly Andolina, Krista Jenkins, and Delli Carpini. *Michael X. A New Engagement?: Political Participation, Civic Life, and the Changing American Citizen*. New York: Oxford University Press, 2006.

Websites

GALLUP/Politics: www.gallup.com/poll/politics.aspx

Pew Research Center: http://pewresearch.org/

15 Concluding Thoughts

This book began with Martin Luther King's dream that one day this nation will do full justice to its creed. Thus, King acknowledged that Americans do in fact have a creed, a set of cherished principles to which they claim to adhere. And, he found that creed to be so excellent that Americans could conquer racism simply by living up to it. He wound his speech around the Declaration of Independence because it is both the simplest and the most profound statement of the creed, "We hold this truth to be self-evident, that all men are created equal and they are endowed by their creator with certain unalienable rights that among these are life, liberty and the pursuit of happiness."

When Lincoln, at Gettysburg, sought to explain to the American people why the Union cause was worth dying for, he gave his own gloss to the Declaration. He proclaimed that the issue at stake was whether a nation "conceived in Liberty, and dedicated to the proposition that all men are created equal" would endure.

Although it may not always be self-evident, the persistence of this creed and its central place in American political culture is the main pillar of American political life. And yet the American creed has been, from the beginning, at odds and in tension with other very powerful contending forces – above all racism, which has also been present in American life from the very beginning. Racial slavery constituted the deepest threat to the predominance of the American creed. After its abolition, the persistence of racial segregation and bigotry mocked the Declaration's fine words.

The American creed has also faced challenge from the centralization and collectivization of power. Concerns about the excessive size and strength of the national government arose as early as the 1790s. Another form of centralization, corporate in nature, came into being following the Civil War, with the rise of the industrial revolution. While this phenomenon was largely responsible for the extraordinary economic growth and prosperity America came to enjoy, it also threatened to undermine the creedal principles of equality, liberty, and the pursuit of happiness.

The growth of the railroads and the rise of massive industrial combinations in such fields as oil, steel, and banking put economic concentration at center stage. A nation of small farmers, merchants, and mechanics came to be dominated by massive factories, financial giants, and interstate railroads owned not by individuals, families, or partnerships but by corporations with hundreds if not thousands of faceless anonymous stockholders and limited liability. Powerful social movements arose among those who felt victimized by the economic giants. The Populists fought the railroads. The Progressives sought to bring all forms of corporate power under the discipline of government.

Today, both liberals and conservatives continue to view centralization and collectivization as a threat to the American creed. They differ, however, about which forms of it are most threatening. Modern Progressives, like their forebears, focus their attention on private economic power. The Obama administration's efforts to exert greater control over banks and investment houses were grounded in that tradition. Modern-day Progressives champion environmental, occupational safety, and consumer protection regulations as necessary means to protect the public interest from abuses stemming from corporate greed. By contrast, Conservatives are more concerned with the expansion of national government. Their opposition to the "nanny state" is grounded in the belief that an impersonal collective entity, the national government, is usurping the liberties, privileges, and obligations that rightfully belong to individuals, families, state, and local government.

President Donald Trump's message does not fit neatly into the liberal versus conservative dichotomy. As we pointed out at the end of Chapter 4, rather than stressing hallowed conservative themes of reducing spending and decentralizing government, he has championed a powerful national government that will restore national greatness, aggressively prosecute illegal aliens, maintain law and order, fight unfair foreign competition, and pressure American companies into building factories at home, not abroad. It remains to be seen whether this viewpoint, labeled as populist but a far cry from the Populist movement of the 1890s, will redefine American politics, or whether it represents no more than a temporary deviation from the previously dominant poles of political debate.

The individualistic premises of the American creed also place it in tension with communitarian principles deeply embedded in American political culture. The Puritans believed that all good Christians were indeed their brothers' keepers and that moral and religious virtue was more fundamental than life and liberty. The antimaterialism expressed in the Sermon on the Mount is not easy to reconcile with the competitive practices and self-regarding impulses emblematic of the "pursuit of happiness."

In the nineteenth and twentieth centuries, the US was transformed from an essentially Anglo-Saxon and African American country to a nation of great ethnic, religious, and racial diversity. Many immigrant groups did not believe that adoption of the American creed required them to abandon their group identity. Their communitarian efforts to stick together often put them at odds with the creed's emphasis on individual freedom. They understood that their ability to cohere required that their children marry within the faith and within the ethnic group. The high rates of religious and ethnic intermarriage that emerged during the twentieth century indicated that parents often lost such battles, but not without a fight.

The current controversy regarding illegal immigration also pits appeals to the creed against communitarian appeals, but here the roles are reversed. Advocates for open borders claim that restriction efforts make a mockery of the American creed while those who seek to reduce illegal immigration decry the stresses it puts on the fiscal stability and social cohesion of impacted communities.

Contemporary political movements also frequently find themselves at odds with individual freedom of choice. Although Christian and Jewish fundamentalists on the one hand and radical environmentalists on the other differ about many things, they would all agree that personal liberty must give ground when it conflicts with transcendent religious, philosophical, and moral principles. The former would argue that people should not always be free to express their sexual preference or abort fetuses. The latter would insist that individuals are not free to use their property as they choose if by so doing they desecrate nature.

But there is also a supportive side to the relationship between these anti-individualist, communitarian values and the American creed. The very survival of such divergent political, religious, and moral outlooks depends upon the civil liberties protections and the limits on government the American creed set in place. No other democratic republic is as permissive of group differences as the United States. In France, Muslim girls and women are forbidden to wear headscarves to school. In the US, they may freely do so. Based on the free exercise of religion clause of the First Amendment, US law permits some Indian tribes to smoke marijuana because it is an intrinsic part of their religious practice. Similarly, the Amish are permitted to use child labor under conditions forbidden to other Americans. Because the government provides fewer services than in most other countries voluntary associations; mutual aid societies and service organizations flourish in the US as in no other place.

To understand how these principles, conflicts, and tensions have found their way into contemporary political life, this book has focused on American political development. The key concepts for understanding and appreciating how that development has taken place are path dependency and critical choice. Path dependency provides a means for coming to grips with the remarkable persistence of the American creed itself and the key constitutional political and institutional principles that have formed around it. Critical choice focuses attention upon the crucial junctures when paths have been decisively altered. Altered but not obliterated. We refer to the most important of these critical choices as conservative revolutions to call attention both to the vital principles and practices they transform as well as those they leave in place. Each conservative revolution was revolutionary in that it brought about a major shift in the understanding of the meaning of democracy and equality and of the role of government. It was conservative in its fidelity to fundamental creedal, constitutional norms and principles.

The first conservative revolution was the American Revolution itself. It was radical not only in declaring itself independent of Britain but in abandoning monarchy in favor of a republic dedicated to securing natural rights. The Sons of Liberty and the local militias that sparked the revolution established a tradition of taking politics "out of doors" that has been perpetuated by social movements seeking radical political changes. These include the abolitionists, suffragists, and Populists of the nineteenth century; the labor, women's, and civil rights movements of the twentieth; and the Tea Party, Occupy Wall Street, and Black Lives Matter movements of the twenty-first. The revolution's conservatism is most evident when it is compared to the later French, Russian, and Chinese revolutions, which crushed the existing social, economic, and religious orders and trampled on human and civil rights.

The adoption of the Constitution was likewise a profound choice based on conservative and revolutionary principles. In the words of *Federalist* 10, it established a "new science of politics" based on the innovative idea that an extensive republic would prove more stable and protective of liberty than a small one. And, it built on the thinking of such great Classic Liberal philosophers as Locke and Montesquieu to create practical governing institutions that would divide power and check one another's tyrannical ambitions. Its conservatism rested in the antidemocratic elements it included in its institutional design – especially the Supreme Court and the Senate – and in the provisions it included protecting property rights. Its central premise – that government should be limited to those powers specifically enumerated – was both conservative and revolutionary. It was radical in that it had never been tried before, but conservative in the limits it placed on government's capacity to interfere with how people led their lives.

Each of the subsequent conservative revolutions profoundly altered American political life without deviating from the essential political principles that the Constitution established. The Jeffersonians promoted democracy by endorsing and nurturing those political institutions and constitutional principles they considered to be most democratic in character: free speech, legislative supremacy, and states' rights. The Jacksonians invented a means for sustaining Jeffersonian principles, the party system. Lincoln and the Republican Party removed the stain of slavery from the American creed. The New Deal expanded the concept of rights to include a right to economic security and established an administrative framework capable of curbing the excesses of private economic power while still preserving property rights and essential free market principles.

The American political development perspective also enables one to appreciate how crucial have been the choices not made and the paths not taken, ones that would have undermined creedal and constitutional principles. In the *Dred*

Scott decision, the Supreme Court, egged on by President James Buchanan, sought to put the Union on the path of permanent acceptance of slavery. That choice was ultimately rejected, albeit at the cost of hundreds of thousands of lives. In a series of decisions made in the late nineteenth and early twentieth centuries, the Supreme Court sought to prevent the national government from regulating the economy. This seemingly critical choice was overturned not on the battlefield but at the ballot box via the election of Progressive presidents and the judicial selections they made. And yet when FDR sought to solidify his New Deal program by packing the Court, Congress and the public defeated this attempt to undermine the hallowed constitutional doctrines of separation of powers and checks and balances.

As these false moves demonstrate, there is plenty of room in political life for folly, narrow mindedness, and just plain evil. But this book is also full of examples of wise and even noble politics. Good politics relies heavily on leadership and rhetoric. For example, John Marshall used his position as Chief Justice of the Supreme Court to succeed in establishing the Court's right to determine the constitutionality of statutes establishing it as a truly coequal branch of the national government (see Chapter 9). As head of the Forest Service, Gifford Pinchot enabled the agency to break the mold of corruption and ineptitude that had enveloped federal public administration and attain a high level of competence, effectiveness, and expertise (see Chapter 10). John L. Lewis spearheaded the creation of the modern labor movement (see Chapter 12). Elizabeth Cady Stanton's Seneca Falls Declaration of Sentiments was critical to launching the women's movement (see Chapter 2).

As we said at the very beginning of this book, in a free society, most of political life is lived through speech. The various forms of speech that politics employs – argument, explanation, exhortation, discussion – are what give it its distinctive character. Just as clay is the medium of sculpture, words are the medium of republican and democratic politics. The book began with Martin Luther King's noble words explaining and defending the cause of racial justice. Likewise, the speeches of Webster and Lincoln gave the public the language and concepts they needed to understand and elevate their devotion to the cause of Union. FDR's fireside chats created homely metaphors enabling ordinary people to make sense of the New Deal's programs. By declaring the Soviet Union to be an "Evil Empire," Ronald Reagan made clear why the sacrifices and fortitude the Cold War required were worth the trouble.

These fine words and deeds are the work of great political men and women, but leadership is not only exerted by the powerful, nor is rhetoric confined to the famous few. The joy and challenge of politics in a free country is that it is open to everyone and it is everyone's obligation. Because the wellbeing of a democratic republic ultimately rests on the shoulders of its ordinary citizens, they too must be leaders and spokespersons. This book has shown that American government rests on strong philosophical and cultural foundations, but also that it is subject to deep stresses and strains. American political development's ability to protect life, liberty and the pursuit of happiness depends on the capacity of its people to nurture and develop the political wisdom and skills that successful democratic-republican citizenship demands.

Index